FREEDOM THROUGH LAW

FREEDOM *through* LAW

PUBLIC CONTROL OF PRIVATE GOVERNING POWER

by *Robert L. Hale*

NEW YORK · COLUMBIA UNIVERSITY PRESS

1952

PUBLISHED IN GREAT BRITAIN, CANADA, AND INDIA BY GEOFFREY CUMBERLEGE
OXFORD UNIVERSITY PRESS, LONDON, TORONTO, AND BOMBAY
MANUFACTURED IN THE UNITED STATES OF AMERICA

To Charles Cheney Hyde

PREFACE

MOST of us Americans are as strongly in favor of individual liberty as Calvin Coolidge's preacher was opposed to sin, but we are not always any clearer as to what we mean specifically by liberty than the preacher was as to sin. No reasonable person demands for himself freedom from all control whatsoever. We all recognize that government must exist, with power to make us pay damages if we fail to observe certain obligations which we owe to our neighbors and with power to denounce certain activities as crimes and to punish the perpetrators by fine, imprisonment, or even death. But because government alone may legally impose such powerful sanctions as these for the coercive control of individual conduct, we are apt to think of liberty narrowly in terms of freedom from restrictions imposed by those official bodies (national, state, or local) which are conventionally regarded as "governmental" and to overlook the existence of private government, which, unless restrained by law, is as capable in some circumstances of destroying individual liberty as is public government itself. Though private persons are not permitted to impose their will by making death, imprisonment, or the seizure of property alternatives to obedience, there are other sanctions which they may lawfully invoke in order to force compliance with their wishes.

When a powerful labor union, for example, threatens to strike against employment of Negroes in an industry, the liberty of the Negroes may be quite as effectually curtailed as if the state had made their employment in that industry a crime. If government steps in to forbid the strike against Negro employment, it is extending the freedom of the Negroes from control by a private governing power, while restricting somewhat the freedom of the union from control by the official government. Freedom of the union to strike against Negro employment conflicts with freedom of the Negroes to obtain employment, but the latter freedom is surely a more vital form of individual liberty than the former. A law which by restricting one liberty gives birth to a more essential one results in a net enlargement of individual liberty.

However, the freedom from private control is not always a more vital liberty than the freedom to exert that control. Such economic bargaining power as each of us possesses is a power to exert some degree of coercion over others, but the freedom to exert that power may be more important to our own liberty than freedom from our coercion would be to the liberty of others. Much depends upon the degree of coercive power involved, as Professor Arthur E. Sutherland has recently pointed out in an illuminating article, "Private Government and Public Policy," in the *Yale Review* for the Spring of 1952 (Vol. 41, p. 405).

Every transaction for the sale of goods involves a certain degree of coercion on each side. A retailer can deny to a customer freedom to use any of the particular goods in his store. Because he can threaten not to sell he can coerce the customer into paying him money. But his coercive power in this respect is limited. It is not likely that the customer, however much he needs the goods, can be compelled to pay appreciably more than some competitor charges. Similarly, the customer can deny his money to the retailer, and by threatening to deny it can coerce the retailer to furnish him with the goods. But the customer's coercive power is likewise limited. It is not likely that the retailer, however much in need of money he may be, can be compelled to furnish the goods for appreciably less than he could obtain from other customers. If the price in which the transaction eventuates is reasonable, the parties presumably have more liberty than they would have if the freedom which each had to coerce the other were more restricted. Though our freedom to make use of material goods is restricted by the property rights and by the coercive bargaining power of others, still, by virtue of our own property rights and our own bargaining power, we each have a far wider range of economic liberty than we would have in a regimented or totalitarian system.

Some of us, however, have a much greater degree of economic liberty and of economic governing power than others. This inequality in liberty and in governing power is based in part on inequality in the specific rights of property which each person enjoys by operation of law, and is reflected in the great inequalities of fortune with which we are familiar. Many of these inequalities may be justified on one ground or another, but some of them may be questionable. One of the principal questions raised by any proposal to employ the power of state or nation to make changes in the distribution of wealth is whether that particular change will bring about a net enlargement or a net diminution of individual liberty. It cannot be assumed without inquiry that it will bring about the one result rather than the other. The common notion that any governmental step toward greater economic equality must necessarily diminish liberty is based on a fallacy.

The present book is concerned primarily with this question of the distribution of economic liberty in the broad sense of freedom from restrictions on one's economic activities as consumer or as producer, regardless of whether those restrictions are attributable to government or to other sources. Part I contains an analysis of the coercive factors in our system of free enterprise and of the economic inequalities which flow from it.

Part II, after a background exposition of the functions of courts, is a study of judicial decisions in which courts have been asked to expand or modify the common law in order to deal with attempts of one party to exert pressure on the other by means which might in other circumstances be held lawful.

Part III explores the protection which the Constitution has been held to afford to economic liberty and equality, commencing with an account of the process of expounding and enforcing the Constitution and of the role which the Supreme Court plays in that process. Specific provisions of the Constitution which can be invoked for the protection of individual economic interests are explained in the light of interpretative judicial decisions. Certain forms of governmental action against which these interests receive constitutional protection and certain other forms against which their protection is less clear are explained. Since most of the constitutional provisions involved refer to official action by state or nation, a discussion follows of the circumstances in which impairment of economic interests by the action of private individuals has been held attributable in some way to the official government and therefore subject to constitutional limitations. While in recent years the Supreme Court has recognized the hand of official government in certain exercises of private governing power where it was not previously recognized, nevertheless, for protection against private power one must for the most part look to political rather than judicial action.

Part IV deals with certain types of political action designed to protect some liberties by restricting others. There are chapters dealing with the rise and fall of constitutional barriers to legislative attempts to redistribute economic liberty through the regulation of wages, prices, and the rates charged by public utilities and railroads. Another chapter discusses some of the economic problems which call for solution when the reasonableness of a company's rates is being determined. The conclusion is reached that the search for a criterion of the reasonableness of rates leads logically to a search for a criterion of the reasonableness of the yield of property outside of the regulated field, as well as within it, and demands the formulation of public economic policy in regard to the distribution of wealth throughout the economy and in regard to the desirability or undesirability of altering that distribution in specific respects by price regulation or corrective taxation.

Part V, the Conclusion, raises the question where among the various organs of official government the lodgment of final authority to determine governmental policy would be the most likely to result in a distribution of economic liberty in harmony with democratic ideals. As will be seen from this outline, there are many vital problems of public economic policy with which this book does not pretend to deal.

Though the book deals largely with judicial decisions, it is hoped that it will be intelligible to serious-minded laymen, as well as to lawyers. It follows a line of thought which I have been pursuing almost ever since my graduation from the Harvard Law School in

1909. That line of thought has been embodied in a course which I have been teaching for many years at the Columbia Law School under the name "Legal Factors in Economic Society." Since 1937 I have received financial aid from the Council for Research in the Social Sciences of Columbia University for the employment of research assistants and stenographic help and for final publication. I have drawn freely for this book on articles which I have published elsewhere, some of them written in preparation for the book. These articles have appeared in the law reviews of Columbia, Harvard, Yale, and Illinois, in the *Political Science Quarterly*, the *American Labor Legislation Review*, the *American Bar Association Journal*, and the *Lawyers Guild Review*.

I am greatly indebted to Miss Ida M. Lynn, of the Columbia University Press, for her editorial work in reading the manuscript and suggesting many improvements in the text. I have profited much from the research and the criticism of those who have worked as research assistants at various times—Mr. Beryl Harold Levy, of the New York Bar, Mrs. Elizabeth W. Weston, of the legal staff of the National Labor Relations Board, and Mr. Daniel Gersen, of the New York Bar. Two of my former students, Mr. Victor G. Rosenblum, of the Political Science Department of the University of California, and Mr. C. Sam Daniels, at present a law clerk to Mr. Justice Black, have read portions of the manuscript and given me invaluable suggestions and criticism. I feel it impossible to give adequate expression to the gratitude I feel to the late Charles Cheney Hyde for the constant encouragement he gave me and the interest he took in the progress of this work up to the day of his death.

ROBERT L. HALE

Columbia University
New York City
April, 1952

CONTENTS

PART ONE

INTRODUCTION

I

ECONOMIC LIBERTY AND THE STATE

"STATISM" is often singled out as the prime enemy of individual liberty. Unrestricted state power can, indeed, crush liberty. History is full of examples, but we need go no further than to contemplate the practices of present-day totalitarian governments to demonstrate the fact. But in our revolt against statism we must not forget that while the state is capable of destroying our liberties it is also essential to their very existence. We must rely on the state to restrain powerful private individuals from unduly restricting the liberty of weaker ones. One who is locked up by a kidnapper is deprived of liberty as completely as if he were imprisoned by the state. One who shuts up his shop to avoid the threatened violence of gangsters has lost his freedom to conduct his business quite as much as if the state had passed a law forbidding him to conduct it. When the state, through its administration of the criminal law, destroys the liberty of kidnappers and gangsters to engage in their activities, it is enhancing, not curtailing, liberty in general.

The liberty to kidnap or to engage in violence which the state represses is not a liberty which anyone would openly condone. In fact, there are many who say that when the state represses such activities it is not repressing liberty at all, but license. This would seem to be an evasion of the issue. The state certainly undertakes to repress liberty to commit "license." It would seem more candid to recognize that there are some liberties that are pernicious and that would, if permitted to exist, destroy other liberties which ought to be protected.

As society grows more complex, acts which in a simpler state were innocent enough may now endanger other people's liberty. In the days of the horse and buggy there was no occasion to install traffic lights. Now that we have the automobile we have found it necessary. Freedom to continue to drive while the light is red is restricted, but the restriction serves to enhance the general freedom of driving, which would otherwise be restricted by traffic snarls.

Turning to the economic sphere, we have a mélange of conflicting liberties. Every person has a certain amount of bargaining power on which he depends for his livelihood. Bargaining power is power to exert pressure on those with whom one carries on transactions—in other words, to coerce them. Each person exerts some degree of coercion over other people's liberty, while at the same time his own liberty is subject to some degree of control by others. For the state to step in and suppress every liberty to restrict other people's liberty would indeed be oppressive. But it is a fallacy to assume that every attempt by the state to control and to revise the economic results of bargaining involves a net curtailment of individual liberty. It may or may not do so. If the liberty of those whom it restrains is less vital than the liberty which those persons would themselves restrain, then state intervention may spell a net gain in individual liberty. As General Eisenhower said at his installation as president of Columbia University, a danger to freedom arises "from too great a concentration of power in the hands of any individual or any group: The power of concentrated finance, the power of selfish pressure groups, the power of any class organized in opposition to the whole. . . . Any one of these, if allowed to dominate, is fully [as] capable of destroying individual freedom as is excessive power concentrated in the political head of the state." [1] To protect individual freedom from the danger to which General Eisenhower alluded, it becomes necessary at times for the

[1] Printed (November, 1948) in 40 *Columbia Alumni News;* 34 Am. Ass'n of Univ'y Professors, *Bulletin* 517, 520 (1948).

political state to curtail the freedom of powerful groups to dominate. Whether any given extension of state control in the economic sphere involves an enlargement or a diminution of individual liberty can be determined only after a careful weighing of alternatives.

Economic liberty has a twofold aspect. On the one hand is freedom in the choice of one's work; on the other, freedom to enjoy the material goods of life—in other words, freedom as a producer and freedom as a consumer. Any force which compels a man to work or restrains him from choosing his work restricts his liberty as a producer; any obstacle to his use of material goods restricts his liberty as a consumer. But neither as producer nor as consumer can everyone achieve complete liberty. The problem is how to secure the greatest practicable degree of liberty for everyone in both roles.

While we have abolished slavery in this country, we cannot abolish all the economic pressures which compel men to work at tasks which may be uncongenial to them. Some men have greater freedom from such pressures than others. A person whose capacities have a high value in the market may be able to obtain a satisfactory livelihood by choosing work which is highly congenial to him, and he may have considerable independence in the manner of its performance. On the other hand, a person capable only of jobs which have low market value may have to work long hours at a disagreeable occupation and under the constant supervision of someone else. Another factor which frees an individual from economic pressure to work is an independent income. The more money a man has, the less is he under the economic necessity to work. If his income is large enough to satisfy him, he may choose to do only such work as appeals to him or, if so inclined, none at all. But this factor of freedom depends on governmental restriction of other people's liberty. An income which does not come from work of some kind comes from some form of property. And property would yield no income unless the law stood ready to enforce property rights—that is, to deny liberty to anyone to act in a way which violates them.

Freedom from compulsion to work is thus relative. Some have more of this freedom, some less. Freedom to consume or to derive benefit from material goods is likewise necessarily relative. In a few cases, it is true, such freedom may be absolute. We may all breathe as much air as we wish without depriving anyone else of freedom to do likewise. We may all make use of the public pavements and enjoy whatever benefits we get from the lighting of the streets without preventing others from getting similar benefits. But few material goods are produced in sufficient quantities to enable everyone to make free use of them. If free use were permitted to the firstcomers until the supply was exhausted, the latecomers would find that their freedom to consume those goods had been effectually blocked. This is not what now restricts freedom to consume. Instead, the law forbids consumption except to the owner and to those to whom the owner gives his consent.

In a thinly settled country, where each family has its own piece of land, each family might rely for its wants on its own productive efforts. As producer of what it needs, it becomes the owner of its own products. Its liberty to consume is then limited only to the amount of what it produces. No other person's consent has to be obtained in order to enjoy this much of freedom, and other people are restrained by law from interfering with it by themselves making use of the family's products. But this sort of family economy would not suffice to produce for the needs of people in a country so thickly settled as is ours. We rely, instead, on a far more efficient, but far more complex, system of collective production and widespread division of labor.

Because of this division of labor scarcely anyone consumes the products of his own labor. He produces what he does, not in order to consume it, but in order to obtain the wherewithal to enable him to consume the products of other people's labor. But to obtain freedom to consume these products, the law requires him to have the consent of the owners. He can get that consent by paying the market price. Indeed, the market price is nothing else than the statement of the conditions which restrict his liberty to consume. He may not make free use of the goods in the market. His liberty to use them is not absolute. It is conditioned on his payment of the going price.

He pays this price in money, not by direct barter of the goods which he himself owns. How does he obtain the money? If he is himself the owner of goods of which he does not care to make personal use, he obtains money by selling them at their market price. If he becomes the owner by producing them with his own efforts alone, his freedom as a consumer depends on the relation between the market prices of the goods he has produced and of those which he wishes to consume. But to obtain such freedom as he gets, he has to forego the exercise of freedom to refrain from working for their production.

Not many people, however, become the owners of goods by producing them. Goods are typically produced by such complex processes by so many participants that generally it would be impossible to identify the producer. The owner of the factory commonly becomes the owner of the goods which it turns out. He is, doubtless, if he takes part personally in organizing or managing the plant, one of the participants in their production, but obviously not the only one. Those who provided him with his raw materials and fuel and his machinery, as well as his employees, have all participated in the collective efforts needed to produce the goods. In consenting to perform these various productive functions, however, these others have either explicitly or tacitly waived all right to participate in the ownership of the finished product. They have waived it in return for money paid them by the owner. While the latter, therefore, has not acquired the ownership by virtue of having produced the goods himself, he has acquired it by virtue of numerous transactions in which the other producers have transferred their shares to him. He has acquired it with the consent of all the other joint producers.

His freedom to consume, then, will depend on the inducements which he can offer these other producers to enter into transactions to co-operate with him in production, on the inducements he can offer consumers to enter into transactions for the purchase of his products, and on his ability to induce other owners to enter into transactions for selling to him what he wants to use. The lower the market price in these transactions for the purchase of his requirements, either for his business or for his personal use, and the higher the market price in the transactions for the sale of his products, the greater will be his liberty to consume.

But ownership of products is not the only source of money for an individual. As already indicated, an employee in a factory waives all claim to ownership. He receives, instead, direct money payment for his work, and this varies with the market value of the work which he is capable of rendering. Like the owner, his money depends on a transaction, and his freedom to consume on further transactions with those who own what he wants.

The owner performs his role in the productive process in anticipation of future transactions for the sale of his goods; the employee, as the result of a transaction already made. We rely on all these numerous bargaining transactions for the production of goods. We all have a common interest in making this collective output as great as possible. If the goods are not there, we cannot enjoy them. No matter how rich a man was during the Second World War, his freedom to consume butter, gasoline, and tires was strictly limited. Moreover, if goods are so scarce that the price is high, each customer's dollar will give him less freedom to consume than otherwise.

On the other hand, a plentiful output of goods is of no benefit to one who is denied access to them. To acquire liberty of access, we again rely on transactions. The more money a man has, given a certain aggregate output of goods, the greater will be his freedom to consume. But the amount of money he can obtain in transactions for the sale of his goods or services will be greater if the supply of similar goods or services is scarce. The introduction of the mechanical cotton picker may increase the general welfare by facilitating access to cheap clothing; at the same time, the human cotton picker in the South may pay a disproportionate price for this improvement in the general welfare by losing his earning power. And the dislocations involved may have such serious repercussions as to nullify the benefit to the general public. Reduction of the tariff to permit the increased importation of cheap foreign goods would promote the general interest of Americans by resulting in greater abundance, were it not for dislocations caused by the impairment of those special interests which thrive on relative scarcity. When we build a highway for the general welfare which involves the use of privately owned land, we compensate the owner so that he does not bear a disproportionate part of the cost of the general improvement. We have as yet devised no practicable system for compensating those whose special interests in scarcity will be sacrificed to the general interest in abundance. Unless and until we can do so, we shall probably have strong political obstacles to an economy of abundance.

The transactions which result in the production of our collective output and in individual freedom to consume some portion of that output when produced are bargains. Their terms depend on the relative bargaining power of the parties. The market prices of goods and services, on which the degree of each person's economic liberties depends, register that relative bargaining power. To call the transactions bargains does not necessarily imply that there is haggling over terms. There may or may not be. In negotiating a new wage agreement by collective bargaining or negotiating for the sale of real estate when the market does not set a definite price the obstinacy and the bargaining skill of the parties may be important factors. In a sale of one hundred shares of United States Steel, on the other hand, the terms are fixed by the quotations on the Stock Exchange. But because the bargaining power of the owner of the shares enables him to collect the market price and because that of the owner of the money enables him to insist on delivery of the shares at a price no higher than that, the transaction takes place according to those terms.

Bargains are made only when both parties consent to them. The process is sometimes referred to as "freedom of contract." But it is not entirely "free." One consents to the terms of a bargain because the other party's consent is necessary to the obtaining of some advantage. The employer can grant or withhold a wage from a prospective employee. It is to avert the withholding of that wage that the employee consents to work. The worker is under no legal obligation to work for this employer, and it is to avert the worker's withholding of his services that the employer consents to transfer to him a specified amount of his money. The worker can act to the disadvantage of the employer by declining to work, and the employer can act to the worker's disadvantage by refusing to hire him. If the transaction is completed, each yields in order to avoid the disadvantage to which the other can subject him. That is, he yields to a threat.

The threat may not invoke resentment. The counterpart of a threat is an offer to act so as not to subject the other party to the threatened disadvantage. The offer may be sufficiently welcome to inspire gratitude and to cause the threat to recede into the background of his consciousness, where it remains, nevertheless, a threat. Intention to act to one's disadvantage is not the less a threat because there is nothing unfriendly about it or because the other party regards it as reasonable. But if one gives up part of his liberty to remain idle or part of his money or other property in order to induce the abandonment of the intention to act disadvantageously toward him, he is responding to a threat. He is coerced into giving his consent to the transaction, as, indeed, are both parties. The more serious the harm which one party can threaten to inflict on the other and the more important the advantages which he can threaten to withhold, the greater will be his bargaining power and the more favorable to him will be the terms of the transaction. And market values reflect the relative force of the threats which buyers and sellers of goods or services can make.

The threats which can be made by some people are more serious than those which can be made by others, and therefore, in the results of the various transactions in which such threats are employed we find great economic inequalities—inequalities with respect to freedom from the necessity of doing disagreeable work and freedom to enjoy the good things of life. That is why one who is capable of rendering service of a kind that is scarce in relation to the demand for it can, by threatening to withhold that service, obtain better terms for not carrying out his threat than can one with no such ability. The latter may be forced to perform one of the humblest jobs, and in return may acquire only as much freedom to consume as is possessed by the ill-fed, the ill-clothed, and the ill-housed. The owner of valuable real estate or industrial plant, on the other hand, can by threatening to withhold it from use succeed in obtaining a large sum of money for consenting to its use, since the law forbids its use without his consent. He may then be able to live as well as he likes, immune from any pressure to enter into a transaction calling for any work which he does not wish to do. Everyone must make bargains for the acquisition of property, in the form of food and clothing. But he who already has much property, whether in the tangible form of physical things or the less tangible form of contract rights (such as bonds, mortgages, and bank deposits), can acquire the things he wishes to consume without rendering personal services in return; he who starts with no property cannot do so. As Justice Pitney once remarked in speaking of "the right to make contracts for the acquisition of property," with special reference to those "by which labor and other services are exchanged for money or other forms of property," "the vast majority of persons have no other honest way to begin to acquire property, save by working for money." [2] Again, pointing out that "inequalities of fortune" are inevitable when private property exists, he said:

> thus it naturally happens that parties negotiating about a contract are not equally unhampered by circumstances. . . . Indeed a little reflection will show that wherever the right of private property and the right of free contract co-exist, each party when contracting is inevitably more or less influenced by the question whether he has much property, or little, or none; for the contract is made to the very end that each may gain something that he needs or desires more urgently than that which he proposes to give in exchange.[3]

The "circumstances" which hamper the parties unequally are law made. The law hampers everyone in the use of things which other

[2] Coppage v. Kansas, 236 U.S. 1, 14 (1915).

[3] *Id.* at 17.

people own. But the hamper works more severely on owners of little than on owners of much. Each enters the negotiation armed with bargaining power in the form of what the law permits him to do (such as withholding his services) and what it *empowers* him to do (such as barring others from the use of his property). The weapons are not of equal force. At the end of the transaction each party has lost some legal advantage which he had before, and gained some which he did not have. As a result of past transactions many people own property which they did not produce; many who produced material things do not own them; some own much property; some, little; some have large amounts of money owing to them; and some are heavily burdened by debt. These economic inequalities are embodied in legal rights which the government enforces. It denies to people the liberty to make unauthorized use of an owner's property or to deviate from obligations incurred by contract. Though the unequal property and contract rights resulted from transactions, many of the transactions were influenced by the fact that the parties were unequally hampered by the previous legal relationships. The unequal property rights which preceded any given transaction, however, were in part acquired by each owner in a still earlier transaction in which he gave in exchange some product of his own industry or some service whereby he contributed to the production of the collective output of the community; they were acquired in part by the owner's direct activities in producing the very things which he finally owned. If they were all so acquired, it might be said with some plausibility that when the government steps in to protect the unequal fruits of bargaining it is merely assuring that the share which each person is enabled to take from the common output of society is the economic equivalent of what he has contributed to that output.

Any such conclusion, however, is only partly true. The government has assigned property rights to many who have neither produced the objects whose ownership is assigned to them nor contributed to the common output anything which they have given in exchange for the assigned property rights.[4] Land and natural resources, which were

[4] John Stuart Mill stressed this fact as long ago as 1848, when his *Principles of Political Economy* was first published. Combatting the theory that repression of force and fraud was the only legitimate function of government, he asked under which of these heads we are to place the operation of the laws of inheritance. Continuing, he said: "Nor is the function of the law in defining property itself, so simple a thing as may be supposed. It may be imagined, perhaps, that the law has only to declare and protect the right of

never produced by anyone, have been assigned to private ownership, not always in an equal manner and not always in exchange for any economic equivalent. He who by virtue of the law of wills or the intestacy law succeeds to the ownership of the property of a deceased person acquires a property right for which he has himself given no economic equivalent in exchange—however desirable the arrangement may be on other grounds. With this advantage to start with, the beneficiary of an unequal grant of public domain or the heir to a fortune has an advantage in future transactions over one who is less "unhampered by circumstances."

Economic inequalities, then—inequalities in freedom as producer and as consumer—are embodied in unequal legal rights. In assigning and enforcing legal rights to the fruits of transactions, the law is doing more than protect the winnings in the game of production and exchange. It is dealing unequal hands to the players. Further state intervention to alter the distribution of rights and liberties, to the advantage of those whose liberty is most restricted as a result, in part, of state action cannot be properly described as "statism" in any obnoxious sense. There may, however, be good reasons of policy against disturbing many of the present inequalities. But elucidation of this matter will require another chapter.

every one to what he has himself produced, or acquired by the voluntary consent, fairly obtained, of those who produced it. But is there nothing recognized as property except what has been produced? Is there not the earth itself, its forests and waters, and all other natural riches, above and below the surface?" The quotation is from bk. V, c. 1, § 2 in the 5th London ed., D. Appleton, 1866.

II

THE LEGAL BASES OF ECONOMIC INEQUALITY

ONCE it is recognized that economic inequalities spring from legal inequality, the question arises, how far they can be justified.

THE NOTION THAT THE LAW SHOULD TREAT ALL PERSONS EQUALLY

The role which the law plays in creating economic inequality is commonly overlooked, because in modern societies it plays that role in a less obtrusive way than it did in feudal times. Then there was no pretense of equality before the law. Laws which applied to serfs or to commoners did not apply to the nobility. One's legal position was largely a matter of status determined by birth. Nowadays, on the other hand, most of the property and contract rights possessed by any person and enforced by the law are rights acquired in a series of transactions. Hence it is often said, following Sir Henry Maine, that the progress of the law has been from status to contract and that inequalities of fortune, being the outcome of contract, are in no way due to any inequality in the legal treatment of the various individuals concerned. Legislative attempts to reduce any of the economic inequalities by protecting the weak from the economic power of the strong are frequently characterized as attempts to introduce inequality into the law and to return it from contract to status. The late Professor John Chipman Gray, writing in 1895, deplored "the reaction against those doctrines of *laissez faire*, of sacredness of contract, and of individual liberty, which were prevalent during the greater part of the [nineteenth] century." Speaking of the system of law and social morality which "had established itself in England and in the most civilized parts of the United States" as the culmination of the change by which "mediaeval feudalism had given way to the industrial and commercial states of modern times," he said:

> The foundation of that system of law and morals was justice, the idea of human equality and of human liberty. Every one was free to make such agreements as he thought fit with his fellow creatures, no one could oblige any man to make any agreement that he did not wish, but if a man made an agreement, the whole force of the State was brought to bear to compel its performance. It was a system in which there was no place for privileges,—privileges for rank, or wealth, or moral weakness. The general repeal of usury laws was the crowning triumph of the system.[1]

To the reaction against this system Professor Gray attributed the enactment of such laws as those regulating the hours of labor—"laws intended to take away from certain classes of the community, for their supposed good, their liberty of action and their power of contract; in other words, attempts to bring society back to an organization founded on status and not upon contract."

In asserting that the idea of human equality and of human liberty were foundations of the system he described, Professor Gray overlooked the fact that in making any of the agreements whose performance would be compelled by "the whole force of the State" the parties were responding to pressures, even though there was no specific legal obligation to make the agreement; that these pressures curtailed the liberty of the parties to an unequal degree; and that they were based in large part on inequality in the property rights which the law assigned to the respective parties.

George W. Alger expressed a somewhat similar point of view in an article published in the *Atlantic Monthly* in 1921.[2] He was deploring the failure of the law to prosecute wheat growers for combining to withhold wheat from the market until their price could be attained,

1 GRAY, RESTRAINTS ON THE ALIENATION OF PROPERTY, Preface to the 2d. ed. (1895).

2 Alger, *The Menace of New Privilege* (February 1921), 127 ATL. MONTHLY, 146.

while he assumed that it would prohibit similar combinations among steel manufacturers.

> What the American people have to consider today [he said] is the return in an entirely new and menacing form, of one of the outworn dogmas that were overthrown by the French Revolution—the doctrine of privileged classes. More precisely, it is the doctrine which in application purports to confer, by form of law, upon certain favored classes, the right to perform with impunity acts expressly declared to be criminal if done by others not of the favored group.

Mr. Alger, like Professor Gray, leaves out of his picture the necessary workings of the law of property. If we are to have any private property at all—and even communists would permit private ownership of some things—it is impossible for the law not to confer upon certain favored classes the right to perform with impunity acts expressly declared to be criminal (or at least illegal) if done by others. In regard to acts which involve the use of those things which I own, the law favors me above everyone else. It permits me to use those things, while if anyone else uses them, unless he is favored by my permission, his act constitutes either the crime of larceny or at least a tortious conversion of my property. True, in regard to acts which involve the use of those things which another person owns, the law reverses its favors. The act of using those things is permitted to him, but is illegal for me. Nevertheless, the fact remains that the same act must be permitted to the owner of the property and forbidden to others if property is to have any significance whatsoever. The doctrine which confers by law upon certain persons the right to perform with impunity acts declared to be criminal if done by others, was never overthrown by the French Revolution or by any other event.

THE UNIQUENESS OF THE RIGHTS CONFERRED ON EACH PERSON BY LAW

The law confers on each person a wholly unique set of liberties with regard to the use of material goods and imposes on each person a unique set of restrictions with regard thereto. The privileges, rights, and duties of each person differ from those of every other person. In some cases they may be equal, but they are never identical. And before pronouncing them equal or unequal, we have to decide with what we are measuring equality. Two things which are equal in weight, for instance, may be vastly unequal in size or value.

Certain obligations the law does put upon all alike. The obligation not to hit another person's face is the same obligation for all. It may be more irksome to a pugnacious person than to one peaceably inclined, but it is the same obligation. When we say that the law imposes on everyone an obligation not to make use of another's property without his consent, we create the illusion that here also the law is imposing the same obligation upon all, but it is the same only verbally and in the abstract. When the law forbids me to hit another person's face, the obligation is sufficiently described without further acts of the law. If I am accused of violating this obligation, the only thing that has to be determined in court is whether certain physical acts took place or not. If the acts are known, there can be no dispute as to whether it was your face which I hit. My obligation to abstain from using your property without consent is entirely different. The physical acts which I commit may be known without question, but I cannot be convicted of larceny or required to pay damages for a conversion merely because it is proved that I performed the physical acts of picking up certain identified objects and walking away with them. Something else must be shown as well as these physical acts. It must be shown that these objects were not my property, but another's. If they are another's, it is by virtue of the law. It is in defining who owns what that the law has to discriminate among persons if there is to be such a thing as private property.

To make a statement of my legal obligations in respect to other people's property sufficiently complete to enable me or a court to know what physical acts are permitted or prohibited in the matter requires something more than the abstract doctrine, which applies to everyone, that a person must not make unauthorized use of another's property. It requires in addition a legal statement of what is my property and what is another's. My obligation, stated with sufficient completeness to define what it is, is an obligation not to make unauthorized use of any physical objects excepting this described object or that described object, which the law defines as mine. Your obligation, stated with similar completeness, is an obligation not to make unauthorized use of anything except—and here would follow an enumeration of the things which the law defines as yours. In defining the exceptions, the law is not treating everyone alike, nor can it. Even if the assignment of property rights conformed to the past achievements of the various owners, in which all had an equal opportunity to participate, the fact would remain that at any given moment the law would be assigning a different set of rights to each person, and in doing so would impose a different set of restrictions on each person's liberty. These different rights and restrictions are by no means equal in their human or economic significance.

THE RELATION OF PROPERTY RIGHTS TO THE LIBERTY OF THE OWNER AND OF NONOWNERS

The significance of a property right to the owner, and the significance to the nonowner of the corresponding restrictions on his liberty vary greatly. Everyone is the owner of some property and the nonowner of other property, but the interests which the rights of ownership promote and the interests which property duties thwart vary greatly with respect to different owners. Private ownership increases the liberty of the owner in diverse ways. With respect to things which he is himself utilizing his rights of ownership protect him against restrictions which nonowners (not the government) might otherwise place on his liberty to use those things. An owner's freedom to use his property the law protects from impairment at the hands of nonowners. At the same time, if everyone owned or could acquire ownership of the goods which he needs to utilize, the restriction which the law places on the liberty of nonowners would be regarded by most people as less important than the restrictions which nonowners might otherwise place on the liberty of the owners.

When a manufacturer of goods, on the other hand, owns those goods, the liberty which his right of ownership promotes is of a different type. Ordinarily he is not interested in the personal use of the products of his factory. He values his right to prevent their use by others merely as a means of enabling him to exact money from those others. If successful, he will not, in fact, deny to all others the liberty of using his products, but because he may deny that liberty he is in a position to impose conditions with which a person who acquires the liberty must comply. These conditions normally consist of the payment of money. The manufacturer, meanwhile, is himself denied the liberty to use any of the goods produced by other manufacturers until he obtains their consent. The money which he obtains for not curtailing the liberty to use his own goods enables him to escape in some degree from the restrictions which the law places upon his liberty to use the goods of other owners. It is in this way that ownership of things which one does not care to use personally enlarges the liberty of the owner. The restrictions to which the property rights of other people subject an owner he can escape, more or less effectively, by owning other goods. However, a man who for one reason or another is unable to acquire property by which he can exact a money income from others cannot easily escape the restrictions which other people's property rights place on his freedom. If he is unable to own sufficient property of this type, he may be compelled to accept employment as the only condition on which he can obtain the money essential to purchase the freedom to eat. Nor can he produce and so become the owner of goods from the sale of which he can derive an income sufficient for a livelihood. Here, again, the restrictions placed on his liberty by other people's property rights prevent him. In more primitive times in the United States a man might acquire without great expense ownership of a piece of land from which he could produce considerable crops and on which he could build a house. By working in his own behalf, rather than for an employer, he could produce and then own a large part of the things of which he would make personal use, and could produce in addition a surplus of which he would likewise be the owner. By exacting money from consumers by threatening to deny them freedom to use this surplus, he might have money with which to purchase freedom to use some of the products of other people's labor. Similarly, at no great expense a man might weave cloth with a hand loom and sell the products for a livelihood.

With the filling up of the country, however, it is no longer possible for anyone to acquire a farm unless he has first accumulated enough money to pay for land, which has risen in price since the early days. He may still weave the same quantity of cloth on a hand loom as before but in view of the introduction of far more efficient power looms, he could not sell the product of his hand loom at prices high enough to furnish a livelihood. Obviously, one who has not already accumulated considerable money cannot produce or buy the expensive type of equipment called for by modern methods of production. He must perforce accept employment of some sort. It is the liberty to work as his own master which in his case the governmental enforcement of property rights curtails.

THE RELATION OF PROPERTY VALUES TO THE PRODUCTIVE CONTRIBUTIONS OF THE OWNERS

If all people were subjected to the same legal restrictions on their liberty to become the owners of salable goods by production, then if some produced and consequently owned goods of greater value than those owned by others, the resulting inequalities in property rights could be said to be the outcome of differences in industry and skill (with perhaps an admixture of luck), not of pre-existing legal inequalities. Empowering each owner to withhold the goods which he had produced, save on his own terms, would merely be to supplement the power of each person to withhold his own labor. The distribution of wealth would then conform to the differences in the value of the productive services rendered by each. But it is not true that all have equal opportunities to produce and to own salable goods. Those who already own more valuable land and equipment or more money are in a position to become the owners of goods produced with the aid of this land or equipment on terms not open to others who do not already have sufficient money to buy it.

Much of the income derived from property rights, however, does measure the economic value of services rendered. A man may refuse to render a service of great economic value of which he is capable until paid the market value thereof. Other types of service cannot be withheld in this manner. They are rendered first in the form of producing goods, and the bargaining for the reward can take place only after the goods have been produced. In such cases the legal right to withhold the goods is the only thing which enables their producer to get a reward for the services he has rendered in the past in producing them. Although not many people in modern life produce the goods which they own unaided, still it would be conceivable that if all had the same legal opportunity to engage in productive activities the net income from the sale of the goods would represent the economic value of the owner's contribution toward their production. From the gross proceeds of the sale he would have paid to all others who participated in the production the value of their services, and what remains would be the value of his own services. If he had been supervising the operations of the factory himself, the net income which he would receive would be greater than if he had hired someone else to supervise it, whose salary would have had to be deducted from the gross receipts.

If he had himself furnished the capital with which the plant was constructed, he need not have deducted interest payments to others. If he had furnished both the service of supervision and the capital, part at least of his net earnings would represent a reward for furnishing those two services. The more efficient his planning and supervision (in other words, the greater the value of the services he renders in that respect), the higher his net earnings are likely to be.

In fact, if planning and supervision are the only services he is himself rendering, whereas he has paid others to render such services as the advancement of the capital, it might be said that his net earnings are the value of his services. They might be supposed to fluctuate with conditions which would normally affect the market for such services. Thus, if the supply of those who possess equal or superior capacities for this type of service were to be increased, the effect would presumably be to increase the output of goods and reduce the net earnings of all those who are rewarded in this form for their supervision of factories. And if the supervisors sought payment in the form of salaries paid by owners, the increased supply of those capacities would similarly bring down the salaries they could command. The rewards which an owner could obtain from the profit on the sale of his goods, in so far as this reward is attributable solely to his services of supervision (what the economists sometimes call "wages of management"), would not deviate appreciably from the salary which a hired superintendent of equal capacity would be likely to obtain, since a superintendent has a choice between the two forms of payment for his services. This being the case, if the net earnings from any factory yielded to its supervising owner no more than the rough equivalent of the value of his supervising services, the right of ownership would be of no advantage and would have no value. A purchaser would pay nothing for it, since the factory would yield him no net earnings if he owned it over and above what he could obtain on a salaried basis. What gives value to the ownership is the power to obtain net earnings over and above the value of any services thereafter to be rendered.

In any successful business the property will yield its owners revenue, and will accordingly have value, wholly apart from any services they may render after they have acquired it. But part, at least, of this income is a payment for services rendered in the past, without which the products could not have been produced so economically. This service consists of advancing the money necessary for the creation of the plant, and perhaps some of it consists of making the plans for starting the business. Investing money in a productive business means diverting the energies of the community into the production of equipment instead of the production of consumable goods which the investor might otherwise have enjoyed. It thus increases the total productive capacity of the community. Those who advance money to a corporation are enabling it to create the plant for the production of its output, and part, at least, of the income which the corporation subsequently pays them, whether in the form of interest on the bonds or dividends on the stock, is a reward for genuine contributions they have made to the production of its output. Similarly, when an unincorporated owner constructs his plant out of his own pocket, part of his earnings corresponds to his service as an investor, though it is less easy in his case to differentiate nicely the returns which he gets for furnishing the capital, from those which he gets for supervising the plant and for planning the enterprise. In all cases the return to the investors has its source in the payments made by the customers. These payments are made in compliance with the compulsory requirements of the owner of the plant, backed up by the threat to exercise the law-given right to forbid the use of those products.

The service rendered by investors consists of advancing a certain amount of money. Hence the value of that service at the time when it was rendered is readily ascertainable. The services rendered by the investors were rendered at one time, but the rewards are spread over a series of years. In a set of books, the services rendered would be entered in the capital account; the rewards, in the income account. There is a market, however, in which lump sums are paid (capital investments made), for opportunities to obtain income payments in the future. If the lump sum which the investor advances is equivalent to the value which the market places upon the prospective series of periodical payments which he takes in exchange, then the reward which he obtains through the exercise of the corporation's property rights is the exact equivalent of the value of the service he has rendered.

It is true that the sum total of the future payments he will receive may vastly exceed the amount which he invested, but since the opportunity to obtain those payments is postponed, the prospect of obtaining them may be worth no more in the market today than the capital sum contributed. Postponed payment is worth less than present payment of the same amount, not only because of the risk that the future payment will not in fact be made but also because of the human reluctance to postpone an enjoyment to the future even if the future is secure. Not every investor, of course, is so reluctant. In fact, many who are well-to-do invest money which would add nothing to their enjoyment if spent at present, since they are spending all the money they can possibly enjoy. Nevertheless, the theory is that the demand which industry makes for capital could not be satisfied by these painless investments alone and that the supply of capital is limited by the fact that those called upon to furnish the additional capital required have a real reluctance to postpone the enjoyment of what they can obtain for their money, a reluctance which can only be overcome by offering them a prospect of obtaining more in the future than they give up now.

Meanwhile, industry is supposed to be in a position to offer more in the future than it receives now, because by constructing equipment at present it can produce goods more cheaply in the future and thus afford to pay the interest. Since the demand for capital enables anyone who has money which he can advance to obtain interest, whether the postponement of consumption represents a sacrifice to him or not, those to whom postponement would be no sacrifice in any other respect are nevertheless, when they advance money to one person, sacrificing the opportunity to obtain interest on it from another. If there were no limit to the funds whose possessors would as readily spend in the future as today, then the fact that they can obtain more in the future by postponing consumption, would induce them to invest more and more. The result would supposedly be an increase in the capital equipment of the country, an increase in the output of this equipment, and a lowering of the price of the output as a consequence. If the price of the products were lowered, presumably manufacturers would be unable to offer investors such high returns as before and the process would continue until interest vanished, except that which represents a risk of loss rather than a return for postponement of enjoyment. What prevents this from happening, according to many economists, is the fact that reluctance to postpone the enjoyment of one's money does in fact operate to prevent the expansion of productive equipment. Hence, the opportunity to obtain an indefinite series of periodical payments in the future does not outweigh in value a much smaller capital payment contributed in the present. If the value of the property rights in a productive industry were no greater than the amount of the contributions made by the investors, it could then be said that the law's intervention against customers and in favor of the owners serves no more than to give the owners rewards equal to the value of their contributions, even though it would be true that much of the value contributed by well-to-do investors is contributed at no sacrifice; for the value of anything does not necessarily conform to its *cost* in terms of human sacrifice.

Operating a plant and contributing the capital with which to construct it are not always the only services rendered by the owners. There is also the original planning and promotion of the enterprise. The promoters may have taken to themselves a number of shares in a corporation without investing, or they may have invested in the hope of obtaining returns higher than those which measure the value of mere investing. If the business earns enough to give the property a value above the value contributed by investment alone, part at least of this excess value may reflect the value of the very real service of promoting the enterprise. To what extent this may be true in any given case cannot be readily determined, since the value of the service of promoting is not so easy to measure as is the value of the service of contributing the capital.

But the earnings which any given productive property yields may often be such as to give the property a value which has no relation to the contributions made by the present owners. Such deviations in the value of property above or below the expense of producing or acquiring it were thought by the traditional economists to be so ephemeral as to deserve no serious consideration. So long as the government made no formal grants of monopoly, competition was supposed to iron them out in short order. If the earnings from a particular plant exceeded the market rate of return (in view of all the risks) on the cost of construction, it was thought that competitors would construct new plants which would bring down the price obtainable for the products. Conversely, if the property yielded less than the market return, some of the existing plants would not be replaced when they wear out, and because of the reduced aggregate output, the price of the products still produced would rise. No owner would continue for long to produce at a cost which exceeds the price he could obtain on the market, nor could any producer long charge a price above what it would cost to add to the supply. If he attempted to do so, he would lose his market to others who would be willing to sell for as little as cost. Only a formal monopolist, who could control the supply, was thought to be in a position to charge a price which in the long run would exceed the cost, without losing his market to someone else.

This may have been substantially true in the early part of the nineteenth century, but is far less true today. Many factors other than a formal grant of monopoly interfere with such a precise working of competition, even in the long run. Because of the growth in large-scale production, it is not always feasible for new competitors to enter the field. Recent writers have stressed the fact that when a certain product is produced by a few large concerns, collusion between them is not necessary to enable each to sell at a price higher than that which would have to be charged to meet the cost of adding to its output. By producing only as much as can be sold at the higher price, and thus not tempting its competitors to produce more, it can reasonably hope that they will not deprive it of its market by expanding their own production. Each concern, acting from the same motives, may feel that it would be unprofitable to expand its output to the point where it would be getting a price which would make the added production itself worth while, for its action in doing so would have the disadvantage of reducing the price of the rest of its product. Hence, with the output restricted by all, prices of goods produced by a few large enterprises are likely to remain high enough to make the yield worth on the capital market more than the original cost of the plants. Though there is no complete monopoly and no collusive action between the competitors, there is, on the other hand, no perfect competition. We have what some writers term "duopoly," or "oligopoly." [3] In addition to such interferences as these with what was supposed to be the precise working of competition, collusion between competitors is by no means unknown. Despite the anti-trust laws, it is notorious that competition is frequently restrained by formal or informal understandings, as well as by what are called "unfair methods of competition" and by combinations of various sorts.[4]

INEQUALITIES IN PROPERTY RIGHTS IN LAND

When the earnings from a particular plant are attributable in large part to the advantages of the site on which it is located or to

[3] See EDWARD H. CHAMBERLIN, THE THEORY OF MONOPOLISTIC COMPETITION (1933); JOAN ROBINSON, THE ECONOMICS OF IMPERFECT COMPETITION (London, 1933).

[4] See ARTHUR ROBERT BURNS, THE DECLINE OF COMPETITION (1936).

the superior productivity of the soil or the natural resources which it owns, then even in the days when the traditional economists wrote competition would have had no tendency to keep prices at the level where the capital value of the returns covered only the cost of producing the plant. In fact, there was no cost in producing sites and natural resources, although the present owner may have incurred expense in acquiring them. This cost he has incurred only because the natural resources had previously attained a value in excess of their cost. This could not have happened had there been an unlimited quantity of equally good sites and resources. In such a case enough of these resources would be devoted to the production of the products to bring their prices down so low that the land would have no value. It would still be useful and essential in order to obtain earnings from the other factors, just as the use of the air is essential for the maintenance of furnaces for the production of steel and the use of the ocean is essential for earning a revenue from transatlantic shipping. But it would have no value, just as the privilege of using air or the ocean forms no part of the assets of any business. The land does have value, however, because if the demand for any of its products increases, as it is likely to increase in general with the growth of population, those who own the better sites and resources cannot add indefinitely to the output without incurring constantly increasing costs of operation and those who attempt to produce from inferior resources must incur greater costs at the outset. And although new factories can be constructed which will be quite as good as the best now in existence, the new natural resources which can be brought into use for production are inferior to the ones already being used. Competition will tend only to keep the price high enough so that the most expensively produced portions of the aggregate output can be sold advantageously when added to the less expensively produced portions. This price, which covers what is called the marginal cost of production, will be obtainable by those whose output is produced at a lower cost as well as by those who produce the marginal portion of the output. Even the classical economists realized that in the case of goods produced in this manner competition would not keep the price at a level with the cost of all the output (even though the word "cost" be taken to include wages of management and interest on the expenses of constructing equipment), but would result in a price equal to the cost of the marginal portion of the output. Those who produce at lower costs because they own superior land would reap a differential advantage which Ricardo, in his well-known analysis, designated the "economic rent." He recognized that it was a return which the owner of the better lands could obtain in excess of the costs of production.

Whenever the demand for the products of any given land increases, the tendency will be to increase the differential advantages of the owners. While the initial rise in the price of the product will be offset somewhat by increased output, it will not be brought back to its former level. The additions to the output will constitute the new marginal portion, whose production cost is higher than the former marginal cost. The ultimate price, which will coincide with the new marginal cost, will therefore be higher than it was before the demand for the product had increased. This will increase the differential which the owners of the better lands can obtain between the price they receive and the costs which they must incur in producing their contributions to the supply. Anyone else who might have owned this better land could likewise have obtained the increased annual return. This makes the right of ownership in the land more advantageous, in pecuniary terms, than it was before. In other words, it increases the value. We thus have the familiar phenomenon of the so-called "unearned increment" in land values in growing communities.

We have seen that in all the many instances in which competition fails to keep the value of the right to own property (which is another expression for the capital value of the series of anticipated future annual returns from the property) down to the level of the contribution made toward the production of the output by those who paid for the construction of the equipment, some persons are empowered by their property rights to exact from the rest of the community more money than their contributions toward production are worth in the market. The economic inequalities of the property rights do not conform to inequalities in the value of services rendered.

Many of the present owners, however, may have paid for their land or other productive equipment the full value which it now has. What they paid in excess of the cost of producing the equipment or making improvements in the land may be thought to form no contribution to the production of the product, for the land would be there even had they incurred no expense, and the equipment, if they had paid only the cost of constructing it. However, the former owner may have lacked the ability or the inclination to use the land productively, and his power to withhold it created an artificial obstacle to its productive use by the present owner—an obstacle which the latter could overcome only by paying the full market value of the land. In this sense, whatever the present owner was required to pay for the land constitutes a necessary contribution he has made toward production of the output.

Any increment in value, however, above what the present owner paid, corresponds to no such contribution—unless the increment, measured in dollars, is apparent rather than real in view of a lower purchasing power of the dollar or unless the increment is a reward without which the owner could not have been induced to incur a risk which had to be incurred if the production was to take place. Apart from these two instances, any increment above what the owner paid reflects the power which the law gives him to compel the consumers of his product to pay him more than the value of anything he has contributed to producing it.

The first owner of a piece of land or a natural resource did not acquire it by contract with other private individuals. The government either made him a special grant of the land, thus creating in him the status of ownership, or else it accorded that status to anyone who would conform to certain conditions. In the early colonial days both methods were used. In some colonies, notably in New York, large grants were made to favored persons. On the other hand, in many colonies the law recognized the status of owner in any one who would occupy and claim a piece of land as a farm. During the nineteenth century great quantities of the public domain passed into private ownership. Some portions were granted to special persons or corporations, ostensibly for services rendered or to be rendered, as in the case of the huge grants made to the transcontinental railroads. On the other hand, under the Homestead Act of 1862 "Congress offered a quarter-section of public land, free of cost, to any citizen who would occupy the land and maintain a residence for at least five years." [5]

At the outset, the operation of the Homestead Act had an equalizing tendency. Not only were many persons of small means given the status of landownership, but the opportunity to go West and acquire this status reduced the pressure on workers in the East to accept jobs on unfavorable terms. While in the beginning the acquisition of

[5] T. W. Van Metre, Economic History of the United States (Henry Holt & Co., 1921) 387.

a quarter section of land under the Homestead Act gave no one any particular advantage over others, the continuance of the legal maintenance of the property rights of the settlers against all others began to produce inequality when the country filled up. At first it may have been true in most cases that the right to exclude others from the use of a particular quarter section caused no hardship to the others, who might themselves acquire equally good quarter sections. The ownership of the crops produced on a particular quarter section would probably enable the owner to exact from consumers no more than the value of the services he had rendered in producing the crops. But as the demand for farm products increased with a growing population, the time came when the supply could no longer keep pace with it, since the best land was already occupied. And when a city grew up in the neighborhood of any quarter section, the demand for the use of the site for urban purposes may have caused tremendous unearned increment, which could not be attributed to any risk undertaken by the owner. The same thing was true later when oil was discovered under any land.

Legal intervention which restricts all but one person from the occupation of a particular quarter section may work with substantial equality at first and as long as other equally good quarter sections are available, but may work with great inequality subsequently. If passengers in a partly filled day coach are permitted to make exclusive use of two seats, there is no inequality in the arrangement at first. A passenger excluded from any two seats in a partly empty coach may himself occupy two others. But when the train fills up, it is obvious that a continuance of the power of the first passengers to keep others from empty seats would force the newcomers to stand in the aisles or to come to terms with the first occupants. So the terms that created a status of landownership in those who occupied quarter sections were at first substantially equal; but they resulted in legal rights which became unequal in their economic significance, as soon as the newcomers found all the best land occupied.[6] This result may be defended on various grounds, but scarcely on the particular ground that it is the outcome of equal legal rights or equality before the law.

[6] Henry George made eloquent use of this analogy in asserting the injustice of private property in land. PROGRESS AND POVERTY (25th anniversary ed., 1909) bk. VII, c. 1, pp. 342–343.

INEQUALITIES IN RIGHTS TO INHERITED PROPERTY

Up to this point we have been examining the rights of ownership in objects for which the owners have paid and in natural resources which have been granted to their owners by law. There is another very important source of ownership, namely, inheritance. Even if property be worth no more than the original cost of constructing it, still, if the man who incurred that cost is dead, there is no way of continuing to reward him for his past services. The person who now owns the property acquired it by operation of law, by status, not by contract. If the previous owner left it to him in a will, it is his only because the law gives effect to the wishes of the decedent so expressed. The law did not always do so. In feudal times property passed on death to those whom the law thought most fitting to acquire it, and the wishes of the former owner could not affect the transmission. At present, if a man dies without making a will the property passes to those relatives whom the intestacy laws of the state favor. Even if it be thought that the present intestacy laws, unlike the laws of inheritance before wills were allowed, are designed to give effect to the wishes which the deceased owner would probably have expressed if he had taken the trouble to make a will, it remains true that the presumed wishes of the decedent, just like the wishes he actually expresses in a will, are effective only by operation of law. The power of the owner of inherited property to exact money from the community cannot be said to result in rewarding the inheritor for any services which he himself ever rendered. Nor can it be said to be the fruit of a system of equal legal rights or of equality of opportunity. There would be no meaning at all to the phrase if it were asserted that everyone has an equal opportunity to acquire the favor of a rich man and so to inherit his property. And when the rich man dies intestate, it is obviously untrue that a person unrelated to him has the same opportunity to inherit as does a relative. If it were true, it could be said with equal truth that in the feudal system itself the son of a serf had an equal opportunity to be born the son of a lord. In determining the transmission of title to the property of a deceased owner, the law is undeniably a respector of persons. The legal institution of inheritance can be justified only on the ground that the inequality which it creates is a desirable inequality, not that it is furnishing equal protection to all in any real sense. Proposals to modify inheritance, either by abolishing it altogether or by taxing it, must meet the objection that they defeat the legitimate purposes of a system of legal inequality. But taxation of inheritance for the benefit of those who inherit least cannot properly be said to be a governmental coddling of the poor at the expense of the rich. It is, on the contrary, an attempt by the law to cease coddling the rich quite so much at the expense of the poor. Those economic inequalities which result from inheritance, however justifiable they may be, are the result of status rather than contract and flow from inequality of legal rights.

INEQUALITIES IN THE MARKET VALUES OF PRODUCTIVE SERVICES

Some of the inequalities in legal rights which the law accords cannot, then, be said merely to reflect inequalities in the value of services rendered in the past. Some of them, however, do. Moreover, payments obtained, not for the use of property, but for the direct rendering of services, normally reflect inequalities in the value of services rendered.

The economic value of a service merely expresses what the person who renders it can induce others to pay him for doing so. He induces the payment by threatening otherwise to subject the rest of the community to a compulsory foregoing of the benefits to be derived. He is thus collecting his reward by a compulsory process. This power to compel other people to pay him money, under threat of not performing services, is, however, an essential element in our economic system. It supplies almost the only means by which a person without property can gain access to the necessities of life. There would be no purpose in maintaining legal arrangements for encouraging the production of wealth unless there were further arrangements for enabling people to make use of it after it is produced. The producer himself cannot ordinarily live by consuming the specific products which he has made. Owing to the widespread division of labor which efficient production necessitates, every producer has to consume many things produced by other people. These things are barred to him by the law of property, and the bars can be lowered only by the offer of money. And ordinarily money can be obtained only by exerting pressure against others by threatening to withhold property or services. When one has no property sufficient for this purpose, the threat to withhold one's services can be exerted effectively only by not carrying out the threat when the condition of payment is met. Thus, the power to exact money in this way from other members of the community can be exercised only by rendering service. The mechanism by which this is made possible thus performs a twofold function in economic life. The person who exercises the power gains access to a certain part of the wealth produced by others. At the same time, he is himself compelled to contribute to the production of wealth and thus add to the amount to which others can obtain access. The amount of money he can obtain by exercising this power is the market value of the services he renders.

It may, of course, be value in a "forced" rather than a "normal" market. A worker may be so needy as to be forced to accept the first job offered without waiting to find out whether higher wages would be obtainable in an open market, or he or she may be ignorant of the fact that the services are worth so much to the employer that the latter would pay a higher wage if he could not obtain this worker's services for less. In such a case the wage actually obtained is less than the value of the service on an open market. On the other hand, an unscrupulous doctor or lawyer or a person who renders the service of underwriting a security issue may be able to take advantage of the needs or the ignorance of the person he is serving and exact more for his services than could be obtained on an open market.

But even if wages, salaries, and fees were strictly commensurate with the values of the services rendered, not on a market restricted by the pressing necessities or ignorance of either party, but on a market in which all potentially interested bidders have sufficient time and information to participate, the power of different persons to exact money from other people for services rendered would still vary greatly. Even on the open market the value of the service that some persons are capable of rendering (and so of withholding) is very slight, while the value of the services which other people are capable of rendering is very great.

If each individual could freely choose whether to render a service of high market value or one of low value, then if he chose the latter it could be assumed with some confidence that he had found some advantage to compensate for the lower wage obtainable. He would have no conceivable grievance against the higher paid worker, since it would be equally open to him to become a higher paid worker himself. To a limited extent, differences in the market value of different services do reflect the choices of the persons affected. If those who work on the night shift of a plant get higher wages than those who perform similar work during the day, and if the latter are free to obtain the night jobs, then presumably the difference in the pay compensates for a difference in the attractiveness of the work. Night labor could be said to be scarcer and hence more valuable on the market than day labor of the same type, because the disadvantages of doing night work keep people from accepting it except at a higher wage. So, too, perhaps, a person capable of acquiring the capacity to render services which require long and expensive preliminary training may prefer to perform services of lower market value which do not require such preliminary sacrifices. In that case it would also be true that the higher pay obtained by those who have undergone the training merely compensates for the disadvantages they suffered because of the expense and the postponement of their earning power. This is on the assumption, of course, that those who chose the less-well-paid occupation had the same financial and other opportunities to secure the training essential for entering the higher paid one.

Adam Smith explained all differences in payments for labor and services on grounds such as these. Later economists, however, have maintained that such differences in sacrifice come far short of explaining all the differences in payments for services. As Professor Taussig had pointed out,

> the movement of labor from grade to grade is not free. Amid the great variety of occupations and of wages which in fact exists, certain broad groups may be distinguished. These may be called, in the phrase introduced by Cairnes, non-competing groups; non-competing in the sense that those born or placed in a given grade or group usually remain there, and do not compete with those in other groups. For most men it is very difficult, for many it is impossible, to move from the group in which they find themselves into one more favored.[7]

In short, a person in a low-paid noncompeting group does not have an opportunity equal to that possessed by one in a higher group to render services of equal value and so to acquire equal wealth. The opportunity may be lacking because the person in the lower group or his parents could not afford the education and training necessary for the development of whatever inborn talents that person may have. Extension of free educational opportunities may level some of the obstacles to equality of opportunity to acquire wealth. Differences in inborn capacity, however, would doubtless remain, and there still would be many who would be incapable of rendering services as valuable in the market as those rendered by others. It can scarcely be said

[7] Frank W. Taussig, 2 Principles of Economics (2d ed. rev., Macmillan, 1920) 134.

that the former have an opportunity equal to that of the latter. "Equality of opportunity" is a deceptive term. If some external obstacle is placed in the way of one's doing remunerative work, who would assert that his opportunity for earning money was equal to that of one who has no such obstacle to overcome? Is there any greater equality of opportunity when the obstacle is an internal one—one's own lack of inborn ability? Is the opportunity of a cripple to win a race equal to that of a well man? In so far as remuneration is based on ability, the opportunities of the able and the less able can be accurately described as proportionate to their respective unequal abilities. It is not accurate to describe them as equal to one another. A distribution of property rights according to the value of services rendered is not the outcome of equality of opportunity.

INEQUALITIES WHICH BENEFIT AND THOSE WHICH HARM THE LESS FAVORED

Not every inequality of opportunity is injurious to those who have the smaller share. Because the blind have no opportunity to enjoy paintings, it would in no way benefit them to deprive those who can see of the opportunity to do so. There is no way in which the greater opportunity of the seeing can be shared with the blind. When it comes to the distribution of wealth, the situation is somewhat different. If the community's output of material goods were a fixed quantity, then it would follow mathematically that if anyone received more than the per capita average of the output, someone else must receive less than his per capita share. But the community's output is not a fixed quantity. If an equalization of the rewards were to diminish the total output, the result might well be to harm rather than to benefit those at the bottom of the economic scale. While one at the bottom would receive a larger proportion of the total, still if the total were sufficiently reduced, this larger proportion would constitute a smaller absolute amount. One percent of one thousand is more than 2 percent of four hundred. If those who have the superior opportunity to render valuable service which increases the aggregate wealth of the community can be induced to render that service only by the hope of obtaining disproportionate rewards, then the allowance of such disproportionate rewards to those who have this superior opportunity will redound to the benefit of those who have less opportunity as well. The latter will receive a smaller relative share of the community's wealth than they would if rewards were more equally distributed, but their absolute share will be greater than it would be if the more fortunate had not been induced to increase the aggregate wealth. At the end of the Second World War it was found that coal miners in Western Europe were incapable of producing the desired output of coal unless they received more than the average rations of food. Giving the miners more meant a smaller proportion for the others, but since the possibility of increasing rations at all depended on an increased output of coal, the increased ration was given to the miners for the sake of the rest—not because miners were thought more deserving than anyone else.

The miners were physically unable to render the services desired of them without obtaining unequal rations. The same principle applies to those who, although able to perform superior services, are unwilling to do so without obtaining the rewards which their bargaining power, based on threats of nonfeasance, enables them to obtain. If there is no practical way of compelling or otherwise inducing them to serve, a system which protects their property rights in the fruits of their bargaining will for the same reasons benefit those whose opportunities are less. Their rewards, in proportion to their needs or their sacrifices, may be much higher than the rewards of the less fortunate, but may be justified from the point of view of the latter, even by one who sees no justification in the mere fact that the market value of their services is higher than the value of services which others can render. In the mid-nineteenth century John Stuart Mill wrote:

> The proportioning of remuneration to work done, is really just, only in so far as the more or less of the work is a matter of choice: when it depends on natural differences of strength or capacity, this principle of remuneration is in itself an injustice: It is giving to those who have; assigning most to those who are already most favoured by nature. Considered, however, as a compromise with the selfish type of character formed by the present standard of morality, and fostered by the existing social institutions, it is highly expedient; and until education shall have been entirely regenerated, is far more likely to prove immediately successful, than an attempt at a higher ideal.[8]

Much of the income derived from the ownership of property, as well as income in the form of salaries and wages, measures the market value of services rendered. Some of it, we have seen, does not. Income from inherited property, for instance, does not reflect any service ever

[8] PRINCIPLES OF POLITICAL ECONOMY, bk. II, c. 1, § 4.

rendered by the recipient. Even here, however, the power to transmit one's property at death doubtless functions to some extent as an incentive, not for the recipient, but for the testator to render services to society which he would not otherwise render. Nevertheless, there is room for the more equal distribution of wealth in a manner which would not significantly impair the incentives to productive service and would enlarge the economic freedom of those who have least. Taxes on inheritances in excess of a certain amount and on unearned increments and graduated taxes on incomes (even incomes which measure the value of services rendered) would not necessarily impair the motives for rendering useful service. The proceeds can be used to subsidize housing or schools or hospitals for the benefit of those whose opportunities are the least favorable. To enlarge the freedom of customers to enjoy their services, rates of railroads and public utilities and perhaps other prices may be regulated if the regulation is not pressed to the point where the service is impaired or the needed capital for extensions and improvements cannot be had. The terms of the labor contract can be regulated to the advantage of the worker. Other methods of rendering bargaining power more equal than it is will readily suggest themselves. Resort to any of these measures raises specific problems of some difficulty. Underlying them all, however, is one fundamental ethical problem.

ETHICAL CONSIDERATIONS RESPECTING INEQUALITY

Even when not required by Mill's principle of expediency, are certain inequalities to be favored on ethical grounds? More specifically should anyone be denied rewards commensurate with the superior value of his services, even if such denial will not reduce the incentive to render them? The answer is clear if one accepts an equalitarian or democratic philosophy, which regards the welfare of every person as equally sacred, without preference for members of one race or one country or one economic class above others, or even of the virtuous above the wicked, or the person endowed by nature with great abilities over one less well endowed. According to this philosophy one who can render great service at no more sacrifice than that incurred by one capable only of rendering service less valuable deserves no more moral credit for rendering it than does the other. If we would pay him more, it is only because we do not see how otherwise to prevent him from withholding the service which he ought to be rendering. Even now we do not conventionally regard everyone as deserving pay commensurate with every benefit he confers. A witness who accidentally is in a position to render unusual service in the administration of justice gets no higher witness fee than one whose testimony is of less value. Because a bystander happens to be the only person capable of directing the firemen to a valuable building which is on fire, who would think him entitled to any exceptional reward for doing so? Why, then, should we regard a man whose services have exceptional value as deserving of exceptional reward, unless he has made an exceptional sacrifice in rendering them?

A philosophy which denies that he deserves an exceptional reward (which, it must be kept in mind, diminishes the reward available to others) is not inconsistent with assigning to him exceptional property rights as a result of his bargaining power, provided his services cannot be otherwise obtained. Mill's grounds of expediency still hold good to a certain extent, the principle on which the coal miners were given exceptional rations. His superior position may be given him, not as an end in itself, but as a means to the ends of the welfare of other persons. To the extent that it does not serve as a means to these other ends, we would transfer the surplus in one way or another to those who need it more urgently—not because the welfare of the able man is not a worthy end itself, but because it conflicts with still worthier ones.

By the same philosophy we might pity rather than denounce the criminal, but at the same time hang him. We may be fully convinced that the criminal is what he is by reason of his heredity and environment and may echo the words attributed long ago to John Bradford when he saw a convict being led to the gallows—"But for the grace of God, there goes John Bradford." [9] At the same time we may believe that hanging the criminal may be the only means of preventing others from committing crimes which if not prevented would cause more misery to others than the hanging causes to the criminal. If that belief is correct, the punishment is consistent with the equalitarian belief in the equal sacredness of every person's personality. While it sacrifices the personality of the criminal, whose personality is sacred, that of others is no less so, and the different ends conflict. If punishment is not a means to other worthy ends, it cannot be justified on the basis

[9] The remark has also been attributed to others. John Bradford lived from 1510 to 1555. See BARTLETT, FAMILIAR QUOTATIONS (11th ed., 1944) 18.

of this philosophy; nor can inequalities in the distribution of wealth, other than those which compensate for inequalities of sacrifice or need and those which serve indirectly to benefit persons who get the least. Many of the existing inequalities do serve in this way, but by no means all.

Since inequalities in wealth result from inequalities in the coercive bargaining power of the different members of the community and since the bargaining power of each individual is conditioned by his legal rights and duties as defined by the courts, it becomes pertinent to inquire into the protection which the courts afford to one man's economic liberty against the coercive power of other individuals or of the government—whether in proclaiming rules of the common law or in giving authoritative interpretation to the provisions of the Constitution.

PART TWO

COMMON-LAW ADJUSTMENTS OF CONFLICTING ECONOMIC LIBERTIES

III

STATE AND FEDERAL COURTS AS SOURCES OF COMMON LAW

EVERYONE'S liberty, we have seen, is subject to a certain degree of restraint at the hands of others, who can inflict unpleasant consequences on one who will not come to terms or withhold benefits from him. Some of the unpleasant consequences may be inflicted without the aid, but with the acquiescence, of the law; others, through the agency of the law, by invoking its aid to enforce contractual obligations or to exclude certain property from use. But there are some threats which the law will not permit one to carry out. The criminal law, in the form of legislation, defines certain acts as crimes, and governmental officials prosecute those who are charged with committing them. Other acts are civil wrongs; they violate somebody's rights, and the government does nothing about them until someone whose right they violate brings action in the courts. The court will then give a remedy to a plaintiff who proves that his right is violated. It may order ejectment of a trespasser or restitution of a chattel which has been wrongfully converted, or it may render a judgment ordering the defendant to pay money to the plaintiff whose right has been violated.

These are called "legal," as distinguished from "equitable," remedies, the distinction stemming from the time when "law" and "equity" were administered by separate courts. Under some circumstances the court will grant the "equitable" remedy of a decree for specific performance of a contract or an injunction restraining threatened wrongful acts. Failure to satisfy a judgment for damages subjects the property of the defendant to a levy of execution at the hands of public officials—if he has sufficient property within the jurisdiction. Disobedience of an equitable decree subjects the defendant to punishment for contempt of court.

The law is constantly being modified—expanded, contracted, clarified, or altogether changed. Who changes it? In the United States, anyone living in a state is subject to two bodies of law—state and federal. Acts of Congress and of the state legislature make and change the federal and state laws. In England, Parliament can make laws. But legislation can seldom be made so precise as to apply clearly to every concrete case which may arise. Statutes have to be construed by courts. The construction which the highest state court places on a state statute, or the United States Supreme Court on an act of Congress, or the House of Lords on an act of Parliament becomes a part of the law, unless and until the appropriate legislative body amends the act.

There is, however, a great mass of law which has never emanated from any legislature. This is what is generally called the common law. The term is also used with other connotations. The whole system of Anglo-American law is sometimes called "common law" to distinguish it from the "civil law" prevalent on the Continent of Europe. Again, suits between private parties are sometimes spoken of as actions at common law, to distinguish them from criminal proceedings. Another distinction is sometimes made between common law and equity. Here, however, the term "common law" will be used to refer to all court law, including equity, which is not based on statutes or constitutions.

The common law is not necessarily the same in all jurisdictions. What it is on any point, lawyers seek to determine from court decisions. In England a decision of the House of Lords is conclusive of the common law of England—though of course it can be changed by statute. In the United States there was for a long time confusion as to what court could speak with final authority on the common law in any state. This confusion arose from the fact that federal, as well as state, courts are sometimes called upon to decide cases involving state law.

The federal judicial power is created by Article III of the Constitution, which defines the "cases" and "controversies" to which it shall extend. It extends, of course, to cases involving federal law but also, among other things, to controversies "between Citizens of different States." The jurisdiction so conferred on federal courts is what is usually called the diversity jurisdiction.[1] Article III itself created no federal courts other than the Supreme Court, on which it conferred no "original," but only "appellate," jurisdiction to hear such cases. But it authorized Congress to create inferior federal courts as well, with original jurisdiction. Congress first did so when it enacted the Judiciary Act of 1789. Section 34 of that Act, which still remains on the books, reads:

> The laws of the several states, except where the Constitution, treaties, or statutes of the United States otherwise provide, shall be regarded as rules of decision in trials at common law, in the courts of the United States, in cases where they apply.

The "trials at common law," to which this section applies, include cases involving statutory as well as common law in its more restricted sense, but do not include criminal cases. The question arose at an early date how far "the laws of the several states" were to be found in the decisions of state courts. From 1842 to 1938 the authoritative answer was found in an opinion rendered by Justice Story in 1842 in the well-known case of *Swift* v. *Tyson*.[2] Story declared that "the laws of the several states" included state statutes, state court decisions construing such statutes, and state court decisions which concerned "rights and titles to things having a permanent locality, such as the rights

[1] It requires that every party on one side of a suit must have a state citizenship different from that of every party on the other side, despite a contention by Justice Bradley in a dissenting opinion in the Removal Cases (Meyer v. Construction Co.), 100 U.S. 457, 486 (Oct. Term, 1879). For purposes of this jurisdiction, corporations are sometimes spoken of as citizens of the state in which they are incorporated, although they are held not to be citizens within the meaning of other clauses of the Constitution. At any rate, the federal courts take jurisdiction of suits between corporations incorporated in one state and citizens of others. For an incisive criticism of this practice see a series of articles by Dudley O. McGovney, *A Supreme Court Fiction: Corporations in the Diverse Citizenship Jurisdiction of the Federal Courts* (1943) 56 HARV. L. REV. 853, 1090, 1225. McGovney points out (*id.* at 894) that the Supreme Court's rationalization is that a suit by or against a corporation "is regarded as a suit by or against its shareholders, *and* they are conclusively presumed to be citizens of the incorporation state." He points out the absurdity of this presumption, especially in cases where a stockholder brings suit against the corporation.

[2] 16 Pet. 1, 18–19 (U.S. 1842).

and titles to real estate, and other matters immovable and intra-territorial in their nature and character." But they did not include, he maintained, and Section 34 did not apply

> to questions of a more general nature . . . as, for example, to the construction of ordinary contracts or other written instruments, and especially to questions of general commercial law, where the state tribunals are called upon to perform the like functions as ourselves, that is, to ascertain, upon general reasoning and legal analogies, what is the true exposition of the contract or instrument, or what is the just rule furnished by the principles of commercial law to govern the case.

Accordingly, where there was no statute applicable to a certain state of affairs, lawyers would have to look to decisions of *federal* courts (ultimately of the Supreme Court) to ascertain what rule of "general commercial law" governed the transaction, if it was to be litigated in a federal court. This rule would be uniform throughout the country. At the same time, they would have to look to decisions of the courts of the particular state to ascertain the governing rule, if the matter was to be litigated in a state court, where it would have to be litigated if the parties to the controversy were citizens of the same state. In that case, the state court would be free to reject the rule of the federal courts, and no appeal would lie to the federal courts, since the federal judicial power does not extend to controversies between citizens of the same state, where no question of federal law is involved. As a result, while the "general" law applied by the federal courts would be uniform throughout the country, there was not necessarily uniformity within any one state between the rule of law which would be applied by a state and that by a federal court to the same transaction, according to whether a controversy over it reached the one court or the other. In fact, the same transaction might be governed by two conflicting rules of law. The conflict could only be removed by state legislation, which might reject the rule of the federal courts. In that event, the federal courts would no longer be free to apply their notions of "general commercial law," for there would admittedly be a law of the state, which Section 34 required them to regard as a rule of decision.

The doctrine of *Swift* v. *Tyson* assumed the existence of some body of commercial law, independent of any statutes or state decisions, which could be ascertained by the federal courts. This assumption Justice Holmes challenged in 1917, when, speaking for the Court in *Southern Pacific Co.* v. *Jensen,*[3] he said that "the common law is not

[3] 244 U.S. 205, 222 (1917).

a brooding omnipresence in the sky but the articulate voice of some sovereign or quasi-sovereign, that can be identified." In 1928 he protested in a dissenting opinion (in which Brandeis and Stone concurred), in *Black & White Taxicab Co.* v. *Brown & Yellow Taxicab Co.*,[4] against extending the doctrine of *Swift* v. *Tyson* to apply to state decisions as to the validity of contracts in which a railroad granted exclusive taxicab privileges in its station premises. While not prepared to overrule *Swift* v. *Tyson*, he insisted that it was founded on a fallacy and "has resulted in an unconstitutional assumption of powers by the Courts of the United States." Explaining his position, he said:

> Books written about any branch of the common law treat it as a unit, cite cases from this Court, from the Circuit Court of Appeals, from the State Courts, from England and the Colonies of England indiscriminately, and criticise them as right or wrong according to the writer's notions of a single theory. It is very hard to resist the impression that there is one august corpus, to understand which clearly is the only task of any Court concerned. If there were such a transcendental body of law outside of any particular State but obligatory within it unless and until changed by statute, the Courts of the United States might be right in using their independent judgment as to what it was. But there is no such body of law. The fallacy and illusion that I think exist consist in supposing that there is this outside thing to be found. Law is a word used with different meanings, but law in the sense in which courts speak of it today does not exist without some definite authority behind it. The common law so far as it is enforced in a State, whether called common law or not, is not the common law generally but the law of that State existing by the authority of that State without regard to what it may have been in England or anywhere else.[5]

Accordingly, Holmes declared at a later point:

> The Supreme Court of a State does something more than make a scientific inquiry into a fact outside of and independent of it. It says with an authority that no one denies except when a citizen of another State is able to invoke an exceptional jurisdiction that thus the law is and shall be. Whether it be said to make or to declare the law, it deals with the law of the State with equal authority however its function may be described.[6]

Ten years later, in 1938, after Holmes had left the Court, an end was put to the doctrine of *Swift* v. *Tyson*, and it was overruled in *Erie Railroad Co.* v. *Tompkins*.[7] In following *Swift* v. *Tyson*, said Justice Brandeis for the majority,[8] the federal courts had "invaded rights

[4] 276 U.S. 518 (1928).
[5] *Id.* at 533–534.
[6] *Id.* at 535.
[7] 304 U.S. 64 (1938).
[8] Concurring with Brandeis were Chief Justice Hughes and Justices Stone, Roberts, and Black. Justice Reed concurred in the overruling of Swift v. Tyson, on the ground

which in our opinion are reserved by the Constitution to the several states." Technically, no act of Congress was held unconstitutional, but Section 34 was held to have been wrongly construed, so as to bring about an unconstitutional result. Said the Court:

Except in matters governed by the Federal Constitution or by acts of Congress, the law to be applied in any case is the law of the state. And whether the law of the state shall be declared by its Legislature in a statute or by its highest court in a decison is not a matter of federal concern. There is no federal general common law. Congress has no power to declare substantive rules of common law applicable in a state whether they be local in their nature or "general," be they commercial law or a part of the law of torts. And no clause in the Constitution purports to confer such a power upon the federal courts.

As a result of this decision, state courts can now make pronouncements on state law, whether commercial or local, with an authority which will be binding on federal courts.[9] No conflicting federal decision, even by the Supreme Court, will have any authority. Supreme Court decisions on state commercial law no longer constitute a body of common law. At most they serve as decisions on the law of a particular state, which state courts may disregard. There may be such decisions in the future, as in the past, for controversies between citizens of different states often reach federal courts, involving questions of state law on which the highest state court has made no pronouncements. Even then, Justice Stone said in 1940 in *West* v. *American Tel. & Tel. Co.:*[10]

There are many rules of decision commonly accepted and acted upon by the bar and inferior courts which are nevertheless laws of the state although the highest court of the state has never passed upon them. In those circumstances a federal court is not free to reject the state rule merely because it has not received the sanction of the highest state court, even though it thinks the rule is unsound in principle or that another is preferable.[11]

---

that the Judiciary Act had been erroneously construed, but doubted whether, as so construed, it was unconstitutional. Justice Butler wrote a dissenting opinion, in which Justice McReynolds concurred. Justice Cardozo, because of illness, took no part in the decision.

[9] But when a state court holds that a statute is not an unconstitutional impairment of the obligation of a contract, on the ground that no obligation was ever created by the contract, the Supreme Court insists on determining for itself whether an obligation was created. It determines the question, however, with reference to state law. This practice probably involves no real departure from the philosophy of Erie Railroad v. Tompkins. See the discussion *infra*, pp. 204–205. And see Hale, *The Supreme Court and the Contract Clause*, III (1944) 57 HARV. L. REV. 852, at pp. 852–872.

[10] 311 U.S. 223 (1940).

[11] To the same effect were two other decisions of the same day, Chief Justice Hughes

But if no state rule at all is to be found, the federal court must perforce improvise one to apply to the case.[12] Any such improvised rule, however, will form no part of the state's common law. Even when a state court makes its pronouncement after the federal proceedings have commenced, and after the federal trial court has given judgment based on what the state law at the time seemed to be, the federal appellate court must follow the latest decision of the highest state court on the question of what the state law was, whether that decision purports merely to "clarify" previous decisions, as the majority thought it did in *Oklahoma Packing Co.* v. *Oklahoma Gas & El. Co.*,[13] or whether it expressly overrules them, as in *Vandenbark* v. *Owens-Illinois Glass Co.*[14]

Erie Railroad Co. v. *Tompkins* held that neither Congress nor the federal courts had power "to declare *substantive* rules of common law applicable in a state." They still have power to declare procedural rules to govern federal courts, even when passing on questions of state law. But, as Justice Reed remarked in his concurring opinion, "the line between procedural and substantive law is hazy." A change in the legal remedy for vindicating a right may reduce the right itself to practical insignificance, when asserted in the court whose procedure has been altered. Perhaps this is the effect of the Norris–La Guardia Act of 1932, by which Congress, exercising its power to promulgate procedural rules for federal courts, provided that no federal court

rendering the opinions. Fidelity Union Trust Co. v. Field, 311 U.S. 169, and Six Companies v. Highway District No. 13, 311 U.S. 180. Two weeks later (December 23, 1940) Justice Murphy followed the same principle in rendering the Court's opinion in Stoner v. New York Life Ins. Co., 311 U.S. 464.

[12] In an interesting article, *Mr. Tompkins Restates the Law* (1941) 27 A.B.A.J. 547, Judge Herbert F. Goodrich suggests that when federal courts face a gap in state law, they might well resort to the "Restatements" of various branches of law prepared by the American Law Institute. These Restatements have "been based on case law but not the case law of any one individual state or group of states."

[13] 309 U.S. 4 (1939).

[14] 311 U.S. 538 (1941). Presumably this rule would not apply when the state court in its latest decision overrules earlier ones as erroneous, but declares that the earlier ones shall, nevertheless, apply to transactions antedating the time when they were overruled. This is what the supreme court of Montana did with respect to a decision construing its railroad statutes in the case which was affirmed in Gt. Northern Ry. Co. v. Sunburst Oil & Ref. Co., 287 U.S. 358 (1932). A state, said Justice Cardozo, "may say that decisions of its highest court, though later overruled, are law none the less for intermediate transactions." That case originated in a state court, and there was no occasion for any federal court to apply state law. The Supreme Court merely held that there was nothing unconstitutional in the state court's action. Had a controversy between citizens of different states involving Montana law reached a federal court, presumably that court, notwithstanding the Vandenbark case, would have followed the state court in holding that the law governing antecedent transactions was that which the earlier decisions held it to be.

should issue an injunction against certain specified acts in labor disputes. This Act did not alter substantive state law. Acts which were illegal before its passage remained illegal. A citizen of another state could still obtain from the federal courts a judgment for damages for such acts. A judgment for damages, however, is seldom worth obtaining against persons unlikely to be able to pay them. A change in procedural law has rendered the unchanged substantive law ineffective for all practical purposes in the federal courts.

While there is no longer any "federal general common law" applicable in cases which reach federal courts only because they involve controversies between citizens of different states, there is none the less plenty of federal case law on subject-matters to which the federal judicial power, regardless of the citizenship of the parties, extends. Apart from authoritative interpretations which the Supreme Court places on the Constitution and federal statutes, there is even a federal common law. The federal judicial power extends to "cases of admiralty and maritime jurisdiction." In deciding such cases, it is not state law that the federal courts follow. It is law which they themselves determine with authority. In "controversies between two or more states" (to which federal judicial power also extends) questions frequently arise which do not depend on the law of any one of the states, and on which there is no federal legislation—such as those involving the respective powers of two states in regard to the diversion of water from an interstate river. In such cases the federal courts have to work out a species of federal common law. On the same day in which Justice Brandeis denied the existence of "federal general common law" of the type recognized in *Swift* v. *Tyson,* he wrote the Court's opinion in another case, *Hinderlider* v. *La Plata River &c. Ditch Co.,*[15] in the course of which he declared that "whether the water of an interstate stream must be apportioned between the two states is a question of 'federal common law' upon which neither the statutes nor the decisions of either state can be conclusive." Likewise, of course, the federal courts declare common law for the District of Columbia and for the territories.

15 304 U.S. 92, 110 (1938).

IV

COURTS AS POLICY-MAKERS IN THE DEFINING OF RIGHTS AND DUTIES

MOST private wrongs were defined originally in some court decision which became a precedent in the development of the common law. They are frequently altered by legislation, and in some states the legislatures have enacted comprehensive codes embodying what was thought to be the common law, with or without amendments. Nevertheless, the origin of most private wrongs and rights is to be found in the common law of the particular jurisdiction, as developed by courts; and courts still feel free to declare acts wrongful which do not fall within any hitherto well-defined category.

Among the well-defined categories of private wrongs are breaches of contract and various kinds of torts. Among the latter are assault and battery, negligent injury, libel and slander, fraud, and the unauthorized use or appropriation of another's property. In defining these acts as torts, and in conferring upon people rights to get legal redress when subjected to them, the courts have doubtless acted on the assumption that it was important to protect people in their bodily safety, or their reputation, or their property, against injury. But not every act which causes harm to a person gives him a cause of action at law. A plaintiff cannot recover a judgment for a bodily injury he has suffered by an act of another who was guilty of no negligence and who did not intend the injury. Nor can he recover for diminution in the value of his property from one who caused it by declining to work for him or to sell him materials essential to his business. Otherwise there would be no bargaining. And the value of his property may be reduced by acts of others which are performed for non-bargaining purposes—such as the act of one who starts competition with him. Such an act is perfectly lawful.

Even when one is harmed by an unlawful act of another, he can have no redress if the act was unlawful only in that it violated a right of someone else. In a well-known case in which the opinion of the New York Court of Appeals was rendered by Chief Judge Cardozo in 1928 (*Palsgraf* v. *Long Island R. Co.*),[1] a conductor had assisted a passenger to board a moving train in such a manner that a package which the passenger was carrying was dislodged and fell onto the platform. There was no outward indication that the package contained fireworks, but such was the fact. The fireworks exploded and upset some scales on the platform, injuring a woman bystander. She sued the railroad, alleging that the conductor's manner of assisting the passenger constituted negligence. It was held that she could not recover, whether the conductor was negligent or not. He may have acted unlawfully in disregard of a duty which he owed to the passenger to use due care. The passenger had a right not to be negligently handled, but he was not suing. The bystander had no right which was violated by negligence toward the passenger. And in view of the fact that the conductor could not have known the explosive character of the package, it was held that he had not shown negligence toward the plaintiff.

The duty to refrain from committing a wrongful act is not a duty owed to everyone who may be harmed by it. But the question of whose right is violated is not rigidly closed. The duty to refrain from physical violence was doubtless first established in order to safeguard an interest in bodily safety. But violence may do harm to persons whose bodily safety is not threatened by it. An employer suffers pecuniary

[1] 248 N.Y. 339 (1928).

loss when his customers or his workers are kept away by threats of violence in a labor dispute. But the customers or the workers who yielded to the threats have violated no rights of the employer. Nor have the pickets violated any right of *his* to bodily safety. It is now well settled, however, that he has a cause of action against the pickets. His right, which they have violated, is a right not to have his freedom to conduct his business interfered with by unlawful means, even if the unlawfulness consists primarily in its violation of someone else's rights, when the purpose of the interference is to harm him. Even without any such purpose, there is one case in which the Massachusetts court held that a woman whose house was burned had a cause of action against physical interference with the freedom of firemen to extinguish the fire. In that case, *Kiernan* v. *Metropolitan Construction Co.*,[2] it was assumed that the firemen were under no duty to do their work. They would have done so, however, if the defendants had not obstructed access to the hydrant and kept it obstructed, although they knew that the plaintiff might lose her house in consequence. Since they knew that the loss was likely to ensue, it can be said that they inflicted it on the plaintiff intentionally. But that does not seem to have been their purpose, which was simply to continue without interruption the work in which they were engaged. Nevertheless, the householder was held to have a right not to have the preservation of her property prevented by acts which were unlawful primarily because they violated a right of the firemen.

In cases like these, unquestionably the acts of the defendants have violated somebody's rights. The only question is whether the plaintiff is one of the persons who had a right in the matter. There are other cases in which it is clear that if anyone's right has been violated it is the plaintiff's, but where it is in dispute whether there has been a violation of *any* right—that is, whether the defendant's conduct was legally wrong. Thus, in the English case of *Fletcher* v. *Rylands*,[3] the defendants had constructed a reservoir on their own land, above some mine workings of which they were unaware and which were connected by underground passages with the plaintiff's colliery. Without any negligence on the defendants' part, the water from the reservoir, when it was filled, flowed through these passages and caused damage to the colliery. It was held in the Exchequer Chamber in 1866, in a

[2] 170 Mass. 378 (1898).
[3] L.R.1 Ex. 265 (1866). Affirmed in Rylands v. Fletcher, L.R.3 H.L. 330 (1868).

decision affirmed in the House of Lords in 1868, that the defendants were liable, on the theory that one who brings on to his land something likely to do harm if it escapes, must keep it there at his peril. But this theory has been generally repudiated by American courts. In *Losee* v. *Buchanan*,[4] the defendant's steam boiler exploded, without any negligence on his part, and portions of it were projected on to the plaintiff's land, where they damaged some of his property. The New York Commission of Appeals (predecessor of the present Court of Appeals) held in 1873, in an opinion by Commissioner Earl, that the defendant was not liable. He based his refusal to follow the English doctrine in part on grounds of economic policy, saying:

By becoming a member of civilized society, I am compelled to give up many of my natural rights, but I receive more than a compensation from the surrender by every other man of the same rights, and the security, advantage and protection which the laws give me. So, too, the general rules that I may have the exclusive and undisturbed use and possession of my real estate, and that I must so use my real estate as not to injure my neighbor, are much modified by the exigencies of the social state. We must have factories, machinery, dams, canals and railroads. They are demanded by the manifold wants of mankind, and lay at the basis of all our civilization. If I have any of these upon my lands, and they are not a nuisance and are not so managed as to become such, I am not responsible for any damage they accidentally and unavoidably do my neighbor. He receives his compensation for such damage by the general good, in which he shares, and the right which he has to place the same things upon his lands. I may not place or keep a nuisance upon my land to the damage of my neighbor, and I have my compensation for the surrender of this right to use my own as I will by the similar restriction imposed upon my neighbor for my benefit. I hold my property subject to the risk that it may be unavoidably or accidentally injured by those who live near me; and as I move about upon the public highways and in all places where other persons may lawfully be, I take the risk of being accidentally injured in my person by them without fault on their part. Most of the rights of property, as well as of person, in the social state, are not absolute but relative, and they must be so arranged and modified, not unnecessarily infringing upon natural rights, as upon the whole to promote the general welfare.[5]

The right to have one's property protected from accidental damage was denied here, not simply because the acts which caused the damage

[4] 51 N.Y. 476 (1873).

[5] *Id.* at 484–485. Later in the same year Justice Doe of the New Hampshire court entered into a searching criticism of the English rule. Brown v. Collins, 53 N.H. 442 (1873). The owner of a runaway horse was held not liable, in the absence of negligence, for property damage caused by the runaway.

did not fall into any clearly defined category of tort, but rather because it was thought that in arranging and modifying rights of property it would upon the whole promote the general welfare to cast the risk of accident on the neighbor rather than on the promoter of the enterprise. It was apparently assumed to be the function of the court to decide what arrangement of the rights of property would best promote the general welfare. Had it been thought that the general welfare would be better promoted, by making the victim of the accident pay no more for his share in that general welfare than others who derived as much benefit as he did, the risk of loss might have been placed on the promoter, who, by taking it into account in fixing his prices, might spread the burden among all those who made use of his products.

There are other cases in which courts have to decide whether acts performed on one man's property, which cause damage to another man's, shall be held actionable. Such cases frequently involve the diversion of water which would otherwise reach the plaintiff's land. It seems to have become a fairly well-recognized legal wrong (at least in many jurisdictions) for an owner of land through which a surface stream runs to divert that stream in such a way as to interfere with its flow to another's land. It seems also to be a wrong to dig in one's own land in such a way as to divert a known subterranean stream. But when the water which feeds a person's well comes from seepage or from an unknown subterranean stream, the operation of pumps by a neighboring landowner, causing the well to go dry, has been held lawful. Such was the holding of the English House of Lords in 1859 in *Chasemore* v. *Richards*.[6] And such was the holding in Pennsylvania in 1863 in *Haldeman* v. *Bruckhart*.[7] In that case Judge Strong (who later became a Justice of the United States Supreme Court) pronounced the plaintiff's loss of the use of his well to be *damnum absque injuria*—that is, damage without "injury" in the etymological meaning of that word, that is, violation of a right. Other instances of *damnum absque injuria* occur when one landowner puts up structures which diminish the value of neighboring property, either by changing the character of the neighborhood or by shutting out light and air from the neighbor. As a general rule, the neighbor has to put up with his economic loss.

The lawfulness of such acts, however, may depend in some juris-

[6] 7 H.L.C. 349 (1859).

[7] 45 Pa. 514 (1863).

dictions on the motive with which they are done. In *Haldeman* v. *Bruckhart* Judge Strong was careful to say, "We are not, however, to be understood as intimating that an owner may maliciously or negligently divert even an unknown subterranean stream to the damage of a lower proprietor." [8] And in what are known as "spite fence" cases, some courts, such as the supreme court of Michigan in *Flaherty* v. *Moran*,[9] have held it wrongful to build and maintain a structure when the only motive for doing so is to work harm to a neighbor by shutting out his light and air—though the same court, speaking by the same judge, held in *Kuzniak* v. *Kozminski* [10] that if the defendant wished to use the structure, its maintenance was lawful, even though "there may have been some malice displayed in putting it so near the complainant's house as to shut off some of the light."

The motive with which an act is done is sometimes, then, the factor which determines whether it is lawful or unlawful. Is malice, in the sense of spite or ill will, the only motive which makes an act unlawful when it would otherwise be lawful? If a man threatens to inflict harm on another by an act which would in ordinary circumstances be lawful for the purpose of bringing him to terms and obtaining some economic advantage, will the courts, as a matter of common law, hold the act illegal because they regard the economic advantage he is seeking unjustified? In other words, will they scrutinize the ends for which bargaining power is employed to determine the legality of its use? These questions will be considered in the next chapter.

[8] 45 Pa. at 521.

[9] 81 Mich. 52 (1890). For a recent case taking a contrary position see Cohen v. Perrino, 355 Pa. 455 (1947).

[10] 107 Mich. 444 (1895).

V

MALICIOUS WRONGS, PRIMA FACIE TORTS, AND CONSPIRACIES

THE circumstances under which usually lawful acts are to be held unlawful because of the motives which actuate them have been discussed at length by the English House of Lords and by numerous American courts and writers.

DECISIONS OF THE ENGLISH HOUSE OF LORDS

The so-called spite fence cases noted in the last chapter raise the question how far the lawfulness of an act may depend upon the motive which actuates it. Rendering one of the opinions of the English Court of Appeal in 1889 in *Mogul Steamship Co.* v. *McGregor, Gow & Co.*,[1] Lord Bowen, by way of dictum, made the following much-quoted statement:

Now, intentionally to do that which is calculated in the ordinary course of events to damage, and which does, in fact, damage another in that per-

1 L.R. 23 Q.B.D. 598, 613 (1889).

son's property or trade, is actionable if done without just cause or excuse. Such intentional action when done without just cause or excuse is what the law calls a malicious wrong.

The doctrine here expressed is sometimes known as the doctrine of prima facie torts: there is a prima facie presumption that the intentional infliction of damage is tortious, but that presumption can be rebutted by showing a justification. Taken without qualification, a "malicious wrong" might be something entirely devoid of malice in the ordinary sense of malevolence or spite. In legal parlance "malice" does not necessarily connote spite, and when one inflicts damage as a means of pressure to bring the other party to terms, courts might hold the infliction tortious if they did not approve the terms. They could hold that the pursuit of some terms constituted "just cause" for the infliction of damage, and the pursuit of other terms not so.

In England, however, the courts have not employed this doctrine to make themselves censors of economic bargaining. If the predominant motive for inflicting damage on another's property or trade is to promote the economic interests of those who inflict it, they seem to regard that motive as a justification—provided, of course, that the damage is inflicted by means that are not unlawful on more conventional grounds. And the members of the House of Lords strongly intimated in the most recent case on the point decided by that body that in the absence of concerted action the motive is wholly irrelevant—the only tort whose existence they regard as depending on motive being the tort of "conspiracy to injure."

Lord Bowen himself regarded economic self-advancement as a complete justification. The defendants, shipowners engaged in the China tea trade, formed a "conference," and, in order to attain a monopoly, engaged in cut-throat competition against any ship not a member of the conference and gave rebates to shippers who boycotted nonconference ships. In the words of Lord Fry, in another opinion rendered in the case, their scheme was "by means of competition in the near future, to prevent competition in the remoter future." [2] Though they were obviously seeking to fetter the trade of their rivals, Lord Bowen insisted that to hold their efforts unlawful would "impose a novel fetter upon trade." [3]

The case was affirmed by the House of Lords in 1891,[4] several of the Lords expressly adopting Bowen's views as their own. It was fol-

[2] L.R. 23 Q.B.D. at 622. [3] *Id.* at 615. [4] [1892] A.C. 25.

lowed by a notable series of House of Lords cases, extending from 1895 to 1941; in most of them divergent reasons were given in the several opinions rendered for reaching the decision.

In *Mayor of Bradford* v. *Pickles*,[5] decided in 1895, it was held that the defendant had an "absolute right" to dig in his own land, regardless of his motive, although his doing so diverted water from the town's reservoir. Assuming that his real object was to blackmail the town into buying his land, Lord Macnaghten remarked: "Well, he has something to sell, or, at any rate, he has something which he can prevent other people enjoying unless he is paid for it. . . . His conduct may seem shocking to a moral philosopher. But where is the malice?"[6] Even had there been malice (in the sense of spite), it would have made no difference, for, said Lord Macnaghten, "if the act, apart from motive, gives rise merely to damage without legal injury, the motive, however reprehensible it may be, will not supply that element."[7] It may be, however, as Justice Holmes suggested later,[8] that the privilege of working on one's own land was regarded as more absolute than other privileges and that the irrelevance of motive was meant to be asserted only for the more absolute privileges.

In *Allen* v. *Flood*,[9] however, decided in 1897, each of the six Lords who formed the majority declared that except in criminal law the motive actuating a single individual had nothing to do with the lawfulness of his act, though five of them intimated that "malice" might determine the lawfulness of combined action. A jury had found that Allen had "maliciously induced" an employer to discharge the plaintiffs, and the trial court had rendered a judgment for damages against him. The Court of Appeal affirmed, but the House of Lords reversed, by a vote of six to three.

Allen, an agent of the union to which the ironworkers engaged in repairing a ship belonged, had told the employer that the men would strike unless the plaintiffs, two shipwrights doing woodwork, were dismissed, because these plaintiffs, who belonged to another union, had previously done ironwork for another employer. It was not certain whether Allen had said he would call the men out or had merely informed the employer that they would quit. Since the president of Allen's union had testified that the union would not have struck

[5] [1895] A.C. 587. [6] *Id.* at 600–601. [7] *Id.* at 601.

[8] Aikens v. Wisconsin, 195 U.S. 194, 204 (1904). Cf. also Hollywood Silver Fox Farm, Ltd. v. Emmett [1936] 2 K.B.D. 468.

[9] [1898] A.C. 1.

The significance which he attached to combined action or to numbers is further revealed in his statement that

> coercion by threats, open or disguised, not only of bodily harm but of serious annoyance and damage, is prima facie, at all events, a wrong inflicted on the persons coerced; and in considering whether coercion has been applied or not, numbers cannot be disregarded.[21]

Lords Halsbury, Macnaghten, and Brampton, on the other hand, attached more weight to the element of combination. Lord Halsbury, who had been with the minority in *Allen* v. *Flood,* maintained that that case could be taken as authority only for what was decided on the hypothesis on which the majority proceeded—namely, "that the defendant there neither uttered nor carried into effect any threat at all." And, "it was further an element in the decision that there was no case of conspiracy or even combination." [22] Whether the existence of a threat in *Quinn* v. *Leathem* would have sufficed to make the defendant liable, even had there been no combination, he did not say; but he did seem to attach some significance to the fact of combination.

Lord Macnaghten agreed with the others that the defendant was liable here, although he considered that *Allen* v. *Flood* stood for the proposition that "an act which does not amount to a legal injury cannot be actionable because it is done with a bad motive." [23] No act of Quinn or his associates, taken singly, amounted to a legal injury; but in combination he held that they did. "That a conspiracy to injure—an oppressive combination—differs widely from an invasion of civil rights by a single individual cannot be doubted." [24]

Lord Brampton was still more explicit in regarding combination as essential to the case. He declared that "the real and substantial cause of action is an unlawful conspiracy to molest the plaintiff, a trader in carrying on his business, and by so doing to invade his undoubted right" to carry it on according to his own free discretion.[25] It is the willful doing of the mischief which the men combined to bring about, "coupled with the resulting damage, which constitutes the cause of action, not of necessity the means by which it was accomplished." [26] The cause of action is there, even if those means were not themselves unlawful. The *Mogul* case is distinguishable, since "competition is not even suggested as a justification for the acts now complained of." [27]

[21] [1901] A.C. at 540. [22] *Id.* at 506–507. [23] *Id.* at 508–509.
[24] *Id.* at 511. [25] *Id.* at 525. [26] *Id.* at 530. [27] *Id.* at 528.

It was nearly a quarter of a century before the House of Lords again had occasion to discuss the matter at length, though in 1909 the defendant in *Conway* v. *Wade* [28] was held liable for wrongfully inducing an employer to dismiss the plaintiff, by threatening to call a strike. In that case, however, the discussion chiefly concerned whether the defendant acted "in contemplation or furtherance of a trade dispute." If he did, his acts would have been lawful under the Trade Disputes Act of 1906. The jury found that he did not so act. The Court of Appeal reversed on the ground that he did. The House of Lords, however, held that the jury's finding should not be disturbed and that the trial court's judgment for the plaintiff should be restored. The "alleged perversity" of the jury's finding was, in Lord Atkinson's view, "the only question raised by the notice of appeal." [29] He did say, however, that, apart from the Trade Disputes Act he thought the plaintiff would be entitled to a verdict, "notwithstanding that the defendant did not conspire with another, or with others, but merely acted alone." [30] The other Lords seemed to take the same position.

In 1925 the case of *Sorrell* v. *Smith* [31] was decided. Here the defendants acted in concert, and it was their threat which caused the damage to the plaintiff; but the defendants were advancing their own economic interests—in fact, they were defending them against an attack instituted by the plaintiff and his associates. The House was unanimous in holding that the plaintiff had no cause of action.

A union (or federation) of retail newsdealers to which Sorrell belonged objected to a newcomer's opening a shop in contravention of the union's "distance limit policy." To drive him out, they sought to induce the wholesaler from whom the newcomer obtained his papers to cease supplying him. When the wholesaler refused to comply with their demands, they sought to bring pressure on him by calling for volunteers to transfer their custom to other wholesalers. Sorrell volunteered, and transferred to Watson & Sons. To counteract this boycott of the original wholesaler and of the newcomer, the Circulating Managers' Committee of the London newspapers, of which Smith was a member, threatened to cut off Watson's supply of papers unless Watson ceased to supply Sorrell. Watson yielded and terminated its contract with Sorrell, who then sued for an injunction.

When two or more men combine to inflict harm on another's trade or property, by means not otherwise unlawful, all the Lords agreed

28 [1909] A.C. 506. 29 *Id.* at 518. 30 *Id.* at 516. 31 [1925] A.C. 700.

that the lawfulness of their acts would depend upon their motive. They disagreed as to whether the lawfulness of harm inflicted by a single individual would depend upon it. They also disagreed somewhat as to what motives would make combined action unlawful.

As to combinations, Lord Cave, in an opinion to which Lord Atkinson subscribed, deduced these two propositions from the cases:

> (1) A combination of two or more persons wilfully to injure a man in his trade is unlawful and, if it results in damage to him, is actionable.
> (2) If the real purpose of the combination is, not to injure another, but to forward or defend the trade of those who enter into it, then no wrong is committed and no action will lie, although damage to another ensues.
> The distinction between the two classes of cases is sometimes expressed by saying that in cases of the former class there is not, while in cases of the latter class there is, just cause or excuse for the action taken.[32]

Malice, in the sense of spite or ill will, would be neither essential to illegality, nor conclusive of it.[33]

Lord Sumner, however, thought that spite was essential and that without it *Quinn* v. *Leathem* would have been decided differently.[34] If defendants act from some motive other than a "coldly selfish" one they will be liable, but "what other motive can there be in such a matter, beyond selfishness and malice, except, indeed, mere irresponsible wantonness?" [35] Sumner agreed with Cave, however, that the presence of spite was not conclusive of illegality. He was not prepared to say that the conduct of a member of a competitive combination, otherwise justifiable, was illegal "if it is proved that he adds to his desire to make money a personal animosity against the rival, against whom he acts, and a personal glee in seeing him overtaken by defeat." [36] He found it beyond his power to draw a definite line "between acts, whose real purpose is to advance the defendants' interests, and acts, whose real purpose is to injure the plaintiff in his trade"—though he seems to have recognized that in *Quinn* v. *Leathem* the latter purpose existed without the former.

Lord Buckmaster was somewhat ambiguous as to whether spite was essential to a holding of illegality. Discussing *Quinn* v. *Leathem*, he said that the case really rested on the jury's finding of "wrongfully and maliciously" in the light of the trial judge's summing up,

32 [1925] A.C. at 712.
33 *Id.* at 714.
34 *Id.* at 735 and 741.
35 *Id.* at 739.
36 *Id.* at 742.

> in which it was pointed out that by "wrongfully" was meant not only with intent to injure the plaintiff, but also not in furtherance of any trade dispute. . . . In other words, the expanded finding of the jury was this. The acts done have for their purpose the plaintiff's injury as distinguished from acts done for advancing the defendants' own interests, and were, therefore, wrongful and malicious.[37]

Perhaps Buckmaster assumed that spite was the only alternative to a motive to advance one's own interests, for at a later point, in criticizing Bowen, he maintained that a combination purposely interfering with a man's trade "was not illegal without malice, and the onus is not on the defendant to justify but on the plaintiff to prove that the act was spiteful and malicious." [38]

Lord Dunedin did not discuss malevolence as such. In determining whether the combined infliction of damage was an unlawful conspiracy, he would ask the jury whether the purpose of injuring the plaintiff was "the real root of the acts that grew from it, or was the true motive something else, such, as for instance, the furtherance of the defendants' own business?" [39] And whether an act is done in the legitimate furtherance of one's own business "is really no more than a piece of evidence which enables the jury to answer" this question.[40] As to the present case, he concluded "as a juryman" [the case had been tried without a jury], that there was no proof of a "conspiracy to injure." The defendants' action "was a defensive action to protect their own trade against being dictated to by the federation; it was, in no sense, a conspiracy to injure Sorrell . . ." He inquired into the facts, not to determine whether there was justification, but to determine "whether there was any proof of illegal action, i.e., a conspiracy to injure." [41]

So long as the motive was a proper one, it seems to have been assumed that it was immaterial that the damage to the plaintiff was brought about by the employment of threats or coercion. Lord Cave said that a threat to withdraw trade is not necessarily illegal,[42] and Lord Dunedin insisted that threats to do lawful acts do not constitute an illegal means.[43] According to Lord Buckmaster, "A threat to do an act which is lawful cannot, in my opinion, create a cause of action, whether the act threatened is to be done by many or by one." [44] In

[37] *Id.* at 744–745.
[38] *Id.* at 748.
[39] *Id.* at 717.
[40] *Id.* at 726.
[41] *Id.* at 729–730.
[42] *Id.* at 714.
[43] *Id.* at 730.
[44] *Id.* at 747.

Lord Sumner's opinion alone does there seem to be any survival of Lord Lindley's belief, in *Quinn* v. *Leathem,* that coercion was in itself illegal. In holding that ill will was essential in *Quinn* v. *Leathem,* Sumner thought it necessary to deny that there were any threats there,[45] which would apparently, in his view, have made the defendants liable even without spite. He denied that in the present case the Circulating Managers' Committee had used threats against the wholesalers, and advanced the untenable contention that the latter had exercised a "free choice" when they preferred doing without Sorrell's trade to losing their supply from the publishers.[46]

Intimidation or coercion, of course, may be relevant to determine whether a plaintiff's loss was in fact brought about by the defendants' threats. This is, perhaps, what Sumner had in mind when, after denying that this was the occasion for expressing any decided opinion "as to the part which combination or concerted action plays in an alleged tort of this kind," [47] he asked:

> Is not there a good deal to be said for thinking that combination in such a connection is really only a particular form of intimidation, and that, where no one is or ought to be frightened, the combined traders are not tortfeasors, unless they would also have been tortfeasors, if they had acted simultaneously, but spontaneously, in identical ways but without concert or combination? [48]

Sumner evidently did not think that the previous decisions had foreclosed inquiry into the motive which actuates a single individual when he intentionally inflicts harm on another. Neither did Cave or Atkinson. Cave said he was not prepared to take a position on the question whether combination was an essential element of illegality,[49] and Atkinson, consistently with his position in *Conway* v. *Wade,* subscribed to Cave's opinion. *Mayor of Bradford* v. *Pickles* was not mentioned in any of the opinions.

Two of the five Lords who participated, however, took a different position. Lord Buckmaster said that one of the propositions established by *Quinn* v. *Leathem* was "that the case of *Allen* v. *Flood* depended upon the fact that the defendant there acted alone and neither uttered nor carried into effect any threat at all." [50] If so, *Allen* v. *Flood* established nothing as to a defendant who acts alone, but does utter or carry into effect some threat. Buckmaster, however, seems to have

[45] [1925] A.C. at 737. [46] *Id.* at 732–733. [47] *Id.* at 739.
[48] *Id.* at 741. [49] *Id.* at 713–714. [50] *Id.* at 744.

thought that *Allen* v. *Flood* established the irrelevancy even of such a defendant's motive. It was on this assumption that he remarked later:

Nor because an act done by an individual if lawful cannot become unlawful when done for the express purpose of injury, does it result that the same rule applies to acts done in combination, for the actual combination to injure lies at the root of the illegality.[51]

He added that he accepted Lord Dunedin's "careful exposition of the law" and had nothing to add to it.

Like Buckmaster and like Brampton in *Quinn* v. *Leathem*, Dunedin regarded the combination to injure as the root of the illegality in torts of this nature. Maintaining that infliction of loss on a plaintiff is actionable only if the means used are illegal, whatever the motive, Dunedin managed to bring in motive by the side door. There was historically a crime known as criminal conspiracy. If defendants inflict loss by means of such a crime, then the means used *are* illegal, and the plaintiff can recover. But as in the case of all crimes, motive, or *mens rea* (here "a desire to injure"), is a determining factor.[52] By this process, Dunedin was able to make recovery turn, as we have seen, on the "true motive" of the defendants' acts. But a single individual, of course, acting alone, could not be guilty of a criminal conspiracy.

In *Sorrell* v. *Smith*, the argument for the defeated party, Sorrell, was made by Sir John Simon, K.C., and Maugham, K.C., who contended unsuccessfully that interference with a plaintiff's "right to carry on his business in his own way" is unlawful and requires justification, and that pursuit of the defendants' own interests is no justification if the interference is effected by "the use of illegal methods—namely, threats and coercion." [53] When in 1941 the House of Lords decided *Crofter Hand Woven Harris Tweed Co.* v. *Veitch*,[54] Simon and Maugham were among the five members of that body who rendered judgments. They did not, however, renew the stand they had taken as counsel for Sorrell. All five Lords addressed themselves to the question whether the tort of "conspiracy to injure" had been made out. All but Lord Wright ignored any question of a "right to carry on business" or of threats and coercion, and Wright declared that such questions were not significant.

Spinning mills had been established on the island of Lewis, in the Outer Hebrides, to spin yarn which was delivered to hand-weaving

[51] *Id.* at 748–749. [52] *Id.* at 725–726. [53] *Id.* at 702–703.
[54] [1942] A.C. 435.

crofters to weave into Harris Tweed, which the mills then "finished." Traffic with the mainland came through the port of Stornoway. Ninety percent of the spinners in the mills and all the dockers at Stornoway were members of the Transport and General Workers' Union. Meanwhile, independent producers, of whom the appellant in this case was one, obtained their yarn from the mainland at prices lower than those charged by the island mills. In the apparent belief that this practice was detrimental to the interests of the union, its Scottish area secretary, Mr. Veitch, after consultation with the secretary of the Mill-Owners' Association (Mr. Skinner), sent word to the Stornoway branch secretary of the union (Mr. Mackenzie), calling an "embargo" on all yarn arriving at Stornoway for the appellants. Mackenzie passed the instructions on to the dockers, who at once complied unanimously. The appellants then sought an interdict (the Scottish term for an injunction) against Veitch and Mackenzie to stop the embargo. An interim interdict was issued, and the embargo was raised, but the Lord Ordinary, who passed on the facts as well as the law, subsequently recalled it, on the ground that an intention to injure the appellants' trade had not been proved. On appeal, this decision was affirmed by the Inner House, and then by the House of Lords. The case presented a question of Scottish law, but, said Lord Simon, "it was not suggested that, as regards the law applicable to the present action, there was any material difference between the Scottish law of delict and the English law of tort." [55]

All agreed that if there was any tort at all it was the tort of conspiracy to injure. The alleged tort, said Lord Wright, "cannot be merely that the appellants' right to freedom in conducting their trade has been interfered with. That right is not an absolute or unconditional right." [56] He distinguished it from such a right as one to have a contract performed, interference with which would be illegal unless justified.[57] As for coercion, there was no coercion of the dockers, but even if there had been, Lord Wright intimated that it would not necessarily have been tortious.

In *Quinn* v. *Leathem* [he said] a wide meaning was given to words like threats, intimidation or coercion, especially by Lord Lindley, but that was not the ratio decidendi adopted by the House. These words . . . are not terms of art and are consistent either with legality or illegality. They are not correctly used in the circumstances of a case like this. . . . There

[55] [1942] A.C. at 438. [56] *Id.* at 463. [57] *Id.* at 465–466.

is nothing unlawful in giving a warning or intimation that if the party addressed pursues a certain line of conduct, others may act in a manner which he will not like and which will be prejudicial to his interests, so long as nothing unlawful is threatened or done.[58]

He proceeded to quote Lord Buckmaster's words on the subject in *Sorrell* v. *Smith.*

The defendants claimed that there was no combination here, and hence that there could be no conspiracy to injure. Had this claim been sustained, it would have been necessary to decide whether there was any other tort. But this claim was not sustained. The Lord Ordinary held that, while it had not been proved that the union officials Veitch and Mackenzie, the only defendants in the case, had combined with the millowners, they had, nevertheless, combined with each other. The Inner House found the evidence sufficient to involve Skinner, of the millowners, in the combination. In the Lords, Lord Simon agreed with the Lord Ordinary that Skinner was not involved,[59] but that the two defendants acted in combination.[60] Lord Porter seemed inclined to agree, but was prepared to treat the case, as did the other three Lords, on the footing that the wider combination had been proved.[61]

Since in the view of all the Lords the harm had been inflicted by combined action, it was not essential to the decision to take any position on the relevance of motive when harm is inflicted by a single individual. All but Lord Thankerton, however, did take a position on this question. Contrary to the intimations of three of the five Lords in *Sorrell* v. *Smith,* and contrary to what seems to have been the holding in *Conway* v. *Wade,* they concluded that, in the absence of combination, motive was irrelevant in English law. Lord Maugham had never "felt any difficulty in seeing the great difference between the acts of one person and the acts in combination of two or of a multitude." [62] Lords Simon, Wright, and Porter, however, felt that the explanation of what they took to be the settled rule was not so easy. The explanation that numbers have more power to inflict damage than has a single individual they found unsatisfactory, as it is not always true. "The power of a big corporation or trader," said Lord Wright, "may be greater than that of a large number of smaller fry in the trade." [63] Yet he maintained that to hold motive material in the

[58] *Id.* at 466–467.
[59] *Id.* at 439.
[60] *Id.* at 441.
[61] *Id.* at 481–482.
[62] *Id.* at 448.
[63] *Id.* at 468.

case of a single individual "seems to be inconsistent with the express rulings in *Allen* v. *Flood*." [64] He suggested, however, that there might be exceptions to the rule, saying, "I need not consider whether any qualification may hereafter be found admissible."

While four at least of the Lords thought motive irrelevant in determining the lawfulness of an act done by a single individual, all five agreed that it was relevant in the case of concerted action. All agreed with Lord Cave's test, to determine whether the "real purpose" of the combination was to injure or damage the plaintiff, or to forward or defend the trade of those in the combination, though Lord Porter objected to Cave's putting it in terms of justification.[65] But if the purpose was to harm the plaintiff only as a means to promote the defendants' own interests, then harming the plaintiff was not the "real purpose." Lord Porter assumed that this was what Cave meant when he spoke of "a threat being to forward trade interests and not wilfully and ultroneously to injure the trade of another, by which I think he means not wilfully to injure the trade of another save for the purpose of forwarding one's own." [66] In this case the damage inflicted by the combination was "but a step to an end. The combination was therefore not to injure but was to defend the interests of the parties to it." [67]

It would be possible, however, that defendants might wish to harm the plaintiff, not merely as a means to forwarding their own interests, but as a separate end in itself. As Lord Sumner said in *Sorrell* v. *Smith*, a member of a competitive combination may "add to his desire to make money a personal animosity against the rival, against whom he acts, and a personal glee in seeing him overtaken by defeat." There was no evidence that such was the case here, and Lord Thankerton did not discuss the question. Lords Simon, Maugham, and Wright, however, declared that in the case of mixed motives, lawfulness would depend on which motive was predominant. If the predominant motive was to advance their own interests, the combiners' acts were lawful, even though there was a subordinate motive of vengeance; if the desire to harm the plaintiff was predominant, their acts were unlawful even though they thought they were at the same time forwarding their own interests.[68] Lord Porter was more noncommittal. "If I

[64] [1942] A.C. at 466. Simon's discussion of the point will be found at 443–444, and Porter's at 487–489.

[65] *Id.* at 495–496.

[66] *Id.* at 491.

[67] *Id.* at 494–495.

[68] Lord Simon at 445; Lord Maugham at 452–453; Lord Wright at 478.

thought," he said, "that in the present case the object of the parties to the combination was to ruin the appellants, even though they hoped thereby each to gain an advantage for himself, I should desire to consider the matter further before deciding that the respondents were not liable, but I do not think that such a case has been proved." [69]

If the predominant motive is malice in the sense of malevolence, however, it seems safe to say that the acts of the combination would be held unlawful by the English courts. Could they be unlawful without malevolence? Lord Simon said they would be unlawful unless the predominant motive was to forward or defend the combiners' interests.[70] Lord Maugham thought that if the real purpose was not to advance those interests, "some other just cause or excuse" must be shown to avoid liability. The mere fact that the predominant motive was not to injure the plaintiff would not suffice.[71] Lord Wright agreed.[72] Lord Porter, after quoting Lord Sumner's question by asking what other motive there could be "beyond selfishness and malice except, indeed, mere irresponsible wantonness," suggested the case "where the defendants desire neither their own business advantage nor the injury of the plaintiff, e.g., where they combine to compel him to subscribe to an extraneous charitable fund." [73] That not being the case here, Lord Porter did not volunteer an opinion as to the lawfulness of such a combination.

Though a predominant motive of self-interest would generally serve to render the combination lawful, certain qualifications were suggested. If it had been proved that the union had acted in response to a bribe from the millowners—whether in the form of a contribution of money or of an offer to employ only union members in the mills—several of the Lords thought that would not be the kind of self-interest which would prevent the defendants' action from constituting a conspiracy to injure. Such "indirect gains," thought Lord Simon, "would not provide a justification." [74] Lord Maugham took the same position.[75] Lord Thankerton doubted "if it would be legitimate for a union to use a means of pressure with which it had no connection except that which was constituted by a money payment, for instance." [76] Lord Wright said that since the facts did not support the appellants' contention "that the respondents or the union were bribed and were mere mercenaries, not interested in the embargo except

[69] *Id.* at 490.
[70] *Id.* at 446.
[71] *Id.* at 450–451.
[72] *Id.* at 470–471.
[73] *Id.* at 491–493.
[74] *Id.* at 446–447.
[75] *Id.* at 451.
[76] *Id.* at 460.

for the reward which was in its nature unrelated to the embargo," he need not discuss whether such a "separate and mercenary" interest could serve as a justification.[77]

The interests which Veitch and Mackenzie were seeking to advance were not their own individual interests, but those of their union. This, however, was held to make their action lawful.[78] The prosperity of the island trade was an interest they had in common with the millowners, with whom most of the Lords thought they were combining. Even if the millowners' interest in obtaining a monopoly of the yarn used on the island be thought distinct from the union's interest in securing better conditions of employment, still, so long as each group in the combination was pursuing its own economic ends, the fact that their interests were not identical made no difference.[79] It is hard to see why the dockers were not parties to the combination; but even so, though their immediate interest did not lie in the conditions of employment in the mills, nevertheless, Lords Thankerton and Wright declared that they had a joint interest in promoting the interests of the union as a whole.[80] Moreover, so long as the defendants honestly believe that their combined action will promote their own interests, the validity of that belief is not to be questioned in the courts.[81]

So, in the English law as expounded in the latest case, the intentional and concerted infliction of harm by means otherwise lawful does not constitute a conspiracy to injure, so long as the predominant motive is to forward the interests of those in the combination—unless the interests are such "indirect" ones as qualifying for a bribe. And the courts will seemingly not weigh the conflicting interests of plaintiff and defendants to determine the legality of the action. Liability cannot be determined, said Lord Simon, "by asking whether the damage inflicted to secure the purpose is disproportionately severe: this may throw doubts on the bona fides of the avowed purpose, but once the legitimate purpose is established, and no unlawful means are involved, the quantum of damage is irrelevant." [82] And in the absence of combination, according to dicta in the *Harris Tweed* case, the purpose itself is irrelevant.

In the *Mogul* case Lord Bowen had rejected the notion that "a

[77] [1942] A.C. at 479–480.
[78] Simon at 447; Maugham at 456; Thankerton at 460; Wright at 478; Porter at 490.
[79] See Lord Porter's discussion at 493–495.
[80] Thankerton at 460; Wright at 480.
[81] Wright at 477–478; Maugham at 455–457.
[82] *Id.* at 447.

combination of capitalists differentiates the case of acts jointly done by them from similar acts done by a single man of capital." If it does, he said,

> one rich capitalist may innocently carry competition to a length which would become unlawful in the case of a syndicate with a joint capital no larger than his own, and one individual merchant may lawfully do that which a firm or a partnership may not. What limits, on such a theory, would be imposed by law on the competitive action of a joint-stock company limited, is a problem which might well puzzle a casuist.[83]

What constitutes a combination does, indeed, present many puzzling problems. Lord Wright in the *Harris Tweed* case, discussing Lord Sumner's "artificial case" in *Sorrell* v. *Smith* of an owner who "conspired" with a partner to whom he had given a small share of his business, said, "For practical purposes the position there is the same as if he had remained a sole trader," and added: "The fact that the sole trader employed servants or agents in the conduct of his business would not per se in my opinion make these other co-conspirators with him." [84] But in the same case, Lord Simon, in holding that a combination existed between Veitch and Mackenzie, said that "even if Mackenzie should be regarded as only obeying orders received from his superior, the combination would still exist if he appreciated what he was about." [85] Then why should not Mackenzie be regarded as combining with the dockers even if he had ordered the embargo on his own initiative, without any direction from Veitch? Such puzzling problems would not arise if the House of Lords had followed Lord Bowen's more sensible views as to the significance of combination.

AMERICAN DECISIONS

Lawfulness of a Harmful Act Dependent on Its Purpose

American courts have shown less reluctance than has the House of Lords to adjudge acts of single individuals unlawful because of their motive. The chief significance of combination in this country, as we shall see, is to supply the element of affirmative action in cases where otherwise it would be held that the defendant inflicted the harm solely by means of "nonfeasance." In this country, too, a motive to advance the defendant's own economic interests has not always served as justification.

[83] L.R. 23 Q.B.D. 598, 617 (1889).
[84] [1942] A.C. at 468.
[85] *Id.* at 441.

However, in deciding whether acts designed to harm the plaintiff, which are otherwise lawful, become unlawful on account of the motive, American courts, like some members of the House of Lords, have sometimes resorted to question-begging language concerning "rights." In holding acts unlawful, the decision is frequently placed on the ground that they are designed to coerce the plaintiff to desist from exercising some "right"—such as the "right" to run a shop nonunion. That was one of the grounds on which the Supreme Court in 1917, speaking through Justice Pitney, affirmed an injunction against officers of the United Mine Workers in *Hitchman Coal & Coke Co.* v. *Mitchell.*[86] To bring about a strike "to compel plaintiff, through fear of financial loss, to consent to unionization of the mine as the lesser evil, was an unlawful purpose." In holding acts lawful, on the other hand, the decision may be placed on the ground that, though the attempt is to induce the plaintiff to forego the exercise of some "right," still the defendant is merely exercising some "right" of his own; and since the plaintiff is free to decline the defendant's terms, he is not being coerced if he accepts them—even though the price of declining may be loss of his job. Thus, in 1915, in *Coppage* v. *Kansas,*[87] the Court in another opinion by Pitney decided not only that an employer had a "right" at common law to discharge a man after threatening to do so if he would not sign a nonunion contract but also that a state legislature could not curtail this "right" without violating the Fourteenth Amendment. There was, in fact, as much compulsion on the worker, "through fear of financial loss, to consent" to the nonunion contract "as the lesser evil," as there was on the employer in the *Hitchman* case to consent to unionization. But Pitney could not see it. The worker, he said, "is free to decline the employment on those terms, just as the employer may decline to offer employment on any other." Elsewhere in the opinion Pitney insisted that there was no coercion of the employee "by means unlawful without the act," [88] while in the *Hitchman* case he did find some of the means used by the union organizers unlawful on other grounds. But he did not there base his finding of compulsion solely on that unlawfulness. The threat of finan-

[86] 245 U.S. 229 (1917). The union was also held to be inducing breach of "yellow dog" contracts, by which the employees agreed not to join a union while in the plaintiff's employ. The injunction, however, went further than enjoining breach of the contracts, and so did Pitney's reasoning. Justice Brandeis wrote a dissenting opinion (*id.* at 263), in which he was joined by Holmes and Clarke. It is not clear whether Pitney was laying down principles of "general" common law or of what he conceived to be the common law of West Virginia, where the acts took place.

[87] 236 U.S. 1 (1915). [88] *Id.* at 8.

cial loss was sufficient. He nowhere explained why fear of economic loss could be said to "compel" an employer to accede to terms, while fear of loss of a job would leave an employee "free" to reject them.[89]

Compulsion, or coercion, of course, is not necessarily unlawful. As long ago as 1842, Chief Justice Lemuel Shaw, of Massachusetts, in the leading case of *Commonwealth* v. *Hunt*,[90] held that the facts alleged in a certain indictment failed to set forth a criminal conspiracy. As to one of the counts in the indictment, which charged that the defendants conspired not to work for anyone who should employ any workman not a member of their society and that by means of this conspiracy they compelled one Wait to discharge one Horne, Shaw held that the purpose of inducing all engaged in the occupation to join the society was not an unlawful purpose and that the means alleged for accomplishing that purpose were not themselves necessarily unlawful. As to whether it was unlawful to "compel," he said,

> it would depend altogether upon the force of the word "compel," which may be used in the sense of coercion, or duress, by force or fraud. . . . If, for instance, the indictment had averred a conspiracy, by the defendants, to compel Wait to turn Horne out of his employment, and to accomplish that object by the use of force or fraud, it would have been a very different case. . . . But whatever might be the force of the word "compel," unexplained by its connexion, it is disarmed and rendered harmless by the precise statement of the means, by which such compulsion was to be effected. It was the agreement not to work for him, by which they compelled Wait to decline employing Horne longer.[91]

In this connection, some remarks in Justice Holmes's dissenting opinion in *Vegelahn* v. *Guntner* [92] are pertinent:

[89] In the Coppage case the threat to sever the employment relationship was carried out by the direct action of the employer who made the threat, while in the Hitchman case it would have been carried out by the employees, at the instigation of the defendant union organizers, who made the threat but would not have been the ones to carry it out. Pitney laid some stress on this distinction in the Hitchman case and intimated that had the employees there, instead of outside instigators, threatened the employer with financial loss unless he unionized the mine, the case might have presented a different question. This may well be, since the justification for the compulsion would have been different. But there would have been fully as much compulsion on the employer to forego his "right" to run nonunion in the one case as in the other.

Justices Holmes, Day, and Hughes dissented in the Coppage case, which is discussed more fully on pp. 390–395, *infra*. The case can no longer be regarded as authoritative. See Phelps Dodge v. NLRB, 313 U.S. 177, 187 (1941).

[90] 4 Metc. 111 (Mass. 1842).

[91] *Id.* at 132–133. Shaw was evidently using the word "force" as synonymous with "violence." For an illuminating account of the circumstances and background of this case see Walter Nelles, *Commonwealth v. Hunt* (1932) 32 COL. L. REV. 1128.

[92] 167 Mass. 92, 107 (1896).

I pause here to remark that the word "threats" often is used as if, when it appeared that threats had been made, it appeared that unlawful conduct had begun. But it depends on what you threaten. As a general rule, even if subject to some exceptions, what you may do in a certain event you may threaten to do, that is, give warning of your intention to do it in that event, and thus allow the other person the chance of avoiding the consequences. So as to "compulsion," it depends on how you "compel." *Commonwealth* v. *Hunt*, ... So as to "annoyance" or "intimidation."

In this case, which involved a dispute over wages, Holmes, disagreeing with the majority, thought that the injunction should not forbid a patrol of two pickets and a refusal of social intercourse with strikebreakers, but only threats of personal violence and physical obstruction of property and inducements to break contracts. The latter would constitute unlawful means for securing an economic advantage. Threats to commit lawful acts would not. But a combination to harm a plaintiff, even by doing lawful acts, would, to Holmes, require a justification.[93] Justification would turn on questions of policy, but Holmes went even further than Lord Bowen in holding competition to be a justification. Justification "is not limited to struggles between persons of the same class competing for the same end. It applies to all conflicts of temporal interests." [94] He declared that "the doctrine generally has been accepted that free competition is worth more to society than it costs, and that on this ground the infliction of the damage is privileged"—adding, in the next paragraph, "when the damage is done not for its own sake, but as an instrumentality in reaching the end of victory in the battle of trade."

While noncommittal in this case as to whether combination is essential to bring the prima facie tort doctrine into play at all, Holmes denied emphatically that when harm is inflicted for the justifiable purpose of competition it becomes unlawful merely because inflicted by concerted action. "Free competition," he said,[95] "means combination," adding:

One of the eternal conflicts out of which life is made up is that between the effort of every man to get the most he can for his services, and that of society, disguised under the name of capital, to get his services for the least possible return. Combination on the one side is patent and powerful. Combination on the other is the necessary and desirable counterpart, if the battle is to be carried on in a fair and equal way.

[93] 167 Mass. at 105. [94] *Id.* at 107. [95] *Id.* at 108.

In 1894, shortly before the decision in *Vegelahn* v. *Guntner*, Holmes had published an article entitled *Privilege, Malice, and Intent,*[96] which has had considerable influence on legal thought. In that article he spoke more at length of the nature of the question which judges must answer in deciding whether there is justification and of their tendency to avoid facing the issue, by begging the question and seeming to make deductions from propositions as to the "rights" or "wrongs" of plaintiff or defendant. On this point he said:

> . . . the intentional infliction of temporal damage, or the doing of an act manifestly likely to inflict such damage and inflicting it, is actionable if done without just cause. When the defendant escapes, the court is of opinion that he has acted with just cause. There are various justifications. In these instances, the justification is that the defendant is privileged knowingly to inflict the damage complained of.
>
> But whether, and how far, a privilege shall be allowed is a question of policy. Questions of policy are legislative questions, and judges are shy of reasoning from such grounds. Therefore, decisions for or against the privilege, which really can stand only upon such grounds, often are presented as hollow deductions from empty general propositions like *sic utere tuo ut alienum non laedas,* which teaches nothing but a benevolent yearning, or else are put as if they themselves embodied a postulate of the law and admitted of no further deduction, as when it is said that, although there is temporal damage, there is no wrong; whereas, the very thing to be found out is whether there is a wrong or not, and if not, why not.[97]

He went on to say that when the question of policy is faced, the answer must be determined by the particular character of the case; "the worth of the result, or the gain from allowing the act to be done, has to be compared with the loss which it inflicts." Then, after giving some illustrations and referring to the English case of *Temperton* v. *Russell,*[98] which had held certain trade union practices unlawful, Holmes added:

> The ground of decision really comes down to a proposition of policy of rather a delicate nature concerning the merit of the particular benefit to themselves intended by the defendants, and suggests a doubt whether judges with different economic sympathies might not decide such a case differently when brought face to face with the issue.[99]

Holmes went on to notice some decisions which held certain acts done in combination unlawful, when the same acts would be privi-

[96] (1894) 8 HARV. L. REV. 1, reprinted in Holmes, COLLECTED LEGAL PAPERS (1921) 117.
[97] *Id.* at 3. [98] [1893] 1 Q.B. 715. [99] 8 HARV. L. REV. at 8.

leged if done by one person, and raised the question "whether the courts are not flying in the face of the organization of the world which is taking place so fast, and of its inevitable consequences." [100]

By 1900 the Massachusetts court had come around to Holmes's approach to the question, though not accepting his view as to the particular justification in the case before it. In *Plant* v. *Woods* [101] a painters' union in Springfield, affiliated with a national organization whose headquarters was in Baltimore, had a jurisdictional controversy with another painters' union, affiliated with a national organization whose headquarters was in Lafayette, Indiana. The Baltimore union threatened to strike unless the employers would require employees of the Lafayette union, under penalty of dismissal, to join the Baltimore union. There was no violence or threat of it, though the court expressed the opinion that a strike would necessarily lead to violence. The Baltimore union was not seeking to obtain for its own members the jobs held by the Lafayette men, but to force the latter to affiliate. It was held that the officers and members of the Lafayette union were entitled to an injunction restraining the activities of the Baltimore union.

The court did not, as in *Vegelahn* v. *Guntner,* place its decision on the ground that knowingly causing the plaintiffs to lose their jobs by coercive methods was necessarily unlawful. Justice Hammond, for the majority, pointed out, it is true, that the defendants' methods were coercive. But it required something more to make them unlawful in his opinion. After citing Holmes's "instructive article" in the *Harvard Law Review,* he pointed out that the court already had had occasion to consider how far such coercive, damaging, and intentional acts are justifiable.[102] Under some circumstances they have been found justifiable; under others not so. Hiş reason for finding the present acts unjustifiable is placed expressly on a policy judgment.

> The necessity [he said] that the plaintiffs should join this association is not so great, nor is its relation to the rights of the defendants, as compared with the right of the plaintiffs to be free from molestation, such as to bring the acts of the defendants under the shelter of the principles of trade competition. Such acts are without justification, and therefore are malicious and unlawful, and the conspiracy thus to force the plaintiffs was unlawful. Such conduct is intolerable, and inconsistent with the spirit of our laws.[103]

100 8 HARV. L. REV. at 9. 101 176 Mass. 492 (1900). 102 *Id.* at 500.
103 *Id.* at 502.

It was only on the point of justification that Holmes (now Chief Justice) dissented. He rejoiced at the court's approach to the question and its abandonment of the doctrine seemingly laid down in *Vegelahn* v. *Guntner*, saying:

> . . . If the decision in the present case simply had relied upon *Vegelahn* v. *Guntner*, . . . I should have hesitated to say anything, although I might have stated that my personal opinion had not been weakened by the substantial agreement with my views to be found in the judgments of the majority of the House of Lords in *Allen* v. *Flood*. . . . But much to my satisfaction, if I may say so, the court has seen fit to adopt the mode of approaching the question which I believe to be the correct one, and to open an issue which otherwise I might have thought closed. The difference between my brethren and me now seems to be a difference of degree, and the line of reasoning followed makes it proper for me to explain where the difference lies.[104]

The difference, he went on to explain, lay in the fact that, although the defendants' immediate purpose of strengthening their union was "one degree more remote" than the raising of wages, Holmes thought "that the threats were as lawful for this preliminary purpose as for the final one to which strengthening the union was a means." [105]

In the foregoing cases, the defendants had sought to induce employees to leave the plaintiff's service (as in the *Vegelahn* case), or employers to dismiss the plaintiffs (as in *Plant* v. *Woods*), by means of some sort of threats; and the defendants had acted in combination. Shortly afterwards, however, the Massachusetts court, in an opinion by Holmes, from which there was no dissent, held that neither of these facts was essential to bring the prima facie tort doctrine into play. It is enough that a defendant, acting alone, persuades an employer to dismiss a plaintiff, if his act is due only to malevolence.

The case is *Moran* v. *Dunphy*,[106] decided in 1901. The Superior Court had sustained a demurrer to the plaintiff's declaration, which contained two counts. The first count alleged that the defendant slandered the plaintiff to his employer, thus inducing the employer to discharge him. Slander, of course, is a tort whose unlawfulness does not rest on the prima facie tort doctrine. The Supreme Judicial Court sustained the demurrer to this count on the technical ground that the declaration should have set forth the alleged slanderous words. But the second count was not for slander. It did not allege any false statements, but merely that the defendant "did maliciously, wilfully

[104] *Id.* at 504. [105] *Id.* at 505. [106] 177 Mass. 485 (1901).

and wrongfully induce and instigate" the employer to discharge the plaintiff and that the employer did so. This count, Holmes held, stated a cause of action, and the demurrer to it should accordingly be overruled. The count alleged that the plaintiff had been working for the employer under an oral contract. If the contract had bound the employer not to dismiss the plaintiff when he did, then the defendant induced the commission of an unlawful act. But the declaration did not state that the dismissal was a breach of the contract. For all that appears, the contract may have bound the employer to pay stated wages only when and if the plaintiff did the prescribed work. And Holmes's reasoning would make the defendant equally liable, whether the dismissal was a breach of contract on the employer's part or not.

After citing a number of Massachusetts cases, including *Vegelahn* v. *Guntner* and *Plant* v. *Woods*, Holmes said:

> . . . we cannot admit a doubt that maliciously and without justifiable cause to induce a third person to end his employment of the plaintiff, whether the inducement be false slanders or successful persuasion, is an actionable tort. . . .
>
> . . . it may be taken to be settled by *Plant* v. *Woods*, . . . that motives may determine the question of liability; that while intentional interference of the kind supposed may be privileged if for certain purposes, yet if due only to malevolence it must be answered for. On that point the judges were of one mind. . . . Finally, we see no sound distinction between persuading by malevolent advice and accomplishing the same result by falsehood or putting in fear. In all these cases the employer is controlled through motives created by the defendant for the unprivileged purpose. It appears to us not to matter which motive is relied upon. If accomplishing the end by one of them is a wrong to the plaintiff, accomplishing it by either of the others must be equally a wrong.[107]

Massachusetts is not the only state in which acts of a single individual have been held unlawful because of the motive. In what are known as "spite fence" cases, we have seen that courts in some states have held it unlawful for a landowner to build a structure for the sole purpose of shutting out a neighbor's light and air.[108] While Holmes

[107] 177 Mass. at 487. This reasoning seems to dispose of the difficulty felt by Judge Florence Allen, speaking for the Supreme Court of Ohio in 1923 in La France El. Cons. & Supply Co. v. International Brotherhood of El. Workers, 108 Ohio St. 61, 93–94. "It is difficult upon principle," she said, "to see how persuading a man to do a thing, which he may do with perfect legality, can be illegal." She seems to have assumed that the considerations of policy which make the law reluctant to constrain a man to work for or to employ another apply with equal force to the question whether the law shall constrain a man to desist from the act of persuasion.

[108] See *supra*, p. 54.

seems to have disagreed with these cases and to have thought that at common law the rightfulness of a man's use of his property did not depend upon his motive,[109] nevertheless, in 1889 he sustained the constitutionality of a statute which made a "private nuisance" of any fence "unnecessarily exceeding six feet in height, maliciously erected or maintained for the purpose of annoying the owners or occupants of adjoining property." He sustained it in *Rideout* v. *Knox* [110] because the common law right

> to use one's property for the sole purpose of injuring others is not one of the immediate rights of ownership; it is not a right for the sake of which property is recognized by the law, but is only a more or less necessary incident of rights which are established for very different ends.

And he contrued the act, as the House of Lords seems to have construed the common law tort of "conspiracy to injure," by saying that "it is not enough to satisfy the words of the act that malevolence was one of the motives, but that malevolence must be the dominant motive,—a motive without which the fence would not have been built or maintained." [111]

There is at least one other notable case in which the damage inflicted by a single individual was held actionable because of the motive. That case, *Tuttle* v. *Buck*,[112] is the more notable in that the damage was inflicted by means of competition. It was held that a good cause of action was set forth in a complaint by a barber which alleged that the defendant, a wealthy banker, had set up a rival barber shop "with the sole design of injuring the plaintiff, and of destroying his said business, and not for the purpose of serving any legitimate purpose of his own." Although competition was the means used to inflict the damage, the damage was nevertheless inflicted, according to the allegation, for its own sake, and not in Holmes's words "as an instrumentality in reaching the end of victory in the battle of trade." [113]

In this case competition was the means used to inflict the harm, though the purpose was not to secure a competitive advantage. But the infliction of harm for the purpose of competitive success, by means which would ordinarily be lawful, is not always sanctioned. The de-

109 Note his explanation of Mayor of Bradford v. Pickles [1895] A.C. 587, as resting on the premise that the use of one's own land is an absolute privilege, apparently one to which the prima facie tort doctrine is not applicable. Aikens v. Wisconsin, 195 U.S. 194, 204 (1904), quoted *infra*, p. 82.

110 148 Mass. 368, 372 (1889).

111 *Id.* at 373.

112 107 Minn. 145 (1909).

113 Vegelahn v. Guntner, 167 Mass. 92, 106 (1896).

fendants in *Plant* v. *Woods* were pursuing a competitive advantage. Moreover, courts have sometimes held acts unlawful, and characterized them as "unfair competition," when the same acts, done for a "legitimate purpose," would have been held lawful; and the element of combination does not seem to be an essential ingredient of "unfair competition." One such case was decided by the United States Supreme Court in 1918, in an opinion by Justice Pitney. The case is *International News Co.* v. *Associated Press.*[114] The A.P. at considerable expense, had been furnishing its members with cable reports of events in Europe during the First World War. After these reports were made public in early editions of A.P. papers, or on their bulletin boards, on the Eastern seaboard, the International News Company made a practice of telegraphing their contents to its constituents in the West, who, taking advantage of the difference in time, published them in their own papers without giving credit to the A.P.—frequently before the A.P. papers in the locality could appear. There was no copyright on the A.P. reports. Nevertheless, the Court held that the practice should be enjoined, on the ground that, although a purchaser of a single copy of an A.P. newspaper may "spread knowledge of its contents gratuitously, for any legitimate purpose not unreasonably interfering with complainant's right to make merchandise of it," that was not what the International News Company was doing. Instead, "it is endeavoring to reap where it has not sown, and . . . is appropriating to itself the harvest of those who have sown. . . . The transaction speaks for itself, and a court of equity ought not to hesitate long in characterizing it as unfair competition in business." [115]

In the preceding year, in the *Hitchman* case, Justice Pitney had also invoked the concept of "unfair competition" in a hypothetical case of his own formulation.

Certainly, [he said] if a competing trader should endeavor to draw custom from his rival, not by offering better or cheaper goods, employing more competent salesmen, or displaying more attractive advertisements, but by persuading the rival's clerks to desert him under circumstances render-

114 248 U.S. 215 (1918).

115 *Id.* at 239–240. Justice Holmes (*id.* at 246) thought the injunction should only restrain publication which failed to give credit to the A.P. Justice Brandeis (*id.* at 248) thought the injunction should be denied, because (among other reasons) the problem was one which could be dealt with more appropriately by legislation. The case is discussed in some detail by Callmann, *He Who Reaps Where He Has Not Sown; Unjust Enrichment in the Law of Unfair Competition* (1942) 55 HARV. L. REV. 595.

ing it difficult or embarrassing for him to fill their places, any court of equity would grant an injunction to restrain this as unfair competition.[116]

Harmful Nonfeasance and Conspiracies

The competing trader in this hypothetical case was inflicting the injury by an affirmative act, and there seems no sound reason why he should not be held to be acting unlawfully, even though there is no concerted action, unless one accepts the view which Holmes suggested in *Vegelahn* v. *Guntner,* that the attempt to gain any sort of economic advantage always justifies the intentional infliction of harm, provided the means used are not unlawful on other grounds. When an employer inflicts harm on a worker, however, by declining to employ him further, or when a worker inflicts harm on an employer by discontinuing his work, neither is doing any affirmative act. The refusal to employ or to work is called "nonfeasance" or an "omission" to act, rather than an act, and many courts find difficulty in holding nonfeasance unlawful unless a person has incurred something like a contractual duty to act. Where there is a combination of several persons for the purpose of concerted nonfeasance, however, the act of combining may be held to supply the missing ingredient of affirmative action. These circumstances, as well as the bad odor attaching to the word "conspiracy," render conduct of a combination of persons more vulnerable to legal attack than similar conduct of a single individual.[117]

Justice Holmes's opinion in *Aikens* v. *Wisconsin* [118] illustrates this point. The immediate question before the Court was whether a Wisconsin criminal statute, as applied to the defendants, was constitutional. It was not a question of rights and wrongs at common law. But in sustaining the conviction under the statute and holding that the Fourteenth Amendment created no constitutional right in the defendants to do what they did, Holmes laid stress on the fact that in many jurisdictions what they did would have been actionable at common law. The branch of the statute under which the defendants were convicted imposed punishment on any two or more persons who combined for the purpose of maliciously injuring another in his reputation, trade, business, or profession. "We interpret 'maliciously in-

[116] 245 U.S. 229, 259 (1917).

[117] Note also the reasons given in the House of Lords, based on the historical accident that "conspiracy to injure" had long been recognized as a crime. *Supra,* pp. 55–71. The English courts seem to lay little, if any, stress on the distinction between feasance and nonfeasance.

[118] 195 U.S. 194 (1904).

juring,'" said Holmes, "to import doing a harm malevolently for the sake of the harm as an end in itself, and not merely as a means to some further end legitimately desired." The defendants were managers of newspapers in Milwaukee. According to the information filed by the District Attorney, whose allegations they were held to have admitted by their pleadings, they combined with the intent of "maliciously" (*i.e.,* as Holmes construed it, malevolently) injuring the *Journal* Company, which published another Milwaukee newspaper. The *Journal* had announced an increase of about 25 percent in its advertising rates. This action is what seems, for some reason not explained in the report of the case, to have aroused the malevolence of the defendants. The way they injured the *Journal* was by agreeing to refrain from publishing the advertisements of anyone who should agree to pay the *Journal* its increased rates, except at a higher rate than that charged to unoffending advertisers. They agreed to refrain from doing something. They did not agree to do anything (other than to announce their terms).

Before coming to the question of nonfeasance, Holmes, in holding that there was no constitutional right to combine to inflict the malicious injury, referred to the common law, reiterating the philosophy he had expounded while on the Massachusetts Court.

> It has been thought by other courts [he said] as well as the Supreme Court of Wisconsin that such a combination followed by damage would be actionable even at common law. It has been considered that, *prima facie,* the intentional infliction of temporal damage is a cause of action, which, as a matter of substantive law, whatever may be the form of pleading, requires a justification if the defendant is to escape. *Mogul Steamship Co.* v. *McGregor,* . . . . If this is the correct mode of approach, it is obvious that justifications may vary in extent according to the principle of policy upon which they are founded, and that while some, for instance, at common law, those affecting the use of land, are absolute, *Bradford* v. *Pickles,* . . . others may depend upon the end for which the act is done. *Moran* v. *Dunphy,* . . .; *Plant* v. *Woods,* . . .; *Squires* v. *Wason Manuf. Co.,* 182 Massachusetts, 137, 140, 141.[119]

After thus restating the common law doctrine of prima facie torts, Holmes went on to deal with its application to harmful nonfeasance, in these words:

> But if all these general considerations be admitted, it is urged nevertheless that the means intended to be used by this particular combination

[119] 195 U.S. at 204.

were simply the abstinence from making contracts, that a man's right so to abstain cannot be infringed on the ground of motives, and further, that it carries with it the right to communicate that intent to abstain to others and to abstain in common with them. It is said that if the statute extends to such a case it must be unconstitutional.

Holmes seemed to concede, at least for the sake of argument, that inflicting harm by abstaining from action, or even by adding to the nonfeasance of abstaining, the affirmative act of announcing the terms on which one would continue to abstain, would be lawful whatever the motive and required no justification; for he met the defendants' argument, not by denying this proposition, but by pointing out the existence of affirmative action, in addition to the act of announcing to advertisers that they could enjoy the lower rates by boycotting the *Journal.* He followed the words we have just quoted with these:

The fallacy of this argument lies in the assumption that the statute stands no better than if directed against the pure nonfeasance of singly omitting to contract. The statute is directed against a series of acts, and acts of several, the acts of combining, with intent to do other acts. "The very plot is an act in itself." *Mulcahy* v. *The Queen,* L.R. 3 H.L. 306, 317. But an act, which in itself is merely a voluntary muscular contraction, derives all its character from the consequences which will follow it under the circumstances in which it was done. When the acts consist of making a combination calculated to cause temporal damage, the power to punish such acts, when done maliciously, cannot be denied because they are to be followed and worked out by conduct which might have been lawful if not preceded by the acts. No conduct has such an absolute privilege as to justify all possible schemes of which it may be a part. The most innocent and constitutionally protected of acts or omissions may be made a step in a criminal plot, and if it is a step in a plot neither its innocence nor the Constitution is sufficient to prevent the punishment of the plot by law.

In the *Harvard Law Review* article already cited, published ten years before this decision, Holmes seemed less ready to concede that mere nonfeasance calculated to interfere with a man's business required no justification. He referred to the English case of *Temperton* v. *Russell,*[120] which held it unlawful, in Holmes's words, "for the officer of a trade union to order the members not to work for a man if he supplies goods to the plaintiff, for the purpose of forcing the plaintiff to abstain from doing what he has a right to do." While "the defendant's act, strictly, was giving an order, not refusing to

120 [1893] 1 Q.B. 715.

contract," still, said Holmes, "perhaps the case would have been decided the same way if the same course had been adopted by unanimous vote of the union." [121] So, without making the point that the element of combination supplied an affirmative act, Holmes went on to say that "the right to abstain from contracting is not absolutely privileged as against interference with business."

However, the harm for which the defendants were held liable in this case was not the harm suffered by the man with whom the defendants abstained from contracting. It was the harm suffered by a third party by reason of that man's conduct, induced by the defendants. The act of inducing him to withdraw his trade from the plaintiff would seem to be what made the defendants liable, in the absence of justification. Such liability would accord with the principles Holmes later enunciated in *Moran* v. *Dunphy*.[122] If mere persuasion would make them liable, they would not be less so because the persuasion was backed up with threats of nonfeasance. Holmes recognized that some such argument could be made, saying:

> It might be said that the defendants were free not to contract, but that they had no right to advise or persuade the contractors who would have dealt with the plaintiff not to do so, and that, by communicating the union's willingness to deal with the contractors, if they would not deal with the plaintiff, the defendants were using such persuasion.[123]

But he suggested that "this refinement [is] . . . a round-about denial of the freedom not to contract, since a man hardly is free in his abstaining unless he can state the terms or conditions upon which he intends to abstain . . ." Without retreating, however, from the proposition that "the right to abstain" is not absolutely privileged, he gave another twist to the argument at a later point in the article, saying:

> What I have called heretofore the privilege not to contract really is only the negative side of a privilege to make contracts. I stated it in the negative way in order to make the claim of an absolute privilege more plausible. But the right not to contract in a certain event, and to say that you will not, means nothing unless it is implied that you offer a contract, that is, an act on your part, in the other event.[124]

But for the offer to act (that is, to work for the employer), the employer would not have complied with the demand to cease supplying

121 8 HARV. L. REV. at 8.
122 177 Mass. 485 (1901). *Supra*, p. 77–78.
123 8 HARV. L. REV. at 8.
124 *Id.* at 13.

goods to the plaintiff, and the latter would have suffered no damage. But when there are only two parties concerned, an offer by one of them to act if the other will come to terms, accompanied by a threat of nonfeasance if he will not, may be highly damaging. The damage, however, unlike that in the three-party cases, comes only from the nonfeasance or the terms exacted by the threat of nonfeasance, not from the offered act. Thus, when an employer omits to continue hiring a man who cannot readily find another job, or when a worker who cannot be easily replaced omits to continue at work for the employer, because in each case the other party will not accede to the terms offered, it is nonfeasance that causes the damage. The worker is not hurt by the employer's offer to continue the affirmative act of hiring, nor is the employer by the worker's offer to continue the act of working. And if either party accepts hard terms from the other, it is because he finds them preferable to the damage he would suffer if the threat of nonfeasance should be carried out. Were it not for the offer to act in each case, the damage would be still greater—the aggrieved party would have no escape from what he himself regards as the more onerous burden of suffering from the nonfeasance itself. Does it follow that in cases where the plaintiff suffers, not from the defendant's act or offer to act, but solely from his nonfeasance or from yielding to the threat of nonfeasance, the nonfeasance must be regarded as absolutely privileged at common law, requiring no justification, whatever its motives?

If so, those who do the act of combining to be followed by concerted nonfeasance, like the defendants in *Aikens* v. *Wisconsin* or the workers in a factory who combine to strike, may be held to answer for the harm inflicted by their nonfeasance if a court finds no justification in their aims, while an employer who without combining with others can inflict as great damage on them by his own nonfeasance escapes judicial scrutiny of his motives. In fact Judge Andrews, speaking for the majority of the New York Court of Appeals in 1927, in *Exchange Bakery & Restaurant Inc.* v. *Rifkin*,[125] a decision on the whole favorable to union activities, assumed that this was the law. Workers may quit work, he said, and employers may hire and discharge, for any reason, good or bad, "so long as they act independ-

[125] 245 N.Y. 260 (1927). Picketing a restaurant to induce it to unionize its shop was held justifiable, although the employees were not members of the picketing union and were not on strike; and "yellow dog" contracts were held invalid.

ently." But if action is concerted, "it is subject to control"; and what may be "lawful in the case of an individual may be unlawful if the joint action of a number." What he did not note was that the pressure that a single large employer may exert against a worker by a threat of discharge cannot be matched by the threat of a single worker to quit; it can as a rule be matched only by the pressure of a concerted threat of a number of them to quit.

By applying a stricter legal control to concerted threats than to unconcerted threats, whether of acts or of nonfeasance, we have an anomaly like that which Lord Bowen pointed out, where

> one rich capitalist may innocently carry competition to a length which would become unlawful in the case of a syndicate with a joint capital no larger than his own, and one individual merchant may lawfully do that which a firm or a partnership may not. What limits, on such a theory, would be imposed by law on the competitive action of a joint-stock company limited, is a problem which might well puzzle a casuist.[126]

When the casuist resolves the puzzle by treating the concerted action of the officers of a corporation as the unconcerted action of a single fictitious legal person, then the discrepancy between the privileged nonfeasance of "the corporation" and the unprivileged combination of unincorporated persons for the purpose of comparable nonfeasance is still more marked.

In *Green* v. *Victor Talking Machine Co.*[127] the Federal Court of Appeals for the Second Circuit took the position that the affirmative act of combining on the part of the officers of a corporation was to be ignored and only the nonfeasance of the corporation itself, resulting from that combination, to be regarded.

> And the allegation [said Judge Swan] that this defendant's conduct was pursuant to a conspiracy between defendant and its own directors adds nothing. It is but a reiteration in another form of the allegation of nonfeasance by the defendant corporation, which can act only through its officers or agents.

And the prima facie tort doctrine was held not to apply to nonfeasance.

The corporation's nonfeasance in this case did not consist of refusal to hire, but of refusal to sell. Mrs. Green, the plaintiff, was the owner of all the stock of another corporation, the Pearsall Company, whose only business was to resell products purchased from the Victor Company. Her complaint was that the Victor Company ceased selling to

[126] L.R. 23 Q.B.D. 598, 617. *Supra*, pp. 70–71.

[127] 24 F. 2d 378, 382 (2d Cir. 1928).

her corporation, completely destroying the value of its stock, in pursuance of a threat made to induce her to sell the stock to a named person. The court held that if there was a tort by the Victor Company, it was a tort against the Pearsall Company, not against the owner of its stock, so that the remedy would lie through a suit by that corporation. But the court thought there was no tort at all. After citing some of Holmes's remarks in *Aikens* v. *Wisconsin,* Judge Swan added:

> But no case has decided, so far as we are aware, that the refusal of one individual to deal with another requires justification. A private trader is privileged to exercise his own pleasure as to parties with whom he will deal. [Citations.] To make his motive in exercising this privilege the subject of judicial inquiry would be a step beyond what the courts have yet done, or what we think they can wisely do in the present stage of our economic order. [Citations.]
>
> Even the most ardent advocates of the principle that the intentional infliction of temporal harm requires a justification have stopped short of asserting that it applies to harm resulting from nonaction, in the absence of facts creating a duty to act. Ames, 18 Harv. Law Rev. 411; Harno, 30 Yale Law J. 145, 156. The defendant owed the Pearsall Company no duty to continue dealing with it, in the absence of a contract so to do, even though its motive in refusing was malicious; i.e. an intention to destroy the Pearsall Company's business without benefit to defendant.[128]

Doubtless Judge Swan did not mean to deny that justification is required for harm resulting from nonaction which follows affirmative acts, such as the affirmative act of a defendant in inducing nonaction by a third party or the act of several defendants in combining for concerted nonaction on their own part. His citation of *Aikens* v. *Wisconsin* would seem to indicate this. And in the article cited,[129] Dean Ames expressly took the position that if a person acted to procure the dismissal of another from employment "from pure malevolence, his conduct would be tortious," citing Holmes's language in *Moran* v. *Dunphy* in support of this proposition. Although the defendant's act in such a case would be affirmative, the harm resulting to the plaintiff would of course be harm resulting from the employer's nonaction. Ames stated his general thesis thus:

> The wilful causing of damage to another by a positive act, whether by one man alone, or by several acting in concert, and whether by direct action against him or indirectly by inducing a third person to exercise a

128 *Id.* at 382.

129 James Barr Ames, *How Far an Act May Be a Tort Because of the Wrongful Motive of the Actor* (1905) 18 HARV. L. REV. 411, 419.

lawful right, is a tort unless there was just cause for inflicting the damage; and the question whether there was or was not just cause will depend, in many cases, but not in all, upon the motive of the actor.[130]

Ames did, however, express an opinion like that which Judge Swan doubtless meant to express—that a defendant's motive for his own nonfeasance cannot affect its lawfulness. He said:

> The discontinuance of a service at will or the refusal to employ a man, to make a lease to him, to buy his goods, to lend him money, to recommend him as a servant, will give him no cause of action, however great the damage to him or however malevolent the attitude of the party refusing to gratify his wish. [Citing cases.] But these and similar cases are foreign to the present discussion, which relates to possible torts. The refusals just mentioned cannot be torts, for they are not acts but failures to act.[131]

Failure to act, however, may be legally wrong even when it is not a tort. It may, of course, amount to breach of a contract. A contract to build a house puts affirmative duties on the contractor. Putting oneself in certain positions of trust to another raises an affirmative duty to do what that relationship requires. A common carrier has a duty, at common law, to serve. Moreover, one who quite innocently sets certain machinery in motion (like an automobile) incurs an affirmative duty to perform whatever further positive acts may be required in the exercise of that care towards others which the law calls "due." Failure to perform such acts is not only legally wrong; it amounts to that particular type of wrong which the law classifies as a tort. He who fails to perform those acts is said to have committed negligence. Yet it must be clear that his wrong consisted, not in his positive act of starting the car, but in his failure to perform those further acts essential to safety. One who enters another's property lawfully, with the owner's consent, is "committing" the tort of trespass if he fails to leave when the owner requests him to. This is the tort which a participant in a sit-down strike commits, and the only tort, if he was guilty of no fraud when he obtained the owner's consent to enter the premises (having at that time no intention to stay after his work was over), and if he has committed no "act" of combining or persuading others, but simply yielded to someone else's persuasion to stay. His tort is clearly one of nonfeasance. His act of entering was not unlawful, but only his failure to perform the act of leaving. This fact is obscured when we say that his wrong was the commission of trespass.

The courts, nevertheless, have been reluctant to admit that affirma-

130 18 HARV. L. REV. at 412.

131 *Id.* at 416 (footnote).

tive action may be legally required save as the consequence of a person's having got into certain positions by way of contract or otherwise. In 1897 the New Hampshire court, in *Buch* v. *Amory Mfg. Co.*,[132] refused to allow recovery for damage to a child resulting from failure of those in charge of certain dangerous machinery to remove him from harm's way. Chief Judge Carpenter insisted that

> there is a wide difference—a broad gulf—both in reason and in law, between causing and preventing an injury. . . . The duty to do no wrong is a legal duty. The duty to protect against wrong is, generally speaking and excepting certain intimate relations in the nature of a trust, a moral obligation only, not recognized or enforced by law.

Illustrating his point, he said:

> I see my neighbor's two-year-old babe in dangerous proximity to the machinery of his windmill in his yard, and easily might, but do not, rescue him. I am not liable in damages to the child for his injuries . . . because the child and I are strangers, and I am under no legal duty to protect him.

The Supreme Court of Alabama made a similar distinction in 1909, in *L. & N.R.R. Co.* v. *Scruggs & Echols*.[133] The railroad company's servants had moved a train to its usual stopping place, which happened to be between the hydrant and the plaintiff's property, without knowing when they moved it that plaintiff's building was on fire. This prevented the fire department from laying a hose across the track to extinguish the fire. Th railroad servants were requested to move the train in order that the hose might be laid, but refused to do so until, in the ordinary course of business, the conductor received the clearance card from the dispatcher, by which time it was too late to put out the fire. There was no intimation that there would have been any hazard in moving the train at once. The majority held, in an opinion by Dowdell, C.J., that there was no legal duty to do so. The court distinguished between an active and a passive use of one's property, and said, "The law imposes no duty on one man to aid another in the preservation of the latter's property, but only the duty not to injure another's property in the use of his own." It was admitted that,

> if, in the present case, the fire hose had been laid from the hydrant, across the tracks of the defendant, to the fire, and the defendant's servants, with knowledge of the existing conditions as to the fire and the laying of the hose, had willfully or negligently run the train of cars over the hose, de-

132 69 N.H. 257 (1897).

133 161 Ala. 97 (1909).

stroying it, and thereby preventing the extinguishing of the fire, a legal liability for such conduct would have arisen. That would have been an active use of one's property in violation of the maxim, "Sic utere tuo ut alienum non laedas."

It is difficult to see why the law should make this distinction. The harm to the plaintiff is the same in the two cases. Nor would there be more hardship to the railroad, as far as appears, in moving its train after it had reached its position, than in stopping it before.

Perhaps judicial reluctance to recognize affirmative duties is based on one or both of two inarticulate assumptions. One of these is that a self-reliant individual needs no help from others, save such as they may be disposed to render him out of kindness or that he can induce them to render by the ordinary process of bargaining, without having the Government step in to make them help. All he is supposed to ask of the Government is that it interfere to prevent others from doing him positive harm. The other assumption is that when a government requires a person to act, it is necessarily interfering more seriously with his liberty than when it places limits on his freedom to act—to make a man serve another is to make him a slave, while to forbid him to commit affirmative wrongs is to leave him still essentially a free man. Neither of these assumptions is universally true. Neither was true in this Alabama case. No matter how self-reliant the owner of the burning building, his property depended for its preservation on the affirmative acts of the railroad employees—acts which they were evidently not disposed to render out of kindness and which he was in no position to induce them to perform by bargaining. Nor would a legal duty to move the train have subjected either the employees or the railroad company itself to anything having the slightest resemblance to slavery.

There are, however, more serious difficulties in the way of imposing legal duties to render help. It would not always be easy to determine on whom such duties should rest, or under what circumstances. Such difficulties do not arise to the same extent with duties to refrain from positive acts which are harmful. Everyone is under a duty to refrain from affirmative wrongs. Whoever causes harm to another by an affirmative act which violates that other's legal right will be held liable. But if a man falls into a river, it cannot be the legal duty of everyone to aid him—a legal wrong to abstain from helping. In the first place, relatively few are in a position to help. Failure on the part of someone to be there and so to be in a position to help can hardly be a legal or even a moral wrong, unless that person has in some way assumed responsibility. Moreover, if there are several passersby, each capable of rescuing the drowning man, it cannot be the legal duty of all to do so. If all attempted, they would get in one another's way and fail in the attempt. If one does the rescuing, the others cannot well be accused of legal wrong because they abstained. But on which of them could the law fasten a duty to help? The one who does help would evidently release all others from any duty in the matter. It is not so when the duty is to refrain from something, such as assault and battery. One person may do his duty by not assaulting, but everyone else remains under a like duty just the same.

This difficulty in selecting the person on whom an affirmative obligation should be placed is not always present. It was not present in the Alabama case. There was no question there of putting a legal duty to move the train on anyone but the conductor who had charge of it —and of course the company, whose servant he was. The owner of the burning building was asserting no right against all the world, but only against one specific person. If there is but one bystander when the man is in the river, it is on that bystander and on him alone that a duty to rescue could conceivably be laid. But here the other difficulty is to be met. How much trouble or risk would we wish to make him take? If the rescue can be effected by simply tossing in a rope, all would agree that he ought, morally, to do it, and there would be only a technical objection to making it his legal duty. But ought he risk his life? If he is a doctor on his way to save a patient's life, ought he risk the patient's life to save that of the drowning man? Is it practicable to formulate any legal rule to cover such cases? [134]

It would, of course, be desirable for people to act to save others from harm, provided that in so acting they do not cause an equal amount of harm to descend on someone else or on themselves. When the law requires people to refrain from committing certain acts or else to pay for the harm caused to others, usually the requirement does not cause harm to the actor comparable to that which his act would cause to others. Any general requirement, on the other hand, that persons must pay damages whenever they might have acted to prevent loss to others

[134] For an interesting discussion of some of the problems that arise in creating affirmative duties, with special reference to the criminal law, see LORD MACAULAY, A PENAL CODE PREPARED BY THE INDIAN LAW COMMISSION, note M (1838).

and failed to do so would cause more harm than it would cure. Even were the requirement confined to making the omission wrongful only when the act would cause less harm to the actor or to someone else than the omission causes to the plaintiff, it would be a requirement impracticable to administer. The law can scarcely be made an instrument to enforce general unselfishness.

It does not follow, however, that the law can never recognize nonfeasance as a tort. We have seen that it does, in the cases of failure of the automobile driver to apply the brakes and the sit-down striker to leave the premises. It is difficult to see why the railroad company's failure to move the train in order that the hose might be connected with the hydrant should not be held to be a tort. Requiring the company to do that affirmative act is not at all like requiring someone to engage in the railroad business because by doing so he may be thought to be benefiting the community.

Even in the case of acts which we generally desire to allow people freedom to decline to perform, why should their omission be permitted when it is clear that the only motive for the omission is a bad one? For one reason or another, we may think it sound social policy to impose no legal obligation on anyone, as a general rule, to enter into any sort of transaction. We may not wish to make it legally obligatory on him to hire or to work for anyone, to buy or to sell—partly because we consider it too great a hardship to make him do these things if he does not wish to do them, and partly because even if he does wish to do the acts he is not likely to obtain such good terms for doing them if he cannot threaten to refuse in the process of bargaining. We assume that the economic results of free bargaining will on the whole be those that are most desirable socially. But how is it when it is clear that the party has no reluctance to enter the transaction and is not holding out in a normal way for better terms, but is motivated by no other purpose than to cause trouble or to exercise coercion for an unjustifiable purpose? An act done for such purposes would be held unlawful by those courts which follow the prima facie tort doctrine. Why not an omission? Particularly since acts, to be held wrongful, may consist of nothing more than a combination to decline to enter into transactions as in *Aikens* v. *Wisconsin?*

Congress has stepped in to do what Judge Swan thought is not wise for courts to do "in the present stage of our economic order." It has in the Wagner National Labor Relations Act [135] made it an "unfair labor practice" for an employer, whose business is sufficiently concerned with interstate commerce to bring him within the control of Congress, to discharge a man if the motive for the discharge is to interfere with his activity or membership in a union. Many states have enacted similar legislation for local businesses. In sustaining an order of the National Labor Relations Board to cease and desist from discharging men for union membership and to reinstate those already discharged, with back pay, Chief Justice Hughes said, in *NLRB* v. *Jones & Laughlin Steel Corp.*:

The [Wagner] Act does not interfere with the normal exercise of the right of the employer to select its employees or to discharge them. The employer may not, under cover of that right, intimidate or coerce its employees with respect to their self-organization and representation, and, on the other hand, the Board is not entitled to make its authority a pretext for interference with the right of discharge when that right is exercised for other reasons than such intimidation and coercion.[136]

Freedom to abstain from the act of employment is still permitted by law to the employer, whenever it is exercised for those "normal" purposes for which it is generally desired; but the statute forbids such abstention when its purpose is to coerce the employees with respect to their self-organization. A particular type of nonfeasance is thus made unlawful when motivated by a forbidden purpose, and this limitation of freedom to abstain is held not to be the kind of deprivation of liberty which the Constitution forbids.[137] There would seem to be no insuperable barrier to prevent a court, without the aid of legislation, from holding wrongful the intentional infliction of harm by means of nonfeasance, whenever the purpose of the nonfeasance is one that would not justify the intentional infliction of similar harm by means of affirmative conduct. The distinction between affirmative conduct and nonfeasance has been termed "out-moded" by the Supreme Court.[138]

It may be, then, that courts, even without the aid of statutes, will

135 The replacement of the Wagner Act by the Taft-Hartley Act does not do away with this provision.

136 301 U.S. 1, 45–46 (1937).

137 For numerous instances where statutes have made nonfeasance a crime see Otto Kirchheimer, *Criminal Omissions* (1942) 55 HARV. L. REV. 615.

138 Frankfurter, J., in Rochester Telephone Corp. v. United States, 307 U.S. 125, 143 (1939).

be more disposed than they were once to scrutinize the motive for the intentional infliction of harm by nonfeasance, as well as by affirmative acts. They may, perhaps, place legal limits on bargaining power when it is based on a corporation's threat of nonfeasance in the form of a refusal to buy, sell, or employ, as well as when it is based on a threat by individual workers to do the affirmative act of combining, followed by the nonfeasance of a refusal to work. And they may refuse to enforce what they regard as unconscionable contracts, when the agreement was induced by threats of nonfeasance. In a recent case, Justice Frankfurter spoke of "the familiar example of the drowning man who agrees to pay an exorbitant sum to a rescuer who would otherwise permit him to drown. No court would enforce a contract made under such circumstances." [139] These remarks were in a dissenting opinion, but the majority, while it thought them inapplicable to the particular contract before the Court, expressed no disagreement with them. Whether they reflect the present state of the law with accuracy or not, they may foreshadow the way it will develop.

[139] United States v. Bethlehem Steel Corp., 315 U.S. 289, 330 (1942).

VI

JUDICIAL MODIFICATION OF LEGAL DUTIES

UNDER the prima facie tort doctrine acts (and perhaps nonfeasances) which are legally wrong only because they intentionally inflict damage on another, lose their wrongful character when properly motivated. Acts which are legally wrong on other grounds, on the other hand, are more apt to be held still wrong, whatever the motive. An exception is made in libel, slander, and false arrest, where certain circumstances may create a privilege, but where the privilege may be defeated by showing that the motive was malevolent. If an act remains wrongful regardless of motive, it would seem that the act of the person whose right it infringes in taking steps to enforce his right will be lawful. When a man enforces his right against another, however, he knows that he is likely to cause damage to the wrongdoer, whether he enforces his right by self-help, as by removing a trespassing object from his property, or by resorting to the courts. If his motive is bad, will his causing of damage to the wrongdoer ever be held to be itself a legal wrong? Or if he resorts to the courts will they ever deny him relief, or will they give him only partial relief, insufficient actually to stop the defendant's wrong, either because he is seeking enforcement of his own right for an improper purpose or because the court feels that the defendant's act, though coming within one of the conventional categories of "wrong," should nevertheless be permitted under the circumstances or at least permitted conditionally if the defendant will pay damages? Dean Ames, in his 1905 article, thought the answer to at least some of these questions should be "no." Some cases decided later, however, suggest a different answer.

Ames distinguished cases in which the courts agree that wrongful motive makes the act unlawful and in which they disagree as to this point, from a group of cases in which "the wrongful motive has no legal significance." Discussing this last group of cases, he said:

A defendant who has caused damage to the plaintiff and been actuated in so doing by the most reprehensible motives escapes liability if the plaintiff is suffering only the consequences of his own breach of duty. For example, the plaintiff refuses to leave the defendant's house, when requested, whereupon the defendant puts him out by force; or the defendant removes the plaintiff's encroaching fence; or his wrongful obstruction to the flow of a stream; or turns the plaintiff's trespassing horse into the highway where it is lost or stolen. It makes no difference that the defendant, in doing these acts, was taking advantage of the opportunity to gratify a vindictive spirit, and would not have done them otherwise. It is still true that he was merely putting an end to the plaintiff's tort. Similarly, a creditor pursues his debtor with all the rigor of the law in order to ruin him, although he knows that with some indulgence he would realize more himself and enable his debtor to avoid bankruptcy; or in a spirit of malevolence he sues a trespasser. Here again the malevolent motive of the defendant is legally of no significance. The debtor and the tort-feasor were legally bound to pay and cannot claim damages because they were brought into court for the breach of their duty. The action is refused in these cases, notwithstanding the reprehensible motive of the defendant, because the court could not without stultifying itself punish him for enforcing his absolute legal rights against his debtor or the wrongdoer.[1]

However, in *American Bank & Trust Co.* v. *Federal Reserve Bank of Atlanta*[2] the Supreme Court of the United States held in 1921 that a certain method pursued by a holder of checks to enforce their payment by the banks on which they were drawn was illegal because of the holder's motive. The plaintiff's allegations, which at this stage

1 18 HARV. L. REV. at 412–413. The footnotes citing supporting cases are omitted.
2 256 U.S. 350 (1921).

of the pleadings were assumed to be true,[3] charged that the Federal Reserve Bank was accumulating checks on country banks with the intention of presenting them in a body, for the purpose of forcing the country banks to keep so much cash in their vaults that they would be driven out of business unless they would submit to the Reserve Bank's insistence that they join the reserve system. It was held that if the allegations could be proved, the Reserve Bank should be enjoined from collecting checks except in the usual manner. To determine whether it was permissible for the Reserve Bank to pursue its alleged practices, said Justice Holmes, "it is not enough to refer to the general right of a holder of checks to present them but it is necessary to consider whether the collection of checks and presenting them in a body for the purpose of breaking down the plaintiff's business as now conducted is justified by the ulterior purpose in view." [4] Yet the Reserve Bank was only taking steps to compel the country banks to perform the legal duties they had incurred by contract, to honor the checks drawn on them. It was because (according to the allegations) the defendant deliberately chose a method of enforcing the country banks' duties which would be most burdensome to them, with an improper motive, that its action was held unlawful.

There are other cases in which courts, while not forbidding a man to enforce duties owed him by others, will refuse their aid to him in making the "wrongdoer" actually perform his duties, and only award the "injured" party damages for the wrong instead—either because of some improper motive actuating the man who sues, or because actual performance of his duties is regarded as too great a hardship to the defendant. The "equitable" remedy of an injunction against the commission of a threatened wrong is, of course, more effective in preventing it than is the mere knowledge of the wrongdoer that he may later have a judgment rendered against him for the payment of damages—the ordinary "common law" remedy. In both cases the prevention takes the form of a threat of some sort of a penalty after the act has been committed. But after an injunction is issued the penalty for disobedience is likely to be severe, even imprisonment for contempt of court, and is relatively certain. It will be imposed by the same judge who issued the injunction, and no jury trial is required.

[3] On the basis of findings by a lower court to which the case had been remanded, it was held at a later stage of the proceedings that the allegations had not been proved. 262 U.S. 643 (1923).

[4] 256 U.S. at 359.

In a suit for damages, on the other hand, the defendant may hope for a light verdict from the jury, the judgment may not be collectible if the defendant has insufficient property on which execution can be levied, and even if collectible the defendant may think commission of the wrong worth the price. For all these reasons a plaintiff may find the equitable remedy highly preferable. But courts of equity have long since adopted a maxim that "he who seeks equity must do equity," or, as sometimes expressed, that equitable relief will be denied a suitor unless he "comes into court with clean hands." This does not mean that equity demands "that its suitors shall have led blameless lives," [5] but only that they shall not be guilty of wrong conduct in respect to the transactions that form the basis of the suit. But unclean hands are no bar to the granting of an award of damages.

Thus, the Supreme Court has held that a court of equity should deny a patentee relief in an infringement suit, so long as he is using his patent as a means of enforcing a monopoly in an unpatented adjunct to his patented machine. Such use of his patent, said Chief Justice Stone in *Morton Salt Co.* v. *G. S. Suppiger Co.,* thwarts "the public policy underlying the grant of the patent"—a policy which "includes inventions within the granted monopoly," but "excludes from it all that is not embraced in the invention." [6]

When a man contracts to render personal services to another, he incurs a legal duty to perform and can be held liable for the payment of damages if he breaks his contract. But courts will not tolerate certain stronger measures to compel performance, not because they find anything improper in the employer's desire to secure the promised services, but because they regard "compulsory" labor as too great a hardship on the employee. In England the courts not only refuse to grant affirmative injunctions to perform the promised services but also to grant negative injunctions forbidding all work for others if the effect is likely to be to compel performance of the contract through fear of starvation. In this country statutes inflicting criminal punishment on the nonperformance of service contracts have been held unconstitutional as creating "involuntary servitude" forbidden by the Thirteenth Amendment. The cases will be examined more fully in a subsequent chapter dealing with that Amendment. But it should be noted here that liability to pay damages for breach of a contract

[5] Brandeis, J., in Loughran v. Loughran, 292 U.S. 216, 229 (1934).

[6] 314 U.S. 488 (1942).

to render services will be effective to compel performance whenever the work seems less onerous to the employee than loss of the money—but not otherwise.

In fact, liability to pay damages for any "wrong" conduct is a restriction on the freedom to engage in it, although such liability serves another purpose too. It affords reparation to plaintiffs for losses they have suffered. Such reparation alone, however, would scarcely justify placing the burden of it on defendants, if we were not ready to place some restriction on freedom to engage in the conduct that we designate as "wrong." As stated by Clarence Morris, in a thoughtful discussion of damages:

> If the reparative use of the law of torts is desirable, there must be reasons for making repairs in plaintiffs' fortunes at the expense of defendants other than the desirability of assuring the economic stability of plaintiffs. For, if money were taken capriciously from defendants by operation of the law of torts, there would be just as many economic bad spots created as cured; and the energy expended in shifting losses would be expended worthlessly.[7]

In those tort cases in which defendant's fault (or wrong) is a prerequisite to liability, Morris finds the reason for making defendants bear the loss in the likelihood that judgments against a defendant will discourage similar conduct on his part or on the part of others. "So, in the liability with fault cases there is an admonitory function as well as a reparative function; and the linkage of these two functions supplies a reason for taking money from the defendant as well as one for giving it to the plaintiff." [8] If the "wrong" for which damages must be paid, however, is something which the law wishes to prevent even if the one who commits it is willing to pay, the device of a money judgment is not always effective. "The sum required to make the plaintiff whole may be much too severe or much too lenient as admonition of the defendant." [9] In laying down rules for the measurement of damages, courts usually focus on the reparative function and measure them by the loss suffered by the plaintiff, although they sometimes add "punitive" damages in order better to serve the admonitory function.

Compensatory damages, however, would never be too lenient if the policy of the law were to prevent the act only where the performer is unwilling to pay for the loss occasioned by its performance. There are cases in which compensatory damages are assessed against a de-

[7] *Punitive Damages in Tort Cases* (1931) 44 HARV. L. REV. 1173.
[8] *Id.* at 1174. [9] *Id.* at 1175.

fendant who has himself been guilty of no wrongdoing. In such cases, the policy of the law is clearly to permit whatever conduct the defendant engaged in, provided he will compensate those who suffer from it. According to an old doctrine known as *respondeat superior,* an employer is liable, though blameless himself, for injury caused by the wrong of his employee—provided that the employee was engaged in the employer's business or was merely making a "detour" therefrom, as distinguished from being "on a frolic of his own," as Baron Parke expressed it long ago.[10] One modern theory for justifying this doctrine is what Morris calls the "entrepreneur theory"—a theory, be it noted, which would justify extending the doctrine so as to make the master liable for the injury even if the servant were guilty of no wrong himself. As Morris explains this theory:

> Roughly the argument is this: The servant is usually judgment proof; if the injured person must look to the servant for reimbursement, he will have no recourse as a practical matter. But if the master is held liable, he can consider the liability as one of the costs of his business, and plan to bear losses by insuring against them and adjusting his prices so that the custom of the business must bear part, if not all, of the burden of insurance. In this way losses are spread and the shock of accident dispersed.[11]

The implications of this justification had been previously explored and elaborated by Young B. Smith in an article cited by Morris.[12] Smith pointed out that the policy underlying this justification is the same as that which underlies workmen's compensation acts, which make an employer liable to compensate injured employees even when no fault can be imputed to the employer.

When the wrongful act of a servant, then, results in economic loss to an outsider, or when an industrial accident causes personal injuries to an employee, the law shifts the economic burden of the loss to the employer who may be entirely innocent of any wrongdoing. The law does not accuse him of violating any duty to refrain, in the one case, from hiring servants who may conceivably (despite the employer's utmost precautions) inflict harm on others or, in the other, from engaging men to work in occupations which involve risk of accidents. Yet as far as its compulsory effect goes, it represses these acts to pre-

10 Joel v. Morrison, 6 C. & P. *501, *503 (1834).

11 44 HARV. L. REV. at 1199.

12 *Frolic and Detour* (1923) 23 COL. L. REV. 444 and 716. See also William O. Douglas (now of the Supreme Court), *Vicarious Liability and Administration of Risk* (1929) 38 YALE L. J. 584 and 720.

cisely the same degree as if it called them breaches of duty for which the sole penalty was liability to pay compensatory damages. The law might, perhaps, be too effective in its persuasive effect if it called these acts "wrongs." A man who would voluntarily try to comply with the law would in that case be more likely to desist from them. But to the man who is not sensitive to the law's reproaches, only to its more tangible sanctions—the man whom Holmes calls the "bad man"—the effect on his decision to hire or not to hire would be the same, whether the law calls the hiring rightful or wrongful. In either case he must pay for the losses which ensue, and that is all. If he can insure against the liability, he will engage in a business which involves hiring men in the supposed circumstances if he thinks he can obtain a satisfactory profit despite payment of the insurance premium, and not otherwise. Some "bad men" will engage in the business even if they have to pay the premium, some will not, even if they do not have to pay; but there are likely to be some to whom the premium will be the determining factor. These are the ones who will be deterred by the liability. Even if it be assumed that the burden will be shifted to the customers in the form of increased prices, presumably the customers will demand fewer of the products at the higher price than they would demand if the price were lower; hence for this indirect reason, manufacturers will be deterred from engaging as fully in the business as if there were no liability. Whether there were said to be a "duty" to abstain from engaging in such businesses, or not, there is in either case a duty to pay for the losses which ensue. This duty serves to discourage people from entering the business unless the customers desire the products sufficiently to pay all the costs which operation of the business entails, including the losses caused by accidents. It may very well be the policy of the law to discourage the business to that extent, and no more. Such a policy would conform to orthodox economic theories: the consumer should be charged a price which covers all the costs of supplying him with the products, and the production of any more than can be sold at such a price is considered economically wasteful.

There are other acts which are regarded as innocent, acts which the law even goes out of its way to facilitate, such as the exercise of the power of eminent domain by a railroad company, but for which damages must be paid; and there are still other acts for which money must be paid, though it is not called damages. The deterrent effect on the "bad man" is the same as if those acts were called wrongs—assuming that no legal consequence other than the payment of the money is involved. Holmes brought the matter out in a discussion in *The Path of the Law,* first published in the *Harvard Law Review* in 1897.[13] Although he began by emphasizing the distinction between a fine and a tax on the same course of conduct, he proceeded to demonstrate that the distinction is insignificant insofar as it affects the "bad man." Despite this inconsistency, his discussion is so illuminating that it is set forth here at some length. His caution against injecting morals into the law, it should be noted, is pertinent to a descriptive study of what the law does, but not to a critical discussion of whether its effects are desirable. The passage follows.

Take again a notion which as popularly understood is the widest conception which the law contains—the notion of legal duty, to which already I have referred. We fill the word with all the content which we draw from morals. But what does it mean to a bad man? Mainly, and in the first place, a prophecy that if he does certain things he will be subjected to disagreeable consequences by way of imprisonment or compulsory payment of money. But from his point of view, what is the difference between being fined and being taxed a certain sum for doing a certain thing? That his point of view is the test of legal principles is shown by the many discussions which have arisen in the courts on the very question whether a given statutory liability is a penalty or a tax. On the answer to this question depends the decision whether conduct is legally wrong or right, and also whether a man is under compulsion or free. Leaving the criminal law on one side, what is the difference between the liability under the mill acts or statutes authorizing a taking by eminent domain and the liability for what we call wrongful conversion of property where restoration is out of the question? In both cases the party taking another man's property has to pay its fair value as assessed by a jury, and no more. What significance is there in calling one taking right and another wrong from the point of view of the law? It does not matter, so far as the given consequence, the compulsory payment, is concerned, whether the act to which it is attached is described in terms of praise or in terms of blame, or whether the law purports to prohibit it or to allow it. If it matters at all, still speaking from the bad man's point of view, it must be because in one case and not in the other some further disadvantages, or at least some further consequences, are attached to the act by the law. The only other disadvantages thus attached to it which I ever have been able to think of are to be found in two somewhat insignificant legal doctrines, both of which might be abolished without dis-

13 (1897) 10 HARV. L. REV. 457, 461–462. Reprinted in Holmes, COLLECTED LEGAL PAPERS (1921) 167, 173–175.

turbance. One is, that a contract to do a prohibited act is unlawful, and the other, that, if one of two or more joint wrongdoers has to pay all the damages, he cannot recover contribution from his fellows. And that I believe is all. You see how the vague circumference of the notion of duty shrinks and at the same time grows more precise when we wash it with cynical acid and expel everything except the object of our study, the operations of the law.

Nowhere is the confusion between legal and moral ideas more manifest than in the law of contract. Among other things, here again the so-called primary rights and duties are invested with a mystic significance beyond what can be assigned and explained. The duty to keep a contract at common law means a prediction that you must pay damages if you do not keep it—and nothing else. If you commit a tort, you are liable to pay a compensatory sum. If you commit a contract, you are liable to pay a compensatory sum unless the promised event comes to pass, and that is all the difference. But such a mode of looking at the matter stinks in the nostrils of those who think it advantageous to get as much ethics into the law as they can.

Committing a tort is usually described in terms of blame; "committing a contract" in terms of praise. But if the contract calls for the payment of money, there is not even the difference which Holmes noted in the practical consequences. True, you do not have to pay the compensatory sum under the name of damages if the promised event comes to pass. But the promised event can come to pass only if you pay the same sum under the name of keeping your contract. The law effectively compels those to abstain from the tort who would rather do so than incur the monetary liability, and it is ineffective as a deterrent to anyone else. The law is also effective in deterring anyone from incurring a debt who would rather refrain from borrowing than incur an obligation to pay, but deters no one else. Yet the tort is called a legal wrong, but not the incurrence of the debt. But deterring people from incurring debts when they do not care to pay them is surely as consistent with legal policy as is deterring them from committing torts for which they will not pay.

Just as there are some acts designated as "rightful" which the law permits only on condition that payments be made to someone else, so there are nominally "wrongful" acts which it seems to be the policy of the law to permit on that same condition. Mooring one's boat without permission to another man's dock is ordinarily a wrongful trespass, and the owner of the dock may lawfully put an end to the wrong by unmooring the boat, even though it may be damaged as a result.

But in *Ploof* v. *Putnam* [14] the Vermont court held that the trespass was justified by a sudden storm which threatened the boat and its occupants, and that it was unlawful for the owner of the dock to unmoor the boat. He was held liable in damages. The question whether the owner of the boat, though his act was "justified," would nevertheless have been liable for any damages which the mooring might have caused to the dock did not arise.

Two years later, however, that question did arise in Minnesota in the case of *Vincent* v. *Lake Erie Transportation Co.*[15] In that case, too, the owners of a vessel tied it to a dock to avoid its destruction by an unusual storm which suddenly arose. The dockowner did not, however, unmoor it, and the court intimated that it would have been unlawful for him to do so; for it cited the Vermont case with approval, justified the action of the owner of the vessel, and remarked that "the situation was one in which the ordinary rules regulating property rights were suspended by forces beyond human control." However, it sustained a verdict of $500 against the owners of the vessel for damage to the dock caused by the moored vessel being knocked against it by the storm. The court seems to have regarded the acts of the vessel-owners as technically "wrongful," though praiseworthy. Holding defendants liable for damages to a dock might deter owners of boats from mooring them in a storm in case they thought the boat not worth the damage they would have to pay; but it would not deter them otherwise. And sound policy would seem to call for this much deterrence and no more.

There are other cases in which courts conceive the actual performance of a duty to be such a hardship that they will deny an injunction against its breach, provided the defendant would rather pay the damages than comply with his duty. In other words, the person who is said to have a "right" to have the duty performed, in reality has no such right, but only a right to a pecuniary substitute in case the other party prefers to violate the so-called right and pay for doing so. In *City of Harrisonville* v. *Dickson Clay Mfg. Co.*,[16] for instance, the lower court had issued an injunction restraining a city from continuing to discharge the effluent from its sewage disposal plant into a stream. The only harm the discharge caused to the plaintiff was pecuniary, and it would cost the city much more to mend its ways. Hence the Supreme Court directed the lower court to withhold the injunc-

[14] 81 Vt. 471 (1908). [15] 109 Minn. 456 (1910). [16] 289 U.S. 334 (1933).

tion, if the amount of the resulting depreciation in the value of the plaintiff's property be paid within a time to be fixed. Justice Brandeis declared that the discharge of the effluent was a tort, but said: "Where substantial redress can be afforded by the payment of money and issuance of an injunction would subject the defendant to grossly disproportionate hardship, equitable relief may be denied although the nuisance is undeniable." [17]

This same doctrine of comparative hardships was applied in the case of *Smith* v. *Staso Milling Co.*[18] There the Circuit Court of Appeals modified an injunction granted by the District Court which restrained a slate-crushing mill from continuing an admitted invasion of the property rights of the owner of a nearby summer residence by polluting the air with dust. Damages were awarded for the past injuries in preventing Smith "from leasing his property as a residence."

In neither the *Vincent,* the *Harrisonville,* nor the *Staso Milling Company* case would the owner have been allowed to prevent the violation of his property right, either by direct action or by obtaining an injunction. The courts substituted for his property right a right to receive money supposed to be its equivalent. But it was not equivalent to what he could have obtained had he been permitted to threaten complete cessation of the technical wrong done him.

In the *Vincent* case it was implied that the dockowner would not have been permitted to exercise his right to keep the vessel from his dock. In the *Harrisonville* and the *Staso Milling Co.* cases the owner of land was not allowed to exercise his right to prevent the invasion of his property by the effluent from the sewer system or the dust from the slate crushing mill. In all three, damage ensued from the failure to exercise the right, and the owner was allowed to recover for this damage. The property right, while not actually exercised, was still of some avail to the owner. The dockowner received compensation for the physical damage to the dock, the Dickson Company for the depreciation in the value of its land, and Smith for the damage to his property as a summer residence. The compensation in each case, however, probably fell far short of what the owner could have exacted in a bargaining transaction as the price of not exercising his right to prevent the intrusion. The owner of the vessel might have been induced to pay far more than the cost of repairing the dock had the alternative been to risk the probable total destruction of the vessel. The City of

[17] *Id.* at 338.

[18] 18 F. 2d 736 (2d Cir. 1927).

Harrisonville might have paid a sum approaching the cost of building a new sewage plant rather than be forced to cease discharging the effluent from its old one, and the Staso Milling Company might have paid nearly the entire value of its plant as a going concern rather than discontinue its operation. Not only did the court not permit Smith actually to exercise his right to prevent the mill from emitting dust over his premises, but it confined the award for not exercising the right to far less than he could have obtained by bargaining not to exercise it.

The deprivation of Smith's bargaining power, which a right to an injunction would have given him, was, in this case, deliberate.

> The very right on which the injured party stands [said Judge Learned Hand] is a quantitative compromise between two conflicting interests. What may be an entirely tolerable adjustment, when the result is only to award damages for the injury done, may become no better than a means of extortion if the result is absolutely to curtail the defendant's enjoyment of his land. Even though the defendant has no power to condemn, at times it may be proper to require of him no more than to make good the whole injury once and for all.[19]

Thus, the court, while denying a formal right to condemn to the Staso Company, affirmed in effect an informal right to do so and to take from Smith, against his will, his right to prevent the emission of dust over his land, on payment of compensation; and the compensation was not measured by what the right would have been worth to Smith had he been permitted to use it as "a means of extortion," but by what he could have exacted from potential summer tenants had the company not interfered with his leasing. The court was really placing a limit, on the ground of economic policy, on the right which the law accords a man to control other people's conduct, just as courts which apply the prima facie tort doctrine place limits, based on policy, on acts which the law ordinarily permits a man to do. And the policy it pursued was one which involved judicial scrutiny of the possible economic fruits of his bargaining power.

In cases in which a governmental body or a railroad resorts to formal condemnation proceedings, courts seem inclined to follow a similar policy. They not only refuse to allow the owner actually to withhold his property from the public use, but in awarding compensation they decline to include what he might have exacted from the taker had he been able to threaten to withhold, insofar as that ex-

[19] 18 F. 2d at 738.

ceeds what he could have obtained from anyone else. "The question is, What has the owner lost? not, What has the taker gained?" [20] And what he has lost apparently includes no power to take advantage of the peculiar needs of the taker. Thus, when the City of New York was condemning certain parcels of land for a reservoir, the commissioners who appraised them for determining the compensation were sustained in taking no account of the fact that the parcels were situated in a natural basin which rendered them peculiarly desirable for reservoir purposes. It might well be, said Justice Holmes in *McGovern* v. *New York*,

> that the Commissioners regarded it as too plain to be shaken by evidence, on the peculiar facts, that the value of the land for a reservoir site could not come into consideration except upon the hypothesis that the City of New York could not get along without it and that its only means of acquisition was voluntary sale by owners aware of the necessity and intending to make from it the most they could. It is just this advantage that a taking by eminent domain excludes.[21]

Here, as in the *Staso Milling Co.* case, exaction of more than will compensate the owner for loss of his opportunity to bargain with other parties than the taker would be regarded as extortionate.

It must not be supposed, however, that the mere fact that an owner exacts more money from another private individual than he could have obtained from anyone else, as the price of not exercising his property right, renders the exaction illegal. In the *Staso* case itself Judge Hand said: "If the plaintiff had filed his bill before the mill was built, the balance of convenience would have been different, and we should not have hesitated to stop what has yet remained only a project." [22] The actual stoppage of the project, in that case, would not deprive the milling company of the entire value of its business as a going concern, for it would not in any event be able to obtain that value without first incurring the expense of constructing the mill. Stopping the mill from operating once it was constructed, however, would involve loss of most of the value of the going business, to avoid which the company might be induced to pay almost any sum less than this. But to avoid stoppage before construction the maximum which the company would presumably be willing to pay would be the an-

[20] Holmes, J., in Boston Chamber of Commerce v. City of Boston, 217 U.S. 189 (1910).

[21] 229 U.S. 363 (1913). For a more detailed discussion of the problem, see Hale, *Value to the Taker in Condemnation Cases* (1931) 31 COL. L. REV. 1, reprinted in part in LEWIS ORGEL, VALUATION UNDER THE LAW OF EMINENT DOMAIN (1936), c. 6.

[22] 18 F. 2d at 738.

ticipated value of the going business, minus the anticipated cost of construction. While this sum, however, would be considerably less than what might have been exacted once the mill was built, nevertheless, it might well exceed any loss which the dust would inflict upon the value of Smith's property as a summer residence. Yet the power to exact such a sum would, apparently, not be regarded as a means of extortion. What, then, does make the exaction of money legally "extortionate"? It will take another chapter to discuss this matter.

VII

EXTORTION AND DURESS

COLLECTING money by threatening to act unlawfully if it is not paid or by offering to act unlawfully if it is would usually be held criminal under statutes which proscribe extortion or blackmail. Thus, if the publication of a libel is threatened, or if one offers to compound a felony by concealing knowledge of it from the authorities, illegality is obvious. But blackmail or extortion includes cases in which there would be nothing unlawful, either in publishing or in failing to publish. The English Larceny Act of 1916 provides that: "Every person who utters, knowing the contents thereof, any letter or writing demanding of any person with menaces, and without reasonable or probable cause, any property or valuable thing . . . shall be guilty of felony." [1] In three different cases a rule of the Motor Trade Association came before three different English courts, to determine whether it violated this statute. The Association had a Stop List. If any member's name was placed on it, other members would not deal with him. A rule of the Association provided that, if any member deviated from list prices, his name should be placed on the Stop List, unless within twenty-one days he pay a "reasonable" fine.

[1] S. 29, sub-sec. I (i).

The Court of Criminal Appeal, in 1926, in *Rex* v. *Denyer*,[2] held that the attempt to collect the fine was a demand for money "with menaces, and without reasonable or probable cause," and therefore violated the statute. The judge went so far as to say: "A person has no right to demand money . . . as a price of abstaining from inflicting unpleasant consequences upon a man." In 1928, however, the same rule came before a civil court (the Court of Appeal), in the case of *Hardie & Lane* v. *Chilton*.[3] That court held the rule to be lawful, and Scrutton, L. J., said that the demand was not "without reasonable cause," since "the threatener has a legal right to do what he threatens." Finally, the same rule came before the House of Lords in 1937, in the civil case of *Thorne* v. *Motor Trade Association*.[4] There the rule was held lawful, the demand being not "without reasonable cause," but the principle enunciated by Scrutton was subjected to adverse criticism, as well as that of the Court of Criminal Appeal.

Lord Wright, who delivered one of the five opinions, referred thus to the latter statement:

> There are many possible circumstances under which a man may say to another that he will abstain from conduct unpleasant to the other only if he is paid a sum of money. Thus he may offer not to build on his plot of land if he is compensated for abstaining. He is entitled to bargain as a consideration for agreeing not to use his own land as he lawfully may, and the other man may think it worth while to pay him, rather than have the amenities of his house destroyed by an eyesore. Or a valued servant may threaten to go to other employment unless he is paid a bonus or increased wages.[5]

To these examples he added later the case "of the owner of multiple stores offering not to open a shop in a particular locality if a tradesman or tradesmen in the locality will compensate him for so doing." [6]

Lord Wright made it clear, however, that not every threat to inflict unpleasant consequences unless money be paid is legal, as Scrutton had held, merely because "the threatener has a legal right to do what he threatens." As to this he said:

> If by "right to do" it is intended to refer to a right of a man to use his property as he desires or to give or withhold his services without any breach of contract as he desires, or to abstain from legitimate competition, the proposition seems to me to be correct. . . . But there are many cases where a man who has a "right," in the sense of a liberty or capacity

[2] [1926] 2 K.B. 258.
[3] [1928] 2 K.B. 306.
[4] [1937] A.C. 797.
[5] *Id.* at 820.
[6] *Id.* at 822.

of doing an act which is not unlawful, but which is calculated seriously to injure another, will be liable to a charge of blackmail if he demands money from that other as a price of abstaining. Such instances indeed are very typical cases of blackmail, . . . Thus a man may be possessed of knowledge of discreditable incidents in the victim's life and may seek to extort money by threatening, if he is not paid, to disclose the knowledge to a wife or husband or employer, though the disclosure may not be libellous. Such is a common type of blackmail. Cases where the non-disclosure to the proper authority is illegal as amounting to compounding a felony or a misdemeanour of public import, or where the publication would constitute a criminal libel, are a fortiori.[7]

In *Keys* v. *United States*[8] the Court of Appeals for the 8th Circuit, in 1942, sustained a conviction under a federal statute which provided punishment for any person who with intent to extort money transmitted in interstate commerce a communication containing a "threat to injure the property or reputation of the addressee." The communication was addressed to the Aluminum Association, and the threat was to distribute a pamphlet alleging that aluminum cooking utensils were a danger to health. It was held not to be "an essential element of the offense" that the threat should be to violate a legal right of the addressee, and the court, speaking through Thomas, Cir. J., dismissed the defendant's contention "that a threat to do something which a person has a right to do is not a threat in a legal sense." Yet it must be that not every threat to injure the property of the addressee contained in an interstate communication would be held to violate this statute. If a man in Connecticut addressed a letter to his neighbor, at the latter's office in New York, telling of his intent to put up a building for his own use which would cut off the neighbor's light and air and offering to abandon the project and grant the neighbor an easement of light and air for a certain price, it is not likely that the writer would be held guilty of attempted extortion. Such a letter, nevertheless, contains what to the addressee amounts to a threat to injure his property and a demand for money for not carrying out the threat. What is the distinction between a lawful and an unlawful demand for money when each demand is accompanied by "a threat to do something which a person has a right to do"? Do we get any clue from the civil cases dealing with "duress," in which criminal statutes against extortion or blackmail do not apply?

In a civil action, one who has parted with possession of property

[7] *Id.* at 822.

[8] 126 F. 2d 181 (8th Cir. 1942).

under duress or paid money because "extortion" has been practiced against him may recover it from the person who subjected him to the duress or extortion; and if he has made a contract under duress, he may "avoid" the contract (have it declared invalid) as against the one who exerted duress. But at first duress was recognized by the law only when coercion was applied by threatening some act which would be unlawful apart from its coercive effect. And if the unlawful act threatened was one for which the victim could obtain satisfaction in an action for damages, it was at one time thought that no contract or deed could be avoided because made under such a threat—possibly because courts took the unrealistic and complacent view that no man need fear a threat of unlawful conduct for which he can get a legal remedy and that it must therefore be assumed that he did not in fact yield to such an empty threat. At any rate, Lord Coke long ago declared that a man could avoid his deed for fear of loss of life, loss of a member, mayhem, or imprisonment, but added, "otherwise it is for fear of battery, which may be very light, or for burning of his houses, or taking away, or destroying of his goods, or the like, for there he may have satisfaction by recovery of damages." [9]

By and by the courts came to apply a test, not of what the particular threat was, but of whether it was sufficient to "overcome the mind" of a "person of ordinary firmness." This test was further revised in some jurisdictions, so that the question became whether the threat was sufficient to overcome the mind, not of a "person of ordinary firmness," but of the particular party who alleged the duress.[10] Courts seem inclined even at the present time, however, to take the position that a threat to do an act for which the other party can sue does not constitute illegal duress and that the threat to subject him to the expense and uncertainty of litigation must be presumed, at least, to have had no coercive effect. In 1943 the District of Columbia Court of Appeals held that when the appellee made a contract under protest because the appellant threatened to have the bid bond forfeited which appellee had furnished under a bid which it claimed a right to rescind because of a mistake, there was no duress, since appellee could have litigated the question.[11] In the same year the Massachusetts court, in

[9] 2 Co. Inst. 483, quoted in 2 E. W. Patterson, Cases and Materials on Contracts, 45 (1935).

[10] For an account of this development see the opinion of Harvey, J., in Riney v. Doll, 116 Kan. 26 (1924).

[11] Edgerton, J., in Board of Trustees of National Training School for Boys v. O. D. Wilson Co., 133 F. 2d 399 (Cir. D.C. 1943).

an opinion by Justice Ronan, denied that an employer's payment of back wages, made to terminate a strike which the employer alleged to be illegal, was made under duress. "If the union was engaged in an illegal strike," said the court, "the plaintiff had a legal remedy." Because the employer settled the strike, instead of pursuing that legal remedy, the court concluded that it had not sustained the burden of proving that, as a question of fact, it "was forced to pay the money through the coercive effect of the strike." [12]

In this case the court was only deciding whether the allegedly illegal strike had in fact had a coercive effect. But, though the present weight of authority may be otherwise, there are courts which have held, and still hold, that coercive effect is not sufficient to constitute duress or even deny that there is any coercion unless "the mind was overcome," so that when the person to whom the duress was applied parted with his property or signed a contract his doing so was not really his act at all, but rather was like the act of one under hypnosis or suffering from senility, who, while able to write his name, scarcely knows what he is doing when subjected to "undue influence." How did this doctrine of "overcoming the mind" arise?

When courts regard a threat to do illegal acts that are less serious than mayhem and the like as an empty threat, because the victim has a legal remedy, it is perhaps natural that they should conclude that no one would yield to such a threat unless his mind or his will had been overcome. This may, perhaps, be the explanation. Or perhaps courts may have been confused by the terminology used in physiological discourse in distinguishing "voluntary" from "involuntary" motions. From the physiological standpoint, wincing when hit, being startled when hearing a sudden noise, breathing while asleep, and the beating of the heart all result from involuntary muscular contractions. But acts committed deliberately, because of signals sent from the brain, are all termed "voluntary." It might avoid confusion to term them "volitional" rather than "voluntary," for they are not all voluntary except in the physiological sense of the word. If a convict breaks rock in a jail to escape some worse punishment, a slave toils to escape the lash, or a man signs a check because a gun is pointed at his head, the acts are all "voluntary" in the physiological sense—but not in any other sense. Statements are frequently to be found, however, to the effect that there can be no duress unless the party to whom

[12] Cappy's, Inc. v. Dorgan, 313 Mass. 170 (1943).

it was applied was so overcome in his will or his mind that what he did was not his "voluntary" act at all, in that he was deprived of the power to make a decision—in short, that it was not volitional.

The converse of this proposition is that once it is established that a man did something under duress, what he did was no more his act than would be the falling of his body if a more powerful man had thrown him out of a window. The legal consequence of such a doctrine is to make a distinction between the parting with property or the making of a contract when induced by fraud and when induced by duress. One who is induced by fraud to part with property or to sign a contract can recover the property or avoid the contract as against the fraudulent party, but not as against an innocent purchaser or transferee. A contract induced by fraud is therefore said to be "voidable," but not "void." But if property is stolen, the true owner can recover it even from an innocent purchaser from the thief. And if signing a contract under duress be taken not to be a volitional act, the contract is not only voidable, but void, so that the defense of duress will prevail even against a bona fide transferee of the contract who is unaware of the duress.

Thus, in *Barry* v. *Equitable Life Assurance Society*,[13] decided by the New York Court of Appeals in 1875, plaintiff had put her signature to an assignment in blank of an insurance policy. In doing so, she was found to have acted "under duress, coercion and undue influence" exercised by her husband. The manner in which he exercised these influences does not appear from the report of the case. The husband then had the blanks filled out so as to purport to assign the policy to one Brune, who gave consideration for the transfer and was unaware of the duress exercised by the husband. In holding that the transfer was void, the court, speaking through Judge Folger, said:

> We do not agree, however, with the learned justice, that a *bona fide* purchaser for value, acquires a good title to a chose in action which he has bought from one who has procured it from the owner of it by undue influence, compulsion and coercion. There is a class of cases which hold that where the owner of property, induced by false representations, sells it and parts with the possession of it with the intention of passing the title to the vendee, there the *bona fide* purchaser for value from the fraudulent vendee obtains a title which he can defend. In such case there is a voluntary parting with the possession of the property and there is an uncontrolled volition to pass the title. But where there exist coercion,

[13] 59 N.Y. 587 (1875).

threats, compulsion and undue influence, there is no volition. There is no intention nor purpose, but to yield to moral pressure, for relief from it. A case is presented more analogous to a parting with property by robbery. No title is made through a possession thus acquired.[14]

But to say that there was no intention but to yield to moral pressure is not the same thing as to say there was no volition. And courts which deem lack of volition essential to a finding of duress frequently make a priori assumptions as to the mental state of the victim. In the English case of *Williams* v. *Bayley*,[15] for example, a man charged his property to secure the amount which his son had obtained by forgeries, when informed that the son had admitted the crime, for which the penalty was transportation for life. Lord Westbury, after stating that "a contract to give security for the debt of another, which is a contract without consideration, is, above all things, a contract that should be based upon the free and voluntary agency of the individual who enters into it," added:

But it is clear that the power of considering whether he ought to do it or not, whether it is prudent to do it or not, is altogether taken away from a father who is brought into the situation of either refusing, and leaving his son in that perilous condition, or of taking on himself the amount of a civil obligation.

I have, therefore, in that view of the case, no difficulty in saying that, as far as my opinion is concerned, the security given for the debt of the son by the father under such circumstances was not the security of a man who acted with that freedom and power of deliberation that must, undoubtedly, be considered as necessary to validate a transaction of such a description.

Was the real objection to the transaction that the father could not deliberate and could not consider whether it was prudent or not, or was the objection rather that no matter how much power of deliberating he retained he would still be faced with the dilemma which would make him consider it prudent to make the contract as the lesser evil? Lord Westbury cited no evidence to show that the father's choice was imprudent, and none but an a priori presumption to show that he was really unable to form a sound judgment as to what was his most prudent course under the circumstances.

Westbury's language was quoted with approval by the Oregon Supreme Court in 1917 in *Rostad* v. *Thorsen*,[16] in which a wife had

[14] *Id.* at 591–592.
[15] 1 L.R. Eng. & Irish App. 200, 218–219 (1866).
[16] 83 Ore. 489 (1917).

signed papers in favor of a bank when suddenly confronted with knowledge that her husband had embezzled from the bank, and had signed them in the hope that he would be saved from prosecution. Chief Justice McBride stressed the woman's presumed nervous condition, speaking of her as "a helpless woman, without counsel, overpowered by the most distressing situation that a woman could be placed in, and terrified for the future of her husband, her own future, and that of her little children." At a previous point in his opinion he said:

> Naturally, in her disturbed condition of mind, by reason of the shock of these revelations and the thought of the disgrace that would be inflicted upon her husband, herself, and her two children, she consented to sign. We think that this was not her voluntary act. Whether we call it duress or undue influence matters little.

The court based the involuntary character of the act on the woman's disturbed state of mind, implying that it was not voluntary in the physiological sense. But even if it could have been shown that she acted calmly and was not "overpowered" in the sense of losing her self-control, could not her act have been held involuntary in the broader meaning of that word?

There are courts which still speak of overcoming the will as an essential element of duress. Even as late as 1942 Justice Black remarked, in an opinion in the Supreme Court in *United States* v. *Bethlehem Steel Corp.*, that "there is no evidence of that state of overcome will which is the major premise of the petitioner's argument of duress." [17] If there must be evidence of an overcome will, courts are presented with a difficult problem in psychology. What sort of evidence would suffice?

In *Gill* v. *Reveley* [18] a federal court was confronted by certain transactions which took place in Kansas, and accordingly applied Kansas law. The plaintiff contended that he had sold certain stock to the defendant at less than its fair value, under duress, because the defendant, some two weeks before the sale, had threatened to have him prosecuted and sent to the penitentiary under the Mann Act, for traveling across state lines with a woman who was not his wife. Judge Bratton, after stating that under the law of Kansas a threat of criminal prosecution does not constitute duress "unless the person to whom the threat was made became so frightened or was placed in such fear as to overcome his judgment and make it impossible for him to exercise his own free will," proceeded to discuss the evidence:

[17] 315 U.S. 289, 301 (1942).

[18] 132 F. 2d 975 (10th Cir. 1943).

Here Gill testified that the threat of Reveley made in the lobby of the hotel frightened him and made him mad; that except for such threat he would not have resigned; and that he did not want to sell his stock and would not have done so had it not been for such threat. But he did not testify that he became deeply moved or upset in mind; that he could not sleep; that his nerves were strained; that he could not think clearly; that he could not control himself; or that he could not exercise his own free will. He did not give any testimony of that nature. And there was no other direct evidence indicating such a condition of mind. Moreover, the testimony that the threat frightened him and made him mad had reference to the time of the conversation in the lobby of the hotel, and the stock was not sold then. The contracts for the sale of the stock were executed more than two weeks later, and the record is utterly bare of any direct evidence with respect to his being frightened or otherwise disturbed in mind at that time.

In the Massachusetts case of *Omansky* v. *Shain*,[19] decided in the same year (1943), the court also described some of the symptoms of an overcome will. In this case the plaintiff was suing on a note which the defendant contended had been obtained by duress. The court held that the evidence justified the finding of the court below that the plaintiff obtained the note "by threats that were in fact sufficient to overcome the will of the defendant, in the condition in which he was, whether or not they would have been sufficient to overcome the will of a person of ordinary courage and firmness." Evidence that was held admissible to show the defendant's state of mind and his fear of the plaintiff, "and thus to show his susceptibility to duress," included letters written by plaintiff to defendant's estranged wife (a sister of the plaintiff's wife), containing "extravagant language of affection," and defendant's testimony "that beginning early in 1928 he did not eat at home, because he feared being poisoned by his wife and the plaintiff." The defendant was in a house of correction under sentence for an offense which the report does not specify when he signed the note in question on December 1, 1930. The court thus summarized the evidence as to the circumstances of the signing:

The plaintiff wished the defendant to pay $500 for a fur coat that the defendant's wife had bought. The plaintiff told the defendant that if he did not pay the money he would be in jail for the rest of his life. The plaintiff shouted that the defendant must do what he was told to do, that "they" had power and influence, and that the defendant should ask no questions but should give "them" the money; that another brother-in-law was an editor of a magazine, and that one word from him would cause the newspapers to print anything he wished. The defendant pleaded with

[19] 313 Mass. 129 (1943).

the plaintiff not to bother him any more, but the plaintiff said, "We will keep you here for life. * * * We can frame you again." At the time the defendant was mentally ill, helpless and confused, and vomiting frequently, and he was afraid that the plaintiff would make good his threats. Accordingly he gave the note to induce the plaintiff to pay for the fur coat.

Of course the defendant's state of mind might have been held relevant even if overcoming the will were not thought essential, since it might throw light on whether in signing the note he was in fact influenced by the plaintiff's threats. It might, perhaps, be assumed that a man in better mental health would not have believed the plaintiff capable of carrying out his threats and that if such a man had signed the note the threats could have played no part in motivating him. Moreover, if one man's threats deprive another of the mental power to exercise his sound judgment, that fact might well be held sufficient to permit him to avoid his contract as against the one who made the threats. But it does not follow that a contract can only be avoided by one who was deprived of the power of sound judgment or that when a man has made a contract under duress while in control of his mental powers it was any less his act than if he had been induced to do so by fraud.

Justice Holmes has several times pointed out the fallacy in thinking that acts done under duress are synonymous with acts which in the physiological sense are "involuntary." In *Fairbanks* v. *Snow,*[20] decided in Massachusetts in 1887, Holmes held that the trial judge was correct in holding that if a note signed under duress came into the hands of one ignorant of the duress, duress (like fraud) would be no defense to a suit on the note. The defendant alleged that she had signed the note under duress brought to bear, not by the plaintiff, but by her husband. The nature of the duress does not appear in the report. She took exception to the trial court's refusal to rule that "if the defendant signed the note under duress, it was immaterial whether the plaintiff knew, when he received the note, that it was so signed." In overruling this exception, and sustaining the trial judge, Justice Holmes said:

> No doubt, if the defendant's hand had been forcibly taken and compelled to hold the pen and write her name, and the note had been carried off and delivered, the signature and delivery would not have been her acts; and if the signature and delivery had not been her acts, for what-

[20] 145 Mass. 153 (1887).

ever reason, no contract would have been made, whether the plaintiff knew the facts or not. There sometimes still is shown an inclination to put all cases of duress upon this ground. *Barry* v. *Equitable Life Assurance Society,* 59 N.Y. 587, 591. But duress, like fraud, rarely, if ever, becomes material as such, except on the footing that a contract or conveyance has been made which the party wishes to avoid. It is well settled that where, as usual, the so-called duress consists only of threats, the contract is only voidable. [Citations.]

This rule necessarily excludes from the common law the often recurring notion, just referred to, and much debated by the civilians, that an act done under compulsion is not an act in a legal sense. *Tamen coactus volui.* D. 4. 2. 21, § 5. See Windscheid, Pandekten, § 80.[21]

Again, in the United States Supreme Court in 1905, in the case of *The Eliza Lines,* Holmes stressed the distinction between "duress by threats" and

overmastering physical force applied to a man's body and imparting to it the motion sought to be attributed to him. In the former case there is a choice and therefore an act, no less when the motive is recognized as very strong or even generally overpowering, than when it is one which would affect the particular person only, and not the public at large. . . . The distinction is as old as the Roman law, *Tamen coactus volui.*[22]

Failure to make the distinction, he said, "is one of the oldest fallacies of the law." That there can be volition, or choice, under duress, Holmes pointed out once more in 1918, in *Union Pacific Ry. Co.* v. *Public Service Commission,* when he said: "It always is for the interest of a party under duress to choose the lesser of two evils. But the fact that a choice was made according to interest does not exclude duress. It is the characteristic of duress properly so called." [23]

Not only may there be duress when a choice was made without the mind being overcome, but duress may be held to exist when the threat upon which it is based is a threat to do what in other circumstances would be lawful. Indeed, to state this goes little (if at all) beyond the prima facie tort doctrine which would make the carrying

21 *Id.* at 154. In the subsequent Massachusetts case of Morse v. Woodworth, 155 Mass. 233, 250 (1892), Knowlton, J., seems to have learned little from Holmes. Explaining the rule as to duress, he said that if an influence is exerted on one of the parties "of such a kind as to overcome his will and compel a formal assent to an undertaking when he does not really agree to it, and so to make that appear to be his act which is not his but another's imposed on him through fear which deprives him of self-control, there is no contract unless the other deals with him in good faith, in ignorance of the improper influence, and in the belief that he is acting voluntarily." Holmes was a member of the court, but the report does not list his name among those present at this stage of the proceedings.

22 199 U.S. 119, 130–131 (1905).

23 248 U.S. 67, 70 (1918).

out of the threats unlawful if they were designed to accomplish what the courts would regard as an improper purpose or the doctrine that to make threats of what would otherwise be lawful conduct may under some circumstances be blackmail or criminal extortion.

In *Silsbee* v. *Webber*[24] we find another discussion by Holmes, where the threatened act, if it had been carried out, would have been lawful (if at all) only because of the administrative difficulty of making it unlawful. The plaintiff had executed an assignment of her share in her father's estate to the defendant. She was suing to recover $1,150 which the defendant had collected under this assignment, alleging that the assignment had been obtained by duress. According to her testimony, she executed the assignment to prevent the defendant from carrying out his threat to tell her husband of their son's theft of defendant's money—the son having been employed by defendant. The husband, according to her testimony, was in such a condition that the knowledge was likely to cause his insanity, and she had told the defendant about her husband's condition. The trial judge directed the jury to return a verdict for the defendant. The majority of the Supreme Judicial Court of Massachusetts, although somewhat skeptical of plaintiff's testimony, thought that if the jury believed it, a verdict for the plaintiff would have been warranted. Accordingly, the verdict was set aside, with a direction that the case stand for trial. In the course of the opinion, Justice Holmes said:

> The strongest objection to holding the defendant's alleged action illegal duress is, that, if he had done what he threatened, it would not have been an actionable wrong. In general, duress going to motives consists in the threat of illegal acts. Ordinarily, what you may do without liability you may threaten to do without liability. See *Vegelahn* v. *Guntner*, . . . ; *Allen* v. *Flood*, ... But this is not a question of liability for threats as a cause of action, and we may leave undecided the question whether, apart from special justification deliberately and with foresight of the consequences, to tell a man what you believe will drive him mad is actionable if it has the expected effect. . . . If it should be held not to be, . . . it would be only on the ground that a different rule was unsafe in the practical administration of justice. If the law were an ideally perfect instrument, it would give damages for such a case as readily as for a battery. When it comes to the collateral question of obtaining a contract by threats, it does not follow that, because you cannot be made to answer for the act, you may use the threat. In the case of the threat there are no difficulties of proof, and the relation of cause and effect is as easily shown

[24] 171 Mass. 378 (1898).

as when the threat is of an assault. If a contract is extorted by brutal and wicked means, and a means which owes its immunity, if it have immunity, solely to the law's distrust of its own powers of investigation, in our opinion the contract may be avoided by the party to whom the undue influence has been applied. Some of the cases go further, and allow to be avoided contracts obtained by the threat of unquestionably lawful acts. *Morse* v. *Woodworth*, 155 Mass. 233, 251. *Adams* v. *Irving National Bank*, 116 N.Y. 606. *Williams* v. *Bayley*, L.R. 1 H.L. 200, 210.[25]

In the three cases last cited, as in some of the others that we have noted, the threat was imprisonment. In the case of this threat, there may be a special reason for releasing the party subjected to it from his contract, which does not apply with equal force to other threats. He may have a right against the party who for the purpose of carrying out a threat instigates the imprisonment, even when he has no right against the authorities who imprison him. As Justice Knowlton said in 1892, in the passage which Holmes cited from *Morse* v. *Woodworth:*

It has sometimes been held that threats of imprisonment, to constitute duress, must be of unlawful imprisonment. But the question is whether the threat is of imprisonment which will be unlawful in reference to the conduct of the threatener who is seeking to obtain a contract by his threat. Imprisonment that is suffered through the execution of a threat which was made for the purpose of forcing a guilty person to enter into a contract may be lawful as against the authorities and the public, but unlawful as against the threatener, when considered in reference to his effort to use for his private benefit processes provided for the protection of the public and the punishment of crime. One who has overcome the mind and will of another for his own advantage, under such circumstances, is guilty of a perversion and abuse of laws which were made for another purpose, and he is in no position to claim the advantage of a formal contract obtained in that way, on the ground that the rights of the parties are to be determined by their language and their overt acts, without reference to the influence which moved them. In such a case, there is no reason why one should be bound by a contract obtained by force, which in reality is not his, but another's.[26]

Of course, the making of the contract is his act, not another's, even though he chose to perform the act as the lesser of two evils. Nevertheless, Knowlton seems to have reached the heart of the matter when he made the lawfulness of certain acts depend on whether they are performed in execution of a threat, and whether the law which generally permits their performance is made for another purpose. The law

[25] *Id.* at 380–381.

[26] 155 Mass. 233, 251 (1892).

creates rights of private property and allows the privilege of declining to work or to enter into transactions, for the benefit of the person to whom these rights and privileges are accorded. Hence, there is ordinarily nothing wrong in his effort to use such rights and privileges "for his private benefit," even by influencing another's conduct by a threat so to use them. It is considered legitimate not only to enforce one's rights and exercise one's privileges of this type but also to bargain with them. On the other hand, the power to cause the imprisonment of a guilty person and the privilege of communicating derogatory information about a person (when it falls short of libel) are allowed for purposes other than to enable one to gain economic benefit. If threatened for the purpose of being bought off, the law may not permit them; and if the threat has induced the victim to pay money or sign a contract, the transaction may be annulled—but not properly on the ground that he entered into it without "volition."

Even privileges which are permitted for the private economic benefit of the possessor may at times be thought to be perverted when he threatens to exercise them for the purpose of gaining some different sort of advantage. A landowner's privilege to sink a shaft may be justified on the ground that he should be permitted to make whatever use of his land he finds advantageous. When his purpose, however, is not to improve his land, but, as in *Mayor of Bradford* v. *Pickles*,[27] to force someone to buy him out, because "he has something which he can prevent other people enjoying unless he is paid for it," it seems questionable whether he should be permitted to realize on a mere nuisance value. Workers are recognized to have the privilege of ceasing work (if not bound by contract) and of combining to cease work in order that by threatening to do so they may force their employer to pay them higher wages or to work them shorter hours. But the threat to combine to cease work may be held unlawful when exerted to secure for the workers certain other advantages, less directly pertaining to their working conditions. Does the mere fact that the threat is used to compel a person to pay money to the union, as punishment for conduct which the union wishes to prevent, render the threat illegal, and give the payer a right to recover the "fine" on the ground that the money was "extorted" from him?

If the threat was to do something which would have been unlawful if done for any other purpose than exacting the money, it would

27 [1895] A.C. 587. Cf. *supra*, p. 57.

seem to be equally unlawful for that purpose, unless the court could find some economic justification for the union obtaining the money —as courts find justification for a strike threat to induce an employer to pay more money, not to the union, but to its members. If, on the other hand, there is certain action which the union can lawfully take to punish a man for conduct they wish to discourage, does their threat to take that action become unlawful merely because they offer him the alternative of paying money and he accepts the alternative? There are intimations in the opinions of the Massachusetts court in *Carew* v. *Rutherford* [28] and of the Connecticut court in *March* v. *Bricklayers' Union* [29] that the demand for the money renders the threat unlawful and the receipt of the money "extortion." In both cases, however, it seems likely that the acts threatened would have been held unlawful if unaccompanied by any money demand, in that they would have inflicted damage without justification; had the acts been performed instead of threatened, the victim could have recovered for the damage suffered; since he averted the damage which the acts themselves would have caused and yielded instead to the demand for money, his damage consisted in the loss of the money, and his appropriate remedy was an action to recover it as having been "extorted" from him. This may account for the two courts speaking in terms of extortion rather than in terms of the prima facie tort.

In the Massachusetts case the fine was levied on a stone-cutting employer for having sent some of his work outside the state to be done. It was collected by threat of a strike. A strike to punish him for having sent work outside the state would very likely have been held unjustified, even had he not been told that the strike would be called off on payment of the fine.

In the Connecticut case a union of bricklayers (who worked for "boss-masons," not for brickmakers), levied a fine on a brickmaker for having sold brick to a nonunion boss-mason. It collected the fine by inducing a certain unionized boss-mason to threaten not to take any more of the plaintiff's brick until the fine was paid, and it induced the boss-mason by threatening to call a strike against him. The plaintiff evidently regarded the payment of the $100 fine as a punishment less drastic than loss of the boss-mason's trade. Had the union insisted on the more drastic punishment, without offering him the less drastic alternative of paying the fine, it is hard to believe that the court

[28] 106 Mass. 1 (1870). [29] 79 Conn. 7 (1906).

would have held its action lawful. The purpose of the fine does not seem to have been the enrichment of the union's treasury, but the punishment of the plaintiff for not participating in a boycott. If such a purpose would not have justified the intentional infliction of harm on the plaintiff, then the fine was exacted by a threat to do an unlawful act, and the case does not elucidate what makes a demand for money unlawful when accompanied by a threat to do an act which would be lawful if not employed for the purpose of collecting money.

Judge Prentice, however, speaking for the court, seemed to intimate that a demand for money as the price of forbearance from a harmful act threatened for the purpose of forcing compliance, is necessarily illegal. He characterized as "palpably unsound" the proposition

> that money demanded and obtained as the price of forbearance from the commission of an act of injury—even when the commission of that act is held over the man to coerce and intimidate him into compliance with the demand—is lawfully obtained, if the threatened act was one which the threatener might lawfully do.[30]

Perhaps all that Prentice meant was that money so obtained was not necessarily lawfully obtained. But if he meant that it is necessarily unlawful to demand and obtain money as the price of forbearance from an act of injury, merely because "the commission of that act is held over the man to coerce and intimidate him into compliance with the demand," he was obviously in error. On such a proposition, it would be unlawful to obtain money in any bargain.

Courts, however, are reluctant to recognize that there is compulsion in all contracts. In *United States* v. *Bethlehem Steel Corp.*, decided in 1942, Justice Black, speaking of the Government's abandonment of one of its demands during preliminary negotiations for a contract in the First World War, in deference to what Black regarded as a reasonable insistence by Bethlehem as to the particular point, said:

> And if the government's abandonment of its position is to be regarded as evidence of compulsion, we should have to find compulsion in every contract in which one of the parties makes a concession to a demand, however reasonable, of the other side.[31]

Well, why not? Each party to a contract must yield something in the transaction, under penalty of being denied something else which he values more. Concession to a demand does not cease to be compulsory

[30] 79 Conn. at 14.

[31] 315 U.S. 289, 302 (1942).

merely because the demand is reasonable. Obedience to a reasonable law is quite as compulsory as is obedience to an unreasonable one. But recognition of the fact that there is compulsion in every contract does not require that all contracts can be avoided on the ground of duress. The question still remains as to what criterion is to be applied in determining when a contract is to be avoided on that ground and when not.

We have seen that courts will sometimes avoid contracts when one party has brought pressure which "overcame the will" of the other and has deprived him of the ability to exercise a sound judgment. For a somewhat similar reason, infants can avoid contracts, because as a class they are thought to be too ignorant or inexperienced to bargain effectively with such rights as they have. Courts will likewise give jealous scrutiny to contracts made by seamen, who are regarded as "wards in admiralty." [32]

Courts have also set aside what they regarded as unconscionable contracts, in which one party had taken advantage of the other party's necessities, regardless of whether the latter was ignorant or inexperienced or whether his mind was overcome. Justice Frankfurter, dissenting in the *Bethlehem* case, thought that this principle applied to the transaction there between the Bethlehem Company and the Government. Stating the principle in general terms, he said:

> Fraud and physical duress are not the only grounds upon which courts refuse to enforce contracts. The law is not so primitive that it sanctions every injustice except brute force and downright fraud. More specifically, the courts generally refuse to lend themselves to the enforcement of a "bargain" in which one party has unjustly taken advantage of the economic necessities of the other. "And there is great reason and justice in this rule, for necessitous men are not, truly speaking, free men, but, to answer a present exigency, will submit to any terms that the crafty may impose upon them." *Vernon* v. *Bethell*, 2 Eden 110, 113. So wrote Lord Chancellor Northington in 1761.[33]

[32] For an interesting explanation of the law's early solicitude for seamen at a time when other workers were left to the mercies of "freedom of contract," see the opinion of Judge Jerome Frank in Hume v. Moore-McCormack Lines, 121 F. 2d 336 (2d Cir. 1941). In a dissenting opinion in M. Witmark & Sons v. Fred Fisher Music Co., 125 F. 2d 949, 954 (2d Cir. 1942), Judge Frank urged a construction of the Copyright Act which would extend the same solicitude to the author of a song, who assigned to a publisher his renewal rights twenty-two years before the copyright expired, for a sum much less than they turned out subsequently to be worth. The Supreme Court, however, affirmed Judge Frank's colleagues in rejecting this construction. Fred Fisher Music Co. v. M. Witmark & Sons, 318 U.S. 643 (1943), Justices Black, Douglas, and Murphy dissenting on the basis of Judge Frank's opinion.

[33] 315 U.S. at 326.

After citing numerous other cases, Frankfurter added:

Strikingly analogous to the case at bar are the decisions that a salvor who takes advantage of the helplessness of the ship in distress to drive an unconscionable bargain will not be aided by the courts in his attempt to enforce the bargain. *Post* v. *Jones*, 19 How. 150, 160; *The Tornado*, 109 U.S. 110, 117; *The Elfrida*, 172 U.S. 186, 193. In *Post* v. *Jones, supra*, it was said that the courts "will not tolerate the doctrine that a salvor can take the advantage of his situation, and avail himself of the calamities of others to drive a bargain; nor will they permit the performance of a public duty to be turned into a traffic of profit." These cases are not unlike the familiar example of the drowning man who agrees to pay an exorbitant sum to a rescuer who would otherwise permit him to drown. No court would enforce a contract made under such circumstances.[34]

Justice Black, speaking for the majority, did not deny these general principles. He thought them inapplicable to the particular contract. In the first place, he denied that the Government had been forced into the contract by its necessities, although when the contract was negotiated there seemed to be danger of losing the war unless the ships in question were promptly built. But Black thought that the Government, which carried on the negotiations through Bowles and Radford of the Government's Emergency Fleet Corporation, need not have yielded to Bethlehem's demands in order to avoid that risk. Part of his reason for thinking so is implied in the statement:

Although there are many cases in which an individual has claimed to be a victim of duress in dealings with government, . . . this, so far as we know, is the first instance in which government has claimed to be a victim of duress in dealings with an individual.[35]

In addition to this a priori assumption that the Government was *ipso facto* invulnerable to duress, Black had a more specific argument. The Government, he contended, was not faced with a choice between risking loss of the war and meeting Bethlehem's terms. It could have commandeered the plant. To the contention that acquisition of the plant would not have assured prompt building of the ships, in case the personnel of the Bethlehem organization should have been unwilling to serve the Government, he replied that there was no evidence that they would have been unwilling to serve, and furthermore, if they had been, the Government could have drafted them. Since any such action, however, would probably have led to prolonged litigation, Frankfurter's reply to Black's insistence that the Government had a third choice, seems effective. Said Frankfurter:

[34] 315 U.S. at 330.

[35] *Id.* at 300.

The contracts were not made by an abstraction known as the United States or by millions of its citizens. For all practical purposes, the arrangement was entered into by two persons, Bowles and Radford. And it was entered into by them against their better judgment because they had only Hobson's choice—which is no choice. They had no choice in view of the circumstances which subordinated them and by which they were governed, namely, that ships were needed, and needed quickly, and Bethlehem was needed to construct them quickly. The legal alternative—that the Government take over Bethlehem—was not an actual alternative, and Bethlehem knew this as well as the representatives of the Government.[36]

In saying that Bowles and Radford acted against their better judgment and that they had no choice, Frankfurter doubtless did not mean to imply that their minds were so overcome or that they labored under such emotions that they did not exercise good judgment in making the choice of accepting the company's terms rather than risk losing the war. That the company took advantage of the Government's necessities to insist on the bargain which it made seems clear.

However, Black gave another reason for thinking that the doctrine as to necessitous men did not apply here. As Frankfurter himself stated that doctrine, it applies only when one party has "unjustly" taken advantage of the necessities of the other or when one takes advantage of distress to drive an "unconscionable" bargain. It is only by reason of someone's necessities or distress that a doctor can collect a fee or a service station charge for rescuing a broken down automobile, yet all would agree that at least some contracts for the payment of the doctor or the service station should be enforced. And though it be admitted that the Government contracted with Bethlehem only because of its necessities, Frankfurter doubtless would not have insisted that the contract be set aside had he thought that it called only for a reasonable payment by the Government. But what test is to be applied to determine the reasonableness of the terms?

The arrangement in this case provided that there should first be an advance estimate of the "actual cost" of building a ship, which should be incorporated in the contract. "Actual cost" was to be computed on an agreed formula, rather generous to the company. It was not the advance estimate, however, that the Government agreed to pay, but the "actual cost" computed on the same formula, as it ultimately turned out to be, plus a stated profit, plus one-half the amount by which the actual "actual cost" fell below the advance estimate thereof.

[36] *Id.* at 331.

This last component in the amount which the Government agreed to pay was provided for in what was known as the "half-savings" clause. It was this clause that was challenged in the present suit.[37]

It was not the company's demand for inclusion of this clause that Justice Black characterized as reasonable in a passage quoted earlier. It was the demand that the Government recede from its insistence on a lump-sum contract. As to the half-savings clause, Black did not insist that it was reasonable or deny that the contract as a whole was "unconscionable." In fact, he implied the contrary. He distinguished some of the cases Frankfurter cited by saying that, "if there was a 'traffic of profit' here, it was not the unanticipated result of an accident as in the salvage cases." [38] Perhaps with the same thought in mind, he said elsewhere that

> high as Bethlehem's 22% profit seems to us, we are compelled to admit that so far as the record or any other source of which we can take notice discloses, it is not grossly in excess of the standard established by common practice in the field in which Congress authorized the making of these contracts.[39]

And again:

> The profits made in these and other contracts entered into under the same system may justly arouse indignation. But indignation based on the notions of morality of this or any other court cannot be judicially transmuted into a principle of law of greater force than the expressed will of Congress.[40]

Even had Black admitted that the Government had been compelled by its necessities to enter into the contract, he would thus seem to deny that it would be proper for courts to set aside contracts induced by the necessities of one party, except when the terms deviate grossly from the standard established by common practice or from the anticipated

[37] The justification given for this clause was that it provided an incentive to the company to reduce the real "actual cost" to the government's advantage. Any such reduction would profit the company by increasing the spread between the real and the estimated "actual cost." But the company could also increase the spread by padding the advance estimate and compelling the government to accept it in the contract.

Justice Douglas agreed with Black that there was no duress, but thought the half-savings clause should be treated as a separate contract, the consideration for which would be the special efforts of the company to reduce costs. In the absence of any evidence of such special efforts, he thought this separate agreement not binding, for want of consideration.

Justice Murphy wrote a separate opinion concurring with Black, but expressing moral disapproval of the company's conduct. Chief Justice Stone and Justice Jackson, "who as former Attorneys General participated actively in the prosecution of these cases," and Justice Roberts took no part in the decision. Black's opinion, therefore, had the full concurrence only of Reed, Byrnes, and Murphy.

[38] 315 U.S. at 304. [39] *Id.* at 305. [40] *Id.* at 308–309.

results of bargaining with respect to necessities. And there is much to be said for this view. The standard established by common practice would ordinarily be the market value, and the market value of a doctor's or a repairman's services would ordinarily result from anticipations as to sicknesses or accidents in general.

Occasions arise, however, when because of unanticipated situations one may be compelled to agree to make what is called a "forced sale" or a "forced purchase." One in immediate need of money to meet an emergency may have to sell real estate for whatever he can get in a hurry, without having an opportunity to resort to the slower processes of the market and to wait for knowledge of the availability of the property to reach those who might be interested and who might bid more. On the other hand, one may be in immediate need of some article for which he cannot shop around or of services, such as those of a physician, and be forced to pay much more than is usually charged or than what he would have to pay if he had an opportunity to find out what he would have to pay others for a similar article or service. In a narrow sense of the word the price agreed to in any of these forced sales or forced purchases may be called the "market value." It is the value fixed by the small market in which the transaction takes place. But the term "market value" is generally used in the broader sense of referring to the price that would be fixed in a market, perhaps hypothetical, in which informed buyers and sellers, under no pressure of unanticipated necessity, would make bids and offers. Frequently the price that would result from such a market cannot be determined with precision, but gross deviations from market value so defined can be detected by courts and the contract invalidated. Many of the cases which Frankfurter cited, in which contracts had been set aside as unconscionable, were cases in which one party, under the stress of necessity, had either sold property for much less or bought property for much more than its normal market value. Courts are appropriate organs for setting aside such gross deviations from market value or established practice. When it comes to inquiring into the reasonableness of the market value or the established practice itself, which results from the various coercive pressures exerted by the bargaining power of the parties, and revising the results to make them conform to the judges' notions of what is reasonable, we have a different question.

In pre-Nazi Germany the courts were presented with a similar problem. In the Civil Code of 1900 was a provision which, in the words of the translation Professor J. P. Dawson made of it in a law review article,[41] declared a transaction void whereby a person, "through exploitation of the necessity, thoughtlessness, or inexperience of another," obtains economic advantages which "exceed the value of the counter-performance to such an extent as to be, under the circumstances, strikingly disproportionate." The implications of this rule of law, says Professor Dawson, were "revolutionary," but it "was deprived of all subversive effects and brought into harmony with basic assumptions of a competitive economy," because the appellate courts limited their inquiries to deviations from current market prices.

In this country, too, courts hesitate to determine whether particular prices are reasonable, when they do not deviate from market values. In applying the prima facie tort theory to labor cases, an attempt to increase wages is always held to justify a strike, if there is no other element of unlawfulness about it, without any inquiry into whether the particular wages demanded are reasonable or not. And in 1927 Justice Stone, speaking for the Supreme Court in *United States* v. *Trenton Potteries Co.,* construed the Sherman Anti-Trust Act as not exempting price-fixing combinations from its scope merely because the particular prices fixed by the combination might be thought reasonable.

> We should hesitate to adopt a construction [he said] making the difference between legal and illegal conduct in the field of business relations depend upon so uncertain a test as whether prices are reasonable—a determination which can be satisfactorily made only after a complete survey of our economic organization and a choice between rival philosophies.[42]

Courts are in no position to make any such complete survey, dealing, as they do, with cases that arise sporadically between two individuals. Nor are judges, chosen as they presumably are for qualifications other than their agreement with the views of constituents, the appropriate officials to make a choice between rival philosophies. That function can better be left to legislators chosen by the people to represent their views. Any attempt to make market prices conform

[41] *Economic Duress and Fair Exchange in French and German Law* (1927) 11 TULANE L. REV. 345, 12 *id.* 42, at 57. For a masterly treatment of the entire subject, see the same author's *Economic Duress—an Essay in Perspective* (1947) 45 MICH. L. REV. 253. For another excellent treatment of the subject see John Dalzell, *Duress by Economic Pressure* (1942) 20 N.C. L. REV. 237 and 341.

[42] 273 U.S. 372 (1927).

to what is thought "reasonable" would require more comprehensive legal changes than courts can effectuate through decisions handed down in individual cases.[43] Legislative organs of Government, with or without the aid of subordinate administrative bodies, are the appropriate officials to deal with such matters. Courts, which mold the common law, can do little to affect market values—they can only remove certain excrescences which result when, in peculiar cases, one party compels the other to pay much more for property or services than market value or to sell them for much less.

Market values themselves, however, result from and register the mutual pressures exerted by buyers and sellers. The amount of pressure which each can exert is very unevenly distributed, with the result that some are economically strong, others economically weak. Each party to a bargain is forced by the bargaining power of the other to surrender certain property in the form of money or otherwise or a certain portion of his freedom to act as he pleases or to be idle. The economically strong retain a considerable residuum of liberty and property; the economically weak, very little.

The Constitution, however, contains various provisions to protect individuals, weak as well as strong, in their economic interests. It protects them from "involuntary servitude," from other deprivations of their liberty or of their property, from impairment of the obligations owed to them in contracts, from abridgment of the privileges and immunities pertaining to their citizenship, and from unequal protection of the laws. The protection afforded by these provisions, however, is not absolute. Moreover, it is protection for the most part against governmental power, state or federal. It leaves individuals exposed to the bargaining power of other private individuals, even when that bargaining power stems from governmental action which denies liberty to make use of those things which the law assigns to the ownership of others, and even though the law by no means treats all individuals equally in its assignment of property rights. Thus, the Constitution by itself does not prevent the weak from being forced by economic pressure into serving others unwillingly or from being deprived of some degree of liberty and much of their property by the superior bargaining power of others or from inequality in their legal

[43] The problem is different when courts review railroad or public utility rates fixed by legislative authority. The decision will apply to all who demand the service, not merely to a single transaction. In these cases, however, courts have by no means refrained from making "a choice between rival philosophies."

property rights. The criminal law and the common law, of course, provide individuals with protection against certain wrongful acts of other individuals which would deprive them of liberty or property. But, as we have seen, this protection does not by any means extend to all coercive acts to which an individual may be exposed. Nor can courts, in the absence of legislation, very well supply this protection by expanding the concepts of "conspiracy to injure" or "prima facie torts" or "duress" or "extortion," even when convinced that the economic fruits of some of these unequal pressures are undesirable. As long as these pressures are registered in the market, courts can do little beyond correcting deviations from the market.

Few would wish to have bargaining abolished or to have all inequalities in bargaining power wiped out. As noted earlier in this work, we rely on coercive bargaining power, not only for distributing the output of our collective processes of production but also for bringing that production into existence. There are many, however, who would alter the bargaining process in this way or in that, in the belief that the market itself can be changed, either directly or indirectly, in such a way that those who are now economically weak may have more freedom from the pressures exerted by the strong, and greater protection for their money or other property from the bargaining power of the strong. When any such belief becomes embodied in legislation, however, we encounter a curious paradox. The legislation gives protection to the liberty and property of some persons against the coercive acts of others. Against such coercion, since it is not recognized as stemming from government, the Constitution by itself affords no protection. But this coercive power of the others is part of the liberty and property which the Constitution does protect against governmental action, and the legislation which curtails it is undeniably governmental action. Therefore, while those who are deprived of liberty or property by the coercive power of other private persons can make no appeal at all to the Constitution for protection, those who deprive them of their liberty or property can invoke it, in the very name of liberty and property, to preserve their power to deprive others of these same things. They cannot always succeed, for the constitutional provisions are so general in their terms that great latitude is permitted the Supreme Court in interpreting them, and the prohibition even of governmental deprivation of liberty or property is not absolute. But they can raise the question as a matter of constitutional law. The legislation which limits their power to deprive others must pass the scrutiny of the Supreme Court, while the power which they themselves exercise to curtail other people's liberty need pass no such scrutiny.

Before discussing these constitutional provisions further, however, we must note the role of courts—particularly federal courts—in our constitutional system.

PART THREE

THE PROTECTION WHICH THE CONSTITUTION AFFORDS TO ECONOMIC LIBERTY AND EQUALITY

VIII

THE PROCESS OF EXPOUNDING AND ENFORCING THE CONSTITUTION

CONSTITUTIONAL guaranties of individual liberties can be understood only in the light of the judicial processes by which they are applied to concrete situations and enforced.

THE ROLE OF THE SUPREME COURT

The federal judicial power, by Section 2 of Article III of the Constitution, extends, among other things, "to all Cases, in Law and Equity, arising under this Constitution, the Laws of the United States, and Treaties made, or which shall be made, under their Authority." This judicial power, by Section 1 of the same Article, is

> vested in one supreme Court, and in such inferior Courts as the Congress may from Time to Time ordain and establish. The Judges, both of the supreme and inferior Courts, shall hold their Offices during good Behaviour, and shall, at stated Times, receive for their Services, a Compensation, which shall not be diminished during their Continuance in Office.

Section 2 of Article II provides for the appointment of federal judges by the President, subject to confirmation by the Senate. Thus the

Supreme Court, composed of judges who are protected from dismissal except by impeachment and from reduction of their salaries, has jurisdiction over cases involving questions as to the interpretation of the Constitution or of federal laws (as well as other matters, some of which have been mentioned). But it has original jurisdiction only in "cases affecting Ambassadors, other public Ministers and Consuls, and those in which a State shall be Party" (Art. III, Sec. 2 of the Constitution). That means that a suit cannot be started in the Supreme Court in other cases, but can only be brought to it to review the decision of a lower court. And in 1803 it was held in one of Chief Justice Marshall's celebrated opinions (*Marbury* v. *Madison* [1]), that Congress could not extend the Supreme Court's original jurisdiction to other cases. This was the first time that the Court held an act of Congress unconstitutional.

It is not in the exercise of its limited original jurisdiction that the significant work of the Supreme Court has been done, but rather in its exercise of appellate jurisdiction. After enumerating the cases in which it shall have original jurisdiction, the Constitution proceeds: "In all the other Cases before mentioned, the Supreme Court shall have appellate Jurisdiction, both as to Law and Fact, with such Exceptions, and under such Regulations as the Congress shall make." In its exercise of appellate jurisdiction the Supreme Court reviews decisions not only of lower federal courts but also of state courts when the case is one to which the federal judicial power extends, such as one arising under the federal Constitution or federal laws. For the Constitution does not preclude state courts from deciding such questions. A party in a state suit frequently raises a question whether some state action or state law conflicts with the federal Constitution or with a federal law, and the state court must decide the question—subject to appellate review of its decision by the Supreme Court, provided for by Section 25 of the Judiciary Act. In fact, the Constitution itself contemplates that state courts may have to decide questions which arise under federal law, for in the so-called Supremacy Clause (the second paragraph of Article VI) it provides that state judges shall be bound by it.

So a case arising under the Constitution or federal laws which reaches the Supreme Court may have originated in a state court. It

[1] 1 Cranch 137 (U.S. 1803).

may also have originated in a lower federal court, for the federal judicial power extends to such cases, and Congress has power to confer original jurisdiction of such cases on "such inferior courts" as it may establish. It has, in fact, conferred it on federal district courts, with appeal to circuit courts of appeal, whose decisions the Supreme Court may in turn review. But the Constitution does not require Congress to confer jurisdiction on any lower federal court or even to create such courts. A case involving the validity of a price regulation made by the Price Administrator is a case arising under the Constitution or laws of the United States, and is clearly one to which the federal judicial power extends. But the Emergency Price Control Act of 1942 set up an Emergency Court of Appeals in which it vested exclusive jurisdiction (subject to review by the Supreme Court) over suits to enjoin enforcement of such regulations—thus withholding jurisdiction from the district courts. The act was unanimously sustained in *Lockerty* v. *Phillips,* Chief Justice Stone saying:

> There is nothing in the Constitution which requires Congress to confer equity jurisdiction on any particular inferior federal court. All federal courts, other than the Supreme Court, derive their jurisdiction wholly from the exercise of the authority to "ordain and establish" inferior courts, conferred on Congress by Article III, § 1, of the Constitution. Article III left Congress free to establish inferior federal courts or not as it thought appropriate. It could have declined to create any such courts, leaving suitors to the remedies afforded by state courts, with such appellate review by this Court as Congress might prescribe. [Citations.] [2]

In deciding questions of federal law, state and lower federal courts follow their own lights if there are no Supreme Court decisions on the point to guide them. It is when the defeated party takes the case to the Supreme Court that the latter makes its decisions on the points in question. These decisions are authoritative, and after they are made, lower courts feel bound to follow them in other cases involving the same points—except in the rare instances when the lower court

[2] 319 U.S. 182, 187 (1943). Nor does the Constitution make it mandatory for the Supreme Court to review all cases decided by lower courts. Under existing legislation, cases of a certain type can be appealed as a matter of right; but in many cases of a different type, the Supreme Court by denying a petition for certiorari may permit the lower decision to stand without implying approval or disapproval of it. For critical discussion of this situation see Fowler V. Harper and Alan S. Rosenthal, *What the Supreme Court Did Not Do in the 1949 Term—an Appraisal of Certiorari* (1950) 99 U. of PA. L. REV. 293; Osmond K. Fraenkel, *Discretionary Review by the United States Supreme Court* (1951) 11 LAWYERS GUILD REV. 31.

thinks it evident that the Supreme Court will overrule its own decision.[8] Though it was once thought a heresy to say that courts make law, instead of ascertaining what it is by studying "a brooding omnipresence in the sky," and though that is still thought heresy by many lawyers, the fact remains that federal law is what the Supreme Court says it is, even though it was not so until the moment the Court spoke. Its pronouncements on state law are not necessarily law, as we have seen, but its pronouncements on federal law are, until changed. The Court itself can change any of this law by overruling its decisions. If the law is federal common law, or admiralty law, or the interpretation of an ambiguous act of Congress, Congress can change it by enacting a new statute—for while the Court makes an authoritative interpretation of an ambiguous statute, it does not feel free to disregard one whose meaning is plain, short of holding it unconstitutional. When, on the other hand, the Court construes the Constitution to mean one thing or another, its interpretation becomes a part of the Constitution,

[8] In 1940 the Supreme Court sustained the constitutionality of the requirement of a board of education that children in the public schools must take part in a flag-saluting ceremony or be expelled. Minersville School District v. Gobitis, 310 U.S. 586. Thereafter the constitutionality of a similar requirement came before a federal district court in Barnette v. West Virginia State Board of Education, 47 F. Supp. 251 (D.W.Va. 1942). In view of the change in views announced by some of the participants in the Gobitis case, and the replacing of some of the other participants, Judge Parker refused to be bound by the Gobitis decision and held the requirement unconstitutional, saying (p. 253), "decisions are but evidences of the law and not the law itself." On appeal, the Supreme Court affirmed Parker's decision and overruled the Gobitis case, Justices Roberts, Reed, and Frankfurter dissenting, in West Virginia State Board of Education v. Barnette, 319 U.S. 624 (1943).

In a five to four decision in United States v. Macintosh, 283 U.S. 605, it was held in 1931 that the oath of allegiance which Congress required as a condition for naturalization was to be construed to deny citizenship to any alien who would not promise to bear arms in any war in which the United States might be engaged. On the authority of this case, the Circuit Court of Appeals for the First Circuit on June 1, 1945, in United States v. Girouard, 149 F. 2d 760, denied naturalization to a Seventh Day Adventist. Circuit Judge Woodbury, however, dissented. Citing Judge Parker in the Barnette case, he maintained (at p. 765) that "on rare occasions, and I think this is one of them, situations arise when in the exercise to the best of our ability of the duty to prophesy thrust upon us by our position in the federal judicial system we must conclude that dissenting opinions of the past express the law of today. When this situation arises and we do not agree with decisions of the Supreme Court I think it our duty to decline to follow such decisions and instead to follow reasoning with which we agree. As I see it this is the situation which confronts us here."

On April 22, 1946, the Court of Appeals was reversed in Girouard v. United States, 328 U.S. 61, and the Macintosh case overruled. The opinion, by Justice Douglas, had the concurrence of Justices Black, Murphy, Rutledge, and Burton. Justice Jackson took no part in the case. Chief Justice Stone (with the concurrence of Justices Reed and Frankfurter) dissented on the ground that Congress, in re-enacting the naturalization law, had acquiesced in the interpretation which the previous decisions had placed upon it.

and unless overruled by a later decision it remains so until changed by a constitutional amendment.[4]

The Constitution is necessarily written in general terms. Its application to concrete circumstances cannot be determined from its text alone. Its specific meaning is supplied by the Supreme Court. But the Supreme Court has always maintained that it can only interpret the Constitution when some "case" or "controversy," properly brought before it, requires it to do so. The reason is that the federal judicial power created by the Constitution (unlike the judicial power of some states) extends only to enumerated "cases" and "controversies." The Supreme Court has jurisdiction over nothing else. And it will make no decision where it has no jurisdiction.

The one exception to this rule arises in the very act of deciding that jurisdiction is lacking. Thus, in *Marbury* v. *Madison,*[5] decided in 1803, in order to decide that it had no original jurisdiction in a case of the character of the one before it, the Court had to hold the statute which attempted to confer such original jurisdiction on it, unconstitutional. And in *Muskrat* v. *United States*[6] the Court, in holding in 1911 that it had no appellate jurisdiction, had to hold another statute unconstitutional, which sought to give original jurisdiction to the Court of Claims, with appellate jurisdiction to the Supreme Court, to decide on the constitutionality of certain *other* statutes, in suits involving no conflicting claims of right and therefore presenting no "cases" or "controversies."

Except in holding that jurisdiction is lacking, however, there must be a case or controversy before the Court will pronounce a statute un-

[4] In two instances, constitutional amendments have been enacted to escape from the interpretations which the Court had placed on the Constitution. Shortly after it had been held in 1793, in Chisholm v. Georgia, 2 Dall. 419, that a state could be sued in a federal court by a citizen of another state, the 11th Amendment was adopted, which reads: "The Judicial power of the United States shall not be construed to extend to any suit in law or equity, commenced or prosecuted against one of the United States by Citizens of another State, or by Citizens or Subjects of any Foreign State."

There is a provision in Section 9 of Article I which reads: "No Capitation, or other direct, Tax shall be laid, unless in Proportion to the Census or Enumeration herein before directed to be taken." In 1895 it was held, in Pollock v. Farmers' Loan & Trust Co., 158 U.S. 601, that a federal tax on income from real estate and personal property was a "direct" tax, and therefore unconstitutional because not apportioned according to population—a requirement which would make any federal income tax utterly impracticable. In 1913 the 16th Amendment was ratified, which reads: "The Congress shall have power to lay and collect taxes on incomes, from whatever source derived, without apportionment among the several States, and without regard to any census of enumeration."

[5] 1 Cranch 137 (U.S. 1803).

[6] 219 U.S. 346 (1911).

constitutional. There is a case or controversy when one is prosecuted for violating a criminal statute which he alleges is unconstitutional. If he is convicted in a trial court, state or federal, the Supreme Court will set aside the conviction if it believes the statute unconstitutional and if the matter has been brought before it by the proper procedure. This it does on the theory that by the "supremacy clause" of the Constitution [7] the Constitution is the "supreme law of the land." Anything inconsistent with it is not law. There is also jurisdiction when a plaintiff sues a public officer or a private citizen for an act which clearly violates some right of the plaintiff unless it is justified by a statute which the plaintiff alleges to be unconstitutional. Here, again, the Court, if it takes jurisdiction, must decide whether the statute is constitutional or not. In short, when any claim of right properly raised in a judicial proceeding can be determined only by deciding on the constitutionality of a statute, the Court must so decide.

The right may be one which the party has by reason of state law, like the right not to be imprisoned except on conviction of violating a valid law, or it may be one which the Court will infer from the very provision in the Constitution which a statute is alleged to violate. But not every limitation which the Constitution places on governmental action is construed as conferring a right on every person adversely affected by such action.

The Tenth Amendment, for instance, is apparently construed as not in itself conferring rights on individuals who may be affected by its violation. It forms part of the Bill of Rights adopted in 1791, and was designed to make explicit what was generally assumed to be implicit in the Constitution from the start. It reads: "The powers not delegated to the United States by the Constitution, nor prohibited by it to the States, are reserved to the States respectively, or to the people." [8] An act of Congress may violate this Amendment, and its

7 "This Constitution, and the Laws of the United States which shall be made in pursuance thereof; and all Treaties made, or which shall be made, under the Authority of the United States, shall be the supreme Law of the Land; and the Judges in every State shall be bound thereby, any Thing in the Constitution or Laws of any State to the Contrary notwithstanding."—Art. IV, par. 2.

It will be noted that valid federal laws, as well as the Constitution, are made supreme over any conflicting state constitutions or laws; but the Constitution is less explicit as to the supremacy of the Constitution over federal laws which conflict with it. Nevertheless, ever since Marbury v. Madison was decided, in 1803, it has been assumed that the Constitution is supreme over such federal laws. This was the view expressed by Hamilton in No. 78 of THE FEDERALIST.

8 In United States v. Curtiss Wright Export Corp., 299 U.S. 304 (1936), this Amendment was said by Justice Sutherland, speaking for the Court, not to apply to powers which

execution may cause loss to some party, but unless he can show that some right of his, derived from some source other than the Amendment itself, depends on the validity or invalidity of the federal act, the courts will not interfere. Thus, in *Alabama Power Co.* v. *Ickes*[9] a power company sought to enjoin federal payments to municipalities for the construction of electrical distribution systems, and in *Tennessee Electric Power Co.* v. *Tennessee Valley Authority*[10] another power company sought to enjoin federal generation, distribution, and sale of power through the TVA. In each case the company asserted that the federal activity in question exceeded any power delegated to the United States by the Constitution and therefore violated the Tenth Amendment. Each company also asserted that it would suffer great loss through the competition of the municipalities or the Federal Government. In each case, however, the Court dismissed the action without passing on the constitutional question. In neither case had state law conferred on the company a right to be free from competition. In the *Alabama Power Company* case Justice Sutherland said:

> The claim that petitioner will be injured, perhaps ruined, by the competition of the municipalities brought about by the use of the moneys, therefore, presents a clear case of *damnum absque injuria*. . . . What petitioner anticipates, we emphasize, is damage to something it does not possess—namely, a right to be immune from lawful municipal competition.[11]

And while the Tenth Amendment does not itself confer a right to avoid ruin by unconstitutional competition, still less does it confer a right to the very problematical reduction in income taxes which might result from a cessation of federal expenditures which violate the Amendment. Hence the Court will not pass on the constitutionality of such expenditures on the suit of an income-tax payer. This was decided in 1923 in *Frothingham* v. *Mellon*,[12] where a payer of the income tax sought to enjoin the Secretary of the Treasury from making payments of grants-in-aid to states under the Maternity Act, which she

---

the states themselves did not possess when the Constitution was adopted. Specifically, it was said that powers to act in relation to foreign affairs were not delegated to the Federal Government by the states, but passed from the British Crown, at the separation from Great Britain, "not to the colonies severally, but to the colonies in their collective or corporate capacity as the United States of America," and that they later passed to the new government set up by the Constitution "as necessary concomitants of nationality."

For a critical discussion of this theory see David M. Levitan, *The Foreign Relations Power: an Analysis of Mr. Justice Sutherland's Theory* (1946) 55 YALE L.J. 467.

9 302 U.S. 464 (1938). 10 306 U.S. 118 (1939). 11 302 U.S. at 479-480.

12 262 U.S. 447 (1923).

alleged was unconstitutional. The Court dismissed the case for want of jurisdiction, Justice Sutherland saying that the taxpayer's interest in stopping the payments

> is shared with millions of others, is comparatively minute and indeterminable, and the effect upon future taxation of any payment out of the funds, so remote, fluctuating and uncertain, that no basis is afforded for an appeal to the preventive power of a court of equity.

The Court, in other words, will not pass on the constitutionality of an act unless the person challenging it can show that if unconstitutional, the act violates some right of his—or unless someone is prosecuted for infringing another person's constitutional right. Its position is similar to that of courts in private actions which refuse to award damages for loss resulting from some act of the defendant merely because that act is unlawful, unless it also appears that the defendant's unlawful act violated some right of the plaintiff.[13] And the mere fact that an act violates the Tenth Amendment does not prove that it violates any right of a person harmed by it.

A party, however, may have a right derived from some other source than the Tenth Amendment, which federal action would infringe if unconstitutional, but not if valid. If in such a case the validity of the federal action is challenged as unconstitutional on the ground that it violates the Tenth Amendment or any other provision of the Constitution, the Court will have to pass on its constitutionality in order to decide the case. Thus, while a person has no right to prevent his income tax from being exacted from him merely because some indeterminate portion of the proceeds will be spent unconstitutionally, since the bulk of the proceeds will go for wholly valid expenditures, still if a special federal tax is levied whose proceeds are to be spent wholly for a purpose alleged to be unconstitutional, the taxpayer can challenge the tax in court. A man has no right against a tax collector who collects a valid tax, but he has a right not to have his money taken from him by a tax that is invalid. This right is derived from the ordinary right of property, and it is also conferred as against a federal tax collector by the Fifth Amendment, which forbids the Federal Government to deprive him of property without due process of law. Now Section 8 of Article I of the Constitution confers on Congress the power to lay and collect taxes, but only for certain specified purposes —namely, "to pay the Debts and provide for the common Defence and

[13] *Cf.* Palsgraf v. Long Island R. Co., 248 N.Y. 339 (1928), discussed *supra*, p. 50.

general Welfare of the United States." It delegates no power to Congress to lay taxes for other purposes. The power to levy taxes for other purposes is therefore reserved to the states by the Tenth Amendment. It follows that a federal law levying a tax for an unpermitted purpose is invalid as violating that Amendment. And, being invalid, its collection violates the taxpayer's common law property right (not to have other people take his property, save when acting under a valid law) and his constitutional right under the Fifth Amendment (not to be deprived of property without due proccess of law). Whether his right derived from these sources is violated can only be determined by deciding whether the use to be made of the proceeds of the tax does or does not violate the Tenth Amendment, even though that Amendment itself confers no right upon him. Hence, when under the first Agricultural Adjustment Act, Congress levied a processing tax, the entire proceeds of which were to be spent for inducing farmers to sign contracts agreeing to limit their production, the payer of the tax was permitted to challenge the validity of the expenditures under the Tenth Amendent in *United States* v. *Butler*.[14] They were held invalid.

If the power companies which challenged federal activities in the other cases cited had been given exclusive rights by state law, the Court would presumably have had to decide whether the federal activities in question violated the Tenth Amendment. A right given by state law to be free from competition would not prevail against valid federal action, for the Constitution and valid federal laws are supreme, "any thing in the constitution or laws of any state to the contrary notwithstanding." But invalid federal laws are not supreme. Therefore, in the first case the power companies would have been asserting state-given rights against the encouragement of municipal competition; in the second, against competition itself. Whether they had such rights or not could only be determined by deciding whether the federal activities in question were or were not valid in the light of the Tenth Amendment. But that question did not arise, because the states had conferred on the companies no rights whatever against competition.

In challenging governmental action as violative of the Tenth Amendment or of certain other provisions of the Constitution, a party must show that the governmental action violates some right of his derived from some source other than that particular constitutional pro-

[14] 297 U.S. 1 (1936)

vision. But such a showing is not essential when the governmental action is challenged as violating certain other provisions of the Constitution. It is generally assumed, for instance, that the Fifth and Fourteenth Amendments not only make certain federal or state actions unconstitutional but also confer rights on persons not to be deprived of life, liberty, or property under given circumstances. Hence, even though the challenger could not show that he had any rights derived from some *other* source than the Amendments themselves, a challenge under the Fifth or Fourteenth could be maintained as it could not be under the Tenth Amendment. In most cases he would have no difficulty in asserting rights from such other sources. If state or federal officials threaten to imprison him or to seize his property under an unconstitutional law, they would be violating some of his common law rights. This may not be true in all cases, however. In *Pierce* v. *Society of the Sisters,*[15] for instance, a state enactment requiring parents to send children of specified ages to public schools was challenged, not by any of the parents, but by a parochial school and by a military academy which would be deprived of pupils. It was not thought necessary to inquire whether under state law the schools had a legal right against unlawful interference with the freedom of parents to send their children to them. They may or may not have had such a right. But on their challenge and without any inquiry on this point, the enactment was held to be an unconstitutional deprivation of the schools' property. The right it was held to infringe was not a mere legal right conferred by state law, but a constitutional right conferred by the Fourteenth Amendment.

Of course, a party who asserts a right under the due process clause of the Fourteenth Amendment must show that he is the person whom the state's act deprives of life, liberty, or property. The Amendment confers on him no right to have the state refrain from depriving someone else. When the various parts of a statute are so integrally related to one another that if part of it is held void the entire statute must fall, then a party whose rights are affected by the statute can challenge its validity on the ground that it violates any provision of the Constitution, even by depriving someone else of property. But if a statute contains several independent provisions, each of which can stand even if the others fall, no one can challenge the provisions which apply to him on the ground that some of the other provisions violate

15 268 U.S. 510 (1925).

the constitutional rights of others to liberty or property. Such a situation is likely to arise in connection with a tax law which provides for various taxes. In *Hatch* v. *Reardon* [16] a taxpayer challenged a state tax law on the ground that it applied to certain transactions which he claimed were outside the state's taxing power and so violated the rights conferred by the Fourteenth Amendment on those engaged in such transactions. But the transactions on which he was taxed were not of that character, and it was held that the possible unconstitutionality of the law as it applied to these other persons did not affect its validity as to him. Justice Holmes declared that

> unless the party setting up the unconstitutionality of the state law belongs to the class for whose sake the constitutional protection is given, or the class primarily protected, this court does not listen to his objections, and will not go into imaginary cases, notwithstanding the seeming logic of the position that it must do so, because if for any reason, or as against any class embraced, the law is unconstitutional, it is void as to all.

This doctrine applies only to cases in which a law can be held valid as to some classes even when unconstitutional as to others or in which the party, as may have been the case in *Pierce* v. *Society of the Sisters,* can assert no right other than one derived from the very constitutional protection itself. In such a case, before challenging the law, he must show that he "belongs to the class for whose sake the constitutional protection is given, or the class primarily protected." And the *Pierce* case was in effect a holding that the proprietary schools belonged to that class.

Even when a person has a "right" which would be infringed by the enforcement of an unconstitutional statute, there is some confusion as to the circumstances in which he can challenge the statute in court. It is generally considered that the mere enactment of the statute does not violate his right. A person who is subjected to criminal prosecution for violation of an unconstitutional statute can, of course, challenge it in the criminal case. But if he is uncertain whether the courts will sustain his contention of unconstitutionality, he runs a great risk in testing it by disobedience. If the penalties for disobedience are heavy and cumulative, he may sometimes secure an injunction against an official who threatens to enforce it, as was done in *Ex parte Young,*[17] in 1908, in which a railroad company enjoined the Attorney-General of the state. In that case, however, the

[16] 204 U.S. 152, 160 (1907).

[17] 209 U.S. 123 (1908).

Court assumed that a suit against the Attorney-General in his official capacity would be a suit against the state, contrary to the Eleventh Amendment, and that the aggrieved party must therefore sue him in his individual capacity—presumably as a private tort-feasor who was threatening to take action which because the statute was unconstitutional he was not authorized to take. Therefore, if the Attorney-General has made no personal threat to enforce the statute, it was held in 1933 in *Ex parte La Prade,*[18] the railroad affected by the statute cannot challenge its validity by a suit to enjoin him. The railroad is thus placed in the position to be obliged, at great expense, to obey the statute which it alleges is unconstitutional or else to violate it, in the hope that the Attorney-General or his successor will not ultimately decide to enforce it or that if they do the Court will hold it unconstitutional. Though there is no threat of immediate prosecution, the risk from disobeying it is great—for if it should ultimately be enforced, and the Court should uphold its validity, the railroad will be subjected to heavy fines. This risk may well be sufficient to force the railroad to obey the statute, without recourse to a judicial determination whether the enforced obedience deprives it of property without due process of law, thus violating its constitutional rights.

For reasons such as these Professor Edwin Borchard, writing in the *Yale Law Journal* for June, 1943,[19] insists that it is the statute itself, not merely the action of the Attorney-General in enforcing it, that subjects the party concerned to jeopardy of his constitutional rights. Such a party, he believes, should in most cases be permitted to challenge the constitutionality of a statute which so jeopardizes him by seeking a declaratory judgment against the appropriate officials in their official capacity. Such a suit would present a real "controversy" between adverse interests. Judicial settlement of the controversy would be appropriate, even though no right had as yet been infringed, and there was no immediate threat of such infringement. In private suits to remove clouds from titles to property, a potential clash of interests is held sufficient to invoke the jurisdiction of courts, without any actual threat to assert the adverse interest. Moreover, a suit for this purpose against an enforcing official in his official capacity should not be considered the type of suit against a state which the

18 289 U.S. 444 (1933).

19 *Challenging "Penal" Statutes by Declaratory Action* (1943) 52 YALE L.J. 445.

Eleventh Amendment removes from federal jurisdiction. That Amendment, says Borchard, "on the basis of plentiful authority," should be construed as only precluding "suits designed to extract money from the public treasury or coerce a state to perform an obligation."[20] Perhaps some day the Supreme Court will act on Borchard's suggestions and overrule such cases as *Ex parte La Prade.*

There are some cases, however, in which the Court has gone a long way in spelling out some "right" which gives a party standing to raise a constitutional issue. Preferred stockholders of a corporation have been held to have a right to prevent the corporation from selling its property to the Government for a use which will violate the Tenth Amendment. In *Ashwander* v. *Tennessee Valley Authority*[21] it was held in a five-to-four decision in 1936 that in a suit to enjoin the corporation from performing its contract to sell its transmission lines to the TVA and to enjoin the TVA from acquiring them, the preferred stockholders could require the Court to decide whether the particular purpose for which the lines were to be used transcended the powers of the Federal Government—though, on the merits, the use was held to be within its powers.[22]

In a five-to-four decision in 1939 in *Coleman* v. *Miller*[23] it was held that state senators had a right (at least when the state court held that they did) not to have their votes against ratification of a constitutional amendment nullified by state officials proclaiming ratification if in fact the ratification did not conform to the procedure required by the Constitution. As we shall see, however, the Court declined to decide whether the ratification was valid on the ground that this

[20] *Id.* at 467.

[21] 297 U.S. 288 (1936).

[22] This decision on the merits did not settle the question which the Tennessee Electric Power Company later sought vainly to have the Court decide—whether the Constitution authorized the Government to engage in the general business of generating, distributing and selling electric power. In the Ashwander case it was held (1) that maintenance of the dam from which the power in question was generated came within the federal power to declare war and to regulate interstate commerce by improving navigable streams; (2) that the sale of the surplus energy there generated came within the power conferred by Art. IV, sec. 3, "to dispose of and make all needful Rules and Regulations respecting the Territory or other Property belonging to the United States"; and (3) that the power to acquire transmission lines was to be inferred from the power of disposing of the surplus energy, as incidental to it. Only Justice McReynolds dissented from the decision on the merits.

The majority opinion was written by Chief Justice Hughes, and on the question whether the preferred stockholders could raise the constitutional issue had the concurrence of Justices Van Devanter, McReynolds, Sutherland, and Butler. On that point Justice Brandeis wrote a dissenting opinion, in which Justices Stone, Roberts and Cardozo joined.

[23] 307 U.S. 433 (1939).

presented a question that was "political," not "justiciable." In an opinion which dissented from the majority view that the senators had any right which was at stake,[24] Justice Frankfurter (with the concurrence of Justices Roberts, Black, and Douglas) pointed out that the senators would have had no right whatever to vote on the question if two of the grounds they advanced for the invalidity of the ratification were to be sustained. These two grounds were that too long a time had elapsed since Congress had proposed the Child Labor Amendment and, apart from this, that since the Kansas legislature had once voted against ratification it had lost all power to ratify. They advanced one other ground, however, which was not inconsistent with their having a power to vote. The state senate had voted twenty to twenty on the question of ratification, and the lieutenant-governor, as presiding officer, had sought to break the tie by casting a vote to ratify. This, the senators claimed, did not constitute ratification by the legislature, for which the Constitution provided. It was the twenty senators who voted against ratification, joined by one other senator and three members of the state house of representatives, who brought mandamus proceedings in the state supreme court to compel the secretary of the senate to endorse the words "was not passed" on the resolution and to restrain other officers from signing and authenticating the ratification. The state court entertained the action, but denied the petition on the merits. The case reached the federal Supreme Court on a writ of certiorari. Chief Justice Hughes for the majority (Justices McReynolds, Butler, Stone, and Reed concurred on this point) declared:

> that at least the twenty senators whose votes, if their contention were sustained, would have been sufficient to defeat the resolution ratifying the proposed constitutional amendment, have an interest in the controversy which, treated by the state court as a basis for entertaining and deciding the federal questions, is sufficient to give the Court jurisdiction to review that decision.[25]

The "interest" of the senators was apparently thought to have been a "right" conferred on them by the Constitution itself by its provisions which authorize state legislatures to vote for or against ratification of proposed amendments.

24 307 U.S. at 460.

25 *Id.* at 446.

POLITICAL RIGHTS AND POLITICAL QUESTIONS

While the majority in *Coleman* v. *Miller* held that the state senators had rights, which they could assert in court, to prevent an unwarranted nullification of their votes on ratification of a constitutional amendment, the Court has sometimes held that it lacked jurisdiction to decide any question on the suit of a party who asserted only a "political" right. Even when the right asserted is not political, the question which has to be decided in determining whether the right has been violated is sometimes held (as indeed it was in *Coleman* v. *Miller*) to be a "political" question, to be decided conclusively by the political branches of the Government, not the judicial. Again, even if the asserted right is one of which a court can take cognizance and even if the subject matter of the controversy is one fit for judicial determination, the court may stay its hand if the remedy sought involves the use of "political" rather than judicial power. These are three distinct situations in which the Supreme Court may decline to pass on a question of constitutionality; but they are sometimes confused with one another.

In the January Term, 1831, there was some discussion of "political" power, "political" rights, and "political" questions in *The Cherokee Nation* v. *The State of Georgia*,[26] though the case went off on another point. The Constitution extends the judicial power to controversies between a state and "foreign states" and confers original jurisdiction on the Supreme Court in cases where a state shall be a party. The Cherokee Nation maintained a tribal government within the boundaries of the state of Georgia. Treaties had been made between it and the United States, recognizing the Cherokees as a political society and assuring them the occupancy of their lands. Claiming the status of "foreign state," the Cherokee Nation brought an original action in the Supreme Court to restrain the state of Georgia from enforcing certain state enactments which, it was alleged, would destroy their tribal government and deprive them of the occupancy of their lands. It was held that the Cherokee Nation was not a "foreign state" within the meaning of the Constitution and that the Court therefore lacked jurisdiction. Justice Thompson dissented, in an opinion in which Justice Story concurred.

While the case was dismissed on this ground, Chief Justice Mar-

[26] 5 Pet. 1 (U.S. Jan. Term, 1831).

shall stated "a serious additional objection" to jurisdiction.[27] On the state laws, he said, "making it criminal to exercise the usual powers of self-government in their own country by the Cherokee nation, this court cannot interpose; at least in the form in which those matters are presented." He conceded that "that part of the bill which respects the land occupied by the Indians, and prays the aid of the court to protect their possession, may be more doubtful."

The mere question of right might, perhaps, be decided by this court in a proper case with proper parties. But the court is asked to do more than decide on the title. The bill requires us to control the legislature of Georgia, and to restrain the exertion of its physical force. The propriety of such an interposition by the court may well be questioned. It savors too much of the exercise of political power to be within the proper province of the judicial department. But the opinion on the point respecting parties, makes it unnecessary to decide this question.

In these dicta Marshall did not hold that the rights asserted by the Cherokees were mere "political" rights or that whether the Georgia laws conflicted with treaties made by the United States was a "political" question unfit for judicial determination. All he suggested was that the means sought to vindicate the rights would involve a use of political power—the suit praying for an injunction against the state of Georgia as such, not against any of its officials.

Justice Johnson, however, in a concurring opinion, maintained that the claim set up "is one of a political character altogether, and wholly unfit for the cognizance of a judicial tribunal." [28] Had he been sitting alone in the case, he declared, he would have waived the point about the Cherokees not being a foreign state (although he agreed with the Court on the matter) and would have put his "rejection of this motion upon the nature of the claim set up exclusively." If the Cherokees were, as they alleged, a sovereign, independent state, their contest with Georgia "is distinctly a contest for empire. It is not a case of *meum* and *tuum* in the judicial but in the political sense. Not an appeal to laws, but to force." These remarks seem to have to do with the character of the rights asserted; but Johnson adduced other grounds for declining jurisdiction. Some of these had to do with the inappropriateness of any action the Court could take to vindicate the Indians' rights. And there is a suggestion that it was for the executive department to determine whether Georgia was

[27] 5 Pet. at 20.

[28] *Id.* at 28–31.

violating any rights secured by treaties or even to ignore the violation if it should find one; for the executive branch of the Government "may often be compelled by the highest considerations of public policy to withhold even the exercise of a positive duty." Thus, Johnson seems to have thought that the question at issue would be political, unfit for determination by a court, even in a case in which a right that a party could properly assert was affected and the remedy sought involved the exercise of judicial power alone.

Thompson, in his dissent, took a different view, not unlike that which the Court itself came later to adopt. He distinguished rights of person and property secured by treaties from certain other rights secured by them, his distinction turning seemingly on whether the remedy appropriate to the enforcement of a particular right involves the exercise of judicial, or of political, power. Much of the matter complained of, he said,

> would seem to depend for relief upon the exercise of political power, and as such, appropriately devolving upon the executive, and not the judicial department of the government.[29]

And again:

> The judiciary is certainly not the department of the government authorized to enforce all rights that may be recognized and secured by treaty. In many instances, these are mere political rights with which the judiciary cannot deal.[30]

Applying this reasoning to the facts of the case, he said at a later point:

> I certainly . . . do not claim, as belonging to the judiciary, the exercise of political power. That belongs to another branch of the government. The protection and enforcement of many rights, secured by treaties, most certainly do not belong to the judiciary. It is only where the rights of persons or property are involved, and when such rights can be presented under some judicial form of proceedings, that courts of justice can interpose relief.
>
> This court can have no right to pronounce an abstract opinion upon the constitutionality of a state law. Such law must be brought into actual or threatened operation, upon rights properly falling under judicial cognizance, or a remedy is not to be had here.
>
> The laws of Georgia set out in the bill, if carried fully into operation, go the length of abrogating all the laws of the Cherokees, abolishing their government, and entirely subverting their national character. Although the whole of these laws may be in violation of the treaties made with this nation, it is probable this court cannot grant relief to the full extent of the complaint. Some of them, however, are so directly at variance with

[29] *Id.* at 51.

[30] *Id.* at 59.

these treaties, and the laws of the United States touching the rights of property secured to them, that I can perceive no objection to the application of judicial relief.[31]

Then, perhaps to refute Johnson's argument that the contest between Georgia and the Cherokees was one of war and also to indicate that the state of Georgia would be likely to obey any injunction issued against it, so that political power against the state would not be required for its enforcement, he went on:

The State of Georgia certainly could not have intended these laws as declarations of hostility, or wish their execution of them to be viewed in any manner whatever as acts of war, but merely as an assertion of what is claimed as a legal right; and in this light ought they to be considered by this court.

He had previously pointed out that the United States had given the Cherokees

a solemn guarantee by treaty of the exclusive right to the possession of their lands. This guarantee is to the Cherokees in their national capacity. Their land is held in common, and every invasion of their possessory right is an injury done to the nation, and not to any individual. No private or individual suit could be sustained; the injury done being to the nation, the remedy must be sought in the name of the nation.[32]

Some of the actions taken to carry out the laws of Georgia "can be considered in no other light than as acts of trespass." [33] And for this trespass he thought an injunction against the state the appropriate remedy to protect the property right of the Cherokee Nation.[34]

Thompson's distinctions were between "political" rights and rights of person or property and between cases calling for the exercise of political power as a remedy and those calling for the exercise of judicial power. He was not describing any particular type of question as unfit for judicial determination if it arose in a case in which rights of person or property were affected and the appropriate remedy would call for the exercise of judicial power.

In *The State of Rhode Island* v. *The State of Massachusetts*,[35] decided at the January Term, 1838, Rhode Island filed an original bill in the Supreme Court, complaining that Massachusetts was exercising sovereignty over land on its southern boundary which properly belonged to Rhode Island.

[31] 5 Pet. at 75. [32] *Id.* at 74. [33] *Id.* at 76.
[34] *Id.* at 78–80. [35] 12 Pet. 657 (U.S. Jan. Term, 1838).

> The prayer of the bill is to ascertain and establish the northern boundary between the States, that the rights of sovereignty and jurisdiction be restored and confirmed to the plaintiffs, and they be quieted in the enjoyment thereof, and their title; and for other and further relief.[36]

Massachusetts moved to dismiss the bill for want of jurisdiction. The motion was overruled in an elaborate opinion by Justice Baldwin.

The questions on the merits were questions of a type familiar to courts. Rhode Island claimed that the line down to which Massachusetts was exercising sovereignty did not in fact conform to the description contained in early colonial charters and that Rhode Island's pre-Revolutionary ratification of a treaty recognizing this *de facto* line was invalid because made under a misapprehension. These were not political questions, thought Baldwin, except in the sense that all controversies between sovereign states are political; but they became judicial when in ratifying the Constitution the sovereign states created the federal judicial power and extended it to controversies between states.

Chief Justice Taney dissented,[37] not because the questions to be decided were political, but because he insisted that the right asserted by Rhode Island was a political right, not one of person or property. After citing the prayers in the bill filed by Rhode Island, he proceeded:

> It appears from this statement of the object of the bill, that Rhode Island claims no right of property in the soil of the territory in controversy. The title to the land is not in dispute between her and Massachusetts. The subject-matter which Rhode Island seeks to recover from Massachusetts in this suit is "sovereignty and jurisdiction," up to the boundary line described in her bill. And she desires to establish this line as the true boundary between the States, for the purpose of showing that she is entitled to recover from Massachusetts the sovereignty and jurisdiction which Massachusetts now holds over the territory in question. Sovereignty and jurisdiction are not matters of property, for the allegiance in the disputed territory cannot be a matter of property. Rhode Island, therefore, sues for political rights. They are the only matters in controversy, and the only things to be recovered; and if she succeeds in this suit, she will recover political rights over the territory in question, which are now withheld from her by Massachusetts.
>
> Contests for rights of sovereignty and jurisdiction between States over any particular territory, are not, in my judgment, the subjects of judicial

[36] *Id.* at 716. The quotation is from the Court's opinion.

[37] *Id.* at 752–754.

cognizance and control, to be recovered and enforced in an ordinary suit, and are, therefore, not within the grant of judicial power contained in the constitution.

In addition, Taney quoted Marshall's language in the *Cherokee* case in regard to the remedy and, paraphrasing it to fit the present case, maintained that it would not be an exercise of judicial power "to 'control the legislature of Massachusetts, and to restrain the exercise of its physical force' within the disputed territory." Taney did not, however, deny the power of the Court to decide disputed questions of state boundaries, whenever necessary to determine rights of property. On this point he was explicit, saying:

I do not doubt the power of this court to hear and determine a controversy between States, or between individuals, in relation to the boundaries of the States, where the suit is brought to try a right of property in the soil, or any other right which is properly the subject of judicial cognizance and decision, and which depends upon the true boundary line.

In *State of Georgia* v. *Stanton,*[38] decided at the December Term, 1867, the Court agreed with Taney that rights of sovereignty are not subjects of judicial cognizance, but it placed claims by states to disputed territory in the category of property rights, on the rather tenuous ground that in the *Rhode Island* case:

The right of property was undoubtedly involved; as in this country, where feudal tenures are abolished, in cases of escheat, the State takes the place of the feudal lord, by virtue of its sovereignty, as the original and ultimate proprietor of all the lands within its jurisdiction.[39]

Following the Civil War the government of Georgia had been revived and reorganized with the permission of President Johnson after his withdrawal of the military government. Congress, however, passed two "Reconstruction Acts" over the President's veto, which would substitute a military government for the one now functioning until a new one should be set up and approved by Congress. The revived state government filed an original bill in the Supreme Court to restrain the Secretary of War and General Grant and General Pope from enforcing the provisions of these Acts. The case was dismissed for want of jurisdiction. Justice Nelson, after distinguishing boundary claims and reciting the prayers in the bill, said:

That these matters . . . call for the judgment of the court upon political questions, and, upon rights, not of person or property, but of a political

[38] 6 Wall. 50 (U.S. Dec. Term, 1867). [39] *Id.* at 73.

character, will hardly be denied. For the rights for the protection of which our authority is invoked, are the rights of sovereignty, of political jurisdiction, of government, of corporate existence as a State, with all its constitutional powers and privileges. No case of private rights or private property infringed, or in danger of actual or threatened infringement, is presented by the bill, in a judicial form, for the judgment of the court.[40]

The "political question" was not whether the Reconstruction Acts were unconstitutional (though perhaps that question would have been called political had the Court's attention been directed to the point), but whether, even granting the Acts to be unconstitutional, the state of Georgia had any justiciable rights which they violated.

In 1923 the Court dismissed another case for want of jurisdiction, on the ground that the rights asserted were "political and not judicial in character." In *Massachusetts* v. *Mellon,*[41] the companion case of *Frothingham* v. *Mellon,* already noted,[42] Massachusetts brought an original suit in the Supreme Court to enjoin the Secretary of the Treasury from making grants of money to the states, under the Maternity Act. These grants were made on condition that any state receiving them enact, in conformity with federal requirements, certain legislation to care for maternity cases. Massachusetts contended that the Maternity Act was an attempt by the Federal Government to exercise powers reserved to the states by the Tenth Amendment. The Court refused to pass on this contention. Stressing the fact that nothing was to be done to any state under the Act without its consent, Justice Sutherland said:

. . . we are called upon to adjudicate, not rights of person or property, not rights of dominion over physical domain, not quasi-sovereign rights actually invaded or threatened, but abstract questions of political power, of sovereignty, of government. No rights of the State falling within the scope of the judicial power have been brought within the actual or threatened operation of the statute and this Court is as much without authority to pass abstract opinions upon the constitutionality of acts of Congress as it was held to be, in *Cherokee Nation* v. *Georgia* of state statutes.[43]

The Court's refusal to decide on the constitutionality of the Maternity Act was not because that question was itself "political" and therefore unfit for judicial determination, but because no right of Massachusetts other than a "political" one was affected by the grants. Had Massachusetts, instead of claiming a right to have the grants

[40] *Id.* at 77.

[41] 262 U.S. 447 (1923).

[42] *Supra,* pp. 143–144.

[43] 262 U.S. at 484–485.

stopped altogether, made a claim for its share of the funds despite failure to conform to the conditions, it would have been asserting a property right, and the Court might have decided the constitutionality of the condition on the merits—as it did in 1947, when a state filed a similar claim in *State of Oklahoma* v. *United States Civil Service Commission,* discussed more fully in a later chapter.[44]

In *Colegrove* v. *Green* [45] the Court, in 1946, dismissed another suit, without passing on the merits of the constitutional issue presented. The suit was brought in a federal district court for a declaratory judgment declaring the 1901 law of Illinois apportioning congressional election districts invalid and for incidental relief preventing state officials from conducting the next election under that law. The result of granting the relief would have been to require Illinois Representatives to be chosen in the election of November, 1946, on a state-wide basis, unless the legislature should enact a new apportionment act in the short time remaining after June 10, the date of the Supreme Court decision. Since 1901 there had been great shifts in the population, so that a voter in the most populated district had a vote which was only one-ninth as effective as that of a voter in the least populated. The suit was brought by voters in one of the largest districts.

The district court's dismissal was affirmed by a vote of four to three, Justice Jackson not sitting, and the late Chief Justice Stone's successor not having yet been appointed. The four who voted for dismissal, however, did not agree on the grounds. Justice Frankfurter spoke for three of them (himself and Justices Reed and Burton), in an opinion which did not purport to be the opinion of the Court. In this opinion there is an intermingling of the distinct questions of whether parties have asserted rights suitable for judicial protection, whether the question to be decided is a political one, and whether the appropriate remedy calls for the exercise of something beyond judicial power. After stating that the issue is "of a peculiarly political nature and therefore not meet for judicial determination," he went on:

> This is not an action to recover for damage because of the discriminatory exclusion of a plaintiff from rights enjoyed by other citizens. The basis for the suit is not a private wrong, but a wrong suffered by Illinois as a polity.

[44] 330 U.S. 127 (1947). See *infra,* pp. 314–315.
[45] 328 U.S. 549 (1946).

. . . In effect this is an appeal to the federal courts to reconstruct the electoral process of Illinois in order that it may be adequately represented in the councils of the Nation.[46]

The basis of the suit, however, seems to have been distinctly a private wrong. As Justice Black pointed out in his dissent (in which Justices Douglas and Murphy concurred), the petitioners claimed that the Illinois law denied to them and to the other citizens of the more heavily populated districts the equal protection of the laws, in violation of the Fourteenth Amendment, and that it violated their rights, conferred by Article I, to an approximately equal vote with other qualified electors for members of Congress. Such rights as these, though in one sense "political," have never been treated as the kind of political rights which the judiciary cannot protect. They are certainly private rights, not rights of "Illinois as a polity."

That the rights asserted were justiciable rights, however, does not prove that the issue to be decided is justiciable rather than political or that an appropriate judicial remedy would be available. Justice Frankfurter advanced other reasons for denying both conclusions. The Constitution, in Article I, Section 4, authorizes Congress to make or alter the regulations prescribed by the states for the manner of holding elections for Representatives, and, in Article I, Section 5, it authorizes each House to judge the qualifications of its own members. From these provisions Frankfurter concluded that "the Constitution has conferred upon Congress exclusive authority to secure fair representation by the States in the popular House and left to that House determination whether States have fulfilled their responsibility." [47] Moreover, "It is hostile to a democratic system to involve the judiciary in the politics of the people." [48]

It is questionable whether it might not be equally hostile to a democratic system to permit the people of Chicago to be governed by a legislative body, in the choice of which they could be outvoted nine to one by the people in rural Illinois, and to remand them to the mercy of that same unequally representative body for relief. As to this, however, the question of the appropriateness of the available remedy comes into the picture. As Justice Frankfurter said:

Of course no court can affirmatively remap the Illinois districts so as to bring them more in conformity with the standards of fairness for a representative system. At best we could only declare the existing electoral system

[46] *Id.* at 552. [47] *Id.* at 554. [48] *Id.* at 553–554.

invalid. The result would be to leave Illinois undistricted and to bring into operation, if the Illinois legislature chose not to act, the choice of members for the House of Representatives on a state-wide ticket. The last stage may be worse than the first.[49]

Thus, the only way the Court could release the voters of the more populous districts from an undemocratic system of representation would be to establish temporarily another undemocratic system; for an election of all the Illinois Representatives at large would, in the words which Frankfurter quoted from Chancellor Kent, "leave the aggregate minority of the people in a state, though approaching perhaps to a majority, to be wholly overpowered by the combined action of the numerical majority, without any voice whatever in the national councils." [50]

These considerations do not relate to any lack of justiciable rights asserted in the complaint, or to the nonjusticiable character of the question of the validity of the Illinois law, but solely to the inappropriateness of the only available judicial remedy. It is on the latter ground that Justice Rutledge, in his separate opinion, concurred in the dismissal. He thought that in view of a former decision [51] the issues were justiciable; but, since a court of equity's power to act is discretionary, he thought this was an occasion for the Court to exercise its discretion and decline to take jurisdiction. The relief sought, he said,

> pitches this Court into delicate relation to the functions of state officials and Congress, compelling them to take action which heretofore they have declined to take voluntarily or to accept the alternative of electing representatives from Illinois at large in the forthcoming elections.[52]

The right to equality in voting can at best be a right to "only a rough approximation" to equality. The right is not absolute. "And the cure sought may be worse than the disease." [53]

In the cases we have examined in which the Court has declined to decide constitutional questions, there was no right other than a "political" right, whose protection depended on a constitutional decision, or else the right was one for which in the circumstances there was no appropriate judicial remedy. There have been other cases, however, in which the Court has had to determine whether a right has been violated and the remedy calls for a proper exercise of judi-

[49] 328 U.S. at 553. [50] 1 Kent, COMMENTARIES (12th ed. 1873) *230–31, n. (c).
[51] Smiley v. Hohn, 285 U.S. 355 (1932).
[52] 328 U.S. at 565. [53] *Id.* at 566.

cial power, but the constitutional question to be decided is one which the Court characterizes as "political" and accepts as conclusive the decision of the question by what it calls the political branch of the Government.

The corporate existence of a state is one of these political questions. The state's own right to corporate existence, as we saw in *Georgia* v. *Stanton,* is not a right of person or property which a court can enforce. It sometimes happens, however, that in a private suit involving rights of person or property and calling for some well-recognized judicial remedy the right which the plaintiff asserts was created by, or revoked by, legislation enacted by a body which purported to be the state. Either the plaintiff or the defendant, as the case may be, may contend that it was not the state which enacted this legislation, but some usurping body, either because some rival body was the authentic state, or because the state did not have a republican form of government as guaranteed by the Constitution. Though the right asserted by the plaintiff (unlike that which the challenged state or its rival might have asserted) is a right of person or property, and though the remedy involves a familiar exercise of judicial power, the Court will not decide whether the "state" whose legislation is challenged is the authentic state. That question it calls a political one. It will not necessarily dismiss the suit for want of jurisdiction, but will accept as conclusive the decision of the political department of the Government.

There are two provisions of the Constitution which are said to give the political branch power to decide such questions. One is the provision in Article I, Section 5, that each House of Congress "shall be the Judge of the Elections, Returns and Qualifications of its own Members." When Senators or Representatives, chosen under the auspices of what claims to be the authentic state government, present themselves to the respective Houses to which they have been elected, each House can decide whether the state under whose auspices they were elected is the authentic one.

The other constitutional provision is Article IV, Section 4, which reads:

> The United States shall guarantee to every State in this Union a Republican Form of Government, and shall protect each of them against Invasion; and on Application of the Legislature, or of the Executive (when the Legislature cannot be convened) against domestic Violence.

At an early date Congress conferred on the President power to decide concerning the necessity of calling out the militia against domestic violence, after application by a state. Accordingly, whenever two rival organizations are contending forcibly for power to function as the government of the state, and the legislature or the governor of one of them applies to the President to protect it against the domestic violence of the other, the President must decide whether the applicant is the authentic government of the state, faced with the rebellion of the rival organization, or whether the applicant is itself in rebellion against the authentic state represented by the rival. In such circumstances the President may decide, as a political question, which is the authentic government of a state. The decision concerning which political branch of the government the Court would regard as conclusive in case the decisions made by the President, the Senate, and the House of Representatives were in conflict has never been made clear.

Some of these matters were discussed in 1849 in the case of *Luther* v. *Borden*,[54] which grew out of Dorr's Rebellion in Rhode Island. Until 1843 Rhode Island had been governed, not under a constitution, but under the charter issued by Charles II in 1663, modified somewhat by acts of its legislature. This charter contained no provisions for its own amendment. It authorized the legislature to prescribe the qualifications for voting, and the legislature confined the right of suffrage to freeholders. This was more than a property qualification, for many wealthy persons whose property took forms other than land were barred. After petitions to extend the suffrage were disregarded by the legislature, those in favor of an extension elected a convention which, though not authorized by any law of the existing government, drew up a new constitution giving the vote to all male citizens of twenty-one or more (with appropriate residence qualifications) and provided for its submission to the same voters. After "ratification" at this informal election, the convention declared that the new constitution was the paramount law of the state and proceeded to elect a legislature and a governor under it —the governor being Thomas W. Dorr. The officers so elected proceeded to organize the new government in May, 1842. The charter government, however, refused to recognize the new one, and repulsed an attempt to take over the state arsenal. It passed an act de-

[54] 7 How. 1 (U.S. 1849).

claring the state under martial law and called out the militia to subdue the rebellion. The charter governor applied to President Tyler to call out the militia of other states to protect the state from domestic violence. The President did not actually call out the militia, but apparently took steps to have them in readiness if necessary, and in doing so he recognized the charter governor as the governor of the state. After this call for federal aid, Dorr urged his followers not to resist, and the rebellion came to an end without bloodshed.

The charter government, meantime, called a convention to draw up a new constitution, which was subsequently ratified by the voters under laws prescribed by the charter legislature. The charter government formally surrendered all its powers to the new one set up under the new constitution, in May, 1843. All parties recognized that the new government was authentic after that date. The Dorr adherents contended, however, that theirs was the authentic government from May, 1842, to May, 1843, and that the charter government had no lawful existence after May, 1842. Dorr was tried for treason against the charter government, in the state courts functioning under the new constitution, which he admitted, therefore, were duly established courts. His defense was that the charter government was not the true government. The same defense was made in other prosecutions. But the state courts ruled against it, the state supreme court saying, in Dorr's case, that the judicial department was bound to follow the political department of the state in its recognition of the charter government as the true one.

One of Dorr's adherents was named Martin Luther. Shortly after resistance to the charter government had ceased, Borden and others, members of the state militia which had been called out when the charter legislature declared martial law, broke and entered Luther's house, at the command of their superior officer, to search for Luther and arrest him. This was in June, 1842. Luther brought an action of trespass against them in the federal Circuit Court. As against their defense that they were acting under proper authority, he contended that the charter government was not the lawful one. The trial court, rejecting Luther's proffered evidence that the Dorr constitution was ratified by a majority of the male voters of twenty-one and more, and also by a majority of those entitled to vote under the old laws, instructed the jury that the laws of the charter government at the time of the breaking and entering were the paramount laws of the state, and justified the acts of the defendants. On writ of error, the Supreme Court affirmed.

There was no question, it will be noted, about the nature of the right asserted or about the appropriate remedy. The right was an ordinary property right, and the remedy a judgment for damages. Borden had violated Luther's right, unless he was acting under the valid laws of a legal government. Justice Woodbury, dissenting, thought that no government could make a valid declaration of martial law in the circumstances, but he agreed with the Court that the validity of the existence of the charter government could not be questioned by the courts.

Chief Justice Taney said that the determination of the proper government related altogether to the constitution and laws of the state and that the federal courts were therefore bound to follow the decisions of the state courts. Since these had held that the charter government was the lawful one during the period in question, the federal courts must so regard it. And the state courts, it will be recalled, had felt bound to follow the decision of the political department of the state.[55]

But Luther contended that the question was not "altogether" one of state law. He contended that

> the guarantee of a government republican in form was the means provided by the Constitution to secure the people in their right to change their government, and made the question whether such change was rightfully accomplished a judicial question determinable by the courts of the United States.[56]

Taney seemed to concede that there was a federal question, despite what he said about the conclusiveness of state decisions, but a question that was political, not judicial. Speaking of Section 4 of Article IV, he said:

> Under this article of the constitution it rests with congress to decide what government is the established one in a State. For as the United States guarantee to each State a republican government, congress must necessarily decide what government is established in the State before it can determine whether it is republican or not. And when the senators and representatives of a State are admitted into the councils of the Union, the authority of the government under which they are appointed, as well as its republican character, is recognized by the proper constitutional authority. And its

[55] 7 How. at 40.

[56] This account of Luther's contention is taken from Chief Justice White's opinion in Pacific States Tel. & Tel. Co. v. Oregon, 223 U.S. 118, 145–146 (1912).

decision is binding on every other department of the government, and could not be questioned in a judicial tribunal. It is true that the contest in this case did not last long enough to bring the matter to this issue; and as no senators or representatives were elected under the authority of the government of which Mr. Dorr was the head, congress was not called upon to decide the controversy. Yet the right to decide is placed there, and not in the courts.[57]

Had Congress decided, by implication, that the charter government was republican in character, Taney stated that its decision would be binding "on every other department of the government." But Congress had made no such decision.[58] The President had made one, however, in Taney's opinion, when upon the application of the governor under the charter government he "took measures to call out the militia to support his authority." [59]

No court of the United States, with a knowledge of this decision, would have been justified in recognizing the opposing party as the lawful government, or in treating as wrongdoers or insurgents the officers of the government which the President had recognized, and was prepared to support by an armed force.

If Dorr's government had elected Senators and Representatives and Congress had admitted them, but the President had nevertheless recognized the charter government, the Court would have faced a dilemma. The decision of Congress would seem to be binding on it and "on every other department of the government," including the President. Yet the Court would not be "justified in recognizing" the Dorr government as the lawful one in defiance of the President's decision. Taney indicated that since the President's act was pursuant to powers Congress had conferred upon him, "if the President, in exercising this power, shall fall into error, or invade the rights of the people of the State, it would be in the power of congress to apply the proper remedy." [60] But would the mere fact that Congress had admitted Representatives and Senators of the Dorr government constitute an application of the remedy, and nullify the President's decision? If not, would not the Court be bound, pending a congressional remedy, by two conflicting authorities? Would it not be so bound in any event should the House admit Representatives chosen under one

[57] 7 How. at 42.

[58] It does not appear how Congress avoided making a decision when it passed on the qualifications of members elected in 1842. Apparently no one challenged the qualifications of those elected under the authority of the charter government.

[59] 7 How. at 44.

[60] *Id.* at 45.

of two opposing governments, and the Senate admit Senators chosen under the other? It would seem that in the case of such a conflict in the political department of the Government, the Court would have to decide the "political" question for itself in order to decide the controversy between the parties properly before it.

The question of the guaranty of a republican form of government was again brought to the Court in the case of *Pacific States Tel. & Tel. Co.* v. *Oregon*,[61] decided in 1912. The state of Oregon provided in its constitution for the initiative and the referendum. A law taxing corporations was passed by the initiative. The telephone company challenged the validity of this tax on the sole federal ground that the initiative and referendum were inconsistent with a republican form of government. After pointing out that, if the contention were sound, there would be no lawful government at all in Oregon, Chief Justice White went on, with copious citations from *Luther* v. *Borden*, to hold that the question was a "political" one for Congress to decide, not a "justiciable" one calling for judicial decision. Congress had been regularly admitting Senators and Representatives from Oregon and had thus, presumably, decided that its government was republican in form. Had it refused to admit them, on the ground that the government was not republican, it would seem that the Court must also hold that there was no state government in Oregon. But suppose the state had thereafter determined to retain the initiative and referendum, even at the price of loss of representation in Congress. Has Congress power to insist, by means more drastic than refusal to admit representatives, that a state conform to the congressional concept of "republican"? Could it, for instance, set up a new state government? Perhaps that power would have to be implied from the constitutional guaranty. If the Court had power to declare the existing government unlawful, said White,

> a power in the judiciary must be implied, unless it be that anarchy is to ensue, to build by judicial action upon the ruins of the previously established government a new one, a right which by its very terms also implies the power to control the legislative department of the Government of the United States in the recognition of such new government and the admission of representatives therefrom.[62]

But if judicial power to dec'are the old government unlawful would imply judicial power to build a new one, it would seem that the

[61] 223 U.S. 118 (1912). [62] *Id.* at 142.

admitted congressional power to do the former would likewise imply congressional power to do the latter—and that implies more congressional power than merely to recognize and admit representatives from some government built by someone else.

If Congress, however, has power to decide what state governments are republican and to set up new ones in conformity with its standards of republicanism, would the Court place no limits at all on its judgment in such matters? Suppose Congress should adopt utterly absurd and arbitrary standards for deciding what form of government is republican—suppose it should hold that no state government is republican in form unless its governor is elected for life or the governorship is made hereditary—would the Court hold that congressional decision based on such standards is binding? In the cases in which the Court has hitherto felt bound by congressional action, Congress has refrained from disturbing an existing and functioning state government. Should it ever in the future disturb one, after making an arbitrary decision that the government in question was not republican in form, it remains to be seen whether the Court will adhere to its position that the republican character of a government never under any circumstances presents a justiciable question.

Other "political" questions which the Court has refused to decide are concerned with the process of amending the Constitution. Article V provides that amendments may be proposed, either by a two-thirds vote of both Houses of Congress or by a convention called by Congress on the application of the legislatures of two-thirds of the states. The former method is the only one that has ever been employed. Proposed amendments are to be valid "when ratified by the Legislatures of three-fourths of the several States, or by Conventions in three-fourths thereof, as the one or the other Mode of Ratification may be proposed by the Congress." Hitherto, Congress has proposed ratification only by legislatures, except in the case of the Twenty-First Amendment, which repealed the Eighteenth. The Constitution is silent concerning any time limit within which an amendment may be ratified and whether a legislature which has once voted against ratification may afterwards ratify.

Both questions were raised in 1939 in the case of *Coleman* v. *Miller*,[63] with respect to the ratification by Kansas of the proposed Child

[63] 307 U.S. 433 (1939). Cf. *supra*, pp. 149–151.

Labor Amendment. Though the Court held that the state senators who brought the suit had rights which were the proper object of judicial protection, it held these two questions to be political, not justiciable, and therefore to be settled by Congress whenever it should be called upon to decide whether to proclaim the adoption of the amendment after the purported ratification by three-fourths of the states. Justices McReynolds and Butler, dissenting, thought the question of an unreasonable lapse of time was justiciable. There was one other question which was thought by half the Court to be political, and by the other half to be justiciable; the Court, therefore, expressed no opinion on the point. This question was whether after a tie in the state senate the Lieutenant-Governor could cast the deciding vote in favor of ratification.[64]

The characteristic of a "political" question is sometimes said to be its concern with the making of laws, rather than with their interpretation. In his minority opinion in *Luther* v. *Borden,* in which he concurred with the Court's disposition of the "political" question, Justice Woodbury said: "Constitutions and laws precede the judiciary, and we act only under and after them, and as to disputed rights beneath them, rather than disputed points in making them." [65] But disputed rights under the Constitution can at times be decided only by inquiring whether a purported amendment has in truth been adopted—an inquiry involving disputed points in the making of the purported amendment. And the Court has not always refrained from deciding such points on their merits.

The late Eighteenth Amendment, prohibiting the sale of liquor, was at least three times challenged in the Court, as not being a part of the Constitution, and each time it was sustained, not on the ground that the challenge presented only political questions, but on the merits. In *National Prohibition Cases* [66] it was definitely held, among other things, in 1920, that "the two-thirds vote in each House which is required in proposing an amendment is a vote of two-thirds of the members present,—assuming the presence of a quorum,—and not a vote of two-thirds of the entire membership, present and absent," and that "the referendum provisions of state constitutions and statutes cannot be applied, consistently with the Constitution of the United States, in the ratification or rejection of amendments

[64] On the mystery of an equal division, in a court of nine members, see Note, *Sawing a Justice in Half* (1939) 48 YALE L.J. 1455.

[65] 7 How. at 52.

[66] 253 U.S. 350 (1920).

to it."[67] In *Dillon* v. *Gloss*[68] it was held in 1921 (on the merits) that ratification was not invalid because Congress, in proposing the Amendment, had declared that it should be inoperative unless ratified within seven years. Finally, in 1931, in *United States* v. *Sprague*,[69] the Court rejected a contention that, since the Amendment dealt with the liberties of the citizen, rather than with changes in federal machinery, Congress must submit it for ratification to state conventions, not to legislatures. This decision, too, was on the merits.

So not every question as to the making of an amendment is regarded as political and nonjusticiable, nor is every question as to the making of a federal statute. In *The Pocket Veto Case*[70] the Court held, in 1929, on the merits, that a bill passed by Congress and presented to the President less than ten days before the adjournment of the session did not become law if the President did not sign it.[71]

It cannot be said, therefore, that every question relating to the *making* of laws and constitutions and constitutional amendments will be treated as nonjusticiable. Whether a bill passed by Congress within ten days of adjournment becomes law without the President's signature, whether a constitutional amendment must be proposed by two-thirds of the entire membership of each House of Congress or only by two-thirds of the members present, whether certain types of amendment must be submitted for ratification to state conventions rather than to legislatures, whether ratification by "legislatures" requires submission to the voters in states which provide for the referendum, and whether in proposing an amendment Congress can provide a time limit for ratification have all been treated as justiciable questions. On the other hand, whether in the absence of a time limit set by Congress too long a time has elapsed to render ratification valid

[67] In this the Court followed Hawke v. Smith, 253 U.S. 221, decided earlier in the same year, in a taxpayer's action to enjoin the secretary of state of Ohio from spending money to submit to a referendum the legislature's action in ratifying the Eighteenth Amendment.

[68] 256 U.S. 368 (1921). [69] 282 U.S. 716 (1931). [70] 279 U.S. 655 (1929).

[71] Art. I, sec. 7, after providing for the presidential veto and the passage of a bill over a veto, says: "If any Bill shall not be returned by the President within ten Days (Sundays excepted) after it shall have been presented to him, the Same shall be a Law, in like Manner as if he had signed it, unless the Congress by their Adjournment prevent its Return, in which case it shall not be a Law." In an opinion by Justice Sanford the Court rejected contentions that "ten days" means, not ten calendar days, but ten legislative days (i.e., when Congress is in session); that "adjournment" means final adjournment, not adjournment of the session; and that the President is not "prevented" from returning a bill when he could hand it to clerks of the two adjourned houses.

and whether a legislature which has once voted against ratification can afterwards validly ratify have been held to be nonjusticiable. And the Court was equally divided as to the justiciable character of the question whether ratification is valid when brought about by the casting vote of the Lieutenant-Governor in an equally divided state senate. Moreover, in sustaining the validity of the Nineteenth Amendment (providing for woman suffrage), the Court declared in 1922, in *Leser* v. *Garnett*,[72] where it was contended that the ratifications of two states were inoperative because in violation of the state rules of legislative procedure, that:

As the legislatures of Tennessee and West Virginia had power to adopt the resolutions of ratification, official notice to the Secretary [of State], duly authenticated, that they had done so, was conclusive upon him, and, being certified by his proclamation, is conclusive upon the courts.[73]

The criterion to be employed in differentiating justiciable questions, on which the Court will form its own judgment, from those which are political, on which it will follow the judgments of the political department of the Government, is thus by no means clear. Justice Woodbury, in his minority opinion in *Luther* v. *Borden,* said that political questions

relate to matters not to be settled on strict legal principles. They are adjusted rather by inclination; or prejudice or compromise often. Some of them succeed, or are defeated even, by public policy alone; or mere naked power, rather than intrinsic right. There being so different tastes as well as opinions in politics, and especially in forming constitutions; some people prefer foreign models, some domestic, and some neither; while judges, on the contrary, for their guides, have fixed constitutions and laws, given to them by others, and not provided by themselves.[74]

Political questions, he added somewhat later in his opinion, are "too dear" to the people

[72] 258 U.S. 130 (1922).

[73] The opinion was by Justice Brandeis. It is not quite clear whether the Secretary's proclamation would be conclusive upon the courts if they thought the notice sent him by the legislature was not "official" or not "duly authenticated."

If one of the thirty-six states whose ratification is essential were to notify the Secretary that it had ratified after once having voted against ratification, or after the lapse of a long period subsequent to Congress's proposal of the amendment, the Court stated in Coleman v. Miller that it would be for Congress to decide whether the amendment had been adopted. Justice Brandeis suggested that it would be for the Secretary of State. If Congress and the Secretary came to opposite conclusions on the "political" questions involved, would not the Court have to choose by which decision of the "political department" of the government it should feel itself bound? The difficulty is like that already suggested in the event that the House and the Senate should come to opposite conclusions as to the republican character of some state government.

[74] 7 How. at 51–53.

for them ever to intrust their final decision, when disputed, to a class of men who are so far removed from them as the judiciary; a class, also, who might decide them erroneously as well as right; and if in the former way, the consequences might not be able to be averted except by a revolution, while a wrong decision by a political forum can often be peacefully corrected by new elections or instructions in a single month. And if the people, in the distribution of powers under the constitution, should ever think of making judges supreme arbiters in political controversies, when not selected by, nor, frequently, amenable to them, nor at liberty to follow such various considerations in their judgments as belong to mere political questions, they will dethrone themselves and lose one of their own invaluable birthrights; building up in this way,—slowly but surely,—a new sovereign power in the republic, in most respects irresponsible and unchangeable for life, and one more dangerous, in theory at least, than the worst elective oligarchy in the worst of times.[75]

These words foreshadow those used by Lincoln in his first inaugural address in 1861, when he said that

the candid citizen must confess that if the policy of the government, upon vital questions affecting the whole people is to be irrevocably fixed by decisions of the Supreme Court, the instant they are made, in ordinary litigation between parties in personal actions, the people will have ceased to be their own rulers, having to that extent practically resigned their government into the hands of that eminent tribunal.[76]

Lincoln would avoid this result, not by having the Court refrain from passing on "vital questions affecting the whole people," but by not regarding such decisions as binding precedents. Woodbury, on the other hand, suggested no limitation on the binding character of judicial decisions when acting "under and after" constitutions and laws; but he would have the courts refrain entirely from making decisions on "disputed points in making them."

[75] When, in Dodge v. Woolsey, 18 How. 331, the Supreme Court held in 1856 that a provision in the Ohio constitution requiring the property of banks to be taxed equally with other property was unconstitutional as impairing the obligation of contracts (the banks having been previously chartered under a law calling for lower taxes), Justice Campbell wrote a vigorous dissenting opinion. In the course of it he said (373): "as to the claim made for the court to be the final arbiter of these questions of political power, I can imagine no pretension more likely to be fatal to the constitution of the court itself. If this court is to have an office so transcendent as to decide finally the powers of the people over persons and things within the State, a much closer connection and a much more direct responsibility of its members to the people is a necessary condition for the safety of popular rights."

Again, speaking of the power of the Court to interfere (376): "The acknowledgment of such a power would be to establish the alarming doctrine that the empire of Ohio, and the remaining States of the Union, over their revenues, is not to be found in their people, but in the numerical majority of the judges of this court."

[76] 6 Nicolay and Hay, Complete Works of Abraham Lincoln (Gettysburg ed. 1905) 180.

But disputed points in making laws do not necessarily involve far-reaching considerations of inclinations or prejudice or compromise, while decisions "under" constitutions not infrequently do. Whether ratification of a constitutional amendment must take place within a reasonable time after submission in order to be effective raises a question of public policy far less fundamental than that raised by a determination whether "under" the commerce clause and the Fifth Amendment Congress has power to forbid a manufacturer to discriminate, in his employment policy, against union membership on the part of his employees. Yet, by Woodbury's criterion and by the Court's own decisions the courts may not pass on the former question, but may on the latter. There would seem to be far less danger of a judicial oligarchy in the exercise of judicial power to decide some of the questions classed as "political" than in the same power to pass on many questions now classed as "justiciable." It may be wise and proper for the Court to accept legislative decisions as conclusive on certain questions which arise under the Constitution. But the wisdom of so doing would not seem to turn on any criterion which the Court has yet employed for distinguishing the "political" from the "justiciable." [77]

ENFORCEMENT BY FEDERAL CRIMINAL LAW

Up to this point we have been dealing with cases in which the Court has been called upon to pass on the complaint of one of the parties that some right of his has been violated or is threatened with violation by unconstitutional means. The victim of unconstitutional action, however, may be given protection, without being a party in a case, by federal statutes providing criminal prosecution of those who have violated his constitutional rights. If a prosecution is based on an allegation that a person's constitutional rights have been violated, the Court must decide whether the Constitution conferred those rights upon him.

As early as 1842 it was held that whenever the Constitution conferred on anyone a right, it impliedly granted power to Congress to provide for the enforcement of that right by criminal sanctions. Hence it was held, in an opinion by Justice Story in *Prigg* v. *Pennsyl-*

[77] *Cf.* Maurice Finkelstein's suggestion that it would be desirable for the Court to include in the category of "political questions," on which the legislative decision shall be final, all questions of the industrial policy of state or nation which may arise under the due process clauses. *Judicial Self-Limitation* (1924) 37 HARV. L. REV. 338.

vania,[78] that since Article IV, Section 2, provided that a slave escaping from a slave state "shall be delivered up on claim" of his master, the federal Act of 1793, providing punishment for obstructing the owner, was within the powers conferred on Congress and that a state statute inconsistent with it was invalid.

The power of Congress to provide punishment for violation of the Civil War amendments (the Thirteenth, Fourteenth and Fifteenth) is more explicit, for each of these amendments confers upon Congress express power to enforce its provisions "by appropriate legislation." This power, of course, does not extend beyond acts relating to what the Court may regard as violations of the amendments. In regard to offenses committed at elections for Senators and Representatives, the power of Congress goes further, by virtue of the provision in Article I, Section 4, that it may "make or alter" the regulations governing such elections. The federal power to make acts committed at congressional elections criminal is not confined to acts which violate constitutional rights. It is only when the statute, as is now the case, defines the election offense in terms of injury to a citizen in the exercise of constitutional rights or the deprivation of such rights, that the Court has to inquire what rights the Constitution confers in regard to elections. No such inquiry is needed when the offense is defined in other terms, as were many offenses in statutes that were repealed in 1894.

Under these earlier statutes there was no need to define the constitutional rights of voters. In 1880 indictments of state-appointed election officers at a congressional election were sustained, in *Ex parte Siebold,*[79] under statutory provisions penalizing interference with federal inspectors and stuffing the ballot box. In the companion case of *Ex parte Clarke,*[80] another federal indictment of a state election officer was sustained under a provision penalizing the violation of any duty required by state or federal law concerning a federal election. The indictment was for violation of a state law. In neither case did the Court have to inquire whose constitutional rights were violated by the defendants. Justice Field's dissent (in which Justice Clifford joined) was based on the contention that state officers were constitutionally immune to federal punishment for their official conduct.

Field (with Clifford) had made the same contention unsuccessfully

[78] 16 Pet. 539 (U.S. 1842). [79] 100 U.S. 371 (1880). [80] 100 U.S. 399 (1880).

earlier in the year, in *Ex parte Virginia*.[81] Here the Court sustained the federal indictment of a state judge for excluding Negroes from a jury because of their race, in violation of a statute which made it a misdemeanor for "any officer or other person charged with any duty in the selection or summoning of jurors" to "exclude or fail to summon any citizen" on account of race, color, or previous condition of servitude. The Court rejected the contention that state officers were immune to federal punishment for their official acts, though it left open the question whether acts done by a judge in the performance of his judicial functions were punishable. Justice Strong, for the majority, insisted that the selection of jurors was a ministerial, not a judicial, function, since it could be performed by a court clerk as well as by a judge. Here, however, unlike the situation with regard to the election cases, no provision of the Constitution conferred power on Congress to penalize state officers for the discriminatory selection of jurors, unless it was the clause in the Fourteenth Amendment granting power to enforce its provisions by "appropriate legislation." To sustain the federal indictment, therefore, it was necessary for the Court to find that the statutory offense constituted a violation of the Amendment. This the Court found, holding that exclusion of Negroes from a jury because of their race was a denial of the equal protection of the laws.

The indicted judge must have known that his acts violated the federal statute; but he may not have known, until the Supreme Court rendered its decision, that they also violated the Fourteenth Amendment and that the statute was therefore a valid one. This suggests the possibility that Congress might bypass the Supreme Court and impose on the states constitutional restrictions according to its own interpretation, which the state might have no opportunity of testing in the Court. Should Congress declare that certain types of state statutes violate the Fourteenth Amendment and make it a crime to enforce them, it might well be that no state official would care to run the risk of doing so, on the chance that the Supreme Court would ultimately hold the state statute in question valid and the federal enactment punishing its enforcement consequently invalid.

In the *Siebold, Clarke,* and *Virginia* cases the prohibited acts were clearly set forth in the statutes. Most of these statutes were repealed

81 100 U.S. 339 (1880).

in 1894. There remain, however, Sections 19 and 20 of the Criminal Code.[82] Section 19 makes it a criminal offense, punishable with a maximum prison sentence of ten years:

If two or more persons conspire to injure, oppress, threaten, or intimidate any citizen in the free exercise or enjoyment of any right or privilege secured to him by the Constitution or laws of the United States, or because of his having so exercised the same.

Section 20 provides:

Whoever, under color of any law, statute, ordinance, regulation, or custom, willfully subjects, or causes to be subjected, any inhabitant of any State, Territory, or District to the deprivation of any rights, privileges, or immunities secured or protected by the Constitution and laws of the United States . . . shall be fined not more than $1,000, or imprisoned not more than one year, or both.

The word "willfully" was inserted in 1909.

In applying these sections, the Court must perforce decide whether anyone's federal rights have been infringed, and, in the absence of a statute conferring rights, the federal right must be a constitutional one. In *Guinn* v. *United States*,[83] decided in 1915, state election officers in Oklahoma had been convicted under Section 19 for conspiring to interfere with the rights of certain Negroes, secured to them by the Fifteenth Amendment, which provides that: "The right of citizens of the United States to vote shall not be denied or abridged by the United States or by any State on account of race, color, or previous condition of servitude." The election officers denied ballots to the Negroes for failure to pass a literacy test required by an amendment to the Oklahoma constitution. The literacy test would have been valid, had it not been accompanied by a familiar "grandfather clause," which exempted from the test those who were entitled to vote anywhere on or before January 1, 1866 (that is, before the adoption of the Fifteenth Amendment) and their lineal descendants.

The Supreme Court was obliged to answer two questions certified to it by the circuit court of appeals, which was entertaining an appeal from the conviction in the district court. The first was whether the state amendment was valid, to which the Court answered "No," since the exemption covered practically all white illiterates, and the

[82] Until 1948 these were sometimes cited as Secs. 51 and 52, respectively, of 18 U.S.C. They are now, respectively, 18 U.S.C. § 241 and § 242 (Supp. 1950).

[83] 238 U.S. 347 (1915).

denial of the vote to colored illiterates would in fact be on account of race. This, however, would not be conclusive, for, with the exemption of the whites stricken out, the literacy test, applicable to white and colored alike, might still be good. But the Court concluded, as a matter of state law on which the state courts had not passed, that the state amendment could not be construed to bar white, as well as colored, illiterates, and it was held bad in its entirety. The Court therefore answered "Yes" to the second question certified to it, namely, whether the Oklahoma amendment was void insofar as it attempted to bar otherwise qualified Negroes from voting because unable to read and write a section of the state constitution. The election officers who obeyed the requirements of the state constitution therefore interfered with the enjoyment of rights secured to the excluded Negroes by the Fifteenth Amendment. Whether they knew they were doing so is another matter. It is difficult to believe that they did, despite the fact that the jury which convicted them had been instructed that "the criminal intent requisite to their guilt is wanting" if their denial of the vote "was due to a mistaken belief sincerely entertained . . . as to the qualifications of the voters." We shall have more to say later on, in connection with other cases, on the requisite intent.

Although Congress, under its power to regulate federal elections, may penalize acts other than those which interfere with constitutional rights and earlier statutes did penalize other acts, those now on the books do not. Accordingly, in prosecutions of federal election offenses under Sections 19 and 20, the Court has found it necessary to define the constitutional rights of federal voters. Article I, Section 2, provides that the electors for the House of Representatives in each state "shall have the Qualifications requisite for Electors of the most numerous Branch of the State Legislature," and the Seventeenth Amendment provides the same qualifications for electors for the Senate. If a person has the requisite state qualifications, he has a federal constitutional right to vote for Representatives and Senators. And this right, said Justice Stone, speaking for the Court in 1941 in *United States* v. *Classic,* "unlike those guaranteed by the Fourteenth and Fifteenth Amendments, is secured against the action of individuals as well as of states." [84]

In 1884 a conspiracy by a mob to prevent a duly qualified elector

[84] 313 U.S. 299, 315 (1941).

from voting in a federal election was held indictable in *Ex parte Yarbrough*,[85] partly on the basis of the statute which subsequently became Section 19, but partly also on the basis of a statute then on the books which applied more specifically to interference with voting. After the repeal of the latter, Section 19 alone was held sufficient in 1915, in *United States* v. *Mosley*,[86] to sustain an indictment of state election officers for conspiring not to receive and count ballots and to falsify returns in a congressional election. Justice Holmes stated that "the right to have one's vote counted is as open to protection by Congress as the right to put a ballot in a box."

In 1944 the right to have one's vote counted was held, in *United States* v. *Saylor*,[87] to include the right to have it honestly counted, which was interfered with by a conspiracy to stuff the ballot box. This, too, was held indictable under Section 19. Previously, the Court held in 1941 in *United States* v. *Classic*,[88] that the right of a voter under Article I was a right to "an effective choice" in the election of a Congressman. Conspiracy by election officers to alter and falsely count and certify ballots, though the ballots were cast at a Democratic congressional primary in Louisiana, not at the general election, was held indictable under Section 19, as "an interference with the effective choice of the voters at the only stage of the election procedure when their choice is of significance." [89] Interference at the primary, it was said, would be interference with the constitutional right, whenever the state has made the primary an integral part of the electoral process or choice at the primary is the practical equivalent of election. Both conditions existed here. The election officers were also held indictable under Section 20, their action being taken "under color of" state law, since taken "in the course of their performance of duties under the Louisiana statute." [90]

Not every offense at a federal election, however, is a federal offense. Congress can make a federal offense of bribery at these elections, but bribery does not interfere with the exercise of the right to vote and to have the vote honestly counted, nor does it deprive anyone of that right. Hence it does not violate Sections 19 or 20. Holding in 1918, in *United States* v. *Bathgate*, that a conspiracy to bribe did not come within the scope of Section 19, Justice McReynolds, speaking for a unanimous Court, said:

[85] 110 U.S. 651 (1884).
[86] 238 U.S. 383 (1915).
[87] 322 U.S. 385 (1944).
[88] 313 U.S. 299 (1941).
[89] *Id.* at 314.
[90] *Id.* at 325–326.

The right or privilege to be guarded, as indicated both by the language employed and context, was a definite, personal one, capable of enforcement by a court, and not the political, non-judicable one common to all that the public shall be protected against harmful acts, which is here relied on.[91]

There is an interference with the exercise of the "personal" constitutional right of a qualified congressional elector when he is prevented from voting, or when his vote is not counted, or when its effectiveness is diluted by the counting of the votes of unqualified or nonexistent electors; but there is no such interference when his choice of a Representative is outweighed by the votes of other qualified electors, correctly counted, however improper their motives may have been.[92]

Sections 19 and 20 provide federal criminal sanctions against certain forms of interference with or deprivations of constitutional rights. They do not, however, make a criminal of everyone who interferes with the exercise of a constitutional right or deprives a person of one. If they did, every member of a legislature who votes for an act later held to be unconstitutional, every judge of a lower court who sustains it, and every executive officer who enforces it would be guilty of a federal crime which he had no means of knowing to be a crime when committed.[93] It was to avoid this result that Justice Douglas gave an unnecessarily strained interpretation to Section 20 in *Screws* v. *United States*,[94] decided in 1945.

A sheriff, a policeman, and a special deputy had arrested a Negro in Georgia on the charge of stealing a tire, had handcuffed him, and had then beaten him to death in the jail yard with an iron blackjack. They were convicted by a jury in a federal district court, under Section 20. The Supreme Court remanded the case for a new trial,

[91] 246 U.S. 220, 226–227 (1918).

[92] See, however, Justice Douglas's statement, dissenting in United States v. Saylor, 322 U.S. 385, 392 (1944): "But he who bribes voters and purchases their votes corrupts the electoral process and dilutes my vote as much as he who stuffs the ballot box." In his dissent in the Classic case he explained United States v. Bathgate as resting on the fact that bribery had only an "indirect" effect on the "personal" right to vote at the general election. Douglas would exclude the offenses committed at the Louisiana primary from the scope of § 19, on the ground that their effect on the right to vote at the general election was equally indirect; 313 U.S. at 333–334. And stuffing the ballot box, he thought in the Saylor case, interfered only indirectly. But bribery was not excluded in the Bathgate case because it had an "indirect" effect on the personal right to an effective choice, but rather because the only right on which it had any effect, direct or indirect, was not that personal right at all.

[93] *Cf.* Justice Field, dissenting, in ex parte Clarke, 100 U.S. 399, 414–415 (1880).

[94] 325 U.S. 91 (1945).

on the ground that the jury had not been properly instructed as to the requisite intent of the defendants. The reasons were given in an opinion by Justice Douglas, which had the concurrence of three other Justices (Stone, Black, and Reed) but which did not purport to be the opinion of the Court.[95] Justices Roberts, Frankfurter, and Jackson wrote a dissenting opinion, in which they contended that Section 20, if applicable to the defendants' acts, was unconstitutional because too vague. They would have ordered the indictment quashed. Justice Murphy dissented for the opposite reason, holding that the conviction had been proper and should have been affirmed. Justice Rutledge agreed with this view, but voted with Douglas in order to break a deadlock.

Justices Roberts, Frankfurter, and Jackson contended that Section 20, if construed so as to make it applicable to official acts which might later be held unconstitutional, would violate the Fifth Amendment, by punishing acts which the performers could not know were illegal at the time of performance, there being no ascertainable standard of guilt. The Government had rashly argued for a construction of the section, which, in the words of this dissenting trio, would make a potential offender of any state official "who as a public service commissioner issued a regulatory order which we should later hold denied due process or who as a municipal officer stopped any conduct we later should hold to be constitutionally protected." [96] Justice Douglas agreed that the section would be unconstitutional if so broadly interpreted that "a local law enforcement officer violates §20 and commits a federal offense for which he can be sent to the penitentiary if he does an act which some court later holds deprives a person of due process of law." [97]

To avoid this result, Douglas stressed the word "willfully," which had been added to the statute in 1909. It would be no innovation, he said, in view of the cases, "if we construe 'willfully' in § 20 as connoting a purpose to deprive a person of a specific constitutional right." [98] As so construed the statute would provide an ascertainable standard of guilt and give adequate warning of what is prohibited.

For the specific intent required by the Act is an intent to deprive a person of a right which has been made specific either by the express terms of the

[95] The official report opens with the words: "MR. JUSTICE DOUGLAS announced the judgment of the Court and delivered the following opinion, in which the CHIEF JUSTICE, MR. JUSTICE BLACK and MR. JUSTICE REED concur." 325 U.S. at 92.

[96] 325 U.S. at 158.

[97] *Id.* at 97.

[98] *Id.* at 101.

Constitution or laws of the United States or by decisions interpreting them. Take the case of a local officer who persists in enforcing a type of ordinance which the Court has held invalid as violative of the guarantees of free speech or freedom of worship. Or a local official continues to select juries in a manner which flies in the teeth of decisions of the Court. If those acts are done willfully, how can the officer possibly claim that he had no fair warning that his acts were prohibited by the statute? He violates the statute not merely because he has a bad purpose but because he acts in defiance of announced rules of law. He who defies a decision interpreting the Constitution knows precisely what he is doing. If sane, he hardly may be heard to say that he knew not what he did. Of course, willful conduct cannot make definite that which is undefined. But willful violators of constitutional requirements, which have been defined, certainly are in no position to say that they had no adequate advance notice that they would be visited with punishment. When they act willfully in the sense in which we use the word, they act in open defiance or in reckless disregard of a constitutional requirement which has been made specific and definite. When they are convicted for so acting, they are not punished for violating an unknowable something.[99]

It is plain that Screws and his companions entertained a purpose to deprive their prisoner of freedom from unjustified physical violence. One would think that the right not to be subjected to it by state officers had been made sufficiently definite by the constitutional provision that no state shall deprive any person of liberty without due process of law. Douglas, however, made no allusion to this right. The purpose with which Screws deprived the victim of two other constitutional rights was not so clear. One was the right not to be deprived of life by the state without due process, a right which had plainly "been made specific by the express terms of the Constitution." The other was a right which Douglas thought specific enough, the right of an accused person to "a trial in a court of law, not a 'trial by ordeal.' "[100] The new trial was ordered, not because these rights had not been made definite, but because additional findings were required in order to prove that when Screws deprived the victim of them his purpose was to do so. It is conceivable, though it strains credulity to think so, that when Screws and his companions continued to beat their handcuffed prisoner with a blackjack from fifteen to thirty minutes after he had been knocked to the ground, their purpose was not to kill him. It is also possible that their purpose was not to punish him for his alleged theft or to prevent him from hav-

[99] 325 U.S. at 104–105.

[100] *Id.* at 106.

ing a fair court trial for it after they had finished torturing him for some other purpose, for "there was evidence that Screws held a grudge against Hall [the victim] and had threatened to 'get' him." [101] Their purpose was obviously to commit a crime, but not necessarily a federal crime; and, said Douglas,

> this question of intent was not submitted to the jury with the proper instructions. The court charged that petitioners acted illegally if they applied more force than was necessary to make the arrest effectual or to protect themselves from the prisoner's alleged assault. But in view of our construction of the word "willfully" the jury should have been further instructed that it was not sufficient that petitioners had a generally bad purpose. To convict it was necessary for them to find that petitioners had the purpose to deprive the prisoner of a constitutional right, e.g. the right to be tried by a court rather than by ordeal. And in determining whether the requisite bad purpose was present the jury would be entitled to consider all the attendant circumstances—the malice of petitioners, the weapons used in the assault, its character and duration, the provocation, if any, and the like.[102]

In a federal court of appeals in 1950 Judge Sibley construed the Douglas ruling to mean that Section 20 could be violated only when "the accused, exercising the power of the State, not only deprived another of a federally secured right, but knew it was such." [103] Some of the language Douglas used lends color to this construction. He said, for instance, that "one who does act with such specific intent is aware that what he does is precisely that which the statute forbids," a statement which he qualified, however, in the next sentence by saying that "he either knows or acts in reckless disregard of its prohibition of the deprivation of a defined constitutional or other federal right." [104] He might act in reckless disregard by not taking the trouble to find out whether the right had been defined. That Douglas did not think knowledge of the right essential would seem to appear from the evidence which he said the jury were to consider in determining whether the acts had been "willful." Neither the malice, the weapons, the character of the assault, nor the provocation would seem to throw any light on whether the defendants knew that the right was federally secured. As Judge Sibley himself had remarked in a dissenting opinion in the lower court in the *Screws* case, "there is no reason to suppose that Screws and Jones once thought of the Fourteenth Amend-

101 *Id.* at 93.
102 *Id.* at 106–107.
103 Williams v. United States, 179 F. 2d 644, 647 (5th Cir. 1950).
104 325 U.S. at 104.

ment, or that they knew much or anything about it." [105] No greater reason to suppose so could be furnished by consideration of the malice, the weapons, or the character of the assault.

Nor was there any evidence of the defendant's knowledge in *Williams* v. *United States*,[106] in which the Supreme Court, in 1951, affirmed a unanimous decision in Judge Sibley's own court,[107] which affirmed a conviction under Section 20 for using torture to obtain confessions. Williams could obviously have had no purpose other than to deprive his victim of the right to be tried fairly by a court. Since that right was well defined, adequate advance notice had been given to Williams, and he was not convicted "for violating an unknowable something." But while the existence of the federally secured right was "knowable," it may not have been "known" by Williams. He may have been unaware of the advance notice. In determining whether his acts were "willful" the jury had been told to consider much the same circumstances as those which Douglas had enumerated in the *Screws* case, and the instructions, said Douglas, "conformed with the rulings of the Court in *Screws* v. *United States.*" [108] Though these circumstances proved nothing at all as to the defendant's knowledge, they satisfied Justice Douglas. In affirming the conviction he said:

> Petitioner and his associates acted willfully and purposely; their aim was precisely to deny the protection that the Constitution affords. It was an arrogant and brutal deprivation of rights which the Constitution specifically guarantees.[109]

Though the purpose was undoubtedly to deprive of the protection which the Constitution affords, there was no evidence that Williams knew that the Constitution affords it.

It was in the companion case, in which Williams and his associates had been convicted under Section 19, that Judge Sibley declared that it was an essential element of the crime that defendant should know that the right was federally secured. If Section 19 applied at all to rights secured by the Fourteenth Amendment (which Sibley did not believe), he held that it would be unconstitutional as so applied unless construed to require that the acts should be done "willfully" in the meaning of the word given in the *Screws* case. And he held that

105 Screws v. United States, 140 F. 2d 662, 666 (5th Cir. 1944).
106 341 U.S. 97 (1951).
107 Williams v. United States, 179 F. 2d 656 (5th Cir. 1950).
108 341 U.S. at 99.
109 *Id.* at 102.

it was error for the trial judge to tell the jury "that knowledge that constitutional rights would be violated is not necessary to the establishment of this crime." [110] When this case reached the Supreme Court, under the name of *United States* v. *Williams*,[111] Justice Douglas in a dissenting opinion indicated that he did not share Sibley's opinion as to the necessity of knowledge, though he did not quote the words which Sibley found objectionable. Believing that "conspiracy" under Section 19 necessarily implied the same thing as "willfully" under Section 20, he held that the charge to the jury "followed the ruling in the *Screws* case."

That Douglas did not regard defendant's knowledge of the existence of the constitutional right as essential is evidenced further by a passage in the *Screws* case, in which he seems to have wavered from his insistence that Section 20 applies only to rights which have been made definite. Explaining why the *Classic* case "met the test we suggest," he said that the charge in the indictment there

> is adequate since he who alters ballots or without legal justification destroys them would be acting willfully in the sense in which § 20 uses the term. The fact that the defendants may not have been thinking in constitutional terms is not material where their aim was not to enforce local law but to deprive a citizen of a right and that right was protected by the Constitution. When they so act they at least act in reckless disregard of constitutional prohibitions or guarantees.[112]

There can be no doubt that the defendants in the *Classic* case aimed to deprive some of the primary voters of an effective choice in the selection of a Congressman; and the Court decided that the right to an effective choice is protected by the Constitution. But this right had not been made definite at the time when the voters were deprived of it. That is one of the reasons why Douglas himself dissented in the case. Until the decision was rendered no one could say with assurance that the Constitution conferred any rights on a voter at a party primary. Yet the defendants were held indictable under Section 20 (as well as under Section 19), and Douglas said the indictment "met the test" of the *Screws* case. It met part of the test in that it charged an aim to deprive the voters of an effective choice, not merely an aimless deprivation thereof, whereas in the *Screws* case the deprivations of life and of a court trial were not shown to

[110] 179 F. 2d 644, 649 (5th Cir. 1950). This is Judge Sibley's accurate paraphrase of the trial judge's language.

[111] 341 U.S. 70, 94 (1951).

[112] 325 U.S. at 106.

have been brought about purposely. But the *Classic* indictment failed to meet that part of the test on which Douglas laid such stress elsewhere in the *Screws* opinion, which requires that the aim must be to deprive a person of "a right which has been made specific either by the express terms of the Constitution or laws of the United States or by decisions interpreting them." The right of which Classic and his associates deprived the voters had not been made specific by either. They aimed to deprive the voters of a right which was definitely enough possessed under state law, but they could not have known that this right was protected by the Constitution.

The Douglas opinion in the *Screws* case is frequently spoken of as the doctrine of the Court, though it represents the view of but four of the nine participating justices. It may be the Court's doctrine, but if so the Court's doctrine is ambiguous. On the one hand the *Classic* case was approved in its application of Section 20 to the purposeful deprivation of a constitutional right which had not been made definite. On the other hand it was declared that Section 20 would not apply to the deprivation, however purposeful, of a right not already made definite. In propounding the ambiguous test of the *Screws* case the Court cannot be thought to have said its last word on the subject.

If the requirement be dropped, as in the *Classic* case, that the right must have been made definite before a person was deprived of it, the Douglas interpretation of the word "willfully" will not save Section 20 from the constitutional vice which he was seeking to avoid. The aim of the defendants in the *Classic* case, as Douglas pointed out, was not to enforce a local law, but to deprive a citizen of a right, and that right was protected by the Constitution. But the two aims are not incompatible. A local administrator, for example, is entrusted by state law with the duty of fixing maximum rents which it will thereafter be illegal for a landlord to charge. He fixes a rent for a certain landlord in the sincere belief that the landlord has no constitutional right to charge more. Until the rent was fixed the landlord had a right under state law which he no longer has. The administrator has purposely deprived him of it, but whether the deprivation in the precise circumstances is valid has never before been definitely determined. The landlord takes the case to the Supreme Court, which holds after much deliberation that the rent order is invalid and that it deprives the landlord of a constitutional right. Is the administrator then guilty of violating Section 20? Though his aim was to enforce local law, it was also to deprive the landlord of a right, and that right was protected by the Constitution. He would seem to have acted "willfully" in the sense which Douglas gave to the word in his explanation of the *Classic* case. But the result is the very thing which he was seeking to avoid, for the administrator "had no adequate advance notice that [he] would be visited with punishment."

To avoid this result, is it necessary to hold that it is only the deprivation of rights that have been made definite that can be punished under Section 20? If so, the *Classic* case must be overruled not only in its affirmance of the indictment under Section 20 but also in its affirmance of the indictment under Section 19, as must the *Guinn, Mosley,* and *Saylor* cases in affirming convictions under that section. Convictions in those cases were for conspiring to "injure, oppress, threaten, or intimidate" citizens in their enjoyment of constitutional rights. In the *Mosley* case the right was to have one's ballot counted in a federal election, in the *Saylor* case to have it honestly counted without stuffing of the ballot box, in the *Classic* case to have it counted in a party primary. It had not been made definite that voters have these precise rights under the Constitution before the Court held in each case that they have. The defendants had adequate advance notice in all three cases that what they were doing violated state law, but not that it violated federal law.

If these cases are still to be considered authoritative (and the Court has shown no disposition to overrule them), it would seem that those who conspire to do acts which state law has definitely made criminal and which necessarily injure citizens in the enjoyment of federally secured rights and those who "under color of law" do acts which likewise violate definite state criminal law and necessarily deprive any inhabitant of a federally secured right, can be convicted of violating Section 19 or Section 20, even though the federal right in question has not yet been "made definite." Such persons have done what Section 19 or Section 20 forbids, and the guilty intent is supplied by their purposeful commission of state crimes already made definite. Those without guilty intent of any sort, like the rent administrator of our illustration, could not be convicted. Enforcers of state or local law would lack the guilty intent requisite to a conviction unless they believed at the time when they enforced the laws that enforcement was unconstitutional, as the defendants in the *Guinn* case were found to have believed when they enforced against Negroes the racially discriminatory suffrage provision of the Oklahoma constitution. As in Justice Rutledge's minority opinion in the *Screws* case, Section 20 would condemn only officials who abuse their official functions, not those who commit an "error of judgment, made in honest effort at once to apply and to follow the law." [113]

This is a far cry from Judge Sibley's philosophy. In addition to his belief that it would be unconstitutional to punish anyone under Section 20 for depriving a person of a federal right unless the defendant knew that the right was federally secured, he apparently believed for similar reasons that it would be unconstitutional to punish anyone under Section 19 for conspiring to injure a citizen in the enjoyment of a federal right unless that right had been made definite. To avoid what he conceived to be unconstitutional results he construed Section 19 not to apply to rights under the Fourteenth Amendment. Since the section referred to conspiracies to injure "any citizen," he maintained that Congress in enacting it "had in mind the federal rights and privileges which appertain to citizens as such and not the general rights extended to all persons by the [due process] clause of the Fourteenth Amendment." Under the misapprehension that "the *citizen's* rights are *specifically* stated in the Constitution and statutes" (his italics), he believed that "the trouble about the vagueness of the Fourteenth Amendment as a standard of individual conduct is thus escaped." [114] There he was wrong. As we shall see in the next chapter there is much controversy as to what the privileges and immunities of citizens of the United States include. And the voting rights, to which Sibley thought the section applies, were vague in their scope until convictions were sustained for injuring citizens in their enjoyment of them.

The conviction of Williams and his associates under Section 19 came after Williams had been convicted and the others acquitted under Section 20. In companion cases the Supreme Court sustained the conviction of Williams under Section 20 (*Williams* v. *United States*) [115] and affirmed the appeals court in setting aside all the convictions under Section 19 (*United States* v. *Williams*).[116] Four of the justices dissented from the setting aside of the latter conviction. Of the five who voted to set it aside, Justice Black did so on the ground

[113] 325 U.S. at 130. [114] 179 F. 2d at 648. [115] 341 U.S. 97.
[116] 341 U.S. 70.

that trial under Section 19 after an acquittal under Section 20 was barred by the principle of *res judicata*,[117] and he found it unnecessary to discuss Section 19. The remaining four reached their conclusion from their interpretation of Section 19, as expressed in an opinion by Justice Frankfurter in which Chief Justice Vinson and Justices Jackson and Minton joined. The dissenting opinion by Justice Douglas had the concurrence of Justices Reed, Burton and Clark. Since the participants were equally divided on the construction of Section 19, neither view can be taken as authoritative.

Frankfurter agreed with the lower court that Section 19 does not apply to what the defendants did, but not "because we fully accept the course of reasoning of the court below." [118] His conclusion was that the rights protected by Section 19, unlike those protected by Section 20, "are those which Congress can beyond doubt constitutionally secure against interference by private individuals." These are not confined to rights appertaining to citizenship, for he thought they included the right to establish a claim under the Homestead Act, which he said did not pertain to United States citizenship.[119] The rights protected by Section 19 include the right to vote in congressional elections, but exclude "those rights which the Constitution merely guarantees from interference by a State." [120] Those punishable under Section 19 are described as "persons." Had Congress intended, thought Frankfurter, to apply the section to rights which the Constitution protects only against the states, it would have spoken of "officials" as well as persons, or at least referred to persons "acting under color of law." [121] Justice Douglas, on the other hand, maintained that the word "persons" includes officials and that Section 19 protects both those rights whose enjoyment private individuals conspire to injure and those whose enjoyment is injured by a conspiracy of state officials.[122] Which view will finally prevail it is too early to predict.[123]

117 *Id.* at 116–117. Black's argument was that unless the defendants (other than Williams) had done the acts for which they were acquitted under Section 20, there was no evidence of their conspiring to do them and their acquittal must be taken as conclusive of their not having done the acts. Furthermore, if Williams alone had done the acts he could not have conspired with himself to do them. Douglas thought that the defendants might have conspired, although not actually doing or abetting in the doing of the acts. 341 U.S. at 95–96.

118 341 U.S. at 72.

119 *Id.* at 80, citing United States v. Waddell, 112 U.S. 76 (1884).

120 341 U.S. at 77.

121 *Id.* at 78.

122 *Id.* at 93.

123 A more detailed discussion of the topic of this section will be found in Hale, *Unconstitutional Acts as Federal Crimes* (1946) 60 HARV. L. REV. 65. The discussion there, however, of the question of purpose seems on further reflection to be unsatisfactory, and of course there is no reference to the subsequently decided Williams cases.

We have been considering in this chapter the process whereby the Supreme Court determines what constitutional rights a person has and the methods by which they are made effective. We must now consider some of the particular constitutional rights affecting a person's economic freedom which have been established by judicial decision.

IX

CONSTITUTIONAL PROVISIONS FOR THE PROTECTION OF INDIVIDUAL ECONOMIC INTERESTS[1]

THE Constitution, of course, cannot guarantee absolute liberty to every individual. It does, however, contain various provisions which an individual can invoke for protection against oppression. Some of these provisions we must now examine.

SLAVERY AND INVOLUNTARY SERVITUDE

The most conspicuous lack of economic freedom is to be found where slavery exists. While it existed in this country it was by virtue of law that Negroes were held in a condition of servitude—state law in the slave states, and federal law in some of the territories and in the District of Columbia. The adoption of the Thirteenth Amendment in 1865 nullified all such slave laws, and it went further. It reads:

[1] The substance of this chapter has been published in an article entitled *Some Basic Constitutional Rights of Economic Significance* (1951) 51 COL. L. REV. 271.

Section 1. Neither slavery nor involuntary servitude, except as a punishment for crime whereof the party shall have been duly convicted, shall exist within the United States, or any place subject to their jurisdiction.

Section 2. Congress shall have power to enforce this article by appropriate legislation.

In addition to nullifying laws which subject any person to slavery, the Amendment protects against enslavement at the hands of private individuals and authorizes Congress to provide punishment for such private enslavement. Compelling a person to work, even when he has incurred a contractual legal duty to do so, comes within the ban on "involuntary servitude" if the compulsion takes the form of private violence or imprisonment by the state for nonperformance. In *Clyatt* v. *United States* [2] a federal law which provided punishment for returning a man to a state of peonage was held applicable to the use of physical force to compel a man to perform the work he had contracted to do [3] and was held to be within the power conferred on the federal government by Section 2 of the Amendment, as "appropriate" to enforcing the ban on involuntary servitude; and in *Bailey* v. *Alabama* [4] a state law construed to punish nonperformance of a service contract with imprisonment was set aside as creating involuntary servitude.

However, though performance of a contract to work for another is involuntary servitude if done under constraint of physical violence or under fear of a jail sentence, performance to avoid a judgment for damages for breach of the contract is not considered such. In the two peonage cases the Court even denied that there was any compulsion involved in a legal duty to perform. In the *Clyatt* case Justice Brewer said that one who contracts to perform services, though "subject like any other contractor to an action for damages for breach of that contract, can elect at any time to break it, and no law or force compels performance or a continuance of the service." [5] And Justice Hughes, speaking of the "debt" to render services in *Bailey* v. *Alabama,* said: "The contract exposes the debtor to liability for the loss due to the breach, but not to enforced labor." [6]

These denials of any coercive character to a liability for damages are too sweeping. As Holmes said in his dissenting opinion in *Bailey*

[2] 197 U.S. 205 (1905).

[3] The conviction, however, was set aside for defects in the indictment. A conviction under the same federal law was affirmed in United States v. Gaskin, 320 U.S. 527 (1944).

[4] 219 U.S. 219 (1911). [5] 197 U.S. at 215–216. [6] 219 U.S. at 242.

v. *Alabama*, "any legal liability for breach of a contract is a disagreeable consequence which tends to make the contractor do as he said he would.' [7] True, the liability of a property-less person such as Bailey to pay damages would have but a negligible tendency to make him do the promised work, for he knew that no damages could be collected from him. But in the case of a solvent person, the motive for performing might often be the desire to escape pecuniary liability. If such desire is strong enough to make him render the services stipulated in his contract, then the law does compel performance and enforce the labor—but not where the desire to avoid performance outweighs the desire to escape the liability to pay.

The real principle underlying the peonage cases seems to be the same as that followed by English courts of equity without the aid of a constitutional provision. They will not issue affirmative injunctions ordering the performance of service contracts. Nor will they enjoin breach of sweeping negative covenants to abstain from every kind of work other than for the employer with whom the contract was made. Their refusal to do so is based on the theory that doing so will in effect enforce affirmative performance under penalty of starvation. But when the movie actress Mrs. Nelson (better known as Bette Davis) covenanted to work for Warner Brothers and made a negative covenant to do no theatrical or motion picture work for anyone else, the King's Bench Division did not hesitate to enjoin breach of that negative covenant. After pointing out that there were other kinds of work which, though less remunerative, would save her from starvation as the alternative to rendering the promised services, Branson, J., observed in *Warner Brothers Pictures, Inc.* v. *Nelson*, "She will not be driven, although she may be tempted, to perform the contract, and the fact that she may be so tempted is no objection to the grant of an injunction." [8] One who performs because "tempted" to do so when the alternative will be less remunerative work, and one who is "driven" to avoid starvation, are both forced to perform. The difference, like the difference between a jail sentence and liability to pay damages, is a difference of degree. There are circumstances in which fear of pecuniary loss (unaccompanied by starvation) will not be strong enough to force performance, while fear of starvation or of imprisonment will suffice. The policy of the Thirteenth Amendment, as expounded in the courts, and the policy

[7] *Id.* at 246.

[8] L.R. [1937] 1 K.B.D. 209, 219–220.

of the English courts as well, is against enforcing promised services in such circumstances. But when reluctance to perform will be overcome by fear of liability for damages or by enforcement of a negative covenant which will not result in starvation, courts do not hesitate to instil such fears merely because they will be effective to enforce performance.

In one sense of the word no labor is "involuntary"—not even that of a slave. It is performed through the voluntary muscular movements of the laborer, who chooses to perform it in order to avoid something worse. Obviously, the word is not used in the Thirteenth Amendment in this restricted sense. In another sense of the word, all labor is "involuntary" unless performed for the sheer pleasure of it. A man works because he must do so if he is to avoid some worse alternative. It is equally obvious that the Amendment was not intended to outlaw all labor performed under economic pressure. Pressure which takes the form of physical violence or threat of imprisonment, however, is banned, even when exerted to force performance of labor which one has incurred a contractual legal "duty" to perform. So, too (American courts would probably hold as well as English), is pressure which takes the form of a court decree which forbids all other opportunity to avoid starvation. But if liability to pay damages suffices to force a man to do his promised work, force of that degree is permissible. Presumably it would not suffice to force performance under conditions which he would regard as extremely intolerable, while threat of imprisonment might.

A court decree is not the only conceivable legal restraint which would prevent a man from performing the type of work which he finds the most remunerative, thus forcing him to work at some less congenial occupation. Justice Field, dissenting in *The Slaughter-House Cases*,[9] in 1873, suggested that the grant of a slaughtering monopoly in New Orleans might be held to subject to involuntary servitude those butchers who were forbidden to practice their trade there. He based his opinion that the monopoly was (contrary to the opinion of the majority) unconstitutional chiefly on the ground that it violated the Fourteenth Amendment; but, speaking of the Thirteenth, he said:

> The words "involuntary servitude" . . . include something more than slavery in the strict sense of the term. The abolition of slavery and involun-

[9] 16 Wall. 36, 90 (U.S. 1873).

tary servitude was intended to make everyone born in this country a freeman. A prohibition to him to pursue certain callings open to others of the same age, condition and sex, or to reside in places where others are permitted to live, would so far deprive him of the rights of a freeman, and would place him, as respects others, in a condition of servitude. A person allowed to pursue only one trade or calling, and only in one locality of the country, would not be, in the strict sense of the term, in a condition of slavery, but probably none would deny that he would be in a condition of servitude. He certainly would not possess the liberties nor enjoy the privileges of a freeman. The compulsion which would force him to labor even for his own benefit only in one direction, or in one place, would be almost as oppressive and nearly as great an invasion of his liberty as the compulsion which would force him to labor for the benefit or pleasure of another, and would equally constitute an element of servitude.

The slaughterhouse monopoly, of course, did not go so far as to allow the unprivileged butchers "to pursue only one trade or calling, and only in one locality of the country." They could operate slaughterhouses anywhere outside the region set aside for the monopoly, and even in that region they could pursue any calling other than that of operating a slaughterhouse. But laws of property not infrequently compel certain persons to labor "only in one direction" and "in one place," and sometimes even for only one employer. The law forbids the pursuit of any trade which requires the use of land or material equipment except to those who own that land or equipment or can induce the owners to grant permission to use it. One who owns no means of transportation and does not have enough money to pay the fares charged by public transportation systems may not travel to another place. One without property and without special abilities may literally be compelled to work for a local employer under conditions as oppressive as those which would prevail if he were compelled by direct legal mandate to work for the same employer. One who can render services that are scarce in relation to the demand for them can secure better terms through the exertion of the bargaining power inherent in his ability to threaten to withhold those services—particularly if there is more than one employer to compete for them. But one who lacks this ability must perforce accept whatever terms of employment are offered, as the alternative to the starvation that will face him by reason of the law's enforcement of his legal duties not to make use of the material necessities of life assigned to other owners.

It has never been held that services rendered to others under compulsion of starvation, even though the starvation be enforced by the law of property, constitute the involuntary servitude forbidden by the Amendment. Nor could it well be so held. The worker chooses the employment, however oppressive it may be, in order to avoid what to him is the worse alternative, starvation. To forbid the employment would condemn him to starvation. The case is different when the work is performed to escape the physical violence of the employer or a jail sentence. In such cases the court can remove the pressure which induces a man to perform the labor. It can punish the employer who uses physical violence or nullify the law which provides for imprisonment. When the alternative to the work, however, is starvation, no mere court decree under a constitutional fiat can remove the pressure. The court cannot itself provide food to avert the starvation which will result from choosing not to work; nor can it well authorize the worker to help himself to other people's food or utilize their land to produce his own food. If the law is to afford the sharecropper or the sweatshop worker more freedom from his compulsory servitude, it must do so either by regulating the conditions of employment or, less directly but perhaps more effectively, by taking steps to increase the worker's bargaining power to resist oppressive terms. Either remedy calls for legislation rather than judicial enforcement of the Thirteenth Amendment.

There are circumstances in which service may be compelled even by threats of imprisonment, despite the Thirteenth Amendment. In *Robertson* v. *Baldwin*,[10] decided in 1897, it was held that the Amendment did not nullify provisions in an early statute, punishing a seaman with imprisonment for deserting a vessel in violation of his contract. After expressing doubt whether the service was "involuntary" at all, within the meaning of the Amendment, since the seaman had entered "voluntarily" into the contract to render it, Justice Brown maintained that "even if the contract of a seaman could be considered within the letter of the Thirteenth Amendment, it is not, within its spirit, a case of involuntary servitude." [11] Pointing out that the first ten amendments have always been considered subject to certain exceptions and adverting to the evils which the Thirteenth Amendment was designed to cure, Brown went on:

It is clear, however, that the amendment was not intended to introduce any novel doctrine with respect to certain descriptions of service which have

[10] 165 U.S. 275 (1897).

[11] *Id.* at 280–281.

always been treated as exceptional, such as military and naval enlistments, or to disturb the right of parents and guardians to the custody of their minor children or wards. The amendment, however, makes no distinction between a public and a private service. To say that persons engaged in a public service are not within the amendment is to admit that there are exceptions to its general language, and the further question is at once presented, where shall the line be drawn? We know of no better answer to make than to say that services which have from time immemorial been treated as exceptional shall not be regarded as within its purview.[12]

Under other circumstances also liberty to withhold services, even when no contract was ever made to render them, can be denied, and the withholding punished by imprisonment. Refusal to testify as a witness or to serve on a jury can be punished, and in *Butler* v. *Perry*[13] a requirement of six days' labor on the public highways by every able-bodied male person between the ages of twenty-one and twenty-five was sustained in 1916.[14] Many other affirmative acts can be required, under criminal penalties, which do not absorb a person's entire time and energies and are in no way akin to slavery. Thus, it can be made a crime for a motorist who runs over a pedestrian to fail to rescue him, even though the accident was in no way the motorist's fault, and landlords can be held criminally for failure to make alterations in their buildings required by safety or health.[15]

Under the war power Congress can go much further and can temporarily deprive persons completely of liberty to withhold military services. The draft law of the First World War was sustained and held not to violate the Thirteenth Amendment, in *Arver* v. *United States*.[16] Whether conscription to work in private factories or mines in order to produce goods essential to the war effort would be held to violate the Amendment, the Supreme Court has never yet been called upon to decide. That Congress could draft the men in control of a business organization was asserted by Justice Black as a ground for holding that when the Government was dealing with the Bethlehem Steel Corporation during the First World War for the building of ships, it was not at the corporation's mercy. In *United States* v. *Bethlehem Steel Corporation*, after referring to the power of Congress to draft men for battle service, he said: "Its power to draft business organiza-

[12] *Id.* at 282.

[13] 240 U.S. 328 (1916).

[14] The act there sustained gave an option to pay the road overseer three dollars in lieu of doing the work, but the Court laid no stress on this provision.

[15] For a general survey of legislation of this type, see Otto Kirchheimer, *Criminal Omissions* (1942) 55 HARV. L. REV. 615.

[16] 245 U.S. 366 (1918).

tions to support the fighting men who risk their lives can be no less." [17]

The Thirteenth Amendment, then, does not afford an absolute guaranty against legal compulsions to work, even when those compulsions are backed up by criminal penalties. There may be occasions when the liberty not to work may conflict with some more important liberty. Workers may strike, for instance, for the purpose of denying to Negroes the liberty to engage in the industry. A law requiring them to go back to work for a reasonable time would not add much to the economic pressures which have already induced them to work in the particular occupation. Whatever oppressive effect such a law would have would lie not so much in any serious involuntary servitude as in a weakening of the bargaining power which the threat to quit carries with it. But such a diminution of their bargaining power would be far less harsh to them than their exercise of it would be to the Negroes they wish to exclude. In deciding whether a law punishing a stoppage under such conditions violated the Thirteenth Amendment, the Court might conceivably hold that protection of the conflicting liberty of the Negroes outweighed the slight and temporary element of involuntary servitude of the strikers. If the law went further and punished a strike for higher wages, the conflicting interests of those who would suffer from a successful strike would doubtless be far less persuasive, particularly in time of peace.

The Thirteenth Amendment affords protection against some forms of involuntary servitude, such as outright slavery or peonage. It can afford little against those economic pressures which compel one man to work for another. Whatever protection anyone has against this form of involuntary servitude rests on his bargaining power. Ability to perform services on which the market places a high value constitutes one form of protection. Ownership of property constitutes another. Hence, whatever protection the Constitution affords to property serves to protect those who have property in their freedom from involuntary servitude as well as in other forms of economic liberty, though perhaps at the expense of those who have less property. There are various provisions in the Constitution which protect property, whether in the form of ownership of physical objects or in the form of contract rights.

[17] 315 U.S. 289, 305 (1942).

EX POST FACTO LAWS AND LAWS IMPAIRING THE OBLIGATION OF CONTRACTS

Laws which work to anyone's economic disadvantage are nowadays frequently challenged as deprivations of liberty or property, in violation of the Fifth Amendment or the Fourteenth Amendment. But before any amendments were adopted, the original Constitution gave some protection to property. Art. I, Sec. 10 provides that no state shall "pass any Bill of Attainder, *ex post facto* Law, or Law impairing the Obligation of Contracts." Bills of attainder and *ex post facto* laws were also forbidden to the Federal Government (Art. I, Sec. 9). A bill of attainder is an act of the Legislature convicting a person of a crime. He can only be convicted by a court. An *ex post facto* law was defined as early as 1798 as a retroactive criminal law—one providing punishment for an act committed before the passage of the law.[18] Justice William Johnson later sought vainly to convince the Court that the term included retroactive changes in civil as well as criminal law and that the contrary pronouncements in *Calder* v. *Bull* were based on error.[19] The constitutional limitation, as he construed it, would serve to protect property rights against impairment by a state. But in 1834 Justice Story, speaking for the Court in *Watson* v. *Mercer,* reiterated that *ex post facto* laws "relate to penal and criminal proceedings which impose punishments or forfeitures, and not to civil proceedings which affect private rights retrospectively." [20] The Court has never swerved from this position. The *ex post facto* clause has never played a vital role in the protection of vested rights.

The framers of the Constitution, however, apparently attached much greater importance to the contract impairment clause. According to Chief Justice Marshall's account in 1810, the "people," in adopting the Constitution, were apprehensive of "the violent acts which might grow out of the feelings of the moment" and "manifested a determination to shield themselves and their property from the effects of those sudden and strong passions to which men are exposed." [21] They shielded themselves, however, not from all attacks on

18 Calder v. Bull, 3 Dall. 386 (U.S. 1798).

19 See his separate opinion in Ogden v. Saunders, 12 Wheat. 213, 286 (U.S. 1827). Johnson restated his views on the matter in his concurring opinion in Satterlee v. Matthewson, 2 Pet. 380, 416 (U.S. 1829), and elaborated them in a note which he appended to the case. In some editions this note appears at the end of the report of the case, in others at the end of the volume, 2 Pet. 681.

20 8 Pet. 88, 110 (U.S. 1834).

21 Fletcher v. Peck, 6 Cranch 87, 137–138 (U.S. 1810).

property in general, but from those with which they were familiar, which consisted chiefly of attacks on property in the form of contracts. As Marshall described the situation vividly in a later case,[22] states had frequently passed laws which provided that debts might be liquidated by tendering worthless property instead of money or depreciated paper money instead of coin. Accordingly, the Constitution took from the states entirely the power over the currency and over legal tender, transferring what at first was an indeterminate part of such power to the Federal Government,[23] and in addition forbade states to pass laws impairing the obligation of contracts. The framers seem to have felt less apprehension of attacks being made on property by the Federal Government.

The contract impairment clause, however, was used from the first as a shield against state legislation hostile to property. In *Sturges* v. *Crowninshield* [24] a state insolvency law was held invalid, in 1819, insofar as it operated to discharge debts incurred before its passage. States were also held incapable of legislating to impair their own contractual obligations, as well as those of private persons, and obligations binding on states were rather freely implied. Thus, in *Fletcher* v. *Peck* [25] it was held, in 1810, that when a state had once made a grant of land, a subsequent act repealing that grant impaired the state's implied obligation not to reassert its rights. And in the famous case of *Trustees of Dartmouth College* v. *Woodward* [26] it was held, in 1819, that a corporate charter granted by the state (in this case by the British King, to whose powers and obligations the state had succeeded) was a contract whose obligation was impaired by a statute providing for additional trustees to be appointed by the governor. Moreover, although not every change in the remedy which the law provides for breach of contract is invalid, nevertheless, many laws changing the remedy have been held to impair the obligation. This

[22] Sturges v. Crowninshield, 4 Wheat. 122, 204 (U.S. 1819).

[23] The power of Congress to make paper money legal tender for the payment of debts was challenged after the Civil War. At first it was held, in 1870, in Hepburn v. Griswold, 8 Wall. 603, that Congress had no such power. The vote was four to three. But the case was overruled by a five to four vote in the following year, in the Legal Tender Cases, 12 Wall. 457. Two new Justices had been appointed by President Grant in the meantime, and charges of court packing were made.

In 1935 it was held, in Norman v. B.&O.R. Co., 294 U.S. 240, that a contract to pay a specified number of dollars in gold could not prevail against Congressional power to provide for the discharge of such contracts by the payment of paper dollars.

[24] 4 Wheat. 122 (U.S. 1819).

[25] 6 Cranch 87 (U.S. 1810).

[26] 4 Wheat. 518 (U.S. 1819).

was made plain in 1843 in *Bronson* v. *Kinzie*,[27] and in 1934 a statute exempting moneys paid on insurance policies from seizure for the payment of debts was held bad in *W. B. Worthen Co.* v. *Thomas*.[28]

Thus, long before the Fourteenth Amendment was enacted the contract clause served to prevent a state from doing many things which since 1868 might be held to be unconstitutional deprivations of property. It must not be supposed, however, that it afforded a rigid guaranty that all promises would be performed.

Not every promise carries with it an obligation that it be literally carried out. Except for that class of contracts for which the courts will decree specific performance, a party may always choose not to perform. If the contract is a valid one, this choice will expose him to liability to pay damages when sued by the other party. If he pays them in full, the obligation is discharged, though the promised act was never performed. The obligation, in effect, was not necessarily to do the promised act, but was to choose between doing it and incurring a liability to pay whatever damages might be awarded for breach.[29] As so understood, the obligation is not "impaired" when the party chooses to break his promise and pay damages instead. Even a state may break its promise and subject itself to an action for damages without impairing the obligation of its contract. It was so held in 1920 in an opinion by Justice Pitney in *Hays* v. *Seattle*.[30]

Moreover, there are many agreements between parties which, by the laws of the state where they are made carry no obligation at all, or an obligation different from that expressed in the words of the agreement. Certain agreements which are considered to be against public policy—gambling agreements, for instance—are commonly said either not to be "contracts" at all, or, if designated as contracts, to be invalid. In either case, they carry no legal obligation. Usury laws commonly prevent any obligation from arising out of agreements to pay more than a specified rate of interest. Statutes of frauds make contracts for the sale of interests in real estate invalid unless in writing. Statutes of limitations provide that no suit can be brought on contracts when a specified period of time has elapsed since the

27 1 How. 311 (U.S. 1843).

28 292 U.S. 426 (1934).

29 And, of course, there is no guaranty that the damages will actually be paid. If not paid, the defendant's property in the jurisdiction can be seized in an execution, and the damages paid from the proceeds of its sale. A certain amount of property, however, is exempted from seizure. If the proceeds are insufficient to pay the judgment, the defendant remains indebted for the balance, but he may never be able to pay it.

30 251 U.S. 233 (1920).

cause of action arose. All such qualifications to an absolute right to enforce contracts, unless retroactive, have always been considered entirely consistent with the contract clause. They do not impair any obligation, for, as Chief Justice Marshall conceded in his dissenting opinion in *Ogden* v. *Saunders:* "The obligation must exist, before it can be impaired; and a prohibition to impair it, when made, does not imply an inability to prescribe those circumstances which shall create its obligation." [31] In that case the majority, distinguishing *Sturges* v. *Crowninshield,* held that when a state insolvency law discharged a debt which had been incurred after the passage of the law, it did not impair any obligation of a contract, for the state law made the debtor's obligation conditional from the start. When the obligation first arose, the state insolvency law was "read into it." In fact the "obligation" of any contract was said to be nothing but what the state law made it at the time when the contract was made. The Constitution is held not to require states to give any obligation at all to future contracts.

In 1848 the Court went further in restricting the scope of the contract impairment clause. In an opinion by Justice Daniel in *West River Bridge Co.* v. *Dix,*[32] it read more into a contract than the law which defined its obligation at the time it was made. Into all contracts, said Daniel, "there enter conditions which arise not out of the literal terms of the contract itself; they are superinduced by the preëxisting and higher authority of the laws of nature, of nations, or of the community to which the parties belong." The right of eminent domain, he held, was one such condition; hence, although the state had granted a franchise to maintain a toll bridge for a definite period of time, it could, before the expiration of that period, appropriate that franchise by exercising the power of eminent domain and compensating for the property taken. In so doing it was not impairing the obligation, but "claiming only the fulfilment of an essential and inseparable condition." [33]

The right to retake by condemnation property which it has granted (whether that property is tangible or intangible, like a franchise) is thus reserved by implications in any grant which a state makes. Dissenting judges have from time to time contended that the right of a state to resume its taxing power is similarly reserved in contracts by

[31] 12 Wheat. 213, 348 (U.S. 1827).

[32] 6 How. 507, 532 (U.S. 1848).

[33] *Id.* at 533.

which the state agrees to exempt specified property or persons from taxation,[34] but this view has not prevailed. It has been held, however, that agreements not to exercise the police power in certain of its forms are not binding. *Stone* v. *Mississippi*[35] held in 1880 that a state could not bargain away its power to forbid lotteries, and *Butchers' Union Co.* v. *Crescent City Co.*[36] held in 1884 that, while a state could grant a monopoly to a slaughtering company, it could not obligate itself by contract to refrain from withdrawing the grant before the expiration of the stipulated term.[37]

Restrictions which the contract clause places on any state legislature because of contracts made by its predecessors have been further relaxed to some extent by the doctrine that any ambiguity in such contracts is to be resolved in favor of the state and against the other party. In an opinion by Marshall in *Providence Bank* v. *Billings*,[38] in 1830, this doctrine was applied to contracts which were alleged to grant tax exemption, and later it was stated more generally in Chief Justice Taney's notable opinion in 1837 in *Charles River Bridge* v. *Warren Bridge*.[39] Moreover, after the *Dartmouth College* decision states have commonly included in their charters clauses reserving to themselves power to alter, amend, or repeal them.

Not only is a state permitted to exercise its police power in many of its aspects, despite its own agreement not to do so (that agreement being said to have no obligation from the start), but it is permitted to exercise its power even when the result is to forbid private parties to fulfill agreements, such as those for the sale of liquor, which did have obligations at the start. As Holmes said in 1924 in *Dillingham* v. *McLaughlin:* "The operation of reasonable laws for the protection of the public cannot be headed off by making contracts reaching into the future." [40] At times the Court has frankly stated that despite the contract clause such contracts are subject to impairment.[41] More frequently it has taken the position exemplified in Justice

[34] See, particularly, Catron, J., dissenting, in Piqua Branch Bank v. Knoop, 16 How. 369 (U.S. 1854); Daniel, J., concurring, in Ohio Life Ins. Co. v. Debolt, 16 How. 416 (U.S. 1854); Campbell, J., dissenting, in Dodge v. Woolsey, 18 How. 331 (U.S. 1856); and Miller, J., dissenting, in The Washington University v. Rouse, 8 Wall. 439 (U.S. 1869).

[35] 101 U.S. 814 (1880).

[36] 111 U.S. 746 (1884).

[37] But that a state may obligate itself not to restore competition with business of a type which can be carried on only by public franchise was decided in an opinion by Harlan, J., in New Orleans Gas Co. v. Louisiana Light Co., 105 U.S. 650 (1885).

[38] 4 Pet. 514 (U.S. 1830).

[39] 11 Pet. 420 (U.S. 1837).

[40] 264 U.S. 370, 374 (1924).

[41] *Cf.* Brown, J., for the Court, in Manigault v. Springs, 199 U.S. 473, 480 (1905).

Sutherland's dissenting opinion in 1934 in *Home Bldg. & Loan Ass'n* v. *Blaisdell,*[42] when he said that if a statute, such as one which forbids the sale of liquor, destroys contracts, "the obligation is not impaired in the constitutional sense. The contract is frustrated—it disappears in virtue of an implied condition to that effect read into the contract itself." [43]

From the beginning, the Court permitted the states to exercise somewhat more leeway in legislating on the remedies for the enforcement of contractual obligations than on other aspects of the obligation. While the Court held in *Sturges* v. *Crowninshield* that discharge of a pre-existing debt by a state insolvency law impaired the obligation of a contract, Marshall declared that there was no impairment in the release of the debtor from imprisonment.

The distinction between the obligation of a contract [he said] and the remedy given by the legislature to enforce that obligation . . . exists in the nature of things. Without impairing the obligation of the contract, the remedy may certainly be modified as the wisdom of the nation shall direct. . . . Imprisonment is no part of the contract, and simply to release the prisoner does not impair its obligation.[44]

Later, Justice Swayne, seeking to minimize the power of a state to legislate as to the remedy, explained the validity of laws releasing from imprisonment for debt, by asserting that such imprisonment "is regarded as penal rather than remedial." [45] However sound this ex-

[42] 290 U.S. 398, 477 (1934).

[43] In East New York Savings Bank v. Hahn, 326 U.S. 230, 232–233, decided November 5, 1945, Justice Frankfurter, for the Court, referred to the protective power of the state, mentioned by Chief Justice Hughes in Home Bldg. & L. Ass'n v. Blaisdell, 290 U.S. 398, 440 (1934), and said: "The formal mode of reasoning by means of which this 'protective power of the State,' 290 U.S. at 440, is acknowledged is of little moment. It may be treated as an implied condition of every contract and, as such, as much part of the contract as though it were written into it, whereby the State's exercise of its power enforces, and does not impair, a contract. A more candid statement is to recognize, as was said in *Manigault* v. *Springs, supra,* that the power 'which in its various ramifications is known as the police power, is an exercise of the sovereign right of the Government to protect the . . . general welfare of the people, and is paramount to any rights under contracts between individuals.' 199 U.S. at 480. Once we are in this domain of the reserve power of a State we must respect the 'wide discretion on the part of the legislature in determining what is and what is not necessary.' *Ibid.* So far as the constitutional issue is concerned, 'the power of the State when otherwise justified,' *Marcus Brown Co.* v. *Feldman,* 256 U.S. 170, 198, is not diminished because a private contract may be affected."

[44] 4 Wheat. at 200–201. To the same effect, see Thompson, J., in Mason v. Haile, 12 Wheat. 370, 378 (U.S. 1827), and Story, J., in Beers v. Haughton, 9 Pet. 329, 359 (U.S. 1835).

[45] Von Hoffman v. City of Quincy, 4 Wall. 535, 553 (U.S. 1867). Swayne elaborated this explanation in Edwards v. Kearzey, 96 U.S. 595, 602 (1878).

planation may be, retroactive changes of remedy have often been declared permissible. The Court has always preserved at least a verbal distinction between them and changes in "substance."

When, in *Bronson* v. *Kinzie,* Taney held a law bad in 1843 which acted on the remedy of a pre-existing mortgage, by forbidding a foreclosure sale for less than two thirds of the value, he was careful to state that if the law "had done nothing more than change the remedy upon contracts of this description" it would have been valid.[46] "And, although a new remedy may be deemed less convenient than the old one, and may in some degree render the recovery of debts more tardy and difficult, yet it will not follow that the law is unconstitutional." It was because the law under consideration, by acting on the remedy, had the effect of impairing the obligation, that it was held bad. No one, he presumed, "would say that there is any substantial difference between a retrospective law declaring a particular contract or class of contracts abrogated and void, and one which took away all remedy to enforce them, or encumbered it with conditions that rendered it useless or impracticable to pursue it." [47] Where to draw the line "between legitimate alterations of the remedy, and provisions which, in the form of remedy, impair the right," he admitted to be difficult. The fact remains that the Court then authoritatively recognized that some changes in the remedy are permissible, even though they have an adverse effect on the person to whom the obligation is owed. Since that time several statutes which affected the obligee adversely have been sustained, on the ground that, while they altered the remedy, they did not impair the "obligation." [48]

[46] 1 How. at 315–316.

[47] *Id.* at 317.

[48] In some of these cases, if not all, it may be that the alteration merely prevented the obligee from obtaining more by way of remedy than he would have obtained had the contract been performed. In Morley v. Lake Shore &c. Ry. Co., 146 U.S. 162 (1892), it was held that the statutory rate of interest for delay in the payment of a judgment based on a contract was no part of the obligation of the contract itself, and could therefore be reduced even after the judgment was rendered. Possibly the earlier rate would have given the plaintiff more than he could have obtained by investing his money if it had been promptly paid. In Curtis v. Whitney, 13 Wall. 68 (U.S. 1872), a statute was sustained which required a person, who had already obtained a contract from the state for the conveyance of property bought at a tax sale, subject to redemption by the former owner within three years, to serve notice on the occupant of the land before obtaining the deed to it. In Gelfert v. National City Bank, 313 U.S. 221 (1941), the Court sustained a law, as applied to a pre-existing mortgage, which provided that after the mortgagee had bought the mortgaged property at a foreclosure sale, a deficiency judgment should be limited to the amount of the debt less the market value of the property, if that exceeded the amount paid at the sale. The effect of the laws sustained in these last two cases would be to lessen the likelihood of profiting from the purchase

From an early time, then, states have been permitted to pass laws which prevented agreements from being enforced or from being enforced effectively. But in permitting such laws, the Supreme Court, for the most part, managed to reconcile its decisions to a doctrine that the passage of every state law impairing a contractual obligation once called into existence was prohibited. The permitted laws were said not to impair it. They either prevented the obligation from arising in the first place or, if applied to pre-existing agreements, the agreement was said to contain no obligation (as when the state agreed not to exercise its police power), or an obligation subject to implied conditions, or else the law was said to apply to the remedy alone, without impairing the obligation.

In deciding whether an agreement was obligatory when made or whether its obligation was subject to implied conditions, the Supreme Court was passing on a question of state, not federal, law. This the Court recognized in 1914 in *Ennis Water Works* v. *Ennis,* when Chief Justice White said that when a contract is alleged to arise from a state law or municipal ordinance, "this court will not give to it a meaning in conflict with the settled rule of the State at the time the law was enacted or the ordinance adopted." [49] But in deciding this question of state law, the Supreme Court has always insisted on reaching its own conclusions, regardless of what the state courts may have held—though recognizing, as in the opinions of Taft, C. J., in *Appleby* v. *New York,*[50] and of Roberts, J., in *Indiana ex rel. Anderson* v. *Brand,*[51] that the decision involved an appraisal of state statutes and decisions. Although *Erie Railroad Co.* v. *Tompkins* [52] held in 1938 that state court decisions on common law were conclusive on the federal courts in diversity cases, the Court has since then, as well as before, refused to be bound by them in cases arising under the contract clause, when they determine the extent, under state law, of the obligation of a contract. The Court's present attitude is expressed in a dictum by Justice Jackson in 1942 in *Irving Trust Co.* v. *Day,*[53] in which he said that "the existence of the contract and the nature and extent of its obligation become federal questions for the

of property at a forced-sale value, and in the Gelfert case to prevent the mortgagee from obtaining property (real estate plus a deficiency judgment) worth more than the money he would have obtained had the contract been performed by payment of the debt.

49 233 U.S. 652 (1914).

50 271 U.S. 364, 380 (1926).

51 303 U.S. 95, 100 (1938).

52 304 U.S. 64 (1938). Discussed *supra*, pp. 45-47.

53 314 U.S. 556, 561 (1942).

purposes of determining whether they are within the scope and meaning of the Federal Constitution, and for such purposes finality cannot be accorded to the views of a state court." The views of state courts in decisions rendered after the making of a contract would not necessarily be conclusive as to what the state law was at the time of the making, even on the theory of the *Tompkins* case; they would be conclusive only of state law from the time of the decision.

Much of the judicial ingenuity displayed in demonstrating that a law which the Court wished to sustain did not really impair the obligation of contracts was necessitated by an effort to enable states to escape from the supposed straitjacket of the Constitution; for it was assumed that the contract clause was to be read with literal exactness as forbidding every impairment. From the earliest time, however, protests against this literal construction have been voiced from the chambers of the Court itself, and finally, in 1934, the Court repudiated such strictness.

The first protest was made by Justice William Johnson in 1810, in his dissenting opinion in *Fletcher* v. *Peck*,[54] and this he followed up in 1827 in his separate opinion in *Ogden* v. *Saunders*.[55] He protested against subjecting the contract clause "to a severe literal construction, which would be better adapted to special pleadings." [56] The right of the creditor, he said,

> to the aid of the public arm for the recovery of contracts, is not absolute and unlimited, but may be modified by the necessities or policy of societies. And this, together with the contract itself, must be taken by the individual, subject to such restrictions, and conditions as are imposed by the laws of the country.[57]

On an earlier page he said:

> The constitution was framed for society, and an advanced state of society, in which, I will undertake to say, that all the contracts of men receive a relative, and not a positive interpretation; for the rights of all must be held and enjoyed in subserviency to the good of the whole.[58]

And,

> it is among the duties of society to enforce the rights of humanity; and both the debtor and the society have their interests in the administration of justice, and in the general good; interests, which must not be swallowed up and lost sight of while yielding attention to the claim of the creditor.[59]

[54] 6 Cranch 87, 145 (U.S. 1810).
[55] 12 Wheat. 213, 271 (U.S. 1827).
[56] *Id.* at 286.
[57] *Id.* at 287.
[58] *Id.* at 282.
[59] *Id.* at 283.

Again, after pointing out that many laws that render something unlawful which was not so when the party contracted to do it remain unquestioned, he said:

It is, therefore, far from being true, as a general proposition, "that a government necessarily violates the obligation of a contract, which it puts an end to without performance." It is the motive, the policy, the object, that must characterize the legislative act, to affect it with the imputation of violating the obligation of contracts.[60]

Justice Johnson's approach to the question was adopted by Chief Justice Hughes, speaking for the majority in 1934, in *Home Building & Loan Ass'n* v. *Blaisdell*,[61] a decision which held the Minnesota Mortgage Moratorium Law to be valid. The decisions on the contract clause, he maintained, "put it beyond question that the prohibition is not an absolute one and is not to be read with literal exactness like a mathematical formula." [62] This statement would seem to relieve the Court from the necessity of reading conditions into the contracts themselves, but Hughes nevertheless resorted to that device, speaking, perhaps, only metaphorically.

Not only are existing laws read into contracts [he said] in order to fix obligations as between the parties, but the reservation of essential attributes of sovereign power is also read into contracts as a postulate of the legal order . . . This principle of harmonizing the constitutional prohibition with the necessary residuum of state power has had progressive recognition in the decisions of this Court.[63]

After giving a history of the litigation concerning the contract clause, he went on:

It is manifest from this review of our decisions that there has been a growing appreciation of public needs and of the necessity of finding ground for a rational compromise between individual rights and public welfare. The settlement and consequent contraction of the public domain, the pressure of a constantly increasing density of population, the interrelation of the activities of our people and the complexity of our economic interests, have inevitably led to an increased use of the organization of society in order to protect the very bases of individual opportunity. Where, in earlier days, it was thought that only the concerns of individuals or of classes were involved, and that those of the State itself were touched only remotely, it has later been found that the fundamental interests of the State are directly

[60] 12 Wheat. at 291.

[61] 290 U.S. 398 (1934). Concurring with Hughes were Brandeis, Stone, Roberts, and Cardozo. Justice Sutherland's emphatic dissenting opinion had the concurrence of Van Devanter, McReynolds, and Butler.

[62] 290 U.S. at 428.

[63] *Id.* at 435.

affected; and that the question is no longer merely that of one party to a contract as against another, but of the use of reasonable means to safeguard the economic structure upon which the good of all depends. . . .

. . . The vast body of law which has been developed was unknown to the fathers, but it is believed to have preserved the essential content and the spirit of the Constitution. With a growing recognition of public needs and the relation of individual right to public security, the court has sought to prevent the perversion of the clause through its use as an instrument to throttle the capacity of the States to protect their fundamental interests. This development is a growth from the seeds which the fathers planted. It is a development forecast by the prophetic words of Justice Johnson in *Ogden* v. *Saunders,* already quoted.[64] And the germs of the later decisions are found in the early cases of the *Charles River Bridge* and the *West River Bridge, supra,* which upheld the public right against strong insistence upon the contract clause.[65]

The statute which was sustained was one passed in 1933 for a two-year period of emergency only. It authorized postponement of a mortgagee's taking possession of property by extending the period for redemption, with a proviso that the mortgagor pay the rental value of the property during the extended period. Hughes agreed[66] with the state court that "the economic emergency which threatened 'the loss of homes and lands which furnish those in possession the necessary shelter and means of subsistence' " justified relief. The relief, however, "could only be of a character appropriate to that emergency and could be granted only upon reasonable conditions." The relief afforded by the Minnesota statute, he thought, was of this character. Pointing out its limited nature and the provision for payment of rent to the mortgagee, he went on:

Also important is the fact that mortgagees . . . are predominantly corporations, such as insurance companies, banks, and investment and mortgage companies. These, and such individual mortgagees as are small investors, are not seeking homes or the opportunity to engage in farming. Their chief concern is the reasonable protection of their investment security. . . . The relief afforded by the statute has regard to the interest of mortgagees as well as to the interest of mortgagors. The legislation seeks to prevent the impending ruin of both by a considerate measure of relief.

The *Blaisdell* case was decided on January 8, 1934. On May 28 of the same year, in *Worthen Co.* v. *Thomas,*[67] the Court held invalid

[64] The words quoted were: "But to assign to contracts, universally, a literal purport, and to exact for them a rigid literal fulfilment, could not have been the intent of the constitution." 12 Wheat. at 286.

[65] 290 U.S. at 442–444.

[66] *Id.* at 444–446.

[67] 292 U.S. 426 (1934).

an Arkansas statute exempting moneys paid on insurance policies from seizure for the payment of debts. Hughes stressed the fact that, unlike the Minnesota statute, "the Act contains no limitations as to time, amount, circumstances, or need." The temporary or permanent nature of a statute, however, does not furnish the sole test of its validity. In *Veix* v. *Sixth Ward Building & Loan Ass'n*[68] permanent legislation was sustained which limited the right of a purchaser of shares in a building and loan association to withdraw them. The power to enact the law was based on the importance of such institutions to the state's economy. As to its permanent character, Justice Reed said, "Such legislation may be classed as emergency in one sense but it need not be temporary." The New York deficiency judgment law, sustained in 1941 in *Gelfert* v. *National City Bank*,[69] was likewise permanent, as was the municipal insolvency law sustained in 1942 in *Faitoute Iron & Steel Co.* v. *Asbury Park*.[70] The existence of an emergency may bear on the reasonableness or unreasonableness of a particular enactment, but would not be conclusive in all cases.

The "governing constitutional principle" yielded by "the *Blaisdell* case and decisions rendered since" was expressed thus by Justice Frankfurter in *East New York Savings Bank* v. *Hahn,* decided November 5, 1945:

> when a widely diffused public interest has become enmeshed in a network of multitudinous private arrangements, the authority of the State "to safeguard the vital interests of its people," 290 U.S. at 434, is not to be gainsaid by abstracting one such arrangement from its public context and treating it as though it were an isolated private contract constitutionally immune from impairment.[71]

This does not mean that every sort of legislative impairment is constitutional. Some of them have been held invalid in cases decided since the *Blaisdell* decision. The test would seem to be whether the Court regards the particular impairment as "unreasonable" or "arbitrary." That is the test applied, as we shall see, in passing on the validity of deprivations of liberty or property. The legislation may be deemed reasonable when the literal enforcement of contract rights would endanger important rights of property, such as those involved in widespread foreclosures of mortgages, which the Minnesota moratorium legislation was designed to prevent. But it is too early to say

68 310 U.S. 32 (1940). 69 313 U.S. 221 (1941). 70 316 U.S. 502 (1942).
71 326 U.S. 230, 232 (1945).

whether the Court would apply the same tests of reasonableness under the contract clause and under the due process clause. In commenting on *Wood* v. *Lovett,*[72] in which a certain act was held invalid as an impairment of the obligation of a contract, it was said in a Note in the *Columbia Law Review:*

> The interesting but open questions whether the test of reasonableness under the contract clause ought to be different from that under the due process clause; and whether, within the category of contract clause cases, there should be a distinction, in this respect, between cases involving contracts with the state and those involving purely private contracts, have not been clarified by the instant decision.[73]

If the test of reasonableness is the same under the two clauses of the Constitution, it would almost seem that the contract-impairment clause is superfluous. If a statute which impairs a contract obligation is considered reasonable, it will be held valid notwithstanding the contract clause. If, on the other hand, such a statute should be considered unreasonable, it could be held invalid as a deprivation of property without due process, even if there were no contract clause, since a contract is regarded as a species of property. The contract clause limits the power of states only, not of the Federal Government; but the due process clause of the Fifth Amendment limits federal power. It could probably be invoked to place the same limitations on federal power that the contract clause places on the power of the states. And if a state impairs the obligation of a contract by means of a judicial decision changing the law, instead of by means of legislation, the impairment can be challenged only under the due process clause, for it is settled that, since the contract clause forbids a state only to "*pass any . . . Law* impairing the Obligation of Contracts," it "is directed only against impairment by legislation and not by judgments of courts." [74] "Legislation," however, includes amendments to the state constitution as well as acts of the legislature, despite a vigorous contention to the contrary by Justice Campbell in his dissenting opinion in 1856 in *Dodge* v. *Woolsey.*[75]

[72] 313 U.S. 362 (1941).

[73] 41 COL. L. REV. 1251, 1255, n. 33 (1941).

[74] Taft, C. J., in Tidal Oil Co. v. Flanagan, 263 U.S. 444, 451 (1924).

[75] 18 How. 331, 378 (U.S. 1856). For a more detailed discussion see Hale, *The Supreme Court and the Contract Clause* (1944) 57 HARV. L. REV. 512, 621, 852.

PRIVILEGES AND IMMUNITIES OF CITIZENS

The Fourteenth Amendment, adopted in 1868, declares that "all persons born or naturalized in the United States, and subject to the jurisdiction thereof, are citizens of the United States and of the State wherein they reside." In the ensuing sentence it declares that "no State shall make or enforce any law which shall abridge the privileges or immunities of citizens of the United States." This is followed by other limitations on the states, which we shall discuss in subsequent sections of this chapter. For the present we are concerned with the question whether the Constitution affords to citizens protection of any of their interests other than those which it protects for persons regardless of their citizenship.

Nowhere does the Constitution specify what the privileges and immunities of citizenship are. At the December Term, 1867, however, the Supreme Court held, in *Crandall* v. *Nevada,* [76] without reference to the Fourteenth Amendment, that the privileges of United States citizenship were immune to attack by state legislation. The particular privilege there protected was the privilege of traveling to other states. A Nevada tax of a dollar on each passenger leaving the state by common carrier was held invalid. The Fourteenth Amendment had been recently adopted, but no mention of it was made in the decision. Justice Clifford and Chief Justice Chase thought the tax invalid as an encroachment on the federal power to regulate interstate commerce. But Justice Miller, for the majority, refused to base its invalidity on this ground. He maintained that, as the Federal Government had a "right" to summon its citizens to the national capital or to other federal offices throughout the country, "the citizen also has correlative rights" [77] to go to federal offices for the purpose of transacting business with the Government. And apparently Miller did not confine this privilege of national citizens to travel for governmental purposes; for he quoted with approval [78] a passage from a dissenting opinion by Chief Justice Taney in 1848 in *The Passenger Cases:* "We are all citizens of the United States, and as members of the same community must have the right to pass and repass through every part of it without interruption, as freely as in our own States." [79]

If passing from state to state is a privilege or immunity of United States citizenship, then, whether by implication, as in the *Crandall*

[76] 6 Wall. 35 (U.S. Dec. Term 1867).
[77] *Id.* at 44.
[78] *Id.* at 49.
[79] 7 How. 283, 492 (U.S. 1849).

case, or by the express terms of the Fourteenth Amendment, no state legislation may abridge it. That it is such a privilege was reasserted by Justice Miller in 1873 in a dictum in the *Slaughter-House Cases*,[80] with a citation of the *Crandall* case. And in *Twining* v. *New Jersey*,[81] Justice Moody, for the Court, in 1908, cited the *Crandall* case as authority for including this privilege in his enumeration of some of the privileges and immunities of United States citizenship.

In 1920, however, in *United States* v. *Wheeler*,[82] where the Fourteenth Amendment was not involved, since there was no state action, Chief Justice White, speaking for the Court, held that the *Crandall* case would not sustain a federal indictment for conspiracy by a private mob to eject citizens from the state, for the additional reason that the Nevada statute

> was held to directly burden the performance by the United States of its governmental functions and also to limit rights of the citizens growing out of such functions; and hence it follows that the observation made in *Twining* v. *New Jersey*, 211 U.S. 78, 97, to the effect that it had been held in the *Crandall Case* that the privilege of passing from State to State is an attribute of national citizenship, may be put out of view as inapposite.

The authority of the *Crandall* case was further weakened in 1929 in *Helson & Randolph* v. *Kentucky*,[83] where it was held that for a state to impose a tax on the transit of passengers between states "is to regulate commerce and is beyond state power." Justice Sutherland added that the doctrine of the *Crandall* case, "so far as it is to the contrary, has not been followed." Very likely he was referring to that part of the *Crandall* doctrine which denied that the tax was forbidden by the commerce clause rather than to the assertion that the right to pass from state to state was a privilege of national citizenship. At any rate, Sutherland himself, writing the majority opinion in 1935 in *Colgate* v. *Harvey*,[84] asserted that it was such a privilege, and from this assertion as a premise he reached the conclusion that a tax which discriminated against income from out-of-state investments was an unconstitutional abridgment of that privilege. Justice Stone, in a dissenting opinion in which Brandeis and Cardozo joined, thought that the conclusion did not follow from the premise. The case was overruled in 1940 in *Madden* v. *Kentucky*.[85]

[80] 16 Wall. 36, 79–80 (U.S. 1873). Though citing the Crandall case, he referred here specifically only to the right to pass from state to state for governmental purposes.

[81] 211 U.S. 78, 97 (1908).

[82] 254 U.S. 281, 299 (1920).

[83] 279 U.S. 245, 251 (1929).

[84] 296 U.S. 404 (1935).

[85] 309 U.S. 83 (1940). The opinion was by Justice Reed. Chief Justice Hughes concurred in the result. Justices McReynolds and Roberts dissented.

But Stone went further in his dissent in *Colgate* v. *Harvey*, and rejected the premise. Although it was Justice Miller's majority opinion in the *Slaughter-House Cases* which produced the situation which enabled Stone to refer to "the almost forgotten privileges and immunities clause of the Fourteenth Amendment," Miller went too far, in Stone's opinion, in referring the protection of interstate passage to that clause, when the passage was not for the purpose of dealing with the Government. He pointed out that the *Helson & Randolph* case had overruled *Crandall* v. *Nevada* so far as the latter "referred the protection of such commerce to the privileges and immunities clause rather than to the commerce clause."

The protection and control [said Stone] of intercourse between the states, not carried on in pursuance of the relationship between the citizen and the national government, has been left to the interstate commerce clause, to the due process and equal protection clauses of the Fourteenth Amendment, and to Article IV, § 2, guaranteeing to the citizens of each state the privileges and immunities of citizens in the several states. [Citation.] In no case since the adoption of the Fourteenth Amendment has the privileges and immunities clause been held to afford any protection to movements of persons across state lines or other forms of interstate transaction.

The reason for this reluctance to enlarge the scope of the clause has been well understood since the decision of the *Slaughter-House Cases, supra.* If its restraint upon state action were extended more than is needful to protect relationships between the citizen and the national government, and it did more than duplicate the protection of liberty and property secured to persons and citizens by the other provisions of the Constitution, it would enlarge judicial control of state action and multiply restrictions upon it to an extent difficult to define, but sufficient to cause serious apprehension for the rightful independence of local government. That was the issue fought out in the *Slaughter-House Cases, supra,* with the decision against the enlargement.[86]

In *Madden* v. *Kentucky,* while Justice Reed for the majority denied that "the right to carry out an incident of trade, business or calling such as the deposit of money in banks" is a privilege of national citizenship, he did not expressly deny that the right to pass from state to state was such a privilege. And in 1941 Justices Black and Douglas, who had joined his opinion, as well as Justices Murphy and Jackson, who had not then been on the Court, asserted emphatically that it was such a privilege. Douglas wrote one concurring opinion, in which he was joined by Black and Murphy, and Jackson wrote another, in *Edwards* v. *California.*[87]

[86] 296 U.S. at 444–445.

[87] 314 U.S. 160 (1941).

Edwards had been convicted in a state court of knowingly bringing into California an indigent citizen of Texas (who was, of course, also a citizen of the United States), named Duncan. The statute made it a misdemeanor to bring or assist "in bringing into the State any indigent person who is not a resident of the State, knowing him to be an indigent person." The Court unanimously set aside the conviction, but Justice Byrnes, speaking for the majority, did so on the ground that the section of the statute was an unconstitutional burden on interstate commerce. He found it "unnecessary to decide whether the section is repugnant to other provisions of the Constitution."[88] The others who made up the majority were Chief Justice Stone and Justices Roberts, Reed, and Frankfurter.

Justice Douglas, expressing no opinion as to whether the statute was repugnant to the commerce clause, insisted that it "runs afoul of the privileges and immunities clause of the Fourteenth Amendment." He was "of the opinion that the right of persons to move freely from State to State occupies a more protected position in our constitutional system than does the movement of cattle, fruit, steel and coal across state lines."[89] Quoting the dictum in the *Twining* case to the effect that one of the rights of national citizenship was "the right to pass freely from state to state," Douglas went on to cite the *Crandall* case for the proposition that this "was recognized as a right fundamental to the national character of our Federal government" before the adoption of the Fourteenth Amendment.[90] He admitted that in that case Justice Miller "emphasized that the Nevada statute would obstruct the right of a citizen to travel to the seat of his national government or its offices throughout the country" and that the dictum in *United States* v. *Wheeler* "attempts to limit the *Crandall* case to a holding that the statute in question directly burdened 'the performance by the United States of its governmental functions,' and limited the 'rights of the citizens growing out of such functions.'" But, said Douglas, "there is not a shred of evidence in the record of the *Crandall* case that the persons there involved were en route on any such mission," and "the point which Mr. Justice Miller made was merely in illustration of the damage and havoc which would ensue if the States had the power to prevent the free movement of citizens from one State to another." He concluded that the dictum in the *Wheeler* case "does not bear analysis."[91] Then, after reviewing

88 *Id.* at 177. 89 *Ibid.* 90 *Id.* at 178. 91 *Id.* at 178–179.

other cases, he declared himself unable to accede to the suggestion in the *Helson & Randolph* case and in the *Colgate* v. *Harvey* dissent that the commerce clause is the appropriate explanation of *Crandall* v. *Nevada*. "Two of the Justices in that case expressly put the decision on the commerce clause; the others put it on the broader ground of *national* citizenship. . . . On that broader ground it should continue to rest." [92]

Justice Jackson, in his separate opinion, stated that the hope of imparting vitality to American citizenship was the purpose of the Fourteenth Amendment's declarations as to citizenship. He went on:

> But the hope proclaimed in such generality soon shriveled in the process of judicial interpretation. For nearly three-quarters of a century this Court rejected every plea to the privileges and immunities clause. . . .
>
> While instances of valid "privileges and immunities" must be but few, I am convinced that this is one. I do not ignore or belittle the difficulties of what has been characterized by this Court as an "almost forgotten" clause. But the difficulty of the task does not excuse us from giving these general and abstract words whatever of specific content and concreteness they will bear as we mark out their application, case by case. That is the method of the common law, and it has been the method of this Court with other no less general statements in our fundamental law. . . . But it has always hesitated to give any real meaning to the privileges and immunities clause lest it improvidently give too much.
>
> This Court should, however, hold squarely that it is a privilege of citizenship of the United States, protected from state abridgment, to enter any state of the Union, either for temporary sojourn or for the establishment of permanent residence therein and for gaining resultant citizenship thereof. If national citizenship means less than this, it means nothing.[93]

Jackson conceded that the citizen's right to migrate might be limited if a state seeks to prevent the entry of fugitives from justice or of persons likely to spread contagion, but insisted that it could not be limited because of indigence. Pointing out that citizenship imposed on Duncan the obligation to render military service, he concluded:

> Rich or penniless, Duncan's citizenship under the Constitution pledges his strength to the defense of California as a part of the United States, and his right to migrate to any part of the land he must defend is something she must respect under the same instrument. Unless this Court is willing to say that citizenship of the United States means at least this much to the citizen, then our heritage of constitutional privileges and immunities is only a promise to the ear to be broken to the hope, a teasing illusion like a munificent bequest in a pauper's will.[94]

[92] 314 U.S. at 179–180. [93] *Id.* at 182–183. [94] *Id.* at 185–186.

It might be thought to be a matter of no moment to Duncan whether the privileges and immunities clause gave him a right not to be barred by his indigence from migrating, as long as the commerce clause, under the majority's interpretation, gave him precisely the same right. Jackson's fervent preference for the privileges clause as the source of Duncan's rights seems to stem from his skepticism as to the reliability of the commerce clause. Opening his opinion, he said:

> I concur in the result reached by the Court, and I agree that the grounds of its decision are permissible ones under applicable authorities. But the migration of a human being, of whom it is charged that he possesses nothing that can be sold and has no wherewithal to buy, do not fit easily into my notions as to what is commerce. To hold that the measure of his rights is the commerce clause is likely to result eventually either in distorting the commercial law or in denaturing human rights.[95]

To a certain extent, however, a holding that the right to pass from state to state is a privilege or immunity of national citizenship would merely duplicate the protection afforded to that right by other constitutional provisions. The same thing is true of another right which Justice Miller included, by way of dictum in the *Slaughter-House Cases*[96] in 1873, in a list of privileges and immunities of national citizens—namely "the right to peaceably assemble and petition for redress of grievances." Miller doubtless meant, assemble "for the purpose of" so petitioning. Chief Justice Waite described it in these more specific terms in a dictum in 1876 in *United States* v. *Cruikshank,*[97] as the "right of the people peaceably to assemble for the purpose of petitioning Congress for a redress of grievances, or for any thing else connected with the powers or the duties of the national government." He, too, spoke of it as "an attribute of national citizenship." This right is protected by the First Amendment from abridgment by Congress, and by the due process clause of the Fourteenth Amendment from abridgment by the states, whether or not it be regarded as a privilege of national citizenship. As we shall see, however, there may be some significance, in so regarding it.

In 1939 three Justices, in *Hague* v. *CIO,*[98] maintained that it was a privilege of national citizenship to assemble peaceably, not only for the purpose of petitioning Congress but also for the purpose of urging people to exercise rights given them by federal legislation—in

95 *Id.* at 181–182. 96 16 Wall. at 79–80. 97 92 U.S. 542, 552–553 (1876).

98 307 U.S. 496 (1939). Justices McReynolds and Butler dissented. Justices Frankfurter and Douglas, who had been recently appointed, took no part in the case.

this case the Wagner Labor Relations Act. A five-to-two majority sustained an injunction of a lower federal court restraining Mayor Hague and other officials of Jersey City from excluding or removing members of the CIO from the city, from interfering with their free access to the streets, parks, and public places, and from interfering with their right to communicate their views as individuals to others in an orderly and peaceable manner. The ordinance under which the officials had been practicing these forbidden acts was declared void on its face. But the majority did not agree on the grounds for the decision.

Justice Roberts, in an opinion joined by Black, thought that the applicable statutes gave a federal court no jurisdiction (in the absence of a showing that more than $3,000 was involved) of a suit to redress a deprivation of a "liberty," but that the court did have jurisdiction of a suit to redress deprivation of a "privilege" or "immunity," regardless of the amount involved. He held the ordinance invalid as an abridgment of the privileges and immunities of national citizenship. Citing the dicta in the *Slaughter-House* and *Cruikshank* cases, he maintained that the right peaceably to assemble and to discuss national legislation and the advantages and opportunities afforded by it, "and to communicate respecting them, whether orally or in writing, is a privilege inherent in citizenship of the United States which the Amendment protects." [99] He added: "Citizenship of the United States would be little better than a name if it did not carry with it the right to discuss national legislation and the benefits, advantages, and opportunities to accrue to citizens therefrom." [100]

Justice Stone, in an opinion in which Reed joined, insisted that the injunction could not be sustained as a protection of the privileges of citizenship, because there was no allegation that the members of the CIO who brought the suit were citizens and it prohibited interference with peaceable meetings, whether or not they were for the purpose of discussing federal legislation. He would sustain it on the different ground that it deprived the plaintiffs of "liberty" without due process; that this protection is given to "persons," whether citizens or not, and to freedom to hold peaceable meetings for any purpose, not merely for discussing federal legislation. The cases made it clear, he thought, that the ordinance was unconstitutional on these grounds, and he interpreted the statutes as giving jurisdiction of

99 307 U.S. at 512.

100 *Id.* at 513.

suits to redress deprivations of liberty, regardless of the amount of money involved.

Referring to the reluctance of Roberts to decide whether the due process clause was violated, Stone said:

> If it be the part of wisdom to avoid unnecessary decision of constitutional questions, it would seem to be equally so to avoid the unnecessary creation of novel constitutional doctrine, inadequately supported by the record, in order to attain an end easily and certainly reached by following the beaten paths of constitutional decision.[101]

Chief Justice Hughes, in a brief concurring opinion, agreed with Roberts that the right to discuss the Wagner Act was a privilege of national citizenship, but agreed with Stone that on the record jurisdiction could be based only on the due process clause.

It may well be that the privileges and immunities clause of the Fourteenth Amendment adds nothing to the protection which any interest receives from other parts of the Constitution. The defining of privileges and immunities may nevertheless have some significance, for it may be that if those privileges and immunities are deemed to have their source elsewhere in the Constitution than in the Fourteenth Amendment Congress will have power to enforce them against private individuals.

Privileges and immunities have also been discussed in cases arising under Article IV, Section 2, Clause 1, of the Constitution which declares: "The Citizens of each State shall be entitled to all Privileges and Immunities of Citizens in the several States." Those entitled to these privileges are described as citizens of a state. What they are entitled to is the privileges and immunities of citizens, not of, but in, the other states. The text does not specify whether it is the privileges and immunities pertaining to citizenship of the other state or those pertaining to citizenship of the United States to which they are entitled. If there were citizens of any state who were not at the same time citizens of the United States, it would scarcely seem likely that the Constitution was intended to confer upon them the privileges of national citizenship. But it seems to have been assumed that Article IV conferred rights only on those "citizens of each state" who were at the same time citizens of the United States.

In the case of *Dred Scott* v. *Sanford*,[102] decided in 1857, there was much discussion of the question whether any state could confer state

[101] *Id.* at 525.

[102] 19 How. 293 (U.S. 1857).

citizenship on a free Negro, so as to enable him to invoke the diversity jurisdiction of a federal court in a suit against a citizen of another state. Chief Justice Taney, in the principal majority opinion, held that while a state could confer state citizenship upon anyone, even an alien, for purely state purposes, still such a person "would not be a citizen in the sense in which that word is used in the Constitution of the United States, nor entitled to sue as such in one of its courts, nor to the privileges and immunities of a citizen in the other States." It is only as a citizen of the United States, thought Taney, that a citizen of one state would be entitled to those privileges in another. A state cannot make a person a national citizen ("introduce a new member into the political community created by the Constitution of the United States") if he is of a class "not intended to be embraced in this new political family, which the Constitution brought into existence, but . . . intended to be excluded from it." [103] And he thought Negroes, whether free or slave, were intended to be excluded.

Justice Curtis, who wrote the principal dissenting opinion, rejected this last proposition. He maintained that a state could make any free native-born person a citizen of that state, and thereby a citizen of the United States, entitled to invoke the diversity jurisdiction of the federal courts and to all privileges and immunities of citizens in the several states.[104] "It cannot be supposed," he said, "that it was the purpose of this article to confer the privileges and immunities of citizens in all the States upon persons not citizens of the United States." [105] Curtis, like Taney, believed that all "the citizens of each state" on whom Article IV conferred rights, were entitled to those rights only because they were at the same time citizens of the United States.

But this does not settle the question whether the privileges and immunities of citizens in the several states to which these national citizens are entitled are those of national or of state citizenship. In the leading case before the adoption of the Fourteenth Amendment, *Corfield* v. *Coryell*,[106] no clear distinction is made between the two, though the claim rejected must have been a claim to a privilege of state, not national, citizenship. The case was decided in 1823, in an opinion by Justice Bushrod Washington, of the Supreme Court, sitting as a circuit judge. Citizens of New Jersey were permitted to

[103] 19 How. at 405–406.
[104] *Id.* at 577 and 580–581.
[105] *Id.* at 580.
[106] 4 Wash. C.C. 371, Fed. Cas. No. 3,230 (C.C.E.D. Pa. 1823).

plant oysters in the waters of the state, but all others were forbidden by a state statute to do so. It was held that Article IV did not entitle citizens of other states to do what New Jersey citizens were thus permitted to do, the common property of the New Jersey citizens not being a privilege or immunity of citizenship within the meaning of the Article. The expressions in Article IV, said Washington, should be confined "to those privileges and immunities which are, in their nature, fundamental; which belong, of right, to the citizens of all free governments; and which have, at all times, been enjoyed by the citizens of the several states which compose this Union, from the time of their becoming free, independent, and sovereign."

In 1877 the Supreme Court followed *Corfield* v. *Coryell* in *McCready* v. *Virginia* [107] and sustained a Virginia statute which forbade anyone but a citizen of Virginia to plant oysters in the state's waters. "The right which the people of the State thus acquire," said Chief Justice Waite, "comes not from their citizenship alone, but from their citizenship and property combined. It is, in fact, a property right, and not a mere privilege or immunity of citizenship." And again, after quoting from the *Corfield* case, it "is not a privilege or immunity of general but of special citizenship." [108]

[107] 94 U.S. 391 (1877).

[108] *Id.* at 395–396. In Toomer v. Witsell, 334 U.S. 385 (1948), Article IV was held to invalidate a South Carolina statute which required payment of a license fee of $25 for each shrimp boat engaged in coastal fishing owned by a resident and a fee of $2,500 for each one owned by a nonresident—the practical effect of which was admittedly to exclude nonresidents from such fishing. Chief Justice Vinson conceded that Article IV did not preclude discrimination between citizens and noncitizens of the state if based on valid reasons other than the mere fact that the latter are citizens of other states. But while the "ownership" theory might justify the decision in McCready v. Virginia, since the statute sustained there "related to fish which would remain in Virginia until removed by man," and also "involved regulation of fishing in inland waters," that theory would not sustain the present statute which dealt "with free-swimming fish which. . . are off the coast of South Carolina only temporarily" and which was "directed at regulation of shrimping in the marginal sea." Justice Frankfurter, in an opinion in which Justice Jackson joined, maintained that the statute did not violate Article IV, but thought that it violated the commerce clause. In Russo v. Reed, 93 F. Supp. 554 (S.D. Maine 1950), a three-judge district court, on the authority of Toomer v. Witsell, invalidated a statute which prohibited nonresidents from fishing for commercial purposes in the coastal waters in the summer months, the only time when whiting can be taken there.

In 1869 it had been held, in Paul v. Virginia, 8 Wall. 168, in an opinion by Justice Field, that the privilege of doing business in corporate form was not a privilege of citizenship to which citizens of other states are entitled. And a corporation is not itself a "citizen" entitled to any privileges or immunities of citizenship, either under Article IV or under the Fourteenth Amendment, though for purposes of federal diversity jurisdiction courts have acted as if a corporation was a citizen of the state of its incorporation. *Cf.* McGovney, *op cit. supra*, p. 43, n. 1

agree with Bradley's characterization of them as rights which could be invaded only by the states, not by individuals. Only a year earlier (1883), speaking through Justice Woods in *United States* v. *Harris*,[114] it had declared that Article IV, Section 2, "like the Fourteenth Amendment, is directed against State action."

But the rights which Bradley so characterized were not what the Court regarded as privileges and immunities of citizens of the United States. For aught that Bradley said, the latter might still be capable of invasion by individuals, though any protection the Constitution affords them against individual invasion must be sought elsewhere than in the Fourteenth Amendment, whose prohibitions are directed only against states.

In the *Slaughter-House Cases* Justice Miller, for the majority, insisted that the "fundamental" rights which Washington enumerated were those pertaining to state citizenship. He misquoted Washington as saying, "The inquiry is, what are the privileges and immunities of citizens of [instead of 'in'] the several States?"[115] Throughout Washington's opinion, said Miller, the rights discussed "are spoken of as rights belonging to the individual as a citizen of a State. They are so spoken of in the constitutional provision which he was construing." There is a certain ambiguity here. Article IV, it is true, confers rights on "the citizens *of* each state." Hence, whatever rights it confers can be said to "belong" to an individual as a citizen of a state. But what are the rights which it confers? They are the privileges and immunities of citizens *in* the several states. Before we can say what rights "belong" to a citizen of one state, by virtue of Article IV, we must determine what rights not derived from Article IV "belong" to citizens *in* the other states. Washington's inquiry was concerned with the latter question, and he said so. The rights with which this inquiry was concerned were not spoken of in Article IV as belonging to citizens "of" the several states, but to citizens "in" them. All that Article IV did was to declare that whatever these rights of citizens "in" the several states might be, they should also be enjoyed by the citizens "of" every other state.

However, though the privileges mentioned in the Constitution were not there spoken of as privileges of citizens "of" the several states, that may have been the meaning intended. Washington himself, it may be recalled, spoke of the privileges which have "been en-

[114] 106 U.S. 629, 643 (1883).

[115] 16 Wall. at 76.

joyed by the citizens of the several states," though that is consistent with their being enjoyed by citizens of the states by virtue of their national citizenship. But since the *Slaughter-House Cases* the Court has adhered to Miller's position that the privileges and immunities protected by Article IV are those of state citizenship, while those protected from state abridgment by the Fourteenth Amendment fall in the distinct category of privileges of national citizenship.

In a lengthy passage in the *Slaughter-House Cases*[116] Miller suggested several privileges and immunities which owe their existence to the Federal Government, "lest it be said that no such privileges and immunities are to be found if those we have been considering are excluded." Among these, we have seen, are the right to pass from state to state and the "right to peaceably assemble and petition for redress of grievances," rights for the protection of which the Court now prefers to resort to other provisions in the Constitution. Though Washington included the right to cross a state in his list of rights which Miller said were privileges of state citizenship, Miller apparently had no objection to including it in the national category. Miller also included the right of a national citizen to protection by the Federal Government on the high seas or abroad, the privilege of the writ of habeas corpus, the right to use the navigable waters of the United States, "however they may penetrate the territories of the several States," and rights secured to American citizens by treaties with foreign nations. He added the right which the citizenship definition in the Fourteenth Amendment itself conferred, to become a citizen of another state by residing there. He also made the rather dubious inclusion of the rights secured by the Thirteenth and Fifteenth amendments and by the other provisions of the Fourteenth.[117]

[116] *Id.* at 79–80.

[117] Rights against involuntary servitude, whether or not they are classified as privileges and immunities of national citizenship, are secured by the Thirteenth Amendment, as we have seen, against both private and governmental action.

The Fifteenth Amendment secures the right of citizens to vote from abridgment by the United States or by any state on account of race, color, or previous condition of servitude. It does not secure it against interference by private individuals. Nevertheless, in the Cruikshank case, Chief Justice Waite declared in 1876 that exemption from discrimination in the exercise of the right to vote on account of race, &c, was "a necessary attribute of national citizenship." He dismissed the counts in the indictment which charged conspiracy to prevent certain Negroes from voting, only because "it does not appear in these counts that the intent of the defendants was to prevent these parties from exercising their right to vote on account of their race, &c." (United States v. Cruikshank, 92 U.S. 542, 555–556). The clear intimation is that, wholly apart from the power conferred on Congress by the Fifteenth Amendment, to enforce its provisions by appro-

When in 1908, in *Twining* v. *New Jersey*, the Court rejected the contention that all rights secured against federal action in the first eight amendments automatically became privileges and immunities of national citizens, protected against state abridgment by the Fourteenth,[118] Justice Moody enumerated some privileges which he said were privileges and immunities of citizens of the United States. In addition to the rights to pass from state to state and to assemble peaceably in order to petition for a redress of grievances, he listed the right of a duly qualified elector to vote for national officers, citing the case of *Ex parte Yarbrough*.[119] The authority for protecting that right against violence, however, by means of a federal statute, rested only in part on the ground that it was a privilege of citizenship, since the Constitution expressly confers upon Congress the power to regulate elections for members of Congress. Moreover, it is a right conferred expressly by Article I. Justice Moody, however, listed three more rights among the privileges and immunities of citizens of the United States. These were: the right to enter public lands for the perfection of a right under the Homestead Act, for which he cited *United States* v. *Waddell;* [120] the right to protection while in the custody of federal officials, for which he cited *Logan* v. *United States;* [121] and the right to inform the federal authorities of violations of federal laws, for which he cited *In re Quarles*.[122]

The inclusion of these three rights is highly significant, for it indicates that the Court regarded the privileges and immunities of national citizens as entitled to protection beyond that which the Fourteenth Amendment affords them and also as capable of being invaded (unlike the rights under Article IV as characterized by Bradley) by private individuals as well as by states. The statute involved in those cases [123] made it a crime to "conspire to injure, oppress, threaten, or

priate legislation, a power which could apply only to governmental discrimination, Congress had power to protect the right to exemption from racial discrimination in the exercise of the right to vote from interference on the part of private individuals.

However, when in James v. Bowman, 190 U.S. 127, a similar indictment was dismissed in 1903, although Justice Brewer noted that no charge was made of discrimination on account of race, he seems to have relied principally on the point that the Fifteenth Amendment confers no power on Congress to "punish purely individual action."

118 211 U.S. 78 (1908). Justice Black later supported this rejected contention with an elaborate review of the intention of the framers of the Amendment in a dissenting opinion in which he was joined by Justice Douglas. Adamson v. California, 332 U.S. 46, 68 (1947).

119 110 U.S. 651 (1884).

120 112 U.S. 76 (1884).

121 144 U.S. 263 (1892).

122 158 U.S. 532 (1895).

123 Rev. Stat. § 5508 (1875), 35 Stat. 1092 (1909), 18 U.S.C. § 51 (1940). The statute is Sec. 19 of the Criminal Code, discussed *supra*, pp. 175–187.

intimidate any citizen in the free exercise or enjoyment of any right or privilege secured to him by the Constitution or laws of the United States, or because of his having so exercised the same." This statute was held to apply (in the *Waddell* case) to a conspiracy to prevent a citizen by violence from perfecting his Homestead Act right; to a conspiracy (in the *Logan case*) to murder citizens in the custody of federal officers; and to a conspiracy (in the *Quarles* case) to murder a citizen for having informed of a violation of federal law. The right protected in the *Waddell* case might be thought entitled to protection as a right conferred by statute, rather than as a privilege of national citizenship. But there was no statute like the Homestead Act to confer the rights protected in the other two cases. Nor did the Fourteenth Amendment confer any rights that had been violated by the conspirators. That Amendment confers no privileges and immunities; it only confers a right not to have any state abridge such privileges as already exist. And there was no violation of the Amendment, for no state had done anything. As Justice Gray said in the *Quarles* case:

> The right of a citizen informing of a violation of law, like the right of a prisoner in custody upon a charge of such violation, to be protected against lawless violence, does not depend upon any of the Amendments to the Constitution, but arises out of the creation and establishment by the Constitution itself of a national government, paramount and supreme within its sphere of action.[124]

If, as Justice Moody declared in the *Twining* case, these rights are privileges and immunities of citizens of the United States, it seems to follow that, as in the *Crandall* case, such privileges do not depend for their existence on the Fourteenth Amendment, but are implied from the general nature of the Constitution; furthermore, that they consist of rights not merely against state action, like the rights secured by the Fourteenth and Fifteenth Amendments, but against invasion by private individuals as well. The power conferred on Congress by the Fourteenth and Fifteenth Amendments, to enforce their respective provisions by "appropriate legislation," would, of course, confer no power to protect against private invasions of any privileges, for those Amendments confer no rights against private individuals. The federal power, which was sustained in the *Logan* and *Quarles* cases, must derive, not from the Fourteenth Amendment, but from the principle that whenever the Constitution confers rights of any

124 158 U.S. at 536.

kind, other than rights against governmental action alone, Congress has implied power to protect them from attack by private individuals as well as by government officials. This principle was enunciated by the Court as long ago as 1842 in *Prigg* v. *Pennsylvania*,[125] when Justice Story declared that the Fugitive Slave Law of 1793, which provided punishment for obstructing an owner in the recovery of a slave who had escaped into another state, was constitutional. The Constitution provided that any "Person held to Service or Labour in one State, under the Laws thereof, escaping into another . . . shall be delivered up on Claim of the Party to whom such Service or Labour may be due." [126] This clause, said Story, "manifestly contemplates the existence of a positive, unqualified right on the part of the owner of the slave," and it must have been contemplated that Congress should have authority to enforce the right.

In the *Cruikshank* case Chief Justice Waite applied this principle more specifically, by way of dictum, to privileges and immunities of national citizenship. Indictments in that case under a federal statute, for conspiring to interfere with the enjoyment of rights secured by the Constitution, were set aside, because the rights with which the conspirators were charged to have interfered, were not rights secured by the Constitution. One of the charges was for conspiring to prevent, by violence, the holding of a meeting. Such a conspiracy was, of course, punishable under state law, but Congress had no power to provide for its punishment, since the Constitution conferred no right to hold meetings free from private interference unless they were "for the purpose of petitioning Congress for a redress of grievances, or for any thing else connected with the powers or the duties of the national government." It was in this connection that Waite declared that "the right of the people peaceably to assemble" for such purposes

> Is an attribute of national citizenship, and, as such, under the protection of, and guaranteed by, the United States . . . If it had been alleged in these counts that the object of the defendants was to prevent a meeting for such a purpose, the case would have been within the statute, and within the scope of the sovereignty of the United States.[127]

In *Hardyman* v. *Collins* [128] it was held in the Ninth Circuit that a conspiracy of private individuals to break up a meeting, one purpose of which was to send a petition to Congress, subjected the conspirators

125 16 Pet. 539 (U.S. 1842). Cf. *supra*, pp. 172–173.

126 Art. IV, § 2, clause 3.

127 92 U.S. 542, 552–553 (1876).

128 183 F. 2d 308 (9th Cir. 1950), reversing 80 F. Supp. 501 (S.D. Cal. 1948).

to liability for damages for depriving the plaintiffs of a privilege and immunity of United States citizenship. The same principle was extended by a district court in *Robeson* v. *Fanelli* [129] to a meeting to discuss issues of national importance, even without an allegation of a purpose to petition Congress. The former case, however, was reversed in June, 1951, in *Collins* v. *Hardyman*,[130] on the ground that the statute under which the action was brought applied only to conspiracies whose purpose was to deprive persons of the equal protection of the laws or of equal privileges and immunities under the law. The Court did not deny that Congress had power to subject private individuals to liability for interference with the exercise of the privileges and immunities of citizenship. In fact Justice Jackson, speaking for the majority, said: "In the light of the dictum in *United States* v. *Cruikshank* . . . we assume, without deciding, that the facts pleaded show that defendants did deprive plaintiffs 'of having and exercising' a federal right." In Justice Burton's dissenting opinion, in which Justices Black and Douglas concurred, it is emphasized that "the source of the right in this case is not the Fourteenth Amendment." Whether the dictum in the *Cruikshank* case is to prevail is still an open question.

The cases seem to support the following propositions: Article IV confers on every citizen of the United States who is also a citizen of some state (this possibly excludes citizens of the District of Columbia and of the territories) a right to enjoy in other states those "fundamental" rights listed by Justice Washington, which citizens in the other states enjoy by reason of their state citizenship. The article protects these rights against invasion by these other states, but not against invasion by private individuals. It affords no protection, even to "fundamental" rights, if the other state denies them to its own citizens, though other provisions in the Constitution would be held to protect many of them, even against the action of a state against its own citizens.

The privileges and immunities clause of the Fourteenth Amendment protects no privileges of *state* citizenship, however fundamental they may be, from state abridgment, though, as we shall see, the due process and the equal protection clauses may protect many of them. It only protects the privileges and immunities of *national* citizenship from state abridgment. In doing so, it apparently adds noth-

[129] 94 F. Supp. 62 (S.D. N.Y. 1950). [130] 341 U.S. 651 (1951).

ing to the protection which other provisions of the Constitution afford to such privileges.

Accordingly, if national citizenship were significant only in that its privileges and immunities might not be abridged by any state, it would be of little moment what those privileges and immunities included. The right of a citizen to pass from state to state on other than government business may or may not be such a privilege or immunity. Whether it is or not, the commerce clause prevents any state from interfering with it. Whether the right peaceably to assemble for the purpose of apprising people of their rights under federal statutes is a privilege of national citizenship would likewise make no difference, as far as state interference with it is concerned, for the privileges and immunities clause adds no protection which the due process clause does not already give. So far as the Fourteenth Amendment is concerned, the sharp divergence of opinion in the Court in *Colgate* v. *Harvey,* in *Edwards* v. *California,* and in *Hague* v. *CIO* would seem to be a battle over words.

But if Waite's dictum in the *Cruikshank* case and Moody's in *Twining* v. *New Jersey* are to be taken seriously, as the lower courts took them in the *Hardyman* and *Robeson* cases, privileges of national citizenship have a significance which transcends the Fourteenth Amendment. Though such privileges may be protected by state law from certain forms of private interference, such as the action of a mob, the Federal Government may provide additional protection; and the Federal Government may be held to have implied power to protect them also against forms of private interference which the states have not made illegal. Should the Federal Government attempt to exercise this implied power extensively, dispute over what should be included in these privileges and immunities might take on less of the appearance of a sham battle.

DUE PROCESS AND EQUAL PROTECTION

Procedural Rights

People are deprived of life, liberty, or property when they are executed or imprisoned, when their property is seized and sold at a sheriff's sale to satisfy a judgment for damages, or when it is taken away from them for a public use. Governments must have power to deprive people of life, liberty, or property. Otherwise laws could not be enforced. But the power to do so is capable of abuse. The Constitution accordingly places certain limitations on the exercise of this power.

Before any amendments were adopted, both state governments and the Federal Government, as we have seen, were forbidden to pass bills of attainder or *ex post facto* laws. That is, a man could not be punished on conviction by an act of the Legislature, nor could he be subjected to criminal punishment for an act which was not made a crime until a statute was subsequently enacted.[131]

The "Bill of Rights," as the first ten amendments adopted in 1791 were called, provided further limitations. Unreasonable searches and seizures were forbidden by the Fourth Amendment, and the right to a jury trial in criminal prosecutions was guaranteed by the Sixth. More significant is the Fifth Amendment, which puts certain specific additional safeguards around a defendant in a criminal trial and provides in more general terms that no person shall be deprived of life, liberty, or property without due process of law, and forbids the taking of private property for public use without just compensation. It is important that we have the full text of the Amendment before us. It reads as follows:

> No person shall be held to answer for a capital, or otherwise infamous crime, unless on a presentment or indictment of a grand jury, except in cases arising in the land or naval forces, or in the militia, when in actual service in time of war or public danger; nor shall any person be subject for the same offence to be twice put in jeopardy of life or limb; nor shall be compelled in any criminal case to be a witness against himself; *nor be deprived of life, liberty, or property, without due process of law;* nor shall private property be taken for public use without just compensation.

It is the so-called "due process clause," which we have italicized, with which we shall be especially concerned. It will be observed that the Amendment does not state by whom "no person shall be deprived," but it was clear from the start that the inhibition was not on

131 In United States v. Lovett, 328 U.S. 303 (1946), an amendment to an appropriation, construed as barring three named individuals permanently from government service, was held unconstitutional as a bill of attainder. The three officials had been accused by the chairman of the Dies Un-American Activities Committee of being "subversive," and the accusation sustained by a special subcommittee of the House Appropriations Committee, after secret hearings. The opinion was by Justice Black. In a concurring opinion, Justice Frankfurter (with the concurrence of Justice Reed) denied that the amendment, as construed by the Court, came within the historical definition of a bill of attainder; but Frankfurter construed it as only denying the three officials compensation out of special funds, not as denying them the right to further government employment or as cutting off the Government's obligation to pay them for that employment. Hence, he concurred in affirming the Court of Claims in giving judgment for them.

private individuals. A thief deprives a person of property without due process of law, but, while he is violating the criminal law of the state in which he steals, he is not violating the Fifth Amendment. It was held, moreover, in 1833, in *Barron* v. *Baltimore*,[132] that this Amendment afforded no guaranty against deprivations by the states. Most state constitutions contained due process clauses, and state deprivations might be held to violate them, but there was no question of federal constitutional law presented when a state was alleged to be depriving someone of life, liberty, or property. In fact, said Chief Justice Marshall, all the limitations in the first ten amendments were to be construed as limitations on the Federal Government alone.

After the Civil War, however, the Thirteenth, Fourteenth, and Fifteenth Amendments were adopted. The Fourteenth, adopted in 1866, contains not only the provisions we have examined concerning privileges and immunities of citizens of the United States, but also a due process clause binding on the states, and furthermore a clause not found in the Fifth Amendment, namely, an "equal protection clause." These are all found in the first section of the Amendment. The second, third, and fourth sections contain matter which does not concern us here. The fifth section confers on Congress "power to enforce, by appropriate legislation, the provisions of this article." The first section follows in full.

All persons born or naturalized in the United States, and subject to the jurisdiction thereof, are citizens of the United States and of the State wherein they reside. No State shall make or enforce any law which shall abridge the privileges or immunities of citizens of the United States; nor shall any State deprive any person of life, liberty, or property, without due process of law; nor deny to any person within its jurisdiction the equal protection of the laws.

Under the due process clauses of the Fifth and Fourteenth Amendments neither federal nor state authorities may deprive a person of life, liberty, or property as a punishment, unless he has been duly convicted by a procedure which conforms to the Supreme Court's conception of "due process of law." A sentence which does not so conform is said to violate his procedural right not to be deprived of life, liberty, or property without due process. Not all of the procedural rights enumerated in the Bill of Rights which run against federal punishments are equally applicable to the states. The right not to be compelled to be a witness against oneself, for instance, which the

132 7 Pet. 243 (U.S. 1833).

Fifth Amendment specifically grants in federal criminal prosecutions, has been held not to be embraced within the "due process" which the Fourteenth Amendment guarantees with respect to state procedure. Accordingly, it was held in *Twining* v. *New Jersey*,[133] a conviction in a state court should be affirmed, notwithstanding that the jury had been instructed that they might draw unfavorable inferences from the defendant's failure to testify. Justice Moody discussed the matter at length. On the other hand, defendants have been held to have procedural rights in state courts against what the Court regards as more fundamental denials of justice. Convictions in state courts were set aside in *Moore* v. *Dempsey*,[134] because the court had been dominated by a mob of American Legionnaires and others; in *Powell* v. *Alabama*[135]—the first of the famous Scottsboro cases—because the defendant had not been permitted adequate representation by counsel; and in *Brown* v. *Mississippi*[136] and *Chambers* v. *Florida*,[137] because the conviction had been based on confessions obtained by torture.

The equal protection clause has been invoked to confer on Negroes accused of crime a procedural right to be tried in a court in which Negroes have not been excluded from the jury panel by reason of their race. This was decided in *Strauder* v. *West Virginia*,[138] where state law excluded them, and in the second Scottsboro case, *Norris* v. *Alabama*,[139] where, though state law did not require it, it was shown that Negroes were systematically excluded from the jury list. But if no Negroes have been kept from the panel because of race, a colored defendant in a criminal case has no right to escape trial by a purely white jury, as was held in *Virginia* v. *Rives*,[140] decided at the same time as *Strauder* v. *West Virginia*.

Substantive Rights and Due Process

Constitutional rights to liberty, property, and equal protection, however, are not confined to procedural rights. "Liberty" means more than keeping out of jail; "property" means more than retention of ownership; and "equal protection" means more than the right to as fair a trial as that accorded to others. There are also substantive rights

[133] 211 U.S. 78 (1908). But see Adamson v. California, 332 U.S. 46, 68 (1947), dissenting opinion by Justice Black.

[134] 261 U.S. 86 (1923).

[135] 287 U.S. 45 (1932).

[136] 297 U.S. 278 (1936).

[137] 309 U.S. 227 (1940).

[138] 100 U.S. 303 (1880). See also Ex parte *Virginia*, 100 U.S. 339 (1880), *supra*, pp. 173–175.

[139] 294 U.S. 587 (1935).

[140] 100 U.S. 313 (1880).

to liberty, property, and equal protection, which the Constitution has been held to guarantee. It took the Court some time, however, after the adoption of the Fourteenth Amendment, to reach this conclusion.[141]

In the *Slaughter-House Cases*,[142] in 1873, the discussion of the validity of the monopoly granted by Louisiana turned chiefly on the question whether the privileges or immunities of citizens of the United States were abridged. Justice Miller, for the majority, did not even discuss whether the statute deprived the independent butchers of "liberty" to maintain slaughterhouses. When the grant of the monopoly was repealed, however, before the expiration of its terms, and when the repeal was sustained in *Butchers' Union Slaughter House &c. Co.* v. *Crescent City Live-Stock &c. Co.*,[143] despite the contract-impairment clause, some of the concurring Justices did discuss the point. Justice Bradley, who had dissented in the earlier case, agreed that the repeal was valid, but on the ground that he still thought the original grant was invalid. It was invalid, he thought, not only as an abridgment of the privileges and immunities of citizens, but also as a denial of equal protection and a deprivation of liberty. "The right to follow any of the common occupations of life," he said, "is an inalienable right," and "is a large ingredient of the civil liberty of the citizen." [144] Then, after discussing privileges and immunities, he went on:

> But if it does not abridge the privileges and immunities of a citizen of the United States to prohibit him from pursuing his chosen calling and giving to others the exclusive right of pursuing it,—it certainly does deprive him (to a certain extent) of his liberty; for it takes from him the freedom of adopting and following the pursuit which he prefers; which, as already intimated, is a material part of the liberty of the citizen.[145]

Although this language was in a minority opinion, Justice Peckham, speaking for the entire Court, quoted it with approval in 1897, in *Allgeyer* v. *Louisiana*.[146] In that case a statute was held unconstitutional which, as construed by the Louisiana court, punished a man for the act of writing within the state a letter to effect insurance on property within the state, addressed to a foreign insurance company

[141] As late as 1891, Charles E. Shattuck insisted that imprisonment was the only kind of deprivation of liberty that the due process clauses forbade. *The True Meaning of the Term "Liberty" in Those Clauses in the Federal and State Constitutions Which Protect "Life, Liberty, and Property"* (1891) 4 HARV. L. REV. 365.

[142] 16 Wall. 36 (U.S. 1873).

[143] 111 U.S. 746 (1884).

[144] *Id.* at 762.

[145] *Id.* at 765.

[146] 165 U.S. 578, 590 (1897).

in New York, which had not complied with the conditions for doing business within Louisiana. As so construed, said the Court,

we think the statute is a violation of the Fourteenth Amendment of the federal Constitution, in that it deprives defendants of their liberty without due process of law. The statute which forbids such acts does not become due process of law, because it is inconsistent with the provisions of the Constitution of the Union. The "liberty" mentioned in that amendment means, not only the right of the citizen to be free from the mere physical restraint of his person, as by incarceration, but the term is deemed to embrace the right of the citizen to be free in the employment of all his faculties; to be free to use them in all lawful ways; to live and work where he will; to earn his livelihood by any lawful calling; to pursue any livelihood or avocation; and for that purpose to enter into all contracts which may be proper, necessary, and essential to his carrying out to a successful conclusion the purposes above mentioned.

Ever since this case, it has been settled that the due process clauses confer constitutional rights to "liberty" which prevail not only against imprisonment based on defective procedure, but also against restrictions on conduct, however faultless the procedure may be for enforcing them. As it is frequently expressed, there are *substantive* as well as *procedural* constitutional rights to liberty.

These substantive rights are not absolute. There are, as we shall see, many forms of liberty that may be restrained, notwithstanding the due process clauses. And a person has no procedural right to a trial before being deprived of a substantive liberty, if the statute is otherwise valid. Even "freedom of contract" may be restricted under certain circumstances. But freedom of contract is one of the liberties, as well as freedom from incarceration, to which the due process clauses afford some protection against adverse legislation. So, too, are freedoms of religion, speech, press, and assembly, though these freedoms, too, have their limitations. Their protection against federal encroachment is given in express terms by the First Amendment, which reads:

Congress shall make no law respecting an establishment of religion, or prohibiting the free exercise thereof; or abridging the freedom of speech, or of the press; or the right of the people peaceably to assemble; and to petition the Government for a redress of grievances.

The Federal Constitution contains no provision explicitly restricting the power of the states in these matters. But ever since *Gitlow* v. *New York* [147] was decided, in 1925, it has been settled that the due

[147] 268 U.S. 652 (1925).

process clause of the Fourteenth Amendment is to be construed as incorporating the same restrictions on the states as the First Amendment places on the Federal Government.

As in the case of liberty, the protection which the due process clauses afford to property is now held to have a wider scope than mere protection against physical invasion or seizure of property by way of penalty, without due procedural safeguards. From the beginning it was assumed to apply to the taking of property, even when the purpose was not to penalize. As Justice Miller remarked by way of dictum in 1878 in *Davidson* v. *New Orleans,*

> a statute which declares in terms, and without more, that the full and exclusive title to a described piece of land, which is now in A., shall be and is hereby vested in B., would, if effectual, deprive A. of his property without due process of law, within the meaning of the constitutional provision.[148]

The Fifth Amendment, it will be recalled, expressly prohibits the Federal Government from taking private property for a public use "without just compensation." And an uncompensated taking by a state would be held to be a deprivation without due process. And in 1872, in *Pumpelly* v. *Green Bay &c. Co.,*[149] where before the adoption of the Fourteenth Amendment a dam had caused water to back onto plaintiff's land, destroying most of its value, Justice Miller had held that the owner was entitled to compensation under a clause in the Wisconsin constitution which prohibited taking without just compensation. The flooding was held to be a "taking," and compensation would now be held due under the due process clause.

In these cases the owner had suffered physical loss of his property. But at that time Justice Miller was not inclined to extend the constitutional protection of property to invasions which took a less physical form. Speaking for the majority in 1873, in the *Slaughter-House Cases,* he summarily dismissed the contention of the independent butchers that the statutory monopoly deprived them of property, by referring to the due process clause of the Fifth Amendment and similar clauses in state constitutions, which had for a long time forbidden deprivations of property without due process. Speaking of such clauses, he said:

> We are not without judicial interpretation, therefore, both state and national, of the meaning of this clause. And it is sufficient to say that under no construction of that provision that we have ever seen, or any that we deem

148 96 U.S. 97, 101 (1878).

149 13 Wall. 166 (U.S. 1872).

admissible, can the restraint imposed by the state of Louisiana upon the exercise of their trade by the butchers of New Orleans be held to be a deprivation of property within the meaning of that provision.[150]

Some of the dissenting judges disagreed on this point as well as on others. Regulations of the use of property, or even of the liberty to contract, have since been held to be deprivations of property as well as of liberty. Justice Field, in his dissenting opinion in 1877 in *Munn* v. *Illinois*,[151] maintained that statutory regulation of grain elevator charges was a deprivation of property, and in later cases, whenever rates have been held "confiscatory," it is "property" of which the company has been held to have been deprived. In 1915 Justice Pitney, in *Coppage* v. *Kansas,* said that "the right to make contracts for the acquisition of property" is "included in the right of personal liberty and the right of private property—partaking of the nature of each." [152]

In cases in which a law regulating the use of property, or forbidding the making of certain contracts for its acquisition, has been held invalid as a deprivation of property, it could equally well have been held invalid as a deprivation of liberty. In such cases it would not seem to matter whether the use of the property or the making of the contract were said to be within the scope of the protection which the due process clauses afford to property as such, or whether a deprivation of property were construed to mean only a physical invasion or a seizure.

There are three reasons, however, why the appellation "property" has significance. In the first place, the appropriate remedy for challenging the constitutionality of an act may be an injunction against its enforcement. But there is an old doctrine of equity that an injunction will not be issued except to protect some right of property. While this doctrine has been subjected to considerable criticism, it still retains some vitality. Accordingly, when a person complains that it is property of which a statute deprives him, not merely liberty, he is in a better position to challenge its validity in a suit for an injunction.

The second reason why a broad definition of "property" matters is that a person whose conduct is not directly regulated by a statute and who might find it difficult to support a claim that it deprives him of "liberty" may nevertheless claim that it deprives him of "prop-

[150] 16 Wall. at 80–81. [151] 94 U.S. 113 (1877). [152] 236 U.S. 1, 14 (1915).

erty." Thus, in *Pierce* v. *Society of the Sisters* [153] the statute which required all children between specified ages to attend public schools imposed legal duties on their parents, but not on the private schools which challenged its validity. It did not deprive the schools of "liberty" in the sense of commanding them to do or to refrain from doing anything. Those whose liberty was most obviously restricted were the parents. But the schools could not challenge it on the ground that it deprived the parents of liberty. The schools' challenge was accepted, however, and the statute held unconstitutional, on the ground that it deprived the schools of property. By calling the schools' opportunity to receive pupils from parents willing to send them "property," the court was able to accept the schools' challenge, without taking the perhaps more dubious position that the loss of pupils was a loss of "liberty."

There is a third reason why it is significant to say that a statute deprives one of property, even if it likewise deprives him of liberty. That is because it is well settled that the property of corporations comes within the protection of the due process clauses, while there is doubt whether their liberty is also protected. Corporations, as we have seen, receive no protection from the privileges and immunities clause, since they are not citizens. The due process clauses, on the other hand, apply to "persons," regardless of their citizenship. Ever since the decision in 1886, in *Santa Clara County* v. *Southern Pacific Railroad,*[154] it has been the settled doctrine of the Court that in forbidding state governments and the Federal Government to deprive any "person" of property without due process, the Constitution uses the word "person" to include corporations, as well as natural persons. Although this doctrine was vigorously challenged by Justice Black in a solitary dissenting opinion in *Connecticut General Life Ins. Co.* v. *Johnson,*[155] and later by Justice Douglas in a dissenting opinion in which Justice Black joined, in *Wheeling Steel Corp.* v. *Glanders,*[156] the Court still clings to it.

When it comes to "liberty," however, the Court has pursued a chequered career. In two opinions, rendered in 1906 and 1907, respectively (*Northwestern Nat. Ins. Co.* v. *Riggs* [157] and *Western Turf Ass'n* v. *Greenberg*),[158] Justice Harlan said that the liberty protected by the due process clauses is "the liberty of natural, not artificial per-

153 268 U.S. 510 (1925). Cf. *supra*, pp. 146–147.

154 118 U.S. 394 (1886).

155 303 U.S. 77, 83 (1938).

156 337 U.S. 562, 576 (1949).

157 203 U.S. 243, 255 (1906).

158 204 U.S. 359, 363 (1907).

sons." When, in the first case, the corporation complained that a statute deprived it of liberty because it prevented it from contracting that its policies should be void on account of misrepresentations unconnected with the cause of death, and in the second case that a statute deprived it of liberty because it made it unlawful to exclude unobjectionable persons from race courses, the Court refused to consider the merits of these contentions. The refusal made no difference, however, for the Court did consider (though on the merits it decided against the corporations) whether the statute in each case was an unconstitutional deprivation of property. And in the case of the *Society of the Sisters* it was only because the business of the incorporated schools was regarded as "property" that they were allowed to maintain the actions. As Justice McReynolds said for the Court:

Appellees are corporations, and therefore, it is said, they cannot claim for themselves the liberty which the Fourteenth Amendment guarantees. Accepted in the proper sense, this is true. *Northwestern Life Ins. Co.* v. *Riggs* . . . *Western Turf Association* v. *Greenberg* . . . But they have business and property for which they claim protection. These are threatened with destruction through the unwarranted compulsion which appellants [state officers] are exercising over present and prospective patrons of their schools.[159]

Freedom of speech and of the press, however, are not property rights. A corporation can therefore challenge a restriction on such freedom only if its "liberty" has constitutional protection. In *Hague* v. *Committee for Industrial Organization*,[160] an ordinance which interfered with freedom of speech and freedom of assembly was held unconstitutional in 1939. It was challenged by the CIO, which was unincorporated. But it was also challenged by the American Civil Liberties Union, a corporation. Justice Roberts, who, it will be recalled, based invalidity on privileges and immunities grounds, of course held that only the unincorporated plaintiffs could maintain the suit, the corporation not being a citizen. But Justice Stone, too, who held the ordinance void as a deprivation of liberty, said:

As to the American Civil Liberties Union, which is a corporation, it cannot be said to be deprived of the civil rights of freedom of speech and of assembly, for the liberty guaranteed by the due process clause is the liberty of natural, not artificial, persons. [Citing the two opinions of Justice Harlan alluded to above.] [161]

159 268 U.S. at 535.

160 307 U.S. 496 (1939).

161 *Id.* at 527. The dismissal of the Union's suit made no practical difference, since the injunction granted on the suit of the CIO was effective in preventing enforcement of the ordinance against anyone.

Before this time, however, in *Grosjean* v. *American Press Co.*[162] the Court (of which Justice Stone was a member) had, on the suit of a corporation, held a penalty which took the form of a tax on newspapers of large circulation to be an unconstitutional abridgment of freedom of the press. The contention was made that the Fourteenth Amendment does not apply to corporations, to which Justice Sutherland replied:

> but this is only partly true. A corporation, we have held, is not a "citizen" within the meaning of the privileges and immunities clause. *Paul* v. *Virginia,* 8 Wall. 168. But a corporation is a "person" within the meaning of the equal protection and due process of law clauses, which are the clauses involved here.[163]

In support of this statement he cited *Covington &c. Co.* v. *Sandford*[164] and *Smyth* v. *Ames.*[165] But on the pages cited in these cases there was no statement that the Fourteenth Amendment protects corporations from deprivations of liberty; only that it protects them from deprivations of property. Nonetheless, the Court in the *Grosjean* case protected a corporation's liberty.

Moreover, on December 8, 1941, in *Bridges* v. *California,*[166] it was held that punishments for contempt imposed by state courts violated the right to a free press, not only of the individual Harry Bridges, but also of the corporation which published the Los Angeles Times. The majority opinion, written by Justice Black and concurred in by Justices Reed, Douglas, Jackson, and Murphy, did not discuss the question whether the Fourteenth Amendment protected the liberty of corporations. In Justice Frankfurter's dissenting opinion, it is true (in which Chief Justice Stone and Justices Roberts and Byrnes concurred), it is said, "Corporations cannot claim for themselves the 'liberty' which the Due Process Clause guarantees. That clause protects only their property. *Pierce* v. *Society of Sisters.*"[167]

The dissenters, however, themselves disregarded this principle. The corporation had been fined for the publication of three editorials. As to one of them, the dissenters thought the fine should stand. But as to the other two, Justice Frankfurter agreed "that the judgment of the state court . . . should not stand."[168] So, despite his statement to the contrary, Justice Frankfurter agreed in practice that corporations

162 297 U.S. 233 (1936).
163 *Id.* at 244.
164 164 U.S. 578, 592 (1896).
165 169 U.S. 466, 522 (1898).
166 314 U.S. 252 (1941).
167 *Id.* at 280–281.
168 *Id.* at 298.

could "claim for themselves the 'liberty' which the Due Process Clause guarantees." The Court, however, has never expressly overruled the *Riggs* and *Greenberg* and *Hague* cases holding that they could not, although it has frequently ignored them. Its future course in the matter cannot be predicted with confidence. Corporate claims under the due process clauses are therefore more apt to prevail if they can be brought within the scope of an enlarged category of "property."

The Police Power and Due Process

While the terms "liberty" and "property" in the due process clauses have been given a wider meaning than they were once thought to have, it must not be supposed that every deprivation of liberty or property by state or federal action is unconstitutional. Every law deprives someone of liberty in some degree, and every tax deprives someone of property. Even the judges who construed the Fourteenth Amendment as placing the strictest limitations on state power conceded that some legislation which deprived persons of liberty or property might be valid, if it came within the scope of the loosely defined "police power." Justice Field, one of the strictest of these judges, who dissented in the *Slaughter-House Cases,* wrote the Court's opinion in 1885 in *Barbier* v. *Connolly,*[169] in which an ordinance was sustained which prohibited the use of laundries at night. In the course of his opinion he said:

> But neither the amendment—broad and comprehensive as it is—nor any other amendment, was designed to interfere with the power of the state, sometimes termed its police power, to prescribe regulations to promote the health, peace, morals, education and good order of the people, and to legislate so as to increase the industries of the state, develop its resources, and add to its wealth and prosperity.

Justice Roberts expressed the same thought in 1934, when, speaking for the majority in *Nebbia* v. *New York,* he said:

> The Fifth Amendment, in the field of federal activity, and the Fourteenth, as respects state action, do not prohibit governmental regulation for the public welfare. They merely condition the exertion of the admitted power, by securing that the end shall be accomplished by methods consistent with due process. And the guaranty of due process, as has often been held, demands only that the law shall not be unreasonable, arbitrary, or capricious, and that the means selected shall have a real and substantial relation to the object sought to be attained.[170]

169 113 U.S. 27, 30–32 (1885).

170 291 U.S. 502, 525 (1934).

The text of the Constitution provides no criteria for determining what is "unreasonable, arbitrary, or capricious." The judges of the Supreme Court have to supply their own criterion in each case; and these criteria, until the Supreme Court overrules them, are binding on lower courts as much as if they had been written into the Constitution itself. This is inevitable, as long as the due process clauses are construed to protect substantive rights. For this reason, Justices Black, Douglas, and Murphy, in a concurring opinion written in 1942 in *Federal Power Commission* v. *Natural Gas Pipeline Co.*,[171] objected to the whole construction of these clauses as authorizing the courts to declare legislative acts unconstitutional when they did not interfere with procedural rights or civil liberties. Under the accepted doctrine, they said, "the conclusions of judges, substituted for those of legislatures, become a broad and varying standard of constitutionality." The accepted doctrine they characterized as one "which makes of 'due process' an unlimited grant to courts to approve or reject policies selected by legislatures in accordance with the judges' notion of reasonableness." Explaining why their objections did not apply to statutes interfering with free speech and the like, they said in a footnote:

> To hold that the Fourteenth Amendment was intended to and did provide protection from state invasions of the right of free speech and other clearly defined protections contained in the Bill of Rights . . . is quite different from holding that "due process," an historical expression relating to procedure . . . , confers a broad judicial power to invalidate all legislation which seems "unreasonable" to courts. In the one instance, courts proceeding within clearly marked constitutional boundaries seek to execute policies written into the Constitution; in the other they roam at will in the limitless area of their own beliefs as to reasonableness and actually select policies, a responsibility which the Constitution entrusts to the legislative representatives of the people.[172]

[171] 315 U.S. 575, 599 (1942).

[172] *Id.* at 600, n. 4. For a somewhat similar reason, Justice Sutherland (with the concurrence of Justices Van Devanter, McReynolds, and Butler) objected to the Court's construction of the contract-impairment clause to permit the passage of laws which impair contract obligations when those laws seem reasonable to the Court. In a concurring opinion in Worthen Co. v. Thomas, 292 U.S. 426, 434–35 (1934), he said, with reference to his dissent in Home Bldg. & Loan Ass'n. v. Blaisdell, 290 U.S. 398 (1934): "We were unable then, as we are now, to concur in the view that an emergency can ever justify, or, what is really the same thing, can ever furnish an occasion for justifying, a nullification of the constitutional restriction upon state power in respect of the impairment of contractual obligations. Acceptance of such a view takes us beyond the fixed and secure boundaries of the fundamental law into a precarious fringe of extraconstitutional terri-

Despite this protest, however, the Fourteenth Amendment is still construed as entrusting the Supreme Court with the duty, if not to "select" policies, at least to reject those which the legislature selects if they seem to the judges to be "unreasonable" beyond the limits of judicial tolerance.

Substantive Rights and Equal Protection

In the *Slaughter-House Cases,* in 1873, the independent butchers attacked the statutory monopoly not only on the ground that it abridged their privileges and immunities and deprived them of liberty and property but also on the ground that it denied to them the equal protection of the laws. This ground availed as little with the majority of the Court as did the others. After tracing the history of the adoption of the Fourteenth Amendment, Justice Miller said:

> We doubt very much whether any action of a state not directed by way of discrimination against negroes as a class, or on account of their race, will ever be held to come within the purview of this provision.[173]

Subsequent decisions, however, proved Miller to have been wrong. In 1886, in *Yick Wo* v. *Hopkins,*[174] a San Francisco ordinance was held invalid as a denial of equal protection. It prohibited the use of wooden buildings as laundries without the assent of the supervisors, who could give or withhold their assent for any reason at all. As to wooden buildings, said Justice Matthews, the ordinance

> divides the owners or occupiers into two classes, not having respect to their personal character and qualifications for the business, nor the situation and nature and adaptation of the buildings themselves, but merely by an arbitrary line, on one side of which are those who are permitted to pursue

---

tory in which no real boundaries exist. We reject as unsound and dangerous doctrine, threatening the stability of the deliberately framed and wise provisions of the Constitution, the notion that violations of those provisions may be measured by the length of time they are to continue or the extent of the infraction, and that only those of long duration or of large importance are to be held bad. Such was not the intention of those who framed and adopted that instrument. The power of this court is not to amend but only to expound the Constitution as an agency of the sovereign people who made it and who alone have authority to alter or unmake it. We do not possess the benevolent power to compare and contrast infringements of the Constitution and condemn them when they are long-lived or great or unqualified and condone them when they are temporary or small or conditioned."

Just what were the "fixed and secure boundaries" that Justice Sutherland thought to exist in the territory into which the Court is taken when it "expounds" the due process clauses he never made clear.

173 16 Wall. at 81.

174 118 U.S. 356 (1886).

their industry by the mere will and consent of the supervisors, and on the other side those from whom that consent is withheld, at their mere will and pleasure.[175]

Then, pointing out that in practice consent was regularly given to white persons and withheld from Chinese, Justice Matthews continued:

In the present cases we are not obliged to reason from the probable to the actual, and pass upon the validity of the ordinances complained of, as tried merely by the opportunities which their terms afford, of unequal and unjust discrimination in their administration. For the cases present the ordinances in actual operation, and the facts shown establish an administration directed so exclusively against a particular class of persons as to warrant and require the conclusion, that, whatever may have been the intent of the ordinances as adopted, they are applied by the public authorities charged with their administration, and thus representing the State itself, with a mind so unequal and oppressive as to amount to a practical denial by the State of that equal protection of the laws which is secured to the petitioners, as to all other persons, by the broad and benign provisions of the Fourteenth Amendment to the Constitution of the United States.[176]

Ever since this decision, it has been settled that the equal protection, like the due process, clause confers substantive as well as procedural rights. To cite a single example, it was held in 1928, in *Quaker City Cab Co.* v. *Pennsylvania,*[177] that a tax on incorporated taxicab companies was a denial of equal protection, since unincorporated taxicab companies were exempt.

Not every law which discriminates, however, is held unconstitutional. If based on a classification which the Court regards as not "unreasonable" or "arbitrary" it will be sustained—as was a heavy tax on butter substitutes, but not on butter, in *Magnano* v. *Hamilton,*[178] a law levying higher license fees on stores constituting parts of chains than on independent stores in *State Board of Tax Commissioners* v. *Jackson,*[179] and a minimum wage law which applied to women, but not to men, in *West Coast Hotel Co.* v. *Parrish.*[180] In the two cases last mentioned the Court was divided on the question. This is not surprising, for in deciding whether a legislative classification is "reasonable" or not, the Court is selecting or rejecting legislative

[175] 118 U.S. at 368. For an application of this principle to a discriminatory suffrage requirement see the discussion *infra,* pp. 352–354 of Davis v. Schnell, 81 F. Supp. 872 (S.D. Ala. 1949), affirmed in 336 U.S. 933 (1949), invalidating the Boswell amendment to the Alabama constitution.

[176] 118 U.S. at 373.

[177] 277 U.S. 389 (1928).

[178] 292 U.S. 40 (1934).

[179] 283 U.S. 527 (1931).

[180] 300 U.S. 379 (1937).

policies, just as it is when deciding on the reasonableness of a deprivation of liberty or property.

In fact, the due process and the equal protection clauses overlap to a great extent. Most of the acts which have been held invalid as a denial of equal protection could equally well have been held so as deprivations of liberty or property. The ordinance in *Yick Wo* v. *Hopkins*, for instance, undoubtedly deprived the Chinese of liberty to operate laundries in wooden buildings. If it had applied to all persons, the Court might have assumed that it was "reasonable," as designed for the purpose of preventing conflagrations. Its discriminatory character proved that it had no such purpose, and therefore made it an "unreasonable" deprivation of liberty. It might have been more difficult to hold the discriminatory tax on incorporated taxicab companies invalid on due process grounds. Yet it might, perhaps, have been held a deprivation of their property, which, although designed in part for a legitimate fiscal purpose, lost its justification by reason of its discriminatory character. There is no equal protection clause binding on the Federal Government, as the Court frequently points out,[181] just as there is no clause expressly forbidding federal laws impairing the obligation of contracts. But it is doubtful whether the absence of either clause makes any practical difference with respect to federal legislation. If Congress were to enact an income tax law, imposing higher rates on Republicans than on Democrats, who can doubt that it would be held invalid? And on what more plausible ground than that it deprives Republicans of property, or perhaps of liberty in political matters, without due process? The deprivation of their property would be valid if the same rate applied to all, but becomes arbitrary when based on a classification which is irrelevant to any legitimate purpose.

As applied to corporations, the equal protection clause differs from the due process in one particular. The due process clause forbids a state to deprive any "person." The equal protection clause forbids it to deny equal protection to "any person within its jurisdiction." A corporation is held to be a "person" entitled to protection of its property, but a foreign corporation (one incorporated in another state) is not a person "within its jurisdiction" unless doing business in the state. The distinction was brought out by Chief Justice Taft in 1926

[181] See, for example, Stone, C. J., in Detroit Bank v. United States, 317 U.S. 329, 337 (1943), with citation of other cases.

in *Hanover Insurance Co.* v. *Harding.*[182] He held that once a foreign corporation was admitted to do business in a state, the state could not tax it more heavily than domestic corporations. But, he added:

With respect to the admission fee, so to speak, which the foreign corporation must pay to become a *quasi*-citizen of the state and entitled to equal privileges with citizens of the state, the measure of the burden is in the discretion of the state and any inequality as between the foreign corporation and the domestic corporation in that regard does not come within the inhibition of the Fourteenth Amendment.[183]

The Government Organs to Which Due Process and Equal Protection Apply

It is states, not private individuals, that are forbidden by the Fourteenth Amendment to deprive persons of life, liberty, or property, and to deny to persons within the jurisdiction the equal protection of the laws. But when is it the "state" that is doing the depriving? It does not have to be the entire organization of the state government. A right under the Amendment is infringed when some officer enforces an unconstitutional statute, or enforces a valid law by unconstitutional means. A conviction in a state court without procedural due process, if followed by execution of the sentence, will result in the state's depriving the defendant of life, liberty, or property in violation of the Amendment, whether or not the legislature has passed a statute authorizing the court to act as it did. When it comes to substantive rights, however, the typical case of unconstitutional action involves the carrying out of legislation. But the legislation does not have to be an act of the Legislature. As Justice Van Devanter said in 1928, in *King Mfg. Co.* v *Augusta:*

It of course rests with each State to determine in what form and by what agencies its legislative power may be exerted. It may legislate little or much in its constitution, may permit the electorate to make laws by direct vote, may entrust its legislature with wide law-making functions and may delegate legislative authority to subordinate agencies, such as municipal councils and state commissions. But whether this power be exerted in one form or another, or by one agency or another, the enactments put forth, whether called constitutional provisions, laws, ordinances or orders, are in essence legislative acts of the State; they express its will and have no force otherwise. As respects their validity under the Constitution of the United States all are on the same plane. If they contravene the restraints which that instrument places on the legislative power of a State they are invalid, no matter what their form or by what agency put forth; for, as this Court has said,

[182] 272 U.S. 494, 510–511 (1926).

[183] For an extension of this principle see Lincoln Nat. Life Ins. Co. v. Read, 325 U.S. 673 (1945).

the protection which these restraints afford applies, "whatever the form in which the legislative power is exerted; that is, whether it be by a constitution, an act of the legislature, or an act of any subordinate instrumentality of the State exercising delegated legislative authority, like an ordinance of a municipality or an order of a commission." *Standard Scale Company* v. *Farrell*, 249 U.S. 571, 577.[184]

What the Court said here about the restraints which the Fourteenth Amendment places on the legislative power of the states is equally applicable to the restraints which the Fifth Amendment places on federal legislative power. An order of the Interstate Commerce Commission fixing rates would be open to whatever constitutional objections would apply to an act of Congress fixing the same rates.

Much of the substantive law, however, which regulates the conduct of people, is common law authoritatively promulgated by courts. A state court decision on procedural law can, of course, be challenged under the due process clause, if it results in a man being sent to jail or in the transfer of his property to another, without the requisite procedural process. But what of a state court's decision on a substantive matter? In *Enterprise Irrigation Co.* v. *Farmers' Mutual Canal Co.*,[185] decided in 1917, the state court had adjudicated conflicting claims of ownership. The losing party maintained that the state court had misconceived the statutory and common law of the state, and had thereby deprived him of property without due process. The Supreme Court dismissed this contention, Justice Van Devanter saying: "The due process clause does not take up the laws of the several States and make all questions pertaining to them constitutional questions, nor does it enable this court to revise the decisions of the state courts upon questions of state law." [186]

In *American Railway Express Co.* v. *Kentucky*,[187] decided in 1927, the Kentucky court had held that under Kentucky law the American Railway Express was liable for the debts of the Adams Express, whose property it had acquired. The Supreme Court declined to review

184 277 U.S. 100, 103–104 (1928). The Court split in this case on the proper interpretation of the Judiciary Act as amended in 1925, which provided for obligatory review by the Supreme Court, on writ of error, of state court decisions upholding the validity of "a statute." This was held to apply to ordinances as well as to acts of the Legislature. Justice Brandeis dissented, in an opinion in which Holmes joined, on the ground that an ordinance was not a "statute" and that therefore a state court decision sustaining it could be reviewed only on certiorari, in which the Supreme Court's jurisdiction is discretionary. There is no indication that he did not fully agree with the paragraph in the text. In fact, it was he who wrote the opinion in the Standard Scale case, which Justice Van Devanter quoted.

185 243 U.S. 157 (1917).

186 *Id.* at 166.

187 273 U.S. 269 (1927).

the decision. Justice McReynolds, citing Justice Van Devanter's language in the previous case, said:

Save in exceptional circumstances, not now present, we must accept as controlling the decision of the state courts upon questions of local law, both statutory and common. . . . We cannot interfere, unless the judgment amounts to mere arbitrary or capricious exercise of power, or is in clear conflict with those fundamental "principles which have been established in our systems of jurisprudence for the protection and enforcement of private rights." [Citing cases.] [188]

The principles referred to seem to be principles of procedure.

These two cases were decided, long before 1938, when *Erie Railroad Co.* v. *Tompkins* [189] established the proposition that in diversity jurisdiction cases a state court's decision on state law is conclusive. Since that time, it is even clearer than before that the two state decisions described above presented no federal question. The claim in the *Enterprise Irrigation* case that the state misconceived state law was based on what is now an obvious fallacy. State law is whatever the state court conceives it to be. A misconception is therefore impossible. Nor can the state court's decision be said to have deprived the losing party of property, unless the state decision effected a change in the state law as it previously existed; for one has no title to a piece of property which he does not own, and what he owns depends wholly on what state law recognizes. And in the Kentucky case, there was no unconstitutional deprivation of property when the American Railway Express was compelled to pay debts which it incurred a contractual obligation to pay under the law of Kentucky, when it acquired the Adams Express property.

If the state decisions in these two cases, however, effected a change in state law, a different question would arise. If the losing party in the *Enterprise* case had a good title under state law as it was before the decision, or if Kentucky law at the time the property was acquired attached to the transaction no obligation to pay debts, then the state decisions might be said to have affected substantive rights quite as much as would an act of the legislature. Would they be equally vulnerable to attack under the due process clause? A state decision, we have seen, is not open to attack under the contract impairment clause, if not based on a statute, for that clause applies only to *the passing of a law*. But the due process clause does not confine its prohibitions to any specified methods by which the state may deprive of property.

188 273 U.S. at 272–273.

189 304 U.S. 64 (1938). See *supra*, pp. 45–47.

When a state court, then, openly avows that it is changing state law retroactively, and thereby depriving a party of a property right he had under the previous law, there seems to be no good reason why the decision should not be open to whatever constitutional attack a statute would be open to which accomplished the same result. State courts, however, do not often avow that they are changing law. They generally purport to be ascertaining it. And it would doubtless take a very clear case to induce the Supreme Court to hold that the previous law was different from what the state court now pronounces it to have been.

State courts do on occasion, however, announce that they are changing the law by a decision. If the change is not made retroactive, there is of course no question of depriving anyone of any specific property right acquired under the previous law. Such was the situation in *Great Northern Railway Co.* v. *Sunburst Oil & Ref. Co.*,[190] where the supreme court of Montana announced its disagreement with one of its earlier decisions, but at the same time declared that it would apply the earlier rule to transactions which had taken place before its present decision. The Supreme Court of the United States held that this procedure presented no constitutional question. A state may say, said Justice Cardozo,

> that decisions of its highest court, though later overruled, are law none the less for intermediate transactions. . . . On the other hand, it may hold to the ancient dogma that the law declared by its courts had a Platonic or ideal existence before the act of declaration, in which event the discredited declaration will be viewed as if it had never been, and the reconsidered declaration as law from the beginning. . . . The choice for any state may be determined by the juristic philosophy of the judges of her courts, their conceptions of law, its origin and nature.[191]

But a state court decision may, unlike the decision of the Montana court, change the law retroactively. Even when it does not, a person's "right" to "property," in the broad sense of a "right" to contract or refuse to contract, and his "right" to "liberty" are rights which, unlike the ownership of a specific piece of property, do not depend on state law, but on the Constitution itself. Law may be said to "deprive" him of such rights, even if state law never purported to admit that he had them. A common-law rule would seem to be as effective a deprivation as a statute, even if it does not depart from the law as laid down in previous decisions of the state court.

[190] 287 U.S. 358 (1932). See *supra*, p. 47 n. 14.

[191] *Id.* at 364–365.

In 1922 a corporation challenged a common-law decision in *Prudential Insurance Co.* v. *Cheek*.[192] The decision was sustained, but not on the ground that the due process clause was inapplicable to substantive court decisions. The state supreme court had sustained a judgment in favor of a former employee, based on two counts. The first count alleged a statutory cause of action, and the second alleged one based on common law, in that the defendant corporation had entered into a monopolistic agreement injurious to the plaintiff. In the Supreme Court of the United States the corporation challenged both the statute and the common-law judgment as depriving it of property without due process. The opinion of the Court was devoted chiefly to its reasons for sustaining the statute. But on the common-law point, Justice Pitney for the majority said briefly:

It seems to us clear that the state might, without conflict with the Fourteenth Amendment, enact through its legislative department a statute precisely to the same effect as the rule of law and public policy declared by its court of last resort. And for the purposes of our jurisdiction it makes no difference, under that amendment, through what department the state has acted. The decision is as valid as a statute would be [193]

The intimation seems to be that if a statute to the same effect would be unconstitutional, so likewise would be a decision. However, it seems that until 1940 the Court had held no decision unconstitutional on this ground. A Note in the *Columbia Law Review* for May, 1934, after pointing out the lack of decisons, adds:

It does seem clear, however . . . that a sufficient minimal standard of substantive due process will be applied to state court decisions, to render unconstitutional a wholly arbitrary exercise of judicial power.[194]

The Note approves the result, provided that the standard is less strict than that applied to statutes. It concludes with the statement that

it would seem that the due process clause should . . . provide some curb upon the judicial lawmaking power. Though the desirable limits of such a restriction are not clear, the great number of judgments assailable is a strong consideration of expediency in favor of the imposition of a lower standard of substantive due process upon judgments than upon statutes.

192 259 U.S. 530 (1922).

193 *Id.* at 548. Chief Justice Taft and Justices Van Devanter and McReynolds dissented without opinion. Whether their dissent extended to the quoted passage does not appear. Concurring with Pitney were Justices McKenna, Holmes, Day, Brandeis, and Clarke.

194 *Due Process as a Substantive Restriction Upon Judicial Decisions* (1934) 34 COL. L. REV. 891, 896.

In support of this conclusion it cites *American Railway Express* v. *Kentucky*. As for the need of some standard, it remarks in a footnote: "The extreme case which suggests itself is that of a court which would decide that citizens of a particular race or creed are barred from the exercise of some substantive right." [195]

In 1940, some six years after the foregoing Note was published, the Supreme Court set aside a conviction on a common-law count, in *Cantwell* v. *Connecticut*.[196] And in 1941, in *American Federation of Labor* v. *Swing*,[197] an injunction against picketing was set aside, which the majority thought was based on a common-law doctrine enunciated by the state supreme court.[198] In each case, the common-law rule in question was held to be an unconstitutional deprivation of freedom of speech. And in the *Cantwell* case it was intimated that a stricter standard would be applied when considering a decision than when considering a statute. While the objection to the vagueness of the rule of common law would apply equally to a statute, Justice Roberts, for the unanimous Court, plainly indicated that in a doubtful case the question whether there had been a "legislative judgment" would be given weight.

Cantwell, besides having been convicted of violating a statute (which the Court held unconstitutional), had been convicted (on the fifth count of the indictment) of the common-law offense of inciting to breach of the peace. As a member of Jehovah's Witnesses, he stopped two men, who were Catholics, on the street and, with their permission, played a phonograph record which attacked their church and incensed them. When they told him to be on his way, he left without argument. In setting aside the conviction on the common-law count, based on these facts, Justice Roberts said:

[195] *Id.*, note 52. [196] 310 U.S. 296 (1940). [197] 312 U.S. 321 (1941).

[198] The doctrine in question was that picketing of an employer by those not in his employ is illegal, however peacefully it may be pursued. Justice Frankfurter for the majority held that even if a more narrowly drawn rule of law might have been sustained as applied to the picketing in question, which was alleged to have involved violence and libel, the broad rule enunciated by the state court was unconstitutional. Justice Roberts in his dissent (in which Chief Justice Hughes joined) maintained that, in the complicated state of the record, "I am unable to say" that the state supreme court's affirmance of the decree without opinion "was an affirmance of any recital in the decree of the [intermediate] appellate court respecting the legality of peaceful picketing disconnected with a continued course of publishing libels, making threats and using force."

Concurring in Frankfurter's opinion were Stone, Reed, and Murphy. Black and Douglas concurred in the result without opinion. McReynolds had retired, and his successor had not yet been appointed.

Conviction on the fifth count was not pursuant to a statute evincing a legislative judgment that street discussion of religious affairs, because of its tendency to provoke disorder, should be regulated, or a judgment that the playing of a phonograph on the streets should in the interest of comfort or privacy be limited or prevented. Violation of an Act exhibiting such a legislative judgment and narrowly drawn to prevent the supposed evil, would pose a question differing from that we must here answer. [Citations.] Such a declaration of the State's policy would weigh heavily in any challenge of the law as infringing constitutional limitations. Here, however, the judgment is based on a common law concept of the most general and undefined nature. . . . Here we have a situation analogous to a conviction under a statute sweeping in a variety of conduct under a general and indefinite characterization, and leaving to the executive and judicial branches too wide a discretion in its application.[199]

In the following year, in setting aside certain convictions for contempt for publications made outside the court room, in *Bridges* v. *California*,[200] Justice Black for the majority remarked:

It is to be noted at once that we have no direction by the legislature of California that publications outside the court room which comment upon a pending case in a specified manner should be punishable. As we said in *Cantwell* v. *Connecticut*, . . . such a "declaration of the State's policy would weigh heavily in any challenge of the law as infringing constitutional limitations." But as we also said there, the problem is different where "the judgment is based on a common law concept of the most general and undefined nature." . . . For here the legislature of California has not appraised a particular kind of situation and found a specific danger [footnote omitted] sufficiently imminent to justify a restriction on a particular kind of utterance. The judgments below, therefore, do not come to us encased in the armor wrought by prior legislative deliberation.

There are not many cases in which state court decisions have been held to deprive persons of substantive rights without due process. The three just noted had to do with civil liberties, and the Court has in recent years indicated that it will apply constitutional restrictions more strictly to deprivations of such rights than to deprivations of economic interests.[201] There may be force in the suggestion found in a "Recent Decision" in the *Harvard Law Review*[202] (published before the decision in the *Bridges* case), which, after noting that the *Cantwell* and *Swing* cases departed (in the writer's view) from the Court's earlier decisions, remarked that they "may indicate that the

199 310 U.S. at 307–308.

200 314 U.S. 252, 260–261 (1941).

201 See, for instance, footnote 4 in Justice Stone's opinion in United States v. Carolene Products Co., 304 U.S. 144, 152 (1938).

202 (1941) 54 HARV. L. REV. 1066.

Court will subject any common law determination which it believes concerned with civil liberties to greater scrutiny." [203]

At any rate the Court is not likely to scrutinize familiar and long-established principles of common law to determine whether in their restriction of liberty they produce arbitrary results or lack equality in their impact. The law of property, which necessarily places unequal restrictions on the liberties of different persons to make use of material goods and subjects, in unequal manner, the liberty and property of some to the coercive bargaining power of others, has rarely been challenged as a deprivation of liberty or property, or as a denial of the equal protection of the laws. There are some recent decisions, however, which hold that in certain circumstances the enforcement of contract or property rights by a state court may violate the Fourteenth Amendment. These will be discussed in Chapter XI.

State Power Exerted in Defiance of State Law

It now seems settled that when a state official, using power with which the state has endowed him, deprives a person of life, liberty, or property, or denies him the equal protection of the laws, it is the state that is acting, even though the official is acting in disobedience to state law. We saw in the previous chapter that a federal indictment of a state judge was sustained in *Ex parte Virginia*,[204] for excluding Negroes from juries by reason of their race and thus denying equal protection of the laws. The fact that he "acted outside of his authority and in direct violation of the spirit of the State statute" [205] did not prevent his act from being regarded as that of the state. As Justice Strong said in that case:

> Whoever, by virtue of public position under a State government, deprives another of property, life, or liberty, without due process of law, or denies or takes away the equal protection of the laws, violates the constitutional inhibition; and as he acts in the name and for the State, and is clothed with the State's power, his act is that of the State.[206]

The Court has not always been consistent on this point, but after considerable vacillation it seems to have come back to Strong's position. In 1904, in *Barney* v. *City of New York*,[207] the bill alleged that

[203] The writer adds, however: "Or the court may mean to reserve this power of review for decisions which it considers flagrantly to disregard vital interests."

[204] 100 U.S. 339 (1880).

[205] *Id.* at 348.

[206] *Id.* at 347.

[207] 193 U.S. 430 (1904).

the transit commission, by taking action forbidden by state law, was about to deprive the complainant of property without due process. The Court unanimously dismissed the bill, on the ground that action forbidden by state law could not be state action, and so could not violate the Amendment. In 1907, however, in *Raymond* v. *Chicago Union Traction Co.*,[208] the Court sustained the company's complaint that the state had deprived it of property and denied it equal protection, when the state board of equalization, in violation of the state constitution, had failed to assess its property for taxation on the same basis as other property. Justice Holmes, dissenting, was

> unable to grasp the principle on which the State is said to deprive the appellee of its property without due process of law because a subordinate board, subject to the control of the Supreme Court of the State, is said to have violated the express requirement of the State in its constitution.[209]

Nevertheless, with Holmes still on the Court and not dissenting, it was held in *Home Telephone & Telegraph Co.* v. *Los Angeles*,[210] in 1913, that the fact that a municipal ordinance might violate the state constitution did not prevent it from being state action. The company sought to enjoin the enforcement of an ordinance fixing what it alleged to be confiscatory rates, as depriving it of property contrary to the due process clause of the Fourteenth Amendment. The lower federal court dismissed the action for want of jurisdiction, on the ground that since the California constitution also forbade deprivations of property without due process no ordinance fixing confiscatory rates could be deemed state action, unless sustained by the highest state court. The Supreme Court reversed, holding that the law of principal and agent does not apply to the relations between a state and its officers, for purposes of the Amendment. Rather, the Amendment "provides . . . for a case where one who is in possession of state power uses that power to the doing of the wrongs which the Amendment forbids . . . if the commission of the wrong itself is rendered possible or is efficiently aided by the state authority lodged in the wrongdoer"—and this "although the consummation of the wrong may not be within the powers possessed." [211] Doubting that the *Barney* case overruled this "settled doctrine" of the Court, Chief Justice White added that if there were room for concluding that it had, "it would be our plain duty to qualify and restrict the *Barney*

[208] 207 U.S. 20 (1907).

[209] *Id.* at 41.

[210] 227 U.S. 278 (1913).

[211] *Id.* at 287.

Case in so far as it might be found to conflict with the rule here applied." [212]

Despite this holding and despite a dictum by Justice Brandeis in 1931,[213] Justice Frankfurter, in a concurring opinion, in 1944, regarded the *Barney* case as still authoritative. In *Snowden* v. *Hughes*,[214] Snowden sued the members of the Illinois state primary canvassing board for damages in a federal district court, for violating their duty under state law to certify his nomination for state senator in a Republican primary, thus depriving him of the election. The district court dismissed the suit, partly on the ground that there was no state action. The Circuit Court of Appeals affirmed on the same ground, citing the *Barney* case.[215] The Supreme Court's affirmation, however, was on the different ground that the rights asserted were not rights secured by the Fourteenth Amendment. Chief Justice Stone found it unnecessary to consider whether the action of the board was state action, adding:

> The authority of *Barney* v. *City of New York* . . . has been so restricted by our later decisions . . . that our determination may be more properly and more certainly rested on the petitioner's failure to assert a right of a nature such as the Fourteenth Amendment protects against state action.[216]

Justice Frankfurter disagreed. After paraphrasing the language of Justice Holmes's dissenting opinion in the *Raymond* case, he said:

> I am clear, therefore, that the action of the Canvassing Board taken . . . in defiance of the duty of that Board under Illinois law, cannot be deemed the action of the State, certainly not until the highest court of the State confirms such action and thereby makes it the law of the State. I agree, in a word, with the court below that *Barney* v. *City of New York* . . . is controlling. . . . Neither the wisdom of its reasoning nor its holding has been impaired by subsequent decisions.[217]

The next year, however, in *Screws* v. *United States*,[218] Justice Frankfurter seems to have given up the fight. Joining Justices Roberts and Jackson in a dissenting opinion, he no longer insisted that a sheriff's act in beating a handcuffed prisoner to death was not state

212 *Id.* at 294.

213 "When a state official, acting under color of state authority, invades, in the course of his duties, a private right secured by the federal Constitution, that right is violated, even if the state officer not only exceeded his authority, but disregarded special commands of the state law." Iowa-Des Moines Nat'l Bank v. Bennett, 284 U.S. 239, 246 (1931).

214 321 U.S. 1 (1944).

215 132 F. 2d 476 (7th Cir. 1943).

216 321 U.S. at 13.

217 *Id.* at 16–17.

218 325 U.S. 91 (1945). Other aspects of the case were discussed in the preceding chapter.

action, because it violated state law; he and his colleagues merely insisted that because it violated state law it could not be said to be "under color of law," within the terms of the statute. Yet, while reluctantly conceding that it might be state action, they seem not to have been convinced. Speaking on this point they said:

It may well be that Congress could, within the bounds of the Fourteenth Amendment, treat action taken by a State official even though in defiance of State law and not condoned by State authority as the action of "a State." It has never been satisfactorily explained how a State can be said to deprive a person of liberty or property without due process of law when the foundation of the claim is that a minor official has disobeyed the authentic command of the State. . . . Although action taken under such circumstances has been deemed to be deprivation by a "State" of rights guaranteed by the Fourteenth Amendment for purposes of federal jurisdiction, the doctrine has had a fluctuating and dubious history . . . *Barney* v. *City of New York* . . . which ruled otherwise, has never been overruled.[219]

The other six Justices felt little difficulty in holding that what the sheriff did was not only action by the state, but was also "under color of law." However innocent may be the state's *voice*, in the form of its "authentic command" to its officials, if its *hand* has sinned, so too has the state.[220] This principle is the counterpart of that which we shall observe in the next chapter—that however offensive the state's voice may be, it is only by its hand that it can violate the Amendment.

There are many different ways, however, in which a state can employ its hand to deprive a person of liberty or property. We shall see in the next chapter that while the Constitution is construed to preclude the states from employing certain methods to deprive persons of specified liberties or property interests, other methods no less effective in depriving them of these same interests are frequently tolerated.

219 325 U.S. at 147–148.

220 For a leading article on this topic, published before the Iowa-Des Moines Bank case and cited therein and in Frankfurter's concurring opinion in Snowden v. Hughes, see Samuel Shepp Isseks, *Jurisdiction of the Lower Federal Courts to Enjoin Unauthorized Action of State Officials* (1927) 40 HARV. L. REV. 969. Isseks maintains that it is fallacious to deny the existence of state action when state officers do what they have power to do only because of their position; but he believes it well for lower federal courts to exercise their discretion to decline jurisdiction until local remedies have been exhausted. Of course, this last would not apply to a criminal prosecution for acting unconstitutionally where the wrongful act is past remedy, as in the Screws case.

For a later discussion of state action which violates state law see R. L. Hale, *Unconstitutional Acts as Federal Crimes* (1946) 60 HARV. L. REV. 65, 78–90.

X

CONSTITUTIONAL AND UNCONSTITUTIONAL METHODS OF DEPRIVING PERSONS OF LIBERTY OR PROPERTY

WHEN a state curtails a man's freedom to engage in certain activities by threatening him with imprisonment, the Court, if it believes the curtailment to be arbitrary, will hold it to be an unconstitutional deprivation of liberty. But if the state curtails the same freedom by the use of other threats, which may be equally effective, such as the threat of adverse publicity or taxation or denial of a special privilege, the constitutional question is not so clear.

DIRECT AND INDIRECT DEPRIVATIONS

There are direct and indirect ways of depriving a person of liberty or property. If a state kills a man, or locks him up, or seizes his property, it is directly depriving him of life, liberty, or property. If, on the other hand, it threatens him with unpleasant consequences unless he conforms to certain regulations, and if he does conform in order to avoid those consequences, it is indirectly depriving him of liberty to act differently, and, if the regulations concern the use of property, it is indirectly depriving him of property. Not every direct deprivation is unconstitutional. A state may, through its officers, shoot a man when necessary to prevent him from committing a murder; it may quarantine persons with contagious diseases and jail suspected criminals pending trial; it may take a person's money by way of taxes or take other property by exercising its power of eminent domain. Moreover, if loss of life, liberty, or property is prescribed as the penalty for violation of a valid statute, it may deprive a person of these, provided he has first been convicted with due regard to all his procedural rights to due process. Deprivation of life, liberty, or property, so effectuated, is deprivation with due process of law, and therefore not forbidden by the Fourteenth Amendment.

But imprisoning a man who has been duly convicted of larceny is a permissible direct deprivation of his liberty-to-be-at-large, because the convicted man, presumably, had it in his own hands to avoid being deprived of this liberty by giving up his liberty-to-commit-larceny; and liberty-to-commit-larceny is of course a liberty to which the Fourteenth Amendment affords no protection. One purpose, at least, of imprisoning a convicted thief is to warn others not to steal. To the extent that this purpose is realized, the law which provides punishment for larceny serves as an indirect previous restraint on the commission of larceny, through fear of subsequent punishment. It serves indirectly to restrict liberty to steal and that is its justification.

If, on the other hand, the law restricted in this indirect way some liberty which, in the Court's view, the Fourteenth Amendment protects—the liberty, for instance, to advocate defeat of the present incumbent of some office—it would be invalid. Under such a law, one could avoid loss of the liberty-to-be-at-large only by losing the liberty-to-advocate-defeat. Since the latter liberty is one which the Fourteenth Amendment protects, there is no constitutional justification for depriving him of liberty-to-be-at-large for having exercised it. If convicted of having violated such a law and sentenced to jail, he can, by appropriate proceedings, secure release from imprisonment. He thus escapes from the state's attempt to deprive him directly of liberty-to-be-at-large if he disobeys the statute, and its attempt to deprive him indirectly of liberty-to-advocate. It was through instilling fear of subsequent punishment that the state sought to exercise a previous restraint of liberty-to-advocate.

THE SUPPOSED DISTINCTION BETWEEN PREVIOUS RESTRAINT AND SUBSEQUENT PUNISHMENT

Some confusion has resulted on this point from an unreal distinction that has been drawn (in cases dealing with freedom of speech and of the press) between previous restraint and subsequent punishment. Blackstone said:

> The liberty of the press is indeed essential to the nature of a free state; but this consists in laying no *previous* restraints upon publications, and not in freedom from censure for criminal matter when published. Every freeman has an undoubted right to lay what sentiments he pleases before the public; to forbid this, is to destroy the freedom of the press; but if he publishes what is improper, mischievous or illegal, he must take the consequence of his own temerity.[1]

To say that the state may not "forbid" the publication of anything, even if it is "improper, mischievous or illegal," but that it may punish such publication afterwards, is a contradiction in terms. Punishment of improper publication is justifiable only because it is a previous restraint and implements a prohibition. Thus, not all previous restraint is precluded by Blackstone's definition. What did he have in mind as the sort of "previous restraint" that he found objectionable? It evidently included more than measures which make future publication impossible, such as padlocking a printing establishment. Both Blackstone's followers and some of his critics apply the term to some governmental restraints which depend for their efficacy on subsequent punishment.[2]

[1] 4 Bl. Com. 151, 152.

[2] In an article published in 1916, *Equitable Relief against Defamation and Injuries to Personality* 29 HARV. L. REV. 640, 651, Roscoe Pound apparently interpreted Blackstone's view as meaning that "all legal action must necessarily come after the act." By "legal action" he evidently meant action in the courts. Passage of a libel law by the legislature would not be legal action, but issuance of an injunction would be, though the punishment comes later. Criticizing Blackstone, he said: "Blackstone's doctrine has usually been criticised as not going far enough in securing against imposition of liability after publication upon arbitrary or unreasonable grounds. Equally it goes too far in denying to the law all power of restraint before publication. Although its best title to consideration is in the history of the subject, it goes beyond what history indicates as the main purpose, namely, freedom from a régime of general censorship and license of printing."

Pound was arguing, as the title to his article indicates, against the reluctance of courts to grant equitable relief against injuries to personality brought about by publication of defamatory matter. In Near v. Minnesota, to be discussed presently, Chief Justice

What they have in mind primarily is the system of licensing and censorship which once prevailed in England. Under this system no one was permitted to print without first obtaining a license, which could only be obtained by submitting to an official censor. One who printed without a license was subject to punishment. That there was previous restraint is clear. But, as with the case of criminal libel, the punishment which made the restraint effectual came only after the unlicensed publication.

An injunction against publication is also regarded as a previous restraint, as Chief Justice Hughes held for a divided court in 1931 in *Near* v. *Minnesota.*[3] The Court there held that a certain state statute was an unconstitutional deprivation of liberty under the Fourteenth Amendment. The statute provided that after a person had published several issues of a periodical, he could be found guilty (if the facts warranted it) of the "nuisance" of engaging in the business of publishing "a malicious, scandalous and defamatory" periodical. Truth of the charges contained would be a defense only if it "was published with good motives and for justifiable ends." Then, after being adjudged guilty of the nuisance, the court could enjoin him "from further committing or maintaining it." There was to be no injunction, it is to be noted, before publication of the first offending issues; but after the initial offense there was to be an injunction against further publication. It was as to this renewed publication that the injunction was said to be a "previous restraint."

The statute [said Hughes] not only operates to suppress the offending newspaper or periodical, but to put the publisher under an effective censorship. When a newspaper or periodical is found to be "malicious, scandalous and defamatory," and is suppressed as such, resumption of publication is punishable as a contempt of court by fine or imprisonment. Thus, where a newspaper or periodical has been suppressed because of the circulation of

---

Hughes remarked, with a reference to Pound's article (283 U.S. at 716): "Nor are we now concerned with questions as to the extent of authority to prevent publications in order to protect private rights according to the principles governing the exercise of the jurisdiction of courts of equity."

Professor Zechariah Chafee, Jr., without noting that subsequent punishment *is* previous restraint, makes an incisive criticism of Blackstone's theory in an article, *Freedom of Speech in War Time* (1919) 32 HARV. L. REV. 932, 938–941, which he reiterates in his two books, FREEDOM OF SPEECH (1920), pp. 8–12, and FREE SPEECH IN THE UNITED STATES (1941), pp. 9–12.

[3] 283 U.S. 697 (1931). Concurring with Hughes were Justices Holmes, Brandeis, Stone, and Roberts. Justice Butler wrote a dissenting opinion, in which Justices Van Devanter, McReynolds, and Sutherland joined.

charges against public officers of official misconduct, it would seem to be clear that the renewal of the publication of such charges would constitute a contempt, and that the judgment would lay a permanent restraint upon the publisher, to escape which he must satisfy the court as to the character of a new publication. Whether he would be permitted again to publish matter deemed to be derogatory to the same or other public officers would depend upon the court's ruling. In the present instance the judgment restrained the defendants from "publishing, circulating, having in their possession, selling or giving away any publication whatsoever which is a malicious, scandalous or defamatory newspaper, as defined by law." The law gives no definition except that covered by the words "scandalous and defamatory," and publications charging official misconduct are of that class. While the court, answering the objection that the judgment was too broad, saw no reason for construing it as restraining the defendants "from operating a newspaper in harmony with the public welfare to which all must yield," and said that the defendants had not indicated "any desire to conduct their business in the usual and legitimate manner," the manifest inference is that, at least with respect to a new publication directed against official misconduct, the defendant would be held, under penalty of punishment for contempt as provided in the statute, to a manner of publication which the court considered to be "usual and legitimate" and consistent with the public welfare.[4]

"This," added Hughes, "is of the essence of censorship." And, "in determining the extent of the constitutional protection, it has been generally, if not universally, considered that it is the chief purpose of the guaranty to prevent previous restraints upon publication." After referring to the struggle in England "directed against the legislative power of the licenser," he quoted Blackstone's statement and some others of similar import. He intimated that constitutional freedom of the press might sometimes extend to subsequent punishments, and he conceded that "the protection even as to previous restraint is not absolutely unlimited." He added at once, however, "but the limitation has been recognized only in exceptional cases," citing such instances as preventing the publication of the sailing dates of transports in time of war. He concluded:

The exceptional nature of its limitations places in a strong light the general conception that liberty of the press, historically considered and taken up by the Federal Constitution, has meant, principally although not exclusively, immunity from previous restraints or censorship.[5]

Throughout the discussion it was assumed that an injunction sanctioned by a subsequent punishment for contempt constitutes a pre-

[4] 283 U.S. at 712–713.

[5] *Id.* at 716.

vious restraint, while a criminal law sanctioned by a subsequent punishment does not.

The criticism upon Blackstone's statement [said Hughes] has not been because immunity from previous restraint upon publication has not been regarded as deserving of special emphasis, but chiefly because that immunity cannot be deemed to exhaust the conception of the liberty guaranteed by State and Federal Constitutions. The point of criticism has been "that the mere exemption from previous restraints cannot be all that is secured by the constitutional provisions," and that "the liberty of the press might be rendered a mockery and a delusion, and the phrase itself a by-word, if, while every man was at liberty to publish what he pleased, the public authorities might nevertheless punish him for harmless publications." 2 Cooley, Const. Lim. (8th Ed.) p. 885. But it is recognized that punishment for the abuse of the liberty accorded to the press is essential to the protection of the public, and that the common-law rules that subject the libeler to responsibility for the public offense, as well as for the private injury, are not abolished by the protection extended in our Constitutions. *Id.* pp. 883, 884. The law of criminal libel rests upon that secure foundation. . . . In the present case, we have no occasion to inquire as to the permissible scope of subsequent punishment. . . . As has been noted, the statute in question does not deal with punishments; it provides for no punishment, except in case of contempt for violation of the court's order, but for suppression and injunction, that is, for restraint upon publication.[6]

At an earlier point in the opinion, Hughes had said, "The object of the statute is not punishment, in the ordinary sense, but suppression of the offending newspaper or periodical." [7] Concerning publication of the issues put out before the publisher is brought into court, Hughes was undoubtedly correct in saying that the object was not punishment. The state provided elsewhere for punishment of those issues, if they violated the criminal libel statute. While fear of conviction for nuisance under the present statute, to be followed by an injunction against further publication, might operate as a previous restraint on the initial publication, the libel law already operated as a restraint.[8] The statute does not seem to have been held bad because the additional penalty operated as a more effective restraint than the libel law on publication of the initial issues. It was restraint of renewed publication that made it bad.

[6] 283 U.S. at 714–715.

[7] *Id.* at 711.

[8] The same circumstances that would bring a publisher within the scope of this statute would seem to bring him also within the scope of the criminal libel law, except possibly where the publication, while not true, was "honestly made, in belief of its truth" or "upon reasonable grounds for such belief, and consists of fair comments etc." In such a case the libel law would not apply. See footnote 3 of the Court's opinion. 283 U.S. at 710–711.

Justice Butler, in his dissenting opinion, construed the statute as authorizing restraint "only in respect of continuing to do what has been duly adjudged to constitute a nuisance. . . . There is nothing in the statute purporting to prohibit publications that have not been adjudged to constitute a nuisance." [9] Hence it "does not operate as a *previous* restraint on publication within the proper meaning of that phrase." Because of the pleadings, the scope of the injunction actually issued by the trial court "is not reviewable here." [10] He also thought that defendants, under this statute, might "interpose any defense or introduce any evidence that would be open to them in a libel case." [11] In this view, there was little more restraint on renewed publication of libelous articles than the libel law already provided on their initial publication.

As we have seen, Hughes construed the statute differently, in the light of the state supreme court's own comments on the scope of the injunction in this very case. According to this view, the injunction restrained the publication, not only of matter punishable under the libel law, or even of matter which would originally subject the publisher to conviction of a nuisance (if the scope of this statute is in that respect wider than that of the libel law). It restrained the further publication of anything which the local court might disapprove; and the local court might disapprove the publication of matter which, in the eyes of the Supreme Court, would not be considered an "abuse" of freedom of the press. The injunction, accordingly, restrains freedom to publish matter which comes within the constitutional guaranty. The law of criminal libel, on the other hand, restrains only freedom to publish what does not come within that guaranty. That law doubtless rests upon a "secure foundation." But the foundation is secure because it restrains only "abuses" of freedom of the press, not because its restraint is any less "previous" in its character than that of the injunction. Each restrains in advance by a threat of subsequent punishment. The distinction between them lies in what they restrain, not in the time when the restraint is imposed. Subsequent punishment by a criminal statute of publication which does not constitute an "abuse," would rest upon no secure foundation. If there is any constitutional objection to an injunction restraining the same thing that can be punished as a crime, it must lie in the fact that the subsequent punishment for disobedience can be imposed without a jury trial. But this is not a difference in the timing. The decision could

[9] 283 U.S. at 735–736. [10] *Id.* at 730. [11] *Ibid.*

well have been based on the nature of what the injunction restrained.

In *Near* v. *Minnesota* Hughes cited,[12] in support of Blackstone's distinction, the previous case of *Patterson* v. *Colorado*,[13] decided in 1907. Patterson had published an attack on the motives of the supreme court of Colorado in rendering a certain decision. At the time of publication, the time had not elapsed for motions for rehearing of that decision. The court cited him for contempt and, rejecting his offer to prove the truth of his allegations, fined him. In sustaining this action, Justice Holmes for the majority [14] accepted Blackstone's distinction at face value. Even assuming that the Fourteenth Amendment places the same restriction on the states that the First places on the Federal Government (a question which had not at that time been settled), Holmes held that there was nothing unconstitutional in the state court's fine.

In the first place [he said], the main purpose of such constitutional provisions is "to prevent all such *previous restraints* upon publications as had been practiced by other governments," and they do not prevent the subsequent punishment of such as may be deemed contrary to the public welfare. *Commonwealth* v. *Blanding*, 3 Pick. [Mass.] 304, 313, 314; *Respublica* v. *Oswald*, 1 Dallas, 319, 325. The preliminary freedom extends as well to the false as to the true; the subsequent punishment may extend as well to the true as to the false. This was the law of criminal libel apart from statute, in most cases, if not in all. *Commonwealth* v. *Blanding*, *ubi sup.*; 4 Bl. Com. 150.[15]

It may well be doubted whether the Court sustained the punishment because it did not operate as a previous restraint on publishing an attack on the judges. There is other language in the opinion that suggests that such punishment was thought permissible because it did serve to prevent such attacks on a decision before the case was concluded and that it might be unconstitutional if the punishment were for an attack made thereafter. After stressing what he deemed the importance of preventing even true publications which might tend to interfere with the decision of a pending case, Holmes said: "When a case is finished, courts are subject to the same criticism as other people, but the propriety and necessity of preventing interference with the course of justice by premature statement, argument or intimidation hardly can be denied." [16]

[12] 283 U.S. at 715.

[13] 205 U.S. 454 (1907).

[14] Justices Harlan and Brewer dissented.

[15] 205 U.S. at 462.

[16] *Id.* at 463. The power of a state to punish for published comment on a pending case has since this decision been considerably narrowed. In Bridges v. California, 314

If the fine is justified as a means of "preventing" interference with the course of justice, how can it be called anything other than a "previous" restraint? And if a fine for criticizing a court "when a case is finished" would be invalid (as Holmes seems to have implied), why is that any less of a subsequent punishment, or any more of a previous restraint, than a fine for a criticism made while a case is still pending?

The truth seems to be that the constitutionality of laws affecting freedom of the press turns, not on whether a restraint is "previous" or a punishment "subsequent," but on whether the law in question punishes publication which the Court holds to be within the scope of the constitutional protection or without that scope. If the latter, the Court characterizes the publication as an "abuse" of freedom of the press, and it receives no constitutional protection against either "previous restraint" or "subsequent punishment." If not an "abuse," subsequent punishment is forbidden. This seems to be the test applied since *Near* v. *Minnesota,* in several cases dealing with what Hughes termed the "cognate" rights of free speech, free press, and free assembly.

In *De Jonge* v. *Oregon,*[17] decided in 1937, Chief Justice Hughes spoke of the possibility of abuse of these cognate rights, and added: "The people, through their legislatures, may protect themselves against that abuse. But the legislative intervention can find constitutional justification only by dealing with the abuse. The rights themselves must not be curtailed."

Applying this test, he set aside a subsequent punishment under a criminal syndicalism law for taking part in a meeting held under the auspices of the Communist Party, at which there was no advocacy of violent overthrow of the government. That the Party might be guilty of advocating such overthrow on other occasions was held to be irrelevant. The particular meeting was not an "abuse" of the right of free assembly. The Court was unanimous.

Again, in *Grosjean* v. *American Press Co.,*[18] decided in 1936, the Court unanimously held a subsequent penalty (which took the form

U.S. 252 (1941), fines were set aside which the California courts had imposed on Harry Bridges for publishing a telegram attacking an injunction issued in a case still pending, and on the Los Angeles *Times* for three editorials commenting on pending cases. There was a strong dissenting opinion by Justice Frankfurter, joined by Chief Justice Stone and Justices Roberts and Byrnes. The dissent was not based on the ground that the punishment was subsequent to the publication. In fact the dissenters concurred in setting aside the fines for two of the editorials.

[17] 299 U.S. 353 (1937).

[18] 297 U.S. 233 (1936).

of a tax) unconstitutional. The law imposing the tax was passed in Louisiana under the regime of the late Huey Long. The tax was on the gross advertising receipts of newspapers whose weekly circulation exceeded 20,000. It was to be computed and assessed after the papers had circulated. Of course, mere circulation of a large number constituted no "abuse" of freedom of the press, and it was apparently for this reason that it was held invalid. The tax had a direct tendency, thought the Court, to restrict circulation. In view of the obnoxious English taxes on newspapers and on advertising, in force when the First Amendment was adopted, Justice Sutherland concluded that the framers of the American guaranties of a free press must have intended to guard against just such restraints. In expressing this view, he used language which indicated that censorship was not the only type of "previous restraint." In fact, he characterized this subsequent tax as a previous restraint also, thus obliterating the distinction between previous restraints and subsequent punishments.

> It is impossible to concede [he said] that by the words "freedom of the press" the framers of the amendment intended to adopt merely the narrow view then reflected by the law of England that such freedom consisted only in immunity from previous censorship; for this abuse had then permanently disappeared from English practice. . . .
>
> In the light of all that has now been said, it is evident . . . that by the First Amendment it was meant to preclude the national government, and by the Fourteenth Amendment to preclude the states, from adopting any form of previous restraint upon printed publications, or their circulation, including that which had heretofore been effected by these two well-known and odious methods.[19]

In 1940 the Court likened a criminal statute (with subsequent punishment) to a licensing system. In *Thornhill* v. *Alabama*[20] it invalidated a statute which made it a misdemeanor to go near a person's place of business for the purpose of inducing others not to deal with him. While leaving open the question whether a statute more narrowly drawn to punish abuses of the right of free speech by picketing might be valid, the present statute was held too broad. Speaking of licensing statutes, Justice Murphy said:

> The power of the licensor against which John Milton directed his assault by his "Appeal for the Liberty of Unlicensed Printing" is pernicious not merely by reason of the censure of particular comments but by reason of the threat to censure comments on matters of public concern. It is not the spo-

[19] 297 U.S. at 248–249.

[20] 310 U.S. 88 (1940). Justice McReynolds dissented, without opinion.

radic abuse of power by the censor but the pervasive threat inherent in its very existence that constitutes the danger to freedom of discussion. See *Near* v. *Minnesota,* 283 U.S. 697, 713. . . . A like threat is inherent in a penal statute, like that in question here, which does not aim specifically at evils within the allowable area of State control but, on the contrary, sweeps within its ambit other activities that in ordinary circumstances constitute an exercise of freedom of speech or of the press . . . It is not any less effective or, if the restraint is not permissible, less pernicious than the restraint on freedom of discussion imposed by the threat of censorship.[21]

When the statute applies to speech whose restriction is not permissible under the Constitution, it makes no difference whether the restriction is to be characterized as "previous restraint" or as "subsequent punishment." As the Court remarked at a later point: "The freedom of speech and of the press guaranteed by the Constitution embraces at least the liberty to discuss publicly and truthfully all matters of public concern without previous restraint *or fear of subsequent punishment.*" [Italics added.] [22]

With any other liberty, too, which the Constitution "embraces," previous restraint by instilling fear of subsequent punishment is precluded—when the punishment takes the form of execution, imprisonment, or fine. Not every liberty, as we have seen, comes within the scope of constitutional protection. The particular liberties which a man has a "constitutional right" to exercise and the circumstances in which he has a "constitutional right" to do so are spelled out by the Supreme Court, case by case. But to say that a man has a "constitutional right" to this or that liberty is to say that neither state nor Federal Government may deprive him of it indirectly, by imposing a criminal punishment for having exercised it.

OFFICIAL PUBLICITY AS A PENALTY FOR SPECIFIED CONDUCT

State governments and the Federal Government, however, may deprive him indirectly of liberties which he has a "constitutional right" to exercise, by attaching certain other unpleasant consequences after he has exercised them. The criterion would seem to be whether the imposition of these other consequences can find constitutional justification apart from their deterrent effect on the conduct to which they are attached. Direct deprivations of life, liberty, or property can be justified, as a rule, only as indirect restraints on the exercise of some liberty which does not come within the scope of constitutional

[21] 310 U.S. at 97–98.

[22] *Id.* at 101–102.

protection. Official expression of disapproval of certain conduct, on the other hand, is not a direct deprivation of life, liberty, or property. It requires no constitutional justification. Hence, it has been held immaterial that the disapproval may fall on the exercise of some liberty which is constitutionally protected.

In *Standard Computing Scale Co.* v. *Farrell*[23] the state Superintendent of Weights and Measures published a bulletin containing a "specification" to the effect that "all combination spring and lever computing scales must be equipped with a device which will automatically compensate for changes of temperature, etc." The Standard Company manufactured computing scales equipped with a compensating device which was not automatic. As a result of the bulletin, local sealers (who were not subject to the Superintendent's authority) refused in many cases to seal the Standard scales, and warned dealers not to use them. The Standard's business fell off in consequence. It thereupon brought suit against the superintendent in the district court, praying that the specifications be declared invalid and their enforcement enjoined. The Supreme Court affirmed the dismissal of the suit for want of jurisdiction, since the function of the specifications was at most advisory. Had they, said Justice Brandeis, "been issued as a regulation, that is, a law, we might have been called upon to enquire whether it was a proper exercise of the police power or was, as plaintiff contends, void because arbitrary and unreasonable." [24]

But the purpose of the bulletin was "instruction and information to dealers and weights and measures officials."

> The information given in the "specifications" complained of may, as the plaintiff contends, be incorrect; the instruction may be unsound, and, if it is so, may be mischievous and seriously damage the property rights of innocent persons. But the opinions and advice, even of those in authority, are not a law or regulation such as comes within the scope of the several provisions of the Federal Constitution designed to secure the rights of citizens as against action by the States.[25]

In *Pennsylvania Railroad Co.* v. *United States Railroad Labor Board*,[26] decided in 1923, the railroad had disobeyed an order of the board directing it to take certain action which, the railroad contended, it had a "constitutional right" not to take. Under then existing statutes the board had no power to impose any punishment for disobedience of its order except by publishing the fact of disobedience. Without

[23] 249 U.S. 571 (1919). [24] *Id.* at 577. [25] *Id.* at 575.
[26] 261 U.S. 72 (1923).

passing on the merits of the company's claim that it had a "constitutional right" to disobey, the Court held that no injunction should be issued restraining the board from publishing the fact. Said Chief Justice Taft:

> The jurisdiction of the Board to direct the parties to do what it deems they should do is not to be limited by their constitutional or legal right to refuse to do it. Under the act there is no constraint upon them to do what the Board decides they should do except the moral constraint . . . of publication of its decision.[27]

"Moral constraint," however, might well be effective. The framers of the act very likely hoped that it would be. The opprobrium resulting from public knowledge that the company was defying the board might conceivably cause such economic loss to the company as to make obedience of the order appear the lesser evil. And in the *Standard Computing Scale* case the "opinions and advice" of the superintendent had already caused the company's business to fall off. Fear that such loss of business would continue might well be quite as effective in compelling the company to install an automatic compensating device on its scales as would be a fine for not doing so. The fine, however, would be unconstitutional, should an order to desist from selling nonautomatic scales be held arbitrary. Not so the loss of business consequent on the superintendent's "advice," however arbitrary that advice might be.

The fine would be bad, because it is a direct deprivation of property. As such, it can be justified only as a deterrent to conduct which it is not arbitrary to forbid. If the prohibition is arbitrary, the fine subjects the manufacturer to a choice of evils, each of which involves loss of a "constitutional right." The superintendent's "advice," on the other hand, makes it possible, though it may not be profitable, for the manufacturer to choose an evil which does not involve an unconstitutional deprivation. If he has indeed a "constitutional right" not to be deprived of the liberty to sell nonautomatic scales, it is not made literally impossible for him to continue to exercise that liberty without loss of anything else to which he has a constitutional right. His right not to be deprived of property does not include a right not to be subjected to loss of business brought about by official advice to customers. By choosing this evil, he has it in his own hands to avoid deprivation of his liberty to sell the nonautomatic scales. Even

[27] *Id.* at 84.

though this is the greater evil, it is one against which he has no constitutional right, since, unlike a fine, it does not constitute an invalid deprivation of property. If it is, however, the greater evil, he will be forced, despite the Fourteenth Amendment, to desist from exercising a liberty which that Amendment guarantees to him as against restraints which operate through fear of subsequent imprisonment or fine.[28]

ASSESSMENT OF DAMAGES AS A PENALTY

If a particular liberty is indeed one which would be held to be within the scope of the Fourteenth Amendment, its restriction through fear of subsequent imprisonment would be equally invalid whether the punishment resulted from conviction under a criminal statute or from disobedience of an injunction which prohibited the exercise of that liberty. Freedom to commit many acts designated as "wrongful," however, is restricted, not by the imposition of criminal penalties, nor by the issuance of injunctions, but by imposing a civil liability to pay damages. If the freedom in question is one which does not enjoy constitutional protection—as is the case with freedom to commit most of the ordinary legal "wrongs,"—the justification for exacting damages of the defendant, thus depriving him of property, may rest on the very fact that this procedure does tend to restrict liberty to commit the wrong. But as we saw in a previous chapter, the law subjects some persons to a liability to pay damages, even when they are not regarded as wrongdoers. The innocent employer may have to pay for wrongs committed by his servants, and under workmen's compensation acts an employer may be required to compensate his injured employees, though he has been guilty of no

[28] We have something more than publicity as a sanction when the governmental announcement is accompanied by a notice of further governmental sanction of a more tangible kind. In Columbia Broadcasting System v. United States, 316 U.S. 407 (1941), the Federal Communications Commission had issued regulations announcing that licenses would be refused to stations making contracts with network organizations on terms typical of those contained in Columbia's contracts, though no license would be denied without an individual hearing. As a result many stations were canceling contracts with Columbia or refusing to renew them. In an opinion by Chief Justice Stone it was held that the regulations constituted an "order" within the meaning of the statute which gave federal courts jurisdiction to review the commission's "orders." Justice Frankfurter, dissenting with Justices Reed and Douglas maintained that the regulations did not constitute an "order," since "they require nobody . . . to do anything." *Id.* at 430–431. The Attorney General's listing of organizations as "subversive" without a hearing under an Executive Order which attached certain consequences to membership in a listed organization amounts to more than "opinions and advice." See the various opinions in Joint Anti-Fascist Refugee Committee v. McGrath, 341 U.S. 123 (1951).

negligence or any other wrong. In sustaining the constitutionality of the New York Workmen's Compensation Act in 1917, in *N.Y. Cent. R. Co.* v. *White,* Justice Pitney said:

> In excluding the question of fault as a cause of the injury, the act in effect disregards the proximate cause and looks to one more remote—the primary cause, as it may be deemed—and that is, the employment itself. For this, both parties are responsible, since they voluntarily engage in it as coadventurers, with personal injury to the employee as a probable and foreseen result.[29]

Evidently Justice Pitney did not regard the "primary cause"—the employment—as a "fault" or a legal wrong. He very likely regarded it as a "constitutional right" in that a law making it a crime to employ people in dangerous occupations would be held to be an unconstitutional deprivation of liberty. Yet he found no constitutional objection to a requirement that one who "exercised" this "constitutional right" should be made to pay for the resulting personal injuries.

The liability to pay this compensation may deter those who will find it unprofitable to incur it from exercising a liberty to engage in dangerous trades. But that is no conclusive reason for holding the act unconstitutional. The liability may be justified either because it does deter people from entering an industry whose customers do not want its products sufficiently to pay all the human costs of its operation or because it does not deter those whose customers do want the products sufficiently, while it does provide compensation to the victims of accidents. We have seen that the Thirteenth Amendment is construed to prohibit imprisonment for breach of a contract to render personal services, but not to forbid imposing a liability to pay damages for the breach. The liability to imprisonment may compel performance on the part even of those to whom the work is especially obnoxious, while liability to pay damages will compel performance on the part only of those to whom it is less so. The liberty to refrain from doing the promised work may not be restricted by the more severe penalty. But it is not an unconditional liberty. Similarly, a law making it a crime to incur debts would doubtless be held to be an unconstitutional deprivation of liberty. But if a man is deterred from exercising that liberty because he will subsequently be held liable to pay the promised money, there is obviously nothing unconstitutional. A "constitutional right" to make contracts does not imply that one

[29] 243 U.S. 188, 205 (1917).

is to be free to make them without incurring subsequent liability for failure to carry them out. If it did, there could be no such thing as a legal obligation of contracts.

A contracting party, it is true, is required to pay *damages* only after he has committed a "wrong" by breaking the contract. But if the contract calls for the payment of money, he is required to pay *money* in order to avoid being held to have committed the wrong. The obligation to pay the debt arises when the debt is due. If it is paid, there is no wrongful act, and the legal obligation to pay it arose from the exercise of the constitutionally protected liberty to make the contract. If it is not paid as a debt, the legal authorities will make the debtor pay it as damages if they can get hold of him and if he is solvent.

While the law can therefore require persons who have done no wrong to pay money to others under certain circumstances, it is not to be supposed that the liability to pay damages can be constitutionally attached to every sort of act or omission. The act of making a contract normally carries with it an obligation to pay damages if it is not performed. Thus, one who agrees to work for another can (if solvent) be made to pay the latter the pecuniary equivalent of the work if he does not do the work. But a law would clearly be unconstitutional if it required a person to work for another when he has made no contract to do so or, in default of the work, to pay the would-be employer the value of the work. To make him work when he has not contracted to do so would, even apart from the Thirteenth Amendment, deprive him of liberty under the Fourteenth, unless he could escape without infringement of some other constitutional right. Here he could only escape by paying money, which would be an unconstitutional deprivation of property in the absence of some justification for making him pay. When the only purpose of requiring the payment is to enrich the employer or to restrict the freedom to refrain from working, there would be no justification. When an employer is required by statute to compensate an injured employee, the deprivation of property is justified by the fact that the injury to the employee is as much a part of the cost of carrying on the business as is the consumption of raw material or the labor of the workers, for which it is taken for granted that he must pay. But if the law required a factory owner to pay the cost of illnesses or accidents to those with whom he has no connection, it might well be held to deprive him of property without due process—unless the payment were required under some general tax law.

When payment is required for any act, whether wrongful or rightful, it tends to prevent that act from being committed as freely as if it cost nothing. People may not be so reckless in making promises if they know they are going to be held responsible for carrying them out. But freedom to make irresponsible promises in the form of contracts it is not the policy of contract law to encourage. And nothing in the Fourteenth Amendment stands in the way of this much of a restriction of liberty.

TAXATION AS A PENALTY

A tax on any activity or transaction is as much of an economic deterrent of freedom to engage in that activity as would be a liability to pay the same sum of money by way of damages. Although Holmes, in a passage already cited,[30] declared that whether a man is under compulsion or free depends on whether "a given statutory liability is a penalty or a tax," he was nearer right when in the same passage he maintained that from the point of view of the "bad man" "it does not matter, so far as the consequence, the compulsory payment, is concerned, whether the act to which it is attached is described in terms of praise or in terms of blame, or whether the law purports to prohibit it or to allow it."

In fact the validity of a tax may be sustained on the very ground that it does suppress or regulate the activity taxed, when that activity is one which the taxing government may constitutionally control by more obvious penalties. The completely repressive federal tax of 10 percent on state banknotes was sustained partly on this ground in 1869, in *Veazie Bank* v. *Fenno*.[31] And in *Board of Trustees of University of Illinois* v. *United States*[32] it was held, in 1933, that a state university, even if regarded as an agency of the state, could be required to pay customs duties on articles which it imports, since in exacting such duties Congress was exercising its power to regulate interstate commerce—though *Collector* v. *Day*,[33] which held state agencies

30 *The Path of the Law* (1897) 10 HARV. L. REV. 457, 461–462; reprinted in COLLECTED LEGAL PAPERS (1921) 167, 173 ff. *Supra*, pp. 102–103.

31 8 Wall. 533 (U.S. 1869).

32 289 U.S. 48 (1933).

33 11 Wall. 113 (U.S. 1871).

immune to federal taxation, had not yet been overruled by *Graves* v. *New York ex rel. O'Keefe.*[34]

When the activity, however, on which the tax is laid is one which the tax-laying government (state or federal) may not constitutionally penalize, some other justification for the tax must be found if it is to be sustained. Ordinarily the fiscal needs of the government will serve as a justification. That a tax deprives the taxpayer of property in the form of money does not necessarily make it unconstitutional. Otherwise governments would be paralyzed. And the fact that some persons will feel forced to refrain from exercising some liberty which enjoys constitutional protection, in order to escape the tax, is irrelevant. Nor does it necessarily matter that the legislature was motivated in part by a desire to control the activity on which the tax is laid. The fiscal motive, even if accompanied by another, makes the exaction valid. As Justice Sutherland said for the Court in 1934, in *Magnano Co.* v. *Hamilton:*

> From the beginning of our government, the courts have sustained taxes, although imposed with the collateral intent of effecting ulterior ends which, considered apart, were beyond the constitutional power of the lawmakers to realize by legislation directly addressed to their accomplishment.[35]

And as Justice Cardozo said for the majority in 1935, in *Fox* v. *Standard Oil Co.,*[36] in sustaining a graduated tax on chain stores which bore most heavily on chain gasoline stations, the state "may make the tax so heavy as to discourage multiplication of the units to an extent believed to be inordinate, and by the incidence of the burden develop other forms of industry."

If, however, the intent to effect ends, beyond the government's power to realize directly, appears to the Court to be not merely a collateral intent, but the sole or dominating intent of the tax, it may come to grief. In *Bailey* v. *Drexel Furniture Co.* (the *Child Labor Tax Case*),[37] decided in 1922, the federal excise tax on persons employing children was held to be an unconstitutional attempt to usurp the regulatory functions of the states. Pointing to several features of the act which seemed to him to indicate a regulatory rather than a

[34] 306 U.S. 466 (1939). Collector v. Day had, however, been qualified so as not to apply to agencies performing a "proprietary," as distinguished from a "governmental," function of the state. Thus, in South Carolina v. United States, 199 U.S. 437 (1905), it was held that a state liquor monopoly was not exempt from federal liquor taxes.

[35] 292 U.S. 40, 47 (1934).

[36] 294 U.S. 87, 100 (1935).

[37] 259 U.S. 20 (1922).

fiscal motive, Chief Justice Taft said that there had been such "an extension of the penalizing features of the so-called tax" that it had lost "its character as such" and had become "a mere penalty." On the same day, in *Hill* v. *Wallace*,[38] a federal tax imposed by the Future Trading Act was set aside as a penalty for certain local dealings.

Later in the same year, in *St. Louis Compress Co.* v. *Arkansas*,[39] Justice Holmes held that a state tax on premiums paid to foreign insurance companies not authorized to do business in the state was indistinguishable from a fine on the same sort of transactions, which had been held invalid in a previous case.

The short question [he said] is whether this so-called tax is saved because of the name given to it by the statute when it has been decided in *Allgeyer* v. *Louisiana*, 165 U.S. 578, that the imposition of a round sum, called a fine, for doing the same thing, called an offense, is invalid under the Fourteenth Amendment. It is argued that there is a distinction because the Louisiana statute prohibits (by implication) what this statute permits. But that distinction, apart from some relatively insignificant collateral consequences, is merely in the amount of detriment imposed upon doing the act. The name given by the state to the imposition is not conclusive. *Child Labor Tax* case, 259 U.S. 20. *Lipke* v. *Lederer*, 259 U.S. 557. In Louisiana the detriment was $1,000. Here it is 5% upon the premiums—which is 3% more than is charged for insuring in authorized companies. It is a prohibition to the extent of the payment required. The Arkansas tax manifests no less plainly than the Louisiana fine a purpose to discourage insuring in companies that do not pay tribute to the state.[40]

In this case the size of the so-called tax seems to have been one of the factors which caused the Court to discern a regulatory rather than a purely fiscal motive in its exaction. And in *United States* v. *Constantine*,[41] decided in 1935, Justice Roberts, for the majority, laid stress on the size of the heavy federal tax on the licenses of liquor dealers who violated state prohibition laws in reaching his conclusion that the tax was not a fiscal measure, but a penalty and therefore beyond the scope of federal authority since the repeal of the Eighteenth Amendment—which had given state governments and the Federal Government concurrent authority to enforce prohibition. In *Carter* v. *Carter Coal Co.*,[42] likewise, which held the first Guffey Coal Act unconstitutional in 1936, the Court may well have been influenced by the size of the 15 percent sales tax on coal, with its rebate of 90

38 259 U.S. 44 (1922).
39 260 U.S. 346 (1922).
40 *Id.* at 348–349.
41 296 U.S. 287 (1935).
42 298 U.S. 238 (1936).

percent of the tax to those who would comply with certain federal regulations, in reaching its conclusion that the tax was a penalty designed to force compliance with those regulations—which were held unconstitutional.

There are cases, however, in which the Court has declared that the size of the tax cannot be taken into account. This doctrine dates back to Marshall's oft-quoted statement in *McCulloch* v. *Maryland,*[43] decided in 1819, that "the power to tax involves the power to destroy." He held there that a state tax on the Bank of the United States was unconstitutional, because if the power to levy the tax in question were to be sustained the state might increase it to the point where it would destroy that instrument of the federal government. By taking this view, he said, "We are not driven to the perplexing inquiry, so unfit for the judicial department, what degree of taxation is the legitimate use, and what degree may amount to the abuse of the power." [44]

This doctrine can be employed either to invalidate a light tax which is not in fact repressive, on the ground that a repressive tax on the same activity would be bad; or to sustain a repressive tax on the ground that a light and nonrepressive tax would fall within the permissible taxing power of the government which imposes it. All depends on which end the Court starts with in making its inquiry. And the Court has used the doctrine both ways.

In *McCray* v. *United States* [45] a federal tax on yellow oleomargarine was sustained, in 1905, although the Court was well aware that its object was not to raise revenue, but to suppress the manufacture of the product—an objective beyond any power conferred on Congress unless it be the power of taxation. The case was defended and distinguished by Chief Justice Taft in the *Child Labor Tax Case,* in that the oleomargarine tax law did not "show on its face as does the law before us the detailed specifications of a regulation of a state concern and business with a heavy exaction to promote the efficacy of such regulation." [46] It is true that there were no detailed specifications in the law, but none were needed to promote the efficacy of the regulation or to reveal that regulation was intended. The size of the tax in relation to the price of the competing products was enough. But that is precisely what the Marshall doctrine inhibited the Court from observing.

[43] 4 Wheat. 316, 431 (U.S. 1819).
[44] *Id.* at 429–430.
[45] 195 U.S. 27 (1905).
[46] 259 U.S. 20, 42 (1922).

In 1934 the Court sustained a state tax of 15 cents a pound on butter substitutes in *Magnano Co.* v. *Hamilton.*[47] It was assumed that direct state repression of the butter-substitute business would have been unconstitutional, and "the point may be conceded," said Justice Sutherland, "that the tax is so excessive that it may or will result in destroying the intrastate business of appellant." [48] But he cited authorities to show that this fact was irrelevant, and went on:

> The statute here under review is in form plainly a taxing act, with nothing in its terms to suggest that it was intended to be anything else. It must be construed, and the intent and meaning of the Legislature ascertained, from the language of the act, and the words used therein are to be given their ordinary meaning unless the context shows that they are differently used. *Child Labor Tax Case, supra* . . . . If the tax imposed had been 5 cents instead of 15 cents per pound, no one, probably, would have thought of challenging its constitutionality or of suggesting that under the guise of imposing a tax another and different power had in fact been exercised. If a contrary conclusion were reached in the present case, it could rest upon nothing more than the single premise that the amount of the tax is so excessive that it will bring about the destruction of appellant's business, a premise which, standing alone, this court heretofore has uniformly rejected as furnishing no juridical ground for striking down a taxing act.[49]

A tax, though purposely made high enough to repress what may not be constitutionally repressed by avowed penalties, must be sustained, then, provided only that it is imposed by an innocently worded statute. The Court acts on the assumption that a repressive tax is no worse than a nonrepressive one. On the other hand, if a tax is laid on an activity which the Court thinks must be protected from destructive taxation, the tax must be held bad even if it is not destructive; for a nonrepressive tax is no better than a repressive one. This is the basis for *McCulloch* v. *Maryland* and *Collector* v. *Day* and the cases stemming from them, which, until modified in recent years, held federal activities and agencies absolutely immune from state taxation, and state agencies from federal, no matter how light the tax or how nondiscriminatory.[50] And it is the basis for Justice Sutherland's intimation in *Grosjean* v. *American Press Co.*,[51] in 1936, that the tax on the gross advertising receipts of publications whose weekly circulation exceeded 20,000 copies would have been bad even

47 292 U.S. 40 (1934). 48 *Id.* at 45. 49 *Id.* at 46–47.

50 For an account of recent changes in this field see T. R. Powell, *The Waning of Intergovernmental Tax Immunities* (1945) 58 HARV. L. REV. 633 and *The Remnant of Intergovernmental Tax Immunities* (1945) 58 *ibid.*, 757. See also New York v. United States, 326 U.S. 572 (1946), discussed *infra*, pp. 288–290. 51 297 U.S. 233 (1936).

if it had not been heavy enough to impede their circulation. If the tax, he said, "were increased to a high degree, as it could be if valid, it might well result in destroying both advertising and circulation." [52]

This doctrine has not gone unchallenged. In *Panhandle Oil Co.* v. *Mississippi ex rel. Knox* [53] a state excise tax of 4 cents per gallon on gasoline sold within the state was held unconstitutional in 1928 as applied to sales made to the Federal Government for the use of its Coast Guard and Veterans' Hospital. The dealer who paid the tax passed it on to its customers, so that the tax was in effect on the Government.[54] Justice Holmes, in a dissenting opinion, in which Justices Brandeis and Stone joined,[55] maintained that "the question of interference with Government . . . is one of reasonableness and degree and it seems to me that the interference in this case is too remote." [56] The Government, he said,

> avails itself of the machinery furnished by the State and I do not see why it should not contribute in the same proportion that every other purchaser contributes for the privileges that it uses. . . . The cost of maintaining the State that makes the business possible is just as necessary an element in the cost of production as labor or coal.[57]

The state supreme court had sustained the tax, and Holmes said:

> It seems to me that the State Court was right. I should say plainly right, but for the effect of certain dicta of Chief Justice Marshall which culminated in or rather were founded upon his often quoted proposition that the power to tax is the power to destroy. In those days it was not recognized as it is today that most of the distinctions of the law are distinctions of degree. If the States had any power it was assumed that they had all power, and that the necessary alternative was to deny it altogether. But this Court which so often has defeated the attempt to tax in certain ways can defeat an attempt to discriminate or otherwise go too far without wholly abolishing the power to tax. The power to tax is not the power to destroy while this Court sits. The power to fix rates is the power to destroy if unlimited, but this Court while it endeavors to prevent confiscation does not prevent the fixing of rates. A tax is not an unconstitutional regulation in every case

[52] 297 U.S. at 245.

[53] 277 U.S. 218 (1928). The case was overruled in Alabama v. King & Boozer, 314 U.S. 1 (1941).

[54] The state was suing for the tax. The company defended on the ground that it had not added the tax to the price charged the Government (as it had presumably added it to the price charged other buyers) and that a tax on the Government was unconstitutional.

[55] Justice McReynolds also dissented, in a separate opinion. The majority opinion, written by Justice Butler, had the concurrence of Chief Justice Taft and Justices Van Devanter, Sutherland, and Sanford.

[56] 277 U.S. at 225.

[57] *Id.* at 224.

where an absolute prohibition of sales would be one. *Hatch* v. *Reardon*, 204 U.S. 152, 162.[58]

Although Justice Stone concurred in this dissenting opinion, nevertheless he said in 1942, in *Jones* v. *City of Opelika*,[59] that one reason among others that "a license tax laid specifically on the privilege of disseminating ideas would infringe the right of free speech" is that "if the state may tax the privilege it may fix the rate of tax and, through the tax, control or suppress the activity which it taxes"—citing the *Magnano* and the *Grosjean* cases. And in 1943 Justice Douglas cited the *Magnano* case in *Murdock* v. *Commonwealth of Pennsylvania*,[60] to support the statement that "the power to tax the exercise of a privilege is the power to control or suppress its enjoyment."

These two cases involved the validity of convictions of Jehovah's Witnesses for engaging in certain activities without first obtaining the licenses required by city ordinances, which could only be obtained on payment of specified charges. The case which is reported under the name of *Jones* v. *Opelika* involved not only the license required in Opelika, Ala., but also those required in Fort Smith, Ark., and Casa Grande, Arizona. The license fee in Opelika was $10 per annum for book agents and $5 for transient agents—it was not quite clear in which category the petitioner fell. He was convicted for displaying religious pamphlets without a license on a city street and selling them two for five cents. In Fort Smith the ordinance required a license for "peddling dry goods, notions, wearing apparel, household goods or other articles." The petitioners were convicted for going from house to house without a license and distributing religious books (held to come under the head of "other articles") in return for a contribution of 25 cents. In some cases they gave them away free. The charge for the license was $25 per month, $10 per week, $2.50 per day. In Casa Grande, a town of 1,545 in 1940, transient street vendors were made subject to a quarterly license fee of $25, payable in advance, and petitioners were convicted for activities similar to those in Fort Smith. In *Murdock* v. *Pennsylvania* the petitioner had been convicted for selling "merchandise" without a license required by an ordinance of the City of Jeanette, which could be procured only by paying $1.50 for one day, $7 for one week, $12 for two weeks, or

[58] *Id.* at 223.

[59] 316 U.S. 584, 607 (1942).

[60] 319 U.S. 105, 112 (1943).

$20 for three weeks. Petitioner "sold" books and pamphlets from door to door for 25 cents and 5 cents, respectively, but accepted smaller sums or donated the literature to those without funds.

The *Opelika* case (with its two companion cases) was first decided on June 8, 1942. By a five-to-four decision the ordinances were held valid. The majority consisted of Justice Reed (who wrote the opinion) and Justices Roberts, Frankfurter, Byrnes, and Jackson. Chief Justice Stone wrote a dissenting opinion in which Justices Black, Douglas, and Murphy joined, and Justice Murphy wrote another dissenting opinion, in which Stone, Black, and Douglas joined.[61] A rehearing was ordered. Before it was held, Justice Byrnes left the Court and was succeeded by Justice Rutledge. On May 3, 1943, in a *per curiam* opinion,[62] the previous decision was overruled and the judgments for conviction were reversed, "for the reasons stated in the opinion of the Court" in *Murdock* v. *Pennsylvania,* "decided this day, and in the dissenting opinions filed in the present cases after the argument last term." Justice Reed wrote a dissenting opinion, appended in the official report to *Murdock* v. *Pennsylvania,* in which Roberts, Frankfurter, and Jackson joined, and Justice Frankfurter another, in which Jackson joined. Jackson meanwhile expressed his dissent to this and to another decision of the same day in his concurring opinion to *Douglas* v. *City of Jeanette,*[63] in which the Court affirmed the dismissal of a suit to enjoin enforcement of the Jeanette ordinance for lack of any evidence that the local authorities were likely to attempt to enforce the ordinance which the *Murdock* case held unconstitutional.[64] Thus, it will be seen that the views of the Court are to be found in the opinion of Justice Douglas in the *Murdock* case and in the separate dissenting opinions of Chief Justice Stone and Justice Murphy in the first *Opelika* case; while those of the minority are to be found in the prevailing opinion of Justice Reed in the first *Opelika* case and his dissenting opinion in the *Murdock* case, in Justice Frankfurter's dissent in that case, and in Justice Jackson's concurring opinion in *Douglas* v. *City of Jeanette.*

[61] A further brief dissenting opinion (at 623) by Black, Douglas, and Murphy states that they now believe that the flag-salute case of Minersville School District v. Gobitis, 310 U.S. 586, in which they concurred, was wrongly decided, and foreshadows the overruling of that case in 1943 in West Virginia State Board of Education v. Barnette, 319 U.S. 624.

[62] 319 U.S. 103 (1943).

[63] 319 U.S. 157, 166 (1943).

[64] The other decision with which Jackson expressed disagreement was Martin v. City of Struthers, 319 U.S. 141, which held an ordinance unconstitutional which made it unlawful to ring doorbells for the purpose of distributing handbills or circulars.

All the judges seemed to agree that since reasonable regulation of the manner of distributing religious literature would be permissible, a nominal fee might be charged in order to defray the expense of such regulation. All except Jackson seemed to agree that this was not such a case. He said, "there is not a syllable of evidence that this amount [in the *Murdock* case] exceeds the cost to the community of policing this activity." [65] He was not explicit on the fees charged in the other cases. Again, all agreed that the distribution of *commercial* advertising matter in the streets could be subjected to a charge not only high enough to cover the expense of regulation but also sufficient to yield a revenue to the city. Such a charge would not be a tax on the exercise of a constitutional right, since it had been held as late as 1942, in the unanimous decision in *Valentine* v. *Christensen*,[66] that such activities could be prohibited outright, even though "a civic appeal, or a moral platitude," were appended to the advertising matter. There was disagreement as to whether this principle applied to the activities of the Witnesses, whose practice was to offer religious pamphlets to those who would make a "contribution" of twenty-five cents or less, but to give them free to those who would not contribute. The "mere fact," said Justice Douglas in the *Murdock* case, "that the religious literature is 'sold' by itinerant preachers rather than 'donated' does not transform evangelism into a commercial enterprise." [67] Justice Reed, on the other hand, said in the first *Opelika* decision:

> If we were to assume, as is here argued, that the licensed activities involve religious rites, a different question would be presented. These are not taxes on free will offerings. But it is because we view these sales as partaking more of commercial than religious or educational transactions that we find the ordinances, as here presented, valid. A tax on religion or a tax on interstate commerce may alike be forbidden by the Constitution. It does not follow that licenses for selling Bibles or for manufacture of articles of general use, measured by extrastate sales, must fall.[68]

But the dispute between the majority and the minority went deeper than a controversy as to whether the activities in question were to be characterized as "religious" or "commercial." Reed here seems to have conceded that any tax at all on religious activities might have been bad.[69] On the other hand, any tax at all, however repressive,

[65] 319 U.S. at 177. [66] 316 U.S. 52 (1942). [67] 319 U.S. at 111.
[68] 316 U.S. at 598.
[69] In his Murdock dissent he was more cautious. "This dissent," he said (319 U.S. at 118–119), "does not express, directly or by inference, any conclusion as to the constitu-

would be valid on purely commercial street activities, since the *Valentine* case held that they could be forbidden outright. Yet Reed did not insist that a tax would be valid which would act as a "substantial clog" on these activities of the Jehovah's Witnesses. He must have thought that they fell in an intermediate category.

In the first *Opelika* decision, he maintained that, since the pleadings had not specifically attacked the size of the fees,

> there is not before us the question of the power to lay fees, objectionable in their effect because of their size, upon the constitutionally protected rights of free speech, press or the exercise of religion. . . . In the circumstances we venture no opinion concerning the validity of license taxes if it were proved, or at least distinctly claimed, that the burden of the tax was a substantial clog upon activities of the sort here involved. [Footnote citations.] The sole constitutional question considered is whether a nondiscriminatory license fee, presumably appropriate in amount, may be imposed upon these activities.[70]

Reed held that the tax was valid because not shown to be excessive in amount. In his dissent in the *Murdock* case, however, he indicated clearly that he would regard an excessive tax on these activities (unlike a repressive tax or even an outright prohibition of street distribution of commercial advertising) as unconstitutional and that he did not share Marshall's belief that the judiciary was unfit to inquire into the question what degree of taxation is the legitimate use, and what degree an abuse, of the taxing power.

> It has never been thought before [he said] that freedom from taxation was a perquisite attaching to the privileges of the First Amendment. . . .
>
> It is urged that such a tax as this may be used readily to restrict the dissemination of ideas. This must be conceded but the possibility of misuse does not make a tax unconstitutional. No abuse is claimed here. The ordinances in some of these cases are the general occupation license type covering many businesses. In the Jeanette prosecutions, the ordinance involved lays the usual tax on canvassing or soliciting sales of goods, wares and merchandise. It was passed in 1898. Every power of taxation or regulation is capable of abuse. Each one to some extent prohibits the free exercise of religion and abridges the freedom of the press but that is hardly a reason for denying the power. If the tax is used oppressively the law will protect the victims of such action.[71]

Frankfurter likewise maintained that the validity of a tax on a privilege protected by the First Amendment depends on its effect. If

tional rights of state or federal governments to place a privilege tax upon the soliciting of a free-will contribution for religious purposes."

[70] 316 U.S. at 592–593.

[71] 319 U.S. at 130.

it discriminates against the particular privilege, or actually suppresses the enjoyment of a constitutional privilege, it is bad, but not otherwise.

A tax upon newspaper publishing [he said] is not invalid simply because it falls upon the exercise of a constitutional right. Such a tax might be invalid if it invidiously singled out newspaper publishing for bearing the burdens of taxation or imposed upon them in such ways as to encroach on the essential scope of a free press. If the Court could justifiably hold that the tax measures in these cases were vulnerable on that ground, I would unreservedly agree. But the Court has not done so, and indeed could not.[72]

And again:

The power to tax, like all powers of government, legislative, executive and judicial alike, can be abused or perverted. The power to tax is the power to destroy only in the sense that those who have power can abuse it. Mr. Justice Holmes disposed of this smooth phrase as a constitutional basis for invalidating taxes when he wrote "The power to tax is not the power to destroy while this Court sits." *Panhandle Oil Co.* v. *State of Mississippi* ex rel. *Knox* . . . The fact that power can be perverted does not mean that every exercise of the power is a perversion of the power. Thus, if a tax indirectly suppresses or controls the enjoyment of a constitutional privilege which a legislature cannot directly suppress or control, of course it is bad. But it is irrelevant that a tax can suppress or control if it does not. The Court holds that "Those who can tax the exercise of this religious practice can make its exercise so costly as to deprive it of the resources necessary for its maintenance." But this is not the same as saying that "Those who do tax the exercise of this religious practice have made its exercise so costly as to deprive it of the resources necessary for its maintenance."

The Court could not plausibly make such an assertion because the petitioners themselves disavow any claim that the taxes imposed in these cases impair their ability to exercise their constitutional rights. We cannot invalidate the tax measures before us simply because there may be others, not now before us, which are oppressive in their effect.[73]

The majority, however, insisted that these particular license taxes actually were restrictive of freedom of the press and of religion. While indicating that any form of tax on these activities would be bad, Chief Justice Stone laid particular stress on the form and size of these particular taxes. Defendants' challenge to the ordinances, he said, "is a challenge to the substantial taxes which they impose, in specified amounts, and not to some tax of a different or lesser amount which some other ordinance might levy." [74] Speaking of some of Reed's contentions that the amount of the tax had not been chal-

[72] *Id.* at 136. [73] *Id.* at 137–138. [74] 316 U.S. at 603.

lenged, that it had not been shown that it acted as a substantial clog on the activities, and the like, he said:

All these are considerations which would seem to be irrelevant to the question now before us—whether a flat tax, more than a nominal fee to defray the expenses of a regulatory license, can constitutionally be laid on a noncommercial, non-profit activity devoted exclusively to the dissemination of ideas, educational and religious in character, to those persons who consent to receive them.[75]

Pointing out that "it is the collection of funds which has been seized upon to justify the extension, to the defendants' activities, of the tax laid upon business callings," [76] he continued:

It lends no support to the present tax to insist that its restraint on free speech and religion is non-discriminatory because the same levy is made upon business callings carried on for profit, many of which involve no question of freedom of speech and religion and all of which involve commercial elements—lacking here—which for present purposes may be assumed to afford a basis for taxation apart from the exercise of freedom of speech and religion. The constitutional protection of the Bill of Rights is not to be evaded by classifying with business callings an activity whose sole purpose is the dissemination of ideas, and taxing it as business callings are taxed. The immunity which press and religion enjoy may be lost when they are united with other activities not immune. *Valentine* v. *Christensen* . . . . But here the only activities involved are the dissemination of ideas, educational and religious, and the collection of funds for the propagation of those ideas, which we have said is likewise the subject of constitutional protection. *Schneider* v. *State* [308 U.S. 147]; *Cantwell* v. *Connecticut,* 310 U.S. 296, 304–307.

The First Amendment is not confined to safeguarding freedom of speech and freedom of religion against discriminatory attempts to wipe them out. On the contrary the Constitution, by virtue of the First and Fourteenth Amendments, has put those freedoms in a preferred position. Their commands are not restricted to cases where the protected privilege is sought out for attack. They extend at least to every form of taxation which, because it is a condition of the exercise of the privilege, is capable of being used to control or suppress it.

Even were we to assume—what I do not concede—that there could be a lawful non-discriminatory license tax of a percentage of the gross receipts collected by churches and other religious orders in support of their religious work, ... we have no such tax here. The tax imposed by the ordinances in these cases is more burdensome and destructive of the activity taxed than any gross receipts tax. The tax is for a fixed amount, unrelated to the extent of the defendants' activities or the receipts derived from them. It is thus the type of flat tax which, when applied to interstate commerce,

[75] 316 U.S. at 604.

[76] *Id.* at 607.

has repeatedly been deemed by this Court to be prohibited by the commerce clause. See *McGoldrick* v. *Berwind-White Coal Mining Co.*, 309 U.S. 33, 55–57, and cases cited; cf. *Best & Co.* v. *Maxwell*, 311 U.S. 454, 456. When applied as it is here to activities involving the exercise of religious freedom, its vice is emphasized in that it is levied and paid in advance of the activities taxed, and applied at rates well calculated to suppress those activities save only as others may volunteer to pay the tax. It requires a sizable out-of-pocket expense by someone who may never succeed in raising a penny in his exercise of the privilege which is taxed.[77]

Stone concluded his opinion by saying:

In its potency as a prior restraint on publication the flat license tax falls short only of outright censorship or suppression. The more humble and needy the cause, the more effective is the suppression.[78]

In the *Murdock* case Douglas repeated some of Stone's reasoning. The contention, he said, "that the fact that the license can suppress or control this activity is unimportant if it does not do so," disregards the nature of this tax.[79]

It is [he continued] a license tax—a flat tax imposed on the exercise of a privilege granted by the Bill of Rights. A state may not impose a charge for the enjoyment of a right granted by the federal constitution. Thus, it may not exact a license tax for the privilege of carrying on interstate commerce (*McGoldrick* v. *Berwind-White Co.*, 309 U.S. 33, 56–58), although it may tax the property used in, or the income derived from, that commerce, so long as those taxes are not discriminatory. Id., 309 U.S. at page 47 and cases cited . . .

Douglas, like Stone, stressed the fact that the license tax "is fixed in amount and unrelated to the scope of the activities of petitioners or to their realized revenues," and that "it restrains in advance those constitutional liberties of press and religion and inevitably tends to suppress their exercise." [80]

So it may not be said [he continued] that proof is lacking that these license taxes either separately or cumulatively have restricted or are likely to restrict petitioners' religious activities. On their face they are a restriction of the free exercise of those freedoms which are protected by the First Amendment.

In the first *Opelika* decision Reed had insisted that "the First Amendment does not require a subsidy in the form of fiscal exemption." [81] And he repeated this objection in his dissent in the *Murdock* case, saying:

[77] *Id.* at 608–609.
[78] *Id.* at 611.
[79] 319 U.S. at 113.
[80] *Id.* at 113–114.
[81] 316 U.S. 599.

This decision forces a tax subsidy notwithstanding our accepted belief in the separation of church and state. Instead of all bearing equally the burdens of government, this Court now fastens upon the communities the entire cost of policing the sales of religious literature. . . . The distributors of religious literature, possibly of all informatory publications, become today privileged to carry on their occupations without contributing their share to the support of the government which provides the opportunity for the exercise of their liberties.[82]

At an earlier point he said, speaking of the First Amendment:

"Free" cannot be held to be without cost but rather its meaning must accord with the freedom guaranteed. "Free" means a privilege to print or pray without permission and without accounting to authority for one's actions.[83]

The majority agreed, it will be recalled, that a fee sufficient to defray the cost of regulating the activities might be charged. If charged less, the participants in such activities might well be said to be subsidized, in that they would be imposing a cost on the community without defraying it. In conceding the propriety of a "nominal" fee, the majority seems to have contemplated defraying the expense which the licensing regulations themselves would involve. They stressed the fact that these particular licenses had no regulatory purpose. Reed, on the other hand, had in mind the additional cost of policing which the activities of the Witnesses imposed on the cities in which they operated; for while these particular petitioners were not accused of conduct other than peaceful, the activities of Jehovah's Witnesses were, to say the least, provocative and might necessitate more policing in order to prevent attacks on them by members of other religious sects whose tenets they were impugning. Murphy, however, considered that the question whether the Witnesses should be made to contribute to such expenses did not arise.

Respondents do not show [he said] that the instant activities of Jehovah's Witnesses create special problems causing a drain on the municipal coffers, or that these taxes are commensurate with any expenses entailed by the presence of the Witnesses. In the absence of such a showing I think no tax whatever can be levied on petitioners' activities in distributing their literature or disseminating their ideas. If the guaranties of freedom of speech and freedom of the press are to be preserved, municipalities should not be free to raise general revenue by taxes on the circulation of information and opinion in non-commercial causes; other sources can be found, the taxation of which will not choke off ideas. Taxes such as the instant

[82] 319 U.S. at 130–131.

[83] *Id.* at 122.

ones violate petitioners' right to freedom of speech and freedom of the press, protected against state invasion by the Fourteenth Amendment.[84]

If the minority thought that the taxes were valid and that immunity from them constituted a subsidy, merely because they were levied to defray the cost of policing the Witnesses' activities, the difference comes down to a question of the burden of proof. The minority insisted that the burden was on the Witnesses to show that the taxes exceeded the cost of policing their activities, while the majority maintained that the burden was on the municipalities to prove that they did not. Justice Frankfurter, however, went further. He maintained that as long as the taxes did not "in fact" cramp religious activities they were justified as a contribution not merely to the expense to the municipalities entailed by the presence of the Witnesses but also to the cost of other municipal activities from which the Witnesses derived benefit, even though their presence added nothing to that cost. He said, in concluding his dissenting opinion:

> The ultimate question in determining the constitutionality of a tax measure is—has the state given something for which it can ask a return? There can be no doubt that these petitioners, like all who use the streets, have received the benefits of government. Peace is maintained, traffic is regulated, health is safeguarded—these are only some of the many incidents of municipal administration. To secure them costs money, and a state's source of money is its taxing power. There is nothing in the Constitution which exempts persons engaged in religious activities from sharing equally in the costs of benefits to all, including themselves, provided by government.
>
> I cannot say, therefore, that in these cases the community has demanded a return for that which it did not give. Nor am I called upon to say that the state has demanded unjustifiably more than the value of what it gave, nor that its demand in fact cramps activities pursued to promote religious beliefs. No such claim was made at the bar, and there is no evidence in the records to substantiate any such claim if it had been made. Under these circumstances, therefore, I am of opinion that the ordinances in these cases must stand.[85]

The majority, however, did not insist that those engaged in religious activities were exempt from contributing to the general expenses of government. "It is one thing," said Douglas, "to impose a tax on the income or property of a preacher. It is quite another thing to exact a tax from him for the privilege of delivering a sermon." [86] Although these Witnesses, being nonresidents, would hardly be likely

[84] 316 U.S. at 620. [85] 319 U.S. at 140. [86] *Id.* at 112.

to pay income or property taxes to the municipalities, nevertheless, should they make purchases in them, they would doubtless have to pay any sales taxes which the municipalities might impose for the purpose of defraying general municipal expenses. Conceding that a license tax may be exacted when "the state has given something for which it can ask a return," Douglas held this principle inapplicable here. Evidently he meant that to be applicable the state must be giving something specifically when it grants the license, not merely general benefits such as the safeguarding of health, which would be available regardless of the license. The tax here, he said, "is not a charge for the enjoyment of a privilege or benefit bestowed by the state. The privilege in question exists apart from state authority. It is guaranteed the people by the federal constitution." [87]

The privilege of selling general merchandise was apparently not regarded as one guaranteed by the Constitution, and the state (or city) could therefore charge for bestowing it by the grant of a license. For this reason, thought Douglas, following Stone's line of reasoning in the *Opelika* case, the "nondiscriminatory" character of the ordinance does not save it. In the preceding paragraph he said:

> A license tax certainly does not acquire constitutional validity because it classifies the privileges protected by the First Amendment along with the wares and merchandise of hucksters and peddlers and treats them all alike. Such equality in treatment does not save the ordinance. Freedom of press, freedom of speech, freedom of religion are in a preferred position.

Under these various ordinances, Jehovah's Witnesses would have been permitted to carry on their activities without a license had they refrained from asking "contributions" in exchange for their literature; and they would have been permitted to ask contributions, had they first paid the taxes for licenses. In either event, activities such as theirs would have been rendered impossible to those who could not afford to do without the contributions on the one hand or to pay the taxes on the other, however feasible it might still be for people of greater means to carry on similar activities. But freedom of speech, press, and religion, said Douglas, "are available to all, not merely to those who can pay their own way." [88] And as Murphy put it,

> It matters not that petitioners asked contributions for their literature. Freedom of speech and freedom of the press cannot and must not mean freedom only for those who can distribute their broadsides without charge.

[87] 319 U.S. at 115.

[88] *Id.* at 111.

There may be others with messages more vital but purses less full, who must seek some reimbursement for their outlay or else forego passing on their ideas. The pamphlet, an historic weapon against oppression,[89] *Lovell* v. *Griffin*, 303 U.S. 444, 452, is today the convenient vehicle of those with limited resources because newspaper space and radio time are expensive and the cost of establishing such enterprises great. If freedom of speech and freedom of the press are to have any concrete meaning, people seeking to distribute information and opinion, to the end only that others shall have the benefit thereof, should not be taxed for circulating such matter.[90]

"The more humble and needy the cause," said Stone in language already quoted, "the more effective is the suppression" of a flat license tax.

There may be good ground for holding that freedom of speech, press, and religion should be construed as precluding governments from imposing taxes, as well as criminal penalties, on the exercise of such freedoms, even when the taxes are imposed for the purpose of raising revenue without any purpose to restrict the freedoms. The effect of even light taxes on any activity, regardless of their purpose, will be to restrict the freedom of those who cannot afford the tax to engage in it. And the policy back of the First Amendment may be thought to make the freedoms which it protects available to the poor as well as to the rich. These particular freedoms, as both Stone and Douglas declared, may occupy "a preferred position." But to say, as did Douglas, that "a state may not impose a charge for the enjoyment of a right granted by the federal constitution," would seem to be going too far when applied to rights outside the First Amendment. Earning a salary in any ordinary occupation would seem to be a right granted by the Constitution, yet a tax on the salary would surely be constitutional. Douglas himself intimated that a state might even tax the salary of a preacher. Yet the tax is a charge for having earned money. In the *Magnano* case a tax was sustained on the manufacture of butter-substitutes, though it was assumed that the privilege of manufacturing them was granted by the Constitution, in that a statute directly forbidding it would be invalid. As Holmes said in his dissent in the *Panhandle* case, "A tax is not an unconstitutional regulation in every case where an absolute prohibition of sales would be one."

It is to be doubted whether Douglas would hold every sales tax bad

[89] He pointed out in a footnote that "the pamphlets of [Thomas] Paine were not distributed gratuitously."

[90] 316 U.S. at 619.

which falls on sales which could not be prohibited absolutely. Yet that would seem to be the logic of his broad generalization. And in a dissenting opinion rendered on January 14, 1946, he applied this principle to reach the conclusion that a federal tax on a state for a privilege guaranteed by the Constitution was bad. The case is *New York* v. *United States*.[91] The majority held that the state of New York and its subordinate agencies, which sold mineral waters from the state reservation at Saratoga Springs, were not immune from the federal tax of two cents a gallon on the sale of mineral waters. Douglas, in his dissenting opinion, in which Black joined, maintained that all state agencies (as distinct from citizens who derived income from the state) were entirely immune from federal taxation and that the earlier case of *South Carolina* v. *United States*,[92] which in 1905 had sustained a federal tax on liquor sold by a state monopoly, should be overruled. If the power of the Federal Government to tax the states is conceded, he said, the states

> must pay the federal government for the privilege of exercising the powers of sovereignty guaranteed them by the Constitution [presumably in the Tenth Amendment], whether, as here, they are disposing of their natural resources, or tomorrow they issue securities or perform any other acts within the scope of their police power.[93]

And to sustain the present tax because it does not impair the state's functions of government "overlooks the fact that the power to tax lightly is the power to tax severely." [94] He quoted Marshall's remarks on the subject in *McCulloch* v. *Maryland*.[95]

Not all the judges who had agreed with Douglas in *Murdock* v *Pennsylvania* went along with him now. Rutledge subscribed to an opinion written by Frankfurter sustaining the tax, and added a few words of his own. Stone wrote another opinion sustaining the tax, and this had the concurrence of Murphy as well as of Reed and Burton (who had meanwhile succeeded Roberts). Jackson, serving in Nuremberg as prosecutor of the German war criminals, took no part in the decision. The six judges who sustained the tax agreed that a federal tax on the state would be bad if it discriminated against the state in favor of private persons similarly situated—if, for instance, it had imposed a higher tax on mineral waters bottled by the state than on those bottled privately. Frankfurter intimated that as long as the fed-

91 326 U.S. 572 (1946).
92 199 U.S. 437 (1905).
93 326 U.S. at 595.
94 *Id.* at 594.
95 *Id.* at 597.

eral tax was nondiscriminatory it would be valid, though he admitted that the state could not be subjected to a federal property tax on its Statehouse, or to a federal income tax on its tax revenues.[96] Stone, pointing out that admittedly invalid taxes such as these might be nondiscriminatory, rejected the proposition that every nondiscriminatory tax on a state must be valid.[97] The test he would apply is the "practical" one of "whether such a non-discriminatory tax unduly interferes with the performance of the state's functions of government." In sustaining this particular tax he said:

> It is enough for present purposes that the immunity of the state from federal taxation would, in this case, accomplish a withdrawal from the taxing power of the nation a subject of taxation of a nature which has been traditionally within that power from the beginning. Its exercise now, by a non-discriminatory tax, does not curtail the business of the state government more than it does the like business of the citizen. It gives merely an accustomed and reasonable scope to the federal taxing power. Such a withdrawal from a non-discriminatory federal tax, and one which does not bear on the state any differently than on the citizen, is itself an impairment of the taxing power of the national government, and the activity taxed is such that its taxation does not unduly impair the state's functions of government. The nature of the tax immunity requires that it be so construed as to allow to each government reasonable scope for its taxing power, *Metcalf & Eddy* v. *Mitchell*, 269 U.S. 514, 524. The national taxing power would be unduly curtailed if the state, by extending its activities, could withdraw from it subjects of taxation traditionally within it. [Citations.] [98]

It is not quite clear whether Stone's conclusion that the taxation of this activity "does not unduly impair the state's functions of government" is based on the smallness of the tax or on the view that the particular function is not a vital one. A tax of two cents a gallon is not likely seriously to curtail the mineral water business, whether carried on by a state or by private individuals. But suppose the purveyors of some competing product induced Congress to raise the tax on mineral waters to a dollar a gallon. Such a tax, being nondiscriminatory, would not, it is true, "curtail the business of the state government more than it does the like business of the citizen." But it would probably completely suppress the business of both. It would be hard to resist the conclusion that such a tax does "unduly impair the state's functions of government," if the sale of the products of its natural resources is one of those functions which is to be protected

96 *Id.* at 582. 97 *Id.* at 587–588. 98 *Id.* at 588–589.

from undue impairment. But the majority could reach such a conclusion only by rejecting the dogma that the power to tax lightly is the power to tax severely. Whether it would do so the opinion does not state.[99]

While the state business of selling mineral water is held not to be immune from a nondiscriminatory federal sales tax, there remain state activities which are immune from federal taxation, and federal activities immune from state taxation. Where the immunity prevails, the fact that the purpose of the tax is to raise revenue rather than to repress the activity does not render the tax valid. Nor does the fact that a tax produces revenue, or was even designed primarily for that purpose, save it, when it is laid on the exercise of one of the privileges protected by the First Amendment. The newspaper tax which was upset in *Grosjean* v. *American Press Co.* would probably have yielded large revenue, and the ordinances held invalid in the various cases affecting Jehovah's Witnesses were designed originally for revenue purposes. But while the income of those who exercise the privileges of free press and free religion may be taxed like other incomes, and the property used in connection with these activities likewise, the act of exercising those privileges may not be taxed at all—whether the motive for the tax be repression or simply revenue. Those privileges occupy a "preferred position."

[99] Stone's rejection of a quantitative test elsewhere in the opinion does not refer to such a test as applied to the size of the tax or the effect on the state's functions. It refers rather to the effect on the federal fiscal resources of the withdrawal of the particular subject from federal taxation. What Stone said in this connection follows (at p. 590): "Since all taxes must be laid by general, that is, workable, rules, the effect of the immunity on the national taxing power is to be determined not quantitatively but by its operation and tendency in withdrawing taxable property or activities from the reach of federal taxation. Not the extent to which a particular state engages in the activity, but the nature and extent of the activity by whomsoever performed is the relevant consideration."

In other words, failure to collect this particular tax on the Saratoga mineral waters might have no very serious effect on federal revenues; for doubtless most of the revenue from the mineral water tax was derived from private sources. But if state immunity were recognized, the states collectively might withdraw these sources from the federal taxing power, by taking over the mineral water business.

Justice Douglas, it should be noted, minimized the fear that increase of state activity would cripple the federal taxing power. Pointing out that we have the federal income tax from which state employees may not claim constitutional exemption (which we did not have when the South Carolina liquor tax case was decided in 1905), he said (at p. 598): "There is no showing whatsoever that an expanding field of state activity even faintly promises to cripple the federal government in its search for needed revenues. If the truth were known, I suspect it would show that the activity of the states in the fields of housing, public power and the like have increased the level of income of the people and have raised the standards of marginal or sub-marginal groups. Such conditions affect favorably, not adversely, the tax potential of the federal government."

But not every right protected by the Constitution is immune from taxation. There are many instances in which prohibition of an act would be unconstitutional, but taxation of it valid. If the purpose of the tax is purely fiscal, it is clearly valid, when laid on activities other than the exercise of "civil liberties," despite the fact that it has the effect of forcing those who cannot afford it to desist from the activity on which it falls. If the fiscal purpose is dominant, even though there be a collateral purpose of discouraging or regulating the activity, the Court has frequently held that it is valid. The tax becomes questionable when the fiscal purpose is merely incidental and the repressive purpose dominant. And it is clearly bad when the enactment itself reveals a purpose to repress what the taxing government may not directly repress—probably even though some revenue would be produced by it. The child labor tax might well have produced some revenue, but the Court thought that the form of the statute itself betrayed the dominance of a regulatory motive.

Whether the mere size of the tax can be considered by the Court is a question which arises in those cases in which the size might reveal a regulatory or repressive purpose and the absence of a fiscal one. If the tax is designed for repression, the more successfully its purpose is realized, the less revenue will it yield. Presumably no federal revenue at all was ever collected from the 10 percent tax on state bank notes, for no state bank would issue notes subject to such a tax. While the Court has frequently professed its inability to draw any inferences from the size of the tax, it has at other times noted the size as evidence of a penal rather than a fiscal purpose. The amount of the tax was one of the factors which in *United States* v. *Constantine*[100] was regarded by Justice Roberts as "significant of penal and prohibitory intent rather than the gathering of revenue." Citing this and other cases in an article published in 1936, Professor J. A. C. Grant reduced the Supreme Court's position to the following paradox:

> In short, "a tax, otherwise lawfully levied, does not become unconstitutional merely because it is unduly burdensome"; *but the fact that it is unduly burdensome may prove that it is not a tax, and hence that it is not lawfully levied.*[101]

100 296 U.S. 287, 47 (1935).

101 *Commerce, Production, and the Fiscal Powers of Congress* (1936) 45 YALE L. J. 751, 760–761. Italics in the original.

Professor Robert E. Cushman also pointed out the Court's ambivalent position in an article published in 1935, from which Professor Grant quoted the following paragraph:

The Magnano case, which relies upon and thus reaffirms the McCray case of 1904, shows that the Court desires to eat its cake and keep it too in the matter of the validity of destructive taxation. No amount of logical analysis will disclose any inherent differences in kind between the child labor tax and the oleomargarine taxes upheld in the McCray case and now in the Magnano case. In both cases the legislative intention was regulation and destruction per se, and all intelligent people, including the Court, were well aware of that fact. But the Court preserves two different techniques for dealing with such statutes. When it wishes to uphold the statute, it utilizes the doctrine of the McCray and Magnano cases, which may be called the doctrine of judicial obtuseness, and refuses to see or know anything about the tax which does not appear in the language of the act. If, however, the act pushes too far and impinges upon interests which the Court feels are entitled to protection, it falls back upon the doctrine of the child labor tax case, takes judicial notice of the palpable legislative intention to destroy rather than to raise money, and declares the act void on the ground that it is not a tax at all but a regulation.[102]

How long the Court will cling to the doctrine that the power to tax lightly is the power to tax severely, or how many of its present members still cling to it, we cannot say. It seems clear that Douglas and Black accept it, while Frankfurter and Reed reject it. The position of the other judges is less clear. Meanwhile it seems certain that if the tax is clearly designed for the raising of revenue, it will be sustained despite the fact that the activity (other than the exercise of a "civil liberty") on which it falls is one which it would be unconstitutional to prohibit outright. That the tax is "a charge for the enjoyment of a right granted by the federal constitution" will not, despite Justice Douglas, be sufficient to render it invalid, provided the right is not protected by the First Amendment. Nor will the fact that the enjoyment of the right will in effect be denied to those to whom its enjoyment is not worth the payment of the tax. In *Sonzinsky* v. *United States*,[103] decided in 1937, it was contended that a federal requirement that every dealer in firearms register with the Collector of Internal Revenue and pay a special excise tax of $200 per year, was an invalid regulation of local matters. But the Court sustained the statute, Justice Stone saying:

102 *Constitutional Law in 1933–34* (1935) 29 AM. POL. SCI. REV. 36, 51.
103 300 U.S. 506 (1937).

Every tax is, in some measure, regulatory. To some extent it interposes an economic impediment to the activity taxed. But a tax is not any the less a tax because it has a regulatory effect [citing cases]; and it has long been established that an act of Congress which on its face purports to be an exercise of the taxing power is not any the less so because the tax is burdensome or tends to restrict or suppress the thing taxed. [Citing cases.] [104]

"One who does a thing," said Justice Sutherland in *Carter* v. *Carter Coal Co.*, in 1936, "in order to avoid a monetary penalty . . . yields to compulsion precisely the same as though he did so to avoid a term in jail." [105] These words are just as applicable to a monetary penalty in the form of a valid fiscal tax as they are to the tax to which Sutherland was referring, which was held invalid. To say, then, that one has a constitutional right to act, or to refrain from acting, in a certain way, does not imply that he is to be free from every kind of governmental compulsion to act differently. In many circumstances a man may be compelled to forego a freedom to which he has a constitutional right in order to avoid a monetary penalty in the form of a valid tax on the activity in question. If he has a constitutional right, a government may not compel him to act differently by subjecting him to imprisonment or a fine for "exercising" his constitutional right; for these penalties themselves violate some of his constitutional rights except when they are justified as means for coercing him to refrain from what he has no constitutional right to do. But for exercising his constitutional right to disobey an order of the Railroad Labor Board, the government may subject him to whatever consequences may flow from publication of his disobedience; for exercising his constitutional right to employ workmen, he may be made to compensate them for accidents for which he is in no way to blame; for exercising his constitutional right to make a contract to pay money, he may be subjected to liability to pay the promised amount; and for exercising a constitutional right to sell or to buy goods, a government may compel him to pay a sales tax. Whoever refrains from doing any of these things in order to avoid the condition which the government attaches to their doing "yields to compulsion precisely the same as though he did so to avoid a term in jail." But the coercion is perfectly valid, notwithstanding his constitutional right.

[104] *Id.* at 513.

[105] 298 U.S. 238, 289 (1936).

EXACTION OF A PRICE AS A PENALTY

Exaction of a price for any article restricts freedom to consume it. Every price, like every tax, is in some measure regulatory and to some extent it interposes an economic impediment to the use of the article for which it is charged. He who refrains from consuming as much as he wishes in order to avoid payment of the price "yields to compulsion precisely the same as though he did so to avoid a term in jail." Whether reasonable or unreasonable, the price acts as "a monetary penalty" on consuming, and it is one which is more effective in restricting the liberty of the poor than of the rich. As we all know, the more money a man has, the freer he is to consume what he wants. Of course, the due process clauses protect liberty only from deprivations practiced by government, not by private individuals. But it is government which makes payment of a price for an article compulsory, in precisely the same way in which it makes payment of a tax levied on the consumer. In either case, the consumer can avoid payment by not consuming the article in question. But if he attempts to consume without paying both the tax and the price which the seller exacts, the government will get after him. But in doing so, it is exercising its fiscal powers in punishing him for failure to pay the tax, and performing its normal function of protecting the seller's property rights in holding the consumer to account for making use of another's property without meeting the owner's terms. The enforcement of a property right, like the collection of a tax, is a valid exertion of governmental power, not because it restricts the consumer's liberty to consume, but for independent reasons. Imprisonment or a fine for making use of specified articles, when not imposed in the course of protecting property or for fiscal reasons, would be bad, unless the Court should hold that under the circumstances there was no constitutional right to use them. While one may have a constitutional right not to be imprisoned or fined for using goods which he can acquire without infringing anyone else's property rights, he has no constitutional right to avoid punishment for infringing those rights, even when they restrict his constitutionally protected liberty.

Taxes which incidentally restrict constitutional liberties have generally been held valid. As we have seen, however, when they have been palpably levied for that express purpose they have sometimes been held void. And even when that is not their purpose, the fact that they restrict liberties protected by the First Amendment has been held to vitiate them. While enforcement of property rights may likewise be held to be ordinarily valid, it is arguable that a state is exceeding its constitutional power when its enforcement of a particular property right enables the owner to exact a highly exorbitant price. As yet, however, the Supreme Court has never so held. Courts have at times, as we saw in a previous chapter, set aside what they have regarded as extortionate contracts or allowed recovery of money paid under the ill-defined concept of duress. But they have done so as a matter of common law, not of constitutional right. Later we shall discuss some cases in which the exertion of private power has been held bad because the power of the private group was thought to have been delegated to it by the state. But it is not generally recognized that the bargaining power to exact a price for the use of property stems from the state's restriction of the liberty of nonowners to make unauthorized use of the property. Such, however, appears to be the fact.

WITHHOLDING A SPECIAL PRIVILEGE AS A PENALTY

State governments and the Federal Government sometimes grant privileges to engage in certain activities which would otherwise be forbidden, or to enjoy certain benefits which would otherwise be withheld. There is no constitutional obligation to grant these privileges. A state does not have to permit its own citizens to do business in corporate form, or to permit a foreign corporation (one incorporated in another state) to do business within its borders, or to permit the use of its streets or highways for business traffic. The Federal Government does not have to operate a post office or to carry periodical literature at a lower rate than that charged for carrying letters. When the states do permit these various activities, or when the Federal Government does carry second class mail at low rates, they are said to be granting privileges which the privileged persons are enjoying by governmental favor, not as a matter of constitutional right. Since the privilege in question can be withheld altogether, it can generally be granted conditionally. The condition may be that the person enjoying the privilege conform to requirements that he would have a constitutional right to resist if they had been imposed upon him by a simple threat of imprisonment. In a decision of the Massachusetts court in 1892 sustaining the power of a city to dismiss a policeman for political activity Holmes made the much-quoted remark that "the petitioner may have a constitutional right to talk politics, but he has no constitutional right to be a policeman." [106] In other words, a state may regulate the activities of the holder of a privilege in a way which would be unconstitutional but for the privilege. Thus, in *Packard* v. *Banton* [107] Justice Sutherland sustained a statute requiring taxicabs to file surety bonds or insurance policies with the state. Declaring that the use of the streets for gain might be prohibited altogether, he added:

> Moreover, a distinction must be observed between the regulation of an activity which may be engaged in as a matter of right and one carried on by government sufferance or permission. In the latter case the power to exclude altogether generally includes the lesser power to condition and may justify a degree of regulation not admissible in the former. [Citation.]

If the regulation which required the filing of surety bonds would not have been admissible with reference to one engaged in an activity as a matter of right, it must be because one has a constitutional right not to be required to file the bonds. But the taxicab owner was not being faced with the alternative of filing the bonds or suffering infringement of some other constitutional right, such as the right to keep out of jail. He could avoid filing the bonds by giving up his taxicab business, which he had no constitutional right to carry on, since the state could have forbidden the use of the streets for gain altogether. Any owner who regarded this alternative as worse than filing the bonds would be forced to do the latter, despite his constitutional right not to do so. Because the state has the greater power to prohibit the use of the streets for gain altogether, it can exert the lesser power to prohibit such use only to those who will not submit to the requirement that they file the bonds. As with the power of taxation, the result is that, to the person to whom the exertion of the state's greater power would be more disastrous, his constitutional right to refuse to file bonds (if he has such a right) is made sterile. There is an incongruity here, because the Constitution is construed to inhibit the state's power to impose the less burdensome restriction, but to permit it full discretion to impose the more burdensome by withholding the privilege. The person affected will therefore yield the enjoyment of the liberty which the Constitution protects (in this case

[106] McAuliffe v. Mayor and Board of Aldermen of New Bedford, 115 Mass. 216, 219 (1892).

[107] 264 U.S. 140, 145 (1924).

the liberty not to file bonds), in order to retain the liberty which he values more highly and holds only on sufferance.

This incongruity Justice Sutherland did not note in 1924 when he rendered the Court's opinion in *Packard* v. *Banton*. In 1926, however, he insisted on the incongruity, speaking for the majority of the Court in *Frost* v. *Railroad Commission of California*.[108] He not only insisted on it; he laid down a doctrine which can in no wise be reconciled with his earlier statement that the power to exclude altogether may justify a degree of regulation not admissible in an activity which may be engaged in as a matter of right.

The Frost brothers were private contract carriers by auto truck. A California statute required every motor carrier for hire to obtain a certificate of convenience and necessity as a condition for the use of the state's highways. Acceptance of such a certificate would subject them to the obligations which the law places on common carriers—obligations to render service (subject to certain exceptions) to all applicants, to charge only "reasonable" rates, etc. Private contract carriers are not subject to such obligations. One incurs them and becomes a common carrier by "dedicating" one's property to a public use or by "professing" to serve the general public as distinct from a particular selected customer. It had been previously held unconstitutional for a state to convert by statute a private carrier into a common carrier.[109] The Frosts failed to apply for a certificate of convenience, and the Railroad Commission issued an order commanding them to desist from transporting property by motor truck over a certain route. They sought a writ of certiorari in the state court to review this order, which writ the state Supreme Court denied. In the words of Justice Sutherland, the state court construed the statute as offering "a special privilege of using the public highways to the private carrier for compensation upon condition that he shall dedicate his property to the *quasi* public use of public transportation." The Frosts brought the case on writ of error to the Federal Supreme Court, which reversed the state court's decision and held invalid the commission's order to desist from the transportation in question. The state's power to condition the grant of a privilege, thought Justice Sutherland for the majority,[110] did not include the power to "impose

108 271 U.S. 583 (1926).

109 Michigan Pub. Utils. Comn. v. Duke, 266 U.S. 570 (1925).

110 Concurring were Taft, C. J., and Van Devanter, Butler, Sanford, and Stone, JJ. Justices Holmes, McReynolds, and Brandeis dissented.

conditions which require the relinquishment of constitutional rights." But to quote him more at length:

That, consistently with the due process clause of the Fourteenth Amendment, a private carrier cannot be converted against his will into a common carrier by mere legislative command, is a rule not open to doubt, and is not brought into question here . . . The naked question which we have to determine, therefore, is whether the state may bring about the same result by imposing the unconstitutional requirement as a condition precedent to the enjoyment of a privilege, which, without so deciding, we shall assume to be within the power of the state altogether to withhold if it sees fit to do so. Upon the answer to this question, the constitutionality of the statute now under review will depend.

There is involved in the inquiry not a single power, but two distinct powers. One of these—the power to prohibit the use of the public highways in proper cases—the state possesses; and the other, the power to compel a private carrier to assume against his will the duties and burdens of a common carrier, the state does not possess. It is clear that any attempt to exert the latter, separately and substantively, must fall before the paramount authority of the Constitution. May it stand in the conditional form in which it is here made? If so, constitutional guaranties, so carefully safeguarded against direct assault, are open to destruction by the indirect, but no less effective, process of requiring a surrender, which, though in form voluntary, in fact lacks none of the elements of compulsion. Having regard to form alone, the act here is an offer to the private carrier of a privilege, which the state may grant or deny, upon a condition which the carrier is free to accept or reject. In reality the carrier is given no choice, except a choice between the rock and the whirlpool—an option to forego a privilege which may be vital to his livelihood or submit to a requirement which may constitute an intolerable burden.

It would be a palpable incongruity to strike down an act of state legislation which, by words of express divestment, seeks to strip the citizen of rights guaranteed by the federal constitution, but to uphold an act by which the same result is accomplished under the guise of a surrender of a right in exchange for a valuable privilege which the state threatens otherwise to withhold. It is not necessary to challenge the proposition that, as a general rule, the state, having power to deny a privilege altogether, may grant it upon such conditions as it sees fit to impose. But the power of the state in that respect is not unlimited, and one of the limitations is that it may not impose conditions which require the relinquishment of constitutional rights. If the state may compel the surrender of one constitutional right as a condition of its favor, it may, in like manner, compel a surrender of all. It is inconceivable that guaranties embedded in the Constitution of the United States may thus be manipulated out of existence.[111]

111 271 U.S. at 592–594.

While a state might demand a surrender of any constitutional right as a condition of its favor, it could only succeed in compelling such a surrender by one who regards it as less vital to him than the favor in question. If the state can withhold its favor altogether, for any reason it sees fit, what harm does it do anyone to be allowed to regain the state's favor in exchange for a constitutional right which he values less? If, to use Sutherland's metaphor, the Constitution permits the state of California to hurl the Frosts on the "rock" (that is, compel them to forego the privilege which is vital to their livelihood), how would it benefit them to have the state forbidden to offer them the alternative of the "whirlpool" (acceptance of the intolerable burden of becoming common carriers)? They may still choose the rock if they prefer. Their real quarrel is not with the fact that the state offered them a burdensome alternative to foregoing their privilege of the use of the highways, but that it could withhold that privilege. What the Court really decided was, not that if the state could withhold the privilege for any reason it saw fit, it could not demand the "relinquishment of a constitutional right" as a condition of granting it, but rather that the state could not withhold the privilege at all when its reason for doing so was to compel acceptance of the condition. What was specifically decided was that the commission's order to desist from use of the highway was unconstitutional. In effect, the holding was that the state was violating, not the constitutional right to avoid the burdens of a common carrier, but the constitutional right to use the highways under the circumstances. This latter constitutional right was not absolute, but neither was the state's power to exclude absolute. Its attempt to exercise the power here was unconstitutional, that is, the Frosts had a constitutional right here not to be excluded, because the only purpose motivating the exclusion was thought to be to exert compulsion to relinquish the enjoyment of another liberty (the liberty to avoid being a common carrier), and that liberty was one of those protected by the Fourteenth Amendment. But because this was the case the Frosts had the other constitutional right to have the state refrain from using its power to exclude for the purpose of penalizing. Had the condition which the state attached to the use of the highways been compliance with some requirement which would have been valid if embodied in a penal statute, there might be no more constitutional objection to enforcing compliance by excluding from the highways than by imprisonment. But since the Frosts had a constitutional right not to be jailed for failing to become common carriers, it was held that they likewise had a constitutional right not to be excluded from the highways for failing to do so.

But if it is beyond the state's power ever to grant a privilege upon conditions "which require the relinquishment of constitutional rights" (more accurately, conditions which require the doing of acts which it would be unconstitutional to require by penal statutes), what becomes of the state's power, which Sutherland admitted "as a general rule," to grant a privilege "upon such conditions as it sees fit to impose"? If the conditions it imposes do not "require the relinquishment of constitutional rights," the state could impose them without granting the privilege. The power to impose them as conditions to the grant of a privilege adds nothing to power which the state otherwise possesses. And the power to exclude altogether, despite *Packard* v. *Banton,* justifies no greater degree of regulation of an activity carried on by government sufferance than would be admissible in the regulation of an activity "which may be engaged in as a matter of right."

But the statement is too broad that a state "may not impose conditions which require the relinquishment of constitutional rights." While the Court has made similar statements in other cases, it has also frequently sustained conditions which required, in the same sense as that in which the phrase was used in the *Frost* case, "relinquishment of constitutional rights." In one such case, *Stephenson* v. *Binford,*[112] Justice Sutherland himself wrote the majority opinion. A Texas statute, among other things, forbade private contract carriers to use the state highways, except on condition that they charge rates no lower than those charged by common carriers. There can be little doubt that Sutherland thought that private carriers, as distinct from common ones, had a constitutional right to charge any rates they saw fit.[113] Thus, the condition which the state imposed upon the grant of the privilege to use the highways was a condition which required the "relinquishment" of a constitutional right. Yet Sutherland sustained it.

112 287 U.S. 251 (1932). Justice Butler dissented, without opinion.

113 See the general tenor of his opinions in Ribnik v. McBride, 277 U.S. 350 (1928) and Williams v. Standard Oil Co., 278 U.S. 235 (1929), and Justice McReynolds's dissenting opinion, in which Sutherland joined, in Nebbia v. New York, 291 U.S. 502 (1934), all of which are discussed *infra*, pp. 418–429.

It is well established law [he said] that the highways of the state are public property; that their primary and preferred use is for private purposes; and that their use for purposes of gain is special and extraordinary, which, generally at least, the legislature may prohibit or condition as it sees fit.[114]

And again,

Here the circumstance which justifies what otherwise might be an unconstitutional interference with the freedom of private contract is that the contract calls for a service, the performance of which contemplates the use of facilities belonging to the state; and it would be strange doctrine which, while recognizing the power of the state to regulate the use itself, would deny its power to regulate the contract so far as it contemplates the use.[115]

And it may be said

that it belongs to the state, "as master in its own house," to prescribe the terms upon which persons will be permitted to contract in respect of the use of the public highways for purposes of gain.[116]

In other words, the fact that the condition imposed on the grant of the privilege requires the relinquishment of a constitutional right is not conclusive of invalidity. Unlike the power to imprison, the power to exclude from the highways (or to control any other privilege) may sometimes be used to penalize noncompliance with a requirement with which one has a "constitutional right" not to comply. The requirement, however, must apparently be one which is in some way germane to the purposes which justify control of the privilege. In this case, Justice Sutherland declared that "the assailed provisions . . . are not ends in and of themselves, but means to the legitimate end of conserving the highways." [117] Any "diversion of traffic from the highways to the railroads must correspondingly relieve the former, and, therefore, contribute directly to their conservation." The provision authorizing the commission to fix minimum rates for private contract carriers not lower than those fixed for railroads "has a definite tendency to relieve the highways by diverting traffic from them to the railroads." [118] The *Frost* case, said the Justice, presented "an entirely different question." This is true. But the difference does not lie in there being any less of a requirement in Texas than in California that a constitutional right be relinquished. There is a narrower difference, which Sutherland proceeded to point out. In the *Frost* case, he said in *Stephenson* v. *Binford*,

[114] 287 U.S. at 264.
[115] *Id.* at 274.
[116] *Id.* at 276.
[117] *Id.* at 272.
[118] *Id.* at 273–274.

the California act, as construed by the highest court of the state, was in no real sense a regulation of the use of the highways. Its purpose was to protect the business of those who were common carriers in fact by controlling competitive conditions. . . . The condition which constrained the private carrier to become a common carrier, therefore, had no relation to the highways. In this view, the use of the highways furnished a purely unrelated occasion for imposing the unconstitutional condition, affording no firmer basis for that condition than would have been the case if the contract carrier were using a road in private ownership.[119]

So an "unconstitutional condition" ceases to be unconstitutional when it is imposed on a "related occasion"—related, that is, to the purposes which generally justify withholding of the privilege. Even when unrelated, it is not really the condition that is unconstitutional, but the denial of the privilege when the purpose of the denial is to enforce acceptance of the unrelated condition, and when the condition requires conduct that could not validly be compelled by threat of imprisonment.

As *Stephenson* v *Binford* demonstrates, however, conduct that could not be compelled by threat of imprisonment may nevertheless be compelled by threat to withhold a privilege, provided it is "related" conduct. A constitutional right not to be coerced into a certain course of conduct by imprisonment may or may not imply a constitutional right not to be coerced into the same course of conduct as a condition to the enjoyment of a privilege, depending on the circumstances, just as it may or may not imply a similar right not to be coerced by fear of taxation.

If it were true, as Sutherland declared in the *Frost* case, that it is always unconstitutional for a state to compel conduct as the condition to the enjoyment of a privilege, whenever that same conduct could not be compelled by threat of imprisonment, then the right of private property would be seriously curtailed. The analogy between conditions which the state attaches to the grant of a privilege and those which a private owner attaches to a lease was pointed out by Justice Field as long ago as 1877 in a dissenting opinion in *Munn* v. *Illinois*.[120] Field

[119] 287 U.S. at 275. The validity of the "non-communist" oath required of officers of a union as a condition to the enjoyment by the union of the privileges granted by the Labor Relations Act was sustained by a divided court in American Communications Ass'n v. Douds, 339 U.S. 382 (1950). On March 3, 1952, the New York Feinberg Law, which conditioned the privilege of teaching in the public schools on refraining from certain "subversive" activities, expressions of opinion and associations, was sustained by a divided court in Adler v. Board of Education, 342 U.S. 485.

[120] 94 U.S. 113, 149 (1877).

was dissenting from the majority decision that a state had power to regulate the charges of grain elevators, these being, in the majority view, "affected with a public interest." In the course of his dissent Field conceded the state's power to regulate the prices charged by those to whom it had granted special privileges, saying:

> The State in such cases exercises no greater right than an individual may exercise over the use of his own property when leased or loaned to others. The conditions upon which the privilege shall be enjoyed being stated or implied in the legislation authorizing the grant, no right is, of course, impaired by their enforcement. The recipient of the privilege, in effect, stipulates to comply with the conditions.

The stipulation, however, is made under compulsion, as Sutherland pointed out in the *Frost* case; but so, too, is the stipulation made in order to enjoy the use of another's property. The compulsion is in both cases supplied by the state. If Frost would not stipulate to become a common carrier, the state was prepared to deny him freedom to use the highways. If one will not stipulate to accept the conditions imposed by a private owner, the state is prepared to deny him freedom to make use of the property in question. And the owner's conditions may require the "relinquishment of constitutional rights" in exactly the same sense as that in which the California law required such relinquishment; that is, they may require the other party to engage in conduct which it would be unconstitutional for the state to require, except as a condition for giving its permission, at the owner's behest, to the use of the property. The owner, for instance, in the normal course of transactions, requires a tenant to pay money which he has a "constitutional right" to keep, or an employee to render services to him and to him alone which he has a "constitutional right" to render to someone else or not to render at all. And if the use of the owner's property happens to be vital to the other person's livelihood, the latter's choice, like that of the Frost brothers, is only "a choice between the rock and the whirlpool." But the constitutional right to use the highways when the state's only purpose in denying that use is to force acceptance of an unrelated condition does not imply a constitutional right to use other people's property, even though the owner's purpose in having the state continue to deny that use is to force acceptance of a condition. Perhaps it could be said that the mere fact that the owner imposes a condition on the use of his property makes that condition one that is "related" to the state's function in enforcing the property right. The main purpose of protecting property rights is to promote the owner's wishes in regard to the use of whatever he owns. It is because the state's enforcement of property rights forces the nonowner to accept conditions laid down by the owner, rather than by the state itself, that no question arises as to the germaneness of those conditions, or as to whether they require the "relinquishment of constitutional rights." The state's power to compel acceptance of "unconstitutional conditions" of its own formulation, while it exists, is nevertheless subject to limitations. The legislature's policy in imposing conditions to be enforced by restrictions on the freedom of those who will not comply with them is subjected to judicial scrutiny on constitutional grounds, from which a private owner's policy is exempt. Delegation to the private owner of the legislative function of formulating policy which the state will enforce renders the state's enforcement valid in some cases in which it would not be had the legislative power not been delegated. As we shall see in Chapter XI, it would be impossible for the courts to observe consistently the maxim often enunciated that delegation makes the legislative power invalid.[121]

WITHHOLDING MONEY AS A PENALTY

There is one particular privilege which a government may withhold entirely or grant conditionally, and that is the privilege of receiving funds from the public treasury. Withholding funds would ordinarily have a fiscal purpose, just as does any tax calculated to yield revenue. It is not often, then, that one can complain because he is offered public money only on condition that he act in a way in which the government could not compel him to act by means of threats to imprison him. He has a right to keep out of jail, whether he exercises his constitutional liberty or not. Ordinarily he has no right to government funds, and accordingly they may be either de-

121 The doctrine of "unconstitutional conditions" had its origin when the courts were confronted with the efforts of states to encroach on what was thought to be the proper sphere of the federal government or of other states. The doctrine was invoked to nullify conditions imposed on the privilege of foreign corporations to do business in the state, when the conditions would require them to refrain from invoking the jurisdiction of federal courts in appropriate cases, or to pay taxes to the state on property located elsewhere.

For a more thorough examination of the doctrine see Gerard C. Henderson, THE POSITION OF FOREIGN CORPORATIONS IN AMERICAN CONSTITUTIONAL LAW (1918); Maurice H. Merrill, *Unconstitutional Conditions* (1929) 77 U. of PA. L. REV. 879; R. L. Hale *Unconstitutional Conditions and Constitutional Rights* (1935) 35 COL. L. REV. 321.

nied to him outright or offered conditionally if he will forego the exercise of some constitutional liberty. This is another of the ways in which a government may validly restrict a liberty to which a man has a constitutional right. If he foregoes the "exercise of his constitutional right" because foregoing it is less of an evil to him than doing without the money, he is not foregoing it freely, but under compulsion.

He may not be aware of the compulsion. As in the case of private bargaining, the offer of money may be so welcome to him that he may not realize that an offer to pay is identical with a threat to withhold. If he expected to have all public funds withheld from him outright, a conditional offer to pay him a certain sum might appear to him to enlarge his liberty rather than to restrict it. And so it does, if the liberty to "exercise his constitutional right" is less important to him than the liberty which he can purchase with the funds. The offer enables him to exchange a liberty of less value to him, to which he has a "constitutional right," for another liberty of more value, to which he has no constitutional right. But he gives up the former liberty, because otherwise he will have that much less money. There is exactly the same monetary penalty on exercising it as there would be if he were taxed a like amount for doing so. And, as Justice Sutherland said in language already quoted, "One who does a thing in order to avoid a monetary penalty . . . yields to compulsion precisely the same as though he did so to avoid a term in jail." [122] But this does not suffice to make the monetary penalty unconstitutional.

Nevertheless, the Supreme Court has felt it expedient in some cases to deny the compulsory character of behavior induced by money payments. In *Massachusetts* v. *Mellon*,[123] decided in 1923, the state of Massachusetts contended that federal grants-in-aid to the states under the Maternity Act, which were conditioned on the states taking certain action prescribed by the Federal Government, were unconstitutional in that they compelled the states to yield some of their sovereign powers. It sought to enjoin the Secretary of the Treasury from making such payments. The Court dismissed the case for want of jurisdiction, on the ground that the rights which the state asserted were not justiciable ones within the scope of the federal judicial power. While this was sufficient ground for disposing of the case,

[122] In Carter v. Carter Coal Co., 298 U.S. 238, 289 (1936). *Supra*, p. 293.
[123] 262 U.S. 447 (1923).

Justice Sutherland added that the state was not being coerced, saying:

Probably, it would be sufficient to point out that the powers of the State are not invaded, since the statute imposes no obligation but simply extends an option which the state is free to accept or reject . . . Nor does the statute require the States to do or to yield anything. If Congress enacted it with the ulterior purpose of tempting them to yield, that purpose may be effectively frustrated by the simple expedient of not yielding.[124]

But freedom to accept or reject does not prove the absence of compulsion. One who does a thing to avoid a monetary penalty has an option which he is free to accept or reject. And he may effectively frustrate the ulterior purpose of the penalty by the simple expedient of paying it.

In 1936 the Court had before it, in *United States* v. *Butler*,[125] the question of the propriety of federal expenditures to induce farmers to agree by contract to limit production. These were challenged, not by the farmers, nor yet by any of the states whose sphere the Federal Government was alleged to be invading, but by a payer of the processing tax whose proceeds were earmarked for the payments in question. By a six-to-three vote [126] it was held that in making the expenditures the Federal Government was regulating crops, that the power to regulate them was reserved to the states by the Tenth Amendment, and that the tax therefore violated the rights of the taxpayer. But the only powers reserved by the Tenth Amendment are those which the Constitution does not delegate to the Federal Government. While no power is specifically delegated to regulate crops, nevertheless, power is delegated to levy taxes (and by implication to spend the proceeds) for the "general welfare of the United States." Madison had held that this power was limited to raising money to implement the other powers delegated to the government—of which crop control was not one. But the Court for the first time expressly rejected this view here, and followed Hamilton and Story in holding that the term "general welfare" was broad enough to empower the raising (and spending) of money for purposes other than those for which Congress was authorized to legislate directly.[127] It would therefore seem incumbent on the Court to determine whether expenditure for

124 262 U.S. at 480.

125 297 U.S. 1 (1936).

126 The majority opinion, written by Justice Roberts, had the concurrence of Chief Justice Hughes and Justices Van Devanter, McReynolds, Sutherland, and Butler. Justice Stone's dissenting opinion had the concurrence of Justices Brandeis and Cardozo.

127 297 U.S. at 66.

the purpose of reducing the supply and raising the price of agricultural products was expenditure for the "general welfare of the United States" and so within the power delegated to Congress, or not for that general welfare and so within the powers reserved to the states by the Tenth Amendment. But this is precisely what the Court said it was not required to determine, and by a tour de force held it to be within the reserved powers, "wholly apart from" the question whether it was a delegated power.[128]

Justice Stone, in his dissent, pointed out the fallacy in this reasoning.

> Expenditures would fail of their purpose [he said] and thus lose their constitutional sanction if the terms of payment were not such that by their influence on the action of the recipients the permitted end would be attained. The power of Congress to spend is inseparable from persuasion to action over which Congress has no legislative control.[129]

And again:

> It is a contradiction in terms to say that there is power to spend for the national welfare, while rejecting any power to impose conditions reasonably adapted to the attainment of the end which alone would justify the expenditure.[130]

Replying to some of Roberts's fears of federal power, he pointed out that the framers of the Constitution were quite aware of what they were doing when they conferred this power on Congress. In this connection he said:

> That the governmental power of the purse is a great one is not now for the first time announced. Every student of the history of government and economics is aware of its magnitude and of its existence in every civilized government. Both were well understood by the framers of the Constitution when they sanctioned the grant of the spending power to the federal government, and both were recognized by Hamilton and Story, whose views of the spending power as standing on a parity with the other powers specifically granted, have hitherto been generally accepted.[131]

Stone was not contending that the Constitution had delegated to the Federal Government power to control the planting activities of farmers by any means other than the offer of money. It is because Congress had been given the power to tax (and spend) for the general welfare that he thought the power to induce restriction of planting by means of offering money was not one of the powers reserved to the states by the Tenth Amendment. Power to control farmers by

[128] *Id.* at 68. [129] *Id.* at 83. [130] *Id.* at 85. [131] *Id.* at 86–87.

tal to the federal spending power from those methods which were incidental to it. He was challenging Roberts's intimation that the farmers were subjected to some pressure "apart from the certainty of cash payments at specified times," and from the withholding of such payments from farmers who would not conform. If one understands it in this way, one can take no exception to the statement that threat of loss, not hope of gain, is the essence of that sort of economic coercion which the spending power does not authorize Congress to employ. Holding out a hope of gain to induce conduct conducive to "the general welfare of the United States" is precisely what is authorized, whether it be regarded as coercive or not. It is an incident of the spending power.

In fact, it is coercive, just as threats of nonfeasance may be. An offer to act on stated conditions is equivalent to a threat to abstain from acting if those conditions are not accepted. An offer to pay money is a threat to withhold it. A person who accepts the conditions on which money is offered may be actuated either by fear or by hope. He may accept in order to avert his fear that the mortgage on his farm will be foreclosed if he does not, or to realize a hope that the dreaded foreclosure may not take place after all. Or he may accept in order, not to avoid a loss of something he now has, but to acquire something he does not yet have. His hope of this "gain" will be thwarted if he does not accept the conditions of the offer, and if he has set his heart on the gain the possibility of not realizing it may inspire fear. The distinction between a coercive and a noncoercive inducement to act cannot be made to turn on any distinction between "threat" and "hope" or between "gain" and "loss." In either case, he who rejects the conditions of the offer will be poorer by the amount of what is offered than if he accepts. The coercive effect is the same as if a tax of like amount were placed on nonconformity. It is only the fact that one takes exclusion from access to public funds as a matter of course that creates the illusion that acceptance of a conditional offer of them is voluntary. One who expects to be subjected to the greater evil may welcome an opportunity to accept a lesser evil instead. But he accepts it only to avert the greater one. And this is the essence of coercion. This is why Roberts's statement, while irrelevant to the constitutional question, is nevertheless true, that, "the power to confer or withhold unlimited benefits is the power to coerce or destroy."

In 1937, however, in *Steward Machine Co.* v. *Davis*,[138] the majority denied that acts done to obtain money were done under compulsion, though the denial was unnecessary for the decision of the case. The Social Security Act levied a federal tax on the pay rolls of employers for unemployment relief, but provided that if the state in which an employer operated enacted an unemployment relief statute which met with the approval of the federal Social Security Board, the taxpayer should be allowed to credit the payments he made under the state law against his federal tax, up to 90 percent of the latter. There was no provision for direct payment to the state, as in *Massachusetts* v. *Mellon*, but the abatement of the federal tax was none the less of monetary benefit to any state which enacted an approved law, since it would be able to finance its own law by imposing a lighter burden on its taxpayers than otherwise.

A taxpayer in Alabama sued to recover the federal taxes he had paid, contending, among other things, that the federal law violated the Tenth Amendment by coercing the states into yielding up some of their reserved powers.

Justice Cardozo, for the majority, denied that there was any coercion. Before the enactment of the federal law, he said, "the freedom of a state to contribute its fair share to the solution of a national problem was paralyzed by fear." Many states "held back through alarm lest in laying such a toll upon their industries, they would place themselves in a position of economic disadvantage as compared with neighbors or competitors." [139] So far, the reasoning does not prove that Alabama made its own law conform to federal standards voluntarily. Alabama might have welcomed the federal law, as freeing it from the fear of the competition of other states which paralyzed its freedom to enact any sort of unemployment law. At the same time it might have preferred to enact some different law not conforming to federal standards. One may welcome a traffic law, because by regulating the driving of other people it increases one's own freedom to

[138] 301 U.S. 548 (1937). The majority opinion, by Justice Cardozo, had the concurrence of Chief Justice Hughes and Justices Brandeis, Stone, and Roberts. Justices McReynolds and Butler wrote separate dissenting opinions, in which they maintained that the action of Congress coerced the states into enacting their unemployment acts. Justice Sutherland wrote another dissenting opinion (concurred in by Van Devanter), in which he conceded that there was no coercion on the states to *enact* their laws, but maintained that the federal Act required the states to surrender their power to *administer* their acts after enactment. This requirement he held to be invalid, even if the states' surrender of their administering power be deemed voluntary.

[139] 301 U.S. at 588.

drive. At the same time, one may comply with a particular requirement of the traffic law only for fear of the penalty for noncompliance.

However, it may well be that Alabama was not only glad to have the federal law enacted but was glad to enact the particular state law which was passed. The state was not coerced, said Justice Cardozo.

> Even now she does not offer a suggestion that in passing the unemployment law she was affected by duress. . . . For all that appears, she is satisfied with her choice, and would be sorely disappointed if it were now to be annulled. . . . There would be a strange irony, indeed, if her choice were now to be annulled on the basis of an assumed duress in the enactment of a statute which her courts have accepted as a true expression of her will.[140]

This may all be true and yet the requirement that Alabama pass a law which satisfies federal criteria, under penalty of her taxpayers' not receiving credit on their federal taxes, may have been a compulsory requirement. As we have already observed, a requirement may be compulsory, like the law forbidding larceny, while many given instances of conformity to the law are voluntary.

Discussing the question of coercion more generally, the Court quoted the statement in *Sonzinsky* v. *United States*, which we have already quoted:

> Every tax is in some measure regulatory. To some extent it interposes an economic impediment to the activity taxed as compared with others not taxed.

After quoting this language Justice Cardozo went on:

> In like manner every rebate from a tax when conditioned upon conduct is in some measure a temptation. But to hold that motive or temptation is equivalent to coercion is to plunge the law in endless difficulties. The outcome of such a doctrine is the acceptance of a philosophical determinism by which choice becomes impossible. Till now the law has been guided by a robust common sense which assumes the freedom of the will as a working hypothesis in the solution of its problems.[141]

The outcome of holding that every motive is equivalent to coercion may well be acceptance of philosophical determinism. But one does not need to be a determinist to hold that there is coercion when one is confronted with a choice between two disagreeable alternatives. Nor would the law be plunged in endless difficulties were this admitted. It may be that Alabama would have enacted its unemployment law in its present form because it wished such a law. But if it

140 301 U.S. at 589–590.

141 *Ibid.*

preferred some other law which would not have had the approval of the federal board, it relinquished its preference in order to avoid the loss of federal tax credit to its citizens, and in doing so it was choosing the lesser of two evils with which the Federal Government was confronting it. But this would be no reason for invalidating the federal law. Had the federal tax been levied without the offer of the rebate, the state would have been forced to accept the greater evil of seeing its citizens pay the full federal tax. The opportunity to choose a lesser one gave the state more freedom than it would have had without that opportunity. But a choice of the lesser evil (if the state did indeed regard it as an evil) in order to escape the greater one was still a coerced choice, not a free one.

Indeed, a subsequent passage in the opinion suggests that the Social Security Act was sustained, not because it exerted no coercion on the state, but because the coercion was exerted for a proper federal purpose. That purpose was to induce the states to take some part of the burden of caring for unemployment from the shoulders of the Federal Government. The motive was related to activities within federal power, including fiscal needs. Had it been otherwise, Cardozo intimated that expenditure conditioned on state compliance might be unconstitutional. He said:

> In ruling as we do, we leave many questions open. We do not say that a tax is valid, when imposed by act of Congress, if it is laid upon the condition that a state may escape its operation through the adoption of a statute unrelated in subject matter to activities fairly within the scope of national policy and power. No such question is before us. In the tender of this credit Congress does not intrude upon fields foreign to its function. The purpose of its intervention, as we have shown, is to safeguard its own treasury and as an incident to that protection to place the states upon a footing of equal opportunity. Drains upon its own resources are to be checked; obstructions to the freedom of the states are to be leveled. It is one thing to impose a tax dependent upon the conduct of the taxpayers, or of the state in which they live, where the conduct to be stimulated or discouraged is unrelated to the fiscal need subserved by the tax in its normal operation, or to any other end legitimately national. The *Child Labor Tax Case,* 259 U.S. 20, and *Hill* v. *Wallace,* 259 U.S. 44, were decided in the belief that the statutes there condemned were exposed to that reproach. *Cf. United States* v. *Constantine,* 296 U.S. 287. It is quite another thing to say that a tax will be abated upon the doing of an act that will satisfy the fiscal need, the tax and the alternative being approximate equivalents.[142]

[142] *Id.* at 590–591.

This appears to be the real ground for the decision. In the *Child Labor Tax* case and in *Hill* v. *Wallace* the tax was recognized as a form of coercion. The Social Security tax is to be distinguished, not in that it is less coercive, but in that it satisfies a fiscal need, not only by the revenue it collects from those who pay it but also by the conduct it stimulates in states which choose to relieve their citizens from paying part of it.

If the condition attached to a statutory grant of funds were held to be unconstitutional, it would seem that the grantee who did not comply with the condition would retain his statutory right to his share. The Hatch Act provides in § 12 that no state officer whose principal employment is in connection with any activity financed by federal grants shall take any active part in politics. The United States Civil Service Commission is to determine whether any violation has taken place and, if so, whether the violation warrants removal of the officer. If he is not removed within thirty days after the Commission has notified the appropriate state agency, the Commission is to issue an order to the appropriate federal agency to withhold from the state agency an amount equal to two years' compensation of the offending state officer. Provision is made for review of any order of the Civil Service Commission in a federal district court. In *State of Oklahoma* v. *United States Civil Service Commission*,[143] decided in 1947, the commission had found that a member of the State Highway Commission had taken an active part in politics, which warranted his removal from office. The state declined to remove him, and the Civil Service Commission made the appropriate order for withholding federal highway funds. The state sought review of the order in accordance with the provisions for review contained in the statute.

The Government contended that the state had no standing to attack the constitutionality of § 12, citing, among other cases, *Massachusetts* v. *Mellon*. But in that case Massachusetts was not protesting any withholding of funds from itself, but the disbursement of funds to other states. The Court held that case not in point and overruled the Government's contention as to the state's standing.

Congress [said Justice Reed] may create legally enforceable rights where none existed before. Payments were not made at the unfettered inclination of a federal disbursing officer or highway agency but according to statutory

[143] 330 U.S. 127 (1947). Justices Black and Rutledge dissented. Justice Frankfurter concurred in the result. Justices Murphy and Jackson took no part in the case.

standards, compliance with which entitled Oklahoma to receive her proper share of the federal appropriations for highway construction through state agencies. If it were not for § 12, Oklahoma would have been legally entitled to receive payments from the federal disbursing office of the sums, including the amount that § 12(b) authorizes the Civil Service Commission to require the disbursing or allocating federal agency to withhold from its loans or grants. . . . The power to examine into the constitutionality of the conditions was given the federal courts by the grant of the authority to review the legality of the Civil Service order. Therefore when by § 12 a right of review of the Civil Service Commission's order is given to Oklahoma, we are of the opinion that the constitutionality of the statutory basis, § 12(a), of the order is open for adjudication.[144]

It would seem possible, therefore, for a withholding of funds to be unconstitutional. In this case, however, the Court held on the merits that it was not so. Pointing out that Oklahoma chose not to remove its offending officer, Justice Reed went on:

We do not see any violation of the state's sovereignty in the hearing or order. Oklahoma adopted the "simple expedient" of not yielding to what she urges is federal coercion. Compare *Massachusetts* v. *Mellon* . . . . The offer of benefits to a state by the United States dependent upon cooperation by the state with federal plans, assumedly for the general welfare, is not unusual. [Citations.][145]

Adoption of the "simple expedient," however, meant loss of the statutory right to part of the federal payments. That the federal coercion was unsuccesful does not make the federal requirement any less coercive, when the only means of avoiding it involves a monetary loss. Like the conditions attached to federal grants in the *Steward Machine* case, the conditions here are valid, not because they are noncoercive, but because they are germane to a proper federal purpose. The general offer of federal highway funds is assumed to be valid, because highway development is assumed to come under the head of "general welfare," which justifies federal taxation. But if highway development at federal expense is justified as part of the general welfare, a requirement that the state cooperate, and cooperate effectively, in highway development is related to a federal end. And it is not too violent an assumption to maintain that highway officers would be less efficient if they engaged actively in politics.

If the condition required for the enjoyment of the federal funds were unrelated to any federal end—if it concerned only matters of local, as distinguished from general, welfare—we should have a dif-

[144] 330 U.S. at 136–137.

[145] *Id.* at 143–144.

ferent question. Suppose, for instance, that a federal statute created rights in the states to federal funds for a proper federal purpose, such as highway construction, but provided that no state should be entitled to its share unless the judges of the state courts were chosen by election rather than by appointment. The offer of benefits in such a case would be "dependent on cooperation by the state with federal plans," but the federal plans for altering the state judicial system could hardly be assumed to be plans "for the *general* welfare." In asserting its statutory right to its share in the highway funds, would not a state be entitled to challenge the constitutionality of the condition which would defeat that statutory right, and should it not be held that the condition, being unrelated to a federal purpose, is unconstitutional and that the statutory right remains in full force even if the state which asserts it has refused to cooperate in federal plans for the selection of state judges?

Even when a specific liberty is one that is held to be within the scope of constitutional protection—one whose exercise could not be punished by imprisonment—still governments may force the surrender of it as the alternative to doing without offered public funds, provided its surrender bears some relation to the purposes for which the funds might validly be withheld (or spent) in the first place. The power of governments to repress constitutionally protected liberties in this manner is not unlike their power to do so by attaching conditions to the grant of other special privileges or by imposing taxes on the exercise of such liberties. A government may generally decline to pay money or to grant special privileges to anyone and may impose taxes on specified activities for fiscal purposes. Having this power, it may use it as a bargaining instrument, and threaten to exercise it against anyone who will not accept named conditions, even if those conditions call for the surrender of liberties for whose surrender the government might not bargain by threats of imprisonment. But limitations have been placed on the use by governments of their conditioning and their taxing powers for bargaining purposes. The withholding of a privilege has been held unconstitutional when the condition of its grant calls for surrender of a liberty which could not be constitutionally repressed by the sanction of imprisonment and which at the same time is unrelated to any of the purposes which would normally justify withholding. And taxes have been held invalid when it has been clear from the form of the taxing statute that the dominant purpose was not fiscal, but penal. And it is even possible that the withholding of a bounty from those who will not surrender a constitutional liberty unrelated to any proper governmental purpose would be held invalid.

These, however, are limitations which the Constitution has been held to place on governmental actions which restrict the liberty of individuals. But private individuals are frequently so circumstanced that they, too, can restrict the constitutionally protected liberties of other individuals, by attaching conditions to the grant of privileges or of funds which are essential to those to whom the grants are made and which the law has placed in the control of those who grant them. Do the due process and equal protection clauses afford any protection to an individual from harm caused him by other individuals or by the judicial enforcement of the will of other individuals? This is the question which underlies the discussion in the next chapter.

XI

CONSTITUTIONAL SAFEGUARDS AGAINST PRIVATE COERCIVE POWER

THE Fifth and Fourteenth amendments are directed against governmental activities (state or federal). They cannot be invoked against private individuals who deprive other individuals of liberty, property, or equality unless government can be shown to have had a hand in the deprivation. We must now explore the circumstances which will lead the Court to recognize a governmental hand in deprivations practiced ostensibly by private individuals alone.

PRIVATE ACTS IN GENERAL

Frequently persons are deprived of life, liberty, or property by the criminal acts of other private individuals. They are murdered, kidnapped, or robbed. Such acts are forbidden, of course, by state law. But they are not forbidden by the Constitution. The due process clause of the Fifth Amendment has long been construed to apply only to deprivations by the Federal Government or some of its agencies. The Fourteenth expressly directs its prohibitions to states. Hence, although it authorizes Congress to enforce its provisions by appropriate legislation, it confers no power on Congress to provide punishment for private acts which deprive persons of life, liberty, or property. In this respect rights not to be deprived of such things by private action differ from rights to vote in a federal election or to be free from involuntary servitude, which are rights secured by the Constitution that can be protected from private attack by federal legislation. As Justice Bradley remarked for the Court in 1883, in the *Civil Rights Cases:*

> Under the Thirteenth Amendment, the legislation, so far as necessary or proper to eradicate all forms and incidents of slavery and involuntary servitude, may be direct and primary, operating upon the acts of individuals, whether sanctioned by State legislation or not; under the Fourteenth . . . it must necessarily be, and can only be, corrective in its character, addressed to counteract and afford relief against State regulations or proceedings.[1]

In 1876 the Court, in *United States* v. *Cruikshank,*[2] had already held a federal statute unconstitutional which punished individuals for conspiring to deprive other individuals of life, liberty, or property, or the equal protection of the laws. And in *United States* v. *Harris,*[3] decided in 1883, shortly before the decision in the *Civil Rights Cases,* a federal indictment under Section 5519 of the Revised Statutes, for conspiring to deprive persons of the equal protection of the laws was held bad. The acts charged consisted of attacking and in one case killing prisoners in the custody of the sheriff. There being no state action, there was no violation of the Fourteenth Amendment, and since the acts charged did not establish involuntary servitude, there was no violation of the Thirteenth either. Justice Woods gave another reason for denying violation of the Thirteenth Amendment, which would seem to apply more plausibly to the Fourteenth. He said:

> A private person cannot make constitutions or laws, nor can he with authority construe them, nor can he administer or execute them. The only way, therefore, in which one private person can deprive another of the equal protection of the laws is by the commission of some offence against the laws which protect the rights of persons, as by theft, burglary, arson, libel, assault, or murder. If, therefore, we hold that sec. 5519 is warranted by the Thirteenth Amendment, we should, by virtue of that amendment, accord to Congress the power to punish every crime by which the right of any person to life, property, or reputation is invaded.[4]

[1] 109 U.S. 3, 23 (1883).
[2] 92 U.S. 542 (1876).
[3] 106 U.S. 629 (1883).
[4] *Id.* at 643.

In the *Civil Rights Cases,* decided later in 1883, the portion of the federal Civil Rights Acts was held invalid which provided punishment for denying to citizens the equal enjoyment of accommodations in inns, public conveyances, or theaters, "subject only to the conditions and limitations established by law, and applicable alike to citizens of every race and color, regardless of any previous condition of servitude." Various owners of inns, public conveyances, and theaters had been indicted for denying accommodations to Negroes because of their race. The Court made no note of the fact that without the aid of the state in enforcing their property rights, the owners who had been indicted might have found it difficult to exclude the Negroes from their accommodations. It assumed that the owners were acting without state aid. It also assumed that the Negroes had rights under state law which they could vindicate in state courts. Discussing the matter, Justice Bradley said:

> In this connection it is proper to state that civil rights, such as are guaranteed by the Constitution against State aggression, cannot be impaired by the wrongful acts of individuals, unsupported by State authority in the shape of laws, customs, or judicial or executive proceedings. The wrongful act of an individual, unsupported by any such authority, is simply a private wrong, or a crime of that individual; an invasion of the rights of the injured party, it is true, whether they affect his person, his property, or his reputation; but if not sanctioned in some way by the State, or done under State authority, his rights remain in full force, and may presumably be vindicated by resort to the laws of the State for redress. An individual cannot deprive a man of his right to vote, to hold property, to buy and sell, to sue in the courts, or to be a witness or a juror; he may, by force or fraud, interfere with the enjoyment of the right in a particular case; he may commit an assault against the person, or commit murder, or use ruffian violence at the polls, or slander the good name of a fellow citizen; but, unless protected in these wrongful acts by some shield of State law or State authority, he cannot destroy or injure the right; he will only render himself amenable to satisfaction or punishment; and amenable therefor to the laws of the State where the wrongful acts are committed. Hence, in all those cases where the Constitution seeks to protect the rights of the citizen against discriminative and unjust laws, it is not the individual offences, but abrogation and denial of rights which it denounces, and for which it clothes the Congress with power to provide a remedy. This abrogation and denial of rights, for which the States alone were or could be responsible, was the great seminal and fundamental wrong which was intended to be remedied.[5]

[5] 109 U.S. at 17–18.

Then, after distinguishing the scope of the Thirteenth Amendment from that of the Fourteenth and rejecting the Government's contention that the denial of the accommodations constituted a badge of slavery and thus violated the Thirteenth, he summarized his conclusions, saying:

> . . . we are forced to the conclusion that such an act of refusal has nothing to do with slavery or involuntary servitude, and that if it is violative of any right of the party, his redress is to be sought under the laws of the State; or if those laws are adverse to his rights and do not protect him, his remedy will be found in the corrective legislation which Congress has adopted, or may adopt, for counteracting the effect of State laws, or State action, prohibited by the Fourteenth Amendment. . . . Innkeepers and public carriers, by the laws of all the States, so far as we are aware, are bound, to the extent of their facilities, to furnish proper accommodation to all unobjectionable persons who in good faith apply for them. If the laws themselves make any unjust discrimination, amenable to the prohibitions of the Fourteenth Amendment, Congress has full power to afford a remedy under that amendment and in accordance with it.[6]

Under state law, every person has certain rights of liberty and property which he can vindicate in state courts against hostile action by private individuals. But these rights are not conferred by the Fourteenth Amendment. That Amendment confers only a right not to have the state "impair," or "deprive of," or "abrogate," or "deny," or "destroy," or "injure" these pre-existing state-given rights. With or without the Amendment, private individuals are thought to be incapable of doing any of these things to rights of liberty or property or equal protection; hence, while they might violate or interfere with the enjoyment of these state-given rights, their doing so would not violate the Amendment. The state-given rights, though violated, would themselves "remain in full force."[7]

The case is different, however, the Court intimated, if the acts of the private individuals are "supported by State authority in the shape of laws, customs, or judicial or executive proceedings," or protected "by some shield of State law or State authority," or "sanctioned in some way by the State, or done under State authority." But what would constitute state "authority," or "protection," or "sanction," or "support" for the acts of individuals which deprive other individuals

[6] *Id.* at 24–25.

[7] As to the Fifteenth Amendment, see James v. Bowman, 190 U.S. 127, 139 (1903). Cf. *supra*, pp. 223–224, n. 117.

of life, liberty, or property, or equal protection, so as to afford constitutional protection to the latter?

ACTS COMMANDED BY GOVERNMENT

In the *Civil Rights Cases* it was the owners of inns, conveyances, and theaters who denied equal opportunities to Negroes. The Court assumed that the denial was contrary to state law and that the Negroes could accordingly have redress in the state courts. But a person may be denied equal opportunity or deprived of some portion of liberty or property by the acts of other private individuals which are perfectly lawful on their part. An employer may discriminate in the giving of jobs by reason of race or citizenship. If most employers make the same discriminations there is no equality of opportunity to obtain employment. Yet, in the absence of fair employment policy acts there is no legal wrong for which those against whom the discrimination is practiced may obtain redress. The liberty to sell one's property or to obtain customers for one's business may disappear if no one will buy or patronize. If a state made it a crime for members of a certain race to obtain employment, it would be an unconstitutional denial of equal protection of the laws. And if the state were to make it a crime to sell, it would be an unconstitutional deprivation of property. Yet private individuals may be able to produce the same result without violating the Constitution or any law, by simply declining to employ or to buy.

We have seen, however, that courts have at times given some relief to those who suffer from the lawful refusal of employers to employ or of customers to buy. If those refusals have been instigated by third parties for purposes which the courts deem to lack justification, redress is sometimes given at common law against the latter. On a somewhat analogous principle, if a state requires an employer to discriminate, or a potential purchaser to refrain from buying, the Supreme Court has held it to be a denial by the state of equal protection to the employee, or a deprivation by the state of the seller's property. The state is held responsible for the discrimination or the deprivation of property, even though it is bringing about those results, not by exerting the force of its own agencies directly against the aggrieved person, but by compelling other private individuals to exert the force which they would have been free to exert even if the state had not acted.

In *Truax* v. *Raich*,[8] decided in 1915, the state of Arizona had enacted a statute forbidding any employer of more than five workers to employ less than 80 percent of his employees from qualified electors or native-born citizens of the United States. Fine and imprisonment were imposed on any employer violating the act, but no penalties were imposed on employees, except for misrepresenting their nativity or citizenship. The act was challenged, not by an employer, but by an Austrian named Raich, who had been told by his employer that he would be discharged, solely by reason of the statute and its penalties. Although he would have had no remedy against being discharged had the employer wished to discharge him for his foreign citizenship or for any other reason, it was held that the statute violated his constitutional right to equal protection. Said Justice Hughes for the Court:

> The fact that the employment is at the will of the parties, respectively, does not make it one at the will of others. The employee has manifest interest in the freedom of the employer to exercise his judgment without legal interference or compulsion, and by the weight of authority, the unjustified interference of third parties is actionable although the employment is at will.[9]

The authorities cited were common law actions against private defendants.

In *Buchanan* v. *Warley*,[10] decided in 1917, the City of Louisville had enacted an ordinance forbidding Negroes or whites to move into and occupy houses in blocks in which a greater number of houses are occupied by members of the other race. A Negro named Warley made a contract, apparently after this ordinance had been enacted, to buy certain real estate from a white man named Buchanan in a "white" block. The contract contained a proviso that Warley should not be required to accept the deed or pay for the property "unless I have the right, under the laws of the state of Kentucky and the city of Louisville, to occupy said property as a residence." He had no such right if the ordinance was valid, and in that case the contract conferred on Buchanan no right to insist on Warley's going through with the purchase. Accordingly, when Buchanan sued for specific performance of the contract, Warley contended that since the ordinance was valid he had no obligation to buy, while the white seller, Buchanan, contended that the ordinance was unconstitutional and that the proviso therefore did not nullify Warley's obligation to buy. The state courts

8 239 U.S. 33 (1915). 9 *Id.* at 38. 10 245 U.S. 60 (1917).

held the ordinance valid and decided in favor of Warley. But the Supreme Court reversed.

Objection was made to reversal, because "the alleged denial of constitutional rights involves only the rights of colored persons, and the plaintiff in error is a white person." Justice Day conceded that "attacks upon the validity of laws can only be entertained when made by those whose rights are directly affected by the law or ordinance in question." But, he added, "this case does not run counter to that principle." [11]

Pointing out that in the state courts "the plaintiff's right to have the contract enforced was denied solely because of the effect of the ordinance," Justice Day went on:

> The right of the plaintiff in error to sell his property was directly involved and necessarily impaired because it was held in effect that he could not sell the lot to a person of color who was willing and ready to acquire the property, and had obligated himself to take it. This case does not come within the class wherein this court has held that where one seeks to avoid the enforcement of a law or ordinance he must present a grievance of his own, and not rest the attack upon the alleged violation of another's rights. In this case the property rights of the plaintiff in error are directly and necessarily involved. See *Truax* v. *Raich* . . . .[12]

In this passage the Court leaned somewhat on the assertion that Warley had obligated himself to take the property and that Buchanan had a right to have the contract enforced. It should be noted, however, that upholding the ordinance would not have diminished any right which Buchanan had acquired by the contract; for if the ordinance was valid, the contract, by its express terms, would have given him no such right. What would have been impaired by the ordinance was not any right created by the contract, but the more general "right" to dispose of the property. It was the enjoyment of this "right" with which the ordinance would have interfered. And it was this "right" to sell, which involved no obligation on anyone's part to buy, which the Court held entitled to protection under the due process clause. "Property [said the Court] is more than the mere thing which a person owns. It is elementary that it includes the right to acquire, use, and dispose of it. The Constitution protects these essential attributes of property." [13]

The Court admitted that "the disposition and use of property may be controlled in the exercise of the police power," and cited illus-

[11] 245 U.S. at 72. [12] *Id.* at 73. [13] *Id.* at 74.

trations, "but these cases do not touch the one at bar." The opinion continued:

The concrete question here is: May the occupancy, and, necessarily, the purchase and sale of property of which occupancy is an incident, be inhibited by the states, or by one of its municipalities, solely because of the color of the proposed occupant of the premises? . . . The question now presented makes it pertinent to inquire into the constitutional right of the white man to sell his property to a colored man, having in view the legal status of the purchaser and occupant.[14]

The Court then proceeded to review the history of the adoption of the Fourteenth Amendment and to quote passages from statutes enacted to implement it. The statutory provisions it quoted proclaimed that all citizens of the United States and all persons within the jurisdiction of the United States should have the same right as is enjoyed by white citizens with respect to the security of property and to its purchase and sale, as well as with respect to other matters enumerated. These provisions would seem to have more to do with equal protection than with due process, but it seems that it is because the Louisville ordinance denied equal protection to the Negroes that it was held to be the kind of control of the white man's disposition of his property that deprived the latter of property without due process. The Court summarized its position by asking the following rhetorical question:

In the face of these constitutional and statutory provisions, can a white man be denied, consistently with due process of law, the right to dispose of his property to a purchaser by prohibiting the occupation of it for the sole reason that the purchaser is a person of color intending to occupy the premises as a place of residence?[15]

There is, of course, no guaranty that an owner of property can actually enjoy his "right" to sell his property to a Negro or to anyone else. No one is under a duty to buy. Refusal to do so is perfectly lawful. The most that *Buchanan* v. *Warley* holds is that the due process clause guarantees to the owner that his opportunity to sell shall not be hindered by any state restriction on the liberty of the buyer to buy or to use the property, if that restriction is one which denies to the buyer the equal protection of the laws. It does not protect the owner from the consequences of the spontaneous refusal of buyers to buy, though those consequences would be identical in their effect with those which

[14] *Id.* at 75.

[15] *Id.* at 78.

the Louisville ordinance would have produced. To protect the owner's "right" to dispose of his property against the refusal of unwilling buyers would obviously subject the latter to a deprivation of their more vital liberty to refuse to buy. But to protect it against the refusal of buyers who are made unwilling by fear of penalties imposed by the state deprives no one else of liberty.

Protection against loss of customers, brought about by state coercion of them, was again afforded, in 1925, in *Pierce* v. *Society of the Sisters*,[16] a case to which we have adverted in previous chapters. Proprietary schools were there held to have a right, under the due process clause, not to be deprived of pupils by legislation which penalized parents for not sending their children to the public schools. The parents themselves were, of course, violating no rights of the private schools by refraining from sending their children there.

The parties whose constitutional rights were held to be infringed in *Truax* v. *Raich*, in *Buchanan* v. *Warley*, and in *Pierce* v. *Society of the Sisters* were suffering from the lawful refusal of private individuals to employ, to buy, and to patronize. The statutes and the ordinance that were held unconstitutional gave the private individuals no more power to refuse than they had had before. Raich's employer could have discharged him, Warley could have refused to contract to buy Buchanan's property, and the parents could have withdrawn their children from the parochial school before the challenged legislation was enacted as well as afterwards. Had they done so, and had no one else come forward to employ Raich, to buy Buchanan's property, or to patronize the school, the loss to the injured party would have been just as great as under the legislation, but he would have had no redress under the Constitution or the laws. The legislation added nothing to the power of the individuals to inflict the harm which ensued from their refusals. It did, however, increase the likelihood of their doing so. Without the legislation, they would all have been free to confer their respective benefits had they been inclined to do so. And, as Justice Hughes said in *Truax* v. *Raich* with respect to the alien who was facing discharge, "The employee has manifest interest in the freedom of the employer to exercise his judgment without legal interference or compulsion." It was interest in the other party's being left free to benefit him (even though he was also free to withhold the benefit) to which the injured party was said to

[16] 268 U.S. 510 (1925).

have a constitutional right; and it was state action which took away one person's freedom in which another person had a constitutionally protected interest. To hold this state action unconstitutional interferes in no way with the liberty of the other individuals to inflict the same loss should they wish to do so.

While one's interest in the freedom of another to act for his benefit without legal "compulsion" receives constitutional protection, it is more doubtful whether the Court would accord one a constitutional right against governmental inducement of unfavorable action by third parties when the inducement does not take the form of subjecting those third parties to legal duties, even though the inducement may be for other reasons unconstitutional. As we have seen in *Alabama Power Co.* v. *Ickes*[17] and *Tennessee Electric Power Co.* v. *Tennessee Valley Authority*,[18] utility companies with nonexclusive franchises were held to have no constitutional rights that were infringed by federal activities which might destroy the value of their properties by causing customers to desert them in order to buy their electricity more cheaply from municipalities encouraged by federal loans or from a federal agency itself. They were held to have no such rights whether or not the federal activities in question violated the Tenth Amendment, and the Court therefore refused to pass on their validity under that Amendment. It was intimated, however, that had the Government been found to be "coercing" the municipalities to go into the power business or to be actuated by a motive to force the power companies to sell out, there might have been a violation of the companies' property rights under the due process clause.

ACTS CONDONED BY THE STATE

In the *Civil Rights Cases* it was assumed that the acts of the innkeepers and carriers which discriminated against the Negroes were acts forbidden by state law. They were not thought to be "sanctioned" or "authorized" by the state. Hence there could be no violation of the Fourteenth Amendment. Could there be a violation if a person were deprived of property by acts of other individuals performed without any help from the state, but by its permission?

In *Truax* v. *Corrigan*,[19] decided in 1921, the owners of a restaurant sought an injunction in a state court in Arizona against picketing. The

[17] 302 U.S. 464 (1938). Discussed *supra*, p. 143.
[18] 306 U.S. 118 (1939).
[19] 257 U.S. 312 (1921).

picketing was noisy and perhaps libelous, but not technically violent. It caused many of their customers to desert them, and they were deprived of a large part of the value of their business. The state court denied the injunction, and the state supreme court affirmed the denial. It declared that until the passage of a recent statute the owners would have been entitled to an injunction against the picketing and that they would now be entitled to one against violent picketing, but that the statute took away their right to an injunction against the sort of picketing that was actually taking place. The owners took the case to the United States Supreme Court, alleging that they were being deprived of property in violation of the Fourteenth Amendment. In a five-to-four decision the Court sustained their contention.[20]

Chief Justice Taft construed the state court's decision as holding that under the statute not only did the plaintiffs have no right to the injunction as a remedy but that the picketing did not invade any of their legal rights—that is, that the statute denied them all remedy, legal as well as equitable, and that it rendered the picketing lawful as long as it was not violent.[21] As so construed, it was held that the owners were being deprived of property in violation of the due process clause.

> It is true [said Taft] that no one has a vested right in any particular rule of the common law, but it is also true that the legislative power of a state can only be exerted in subordination to the fundamental principles of right and justice which the guaranty of due process in the Fourteenth Amendment is intended to preserve, and that a purely arbitrary or capricious exercise of that power whereby a wrongful and highly injurious in-

20 Chief Justice Taft's majority opinion had the concurrence of Justices McKenna, Day, Van Devanter, and McReynolds. Justices Holmes, Pitney, Brandeis, and Clarke dissented. Holmes wrote one dissenting opinion, Pitney another (in which Clarke concurred), and Brandeis a third. Holmes expressed agreement with Pitney's and Brandeis's opinions, and Brandeis with Holmes's and Pitney's.

21 After holding that the statute, so construed, deprived the plaintiffs of property without due process, Taft added (at p. 330): "If, however, contrary to the construction which we put on the opinion of the Supreme Court of Arizona, it does not withhold from the plaintiffs all remedy for the wrongs they suffered but only the equitable relief of injunction, there still remains the question whether they are thus denied the equal protection of the laws."

Taft held that they *were* thus denied equal protection, on the strange ground that the statute, on this construction, still left them the equitable remedy against similar picketing by those not engaged in a labor dispute—such as rival restaurant owners. Had they been denied injunctive relief against *all* picketing, they would have lacked this ground for asserting a denial of equal protection. Pitney pointed out incisively the fallacy of this position. If anyone was denied equal protection in this respect, it was not the plaintiffs, but the hypothetical competing restaurant owners. The plaintiffs were in no position to challenge a violation of the constitutional rights of other people.

vasion of property rights, as here, is directly sanctioned and the owner stripped of all real remedy, is wholly at variance with those principles.[22]

The "invasion" was carried out by private individuals (the pickets), not by the state. The state was not requiring them to act as they did, nor was it in any way assisting them otherwise than by ceasing to prohibit their activities. Did the state's legislative power "sanction" their acts by merely permitting them? If so, it would seem that any action by a private individual which deprives another of liberty or of part of the value of his property is state action and within the scope of the Fourteenth Amendment if state law does not make it illegal; for the Fourteenth Amendment applies to any state action, not alone to the enactment of statutes by the legislature. If this is the case, whenever an employer uses his bargaining power to induce an employee to part by contract with his liberty to work for another or a union induces an employer to establish a closed shop and the state courts hold the action legal, a question could be raised under the due process clause; for if an act permitted by the state is to be regarded as sanctioned by it, it is state action. Any decision by a state court which upholds private acts as "justified" when they restrict the freedom of someone else or reduce the profits of his business could be taken up to the Supreme Court, which would have to decide whether it was "arbitrary or capricious" of the state to permit them. The law of prima facie torts would become a branch of constitutional law, beyond the power of state courts or state legislatures to alter it.

It is not likely, however, that mere state permission of private acts will be regarded as state sanction for them. The existence of state action in *Truax* v. *Corrigan* can be placed on a more plausible basis. If the prior law of Arizona had permitted picketing of the character in question, it might be held that there was no state action. But since the previous Arizona law did confer on the owners a right against that sort of picketing, the statute which extinguished that right could be called state action. One ingredient in the owners' rights of property was their right under the state's common law to have the state protect them, through the courts, against loss of profits by the picketing. According to this view, the state's invasion of the property consisted of the statutory extinction of that right. That extinction being invalid, the owners still possessed the right against the pickets which state law had previously conferred on them. But the pickets' invasion

[22] 257 U.S. at 329–330.

of the property was an invasion of a state-given right, not of a right under the Fourteenth Amendment. In directing the state court to issue the injunction, the Supreme Court would be directing them to enforce the state-given right. It would not be holding that the Fourteenth Amendment created the right against the pickets on the dubious ground that the state was "sanctioning" their activities. It would be holding merely that the Fourteenth Amendment placed a limit on the state's "abrogation and denial of rights" (to use Justice Bradley's words). "Denial" of a right which never existed would apparently raise no question involving the Fourteenth Amendment; and of course there could be no such thing as "abrogation" of a nonexistent right.

While a legislative attempt to abolish a right against private acts which result in deprivation of property is state action, it is not necessarily unconstitutional even if the private acts which the statute permits result in a deprivation of property or liberty such as the state could not effect by direct penal sanctions. Because it might be thought arbitrary for the state to forbid certain actions, it does not necessarily follow that it is arbitrary for it to extinguish a right against private power to curtail those same actions. The distinction is brought out in a case decided in 1937, *Senn* v. *Tile Layers Protective Union.*[23]

Paul Senn had a small tile contracting business, in which he employed one or two journeyman tile layers and one or two helpers and in which he worked with his own hands. Without doing that, he could not have earned a livelihood. His employees were not members of the union, and he was not himself eligible for membership. The union requested him to execute an agreement substantially identical with that entered into with those contractors who employed union men. He expressed willingness to do so if Article III were eliminated, which would have prevented him from working in the business with his own hands. The unions (one of tile layers, the other of helpers) refused to eliminate this article, and Senn refused to sign. The unions thereupon picketed his place of business peacefully, carrying banners proclaiming him unfair to the tile layers union. He sought an injunction, which the trial court denied on the ground that the Labor Code of Wisconsin declared peaceful picketing in labor disputes legal and provided that no court should have jurisdiction to issue an injunction against it. The state supreme court affirmed.

23 301 U.S. 468 (1937).

He took the case to the United States Supreme Court, alleging that the Labor Code, as construed by the state courts, violated his constitutional right to work with his own hands in the business. By a five-to-four decision, his contention was rejected.[24]

Senn's contention was rejected, not on the ground that there was no state action, but on the ground that the state action was a reasonable exercise of the police power. While the Court affirmed the decision of the state court, it denied the defendants' motion to dismiss the appeal for want of jurisdiction. That motion was based on the contention "that there is nothing to show that the provisions of the Wisconsin Labor Code here questioned are not merely declaratory of the common law of Wisconsin as it existed prior to the statute." To this contention Brandeis replied:

> But it sufficiently appears that the provisions of the Labor Code were relied upon; that their validity under the Fourteenth Amendment was duly challenged below; and that the rulings of the state courts were based ultimately on the Labor Code. Whether the statute as construed and applied violated the Fourteenth Amendment presents issues never expressly passed upon by this Court. We deny the motion to dismiss.[25]

In passing on the merits, the Court distinguished *Truax* v. *Corrigan*, on the ground that the means employed there, including "threats and intimidation directed against customers and employees,"

> were deemed to constitute "an admitted tort," conduct unlawful prior to the statute challenged. . . . In the present case the only means authorized by the statute and in fact resorted to by the unions have been peaceful and accompanied by no unlawful act. It follows that if the end sought is constitutional—if the unions may constitutionally induce Senn to agree to refrain from exercising the right to work in his business with his own hands, their acts were lawful.[26]

Peaceful picketing was evidently thought to have been lawful in Wisconsin before the enactment of the statute, unless used to gain an end for which Wisconsin law did not permit its use. Brandeis seems to have assumed that the prior law did not permit its use to induce a person like Senn to agree to refrain from working in his business with his own hands; for if it did, the statute effected no change in the law. And it was only by "exercising its police power" that "Wisconsin has

[24] The majority opinion, by Justice Brandeis, had the concurrence of Chief Justice Hughes and Justices Stone, Roberts, and Cardozo. Justice Butler's dissenting opinion had the concurrence of Justices Van Devanter, McReynolds, and Sutherland.

[25] 301 U.S. at 476–477.

[26] *Id.* at 480.

declared that in a labor dispute peaceful picketing and truthful publicity are means legal for unions." They must have been legal before for some purposes, or else they would have constituted a tort, as in *Truax* v. *Corrigan*. But if they had been legal for this purpose, there would seem to be no occasion to inquire into the constitutionality of the Labor Code. And there would have been no state action affecting Senn—unless the acts of private individuals are regarded as "sanctioned" by the state merely because they were not forbidden.

Assuming that the statute took away a right which Senn previously possessed, not to be subjected to peaceful picketing designed to induce him to abandon his working with his own hands, the Court sustained the statute on the ground that the "end" sought by the unions was not unconstitutional. The unions were said to be actuated by no malice in seeking this end, but to be competing for the work. There were more workers than jobs. If Senn continued to work with his own hands, some union worker would be out of a job. If some union worker got a job because of Senn's ceasing to work, then Senn would be out of a job. Someone would be deprived of liberty to work with his hands at tile laying in any event. By taking away Senn's right to be protected from this sort of private pressure to give up his job for the benefit of someone else, the state was not decreeing whether Senn or the union members should have preference in obtaining the limited number of jobs. In holding that state action which exposed Senn to private pressure to yield his job was not arbitrary, the Court was by no means implying that state pressure to make him yield would be reasonable and therefore valid. The state was not forbidding him to work with his hands, and very probably he would be held to have a constitutional right against any such action on the part of the state.

The fact that private pressure may restrict a particular liberty as effectively as public pressure which the Constitution forbids is no anomaly "Relinquishment of constitutional rights," as the Supreme Court inaccurately describes the process when the government attaches a condition to the grant of a privilege, takes place every day in response to private bargaining power. And many an employee is "compelled to hold his life or the means of living at the mere will of others," although Justice Butler in his dissenting opinion, citing *Yick Wo* v. *Hopkins,* declared it to be "a principle of fundamental law" that no one should be so compelled, a principle which this decision, he said, violates.[27] Yet Butler and his fellow dissenters had always been among the first to hold legislative attempts to carry out that principle unconstitutional, as deprivations of the liberty or property of the "others" at whose will the employee holds his means of living.[28]

The principle of *Truax* v. *Corrigan* might, perhaps, serve to justify federal legislation providing punishment for private individuals who engage in lynching. Let us make the improbable assumption that some state legislature passed a statute repealing the law against homicide in so far as it affects lynching. By enacting such a statute, the state has potentially deprived persons of life. If lynching can be stopped, however, the potential deprivation will not ripen into an actual one. The Supreme Court cannot stop it, as it could stop the picketing in *Truax* v. *Corrigan,* by the simple process of reversing a state court decision in a suit which has already been brought by an aggrieved party. Under our supposed statute, no suit will be brought, and the Supreme Court can scarcely take any steps to compel the state prosecuting authorities to act. Legislation, however, which makes lynching a federal crime or authorizes federal authorities to prosecute it in federal courts as a crime under state law as it was before the enactment of the unconstitutional statute would tend to prevent the state's withdrawal of this protection to life from resulting in an actual deprivation of life. Such federal legislation would seem to be appropriate for the enforcement of the Amendment.

It might be argued that it is not the lynchers, but the state that violated the Amendment. To this it might be replied that the lynchers, like the Arizona pickets, were in fact violating the Amendment by bringing to fruition the state's potential deprivation. If the lynchers were not themselves violating the Amendment, neither were the pickets in Arizona. Holding that their acts were still criminal under state law, the repealing statute being unconstitutional, would be going no further than the Court went in the Arizona case, when it held that the picketing was still illegal under state law, notwithstanding the statute.

In Arizona, however, to prevent the statute having an unconstitutional effect it was sufficient to return the case to the state courts with

27 *Id.* at 491.

28 *Cf.* for instance their dissent in West Coast Hotel Co. v. Parrish, 300 U.S. 379 (1939), in which they maintained, contrary to the majority, that minimum wage legislation was unconstitutional.

a directive to enforce the plaintiff's rights. In the case of the lynching, something more would be needed. There must be proceedings in federal courts. And federal courts can be authorized to try prosecutions for violation of state criminal laws. In *Tennessee* v. *Davis* [29] a statute was sustained under which a federal revenue officer charged with murder in a state court could remove the case to a federal court when he alleged that the killing was done in the performance of his federal duties. The federal court, said Justice Strong, would administer the criminal law of the state. On the same day, it was held in *Strauder* v. *West Virginia* [30] that a Negro indicted for murder in a state court could remove the case to a federal court when by reason of a state statute barring Negroes from jury panels his rights under the Fourteenth Amendment would be jeopardized by a trial in a state court. The statute authorizing the removal was said to be legislation appropriate to the enforcement of the Amendment. The federal court would in his case, too, presumably administer the state criminal law and if he were found guilty would order his punishment under it. To prevent a violation of the Amendment, it was held, Congress was authorized to provide for convictions in federal courts of persons who were not themselves the violators of the Amendment.

In *Tennessee* v. *Davis* and *Strauder* v. *West Virginia* the cases that were held removable to federal courts were cases in which the state prosecution had already begun. It is, perhaps, taking a step further to hold that Congress may provide that a federal prosecutor may start the prosecution for a state crime in a federal court. But, since it was held in the *Strauder* case that legislation does not cease to be "appropriate" merely because it provides punishment for persons other than the violators of the Amendment, it seems clear that should any state have the temerity formally to withdraw the protection of life by legislation, a statute would be valid which would make lynching in that state a federal crime.

Of course, no state is likely to make any such formal withdrawal. But in many states prosecutions for lynching have been rare, and convictions still more so, if, indeed, there have been any. Failure to punish for a given murder cannot, of course, be construed as the equivalent of a statute condoning murder. No state can be expected to give absolute protection to life. Unsolved murders occur everywhere. But systematic failure to prosecute for the lynching of Negroes is the

[29] 100 U.S. 257, 271–272 (1880).

[30] 100 U.S. 303 (1880).

practical equivalent of a formal withdrawal of penalties for such crimes. Exclusion of one or two Negroes from a jury panel does not necessarily amount to a denial of equal protection to a Negro who is to be tried by a jury selected from that panel. But when it is shown that a substantial number of Negroes exist whose qualifications for jury duty are unchallenged and that over a considerable period of time no Negro has ever been placed on the panel, the Supreme Court may infer that Negroes were systematically excluded because of their race. This was the holding in *Norris* v. *Alabama*,[31] the second Scottsboro case. Similarly, if in a region where numerous lynchings have occurred, no one has been prosecuted, it might be inferred that condonation of lynching by the state was deliberate and systematic. That the prosecuting officials, in failing to prosecute, violate the duties which state law places upon them does not prevent their failure from being attributable to the state. As we have seen, it is what the state does, not what it says, that counts. A federal statute providing for the punishment of individual lynchers in any such region would seem to be authorized as legislation appropriate to the enforcement of that provision of the Fourteenth Amendment which forbids a state to deprive any person of life without due process of law. It might also be deemed appropriate to the enforcement of that provision which forbids a state to deny the equal protection of the laws. When a state systematically fails to enforce the law which protects Negroes from murder, it can scarcely be said to be giving Negroes the same protection by law as it gives to other potential victims. "Culpable official inaction" on the part of an arresting officer who voluntarily delivered his colored prisoners to a mob "with a willful intent that the prisoners would be beaten by the mob" has recently been held by a federal circuit court to "constitute a denial of equal protection." [32]

ACTS WHICH PUT STATE MACHINERY IN MOTION OR INVOLVE PERFORMANCE OF ESSENTIAL STATE FUNCTIONS

When a state not merely permits private individuals to act, but gives to their acts an effect which they would not otherwise have on the constitutionally protected interests of others, an effect which would be held unconstitutional if produced by the state directly, the Supreme Court has at times pronounced the result to be state action

[31] 294 U.S. 587 (1935).
[32] Lynch v. United States, 189 F. 2d 476 (5th Cir. 1951).

and invalid. This has been done in cases in which the Supreme Court has recognized that the state played a role in the process. The Court has been blind, however, to the state's role in giving to many private acts the effect of depriving other persons of liberty or property or denying them equal opportunities. Recognition of that role would call for reconsideration of tests for determining the constitutional validity of state action.

After it was held in *Nixon* v. *Herndon*[33] that a Texas statute which expressly barred Negroes from voting in the Democratic party primaries was an unconstitutional denial of equal protection,[34] the statute was repealed, and a new one was substituted which provided that "every political party in this State through its State Executive Committee shall have the power to prescribe the qualifications of its own members and shall in its own way determine who shall be qualified to vote or otherwise participate in such political party." The State Executive Committee then passed a resolution disqualifying Negroes from participating. Nixon, the same Negro who had been barred from voting under the previous statute, was barred again and brought suit against the primary election judges for damages for refusing to furnish him with a ballot. The suit was dismissed in the lower federal courts, but their judgment was reversed by the Supreme Court in 1932, in *Nixon* v. *Condon*.[35] As Justice Cardozo pointed out in the majority opinion, the result for Nixon "is no different from what it was when his cause was here before."[36] He was denied the ballot because of his race quite as effectually by the election judges who obeyed the mandate of the Executive Committee as he had been before by the election judges who obeyed the statute. But it was contended that while the Constitution afforded him protection against the first denial, it afforded him none against the equally effective second denial, since the latter denial was not by the state.

The Supreme Court, however, detected state action. It found it, not in the state's permitting the party to practice a racial discrimination which the legislature was forbidden to practice, but in the statu-

[33] 273 U.S. 536 (1927).

[34] For a contention that this decision "was not in accord with the original understanding of equal protection," see John P. Frank and Robert F. Munro, *The Original Understanding of "Equal Protection of the Laws"* (1950) 50 COL. L. REV. 131, 148, n. 89.

[35] 286 U.S. 73 (1932). Concurring in Justice Cardozo's majority opinion were Chief Justice Hughes and Justices Brandeis, Stone, and Roberts. Justice McReynolds wrote a dissenting opinion, in which Justices Van Devanter, Sutherland, and Butler concurred.

[36] 286 U.S. at 83.

tory transfer of power to do so from the party itself to the State Executive Committee.

Whatever inherent power [said Cardozo] a state political party has to determine the content of its membership resides in the state convention. Bryce, *Modern Democracies*, vol. 2, p. 40. . . . Never has the state convention made declaration of a will to bar negroes of the state from admission to the party ranks. . . . Whatever power of exclusion has been exercised by the members of the committee has come to them, therefore, not as the delegates of the party, but as the delegates of the state. Indeed, adherence to the statute leads to the conclusion that a resolution once adopted by the committee must continue to be binding upon the judges of election though the party in convention may have sought to override it, unless the committee, yielding to the moral force of numbers, shall revoke its earlier action and obey the party will. Power so intrenched is statutory, not inherent. If the state had not conferred it, there would be hardly color of right to give a basis for its exercise.[37]

But surely the fact that the statute permitted the committee to draw up resolutions was not what made the committee's action an exercise of state-given power. Anyone may draw up resolutions without statutory authorization. What made the committee's action an exercise of state-given power was the fact that the statute gave force to those resolutions once they were adopted. It gave force to them by making them "binding upon the judges of election." It was the statutory duty of those judges to give ballots at a primary election to all qualified primary voters who applied and to deny them to all others. And the duties of the judges were enforceable by mandamus proceedings in the state courts.[38] In other words, state officials, in the persons of state judges, stood ready to compel the election judges to withhold the primary ballots from Negroes because of their race, in obedience to the discriminatory resolution of the committee, just as state courts had stood ready to compel employers to withhold employment from aliens, or to compel Negroes to refrain from buying Buchanan's property, or to compel parents to withdraw their children from parochial schools.

This constitutes state action, even though the primary election judges be regarded as private individuals rather than state agents (they were chosen and paid by the party) and the executive committee be not regarded as an agent of the state. Compelling the election officers to practice a discriminatory policy is no less state action be-

37 *Id.* at 84–85.

38 Vernon's Texas Statutes, Art. 3142.

cause that policy was formulated by a group of private individuals rather than by the legislature. We shall have occasion presently to note several cases in which state enforcement of policies formulated by private groups has been treated as being within the scope of the Fourteenth Amendment, and the very fact that it was a private group rather than the legislature that formulated the policy which the state was enforcing was held to invalidate it.

If the state action, then, consisted in its enforcement of the discriminatory policy, regardless of who formulated it, there would equally be state action had the policy been formulated by the party convention instead of by the committee. And if the enforcement did not make it state action, then the mere fact that the committee spoke for the state did not make its resolution the type of state action which comes within the scope of the Fourteenth Amendment. The voice of the committee may have been by virtue of the statute the voice of the state. But if it had been only a voice, accompanied by no state action to compel the election judges to obey it, it would have fallen in the class of "opinions and advice" of those in authority, which, as Justice Brandeis had said in *Standard Computing Scale Co.* v. *Farrell*, "are not a law or regulation such as comes within the scope of the several provisions of the federal Constitution designed to secure the rights of citizens as against action by the states." [39] Had there been no constraint upon the election judges to do what the committee decided they should do except moral constraint, then the power of the committee to direct the judges, like that of the Railroad Labor Board in *Pennsylvania Railroad Co.* v. *U.S. Railroad Labor Board*, would not "be limited by their constitutional or legal right to refuse to do it" [40]—or, presumably, by the constitutional right of the Negroes that the judges should be free to refuse to obey the committee. It was only because the state compelled the judges to obey the committee that the case did not fall within the rule laid down in these two last-named cases. And it would have been no less state action had the state required the election judges to respect the voting qualifications formulated by the party itself, instead of those formulated by the executive committee.

The Court's majority, however, did not think that this conclusion necessarily followed. It expressly declined to pass on the question whether a racial qualification for voting adopted by the party itself

[39] 249 U.S. 571, 575 (1919).

[40] 261 U.S. 72, 84 (1923). See *supra*, pp. 266–267.

would be invalid. It supposed that the question of the presence or absence of state action when the election officials were required to carry out a policy of the party was not the same as the question of the presence of state action when the officials were required to carry out a policy of the committee.

Whatever our conclusion might be [said Justice Cardozo] if the statute had remitted to the party the untrammeled power to prescribe the qualifications of its members, nothing of the kind was done. Instead, the statute lodged the power in a committee, which excluded the petitioner and others of his race, not by virtue of any authority delegated by the party, but by virtue of an authority originating or supposed to originate in the mandate of the law.[41]

Cardozo recognized that the statute made the committee's resolution "binding upon the judges of election." But it was not the obligation which state law laid upon the election judges that he identified as the act of the state which denied Nixon equal protection. The act of the state was taken to be, not the enforcement of the committee's resolution, but the committee's act in passing it. And the committee's act was taken to be state action, not because the state enforced it, but because the legislature had transferred the power to pass an enforceable resolution from the convention, where the power would have been "inherent," to the committee. Hence the stress laid on the fact that the committee was given authority independent of the will of the party.

We do not impugn [he said] the competence of the Legislature to designate the agencies whereby the party faith shall be declared and the party discipline enforced. The pith of the matter is simply this, that, when those agencies are invested with an authority independent of the will of the association in whose name they undertake to speak, they become to that extent the organs of the state itself, the repositories of official power. They are then the governmental instruments whereby parties are organized and regulated to the end that government itself may be established and continued. What they do in that relation, they must do in submission to the mandates of equality and liberty that bind officials everywhere. They are not acting in matters of merely private concern like the directors or agents of business corporations. They are acting in matters of high public interest, matters intimately connected with the capacity of government to exercise its functions unbrokenly and smoothly.[42]

Whether they are acting in matters of merely private concern or in matters of high public interest does not determine whether it is the

[41] 286 U.S. at 84.

[42] *Id.* at 88.

state that is giving them the power. And if it did so determine, the members of a party convention who determine whether Negroes may vote or not in the primary are acting in the same matter of high public interest as are the committee members who determine the same thing.

Neither the fact that it is a matter of high public interest, nor the fact that it was the state that made the act effective, availed to convince the Court in 1935, in *Grovey* v. *Townsend*,[43] that state enforcement of a resolution of the party convention was state action. That case was decided by a Court whose personnel had not changed since the decision in *Nixon* v. *Condon*. The decision was unanimous, Justice Roberts writing the opinion.[44]

That in *Nixon* v. *Condon* the Court had ignored the enforcement of the committee's resolution as the determining feature of state action is evidenced by Justice Roberts's account of that case in *Grovey* v. *Townsend*. After quoting the statutory provision that was before the Court in *Nixon* v. *Condon*, he said:

> We held this was a delegation of state power to the state executive committee and made its determination conclusive irrespective of any expression of the party's will by its convention, and therefore the committee's action barring negroes from the party primaries was state action prohibited by the Fourteenth Amendment.[45]

It was state action, then, because the state had made the committee's determination conclusive "irrespective of any expression of the party's will by its convention." But why was it not state action merely because the state made the action "conclusive," no matter by whom it was taken? The state had made the committee's determination conclusive only by requiring the election judges to obey it. In *Grovey* v. *Townsend* it made the "expression of the party's will by its convention" equally conclusive and by the same method. In fact the state's hand in enforcing the discriminatory resolution was more apparent than in the previous case, since the defendant who refused to give the ballot was a public official—a county clerk. It was his duty, under state law, to furnish a ballot to anyone qualified to vote in the primary who expected to be absent on the day of the primary election, and to decline to furnish ballots to those not qualified. It was in pursuance of this duty that he refused to give Grovey the absentee ballot,

[43] 295 U.S. 45 (1935).

[44] The other members of the Court were Hughes, Van Devanter, McReynolds, Brandeis, Sutherland, Butler, Stone, and Cardozo.

[45] 295 U.S. at 48.

because of his race, which disqualified him according to the resolution of the convention, which the county clerk was required by the state to obey. Yet the Court sustained his action and concluded its opinion by saying: "We find no ground for holding that the respondent has in obedience to the mandate of the law of Texas discriminated against the petitioner or denied him any right guaranteed by the Fourteenth and Fifteenth Amendments." [46]

Justice Roberts cannot have thought that the county clerk did not discriminate against the Negro. How can he have thought that in doing so the clerk was not acting in obedience to the mandate of the law of Texas which required him to obey the resolution of the convention? Perhaps all he meant was that the legislature had delegated to the convention the formulation of the qualifications for voting which the state was to enforce, instead of formulating the qualifications itself. But this fact hardly makes it any the less state action.

As a result of the decision, Negroes were excluded from participation in the Democratic primary in Texas, in conformity with the resolution of the convention. Because the fact that it was state action that made that resolution effective was ignored, it was concluded that there was no violation of the Fourteenth Amendment. And in the absence of state or federal action there could be no violation of the Fifteenth Amendment either, which provides that "the right of citizens of the United States to vote shall not be denied or abridged by the United States or by any State on account of race, color, or previous condition of servitude."

It was argued on behalf of Grovey, however, that "if exclusion from the primary renders his vote at the general election insignificant and useless, the result is to deny him the suffrage altogether." [47] This argument could not prevail as far as the Fourteenth and Fifteenth amendments were concerned, as long as the Court maintained that it was not state action that denied him the suffrage. But the primary from which he was excluded was one at which candidates for United States Senator and Congressman were to be nominated. Grovey's right to vote for such officers was derived not only from the Fourteenth and Fifteenth amendments but also from the Seventeenth Amendment and from Article I, Section 2, which provide the qualifications for voting for Senators and for Congressmen, respectively. It may be that Justice Roberts thought (as the *Classic* case held later) that this right

[46] *Id.* at 55.

[47] *Ibid.*

was secured against the actions of private individuals as well as states, for his answer to Grovey's argument on this point was not based solely on the supposed absence of state action. To argue, he said, that the result of excluding him from the primary is to deny him the suffrage altogether "is to confuse the privilege of membership in a party with the right to vote for one who is to hold a public office." [48] This hardly meets the argument that the decision denied Grovey that effective choice in the election of Congressmen to which the Court later held he had a constitutional right.

Grovey v. *Townsend* was decided in 1935. In 1941 the Court handed down its decision in *United States* v. *Classic*.[49] In that case the Court took a more realistic view of a Democratic primary in a southern state and insisted that "the privilege of membership" in the Democratic party (and the right to have one's vote counted in the primary) was, under state primary laws, part and parcel of "the right to vote for one who is to hold public office." As we saw in Chapter VIII, it held that primary election officers in Louisiana who willfully and falsely counted and certified primary ballots were indictable under § 19 (now § 241) for conspiring to injure or oppress citizens in the exercise of rights or privileges secured to them by the Constitution and under § 20 (now § 242) for subjecting inhabitants, under color of any law, to the deprivation of any rights secured or protected by the Constitution. The right in question was the right of a qualified voter to an effective choice in the election of Congressmen, which right was infringed, the Court held, if his vote was interfered with in the primary, when the state has made the primary a necessary step in the election or the primary effectively controls the choice at the general election. And this right, said Justice Stone, "unlike those guaranteed by the Fourteenth and Fifteenth Amendments, is secured against the action of individuals as well as of states." [50]

The right not to be denied a vote for *state* officers on racial grounds, on the other hand, is secured only against the action of states and of the Federal Government. But if the primary has been made a necessary step in the election, or if it effectively controls the choice at the general election, then if the doctrine of *Grovey* v. *Townsend* were to prevail the Negro would be denied, because of his race, an effective choice for state officers, while retaining only a barren right under the Fifteenth Amendment to cast an ineffectual vote at the general elec-

[48] 295 U.S. at 55. [49] 313 U.S. 299 (1941). [50] *Id.* at 315.

tion. The Fourteenth and Fifteenth amendments would afford Negroes no protection at all at what Justice Stone characterized in the *Classic* case as "the only stage of the election procedure when their choice is of significance," [51] because the discrimination is said to be practiced by private persons, not by the state. Realizing that the doctrine of *Grovey* v. *Townsend* would render the Fifteenth Amendment impotent at the only stage of elections that matters, the Court, in *Smith* v. *Allwright*,[52] decided in 1944, searched more intently for the state's hand in the exclusion of Negroes from the Texas primary. The *Classic* case, said Justice Reed for the majority,

> bears upon *Grovey* v. *Townsend* not because exclusion of Negroes from primaries is any more or less state action by reason of the unitary character of the electoral process but because the recognition of the place of the primary in the electoral scheme makes clear that state delegation to a party of the power to fix the qualifications of primary elections is delegation of a state function that may make the party's action the action of the state. When *Grovey* v. *Townsend* was written, the Court looked upon the denial of a vote in a primary as a mere refusal by a party of party membership. . . . . As the Louisiana statutes for holding primaries are similar to those of Texas, our ruling in *Classic* as to the unitary character of the electoral process calls for a reexamination as to whether or not the exclusion of Negroes from a Texas party primary was state action.[53]

After outlining some of the provisions of the Texas statute relating to primaries, Justice Reed went on:

> We think that this statutory system for the selection of party nominees for inclusion on the general election ballot makes the party which is required to follow these legislative directions an agency of the State in so far as it determines the participants in a primary election. The party takes its character as an agency of the State from the duties imposed upon it by state statutes; the duties do not become matters of private law because they are performed by a political party. The plan of the Texas primary follows substantially that of Louisiana, with the exception that in Louisiana the State pays the cost of the primary while Texas assesses the cost against candidates. In numerous instances, the Texas statutes fix or limit the fees to be charged. Whether paid directly by the State or through state requirements, it is state action which compels. When primaries become a part of the machinery for choosing officials, state and national, as they have here, the same tests to determine the character of discrimination or abridgement should be applied to the primary as are applied to the general election. If the State requires a certain electoral procedure, prescribes a general election ballot made up of party nominees so chosen, and limits the choice of

[51] *Id.* at 314.
[52] 321 U.S. 649 (1944).
[53] *Id.* at 660–661. Justice Roberts wrote a dissenting opinion.

the electorate in general elections for state offices, practically speaking, to those whose names appear on such a ballot, it endorses, adopts and enforces the discrimination against Negroes, practiced by a party entrusted by Texas law with the determination of the qualifications of participants in the primary. This is state action within the meaning of the Fifteenth Amendment. *Guinn* v. *United States,* 238 U.S. 347, 362.

The United States is a constitutional democracy. Its organic law grants to all citizens a right to participate in the choice of elected officials without restriction by any State because of race. This grant to the people of the opportunity for choice is not to be nullified by a State through casting its electoral process in a form which permits a private organization to practice racial discrimination in the election. Constitutional rights would be of little value if they could be thus indirectly denied. *Lane* v. *Wilson,* 307 U.S. 268, 275.

The privilege of membership in a party may be, as this Court said in *Grovey* v. *Townsend,* . . . no concern of a State. But when, as here, that privilege is also the essential qualification for voting in a primary to select nominees for a general election, the State makes the action of the party the action of the State.[54]

Grovey v. *Townsend* was expressly overruled.

The chief evidence which Justice Reed saw of state action seems to have been its limitation of the choice of the electorate at general elections to those who have been nominated at the primaries. This limitation converted the party's racial discrimination in the primary into racial discrimination at the general election. It was not by mere non-action that the state "permitted" a private organization to practice racial discrimination in the election; it was "through casting its electoral process" in the form which it adopted. The state did more than "permit." It gave to the party's withholding of "the privilege of membership" the effect of denying to the Negro an effective right to vote at all.

This would constitute state action even were there nothing more. But there was more. Justice Reed spoke of the duties imposed upon the party by state statutes. But it was not any duty imposed on the party that required the party to exclude Negroes; it was, rather, the duty imposed upon the primary election judges to withhold ballots from those not qualified under the convention's resolutions. This was the state action which compelled the election judges to obey the resolution of the convention and so denied the Negro the ballot on racial grounds. And it would have been equally state action even if the state had not likewise acted further to make the primary a part of a unitary

[54] 321 U.S. at 663–665.

electoral process. Tying the primary to the general election made the party's racial discrimination applicable, in effect, to the general election, and so brought the Fifteenth Amendment into the picture. But compelling the election judges to withhold primary ballots from those disqualified by party resolution was in itself state action; and since the party resolution disqualified Negroes by reason of their race, it was state action which enforced a racial ban on primary voting. Even without the tie-up which brought the Fifteenth Amendment into play, a question would arise whether the state action violated the equal protection clause of the Fourteenth. It was that clause, not the Fifteenth Amendment, which was held to be infringed in *Nixon* v. *Herndon* by the statute which expressly barred Negroes from voting at the Democratic primary.

There seems clearly to be state action, then, when a clerk at a primary election, in obedience to state law, refuses a ballot to one whom the party disqualifies. Even though the state law imposed no duty on the clerk to observe the qualifications laid down by the party, there would still be state action if the state's election laws gave preference to primary nominees at the general election. Hence, if there were a legal duty on the primary clerk to obey the party, or if the election laws gave preference to primary nominees, a Negro would have a constitutional right not to be denied a primary ballot by reason of his race. Does he have such a right even when these two conditions are absent?

Immediately after the decision of *Smith* v. *Allwright* the governor of South Carolina called an extraordinary session of the legislature for the avowed purpose of circumventing the decision. All laws relating to primaries were repealed in 1944. Under the rules of the Democratic party which restricted primary voting to whites, a duly qualified Negro voter named George Elmore was not permitted to vote at a county primary held in 1946 for the nomination of candidates for Congress and for various state offices. He brought suit against the precinct election managers and members of the county executive committee, praying for a declaratory judgment with injunction. In the federal district court Judge J. Waties Waring decided in his favor on July 12, 1947, in *Elmore* v. *Rice*;[55] the decision was affirmed under the name of *Rice* v. *Elmore*[56] by the Court of Appeals for the Fourth Circuit on December 30, 1947, in an opinion by Judge Parker (sitting with Judges

[55] 72 F. Supp. 516 (D. S. Car., 1947).

[56] 165 F. 2d 387 (5th Cir. 1947).

Soper and Dobie); and the Supreme Court denied certiorari in 1948.[57]

No one questioned the fact that nomination at the primary was the practical equivalent of election. The defense rested entirely on the alleged absence of state action, contending that since the repeal of the primary laws in 1944, action of the Democratic party was no more state action than would be the action of a private club. Absence of state action, if it could be made out, would, of course, be a good defense to a charge of violating rights secured by the Fourteenth and Fifteenth amendments, but not to a charge of violating the right to an effective choice for Congressmen, which, we have seen, is a right secured against the action of private individuals as well as states. Neither court rested its decision on this ground, however. Both held that there was state action and a violation of the two amendments. Even had the primary been held for the purpose of nominating candidates for state office alone, the exclusion of Elmore would have been unconstitutional.

The state imposed no duties on the election officers to obey the rules of the party, nor did it provide for a preferential position of primary nominees on the ballot at the general election. The two features of the Texas law which indicated state action were lacking. Nevertheless, state action could be found on the principle of *Truax v.Corrigan*.[58] Before 1944, by virtue of the law, a qualified voter had a right to vote in the primary. If the repeal extinguished this right it was as much state action as was the enactment of the anti-injunction statute in Arizona. Judge Waring, in the district court (without mentioning the *Truax* case), noted this argument, but did not rely upon it. On this point he said:

> The argument is that under the law of South Carolina, as it stood before April 1944 and as construed by the Supreme Court decisions, Negroes had a right to vote in the primary as then constituted. And, therefore, when the legislature took action, although this action was in the form of repeal, it deprived these citizens of a right which they then had, and that the act of the legislature, while negative in form, was really positive. . . . However, I think it unnecessary to elaborate this further as this opinion will rest upon entirely different grounds.[59]

The different grounds upon which the opinion rested were briefly these: Title 8 U.S.C.A. § 31 refers to any "constitution, law, custom, usage, or regulation of any State." The method used by the Demo-

[57] 333 U.S. 875 (1948). [58] See *supra*, pp. 327–330. [59] 72 F. Supp. at 524.

cratic party of South Carolina is the same "custom and usage" as the one that had existed before the repeal of the statutes. After the repeal the State Convention

> adopted rules that were almost verbatim to the statutes that had been repealed. While the *General Assembly* repealed the laws governing the primaries, *the people of the State* assembled in convention and enacted practically the same rules. These may not be laws or statutes in name but they certainly amount to *"custom, usage, or regulation"* and are the acts of the *people.*[60]

He was "of the opinion that the present Democratic Party in South Carolina is acting for and on behalf of the people of South Carolina." [61]

In affirming, Judge Parker adopted substantially the same reasoning as Judge Waring. After stating in a footnote that where adoption of the primary as a part of the public election machinery "is done as a matter of fact and custom, the presence or absence of statutory regulation of the primary does not seem a matter of controlling importance," he proceeded to say in the text:

> State law relating to the general election gives effect to what is done in the primary and makes it just as much a part of the election machinery of the state by which the people choose their officers as if it were regulated by law, as formerly. Elections in South Carolina remain a two step process, whether the party primary be accounted a preliminary of the general election, or the general election be regarded as giving effect to what is done in the primary; and those who control the Democratic Party as well as the state government cannot by placing the first of the steps under officials of the party rather than of the state, absolve such officials from the limitations which the federal Constitution imposes. When these officials participate in what is a part of the state's election machinery, they are election officers of the state de facto if not de jure, and as such must observe the limitations of the Constitution. Having undertaken to perform an important function relating to the exercise of sovereignty by the people, they may not violate the fundamental principles laid down by the Constitution for its exercise.[62]

There can be no question that the election officers of the party were exercising a power which was quite as effective as if they had been state officers *de jure*. Though this power did not owe its effectiveness to any action by the state (apart from its action in extinguishing a right against its discriminatory use), its was a power employed in the performance of an essential state function, and was accordingly held to be *de facto* state power, subject to whatever limitations the Consti-

60 *Id.* at 527. Italics in original.
61 *Id.* at 528.
62 165 F. 2d at 390–391.

tution places on the states. It is very doubtful, however, that these limitations would be held to apply to private individuals other than those performing functions essential to the operation of the state, no matter how effective their power to coerce those weaker than themselves, unless the Court could recognize the derivation of their power from the law.[63]

In the case of unions which discriminate against Negroes and effectively bar them from jobs, the Court has in some circumstances found that they were exercising power derived from the law and held, or clearly intimated, that constitutional limitations apply. In *James* v. *Marinship Corp.*[64] the California supreme court held, in 1944, that it was illegal for a union to insist that an employer comply with a closed shop agreement, when the union did not admit Negroes to full membership. Denial of employment to Negroes, because of nonmembership in a union which would not admit them on reasonable terms, was said by Gibson, C.J., to violate the spirit of the Fourteenth Amendment. But the decision was based on common law grounds. Earlier in the year the United States Supreme Court intimated, in *Steele* v. *L. & N.R. Co.,*[65] that if the Railway Labor Act were construed to confer power on the union which was chosen as bargaining representative to bargain for a contract which discriminates against Negro employees who were not eligible to membership in the union, it might well be held to violate the Fifth Amendment. To avoid the constitutional issue, the Court construed the Act differently. Said Chief Justice Stone:

> If . . . the Act confers this power on the bargaining representative of a craft or class of employees without any commensurate statutory duty toward its members, constitutional questions arise. For the representative is clothed with power not unlike that of a legislature which is subject to constitutional limitations on its power to deny, restrict, destroy or discriminate against the rights of those for whom it legislates and which is also under an affirmative constitutional duty equally to protect those rights. If the Railway Labor Act purports to impose on petitioner and the other Negro members of the craft the legal duty to comply with the terms of a contract whereby the representative has discriminatorily restricted their employment for the benefit and advantage of the Brotherhood's own members, we must decide the constitutional questions which petitioner raises in his pleadings.

63 On the general topic see Note, *Negro Disenfranchisement—a Challenge to the Constitution* (1947) 47 Col. L. Rev. 76.

64 25 Calif. 2d 721, 155 P. 2d 329 (1944).

65 323 U.S. 192, 198–199 (1944).

Had the Act conferred the powers which the Court held it did not confer on the union, the intimation is that the union's action in negotiating the discriminatory contract would have been federal action and as such a violation of the Fifth Amendment. The intimation is made explicit in Justice Murphy's concurring opinion. It would have been federal action because it was the federal statute which deprived the Negro employees of power to bargain to protect themselves from the union's actions. In 1946 the Kansas supreme court went further in *Betts* v. *Easley*.[66] It held not only that a contract of this discriminatory character would be unconstitutional if the statute permitted it, but that it was unconstitutional, as a violation of the Fifth Amendment, for a union, chosen under the Railway Labor Act to represent the employees, to refuse to let the Negro employees participate in the bargaining. According to this Kansas decision the union on which the federal statute conferred power over the conditions of employment must not only refrain from imposing unfair conditions on the Negro employees; it must let them participate in determining the conditions of employment. The Federal Supreme Court has not yet passed on this precise question.

THE DOGMA OF NONDELEGABILITY OF LEGISLATIVE POWER

When the Court, in *Nixon* v. *Condon,* recognized that the power of the executive committee had been delegated to it by the state, it held the committee's discriminatory resolution unconstitutional, because inconsistent with "the mandates of equality and liberty that bind officials everywhere." There have been other cases in which the power conferred by the legislature on others to formulate policies to be enforced by the state has been held unconstitutional, even though the particular policy has not violated any constitutional mandate that binds the legislature itself. It is the very fact that someone other than the legislature—whether administrative officials of the Government or selected groups of private persons—has been empowered to formulate policy which the Government will enforce, that has been held to make the delegation invalid. There have been other cases, however, in which the delegation of legislative power has been equally demonstrable, but the Court has called it by some other name and sustained it, as indeed it must do in some cases, if only in the routine enforcement of contract and property rights. It would be impossible for the

[66] 161 Kan. 459, 169 P. 2d 831 (1946).

Court to adhere consistently to the dogma that the delegation of legislative power is necessarily unconstitutional, or even to hold that the policy which the state enforces at the behest of private individuals must always be confined within the limits that confine the policies which the legislature is free to adopt.

Delegation of federal legislative power, whether to executive or administrative officials or to private persons, has to meet one particular obstacle which does not stand in the way of delegation of state legislative power. In Article I, Section 1, the constitution declares that "all legislative powers herein granted shall be vested in a Congress of the United States." This provision has been held inapplicable to legislative power to deal with foreign affairs, on the ground that such power was not "herein granted" by the states which ratified the Constitution, but was one which the Federal Government had already inherited from the British Crown at the moment when the United States achieved its independence. Hence, a delegation to the President of power to make effective a prohibition of the sale of munitions to the countries engaged in war in the Chaco, if he should find that the prohibition "may contribute to the reëstablishment of peace between those countries," was sustained in 1936 in *United States* v. *Curtiss-Wright Export Corp.*[67] On the other hand, in 1935 the Court held certain provisions of the National Industrial Recovery Act bad which conferred on the President power to decide when the interstate shipment of "hot oil" (oil produced in contravention of state conservation laws) should be prohibited (*Panama Refining Co.* v. *Ryan*) [68] and power to draw up codes of fair competition which industries should be compelled to obey (*Schechter Poultry Corp.* v. *United States* [69]). Congress had failed, thought the Court, to declare with sufficient definiteness the policy which was to guide the President in making his determinations. The provision regarding hot oil, in the words of Chief Justice Hughes in the *Panama* case, "permits such a breadth of authorized action as essentially to commit to the President the functions of a legislature rather than those of an executive or administrative officer executing a declared policy." [70]

In this case, however, Hughes admitted that Congress, after laying down policies, may leave to others the duty to make "subordinate

[67] 299 U.S. 304 (1936). *Cf.* David M. Levitan, *The Foreign Relations Power: an Analysis of Mr. Justice Sutherland's Theory* (1946) 55 YALE L.J. 467.

[68] 293 U.S. 388 (1935). [69] 295 U.S. 495 (1935). [70] 293 U.S. at 418–419.

rules within prescribed limits." "Upon this principle," he said, "rests the authority of the Interstate Commerce Commission, in the execution of the declared policy of the Congress in enforcing reasonable rates, in preventing undue preferences and unjust discriminations," and so forth.[71] But the rules of the Commission are not really "subordinate" to any "declared policy" of Congress. Congress has declared that rates shall be "reasonable" and that preferences shall not be "undue" or discriminations "unjust." But it has not declared any policy for determining what shall be considered "reasonable" or "undue" or "unjust." In determining these matters the Commission is legislating. But the legislative power can still be regarded as "vested" in Congress, which is exercising it through administrative officers who formulate policies of "reasonableness" which Congress can at any time alter. Without such delegation, Congress would be unable to legislate at all for a complex society. Delegation is not inherently objectionable, as long as Congress, by retaining the power to alter the legislation of the bodies to whom the power to legislate has been delegated, retains control of the matter, and as long as it does not delegate power to legislate for purposes which would vitiate Congressional legislation itself. After all, federal courts have always exercised federal legislative power in developing rules of law to govern admiralty cases or cases involving the apportionment of the waters of interstate streams.

But delegation of legislative power, whether state or federal, may be held bad for reasons other than the constitutional vesting of federal legislative power in Congress. Under the Fifth and the Fourteenth Amendments, the validity of legislation which restricts liberty or curtails the exercise of property rights or which produces a certain degree of inequality may depend upon the purpose for which it is enacted. And if the legislation has been enacted by the legislative body itself (Congress, or the state legislature, or the city council), there may be a presumption that it was enacted for a proper purpose. But if the restriction is to be imposed at the mere will of some administrative body or some selected private group, uncontrolled by standards furnished by the legislature, the presumption that it was enacted for a proper purpose may be rebutted.

Thus, an ordinance forbidding the operation of laundries in wooden buildings might be sustained on the presumption that the city council had found it necessary as a means of preventing conflagra-

[71] *Id.* at 427.

tions. So, too, might an ordinance forbidding their operation in any building found by the fire department to constitute a fire hazard. But when, in *Yick Wo* v. *Hopkins*,[72] an ordinance forbade the operation of laundries in wooden buildings without first obtaining the consent of the Board of Supervisors, and provided no standards for the guidance of the Board and no judicial review of their decisions, it was held to amount to a denial of equal protection to those who were refused permits. The facts revealed that permits were withheld from every Chinese applicant and granted to every white applicant. The purpose was thus shown to be, not to prevent fire hazards, but to discriminate against the Chinese—a purpose which, if openly admitted, would have been unconstitutional. But even had there been no evidence of this discrimination in practice, the Court was evidently prepared to hold it invalid, because it conferred power on the board to withhold consent "without reason and without responsibility." The fact that the ordinance authorized operation in wooden buildings by those favored by the board indicated that the legislative body had not found their operation to constitute a fire hazard.

In the *Yick Wo* case no standard at all was provided by the lawmakers to guide the actions of the supervisors. Even when a statute provides an ostensible standard, the delegation may be held bad if the standard is so vague or ambiguous that in effect it gives arbitrary power to administrative officers to discriminate.

In 1946 the so-called Boswell Amendment to the Alabama constitution was adopted at the state-wide general election. It provided that no one might register as a voter unless he could "understand and explain any article of the constitution of the United States in the English language." A statute provided that an applicant for registration must establish his qualifications "to the reasonable satisfaction of the board of registrars." In 1949 the Boswell Amendment was held unconstitutional by a three-judge federal district court in *Davis* v. *Schnell*,[73] a suit for a declaratory judgment and injunction. The words "understand" and "explain," said Judge Mullins, are too indefinite to provide a reasonable standard. Elaborating, he went on:

> To state it plainly, the sole test is: Has the applicant by oral examination or otherwise understood and explained the Constitution to the satisfaction of the particular board? To state it more plainly, the board has a right to

[72] 118 U.S. 356 (1886).

[73] 81 F. Supp. 872 (S.D. Ala. 1949). The court consisted of McCord, Cir. J., and Mullins and McDuffie, D.JJ.

reject one applicant and accept another, depending solely upon whether it likes or dislikes the understanding and explanation offered. To state it even more plainly, the board, by the use of the words "understand and explain," is given the arbitrary power to accept or reject any prospective elector that may apply, or to use the language of Yick Wo v. Hopkins, ... these words "actually do confer, not a discretion to be exercised upon a consideration of the circumstances of each case, but a naked and arbitrary power to give or withhold consent * * * ." The board has the power to establish two classes, those to whom they consent and those to whom they do not—those who may vote and those who may not. Such arbitrary power amounts to a denial of equal protection of the law within the meaning of the Fourteenth Amendment to the Constitution, and is condemned by the *Yick Wo* and many other decisions of the Supreme Court.[74]

Judge Mullins went on to say that while it is a court's duty to determine whether an exact meaning was intended for an ambiguous word or phrase, the history of the adoption of the Boswell Amendment "discloses that the ambiguity inherent in the phrase 'understand and explain' cannot be resolved, but, on the contrary, was purposeful and used with a view of meeting the decision of the Supreme Court of the United States in Smith v. Allwright." He showed that the campaign for the adoption of the Amendment had been conducted with the avowed purpose of disfranchising Negroes and concluded that the legislative history "only reinforces the conclusion that the provision in question was incorporated for the purpose of allowing arbitrary action, and not for the purpose of providing a definite and reasonable standard." [75]

Then, pointing out that the practical administration of the Amendment demonstrated that the ambiguous standard had, in fact, been arbitrarily used to discriminate against Negroes, he went on:

It, thus, clearly appears that this Amendment was intended to be, and is being used for the purpose of discriminating against applicants for the franchise on the basis of race or color. Therefore, we are necessarily brought to the conclusion that this Amendment to the Constitution of Alabama, both in its object and the manner of its administration, is unconstitutional, because it violates the Fifteenth Amendment. While it is true that there is no mention of race or color in the Boswell Amendment, this does not save it. The Fifteenth Amendment "nullifies sophisticated as well as simple-minded modes of discrimination," and "It hits onerous procedural requirements which effectively handicap exercise of the franchise by the colored race although the abstract right to vote may remain unrestricted as to race." Lane v. Wilson, 307 U.S. 268, 275.

[74] *Id.* at 878.

[75] *Id.* at 880.

On appeal, the Supreme Court affirmed in a *per curiam* opinion, citing *Lane* v. *Wilson* and *Yick Wo* v. *Hopkins.*[76]

It should be noted that even without the racial motivation which characterized the adoption and the administration of the Boswell Amendment, which made it vulnerable to the Fifteenth Amendment, the district court clearly indicated that it would violate the equal protection clause of the Fourteenth by classifying voters according to the likes and dislikes of the registrars. The racial motivation merely "reinforced" this conclusion and made the Fifteenth Amendment applicable. The Supreme Court's citation of the *Yick Wo* case seems to indicate that it holds like views as to the Fourteenth Amendment.

There are other cases in which a restriction which might be valid if imposed by the legislative body for some presumably public purpose has been held bad because a selected group of private persons was to determine whether it was to be imposed or removed. In *Eubank* v. *City of Richmond,*[77] decided in 1912, an ordinance provided that

> whenever the owners of two-thirds of the property abutting on any street shall, in writing, request the Committee on Streets to establish a building line on the side of the square on which their property fronts, the Street Committee [an official body] shall establish such line so that the same shall not be less than 5 feet nor more than 30 feet from the street line. . . . And no permit for the erection of any building upon such front of the square upon which such building line is so established shall be issued except for the construction of houses within the limits of such line.

Violation of the ordinance was punishable by a fine. On the petition of the owners of two thirds of the property on the side of a certain square, the Street Committee established a line beyond which a bay window in a house owned by Eubank projected about three feet. Eubank was ordered to make his building conform to the line. He refused and was fined $25 in the local court, and the judgment was affirmed by the highest state court. He brought the matter to the Supreme Court, which held that the ordinance was invalid.

The Court did not deny the power of the city itself to establish such a building line, but held the ordinance invalid because of the power which it conferred on some property holders to control the property rights of others at will. Said Justice McKenna for the unanimous Court:

[76] Under the name of Schnell v. Davis, 336 U.S. 933 (1949). Justice Reed thought that the case should be set down for argument.

[77] 226 U.S. 137 (1912).

The statute and ordinance, while conferring the power on some property holders to virtually control and dispose of the proper[ty] rights of others, creates no standard by which the power thus given is to be exercised; in other words, the property holders who desire and have the authority to establish the line may do so solely for their own interest or even capriciously.[78]

Then, after pointing out that under the ordinance the line might be established in different blocks on different principles, he added: "It is hard to understand how public comfort or convenience, much less public health, can be promoted by a line which may be so variously disposed."

In 1928 the Court reached the same conclusion as to a somewhat similar ordinance in the case of *State of Washington ex rel. Seattle Title Trust Company* v. *Roberge*.[79] In that case a zoning ordinance provided that no building should be erected except for certain specified purposes in the district in question. The specified purposes did not include philanthropic homes, but by an amendment it was provided that a philanthropic home for children or for old people should be permitted in that district "when the written consent shall have been obtained of the owners of two-thirds of the property within four hundred (400) feet of the proposed building." The trustee of a philanthropic home for aged poor which already existed in this district proposed to remove the old building and erect a new one in its place. A permit to erect the new building was denied by the Superintendent of Building of the city, on the sole ground that the trustee had not secured the written consents of the owners of two thirds of the property within four hundred feet.

Here, too, the Court held the ordinance invalid under the Fourteenth Amendment, without denying the power of the city to exclude such a new home from the district by a general zoning law. Had there been such a general law, it might have amounted to a legislative determination that public health, safety or the like required the exclusion, just as in the case of *Yick Wo* a general ordinance forbidding the carrying on of the laundry business in wooden buildings might have been presumed to have been enacted in pursuance of a legislative determination that protection from fire hazards required it. In both cases, the power of certain designated persons to release anyone from the restriction, indicated that there was no legislative

[78] *Id.* at 143–144.

[79] 278 U.S. 116 (1928).

determination which would have justified the restriction. Justice Butler, speaking for the unanimous Court, said:

The facts disclosed by the record make it clear that the exclusion of the new home from the First District is not indispensable to the general zoning plan. And there is no legislative determination that the proposed building and use would be inconsistent with public health, safety, morals, or general welfare. The enactment itself plainly implies the contrary. The grant of permission for such building and use, although purporting to be subject to such consents, shows that the legislative body found that the construction and maintenance of the new home was in harmony with the public interest and with the general scope and planning of the zoning ordinance. The section purports to give the owners of less than one-half the land within 400 feet of the proposed building authority—uncontrolled by any standard or rule prescribed by legislative action—to prevent the trustee from using its land for the proposed home. The superintendent is bound by the decision or inaction of such owners. There is no provision for review under the ordinance; their failure to give consent is final. They are not bound by any official duty, but are free to withhold consent for selfish reasons or arbitrarily and may subject the trustee to their will or caprice. *Yick Wo* v. *Hopkins,* 118 U.S. 356, 366, 368. The delegation of power so attempted is repugnant to the due process clause of the Fourteenth Amendment. *Eubank* v. *Richmond,* 226 U.S. 137, 143; *Browning* v. *Hooper,* 269 U.S. 396.[80]

In *Carter* v. *Carter Coal Company,*[81] which we have already noted on other points, the majority of the Court held that the labor provisions of the Guffey Coal Act were invalid, not only because they fell outside the scope of the power conferred on the Federal Government but also for the reason that they delegated legislative power to private individuals. The labor provisions provided that whenever maximum hours of labor should be agreed upon in any contract negotiated between the producers of more than two thirds of the annual national coal tonnage production for the preceding year and the representatives of more than one half the mine workers employed, "such maximum hours of labor shall be accepted by all the code members." They also provided that when any wage agreement should be negotiated by

80 278 U.S. at 121.

81 298 U.S. 238 (1936). Chief Justice Hughes agreed that the labor provisions were unconstitutional for the reasons given by the majority, but maintained that the requirement was valid that the operator accept the code (under penalty of loss of the tax rebate), since the provisions concerning prices were in his opinion valid, and separable from the wage provisions. Justices Cardozo, Brandeis, and Stone also thought the price provisions valid and thought it improper for the Court to pass judgment on the labor provisions. Justices Van Devanter, McReynolds, Butler, and Roberts, however, agreed with Sutherland, who wrote the prevailing opinion, that the labor provisions were properly before the Court, being, as they thought, inseparable from the other provisions of the Act.

collective bargaining in any district or group of districts between representatives of producers of more than two thirds of the annual tonnage production of the district or group of districts during the preceding year and the representatives of the majority of the mine workers therein, the wages provided for in such agreement "shall be accepted as the minimum wages for the various classifications of labor by the code members operating in such district or group of districts." "The effect," said Justice Sutherland, "in respect to wages and hours, is to subject the dissentient minority, either of producers or miners or both to the will of the stated majority . . ." Discussing the matter more fully, he said:

The power conferred upon the majority is, in effect, the power to regulate the affairs of an unwilling minority. This is legislative delegation in its most obnoxious form; for it is not even delegation to an official or an official body, presumptively disinterested, but to private persons whose interests may be and often are adverse to the interests of others in the same business. . . . Some coal producers favor the code; others oppose it; and the record clearly indicates that this diversity of view arises from their conflicting and even antagonistic interests. The difference between producing coal and regulating its production is, of course, fundamental. The former is a private activity; the latter is necessarily a governmental function; since, in the very nature of things, one person may not be entrusted with the power to regulate the business of another, and especially of a competitor. And a statute which attempts to confer such power undertakes an intolerable and unconstitutional interference with personal liberty and private property. The delegation is so clearly arbitrary and so clearly a denial of rights safeguarded by the due process clause of the Fifth Amendment, that it is unnecessary to do more than refer to decisions of this Court which foreclose the action. [Citing the *Schechter Poultry*, the *Eubank* and the *Roberge* cases.] [82]

Chief Justice Hughes, in his separate opinion, based his conclusion that the labor provision of the Code was invalid in part on the delegation of legislative power, as did Sutherland. The Code, he said,

attempts a broad delegation of legislative power to fix hours and wages without standards of limitation. The government invokes the analogy of legislation which becomes effective on the happening of a specified event, and says that in this case the event is the agreement of a certain proportion of producers and employees, whereupon the other producers and employees become subject to legal obligations accordingly. I think that the argument is unsound and is pressed to the point where the principle would be entirely destroyed. It would remove all restrictions upon the delegation of legisla-

[82] 298 U.S. at 311–312.

tive power, as the making of laws could thus be referred to any designated officials or private persons whose orders or agreements would be treated as "events," with the result that they would be invested with the force of law having penal sanctions.[83]

But there are other cases in which legislation has been sustained despite the fact that the restrictions which it imposed were imposed at the will of a private group or were removable with the consent of a private group.

In 1917, after the *Eubank* and before the *Roberge* decisions, a Chicago ordinance was sustained in *Cusack Co.* v. *City of Chicago*.[84] This ordinance forbade the erection of billboards in any residence block "without first obtaining the consent in writing of the owners or duly authorized agents of said owners owning a majority of the frontage of the property on both sides of the street in the block in which such billboard or signboard is to be erected, constructed or located." Most of Justice Clarke's opinion for the majority is devoted to showing the evils which might justify an outright prohibition of billboards. But, like the city of Richmond in the earlier case and the city of Seattle in the subsequent one, Chicago did not forbid them outright. It permitted their erection if the requisite consents of the owners could be obtained. Turning to this provision, Clarke said: "The plaintiff in error cannot be injured, but obviously may be benefited by this provision, for without it the prohibition of erection of such billboards in such residence sections is absolute." [85]

Of course! But this has no bearing on the constitutional question. Eubank was not injured by the fact that the city of Richmond, instead of providing for a building line in all cases, provided for it only in those cases in which the neighboring owners demanded it. Nor was the trustee of the home injured because Seattle, instead of prohibiting absolutely the building of philanthropic homes in the zone in question, permitted the building of them if the specified owners of nearby property consented. The fact that the restriction in those cases was provisional rather than absolute did not, of course, make it more severe. But it was held to make it bad, because it revealed that the purpose of the restriction was not to benefit the public generally, but to benefit a selected group of private persons. And this was equally true of the Chicago ordinance.

[83] 298 U.S. at 318.
[84] 242 U.S. 526 (1917). Justice McKenna dissented without opinion.
[85] 242 U.S. at 530.

Justice Clarke sought to distinguish the *Eubank* case by pointing out that the Richmond ordinance

left the establishment of the building line untouched until the lot owners should act, and then made the street committee the mere automatic register of that action, and gave to it the effect of law. The ordinance in the case at bar absolutely prohibits the erection of any billboards in the blocks designated, but permits this prohibition to be modified with the consent of the persons who are to be most affected by such modification.[86]

It is, of course, arguable that the neighboring owners were more peculiarly affected by the erection of billboards than they were by the establishment of a building line or the construction of a philanthropic home and that therefore it was more reasonable for the city to delegate to them the power to decide whether the billboards should be allowed than to decide whether the building line should be established or the home constructed. But this is an argument for the propriety of delegation in the particular circumstances. Justice Clarke, however, denied that there was any delegation at all. Following the language we have just quoted, he added:

The one ordinance permits two thirds of the lot owners to impose restrictions upon the other property in the block, while the other permits one half of the lot owners to remove a restriction from the other property owners. This is not a delegation of legislative power, but is, as we have seen, a familiar provision affecting the enforcement of laws and ordinances.

If the distinction turns on the difference between allowing the private group to initiate the procedure and allowing it to remove the restriction rather than on the difference in the appropriateness of the group to exercise legislative power, it breaks down. In both cases the private group had the determining voice as to whether the restriction should be effective or not. And if Clarke meant to intimate that the private group in Richmond had more power than that in Chicago, because it was to take the initiative or because it comprised the owners of two thirds rather than slightly more than one half of the neighboring property, he was clearly wrong. The Richmond group would have to take affirmative action before it could impose the restriction, while the Chicago group could keep the restriction on by mere inertia; and those in the Richmond group who wished to impose the restriction could be thwarted by the owners of slightly more than one third of the property, while it would take the owners of more than

[86] *Id.* at 531.

one half of the Chicago property to thwart the desire of the remainder to keep the restriction in force. Moreover, in the subsequent *Roberge* case the Court ignored any distinction between initiating and removing a restriction. The ordinance there, before it was amended, absolutely forbade the construction of philanthropic homes in the district. The amendment permitted the owners of two thirds of the property within 400 feet to repeal the prohibition. The Court called it a delegation of power. It would have been at least as much of a delegation had the owners of more than one half, instead of two thirds, been permitted to repeal it.

In the *Roberge* case Justice Butler distinguished the *Cusack* case on the ground that the facts there found "were sufficient to warrant the conclusion that such billboards would or were liable to endanger the safety and decency in such districts," whereas "it is not suggested that the proposed new home for aged poor would be a nuisance." [87] But the ground for holding the Seattle prohibition bad was not that an outright prohibition of the home by a general zoning ordinance would be unconstitutional—the Court said it need not decide that question—but that a delegation of the power to prohibit it would be bad. And if private individuals are given power to repeal a restriction on the use of property, there is as much of a delegation to them when what they may repeal is a restriction of a nuisance as when it is a restriction of something else.

Earlier in the year in which the *Roberge* case was decided (1928) Chief Justice Taft, speaking for the unanimous Court in *Hampton & Co.* v. *United States,*[88] had something to say about state legislation delegating legislative power to the residents of a district. His remarks were made for illustrative purposes. The case concerned the validity of the "flexible tariff provision" of the Act of 1922, which authorized the President, after an investigation by the Tariff Commission, to raise or lower the duty on imported products by not more than 50 percent in order to equalize the differences in cost between the chief foreign producer and the United States. The provision was challenged as an unconstitutional delegation of legislative power to the President, but the Court sustained it. Pointing out that Congress had laid down the governing principle, Taft said:

> Congress may feel itself unable conveniently to determine exactly when its exercise of the legislative power should become effective, because de-

[87] 278 U.S. at 122.

[88] 276 U.S. 394, 407 (1928).

pendent on future conditions, and it may leave the determination of such time to the decision of an Executive, or, as often happens in matters of state legislation, it may be left to a popular vote of the residents of a district to be affected by the legislation. While in a sense one may say that such residents are exercising a legislative power, it is not an exact statement, because the power has already been exercised legislatively by the body vested with that power under the Constitution, the condition of its legislation going into effect being made dependent by the legislature on the expression of the voters of a certain district. [Citing cases from state courts.]

By this test there was no delegation in the *Eubank* or in the *Roberge* case, because the power to make buildings conform to a line or to forbid philanthropic homes had already been exercised legislatively by the respective city councils, the condition of the legislation going into effect or remaining in effect being made dependent by the council—in the one case on the expression of designated property owners, in the other on their continued silence. Taft's argument is essentially the same as that which the Government made later in the *Carter Coal* case and Hughes so effectively demolished in his concurring opinion there. The argument that legislation is valid

which becomes effective on the happening of a specified event [said Hughes, is an argument which] would remove all restrictions upon the delegation of legislative power, as the making of laws could thus be referred to any designated officials or private persons whose orders or agreements would be treated as "events," with the result that they would be invested with the force of law having penal sanctions.

The fact that legislation could be described as becoming effective on the happening of a specified event did not blind Hughes to the fact that it might also constitute a delegation of legislative power, whether the "event" was the drafting of the details of the legislation by a private group, as in the *Carter* case, or the mere decision by the President that legislation already drafted by Congress should take effect, as in the "hot oil" case.

In 1939, however, Hughes employed the very same argument whose fallacy he had exposed to deny that there was any delegation in *Currin v. Wallace*.[89] The only difference is that he called the consent of the designated private persons a "condition" of the application of a law, instead of an "event," on the happening of which it should be effective.

The law in question was the federal Tobacco Inspection Act. It provided that no tobacco was to be offered for sale at auction at

[89] 306 U.S. 1 (1939).

markets designated by the Secretary of Agriculture until inspected and certified according to established federal standards. But the Secretary was not to designate any market for this control unless at a prescribed referendum two thirds of the growers favored the designation. The act was sustained over various objections to its validity, Justices McReynolds and Butler dissenting without opinion. As to the objection that there was a delegation of legislative power to the growers, Chief Justice Hughes said:

So far as growers of tobacco are concerned, the required referendum does not involve any delegation of legislative authority. Congress has merely placed a restriction upon its own regulation by withholding its operation as to a given market "unless two-thirds of the growers voting favor it." Similar conditions are frequently found in police regulations. *Cusack Co.* v. *Chicago* . . . . This is not a case where a group of producers may make the law and force it upon a minority (see *Carter* v. *Carter Coal Co.* . . . .), or where a prohibition of an inoffensive and legitimate use of property is imposed not by the legislature but by other property owners (see *Washington ex rel. Seattle Trust Co.* v. *Roberge* . . .). Here it is Congress that exercises its legislative authority in making the regulation and in prescribing the conditions of its application. The required favorable vote upon the referendum is one of these conditions. The distinction was pointed out in *Hampton & Co.* v. *United States.*[90]

Hughes proceeded to quote the passage from Taft's opinion which we have already examined. However inoffensive the building of the philanthropic home may have been, the prohibition of the use of the property for that purpose was imposed by the legislative body in exactly the same way as that in which the prohibition of the auction sale of uninspected tobacco was imposed by Congress. The municipal council exercised its legislative power and prescribed the conditions of its application. The silence of the other property owners was one of those conditions. And in the "hot oil" case Congress had exercised its legislative power by forbidding the shipment and had prescribed the condition of the application of the prohibition. The decision of the President was the condition. It was precisely because the condition of the application was the decision of the President there and because the condition in the Seattle case was the silence of the other owners that there was delegation of legislative power. And that is equally true in *Currin* v. *Wallace.*

In these cases, however, the power that was delegated was only

[90] 306 U.S. at 15–16.

to make effective or ineffective legislation ready-made by the legislative body; whereas in *Carter* v. *Carter Coal Co.* power was delegated to a private group to draw up its own legislation. But even power to draw up legislation which others must obey was held to be no delegation, or at least no "unlawful delegation," in *Old Dearborn Distributing Co.* v. *Seagram-Distillers Corp.*[91] This case was decided in 1936, some years before the decision in *Currin* v. *Wallace*. It sustained an injunction issued by a state court under the Illinois Fair Trade Act. The injunction restrained a retailer from willfully and knowingly selling a commodity identified by a trade mark (in this case whiskey) at a price below that fixed in a contract between the wholesaler and other retailers. The price restriction was said to be an appropriate means to the legitimate end of protecting the "property—namely, the good will—of the producer, which he still owns." Distinguishing the *Eubank, Roberge,* and *Carter* cases and denying that "there is an unlawful delegation of power to private persons to control the disposition of the property of others," Justice Sutherland said:

> In those cases the property affected had been acquired without any pre-existing restriction in respect of its use or disposition. The imposition of the restriction in invitum was authorized after complete and unrestricted ownership had vested in the persons affected. Here, the restriction, already imposed with the knowledge of appellants, ran with the acquisition and conditioned it.[92]

The argument may prove that there was no control at all of property which had been acquired without strings and that it was reasonable to delegate to the designated private persons the power to restrict the liberty of the other retailer as to the price at which he might resell, by attaching strings to his property at the time of its acquisition in order to protect the producer's property in his good will. The fact remains that one group of private persons was enabled by the statute to draw up a minimum price requirement which the state would enforce by injunction against a retailer who was not a member of that group. If this is not a delegation of legislative power, it is difficult to see what could be.

But the Court could have sustained this Illinois Fair Trade Act, as well as the Chicago billboard ordinance and the federal Tobacco Inspection Act, without denying that all three involved a delegation of legislative power to designated groups. Legislation which restricts

[91] 299 U.S. 183 (1936). [92] *Id.* at 194.

liberty or property for the benefit of designated groups is not necessarily arbitrary; nor does it become arbitrary because the groups whom it is desired to benefit are permitted to waive the benefits. In the *Cusack* case the Chicago billboard ordinance was supported because billboards in residential districts were thought to increase the risk of fire, bad sanitation, and crime. But if that was its purpose, it is difficult to see why it was thought proper to permit its waiver by the owners of neighboring property, who most likely did not even reside in the district where their property was located. The ordinance could reasonably have been supported, however, as Professor Howard Lee McBain maintained in an article published in 1921,[93] as a protection of property values. If that was its basis, it would be reasonable to delegate to the owners of the property it was designed to protect the power to waive that protection. On the other hand, the justification for an ordinance which requires buildings to conform to a street line may be thought to lie, not in the protection of the value of property abutting on the same street, but in the general convenience or beauty of the city. When the ordinance makes the effectiveness of the requirement depend on the action of the abutting owners, its purpose is revealed to be one which would not justify the restriction on the owner's use of his property. Perhaps prohibiting the erection of a philanthropic home, unlike prohibiting billboards, could not be justified out of concern for neighboring property values, but only by more general considerations of legislative policy. These were shown not to have moved the municipal council; for if they had been the moving consideration, the neighboring owners would not have been empowered to permit the erection. And the regulation of the hours and wages of coal miners might be thought to be valid, if at all, only when enacted for the promotion of some general public interest, as distinguished from the particular interests of competing operators and miners. But the particular interests of tobacco growers might be thought sufficient to justify a regulation which would protect them from competing sales at uninspected and unstandardized auctions; and the referendum provisions were entirely consistent with a purpose to protect these interests. In the *Old Dearborn Distributing Co.* case it was the particular interest of the producer in the protection of his property (his good will) that was expressly adduced as the justification for restricting the liberty of the retailer.

[93] *Law-Making by Property Owners* (1921) 36 Pol. Sci. Q. 617.

In this case the state law enforced a minimum price policy on the retailer of the trade-marked whiskey. This price requirement was made effective, not by the mere passage of the Fair Trade Act, but by the subsequent act of two private parties. The legislature had left it to these parties to determine whether a retailer should be subjected to any minimum price restriction at all. It had no policy of its own on the matter. Nor had it any policy as to what the price should be below which the retailer might not sell in case he should be subjected to a restriction. The policy as to what the minimum price should be, as well as the policy as to whether there should be any minimum price at all, was left to private parties to formulate. The state merely enforced the privately formulated policies. The only policy which the legislature formulated was the policy that whatever private policies should be adopted pursuant to the act were to be enforced. But this delegation of policy-making or legislative power to private groups was sustained (though it was scarcely recognized as such), as a means to the protection of a property right.

While the Court has frequently declared that the delegation of legislative power without definite standards to guide its exercise is unconstitutional, the cases we have been examining demonstrate that it has by no means adhered to that dogma. Nor could it. It would make more sense were the Court to declare that delegation is valid if made to a group that is the appropriate one to exercise the policy-making power. And to be realistic, the Court would have to concede that governmental enforcement of a policy of an appropriate group may be valid, even though enforcement of that same policy, if formulated by the legislative body itself, would be unconstitutional. It may be doubted whether in the *Old Dearborn* case Justice Sutherland thought that a formulation by the legislature of a minimum price for trade-marked whiskey would be valid.[94] Yet the state's enforcement of a privately formulated minimum price was sustained, in pursuance of the legislature's policy of protecting the producer's property right in his good will. And in the routine enforcement of contract and property rights, the state enforces as a matter of course private policies

[94] Despite the decision in 1934, in Nebbia v. New York, 291 U.S. 502 (from which Sutherland dissented), he apparently thought even in 1936 that governmental fixing of either a maximum or a minimum price was unconstitutional, except in the case of a business "affected with a public interest." He reiterated this view in 1937 in his dissenting opinion in the minimum wage case of West Coast Hotel Co. v. Parrish, 300 U.S. 379. He surely cannot have thought the business of selling whiskey was "affected with a public interest."

which it would be held unconstitutional to enforce had they been formulated by the legislature.

ENFORCEMENT OF CONTRACT AND PROPERTY RIGHTS AS A DELEGATION TO PRIVATE INDIVIDUALS

Professor Joseph H. Beale once likened two persons who make a contract with each other under certain circumstances to a legislative body. He was discussing a question which arises in a branch of law known as "conflict of laws." When a suit is brought on a contract, a dispute frequently arises as to whether the court in which it is brought should apply the law of its own state, or that of the state in which the contract was made, or that of the state in which it was to be performed, or that of some other state. Which law should govern is itself a question of the law of the state in which the suit is brought (the "law of the forum"). When in making the contract the parties have chosen the law of some particular state to govern it, some courts apply the law which the parties have chosen. The objection to this, said Professor Beale,

> is that it involves permission to the parties to do a legislative act. It practically makes a legislative body of any two persons who choose to get together and contract. The adoption of a rule to determine which of several systems of law shall govern a given transaction is in itself an act of the law. . . . So in the case of the adoption of a law to govern the nature and obligation of a contract, it is entirely possible from the point of view of any one state that the law of that state or of some other state should be applied to the determination of the question; but if the law of that state is not applied, it is a result of the sovereign will of the state which controls the contract. Now, if it is said that this is to be left to the will of the parties to determine, that gives to the parties what is in truth the power of legislation so far as their agreement is concerned.[95]

It is doubtless true that the adoption of a rule to determine which system of law shall govern is in itself an act of the law. But is not the prescription of a legal duty equally an act of the law? In so far as it is left to the will of the parties to determine what their respective legal duties shall be under the contract which they make, are they not likewise given the power of legislation?

Enforcement of the obligations of a contract must be regarded as a compulsory act of government, even if we ignore the compulsory

[95] *What Law Governs the Validity of a Contract* III (1910) 23 HARV. L. REV. 260, 261. For an acute criticism of Beale's position see Walter Wheeler Cook, *"Contracts" and the Conflict of Laws: "Intention" of the Parties* (1938) 32 ILL. L. REV. 899.

factors which induced the parties to make the contract in the first place and assume that they made it voluntarily. Compulsion to render services which one has contracted to perform, said Justice Hughes in *Bailey* v. *Alabama,* "would be not less involuntary because of the original agreement." [96] Although Hughes thought that liability to pay damages for breach of the contract did not expose one to enforced labor, it must be clear that one who does what he has promised only to avoid a suit for damages is acting under compulsion. In acting to avoid a monetary penalty he is, in words which Justice Sutherland used in another connection, yielding "to compulsion precisely the same as though he did so to avoid a term in jail." [97] And if conformity to contractual obligations is enforced by an injunction or a decree of specific performance, backed by a threat of punishment for contempt of court, the compulsory nature of the government's pressure is still more evident.

Government, then, is forcing individuals to act in certain ways, not because the legislature has declared a policy that they should be required to act in those specific ways, but because the contracting parties have prescribed the conduct to be observed. The state's only policy is that contracts shall be enforced; in other words, that the legislative power to prescribe conduct shall be exercised by private groups whenever those groups can agree on the terms.

Moreover, in exercising this legislative power the contracting parties are by no means bound to act "in submission to the mandates of equality and liberty that bind officials everywhere." [98] They may subject each other to obligations to which the legislature could not validly subject them. That is, they may induce each other to give up some of their constitutional rights, and, having given up a constitutional right by contract, a person's conduct may be forcibly controlled by law in a way in which it could not otherwise be controlled. As Justice Holmes once remarked in a dissenting opinion,

> In order to enter into most of the relations of life people have to give up some of their Constitutional rights. If a man makes a contract he gives up the Constitutional right that previously he had to be free from the hamper that he puts upon himself. Some rights, no doubt, a person is not allowed to renounce, but very many he may. . . . Every contract is the acceptance of some inequality.[99]

[96] 219 U.S. 219, 242 (1911). See *supra*, pp. 190–191.
[97] Carter v. Carter Coal Co., 298 U.S. 238, 289 (1936). See *supra*, p. 293.
[98] Cardozo, J., in Nixon v. Condon, *supra*, p. 339.
[99] Power Mfg. Co. v. Saunders, 274 U.S. 490, 497 (1927).

As Justice Pitney, speaking for the Court in *Coppage* v. *Kansas*, asked: "Can the right of making contracts be enjoyed at all, except by parties coming together in an agreement that requires each party to forego, during the time and for the purpose covered by the agreement, any inconsistent exercise of his constitutional rights?" [100]

Thus, a man cannot ordinarily complain that a state is depriving him of liberty when it compels him to abide by his contract. But, while he can surrender his own constitutional right, can he by making a contract surrender the constitutional right which someone else has in his freedom?

We have seen that (in *Buchanan* v. *Warley*) [101] a law forbidding a Negro to buy (or to occupy) real estate owned by a white man who wished to sell it to him was held to violate the white man's property right. On the same principle, a law which forbade a white owner to sell to a Negro would undoubtedly be held to violate a constitutional right of the Negro. However, a widespread practice grew up whereby owners of neighboring pieces of real estate entered into restrictive covenants, each agreeing not to sell his property to Negroes, or in some cases merely not to permit its occupancy by Negroes. State courts enforced these covenants by enjoining owners from selling to Negroes or enjoining Negroes from occupying certain property even though bought from a willing seller. The result was that Negroes were prevented from residing in extensive urban regions covered by these covenants and were crowded into slum ghettos. They were segregated by state action just as effectually as they would have been had a segregation ordinance been enforced. State enforcement of a segregation policy formulated by a legislative body would clearly have been unconstitutional; but state courts apparently thought that state enforcement of the very same policy would be valid, provided it was formulated by a group of private individuals in the form of a covenant. Here was delegation of legislative policy with a vengeance.

In 1948, however, in *Shelley* v. *Kraemer*,[102] the Supreme Court held that judicial enforcement of such covenants was unconstitutional and was a denial to the Negroes of equal protection of the laws. Two cases were decided together. In the *Kraemer* case the Missouri su-

[100] 236 U.S. 1, 13 (1915). [101] *Supra*, pp. 323–326.

[102] 334 U.S. 1 (1948). Justices Reed, Jackson, and Rutledge, for some reason, felt themselves disqualified and took no part in the case. Otherwise Chief Justice Vinson's opinion had the Court's unanimous support.

preme court had directed the trial court to restrain the Negro petitioners from taking possession of the property they had bought and to divest title from them. In the other case (*McGhee* v. *Sipes*) the Michigan supreme court had sustained a decree directing the Negro petitioners, who had acquired title and entered into occupancy, to remove from the property within ninety days and enjoining them from using or occupying the premises in the future. In this case the covenant prohibited occupancy, but not ownership, by persons not "of the Caucasian race." The petitioners brought the cases to the Supreme Court on certiorari.

After citing many cases involving procedural matters to show that the action of state courts had long been held to be state action within the meaning of the Fourteenth Amendment, Chief Justice Vinson cited *A.F.L.* v. *Swing, Cantwell* v. *Connecticut,* and *Bridges* v. *California* [103] to support the proposition that state judicial action may violate the Fourteenth Amendment even when not procedurally unfair.

> It has been recognized [he said] that the action of state courts in enforcing a substantive common-law rule formulated by those courts, may result in the denial of rights guaranteed by the Fourteenth Amendment, even though the judicial proceedings in such cases may have been in complete accord with the most rigorous conceptions of procedural due process.[104]

Coming to the merits, he proceeded:

> We have no doubt that there has been state action in these cases in the full and complete sense of the phrase. The undisputed facts disclose that petitioners were willing purchasers of properties upon which they desired to establish homes. The owners of the properties were willing sellers; and contracts of sale were accordingly consummated. It is clear that but for the active intervention of the state courts, supported by the full panoply of state power, petitioners would have been free to occupy the properties in question without restraint.
>
> These are not cases, as has been suggested, in which the States have merely abstained from action, leaving private individuals free to impose such discriminations as they see fit. Rather, these are cases in which the States have made available to such individuals the full coercive power of government to deny to petitioners, on the grounds of race or color, the enjoyment of property rights in premises which petitioners are willing and financially able to acquire and which the grantors are willing to sell. The difference between judicial enforcement and nonenforcement of the restrictive covenants is the difference to petitioners between being denied rights

103 These cases were discussed *supra*, pp. 249–250.
104 334 U.S. at 17.

of property available to other members of the community and being accorded full enjoyment of those rights on an equal footing.

The enforcement of the restrictive agreements by the state courts in these cases was pursuant to the common-law policy of the States as formulated by those courts in earlier decisions. . . . The judicial action in each case bears the clear and unmistakable imprimatur of the State. . . . Nor is the Amendment ineffective simply because the particular pattern of discrimination, which the State has enforced, was defined initially by the terms of a private agreement. State action, as that phrase is understood for the purposes of the Fourteenth Amendment, refers to exertions of state power in all forms. And when the effect of that action is to deny rights subject to the protection of the Fourteenth Amendment, it is the obligation of this Court to enforce the constitutional commands.[105]

State action in enforcing the will of private persons, however, does not always have important public consequences. In a dissenting opinion in *Nixon* v. *Condon* Justice McReynolds sought to reduce to absurdity the Court's position that the Texas statutes gave to the resolution of the party executive committee the effect of action by the state. If they do, he maintained, "it would be difficult logically to deny like effect to the rules and by-laws of social or business clubs, corporations, and religious associations, etc., organized under charters or general enactments." [106] He might have gone further. It is state action when state law forbids an unwelcome guest to enter my house. But if the state, by enforcing my property right, gives effect to my arbitrary refusal to have a Catholic or a Protestant or a Jew or a Negro or a Republican in my house, the sound reason why the Fourteenth Amendment is not violated is not that state action is lacking, but that state action to enforce property rights cannot be regarded as arbitrary, however arbitrary the whim of the owner, provided that carrying out the owner's will does not involve some matter of high public importance. In the case of *Nixon* v. *Condon* itself Justice Cardozo, perhaps to meet McReynolds's objection, thought it necessary to

[105] 334 U.S. at 19–20. For a definitive treatment of the problem, published before the decision in Shelley v. Kraemer, see Dudley O. McGovney, *Racial Residential Segregation by State Court Enforcement of Restrictive Agreements, Covenants or Conditions in Deeds Is Unconstitutional* (1945) 33 CALIF. L. REV. 5. For another excellent discussion published almost contemporaneously and reaching the same conclusions see Harold I. Kahen, *Validity of Anti-Negro Restrictive Covenants: a Reconsideration of the Problem?* (1945) 12 U. of CHI. L. REV. 198. In what ought to prove an unsuccessful attempt to emasculate Shelley v. Kraemer, the supreme court of Missouri held, in Weiss v. Leaon, 359 Mo. 1054, 225 S.W. 2d 127 (1949), that a judgment for damages for breach of a racial restrictive covenant was not unconstitutional. A contrary conclusion was reached by Judge Holtzoff in the district court for the District of Columbia in Roberts v. Curtis, 93 F. Supp. 604 (D.C. 1950).

[106] 286 U.S. at 103–104.

allude to the public importance of the functions of the agencies which the state had invested with authority independent of the will of the party. These agencies, he said (in words already quoted),

are then the governmental instruments whereby parties are organized and regulated to the end that government itself may be established or continued. What they do in that relation, they must do in submission to the mandates of equality and liberty which bind officials everywhere. They are not acting in matters of merely private concern like the directors or agents of business corporations. They are acting in matters of high public interest, matters intimately connected with the capacity of government to exercise its functions unbrokenly and smoothly.[107]

Ordinarily the property owner, in deciding whom to admit or to exclude from his property, is not acting in any matter of "high public interest." Hence, though the state enforces his decision, the person excluded can ordinarily raise no constitutional issue. A person has a constitutional right not to have a state, for arbitrary reasons of its own, bar him from the use of property. He has no constitutional right not to have the state bar him from the use of property when the owner will not consent, no matter how arbitrary the owner's reasons may be. And, as we have seen, the owner may impose conditions which had the state imposed them would have been called "unconstitutional," since they require what the Supreme Court inaccurately calls "relinquishment of constitutional rights."

That the owner of property may render certain action unlawful which the legislature could not forbid in pursuance of some policy of its own, was brought out in a remark by Justice Black, in the majority opinion in *Martin* v. *City of Struthers*,[108] decided in 1943. In holding unconstitutional an ordinance which made it unlawful to ring the doorbell or knock on the door of a residence for the purpose of distributing handbills and the like, Black conceded that it might be permissible to

make it an offense for any person to ring the bell of a householder who has appropriately indicated that he is unwilling to be disturbed. This or any similar regulation leaves the decision as to whether distributors of literature may lawfully call at a home where it belongs—with the homeowner himself.

In other words, the owner of property is ordinarily the person to whom the legislative policy of determining the lawfulness of other

[107] *Id.* at 88.

[108] 319 U.S. 141, 148 (1943).

people's conduct with reference to that property may appropriately be delegated. In exercising such legislative power he is not bound by the same mandates of equality and liberty which bind those who determine official policy. An official policy of enforcing the owner's will would not ordinarily be deemed an arbitrary restriction of the nonowner's liberty.

When, however, the owners of all the property in a region covenant, as in *Shelley* v. *Kraemer,* to bring about a result as to that entire region, not merely each as to his own property, a result which involves the state's enforcement of what in effect is an unconstitutional segregation ordinance, the state's enforcement of the covenant is unconstitutional, and thus some vitality is given to the constitutional rights recognized in *Buchanan* v. *Warley*.

There is one recent case in which the state's enforcement of a property right by a criminal statute was held unconstitutional. In *Marsh* v. *Alabama,*[109] decided in 1946, a Jehovah's Witness was convicted under a statute which made it a crime to enter or to remain on the premises of another after having been warned not to do so. She undertook to distribute religious literature on the sidewalk of the town of Chickasaw, which was the property of the Gulf Shipbuilding Corporation. Though privately owned, the sidewalk was used by the general public in the same manner as sidewalks in other towns. The corporation had, however, posted the following notice in the stores adjacent: "This Is Private Property, and Without Written Permission, No Street, or House Vendor, Agent or Solicitation of Any Kind Will Be Permitted." She was warned that she could not distribute the literature without a permit and that no permit would be issued to her.

The Alabama Court of Appeals sustained the conviction, and held that the public use of the sidewalk had not been such as to give rise to a presumption under Alabama law of its irrevocable dedication to the public. The state supreme court denied certiorari, and the case was appealed to the federal Supreme Court.

In reversing, Justice Black, for the majority, accepted the state court's determination of the issue of dedication, which determination, he said, "means that the corporation could if it so desired, entirely close the sidewalk and the town to the public." [110] But he refused to accept the state's contention "that the corporation's right to control the inhabitants of Chickasaw is coextensive with the right of

[109] 326 U.S. 501 (1946).

[110] *Id.* at 505, n. 2.

a homeowner to regulate the conduct of his guests." [111] "The managers appointed by the corporation," he said, "cannot curtail the liberty of press and religion of these people [the people in the area and those passing through] consistently with the purposes of the Constitutional guarantees." [112] He added:

> When we balance the Constitutional rights of owners of property against those of the people to enjoy freedom of press and religion, as we must here, we remain mindful of the fact that the latter occupy a preferred position. [Citations] . . . In our view the circumstance that the property rights to the premises where the deprivation of liberty here involved, took place, were held by others than the public, is not sufficient to justify the State's permitting a corporation to govern a community of citizens so as to restrict their fundamental liberties and the enforcement of such restraint by the application of a State statute. In so far as the State has attempted to impose criminal punishment on appellant for undertaking to distribute religious literature in a company town, its action cannot stand.[113]

If the state's imposition of criminal punishment on the distribution of religious literature is a violation of constitutionally protected civil liberties, any other effective enforcement of the company town owner's right to exclude distributors from its property would seem to be as much of a violation. The enforcement might be quite as effective if the property right were protected by the ordinary civil remedies of injunction or ejectment procedure. The enforcement must have been unconstitutional, not because it took the form of a criminal penalty,

[111] *Id.* at 506. [112] *Id.* at 508.

[113] *Id.* at 509. Justice Jackson (being at Nuremberg) took no part in the case. Justice Frankfurter wrote a concurring opinion, in which he expressed agreement with Black's opinion except for a portion not pertinent here. He said (at 511): "Title to property as defined by State law controls property relations; it cannot control issues of civil liberties which arise precisely because a company town is a town as well as a congeries of property relations." Those who concurred with Black were Douglas, Murphy and Rutledge.

Justice Reed wrote a dissenting opinion, in which Chief Justice Stone and Justice Burton concurred. He objected (p. 512) to the principle which he said the decision establishes, namely, "that one may remain on private property against the will of the owner and contrary to the law of the state so long as the only objection to his presence is that he is exercising an asserted right to spread there his religious views." He objected to this principle even though the Court should subsequently restrict it "to the precise facts of this case—that is to private property in a company town where the owner for his own advantage has permitted a restricted public use by his licensees and invitees." He also laid some stress on the fact that appellant could have distributed her literature on the state's public highway, only thirty feet from where she insisted on distributing it. His opinion concluded (pp. 516–517): "Even though we have reached the point where this Court is required to force private owners to open their property for the practice there of religious activities or propaganda distasteful to the owner, because of the public interest in freedom of speech and religion, there is no need for the application of such a doctrine here. Appellant, as we have said, was free to engage in such practices on the public highways, without becoming a trespasser on the company's property."

but because it would delegate to the owner a power over public affairs which the owner was not the appropriate party to exercise and which, in fact, it was thought that no one should exercise. The power of this owner had ramifications far wider than those which the powers of ordinary property owners would have.

In *Dorsey* v. *Stuyvesant Town Corporation* [114] the corporate owner also had power which had a broader impact than that of the ordinary property owner, but the Court of Appeals of New York held, in 1949, by a vote of four to three that there was no state action involved in the corporation's policy of choosing its tenants on a racial basis and excluding Negroes. For some reason best known to itself the Supreme Court, in 1950, denied certiorari.[115]

Stuyvesant Town Corporation was created in 1943 as a wholly owned subsidiary of the Metropolitan Life Insurance Company, pursuant to the housing provisions of the state constitution adopted in 1938 and the Redevelopment Companies Law. In further pursuance of these provisions, Stuyvesant and Metropolitan negotiated with the city of New York a contract which embodied, in the words of Judge Fuld's dissenting opinion,

> a plan for the rehabilitation of a substandard area comprising eighteen city blocks in Manhattan . . . . The plan and the proposed contract received the requisite approval from the State Superintendent of Insurance, from the Planning Commission and from the Board of Estimate of the City of New York. Following closely the contours of the Redevelopment Companies Law, the contract called for condemnation by the City of the site and its conveyance to Stuyvesant at cost; for grant by the City to Stuyvesant of all public streets within the project in return for an equivalent area on its periphery; and for tax exemption on improvements for twenty-five years. For its part, Stuyvesant agreed to acquire the area, demolish the old buildings and construct the Stuyvesant project. Metropolitan was to advance the necessary funds and to guarantee performance by Stuyvesant.
>
> Condemnation of the land and its transfer to Stuyvesant, along with public streets, was accomplished in 1945, and construction of Stuyvesant Town began in that same year. The Town is now virtually completed, at a cost of over $90,000,000. It occupies eighteen city blocks and, with its thirty-five buildings, houses a population of about twenty-five thousand people. Streets in the area are "private" and signs at all entrances give the public notice of that fact.
>
> Almost from the beginning, the question of exclusion of Negroes from

[114] 299 N.Y. 512 (1949). Judge Bromley wrote the Court's opinion, in which Judges Lewis, Conway, and Dye concurred. Judge Fuld wrote a dissenting opinion, in which Chief Judge Loughran and Judge Desmond concurred.

[115] 339 U.S. 981 (1950).

the community was debated. While the project was under consideration by the Board of Estimate, Stuyvesant and Metropolitan insisted that they be given free choice in the selection of tenants and indicated that they planned to bar Negroes. Despite opposition to the contract on that ground, its execution was authorized. A local law was thereafter passed by the city forbidding racial discrimination in tax-exempt developments, but it expressly excepted from its coverage any project "hitherto agreed upon or contracted for" . . . an exception which could relate only to Stuyvesant Town.[116]

The plaintiffs, Negro veterans who had applied for apartments, sought to enjoin Stuyvesant and Metropolitan from denying any of their accommodations in Stuyvesant Town to any person because of race or color.

Judge Bromley, for the majority, recognized that Supreme Court decisions had held the acts of private individuals to be subject to the limitations of the Fourteenth Amendment (1) "if they act under constraint of State law;" (2) "when they perform functions of a governmental character in matters of great public interest," even if, as in *Rice* v. *Elmore,* the state has "cast off all fetters upon their discretion"; or (3) if, as in *Shelley* v. *Kraemer* and *Marsh* v. *Alabama,* "the State has lent its power in support of private individuals or corporations, and in so doing has clothed the private act with the character of State action." [117]

In the absence of state constraint or state support, the fact that private individuals were acting in matters of great public interest would apparently not suffice to bring them within the scope of the Amendment unless they were at the same time performing governmental functions, and not only that, but functions which the state government, not the Supreme Court, recognized as governmental. Since the New York statute "has declared that the public purpose has been fulfilled by the rehabilitation of the substandard area," control of that area, once it had been rehabilitated, could not be deemed a governmental function. How this position could be reconciled with the South Carolina primary case he did not explain.

Stuyvesant was, of course, not constrained by the state to discriminate against Negroes, and Judge Bromley denied that the state was lending its power to the corporation to do so. He said that "the State has remained silent," and he rejected the contention that state aid in condemning the property which it turned over to the corpora-

[116] 299 N.Y. at 537–538. This account does not differ materially from that of the majority.

[117] The quotations from the Bromley opinion are to be found at 532–535.

tion and in granting it tax exemption was the kind of support which would bring the Fourteenth Amendment into play.

It is hard to see, however, why the state, as in *Marsh* v. *Alabama,* was not lending its power in support of Stuyvesant by assigning to it the ownership of the eighteen blocks and holding itself ready to enforce the property rights so assigned. It was only by virtue of its power to call on the state's intervention to enforce its property right that Stuyvesant could keep Negroes or anyone else from occupying its apartments. When the state acts to gratify the ordinary property owner's whims against use of his property by undesired occupants, it is not "a matter of high public interest," and so not within the scope of the Fourteenth Amendment. But the ordinary property owner cannot, in effect, govern a large area of a city with a population of 25,000 and control the streets within that area.

Judge Bromley, however, assumed that the state was merely tolerating, not supporting, the discrimination; for he supposed that he had disposed of the matter when he rejected the suggestion that state action can be "discerned in any case where the State has tolerated discrimination respecting a matter of high public importance." In rejecting this suggestion he said:

> Such a development in constitutional law would clash with a fundamental policy inherent in the Fourteenth Amendment and the decision of the *Civil Rights Cases* . . . . Both are instinct with the idea that the rights defined in the amendment are to be protected by the States against the actions of private individuals. That high responsibility of the States, implicit in our Federal system, indicates that the political processes must furnish the appropriate means for extension of those rights in areas wherein they have not been heretofore asserted. The unquestioned value of that system suggests the limits to the expanding concept of State action, which has hitherto been found only in cases where the State has consciously exerted its power in aid of discrimination or where private individuals have acted in a governmental capacity so recognized by the State.

It can hardly be said that when South Carolina repealed its primary laws it "recognized" that the individuals who composed the Democratic party would thereafter be acting in a governmental capacity. In fact, the state implicitly denied that they would be.[118] Nor can it be said that when Texas authorized the party to determine the quali-

118 As Judge Fuld pointed out in his dissent, at p. 540, speaking of Rice v. Elmore, "Not even the formal disavowal on the part of the State of all interest in the process of selecting political candidates—by repealing all of its pertinent statutes—served to free 'private' political parties from the duty to function without discrimination."

fications for primary voting its power was exerted any more "consciously" in aid of discrimination than was the power of New York in the *Stuyvesant* case. Of course, the Texas legislature was well aware that the party would discriminate, but so, too, were the New York authorities. As Judge Fuld said in his dissent:

That there is "state action" here is supported and established, however, by more than the constitutional and statutory provisions which made the development possible, by more than the city and state participation and aid that brought Stuyvesant Town into being. In addition, there is the exceedingly significant fact that the City's Board of Estimate approved and authorized the contract for the construction of Stuyvesant Town after having been apprised by city representatives and company officials that Negroes would be excluded from the development. Beyond that, the City Council deliberately excepted Stuyvesant from the coverage of the law, subsequently enacted, which barred discrimination in tax-exempt projects. In a most literal sense, in a most direct way, here was "action," and—if such a showing were necessary, but see, contra, *Steele* v. *Louisville & Nashville R. R. Co.*, 323 U.S. 192, *supra*—action, "consciously exerted," by the State "in aid of" the discrimination being practiced.[119]

Apart from such "conscious" support to the discrimination, the state and city aid to the project and the constitutional and statutory provisions under which it was extended not only (in Fuld's view) showed the hand of the state in the discrimination but also disclosed that (contrary to Judge Bromley) the state recognized the operation of the completed project, as well as the preliminary clearing of the slum, as a governmental function. To quote Judge Fuld at some length on this point:

Respondents' main defense to the charge of constitutional violation is that they, rather than the City, are behind the discrimination, and that they, as private corporations, are not answerable for it. Their premise is faulty. Stuyvesant is in no sense an ordinary private landlord. Its title bespeaks its character. With buildings covering many city blocks, housing a population of twenty-five thousand persons, Stuyvesant is a "Town" in more than name. Its very being depended upon constitutional amendment, statutory enactment and city contract. The exercise of a number of governmental functions was absolutely prerequisite to its existence. As a geographic entity, Stuyvesant Town was created by the City's exercise of its eminent domain and street-closing powers and by its act of transferring such condemned land and public property to respondents. As an economic enterprise, Stuyvesant Town was made possible by the acquisition of this land at its cost to the City—not augmented by reason of any increase in

[119] 299 N.Y. at 543.

value through assembly of the entire tract under single ownership—and by the City's grant of tax exemption. As a going community, Stuyvesant Town functions subject to supervision by governmental agencies. Upon dissolution, its surplus assets revert to the public. All in all, the resemblance between Stuyvesant Town and the company town of *Marsh* v. *Alabama* . . . is strong, the analogy between this case and that one, clear.

To intimate that this is just another instance of a government subsidy is to misconceive the case. To claim that the construction and operation of a project such as Stuyvesant is a matter of but private concern is to disregard the obvious. Unmistakable are the signs that this undertaking was a governmentally conceived, governmentally aided and governmentally regulated project in urban redevelopment. Everywhere in evidence are the voice and authority of the State and the City. Approval of the underlying constitutional housing article set in motion numerous governmental acts necessary to accomplish the "reconstruction and rehabilitation" of slum areas and to provide "incidental * * * facilities." § 1. Proceeding under that authority, the Legislature had in view more than merely the effacement or razing of blighted substandard buildings; their "modernization" and "reconstruction" to provide "adequate, safe, sanitary and properly planned housing accommodations in effectuation of official city plans" were declared to be "public uses and purposes." § 2. And it was to achieve all these ends—not merely the clearance of a slum area—that the plans for Stuyvesant Town were conceived and executed, that the City condemned property for use by defendants, closed public streets and turned over their land area—comprising 19% of the total area of the project—granted tax exemption upon improvements and insisted upon regulation of the rents, profits and financing methods of the redevelopment corporation.[120]

Finally, after pointing out that the discrimination would clearly have been held unconstitutional if the city had zoned the site and closed it to Negroes or had built the development and leased it to private operators for white occupancy only, Judge Fuld added that

it may not be gainsaid that the development plan, the contract and the local law brought about precisely the same situation as if the City had zoned or leased a "white" development. We draw distinctions too fine and too subtle when we say that the several cases are different or that they merit different consideration.[121]

The Court did, however, draw these fine and subtle distinctions, and the Supreme Court denied certiorari. The case seems irreconcilable with *Rice* v. *Elmore,* in which the Supreme Court likewise declined certiorari. Such denial, as the Court has often insisted, implies nothing as to its own views on the question decided below. Accordingly, the denial of certiorari in these two cases in no way indicates

120 299 N.Y. at 542–543.

121 *Id.* at 544.

whether the one case or the other establishes a doctrine which the Supreme Court holds. The *Stuyvesant* doctrine, however, seems to conflict with the principle which the Supreme Court clearly intimated in *Steele* v. *Louisville & Nashville R. Co.*,[122] which has already been discussed. It was there intimated that a statute authorizing the choice of a union as sole bargaining agent, if construed to place no statutory limitations on the union's acts, would subject any discriminatory action of the union to the constitutional limitations of the Fifth Amendment, regardless of the fact that Congress, in enacting the statute, was not "consciously" aiding the discrimination.

The question arises whether Negroes have any constitutional protection against unions which exclude them from membership and deny them employment opportunities in the absence of legislation, such as existed in the *Steele* case, conferring special powers on the union. Must the Negroes rely on the states to protect their right to employment against the union through the "political processes" mentioned by Judge Bromley, or can the Court protect them by spelling out a right under the Fourteenth Amendment? It is, perhaps, unlikely that the Court will do so, but were it so inclined it would not be too difficult to find state action. Whatever economic pressure the union can bring against the employer to compel him to deny employment to the Negroes would, of course, be ineffective for that purpose if the employer did not himself have power to deny employment. He has that power, but only because state law assigns to him the ownership of his plant and stands ready to enforce his property right in it. If the effect of union pressure on all the employers in the trade is to coerce Negroes to keep out of that trade—a result which would be unconstitutional if brought about by statutory prohibition—the owners might be held, as in the *Marsh* case, to be acting in matters of "high public interest," with the aid of the state, and hence to be acting unconstitutionally. And the union, acting through the employers and through them with the aid of the state, might be held to be violating the Fourteenth Amendment. Such a result, however, does not seem to be foreshadowed by any cases yet decided.[123]

122 323 U.S. 192 (1944). *Supra*, pp. 348–349.

123 For a more complete discussion of the exclusionary practices of unions see Clyde W. Summers, *The Right to Join a Union* (1947) 47 COL. L. REV. 33. For an excellent discussion of the same topic, covering a wider field, see Pauli Murray, *The Right to Equal Opportunity in Employment* (1945) 33 CALIF. L. REV. 388.

THE PRIVATE COERCIVE POWER AGAINST WHICH THE CONSTITUTION FURNISHES NO GUARANTY

In enforcing contract and property rights the state is restricting the liberty of those who have incurred contractual obligations and of nonowners. When the owners are in a position to require nonowners to accept conditions as the price of obtaining permission to use the property in question, it is the state that is enforcing compliance, by threatening to continue to forbid the use of the property unless the owner's terms are met. When the state threatens to withhold other privileges unless its own terms are met, its enforcement of the terms by this threat is sometimes recognized as state compulsion, subject to the limitations of the Fourteenth Amendment—as in those cases in which it has been stated that a state may not condition the grant of a privilege on "the relinquishment of a constitutional right." [124] It is just as much governmental action when the conditions are formulated by a private owner, to whom the state, in the routine enforcement of property rights, has delegated the power to formulate them.

Only in extreme cases, however, does the Supreme Court recognize the role played by the state. If that role were fully recognized, the dogma of the nondelegability of legislative power would have to be overhauled. So, too, would the dogma of unconstitutional conditions; for owners can frequently insist that others, as a condition of acquiring or using property, must pay them money, or render them services, or do other acts which the state could not constitutionally compel them to do by direct sanctions. To hold such state implementation of property rights unconstitutional would leave little of the whole system of bargaining on which we largely rely, both for calling forth the efforts essential for the collective production of goods and for each individual's acquisition of such liberty as he may attain to consume material goods once they have been produced.

Constitutional rights protect us from being deprived of certain of our liberties and property rights by state action when it takes the form of imposing direct sanctions, or in some circumstances when it takes the form of taxation or the attachment of conditions to the grant of privileges, or perhaps even to the grant of public funds. But these constitutional rights cannot safely be construed to protect us from

[124] As pointed out in Chapter X, the Court has not been consistent in applying this doctrine.

being deprived of these same liberties and property rights by state action when it takes the form of enforcing other people's property rights—save in extreme cases. Still less can constitutional rights be construed to protect our liberty and property from whatever private coercion there may be which does not depend on the enforcement of property rights or other forms of state intervention—such coercion, for instance, as that practiced by labor unions when they threaten an employer with a cessation of work.[125] In such cases the state is doing nothing.

Some of the economic results of the conflicting bargaining powers of the various members of the community may well be deemed unfortunate and may seem to call for correction. That correction may call for strengthening or weakening this or that element of bargaining power, or altering the conditions of labor, or increasing or diminishing particular fruits of bargaining—as by establishing a floor under wages or farm prices or a ceiling over other prices, or by taxing excess profits or excess incomes and using the proceeds to distribute the benefits more widely. But whatever rearrangements may be called for can be brought about more appropriately by legislation than by judicial action—whether that action take the form of common law development of the doctrines of prima facie torts and duress or constitutional development of the concepts of due process and equal protection.

Legislation which alters the relative economic powers of different classes in the community may often be accurately characterized as protecting the liberty, or property, or equality of some individuals against the actions of others. It falls within Judge Bromley's formula, in the *Stuyvesant* case,[126] of protection by the states of rights defined in the Fourteenth Amendment against the actions of private individuals. It may be, as Judge Bromley said, the "high responsibility of the States" to afford this protection. It can only do so, however, by curtailing some of the rights of other members of the community, which are also "defined in the amendment." For a long time the Supreme Court read into the Fourteenth Amendment barriers to the assumption by states of this "high responsibility." Liberty of the strong, it was once thought, could not be restricted by legislation for the mere purpose of protecting the liberty of the weak from that of the strong. It could only

125 The situation may, of course, be different when the union is compelling the employer to exercise his property right, to the detriment of would-be employees. See the discussion *supra*, p. 379.

126 299 N.Y. at 534, *supra*, p. 376.

be restricted for the promotion of such things as safety, health, or morals. Prices could not be controlled, however much they restricted the liberty of consumers, except in the case of an artificial category of businesses. Wages could not be controlled at all, however slight the liberty they permitted to the worker. Even in those businesses in which some degree of price control was held permissible, an artificial and unworkable limitation was placed on the extent of the permissible control. Gradually, after long and uphill fights, many of these barriers have been reduced by judicial action, as will be set forth in the ensuing chapters.

PART FOUR

POLITICAL PROCESSES FOR ADJUSTING CONFLICTING LIBERTIES

XII

THE POWER TO RESTRICT ONE LIBERTY IN ORDER TO EXPAND ANOTHER

INEQUALITIES of fortune, based ultimately on governmental assignment and protection of property rights and enforcement of contracts, are inequalities in individual liberty. Legal obligations to respect other people's property rights bear more heavily on those to whom the law assigns little property than on those to whom it assigns much. A rich man has more economic freedom than a poor man, both in respect to his choice of work and in respect to his enjoyment of the material goods of the community. In assigning and enforcing property and contract rights, however, government has not planned the specific economic inequalities which ensue. It has conceived itself as hewing to a narrow line of governmental activities, letting the economic chips fall where they may. As a rule, it is not when it assigns property rights, but when it legislates, that it has had any economic aims. Even then, the aim of certain legislative restrictions on "freedom of contract" has not always been to redistribute economic liberty, but rather to promote such supposedly noneconomic public interests as health or safety.

For a time the Supreme Court was disposed to deny the constitutionality of legislation dealing with employment relations except when it could be seen to further such noneconomic interests. As Justice Pitney remarked in 1915, state exertions of the police power to preserve public health and safety had been sustained, "even though the enjoyment of private rights of liberty and property be thereby incidentally hampered." [1] But the mere fact that some people's "private rights of liberty and property" were used to restrict the liberty of those whose private rights were less significant was not thought sufficient to justify interference with the former.

In *Holden* v. *Hardy*,[2] decided in 1898, the Court sustained (over the silent dissent of Justices Brewer and Peckham) a Utah statute forbidding employment for more than eight hours a day in underground mines or smelters, save in cases of emergency. These employments, said Justice Brown for the Court,

> when too long pursued, the legislature has judged to be detrimental to the health of the employees; and, so long as there are reasonable grounds for believing that this is so, its decision upon this subject cannot be reviewed by the Federal courts.[3]

The statute, he thought, was a justifiable measure to protect the worker's health "against himself." [4] The implication seems to be that the statute curtailed the employee's liberty on behalf of his health.

Elsewhere in the opinion, however, Brown intimated that the statute did not impair the employee's liberty at all, but rather accorded to him a liberty he did not have before—a freedom from restraints imposed upon him by the employer.

> The legislature [said Brown] has also recognized the fact . . . that the proprietors of these establishments and their operatives do not stand upon an equality, and that their interests are, to a certain extent, conflicting. The former naturally desire to obtain as much labor as possible from their employees, while the latter are often induced by the fear of discharge to conform to regulations which their judgment, fairly exercised, would pronounce to be detrimental to their health or strength. In other words, the proprietors lay down the rules, and the laborers are practically constrained to obey them. In such case self-interest is often an unsafe guide, and the legislature may properly impose its authority.[5]

This was in 1898. But by 1905, when *Lochner* v. *New York*[6] was decided, Brown had apparently forgotten that there was any con-

[1] Coppage v. Kansas, 236 U.S. 1, 18 (1915). [2] 169 U.S. 366 (1898).
[3] *Id.* at 395. [4] *Id.* at 397. [5] *Ibid.* [6] 198 U.S. 45 (1905).

straint on the laborers. So, too, had Chief Justice Fuller and Justice McKenna, who had subscribed to Brown's earlier opinion. All three joined Justices Brewer and Peckham, who had dissented in the earlier case, in holding unconstitutional a New York statute which limited to ten the number of hours in which a person could be employed daily in bakeries or confectionary establishments. The majority opinion was by Justice Peckham. Justices Harlan and White, who had joined in sustaining the Utah law, now dissented, as did Holmes and Day, who had not been on the Court when that law was sustained. The dissenting opinion was written by Justice Harlan.

Here the Court seemed to depart from the principle enunciated in the earlier case, that the legislative determination of a detriment to health was not reviewable in a federal court if there are reasonable grounds for belief in the detriment. Or perhaps the Court here thought, despite the impressive medical evidence adduced in Justice Harlan's dissent, that there were no reasonable grounds. At any rate, Justice Peckham thought

> that there could be no fair doubt that the trade of a baker, in and of itself, is not an unhealthy one to that degree which would authorize the legislature to interfere with the right to labor, and with the right of free contract on the part of the individual, either as employer or as employee.[7]

Disregarding what Justice Brown had pointed out seven years before, that in working more than ten hours the bakers were doing so because constrained to obey rules laid down by the proprietors and that the statute freed them from that constraint, the Court said:

> There is no contention that bakers as a class are not equal in intelligence and capacity to men in other trades or manual occupations, or that they are not able to assert their rights and care for themselves without the protecting arm of the state interfering with their independence of judgment and of action. They are in no sense wards of the State.[8]

When in 1908 the Court sustained a ten-hour law for women in *Muller* v. *Oregon*,[9] it was partly on the ground that women were thought to be less capable of asserting their rights than men and partly because the famous factual brief prepared by Louis D. Brandeis, as counsel for the state, had convinced the Court that overwork impaired the health of women and their offspring. As to the first point, Justice Brewer, speaking for the Court, observed that though limitations upon woman's personal and contractual rights may be removed

[7] *Id.* at 59. [8] *Id.* at 57. [9] 208 U.S. 412 (1908).

by legislation, "there is that in her disposition and habits of life which will operate against full assertion of those rights. She will still be where some legislation to protect her seems necessary to secure a real equality of right." [10] The implication seems to be that when men, being capable of fully asserting their rights, work more than ten hours, they could never be supposed to be doing so under constraint.[11]

The statute, however, was sustained, not merely because it was thought to enable a woman to enjoy the liberty she was supposed to have to work as short a time as she wished but also because, whatever her own wishes might be, her health was of concern to the public. "As healthy mothers," said Justice Brewer, "are essential to vigorous offspring, the physical well-being of woman becomes an object of public interest and care in order to preserve the strength and vigor of the race." [12] And the limitations which the statute places upon woman's contractual powers "are not imposed solely for her benefit, but also largely for the benefit of all." [13]

These grounds could not be adduced to sustain the other Oregon statute which came before the Court in 1917, in *Bunting* v. *Oregon*.[14] That law applied to men as well as women, nor was it confined to occupations deemed peculiarly deleterious to health—like the smelters in Utah and the bakeries in New York. It prohibited employment of anyone in any factory for more than ten hours per day, with a provision, however, that employment might be continued for three additional hours on condition that time and one-half overtime be paid for them. Though this provision caused the statute to be challenged as a regulation of wages, the Court held it to be, instead, a penalty for exceeding ten hours, and sustained the statute as tending, by limiting the hours, to the preservation of the health of employees.[15] There was no suggestion, as in *Holden* v. *Hardy,* that it tended to increase their liberty.

10 208 U.S. at 422.

11 Justice Brown, who had asserted the contrary in Holden v. Hardy, but had ignored the assertion in the Lochner case, was no longer on the Court.

12 208 U.S. at 421. 13 *Id.* at 422. 14 243 U.S. 426 (1917).

15 There was a curious shift in the alignment of those Justices who had participated in the Lochner case. McKenna, who had been with the majority in holding the New York bakeshop law unconstitutional, wrote the opinion sustaining the Oregon law. White (now Chief Justice), who by joining the dissent had voted to uphold the New York law, now joined Van Devanter and McReynolds in dissent, thus holding the Oregon law to be invalid. Holmes and Day maintained the position they had taken in their dissent in the Lochner case and were with the majority in sustaining the Oregon law. The other three members of that majority were Pitney, Brandeis, and Clarke.

Of course these laws limiting hours of work do restrict an employee's liberty in one respect, but they enlarge it in another. Under a ten-hour law he is no longer free to work for twelve hours. The liberty to do so, however, is of no value to him if his daily wages under the ten-hour law are no less than when he was working twelve. He then gains a liberty to dispose of the additional two hours in a more agreeable way. It is the employer's liberty that has been reduced by an increase in his labor costs—unless, as may be the case, the employee, being less fatigued, turns out as much in ten hours as he formerly did in twelve. If, however, the reduction in hours brings about a reduction in daily wages, then the worker's freedom to dispose of the additional hours is obtained at the cost of part of the liberty-to-consume which he might have purchased with the higher wage. The law has compelled him to forego one freedom in order that he may have the other, and he may not choose which freedom to enjoy. But before the enactment of the statute, he probably had no choice either. If the prevailing hours of factory work were twelve, it is not likely that he could have obtained a ten-hour job by agreeing to take less pay. He had to forego freedom to do what he liked in the extra two hours, though in doing so he acquired more freedom to do what the extra wages might enable him to do. Under the statute if a drop in wages ensued he had to forego the freedom which the extra wages could purchase, but acquired a freedom to dispose of the two hours of his time. One cannot say a priori whether there was a net enlargement or net diminution of his liberty. If his daily wages did not fall when the hours were shortened, clearly there was an enlargement.

Although the *Lochner* case was cited as authoritative in 1923, in *Adkins* v. *Children's Hospital* [16] Chief Justice Taft, dissenting in that case, said "it is impossible for me to reconcile the *Bunting* case and the *Lochner* case, and I have always supposed that the *Lochner* case was thus overruled *sub silentio*." [17] And since the overruling of the *Adkins* case this has clearly become the doctrine accepted by the Court. Speaking in 1941 for the unanimous Court in *United States* v. *Darby Lumber Co.*, Justice Stone, referring to due process objections, cited *Holden* v. *Hardy* and the *Muller* and *Bunting* cases for the statement that it was no longer "open to question that it is within the legislative power to fix maximum hours." [18]

[16] 261 U.S. 525, 548 (1923).

[17] *Id.* at 564.

[18] 312 U.S. 100, 125 (1941).

Laws limiting hours of work were sustained primarily on the ground that they were deemed essential to health. That they also might be thought to give the employee greater freedom from the coercive power of the employer was either ignored or given secondary importance. Statutes designed primarily to enlarge the employee's freedom, by restricting the employer's freedom to coerce him, were for a time frowned upon by the Court as unwarranted deprivations of liberty and property and disturbances of equality of right.

Typical of such statutes were those forbidding an employer to discharge, or threaten to discharge, a man for belonging to a union. An Act of Congress of 1898 made it a misdemeanor for any interstate carrier or any of its agents to require any employee, present or prospective, as a condition of employment, to agree not to become or to remain a member of a union or to "unjustly discriminate against any employee because of his membership" in a union. Adair, an agent of an interstate carrier, was convicted of unjustly discriminating against a certain employee by discharging him because of union membership. The conviction was set aside in 1908, and the statute was held unconstitutional under the Fifth Amendment in *Adair* v. *United States*.[19] Justice Harlan, speaking for the majority, declared that the "right" of the employee to quit for any reason he saw fit was "the same" as the "right" of the employer to discharge for any reason. Without noting that the two "rights" might differ greatly in their practical significance to their possessors, he added: "In all such particulars the employer and the employee have equality of right, and any legislation that disturbs that equality is an arbitrary interference with the liberty of contract which no government can legally justify in a free land." [20]

Later, a Kansas statute came before the Court which made it a misdemeanor for any officer or agent of a company "to coerce, require, demand or influence any person" to enter into any agreement not to join or remain a member of a union, as a condition of employment. Coppage, the superintendent of a railroad, asked a certain switchman to sign an agreement to withdraw from the Switchmen's Union while in the company's employ and told him he would lose his job if he did not sign. The switchman refused, and Coppage discharged him. He was then convicted in a state court of violating the statute, and the conviction was affirmed by the Kansas supreme court.

The United States Supreme Court reversed the conviction in 1915

19 208 U.S. 161 (1908).

20 *Id.* at 174.

in *Coppage* v. *Kansas*,[21] and held the case indistinguishable from *Adair* v. *United States*. Referring to *Holden* v. *Hardy* and other cases in which exercises of the police power had been sustained, Justice Pitney, speaking for the majority, said:

An evident and controlling distinction is this: that in those cases it has been held permissible for the States to adopt regulations fairly deemed necessary to secure some object directly affecting the public welfare, even though the enjoyment of private rights of liberty and property be thereby incidentally hampered; while in that portion of the Kansas statute which is now under consideration—that is to say, aside from coercion, etc.—there is no object or purpose, expressed or implied, that is claimed to have reference to health, safety, morals, or public welfare, beyond the supposed desirability of leveling inequalities of fortune by depriving one who has property of some part of what is characterized as his "financial independence." In short, an interference with the normal exercise of personal liberty and property rights is the primary object of the statute, and not an incident to the advancement of the general welfare. But, in our opinion, the Fourteenth Amendment debars the States from striking down personal liberty or property rights, or materially restricting their normal exercise, excepting so far as may be incidentally necessary for the accomplishment of some other and paramount object, and one that concerns the public welfare. The mere restriction of liberty or of property rights cannot of itself be denominated "public welfare," and treated as a legitimate object of the police power; for such restriction is the very thing that is inhibited by the Amendment.[22]

The liberty which Pitney upheld was a liberty to restrict the switchman's liberty far more drastically than the statute restricted that of the employer. But Pitney would not recognize that the railroad was in any way restricting the switchman's liberty or coercing him. Referring to the term "coerce" in the statute he said, "we have nothing to do with any question of actual or implied coercion or duress, such as might overcome the will of the employé by means unlawful without the statute." [23] It is true that the threat of discharge was not unlawful apart from the statute, but it was hardly less coercive for that reason. The effect of the statue would have been a more equal distribution of liberty. Yet at one point Pitney characterized it as "so disturbing of equality of right." [24] At another, failing to recognize that inequalities of fortune are inequalities of legal rights, he insisted that existing inequalities of fortune may not be disturbed, except as incidental to some other and "paramount" object. He referred to a state-

[21] 236 U.S. 1 (1915). [22] *Id.* at 18. [23] *Id.* at 8.
[24] *Id.* at 14.

ment by the Kansas court that "employés, as a rule, are not financially able to be as independent in making contracts for the sale of their labor as are employers in making contracts of purchase thereof." Commenting on this statement, Pitney said:

No doubt, wherever the right of private property exists, there must and will be inequalities of fortune; and thus it naturally happens that parties negotiating about a contract are not equally unhampered by circumstances. This applies to all contracts, and not merely to that between employer and employé. Indeed a little reflection will show that wherever the right of private property and the right of free contract co-exist, each party when contracting is inevitably more or less influenced by the question whether he has much property, or little, or none; for the contract is made to the very end that each may gain something that he needs or desires more urgently than that which he proposes to give in exchange. And, since it is self-evident that, unless all things are held in common, some persons must have more property than others, it is from the nature of things impossible to uphold freedom of contract and the right of private property without at the same time recognizing as legitimate those inequalities of fortune that are the necessary result of the exercise of those rights. But the Fourteenth Amendment, in declaring that a State shall not "deprive any person of life, liberty, or property without due process of law," gives to each of these an equal sanction; it recognizes "liberty" and "property" as co-existent human rights, and debars the States from any unwarranted interference with either.

And since a State may not strike them down directly it is clear that it may not do so indirectly, as by declaring in effect that the public good requires the removal of those inequalities that are but the normal and inevitable result of their exercise, and then invoking the police power in order to remove the inequalities, without other object in view. The police power is broad, and not easily defined, but it cannot be given the wide scope that is here asserted for it, without in effect nullifying the constitutional guaranty.[25]

Here it is recognized that the economic inequalities which result from the exercise of "freedom of contract" are due, in part at least, to the fact that the different contracting parties do not have equal freedom. They are "not equally unhampered by circumstances." A switchman, dependent on his job for his livelihood and hampered by the "circumstance" that he had little property, had no great freedom to bargain effectively so as to retain his union membership. The railroad superintendent, because of the "circumstance" that the law, in assigning to his corporation the ownership of its property, enabled him to dictate who might work and who might not on his railroad,

[25] 236 U.S. at 17.

had extremely effective power in the exercise of his "freedom of contract" to compel withdrawal from the union. It is true that these inequalities were the result of the coexistence of "the right of private property and the right of free contract." But they were not the "necessary" or "inevitable" results. Property acquired by government grant or by inheritance is not acquired as a result of freedom of contract. Had government pursued a different policy for the assignment to private ownership of natural resources or the distribution of decedents' estates, the coexistence of private property and freedom of contract would have resulted in quite a different pattern of economic inequalities. Under such circumstances that different pattern would have been quite as "inevitable" a result of private property and freedom of contract, as the present pattern was under existing circumstances. But any legislative restriction of liberty or of property rights for the purpose of removing any specific inequality, Pitney held was barred by the Fourteenth Amendment, as "disturbing of equality of right."

Three Justices dissented. Justice Holmes, in a brief opinion, recognized that the statute might promote, not restrict, liberty of contract.

> In present conditions [he said] a workman not unnaturally may believe that only by belonging to a union can he secure a contract that shall be fair to him. . . . If that belief, whether right or wrong, may be held by a reasonable man, it seems to me that it may be enforced by law in order to establish the equality of position between the parties in which liberty of contract begins.[26]

He thought that *Adair* v. *United States* and *Lochner* v. *New York* should be overruled.

Justice Day wrote a longer dissent, in which Justice Hughes concurred. Day did not advocate overruling the *Adair* case, but distinguished it. Adair had been convicted of discharging a man because of union membership. It did not appear that he had threatened to discharge him before actually doing so or that he had asked him to enter into a nonunion agreement. Day agreed that an employer had a constitutional right to discharge a man for union membership or for any other reason and that the section of the federal statute providing punishment for doing so was unconstitutional. The section of the Kansas statute here invoked, however, did not provide punishment for the discharge. Coppage was convicted, not of discharging

[26] *Id.* at 26–27.

the switchman, but of threatening to discharge him; and of threatening to do so not merely to induce him to withdraw from his union but also to sign an agreement to keep out. Day emphasized both points.

There is a real and not a fanciful distinction [he said] between the exercise of the right to discharge at will and the imposition of a requirement that the employee, as a condition of employment, shall make a particular agreement to forego a legal right. The *agreement* may be, or may be declared to be, against public policy, although the right of discharge remains. When a man is discharged, the employer exercises his right to declare such action necessary because of the exigencies of his business, or as the result of his judgment for other reasons sufficient to himself. When he makes a stipulation of the character here involved essential to future employment, he is not exercising a right to discharge, and may not wish to discharge the employee when, at a subsequent time, the prohibited act is done. What is in fact accomplished, is that the one engaging to work, who may wish to preserve an independent right of action, as a condition of employment, is coerced to the signing of such an agreement against his will, perhaps impelled by the necessities of his situation.[27]

Had the switchman signed the proposed agreement, he would have incurred a contractual obligation to keep out of the union—he would have signed away his legal "right" to belong. Had he merely been required to leave the union, without making any agreement, he would still have retained his "right," but would have been forced to refrain from "exercising" it. Had the Court had before it a statutory provision forbidding an employer to make such a requirement, it is not quite clear whether Day would have sustained it. His adherence to the *Adair* case and his emphasis on the agreement that was required suggest that he would not. In a somewhat ambiguous passage, he justified the statute as protecting the employee from being "deprived" of a right, but also as protecting him in its "exercise." The right to join unions, he said,

as against coercive action to the contrary may be the legitimate subject of protection in the exercise of the police authority of the States. This statute . . . has for its avowed purpose the protection of the exercise of a legal right, by preventing an employer from depriving the employee of it as a condition of obtaining employment. I see no reason why a State may not, if it chooses, protect this right, as well as other legal rights.[28]

Elsewhere he said:

The penalty imposed is not for the discharge but for the attempt to coerce an unwilling employee to agree to forego the exercise of the legal right

[27] 236 U.S. at 37–38. Italics in original.

[28] *Id.* at 32–33.

involved as a condition of employment. It is the requirement of such agreements which the State declares to be against public policy.[29]

It may well be that Day would have sustained a statutory provision which went further and penalized attempts to coerce an employee simply to forego, without coercing him to agree to forego, the exercise of the legal right. Foregoing the exercise would be coercive, even without signing away the privilege to exercise it. Day recognized that the attempt to make him sign was coercive, and an attempt to make him leave the union without signing would seem equally so. "In view of the relative positions of employer and employed," he asked at another point, "who is to deny that the stipulation here insisted upon and forbidden by the law is essentially coercive?" [30] "A principal object of this statute," he said later, "is to protect the liberty of the citizen to make such lawful affiliations as he may desire with organizations of his choice." [31] And "it ought not to be a reasonable objection that one motive which impelled an enactment was to protect those who might otherwise be unable to protect themselves." [32] So, in his view, an exercise of a right of liberty or property in such a way as to restrict another's liberty, even though Pitney characterized such exercise as "normal," may in some circumstances at least be properly curtailed by law.

Justice Hughes, who concurred in Day's dissent, left the bench in 1916 when nominated for President, but returned as Chief Justice in 1930. Soon after his return, he had occasion to deny Pitney's appellation of "normal" to an employer's exercise of a right to discharge for the purpose of interfering with union activities. The Railway Labor Act of 1926 set up a scheme for negotiation and mediation of labor disputes on railroads, and contained the following provision:

Representatives, for the purpose of this Act, shall be designated by the respective parties in such manner as may be provided in their corporate organization or unincorporated association, or by other means of collective action, without interference, influence, or coercion exercised by either party over the self-organization or designation of representatives by the other.

In *Texas & New Orleans R. Co.* v. *Brotherhood of Railway & S.S. Clerks* [33] the Court, in 1930, construed this section as authorizing a union to secure an injunction to restrain a railroad company from coercing its employees to withdraw from the union, and from promot-

[29] *Id.* at 40. [30] *Id.* at 38. [31] *Id.* at 40. [32] *Id.* at 42.
[33] 281 U.S. 548 (1930).

ing another union of its own to represent the men, instead of the union which sought the injunction. Such an injunction had been granted in a lower federal court, and when the railroad disobeyed it, that court ordered the railroad, in order to purge itself of contempt, to reinstate members of the union who had been discharged and to disestablish the company union.

In discharging men for union activity, the railroad was not (as in the *Coppage* case) requiring them to make any agreement whereby they were to sign away their "right" to belong to unions. It was merely exercising its right of discharge for the purpose of preventing the men from exercising their "right" to belong (as in the *Adair* case). But, as the statute was construed, such exercise of the right to discharge was prohibited by Congress. And, by unanimous vote of the Justices who participated in the case,[34] the Supreme Court, speaking through Chief Justice Hughes, sustained not only the construction of the statute as forbidding the company's acts, but its constitutionality. In doing so, it denied that the company's exercise of its right to discharge was a "normal" exercise of that right or that it had a constitutional right to exercise it in such a way as to interfere with the freedom of the employees. In other words, the mere fact that one liberty is used to restrain another one may be a sufficient ground for sustaining a legislative curtailment of the former, without regard to any extraneous "paramount" object, such as health or safety. Little was left of the doctrines of the *Adair* and *Coppage* cases, though the Court made a lame attempt to distinguish them. The reasoning, however, is far more consistent with that of Justice Day's dissent in the *Coppage* case (to which Hughes had subscribed) than with that of Pitney's prevailing opinion. On the constitutional point, Hughes said:

> We entertain no doubt of the constitutional authority of Congress to enact the prohibition. . . . The legality of collective action on the part of employees in order to safeguard their proper interests is not to be disputed. It has long been recognized that employees are entitled to organize for the purpose of securing the redress of grievances and to promote agreements with employers relating to rates of pay and conditions of work . . . Congress was not required to ignore this right of the employees but could safeguard it and seek to make their collective action an instrument of peace rather than of strife. Such collective action would be a mockery if representation were made futile by interference with freedom of choice. Thus the prohibition by Congress of interference with the selection of representa-

[34] Justice McReynolds took no part in the case.

tives for the purpose of negotiation and conference between employers and employees, instead of being an invasion of the constitutional right of either, was based on the recognition of the rights of both. The petitioners invoke the principle declared in *Adair* v. *United States* . . . and *Coppage* v. *Kansas* . . . but these decisions are inapplicable. The Railway Labor Act of 1926 does not interfere with the normal exercise of the right of the carrier to select its employees or to discharge them. The statute is not aimed at this right of the employers but at the interference with the right of employees to have representatives of their own choosing. As the carriers subject to the act have no constitutional right to interfere with the freedom of the employees in making their selections, they cannot complain of the statute on constitutional grounds.[35]

The *Adair* and *Coppage* cases certainly held that an employer did have a constitutional right to interfere with the freedom of his employees to belong to unions if the interference took the form of discharging them because of their membership or threatening to discharge them. That holding was clearly rejected here, unless interference with freedom to belong to unions can be distinguished from interference with freedom to select representatives.

No such distinction was made in 1937, when the Court sustained the Wagner Labor Relations Act in *National Labor Relations Board* v. *Jones & Laughlin Steel Corp.*[36] In holding valid an order of the Board to cease and desist from discriminating against union members by discharging them and to reinstate those already discharged, with back pay, Chief Justice Hughes said:

The act does not interfere with the normal exercise of the right of the employer to select its employees or to discharge them. The employer may not, under cover of that right, intimidate or coerce its employees with respect to their self-organization and representation, and, on the other hand, the Board is not entitled to make its authority a pretext for interference with the right of discharge when that right is exercised for other reasons than such intimidation and coercion.

Not much was left of the constitutional right asserted in the *Adair* and *Coppage* cases, and Justice Frankfurter, speaking for the Court in 1941, in *Phelps Dodge* v. *NLRB,* said: "The course of decisions in this Court since *Adair* v. *United States* . . . and *Coppage* v. *Kansas* . . . have completely sapped those cases of their authority." [37] The fact that one liberty or property right is used to interfere with some other liberty may suffice to permit the legislature to extend to the

35 281 U.S. at 570–571.

36 301 U.S. 1, 45–46 (1937).

37 313 U.S. 177, 187 (1941).

latter liberty a protection which the Constitution by itself does not afford.

It is not only governments that are capable of depriving persons of liberty or property. Other private individuals can do so as well. But the due process clauses afford no guaranty against deprivations by private individuals. Liberty and property which are jeopardized by private actions may, however, be preserved by legislation, state or national. In protecting some forms of liberty or property from deprivation at the hands of others the legislature is itself depriving those others to some extent of their liberty or property, and whether it may do so presents a constitutional question. But, as in the *Jones & Laughlin* case, the Court does not now consider it arbitrary for the legislature to prefer the preservation of the one liberty over the other. The same is true when two property rights conflict.

Thus, in Virginia, where apple growing was one of the principal industries of the state, apple orchards were being menaced by the cedar rust disease, which was carried by a fungus from infected ornamental red cedar trees within two miles. Owners of apple orchards were thus being threatened with deprivation of their property, but not by the state. Accordingly, the Fourteenth Amendment gave them no protection. The state legislature, however, extended it to them, by enacting a law, under which the state entomologist was required to order the destruction of any ornamental red cedars within two miles of apple orchards if he found them to constitute a menace to the health of the orchards. If the owner of the cedars failed to destroy them, the entomologist was to do so himself. No compensation was to be given to the owners of the cedars for the value of the standing timber, though they were to be allowed to use the trees when felled. An appeal was provided from the entomologist's order to the courts. The statute declared it to be unlawful for any person to "own, plant or keep alive and standing" on his premises any red cedar tree which might be the source of the "host plant" of the cedar rust disease.

Before the act was passed, a person who kept a cedar tree standing on his premises was only "exercising a property right." The act forbade him to do so. It also required the entomologist to deprive him of his standing trees. The state was clearly depriving him of property, but was doing so in order to prevent the owner of orchards from being deprived of property by means other than state action. An owner whose cedars were ordered destroyed challenged the constitutionality of the act and, after being defeated in the Virginia supreme court of appeals, took the case to the United States Supreme Court.

That Court unanimously sustained the act in 1928, in *Miller* v. *Schoene*,[38] Justice Stone saying:

On the evidence we may accept the conclusion of the Supreme Court of Appeals that the state was under the necessity of making a choice between the preservation of one class of property and that of the other wherever both existed in dangerous proximity. It would have been none the less of a choice if, instead of enacting the present statute, the state, by doing nothing, had permitted serious injury to the apple orchards within its borders to go on unchecked. When forced to such a choice the state does not exceed its constitutional powers by deciding upon the destruction of one class of property in order to save another which, in the judgment of the legislature, is of greater value to the public. It will not do to say that the case is merely one of a conflict of two private interests and that the misfortune of the apple growers may not be shifted to cedar owners by ordering the destruction of their property; for it is obvious that there may be, and that here there is, a preponderant public concern in the preservation of the one interest over the other. [Citations.] And where the public interest is involved preferment of that interest over the property interest of the individual, to the extent even of its destruction, is one of the distinguishing characteristics of every exercise of the police power which affects property. [Citations.]

So, while the due process clause does not itself forbid those who have greater economic power to deprive those who have less, of liberty or property, neither does it, on the other hand, preclude the states from doing so, even by a state restriction of conflicting liberties or property rights. Within wide limits, a state may choose which of various forms of liberty or property are to be preserved in preference to conflicting forms. Inequalities of fortune, resulting from the coexistence of private property and freedom of contract, may be scrutinized, and to some extent property rights and freedom of contract may be modified so as to reduce particular inequalities, not merely as an incident to the promotion of health or safety but also because the legislature adjudges the particular inequality to be undesirable.

38 276 U.S. 272, 279–280 (1928).

XIII

THE PRICES WHICH A STATE MAY CONTROL [1]

WHATEVER pattern the law may follow in assigning to each his particular property rights, the economic inequalities which follow are determined almost entirely by price relationships. Everyone must consume many things which he does not yet own, and, with a given money income his material welfare obviously depends on the prices he must pay for goods and services. But no one has a given money income except as the outcome of other price relationships. This is true not only of the man whose income is derived directly from the sale of goods but also in the less obvious case of the recipient of a so-called independent income. Interest on corporate bonds can be enjoyed only so long as the corporation is able to pay it, which depends on the relationship between the prices of what it sells and those which it must pay for materials and labor. Dividends clearly depend on the same relationship. The wage-earner's income is the price of labor, and the landowner's rent is the price of the right of temporary use.

1 I have drawn freely for this chapter from my article *The Constitution and the Price System: Some Reflections on Nebbia v. New York* (1934) 34 COL. L. REV. 401.

These incomes, moreover, which are themselves prices, depend in part on other prices. Thus, the interest that can be obtained on new loans, the wages in new labor bargains, and the rent that can be obtained in new leases will be influenced by the advantages which the payers of interest or of wages or of rent anticipate from the borrowing of funds, the employment of labor, or the use of land; and these advantages depend on profitability, which depends on price relationships. Any power to control prices, therefore, whether exercised by government or by private groups, is a power to affect the economic relations between different members of the community and to accentuate or mitigate those inequalities of fortune which flow from the exercise of freedom of contract and the right of private property.[2] It determines the relative economic freedom of buyers and sellers.

In this country, until the latter part of the nineteenth century, governments were but little concerned with the direct regulation of prices. Those fixed by the impersonal forces of the market were thought to be satisfactory. With the growth of trusts, there was some complaint of exorbitant charges, but the remedy which first suggested itself was, not direct regulation of the prices, but the enactment of anti-trust laws designed to restore free competitive conditions. In some few businesses, however, governments did concern themselves directly with prices. When special privileges had to be granted to a business before it could operate, such as the privilege of laying tracks in a city's streets or tearing up the streets to lay gas mains, it was realized that competition could not be relied upon. In fact, the opinion came to prevail that competition in some of these cases might be a positive evil, resulting in wastefulness such as the laying of duplicate gas mains. Accordingly, exclusive franchises were frequently granted, and it was not unusual to include in such franchises provisions binding the company to charge no more than a specified rate. Since conditions might change, however, such contractual rates might prove later to be too high or too low. Attempts to fix rates by contract have largely been abandoned, and at the present time rates of public utilities are regulated in most states by commissions.

Meanwhile, many states regulated the rates of railroads by direct legislation or by means of commissions. Since 1887 their interstate rates have been under the control of the federal Interstate Commerce Commission. Railroads were not free from all competition, but they

[2] *Cf.* Pitney, J., in Coppage v. Kansas, 236 U.S. 1, 17 (1915), discussed *supra*, pp. 390–397.

had been given special privileges in the form of authority to exercise the power of eminent domain and sometimes in the form of land grants. Moreover, railroads are common carriers, and the business of the common carrier was one of the few for which there was supposed to be a common law obligation to charge only "reasonable" rates. Accordingly it seemed natural to supplement the common law duty with statutory regulation.

Railroads and public utilities were thought to be businesses "affected with a public interest," though the precise meaning of that phrase was never clear. The due process clause was thought to preclude any governmental regulation whatsoever of the prices charged by businesses not so "affected," until that notion was dispelled in 1934 in *Nebbia* v. *New York*.[3] The since-repudiated constitutional doctrine had its origin in Chief Justice Waite's majority opinion in 1877 in the leading case of *Munn* v. *Illinois*.[4]

Munn and Scott were lessees and managers of a grain elevator in Chicago. Wheat shipped from the Western wheat fields to the Atlantic seaboard had to be transshipped at Chicago, and while waiting transshipment, had to be stored in elevators located near the terminals of the western and eastern transportation systems. There were fourteen such elevators, including Munn's, but because the area available for the purpose was very limited in extent, they had no fear of outside competition. The nine firms which controlled them agreed each year on the prices they would charge for storage. They had a virtual monopoly; their rates were not fixed by impersonal market forces. The legislature of Illinois sought to protect the shippers from this monopoly control by enacting a statute fixing maximum storage rates. Munn and Scott, after challenging the constitutionality of the statute unsuccessfully in the Illinois supreme court, took the case to the federal Supreme Court, where they were again defeated. In sustaining the statute, however, Chief Justice Waite used language taken from words uttered some two hundred years previously in another connection by Lord Chief Justice Hale in England, and clearly intimated that governmental power over prices was confined to the narrow circle of businesses "affected with a public interest."[5]

[3] 291 U.S. 502 (1934).
[4] 94 U.S. 113 (1877).
[5] For an account of the circumstances which led Waite to rely on this concept and for a contention that he misapplied it see an interesting article by Walton H. Hamilton, *Affectation with a Public Interest* (1930) 39 YALE L.J. 1089.

Looking, then, to the common law [said Waite], from whence came the right which the Constitution protects, we find that when property is "affected with a public interest, it ceases to be *juris privati* only." This was said by Lord Chief Justice Hale more than two hundred years ago, in his treatise *De Portibus Maris,* 1 Harg. Law Tracts, 78, and has been accepted without objection as an essential element in the law of property ever since. Property does become clothed with a public interest when used in a manner to make it of public consequence, and affect the community at large. When, therefore, one devotes his property to a use in which the public has an interest, he, in effect, grants to the public an interest in that use, and must submit to be controlled by the public for the common good, to the extent of the interest he has thus created. He may withdraw his grant by discontinuing the use; but, so long as he maintains the use, he must submit to the control.[6]

After further quotations from Lord Hale and from others in support of this principle, Waite came to the question whether Munn's property and business came within its operation. Quoting from the statement of facts in Munn's brief, he went on:

In this connection it must also be borne in mind that, although in 1874 there were in Chicago fourteen warehouses adapted to this particular business, and owned by about thirty persons, nine business firms controlled them, and that the prices charged and received for storage were such "as have been from year to year agreed upon and established by the different elevators or warehouses in the city of Chicago, and which rates have been annually published in one or more newspapers printed in said city, in the month of January in each year, as the established rates for the year then next ensuing such publication." Thus it is apparent that all the elevating facilities through which these vast productions "of seven or eight great States of the West" must pass on the way "to four or five of the States on the seashore" may be a "virtual" monopoly.

Under such circumstances it is difficult to see why, if the common carrier, or the miller, or the ferryman, or the inn-keeper, or the wharfinger, or the baker, or the cartman, or the hackney-coachman, pursues a public employment and exercises "a sort of public office," these plaintiffs in error do not. They stand, to use again the language of their counsel, in the very "gateway of commerce," and take toll from all who pass. Their business most certainly "tends to a common charge, and is become a thing of public interest and use." Every bushel of grain for its passage "pays a toll, which is a common charge," and, therefore, according to Lord Hale, every such warehouseman "ought to be under public regulation, viz., that he . . . take but reasonable toll." Certainly, if any business can be clothed "with a public interest, and cease to be *juris privati* only," this has been. It may not

[6] 94 U.S. at 125–126.

be made so by the operation of the Constitution of Illinois or this statute, but it is by the facts.[7]

The fundamental basis, then, for holding that this business was "affected with a public interest" was that it was a virtual monopoly. Waite was here speaking of the common law, under which the reasonableness of the charge made by such a business presented a judicial, not a legislative, question. But after pointing out that the common-law rule "is itself a regulation as to price," he added:

> But a mere common-law regulation of trade or business may be changed by statute. A person has no property, no vested interest, in any rule of the common law. . . . To limit [by statute] the rate of charge for services rendered in a public employment, or for the use of property in which the public has an interest, is only changing a regulation which existed before. It establishes no new principle in the law, but only gives a new effect to an old one.
>
> We know that this is a power which may be abused; but that is no argument against its existence. For protection against abuses by legislatures the people must resort to the polls, not to the courts.[8]

Justice Field wrote a dissenting opinion, in which Justice Strong joined.[9] Ignoring the basis of virtual monopoly on which Waite based his conclusion, and seizing on the more general statements that a business may be subject to price regulation when it "affects the community at large" or when the owner has devoted his property to a use "in which the public has an interest," Field maintained that "there is hardly an enterprise or business engaging the attention and labor of any considerable portion of the community, in which the public has not an interest in the sense in which that term is used by the court in its opinion." [10] Continuing on the same page, he said:

> The doctrine of the State court, that no one is deprived of his property, within the meaning of the constitutional inhibition, so long as he retains its title and possession, and the doctrine of this court, that, whenever one's property is used in such a manner as to affect the community at large, it becomes by that fact clothed with a public interest, and ceases to be *juris privati* only, appear to me to destroy, for all useful purposes, the efficacy of the constitutional guaranty. All that is beneficial in property arises from its use, and the fruits of that use; and whatever deprives a person of them deprives him of all that is desirable or valuable in the title and possession. If the constitutional guaranty extends no further than to prevent a depriva-

[7] 94 U.S. at 131–132.

[8] *Id.* at 134.

[9] The other members of the Court (who presumably concurred with Chief Justice Waite) were Justices Clifford, Swayne, Miller, Davis, Bradley, and Hunt.

[10] 94 U.S. at 141.

tion of title and possession, and allows a deprivation of use, and the fruits of that use, it does not merit the encomiums it has received.

And again:

If the legislature of a State, under pretence of providing for the public good, or for any other reason, can determine, against the consent of the owner, the uses to which private property shall be devoted, or the prices which the owner shall receive for its uses, it can deprive him of the property as completely as by a special act for its confiscation or destruction. If, for instance, the owner is prohibited from using his building for the purposes for which it was designed, it is of little consequence that he is permitted to retain the title and possession; or, if he is compelled to take as compensation for its use less than the expenses to which he is subjected by its ownership, he is, for all practical purposes, deprived of the property as effectually as if the legislature had ordered his forcible dispossession. If it be admitted that the legislature has any control over the compensation, the extent of that compensation becomes a mere matter of legislative discretion. The amount fixed will operate as a partial destruction of the value of the property, if it fall below the amount which the owner would obtain by contract, and, practically, as a complete destruction, if it be less than the cost of retaining its possession. There is, indeed, no protection of any value under the constitutional provision, which does not extend to the use and income of the property, as well as to its title and possession.[11]

Field admitted, however, that

there is no end of regulations with respect to the use of property which may not be legitimately prescribed, having for their object the peace, good order, safety, and health of the community, thus securing to all the equal enjoyment of their property; but in establishing these regulations it is evident that compensation to the owner for the use of his property, or for his services in union with it, is not a matter of any importance.[12]

Whether Field recognized the fact or not, such admittedly valid regulations deprive the owner of some part of the use of his property and hence some part of its benefits and value. They do not, however, deprive him of any of his power to exclude others from its use, or to impose such conditions on its use as he may see fit to impose in the form of prices.

It is only [said Field] where some right or privilege is conferred by the government or municipality upon the owner, which he can use in connection with his property, or by means of which the use of his property is rendered more valuable to him, or he thereby enjoys an advantage over others, that the compensation to be received by him becomes a legitimate matter of regulation.[13]

[11] *Id.* at 142–143. [12] *Id.* at 146. [13] *Ibid.*

Expanding on this point and maintaining that the enjoyment of a special privilege is the only factor which justifies the fixing of prices in the cases cited by the Court, from Lord Hale and elsewhere, Field said at a later point:

The several instances mentioned by counsel in the argument, and by the court in its opinion, in which legislation has fixed the compensation which parties may receive for the use of their property and services, do not militate against the views I have expressed of the power of the State over the property of the citizen. They were mostly cases of public ferries, bridges, and turnpikes, of wharfingers, hackmen, and draymen, and of interest on money. In all these cases, except that of interest on money, which I shall presently notice, there was some special privilege granted by the State or municipality; and no one, I suppose, has ever contended that the State had not a right to prescribe the conditions upon which such privilege should be enjoyed. The State in such cases exercises no greater right than an individual may exercise over the use of his own property when leased or loaned to others. The conditions upon which the privilege shall be enjoyed being stated or implied in the legislation authorizing its grant, no right is, of course, impaired by their enforcement. The recipient of the privilege, in effect, stipulates to comply with the conditions. It matters not how limited the privilege conferred, its acceptance implies an assent to the regulation of its use and the compensation for it. The privilege which the hackman and drayman have to the use of stands on the public streets, not allowed to the ordinary coachman or laborer with teams, constitutes a sufficient warrant for the regulation of their fares. In the case of the warehousemen of Chicago, no right or privilege is conferred by the government upon them; and hence no assent of theirs can be alleged to justify any interference with their charges for the use of their property.[14]

Not unnaturally, Field held the conventional view that in assigning

[14] 94 U.S. at 148–149. Field explained the validity of usury laws on the same principle. On p. 153 he said: "The practice of regulating by legislation the interest receivable for the use of money, when considered with reference to its origin, is only the assertion of a right of the government to control the extent to which a privilege granted by it may be exercised and enjoyed. By the ancient common law it was unlawful to take any money for the use of money: all who did so were called usurers, a term of great reproach, and were exposed to the censure of the church; and if, after the death of a person, it was discovered that he had been a usurer whilst living, his chattels were forfeited to the king, and his lands escheated to the lord of the fee. No action could be maintained on any promise to pay for the use of money, because of the unlawfulness of the contract. Whilst the common law thus condemned all usury, Parliament interfered, and made it lawful to take a limited amount of interest. It was not upon the theory that the legislature could arbitrarily fix the compensation which one could receive for the use of property, which, by the general law, was the subject of hire for compensation, that Parliament acted, but in order to confer a privilege which the common law denied. The reasons which led to this legislation originally have long since ceased to exist; and if the legislation is still persisted in, it is because a long acquiescence in the exercise of a power, especially when it was rightfully assumed in the first instance, is generally received as sufficient evidence of its continued lawfulness." 10 Bac. Abr. 264.

and enforcing property rights the government is conferring no rights or privileges on the owner—or at least no privilege "by means of which . . . he thereby enjoys an advantage over others." In fact, however, the virtual monopoly of the nine businessmen who operated these warehouses was rooted precisely in their legal right to keep competitors from competing. No one could, as a practical matter, engage in the business without maintaining a warehouse in the narrow area, all the land of which was owned by these nine men or leased by them or by the corporations which they managed. Maintaining such a warehouse would have been forbidden by law, since it would have involved trespass on someone else's property. The legal prohibition of trespass on this area was in effect, though not in name, a prohibition of competition. The result was the same as if the law had, in so many words, conferred on the nine businessmen a legal monopoly—in which case Field would have admitted the legitimacy of regulating their charges.

Some fifteen years later, in *Budd* v. *New York*,[15] an unsuccessful attempt was made to induce the Court to repudiate the doctrine of *Munn* v. *Illinois* and to declare unconstitutional a New York statute which regulated the charges of grain elevators in the harbors of New York, Brooklyn, and Buffalo. While the statute was sustained, Justice Brewer wrote a vigorous dissent, in which Justices Field and Brown joined.

> Property [said Brewer] is devoted to a public use when, and only when, the use is one which the public in its organized capacity, to wit, the state, has a right to create and maintain, and, therefore, one which all the public have a right to demand and share in. The use is public because the public may create it, and the individual creating it is doing thereby and *pro tanto* the work of the state.[16]

He gave here no economic reason for supposing either that prices fixed by an individual doing *pro tanto* the work of the state would be unsatisfactory in their consequences or that prices fixed by other individuals would be satisfactory. Nor did he indicate how to determine

---

Field added this interesting footnote:

"The statute of 13 Eliz. c. 8, which allows ten per cent interest, recites 'that all usury, being forbidden by the law of God, is sin, and detestable'; and the statutes of 21 James the First, reducing the rate to eight per cent, provided that nothing in the law should be 'construed to allow the practice of usury in point of religion or conscience,' a clause introduced, it is said, to satisfy the bishops, who would not vote for the bill without it."

[15] 143 U.S. 517 (1892). The majority opinion was written by Justice Blatchford.

[16] *Id.* at 549.

what is properly the work of the state, beyond remarking that the creation of all highways is a public duty and that railroads are highways. In this part of his argument he seemed concerned, not with economic results, but with what he conceived to be absolute rights of property, with which "men are endowed by their Creator." These absolute rights he thus epitomized:

That property which a man has honestly acquired he retains full control of, subject to these limitations: First, that he shall not use it to his neighbor's injury, and that does not mean that he must use it for his neighbor's benefit; second, that if he devotes it to a public use, he gives to the public a right to control that use; and, third, that whenever the public needs require, the public may take it upon payment of due compensation.[17]

If we accept these dogmas, we may inquire whether any active use of physical property is harmful to others and may properly be prohibited, but not whether the owner's withholding from use is harmful or the conditions on which he consents not to withhold it (the prices) are reasonable; for when the owner insists on withholding, he is regarded as merely exercising his divine right (the right with which he is "endowed by his Creator") not to use it for his neighbor's benefit. The sole exception is when he is doing *pro tanto* the work of the state, in which case, apparently, the state may fix his price even if there is no element of special privilege or monopoly. Perhaps Brewer assumed that some special privilege would necessarily be enjoyed by anyone doing *pro tanto* the work of the state. And he may have assumed that law-made monopolies would not be conferred on anyone else, for in the next paragraph he conceded that the rates of such monopolies could be controlled. He said:

There are two kinds of monopoly; one of law, the other of fact. The one exists when exclusive privileges are granted. Such a monopoly, the law which creates alone can break; and being the creation of law justifies legislative control. A monopoly of fact any one can break, and there is no necessity for legislative interference.[18]

Here Brewer was no longer basing his judgment on his knowledge of the mind of the Deity, but rather on what he assumed to be economic facts. He can hardly have thought that anyone of the victims of a monopoly of fact (the ones to be protected by price regulation) could break it. He must have thought that some competitor would be likely to break any such monopoly in the near future, and that

[17] 143 U.S. at 550.

[18] *Id.* at 550–551.

therefore any monopoly power it might possess would be shortlived. It may not have been as evident in 1892 as it has become since that many monopolies of fact are not likely to be broken in any foreseeable future. Believing that customers were never likely to be left long at the mercy of a monopoly of fact, he may have assumed that a legislative power to reduce the rates to the point where the short-lived monopoly advantage would be eliminated involved a dangerous power to reduce them much further. The doctrine that, even in businesses whose rates are admittedly subject to regulation, the legislative power over them is subject to a drastic "vertical" limit, had been expressed by 1892 only in rather vague dicta.

To the majority, however, the existence of a monopoly of fact or a virtual monopoly seems to have sufficed to justify the power to regulate the rates. In fact, in both the *Munn* and the *Budd* cases, the conclusion that the elevators were "affected with a public interest" was based on the virtual monopoly of those elevators and their position as links in the chain of transportation. Two years after the *Budd* case, however, in *Brass* v. *Stoeser*,[19] the Court seems to have regarded those peculiarities as irrelevant. It sustained a North Dakota statute regulating the charges of grain elevators, though on the record it appeared that there was no element of monopoly in the elevators in the state and that land was available for the construction of elevators almost anywhere in the state. The absence of monopoly, said Justice Shiras for the majority, may be a matter for the legislature to consider, but not the courts.

> When it is once admitted, as it is admitted here, that it is competent for the legislative power to control the business of elevating and storing grain, whether carried on by individuals or associations, in cities of one size and in some circumstances, it follows that such power may be legally exerted over the same business when carried on in smaller cities and in other circumstances.[20]

On this mechanical approach to the problem, one wonders what would have happened if the North Dakota statute had reached the Court before the statute which regulated the Chicago elevators. Looking at the North Dakota elevators and finding no monopoly, the Court might well (having no precedent like the *Munn* case before it) have held that the elevators were not affected with a public interest. Then, if a statute regulating the monopolistic elevators in Chicago had

19 153 U.S. 391 (1894).

20 *Id.* at 403.

reached the Court subsequently, Justice Shiras's reasoning would have held the monopoly irrelevant, and would have concluded that when it is once admitted that it is incompetent for the legislative power to control the business of storing grain in circumstances of competition, it must follow that such power may not be legally exerted over the same business in circumstances of monopoly.

Justice Brewer again wrote a dissenting opinion, in which he was joined, as before, by Justice Field (the only survivor of the Court which decided *Munn* v. *Illinois*) and by two new Justices, Howell E. Jackson and White, who had succeeded two of the majority Justices in the *Budd* case, L. Q. C. Lamar and Blatchford, respectively. Justice Brown deserted the dissenters here and went over to the majority.

The next case of significance in which the Supreme Court dealt with the power to fix prices was *German Alliance Insurance Co.* v. *Kansas,*[21] decided in 1914. Here the power to regulate fire insurance rates was sustained. Justice McKenna, for the majority, declared that the business was affected with a public interest, although it had no special privileges and no monopoly. His argument rested primarily on an economic analysis of the position of fire insurance companies in the community and the interdependence of the various contracts made by the policyholders. After denying the necessity that there must be a monopoly to justify regulation, however, he added a paragraph which seemed to imply that this business was monopolistic, at least in its control of rates.

We may venture to observe [he said] that the price of insurance is not fixed over the counters of the companies by what Adam Smith calls the higgling of the market, but formed in the councils of the underwriters, promulgated in schedules of practically controlling constancy which the applicant for insurance is powerless to oppose and which, therefore, has led to the assertion that the business of insurance is of monopolistic character and that "it is illusory to speak of a liberty of contract." It is in the alternative presented of accepting the rates of the companies or refraining from insurance, business necessity impelling if not compelling it, that we may discover the inducement of the Kansas statute, and the problem presented is whether the legislature could regard it of as much moment to the public that they who seek insurance should no more be constrained by arbitrary terms than they who seek transportation by railroads, steam or street, or by coaches whose itinerary may be only a few city blocks, or who seek the use of grain elevators, or to be secured in a night's accommodation at a wayside inn, or in the weight of a five-cent loaf of bread. We do not say this to belittle such

[21] 233 U.S. 389 (1914).

rights or to exaggerate the effect of insurance, but to exhibit the principle which exists in all and brings all under the same governmental power.[22]

Only four other Justices concurred in Justice McKenna's opinion —Holmes, Day, Hughes, and Pitney. Justice Lurton took no part in the decision, and Justice J. R. Lamar dissented, in an opinion in which he was joined by Chief Justice White and Justice Van Devanter. He made a sharp distinction, as Field had done in the *Munn* case, between the power to regulate the uses of property in other respects and the power to regulate the prices for the use of it. The latter "is as much a taking as though the fee itself had been condemned for a lump sum— that taking, whether by fixing rates for the use or by paying the lump sum for the fee, has always heretofore been thought to be permissible only when it was for a public use." [23] This use was not thought to be a public one, it seems, because, as the company contended, it was under no legal obligation (as public utilities and railroads were) to render its services to anyone to whom it did not wish to render them.

The likening of rate regulation to condemnation overlooks the fact that when property is condemned, the owner is entitled, by way of compensation, to its market value—what he could have obtained in a private sale; whereas if the owner whose prices are regulated is entitled to rates equal to what he could have obtained in the absence of regulation, there could obviously be no regulation. In making the analogy, however, Lamar was merely acting on a theory which was (until recently) orthodox with the Court in determining the limitations on a state's power to reduce the rates of companies which were admittedly subject to regulation. That theory, based on the eminent domain analogy, was that while the earnings of a company may be reduced in some circumstances by the regulation of its rates, still the value of its property must not be impaired. The proposition is self-contradictory, and, as we shall see, the Court has repudiated it in recent cases.

Lamar also insisted that this case "presents no question of monopoly in a prime necessity of life," and since it relates to purely personal contracts "it is evident that the decision is not a mere entering wedge, but reaches the end from the beginning and announces a principle which points inevitably to the conclusion that the price of every service offered can be regulated by statute." [24]

Neither White nor Van Devanter, who joined in this dissent, nor

22 *Id.* at 416–417. 23 *Id.* at 419. 24 *Id.* at 420.

McKenna, who wrote the prevailing opinion, seems to have thought in 1921 that the case established any such principle; for they all, together with McReynolds, who had since joined the Court, dissented from the cases of *Block* v. *Hirsh* [25] and *Marcus Brown Holding Co.* v. *Feldman*,[26] in which the Court sustained the validity of the emergency rent laws of the District of Columbia and of New York. These were sustained on the basis of the existence of an emergency.

By this time it was by no means clear what it was that might so "affect" a business with a public interest that its prices might be regulated. It was not essential that the business should be doing the work of the state or that it should be enjoying special privileges or a law-made monopoly; a virtual monopoly was apparently sufficient, but not essential, since there was no monopoly in the case dealing with the North Dakota elevators, and the Court declared that monopoly was not essential (though it seems to have existed) in the *German Alliance* case. The decision rendered on April 9, 1923, in *Adkins* v. *Children's Hospital*,[27] since overruled, which held the minimum wage law for the District of Columbia unconstitutional, threw no additional light on the problem. While Justice Sutherland maintained that a person selling his labor was to be distinguished from a company affected with a public interest, it was not quite clear at the time whether the Court meant to hold that any regulation of wages whatsoever would be unconstitutional, or only that the particular regulation in question was so, because arbitrary.

Two months later, on June 11, 1923, Chief Justice Taft, who had been one of the dissenters in the *Adkins* case, handed down the unanimous decision of the Court in *Wolff Packing Co.* v. *Court of Industrial Relations*,[28] and in doing so sought to clarify the question. In holding the Kansas compulsory arbitration act unconstitutional as applied to the meat packing business, he intimated that that business, as carried on in Kansas, was not affected with a public interest. Businesses which are so affected he divided into three classes: (1) Those carried on under the authority of a public grant of privileges. (2) "Certain occupations, regarded as exceptional, the public interest attaching to which, recognized from earliest times, has survived the period of arbitrary laws by Parliament or colonial Legislatures for regulating all trades and callings. Such are those of the keepers of inns, cabs, and

25 256 U.S. 135 (1921). 26 256 U.S. 170 (1921). 27 261 U.S. 525 (1923).
28 262 U.S. 522 (1923).

gristmills." (3) "Businesses which, though not public at their inception, may be fairly said to have risen to be such and have become subject in consequence to some government regulation. . . . In the language of the cases, the owner by devoting his business to the public use, in effect grants the public an interest in that use and subjects himself to public regulation to the extent of that interest although the property continues to belong to its private owner and to be entitled to protection accordingly." [29]

"In nearly all the businesses included under the third heading above," he said after some further discussion, "the thing which gave the public interest was the indispensable nature of the service and the exorbitant charges and arbitrary control to which the public might be subjected without regulation." [30] Because it was admitted that there was no monopoly in the preparation of food and that its prices were fixed by competition, he indicated a belief that it did not fall in this third category. But since the statute under consideration was not one which regulated the prices charged by the business, but rather the wages paid by it, which he found objectionable on other grounds, which we shall examine later, he went on to say:

> We are relieved from considering and deciding definitely whether preparation of food should be put in the third class of quasi public businesses noted above, because, even so, the valid regulation to which it might be subjected as such, could not include what this Act attempts.[31]

In fact, he threw doubt on the entire significance of the category of businesses affected with a public interest when he added:

> To say that a business is clothed with a public interest is not to determine what regulation may be permissible in view of the private rights of the owner. . . . It depends on the nature of the business, on the feature which touches the public, and on the abuses reasonably to be feared. . . . The extent to which the regulation may reasonably go varies with different kinds of businesses. The regulation of rates to avoid monopoly is one thing. The regulation of wages is another.[32]

[29] *Id.* at 535. [30] *Id.* at 538. [31] *Id.* at 539.

[32] It should be noted that Taft rather definitely rejected the test which Brewer had thought the correct one—that "property is devoted to a public use when, and only when, the use is one which the public in its organized capacity, to wit, the state, has a right to create and maintain." Budd v. New York (diss.) 143 U.S. at 549 (1892). Since those words were enunciated, the concept of what the public had a "right" to do in its organized capacity had been considerably expanded; and in 1923 Taft maintained that the term "public use," as employed in cases deciding the purposes for which property could be condemned or taxes levied, "would seem to be a term of wider scope than where it is used to describe that which clothes property or business 'with a public interest.'" 262 U.S. at 537.

This language would seem to indicate that whether the prices charged by any particular business might validly be regulated is a question which depends, not upon any esoteric inquiry into whether that business could be described as one "affected with a public interest," but on the pragmatic inquiry whether unregulated prices might lead to some abuse. The chief source of abuse which the Court contemplated seemed to have lain in the absence of competition. This economic test of the power to regulate is not essentially different from that which the Court finally adopted in 1934 in the *Nebbia* case. But in the meantime the majority of the Court (including Taft himself) ignored it, and turned instead to the unreal inquiry whether a particular business was or was not "affected with a public interest" in some more metaphysical sense.

In *Tyson & Bro.* v. *Banton* [33] the Court, on February 28, 1927, held unconstitutional a New York statute which limited the resale price of theater tickets to fifty cents in excess of the box office price. There was no attempt to regulate what the theater itself might charge for admission. Justice Sanford, accordingly, in a dissenting opinion, thought that the question to be decided was whether the ticket broker, not the theater, was affected with a public interest—and he thought the broker was so affected. Justice Sutherland, on the other hand, speaking for the majority (which included Chief Justice Taft and Justices Van Devanter, McReynolds, and Butler), insisted that

> since the ticket broker is a mere appendage of the theatre, *etc.*, and the *price of* or *charge for admission* is the essential element in the statutory declaration, it results that the real inquiry is whether every public exhibition, game, contest or performance, to which an admission charge is made, is clothed with a public interest, so as to authorize a lawmaking body to fix the maximum amount of the charge, which its patrons may be required to pay.[34]

After discussing some of the cases sustaining price regulation in other businesses, Sutherland said:

> From the foregoing review it will be seen that each of the decisions of this court upholding governmental prices and regulation, aside from cases involving legislation to tide over temporary emergencies, has turned upon the existence of conditions, peculiar to the business under consideration, which bore such a substantial and definite relation to the public interest as to justify an indulgence of the legal fiction of a grant by the owner to the public of an interest in the use.[35]

[33] 273 U.S. 418 (1927). [34] *Id.* at 429. Italics in the opinion. [35] *Id.* at 438.

It is difficult to discern the precise grounds on which it was held that conditions failed to justify indulgence of the legal fiction of a grant by the owner of the theater to the public. Of course there was no actual grant, but Sutherland was speaking of a fictitious one. He pointed out how a theater differs from a grain elevator, a stockyard, and an insurance company. "Sales of theatre tickets bear no relation to the commerce of the country, and they are not interdependent transactions." He quoted from the *Wolff Packing Co.* case the statement that

> It has never been supposed, since the adoption of the Constitution, that the business of the butcher, or the baker, or the tailor, the woodchopper, the mining operator or the miner was clothed with such a public interest that the price of his product or his wages could be fixed by state regulation.[36]

> As we have shown, [said Sutherland, apparently referring to this quotation,] there is no legislative power to fix the prices of provisions or clothing or the rental charges of houses or apartments, in the absence of some controlling emergency; and we are unable to perceive any dissimilarities of such quality or degree as to justify a different rule in respect of amusements and entertainments.[37]

He quite ignored Taft's explanation in the *Wolff* case of the reasons for denying the power to regulate food prices. A few paragraphs after the language which Sutherland quoted, Taft said:

> But never has regulation of food preparation been extended to fixing wages or the prices to the public, as in the cases cited above where fear of monopoly prompted, and was held to justify regulation of rates. There is no monopoly in the preparation of foods. The prices charged by the plaintiff in error are, it is conceded, fixed by competition throughout the country at large.[38]

The price of theater tickets, on the other hand, was admittedly fixed by a collusive monopoly between the managers and the brokers. If this is no "dissimilarity," what becomes of Taft's test of "the indispensable nature of the service and the exorbitant charges and arbitrary control to which the public might be subjected without regulation"?

It might be said, of course, that the service rendered by a theater is not indispensable and that it therefore does not meet Taft's test. But it is not easy to understand why the Fourteenth Amendment should be so construed as to give one a constitutional right to charge

[36] 262 U.S. at 537. [37] 273 U.S. at 440. [38] 262 U.S. at 538.

an exorbitant price for a luxury. Is there a constitutional right to "soak the rich"? Sutherland did not stress the fact that the service was not indispensable. He did, however, suggest that the evil of exorbitant prices might be eliminated by statutes aimed at the collusion, without regulating the prices themselves. If the case were limited to these circumstances it might amount to no more than a holding either that the state has no power to regulate the price of luxuries or that it has power only where the evil of extortionate prices can be eliminated by no other method. But the next case which we shall discuss indicates that the holding was not so limited. And in this very *Tyson* case, Sutherland himself said:

> But the difficulty or even the impossibility of thus dealing with the evils, if that should be conceded, constitutes no warrant for suppressing them by methods precluded by the Constitution. . . . Constitutional principles, applied as they are written, it must be assumed, operate justly and wisely as a general thing, and they may not be remolded by law makers or judges to save exceptional cases of inconvenience, hardship or injustice.[39]

There is no principle "written" in the Constitution which expressly precludes resort to price fixing as a means of dealing with the evil of exorbitant prices. Whether the general language of the due process clause impliedly precludes such resort might seem to depend on whether there was any other method of dealing with the evil.

Justice Holmes wrote a brief dissent (joined by Brandeis), in which, among other things, he thought

> that the notion that a business is clothed with a public interest and has been devoted to the public use is little more than a fiction intended to beautify what is disagreeable to the sufferers. The truth seems to me to be that, subject to compensation when compensation is due, the legislature may forbid or restrict any business when it has a sufficient force of public opinion behind it.[40]

Justice Stone wrote a longer dissent, with which Holmes and Brandeis concurred. He, too, pointed out the barrenness of the fiction, saying:

> The phrase "business affected with a public interest" seems to me to be too vague and illusory to carry us very far on the way to a solution. It tends in use to become only a convenient expression for describing those businesses, regulation of which has been permitted in the past. To say that only those businesses affected with a public interest may be regulated is but another way of stating that all those businesses which may be regulated are affected

[39] 273 U.S. at 445.

[40] *Id.* at 446.

with a public interest. It is difficult to use the phrase free of its connotation of legal consequences and hence when used as a basis of judicial decision, to avoid begging the question to be decided.[41]

Having cleared the ground of this illusory test, he proceeded:

The constitutional theory that normally prices may not be regulated rests upon the assumption that the public interest and private right are both adequately protected when there is "free" competition among buyers and sellers, and that in such a state of economic society, the interference with so important an incident of ownership of private property as price fixing is not justified and hence is a taking of property without due process of law.

Statutory regulation of price is commonly directed toward the prevention of exorbitant demands of buyers or sellers. An examination of the decisions of this court in which price regulation has been upheld will disclose that the element common to all is the existence of a situation or a combination of circumstances materially restricting the regulatory force of competition, so that buyers or sellers are placed at such a disadvantage in the bargaining struggle that serious economic consequences result to a very large number of members of the community. Whether this situation arises from the monopoly conferred upon public service companies or from the circumstance that the strategical position of a group is such as to enable it to impose its will in matters of price upon those who sell, buy or consume, as in *Munn* v. *Illinois, supra;* or from the predetermination of prices in the councils of those who sell, promulgated in schedules of practically controlling constancy, as in *German Alliance Ins. Co.* v. *Kansas, supra;* or from a housing shortage growing out of a public emergency [citing the emergency rent cases]—the result is the same.

The question in the case, he added, "is not one of reasonable prices, but of the constitutional right in the circumstances of this case to exact exorbitant profits beyond reasonable prices."

The Taft test, thus articulated, Stone would broaden by eliminating the requirement that the service should be indispensable. In this connection he said:

Nor is the exercise of the power less reasonable because the interests protected are in some degree less esesntial to life than some others. Laws against monopoly which aim at the same evil and accomplish their end by interference with private rights quite as much as the present law are not regarded as arbitrary or unreasonable or unconstitutional because they are not limited in their application to dealings in the bare necessities of life.[42]

Justice Sanford, who thought the question was whether the brokers, not the theaters, were immune from regulation, wrote a separate dis-

[41] *Id.* at 451–452.

[42] *Id.* at 453.

senting opinion. Stressing the fact that the elevators in *Munn* v. *Illinois* had been held subject to regulation, without holding the sale of grain to be subject to it, he added:

So, I think. that here—without reference to the character of the business of the theatres themselves—the business of the ticket brokers, who stand in "the very gateway" between the theatres and the public, depriving the public of access to the theatres for the purchase of desirable seats at the regular prices, and exacting toll from patrons of the theatres desiring to purchase such seats, has become clothed with a public interest and is subject to regulation by the Legislature limiting their charges to reasonable exactions and protecting the public from extortion and exorbitant rates.[43]

Sanford evidently did not think that the power to control rates was limited to rates for indispensable services.

Even if the state has no power to control the prices of services which are not indispensable or to control prices at all when some other method of dealing with the evil of extortion is available, that is no reason for denying the power to control the fees charged by employment agencies in order to suppress the evil of extortionate charges. Yet a year and a quarter later, on May 28, 1928, the Court did deny that power in *Ribnik* v. *McBride,*[44] a case which has since been expressly overruled.[45] There was no contention that the services were luxuries; no denial that they were indispensable to those seeking employment. Nor was there any suggestion, as in the *Tyson* case, that the evil could be dealt with in any manner other than by regulating the fees. All this made no difference to Justice Sutherland, who again spoke for the majority.

To urge [he said] that extortion, fraud, imposition, discrimination, and the like have been practiced to some, or to a great, extent in connection with the business here under consideration, or that the business is one lending itself peculiarly to such evils, is simply to restate grounds already fully considered by this court. These are grounds for regulation, but not for price fixing as we have already definitely decided. [Citing *Tyson* v. *Banton.*] [46]

To this Justice Stone made the pertinent reply that

if the business is subject to regulation, as seems to be admitted, the regulation which is appropriate and effective is some curtailment of the exorbitant fees charged and not some other form of control which would have no tendency to correct the evils aimed at.[47]

[43] 273 U.S. at 455.
[44] 277 U.S. 350 (1928).
[45] See Olsen v. Nebraska, 313 U.S. 236 (1941).
[46] 277 U.S. at 358.
[47] *Id.* at 373.

We have here, then, the thing which Taft had said gave the public interest "in nearly all the businesses included under the third head" —namely, "the indispensable nature of the service and the exorbitant charges and arbitrary control to which the public might be subjected without regulation." Yet it was here held, with Taft's concurrence, that this was insufficient to give the state power to regulate the prices!

If Sutherland rejected the Taft test, what were his positive reasons for holding the regulation of employment agency fees unconstitutional? He had two of them. One is similar to that which he employed in the *Tyson* case. Since it is established that "the fixing of prices for food or clothing, or house rental or of wages to be paid, whether minimum or maximum, is beyond the legislative power" ["at least in the absence of a grave emergency"—he said nothing of the absence of arbitrary control by the owner or monopoly], "we perceive no reason for applying a different rule" in the case at bar.[48] This is reminiscent of Shiras's reasoning in *Brass* v. *Stoeser:* Since the existence of a monopoly justified the power to regulate the charges of the Chicago grain elevators, the state must have power to regulate such charges even when there is no monopoly.[49] So here, since it is unconstitutional to regulate food prices when, because of competition, the sellers have no power to make them exorbitant, therefore it is unconstitutional to regulate the prices charged by those who have such power.

The other ground for finding the regulation of the agency fees unconstitutional was that the *Tyson* case had settled a question which Sutherland himself had in that case said was not the question before the Court. In that case, as we have seen, he insisted that "since the ticket broker is a mere appendage of the theatre" the "real inquiry" is whether the theater, not the broker, is affected with a public interest. He now turned around and maintained that the *Tyson* case had concerned brokers—not merely ticket brokers but brokers of any sort. He said:

The business of securing employment for those seeking work and employees for those seeking workers is essentially that of a broker; that is, of an intermediary. While we do not undertake to say that there may not be a deeper concern on the part of the public in the business of an employment agency, that business does not differ in substantial character from the business of a real estate broker, ship broker, merchandise broker or ticket broker. In the *Tyson* case, *supra*, we declared unconstitutional an act of the New York Legislature which sought to fix the price at which theatre tickets should be

[48] *Id.* at 357.

[49] *Supra,* pp. 409–410.

sold by a ticket broker, and it is not easy to see how, without disregarding that decision, price-fixing legislation in respect of other brokers of like character can be upheld.[50]

In other words, the theater is not affected with a public interest; therefore a theater-ticket broker, being "a mere appendage of the theatre," is not so affected; therefore brokers who are not appendages of the theater are not affected with a public interest either. The logic is curious. As Justice Stone said in his dissent, "Ticket brokers and employment brokers are similar in name; in no other respect do they seem alike to me." [51]

Justice Sanford, more logical than Sutherland, had thought that the inquiry in the *Tyson* case concerned brokers, not theaters, and he therefore concurred here in the result on the authority of that case, "which as applied to the question in this case, I am unable to distinguish." Justice Stone, however, distinguished it, in a dissenting opinion in which he was joined by Holmes and Brandeis, on the ground that "to overcharge a man for the privilege of hearing the opera is one thing; to control the possibility of his earning a livelihood would appear to be quite another." [52] While he had maintained in the previous case that the state could forbid overcharges for the former, he did not believe that the Court's contrary decision precluded the possibility of regulating the latter.

Apart from this distinction, and from a thoroughgoing review of the facts connected with employment agencies, Stone's opinion is largely a reiteration of the considerations he had advanced in the *Tyson* case. He was more explicit here, however, in his reasons for not regarding price regulation as necessarily more drastic than other regulations of property, saying:

> I cannot accept as valid the distinction on which the opinion of the majority seems to me necessarily to depend, that granted constitutional power to regulate there is any controlling difference between reasonable regulation of price, if appropriate to the evil to be remedied, and other forms of appropriate regulation which curtail liberty of contract or the use of property. Obviously, even in the case of businesses affected with a public interest, other control than price regulation may be appropriate, and price regulation may be so inappropriate as to be arbitrary or unreasonable, and hence unconstitutional. To me it seems equally obvious that the Constitution does not require us to hold that a business, subject to every other form of reasonable regulation, is immune from the requirement of reasonable

[50] 277 U.S. at 356–357. [51] *Id.* at 373. [52] *Id.* at 373.

prices, where that requirement is the only remedy appropriate to the evils encountered. In this respect I can see no difference between a reasonable regulation of price and a reasonable regulation of the use of property, which affects its price or economic return. The privilege of contract and the free use of property are as seriously cut down in the one case as in the other.[53]

On January 2, 1929, in *Williams* v. *Standard Oil Co.,*[54] the Court (with its personnel unchanged) held that a state has no power to regulate the prices at which gasoline is sold. The opinion was again by Sutherland. Holmes dissented without opinion, and Brandeis and Stone concurred in the result, likewise without opinions. Unlike the two preceding cases, there is nothing in the report to indicate monopoly or exorbitant prices.

There is nothing in the point [said Sutherland] that the act in question may be justified on the ground that the sale of gasoline in Tennessee is monopolized by appellees, or by either of them, because, objections to the materiality of the contention aside, an inspection of the pleadings and of the affidavits submitted to the lower court discloses an utter failure to show the existence of such monopoly.[55]

This is doubtless why Brandeis and Stone concurred.

Summarizing his position on the general question, Sutherland declared that "a business or property, in order to be affected with a public interest, must be such or be so employed as to justify the conclusion that it has been *devoted* to a public use and its use is thereby in effect *granted* to the public." [56] [Italics in the opinion.] It is to be noted that he no longer spoke of the "fiction" of a grant, but of the conclusion that there was a grant "in effect."

There is a suggestion in the case that if a business is not within the "public" category, not only is price regulation invalid when designed to prevent extortion, but the state is powerless to penalize any sort of price practice. The state contended that certain provisions of the statute which made discriminatory prices unlawful could be sustained even if the main feature could not be, these provisions being severable. Sutherland did not agree, "but," he added, "if treated as separable, they are unconstitutional restrictions upon the right of the private dealer to fix his own prices and fall within the principle of the decisions already cited. See especially *Fairmont Creamery Co.* v. *Minnesota.*" [57]

[53] *Ibid.*
[54] 278 U.S. 235 (1929).
[55] *Id.* at 240.
[56] *Id.* at 239–240.
[57] *Id.* at 244.

In the *Fairmont* case [58] the Court had before it a statute which in its original form penalized price discriminations whose purpose was to monopolize. It had been amended, however, so as to strike out any reference to the purpose and to penalize discriminations regardless of their purpose. Justice McReynolds, speaking for the majority (Holmes, Brandeis, and Stone dissented without opinion), stressed this fact, and said, "We think the inhibition of the statute has no reasonable relation to the anticipated evil—high bidding by some with purpose to monopolize or destroy competition." [59] Moreover, in the *Fairmont* case the Court did not purport to overrule nor did it mention the earlier case of *Central Lumber Co.* v. *South Dakota,*[60] in which a unanimous Court had sustained an act which prohibited similar discriminations where the purpose to monopolize was an element of the offense. The Clayton Act also contains a prohibition against charging discriminatory prices for the purpose of monopolizing, and on the same day in which *Williams* v. *Standard Oil Co.* was decided, Justice Sutherland himself, speaking for a unanimous Court in *Van Camp & Sons* v. *American Can Co.,*[61] gave a broad interpretation to this provision, without even questioning its constitutionality. So, despite the implication which his language in the *Williams* case might suggest, it would seem that Sutherland did not regard the prices charged by a business not affected with a public interest as wholly immune to legislative control.

Before the *Nebbia* case there were a few others which whittled away somewhat the supposedly absolute constitutional rights of strictly private businesses to fix their own prices. In *Highland* v. *Russell Car & Snowplow Co.,*[62] decided April 8, 1929, the Court, in an opinion by Justice Butler, unanimously sustained the power of the President under the war power to fix the price of coal when bought for the production of railroad equipment, such production being in the state of war a public use. There was no suggestion that the business of selling coal was affected with a public interest. Again, on December 5, 1932, in *Stephenson* v. *Binford,*[63] in an opinion by Justice Sutherland, who spoke for the entire Court except Justice Butler (who dissented without opinion), a statute was sustained which authorized the fixing of minimum rates for private contract carriers using the state's high-

[58] 274 U.S. 1 (1927). [59] *Id.* at 9. [60] 226 U.S. 157 (1912).
[61] 278 U.S. 245 (1929). [62] 279 U.S. 253 (1929). [63] 287 U.S. 251 (1932).

ways. Such carriers, as distinct from common carriers, had been emphatically declared to be not affected with a public interest. The regulation was probably sustained, as we saw in Chapter X, only because it was attached as a condition to the use of publicly owned highways—a reason quite in accord with Justice Field's philosophy in the *Munn* case dissent, but which required qualification of some of the more extreme views Sutherland had expressed in 1926 in *Frost* v. *Railroad Commission of California*.[64] Some of the language used in the *Stephenson* case, however, suggests that the same result might possibly have been reached apart from reliance on the conditioning power. The assailed provisions, said Sutherland, "are not ends in and of themselves, but means to the legitimate end of conserving the highways." [65] The rate provision "has a definite tendency to relieve the highways by diverting traffic from them to the railroads." "The principle that Congress may regulate private contracts whenever reasonably necessary to effect any of the great purposes for which the national government was created, *Highland* v. *Russell Car Co.* . . . applies to a state under like circumstances." This language is broad, and the *Highland* decision did not rest on the Government's power to attach conditions to the grant of a privilege. But in view of the other reasons advanced for the decision, not too much weight should be accorded to these words.

The inflexibility of the *Ribnik* doctrine had meanwhile been somewhat relaxed in the Court's unanimous decision of February 24, 1930, in *Tagg Bros. & Moorhead* v. *United States*.[66] This decision sustained the power of Congress to authorize the Secretary of Agriculture to fix "just and reasonable" charges for the services of stockyard brokers engaged in interstate commerce. The only ground, it will be recalled, for holding that the decision in *Ribnik* v. *McBride* necessarily followed from that in *Tyson* v. *Banton* was that brokers of all sorts were immune from price regulation. Yet there was no dissent to Justice Brandeis's statement, in which he said:

> There is nothing in the nature of monopolistic personal services which makes it impossible to fix reasonable charges to be made therefor; and there is nothing in the Constitution which limits the Government's power of regulation to businesses which employ substantial capital. This Court

[64] 271 U.S. 583 (1926). See *supra*, pp. 297–304.

[65] 287 U.S. at 272–275.

[66] 280 U.S. 420 (1930).

did not hold in *Tyson & Bro.* v. *Banton* and *Ribnik* v. *McBride* that charges for personal services cannot be regulated. The question upon which this Court divided in those cases was whether the services there sought to be regulated were then affected with a public interest.[67]

There is one other case prior to *Nebbia* v. *New York* which deserves attention. That case is *New State Ice Co.* v. *Liebmann*,[68] decided March 21, 1932. The personnel of the Court had changed since the trilogy of the *Tyson, Ribnik,* and *Williams* cases. Taft had been succeeded by Hughes, Sanford by Roberts, and Holmes by Cardozo. Sutherland's views still prevailed, and he wrote the Court's opinion. Cardozo took no part, and Brandeis and Stone dissented, in an opinion written by the former. The case did not directly involve price fixing, but rather the power of the state to require a certificate of convenience and necessity as a prerequisite to engaging in the business of manufacturing ice. There is discussion, however, of the concept of businesses affected with a public interest.

Justice Sutherland began by distinguishing the ice business from that of cotton ginning, which he conceded to be in the public category, because "the cotton gin bears the same relation to the cotton grower that the old gristmill did to the grower of wheat," and cotton growing was the chief industry of Oklahoma (whose statute was in question). Ice, on the other hand, while indispensable in a southern climate, was no more so than food. He gave additional reasons, however, which may account for the concurrence of Hughes and Roberts, without implying their agreement with his price fixing views, or their disagreement with those expressed by Brandeis. He denied that the public would be at the mercy of the ice manufacturer, because of the possibility of installing a gas or electrical refrigerating plant "for a comparatively moderate outlay." [69] He added:

> Moreover, the practical tendency of the restriction . . . is to shut out new enterprises, and thus create and foster monopoly in the hands of existing establishments, against, rather than in aid of, the interest of the consuming public.

And later:

> There is no question now before us of any regulation to protect the consuming public.[70]

[67] 280 U.S. at 438–439. [68] 285 U.S. 262 (1932).
[69] *Id.* at 278. Brandeis challenged the moderateness of the outlay. *Id.* at 290.
[70] *Id.* at 278–279.

Justice Brandeis, in his dissenting opinion, made an exhaustive examination of the economic situation and discussed eloquently the relevant constitutional principles. In the course of the discussion, he set forth views similar to those which Stone had previously set forth, and to those which the Court was later to adopt in the *Nebbia* case. He said:

> A regulation valid for one kind of business may, of course, be invalid for another; since the reasonableness of every regulation is dependent upon the relevant facts. But so far as concerns the power to regulate, there is no difference, in essence, between a business called private and one called a public utility or said to be "affected with a public interest." . . . The notion of a distinct category of business "affected with a public interest," employing property "devoted to a public use," rests upon historical error. . . . In my opinion, the true principle is that the state's power extends to every regulation of any business reasonably required and appropriate for the public protection. I find in the due process clause no other limitation upon the character or the scope of regulation permissible.[71]

The *coup de grace* to what Brandeis called "historical error" was administered on March 5, 1934, in *Nebbia* v. *New York*.[72] The opinion was written by Justice Roberts and had the concurrence of Chief Justice Hughes and Justices Brandeis, Stone, and Cardozo. Justice McReynolds wrote a dissenting opinion, in which he was joined by Justices Van Devanter, Sutherland, and Butler, all of whom had been with the majority in the *Tyson* and *Ribnik* cases, while Brandeis and Stone had been with the dissenters. Hughes, Roberts, and Cardozo were not members of the Court when those cases were decided.

In its narrowest scope the decision only sustained the conviction of Nebbia for selling milk at less than nine cents a quart in violation of an order of the Milk Control Board, made in the exercise of statutory authority. The statute had been enacted after extensive research by a joint legislative committee with the cooperation of experts and pursuant to a report of that committee "covering 473 closely printed pages." It was enacted "as a method of correcting the evils, which the report of the committee showed could not be expected to right themselves through the ordinary play of the forces of supply and demand." [73] After reviewing the facts concerning the milk industry, the Court concluded:

[71] *Id.* at 301–303. [72] 291 U.S. 502 (1934). [73] *Id.* at 518.

In the light of the facts the order appears not to be unreasonable or arbitrary, or without relation to the purpose to prevent ruthless competition from destroying the wholesale price structure on which the farmer depends for his livelihood, and the community for an assured supply of milk.[74]

But the Court could not confine its attention to the question whether the particular order was arbitrary. It proceeded to deal with the argument "that the public control of rates or prices is *per se* unreasonable and unconstitutional, save as applied to businesses affected with a public interest" and that the milk industry is not so affected.[75] It is in dealing with this argument that the Court definitely struck from the price fixing power the limitation which had been thought to confine its exercise to a peculiar class of businesses. Said Roberts:

We may as well say at once that the dairy industry is not, in the accepted sense of the phrase, a public utility. We think the appellant is also right in asserting that there is in this case no suggestion of any monopoly or monopolistic practice. It goes without saying that those engaged in the business are in no way dependent upon public grants or franchises for the privilege of conducting their activities. But if, as must be conceded, the industry is subject to regulation in the public interest, what constitutional principle bars the state from correcting existing maladjustments by legislation touching prices? We think there is no such principle. The due process clause makes no mention of sales or of prices any more than it speaks of business or contracts or buildings or other incidents of property. The thought seems nevertheless to have persisted that there is something peculiarly sacrosanct about the price one may charge for what he makes or sells, and that, however able to regulate other elements of manufacture or trade, with incidental effect upon price, the state is incapable of directly controlling the price itself. This view was negatived many years ago. *Munn* v. *Illinois*, 94 U.S. 113.[76]

Discussing the so-called Granger cases, in the same volume of the reports which contains *Munn* v. *Illinois*, which sustained the regulation of railroad rates, Roberts referred to such regulation as an exercise of the police power—not, as had Lamar, as an exercise of the power of eminent domain.

Plainly [said Roberts], the activities of railroads, their charges and practices, so nearly touch the vital economic interests of society that the police power

[74] 291 U.S. at 530.

[75] The specific regulation in question was a regulation not of the prices charged by the milk industry, but of those charged by a retailer—an intermediary. The discussion is none the less relevant to the general price fixing power of the state.

[76] 291 U.S. at 531–532.

may be invoked to regulate their charges, and no additional formula of affection or clothing with a public interest is needed to justify the regulation. And this is evidently true of all business units supplying transportation, light, heat, and power and water to communities, irrespective of how they obtain their powers.[77]

The distinction between the police power and the power of eminent domain has an important bearing, as we shall see in Chapter XV, on the vertical limit to the power to regulate rates which are admittedly subject to some form of regulation; for when property is condemned, the Constitution guarantees the owner against all loss of value; when the police power is exercised, it does not. This fact Roberts overlooked in an opinion rendered the following year, to be discussed in Chapter XV.

Returning to the *Nebbia* case, Roberts denied that in order that the price may be regulated the business must have a franchise from the state or be a monopoly. Munn & Scott had no franchise, and, said Roberts, their "enterprise could not fairly be called a monopoly." This statement seems inaccurate, but it was true of the enterprise regulated in the *Brass* case, which Roberts also cited on the point. Nor, said Roberts, is it essential that the owner should have voluntarily devoted his property to a known public use. Obviously Munn & Scott

had not voluntarily dedicated their business to a public use. They intended only to conduct it as private citizens, and they insisted that they had done nothing which gave the public an interest in their transactions or conferred any right of regulation. The statement that one has dedicated his property to a public use is, therefore, merely another way of saying that if one embarks in a business which public interest demands shall be regulated, he must know regulation will ensue.[78]

After reviewing some of the cases, Roberts went on:

It is clear that there is no closed class or category of businesses affected with a public interest, and the function of courts in the application of the Fifth and Fourteenth Amendments is to determine in each case whether circumstances vindicate the challenged regulation as a reasonable exertion of governmental authority or condemn it as arbitrary or discriminatory. *Wolff Packing Co.* v. *Court of Industrial Relations* . . . . The phrase "affected with a public interest" can, in the nature of things, mean no more than that an industry, for adequate reason, is subject to control for the public good. In several of the decisions of this court wherein the expressions "affected with a public interest," and "clothed with a public use,"

[77] *Id.* at 534.

[78] *Id.* at 533–534.

have been brought forward as the criteria of the validity of price control, it has been admitted that they are not susceptible of definition and form an unsatisfactory test of the constitutionality of legislation directed at business practices or prices. These decisions must rest, finally, upon the basis that the requirements of due process were not met because the laws were found arbitrary in their operation and effect.[79] But there can be no doubt that upon proper occasions and by appropriate measures the state may regulate a business in any of its aspects, including the prices to be charged for the products or commodities it sells.

So far as the requirement of due process is concerned, and in the absence of other constitutional restriction, a state is free to adopt whatever economic policy may reasonably be deemed to promote public welfare, and to enforce that policy by legislation adapted to its purpose.[80]

Summarizing his conclusions, Roberts declared that "price control, like any other form of regulation, is unconstitutional only if arbitrary, discriminatory, or demonstrably irrevelant to the policy the Legislature is free to adopt, and hence an unnecessary and unwarranted interference with individual liberty." [81] The regulation here in question was held not to be vulnerable in these respects.

Justice McReynolds, in his dissent, advanced strong reasons for thinking this particular regulation arbitrary, and irrelevant to the professed purpose of the legislation. But his dissent was not only to the conclusion that the regulation was not arbitrary, but to the Court's departure from the older doctrine. He thundered a warning that "the adoption of any 'concept of jurisprudence' which permits facile disregard of the Constitution as long interpreted and respected will inevitably lead to its destruction." [82] At an earlier point, referring to *Munn* v. *Illinois,* he protested that "to undertake now to attribute a repudiated implication to that opinion is to affirm that it means what this Court has declared again and again was not intended." [83] And so it does. The Court in effect held here that if *Munn* v. *Illinois* meant what the subsequent cases had declared it to mean then those cases were wrong in supposing that it stated the true constitutional principle. *Nebbia* v. *New York* certainly did disregard the Constitution "as long interpreted"—but not "as written." It was the cases which had so "long interpreted" the Constitution as confining the

[79] A footnote at this point cites the Wolff, Tyson, Ribnik, and Williams cases without comment. But the decisions holding the regulation of resale ticket prices and of employment agency fees invalid were distinctly not based on findings that such regulations were arbitrary, but solely on the doctrine which Roberts here repudiated.

[80] 291 U.S. at 536–537.

[81] *Id.* at 539.

[82] *Id.* at 558.

[83] *Id.* at 555.

power to regulate prices to the closed category of businesses affected with a public interest that the Court now in effect held had been decided in facile disregard of the Constitution. The due process clauses themselves did not require the Court to bind the legislatures in any such straitjacket.

Three matters remain for further inquiry. The first concerns the applicability of the principles of the *Nebbia* case to governmental regulation of wages. The second concerns the constitutional limitations on the power of the state, through regulation, over the earnings of businesses admittedly subject to some degree of price regulation. The third concerns the principles employed or suggested as matters of economic policy for determining how much regulated companies should be permitted to earn and involves a further inquiry into the applicability of those principles to the correction of economic maladjustments elsewhere in our economy by means of price control or taxation. These questions are discussed in the next three chapters.

XIV

THE CONSTITUTIONALITY OF WAGE REGULATION

THERE are two types of wage regulation, each of which raises constitutional questions. Minimum wage laws leave undisturbed the bargaining processes for arriving at wages above the established minimum. "Fair" wage laws, on the other hand, call for compulsory arbitration of wage disputes and substitute wages fixed by public authority for those arrived at by strikes and lockouts.

THE MINIMUM WAGE CASES

As long as the doctrine prevailed that the due process clause precluded any regulation of prices, except in businesses affected with a public interest, it was not surprising that the Court should have held a minimum wage law unconstitutional, as it did in 1923 in *Adkins* v. *Children's Hospital.*[1] Even then, however, there was dissent. It is rather more surprising that in 1936, two years after the concept of a "closed class" of businesses affected with a public interest had been repudiated in *Nebbia* v. *New York,*[2] the Court should have again

1 261 U.S. 525 (1923).

2 291 U.S. 502 (1934). Discussed in Chap. XIII.

held a minimum wage law invalid. This it did in a five-to-four decision in *Morehead* v. *New York ex rel. Tipaldo.*[3] The majority in that case, however, thought that the question of overruling the *Adkins* case had not been properly presented; and in 1937, when the question was properly before it, the Court, by another five-to-four decision, definitely overruled the *Adkins* case—in *West Coast Hotel Co.* v. *Parrish.*[4]

The law held invalid in the *Adkins* case, as violating the due process clause of the Fifth Amendment, was an act of Congress forbidding the payment of lower wages to women in the District of Columbia than those fixed by a board, based on the cost of living. Justice Sutherland wrote the majority opinion, in which Justices McKenna, Van Devanter, McReynolds, and Butler concurred. Chief Justice Taft wrote a dissenting opinion, in which Justice Sanford joined, and Justice Holmes wrote a separate dissenting opinion. Justice Brandeis, whose daughter had participated in the litigation, took no part in the case, but he dissented in 1925 from the *per curiam* decision in *Murphy* v. *Sardell,*[5] in which a state minimum wage law was held, on the authority of the *Adkins* case, to violate the Fourteenth Amendment.

Justice Sutherland enumerated four classes of cases in which legislative interference with freedom of contract had been sustained, and concluded that the fixing of wages for women fell within none of the four. The four classes were: (1) "those dealing with statutes fixing rates and charges to be exacted by businesses impressed with a public interest"; (2) "statutes relating to contracts for the performance of public work"; (3) "statutes prescribing the character, methods, and time for payment of wages"; (4) "statutes fixing hours of labor."[6]

Cases sustaining the fixing of charges for businesses impressed with a public interest furnished no precedent for sustaining wage-fixing, for the sale of labor was not a business so impressed in the conventional sense. Nor did this law relate to contracts for the performance of public work. As to statutes prescribing the character, method, and time for payment of wages, he said:

> Their tendency and purpose was to prevent unfair and perhaps fraudulent methods in the payment of wages and in no sense can they be said to be, or to furnish a precedent for, wage-fixing statutes.[7]

[3] 298 U.S. 587 (1936). [4] 300 U.S. 379 (1937). [5] 269 U.S. 530 (1925).
[6] 261 U.S. at 546–547. [7] *Id.* at 547.

Statutes sustained in this category, and those fixing the hours of labor, he said,

> deal with incidents of the employment having no necessary effect upon the heart of the contract; that is, the amount of wages to be paid and received. A law forbidding work to continue beyond a given number of hours leaves the parties free to contract about wages and thereby equalize whatever additional burdens may be imposed upon the employer as a result of the restrictions as to hours, by an adjustment in respect of the amount of wages. Enough has been said to show that the authority to fix hours of labor cannot be exercised except in respect of those occupations where work of long-continued duration is detrimental to health. This Court has been careful in every case where the question has been raised, to place its decision upon this limited authority of the legislature to regulate hours of labor and to disclaim any purpose to uphold the legislation as fixing wages, thus recognizing an essential difference between the two. It seems plain that these decisions afford no real support for any form of law establishing minimum wages.[8]

It is true that in *Bunting* v. *Oregon*[9] the Court placed its decision upon the authority to regulate hours and disclaimed any purpose to uphold the law as a regulation of wages. But, having decided that the law in question was one which regulated hours, not wages, it had no occasion to make any pronouncement on the validity of a wage law. Moreover, far from holding that authority to fix hours can be exercised only in respect of those occupations which Sutherland specified, the Court, in the *Bunting* case, sustained a law regulating hours in all factories.

The minimum wage law upset by the *Adkins* case applied only to women. So, too, did the law regulating hours which had been sustained earlier in *Muller* v. *Oregon*.[10] In that case, as we saw in Chapter XII, Justice Brewer had indicated that a law relating to women might be sustained, whereas a similar one relating to men would not be. He stressed the fact that healthy mothers are essential to vigorous offspring, and he thought that, despite legislation which had removed many of the older legal disabilities of women, women were still not disposed to assert their rights fully and needed legislative protection. But this singling out of women for special protection did not appeal to Sutherland. Stressing the changes in the contractual, political, and civil status of women, "culminating in the Nineteenth Amendment," he said:

[8] *Id.* at 553–554.

[9] 243 U.S. 426 (1917). *Cf. supra*, pp. 388–389.

[10] 208 U.S. 412 (1908). *Cf. supra*, pp. 387–388.

In this respect of the matter, while the physical differences must be recognized in appropriate cases and legislation fixing hours or conditions of work may properly take them into account, we cannot accept the doctrine that women of mature age, *sui juris,* require or may be subjected to restrictions upon their liberty of contract which could not lawfully be imposed in the case of men under similar circumstances.[11]

He ignored any notion such as that expressed in *Holden* v. *Hardy*[12] that the parties might not be equally free in negotiating about a labor contract. And he quoted as authoritative Justice Peckham's opinion as to the limits of the police power in *Lochner* v. *New York,*[13] without purporting to overrule *Muller* v. *Oregon* and *Bunting* v. *Oregon,* though those later cases can scarcely be reconciled with the *Lochner* case.

After concluding that none of the four categories of cases sustaining statutory interference with freedom of contract were applicable to minimum wage laws, he went on to adduce more specific reasons for holding this law arbitrary. In the first place he insisted that

The standard furnished by the statute for the guidance of the board is so vague as to be impossible of practical application with any reasonable degree of accuracy. What is sufficient to supply the necessary cost of living for a woman worker and maintain her in good health and protect her morals is obviously not a precise and unvarying sum—not even approximately so. The amount will depend upon a variety of circumstances: the individual temperament, habits of thrift, care, ability to buy necessaries intelligently, and whether the woman live alone or with her family.[14]

Another objection to this particular law was that under it the minimum wage fixed by the board might exceed the value of the services rendered. On this point Sutherland remarked:

The law takes account of the necessities of only one party to the contract. It ignores the necessities of the employer by compelling him to pay not less than a certain sum, not only whether the employee is capable of earning it, but irrespective of the ability of his business to sustain the burden, generously leaving him, of course, the privilege of abandoning his business as an alternative for going on at a loss. Within the limits of the minimum sum, he is precluded, under penalty of fine and imprisonment, from adjusting compensation to the differing merits of his employees. . . . To the extent that the sum fixed exceeds the fair value of the services rendered, it amounts to a compulsory exaction from the employer for the support of a partially indigent person, for whose condition there rests upon him no peculiar responsibility, and therefore, in effect, arbitrarily shifts to his

11 261 U.S. at 553.

12 169 U.S. 366 (1898). *Cf. supra,* p. 386.

13 198 U.S. 45 (1905). *Cf. supra,* pp. 386–387.

14 261 U.S. at 555.

shoulders a burden which, if it belongs to anybody, belongs to society as a whole.

The feature of this statute which, perhaps more than any other, puts upon it the stamp of invalidity is that it exacts from the employer an arbitrary payment for a purpose and upon a basis having no causal connection with his business, or the contract or the work the employee engages to do. The declared basis, as already pointed out, is not the value of the service rendered, but the extraneous circumstance that the employee needs to get a prescribed sum of money to insure her subsistence, health and morals. The ethical right of every worker, man or woman, to a living wage may be conceded. One of the declared and important purposes of trade organizations is to secure it. And with that principle and with every legitimate effort to realize it in fact, no one can quarrel; but the fallacy of the proposed method of attaining it is that it assumes that every employer is bound at all events to furnish it. The moral requirement implicit in every contract of employment, viz. that the amount to be paid and the service to be rendered shall bear to each other some relation of just equivalence, is completely ignored. The necessities of the employee are alone considered and these arise outside of the employment, are the same when there is no employment, and as great in one occupation as in another. Certainly the employer by paying a fair equivalent for the service rendered, though not sufficient to support the employee, has neither caused nor contributed to her poverty. On the contrary, to the extent of what he pays he has relieved it. . . . A statute requiring an employer to pay in money, to pay at prescribed and regular intervals, to pay the value of the services rendered, even to pay with fair relation to the extent of the benefit obtained from the service, would be understandable. But a statute which prescribes payment without regard to any of these things and solely with relation to circumstances apart from the contract of employment, the business affected by it and the work done under it, is so clearly the product of a naked, arbitrary exercise of power that it cannot be allowed to stand under the Constitution of the United States.[15]

Sutherland also seemed to question whether the law would prove of economic benefit to the women themselves, or whether, on the other hand, it might lead to unemployment among them. Their increased earnings since the enactment of the statute may have been due to other causes.

No real test [he said] of the economic value of the law can be had during periods of maximum employment, when general causes keep wages up to or above the minimum; that will come in periods of depression and struggle for employment when the efficient will be employed at the minimum rate while the less capable may not be employed at all.[16]

[15] 261 U.S. at 557–559.

[16] *Id.* at 560.

Disregarding the fact that whatever argument there may be for fixing maximum wages must rest on grounds entirely different from those adduced to support the fixing of minimum wages, Sutherland thought that the power to fix the one must imply power to fix the other. He said:

> Finally, it may be said that if, in the interest of the public welfare, the police power may be invoked to justify the fixing of a minimum wage, it may, when the public welfare is thought to require it, be invoked to justify a maximum wage. The power to fix high wages connotes, by like course of reasoning, the power to fix low wages.[17]

Turning to more general considerations regarding freedom of contract and the police power, he concluded his opinion with these remarks:

> It has been said that legislation of the kind now under review is required in the interest of social justice, for whose ends freedom of contract may lawfully be subjected to restraint. The liberty of the individual to do as he pleases, even in innocent matters, is not absolute. It must frequently yield to the common good, and the line beyond which the power of interference may not be pressed is neither definite nor unalterable but may be made to move, within limits not well defined, with changing need and circumstance. Any attempt to fix a rigid boundary would be unwise as well as futile. But, nevertheless, there are limits to the power, and where these have been passed, it becomes the plain duty of the courts in the proper exercise of their authority to so declare. To sustain the individual freedom of action contemplated by the Constitution is not to strike down the common good but to exalt it; for surely the good of society as a whole cannot be better served than by the preservation against arbitrary restraint of the liberties of its constituent members.
>
> It follows from what has been said that the act in question passes the limit prescribed by the Constitution . . .[18]

This passage, it will be noted, ignores the possibility that a minimum wage law may increase the individual freedom of the worker in a manner which outweighs the limitation which it imposes on her individual freedom or that of her employer.

Chief Justice Taft, however, in his dissenting opinion, did not ignore this possibility. He recognized that employees who accept extremely low wages may not be doing so voluntarily, saying:

> Legislatures in limiting freedom of contract between employee and employer by a minimum wage proceed on the assumption that employees,

17 *Ibid.*

18 *Id.* at 561–562.

in the class receiving least pay, are not upon a full level of equality of choice with their employer and in their necessitous circumstances are prone to accept pretty much anything that is offered. They are peculiarly subject to the overreaching of the harsh and greedy employer. The evils of the sweating system and of the long hours and low wages which are characteristic of it are well known. Now, I agree that it is a disputable question in the field of political economy how far a statutory requirement of maximum hours or minimum wages may be a useful remedy for these evils, and whether it may not make the case of the oppressed employee worse than it was before. But it is not the function of this Court to hold congressional acts invalid simply because they are passed to carry out economic views which the Court believes to be unwise or unsound.

Legislatures which adopt a requirement of maximum hours or minimum wages may be presumed to believe that when sweating employers are prevented from paying unduly low wages by positive law they will continue their business, abating that part of their profits, which were wrung from the necessities of their employees, and will concede the better terms required by the law; and that while in individual cases hardship may result, the restriction will inure to the benefit of the general class of employees in whose interest the law is passed and so to that of the community at large.[19]

After expressing surprise that the *Lochner* case should have been cited as authoritative,[20] Taft questioned the assertion that the wage term goes any more to the heart of the contract than does the term concerning hours.

In absolute freedom of contract the one term is as important as the other, for both enter equally into the consideration given and received, a restriction as to one is not any greater in essence than the other, and is of the same kind. One is the multiplier and the other the multiplicand.[21]

Nor did Taft think that the Court could say that Congress was not warranted in taking the view that a low wage may be quite as harmful to health as long hours.[22] He also insisted that *Muller* v. *Oregon* controlled this case in justifying the application to women of regulations which were not applied to men.[23]

As to Sutherland's contention that power to fix a minimum wage implies power to fix a maximum, Taft said:

This, I submit, is a *non sequitur*. A line of distinction like the one under discussion in this case is, as the opinion elsewhere admits, a matter of degree and practical experience and not of pure logic. Certainly the wide difference between prescribing a minimum wage and a maximum wage could as a matter of degree and experience be easily affirmed.[24]

19 261 U.S. at 562–563.
20 *Id.* at 564.
21 *Ibid.*
22 *Ibid.*
23 *Id.* at 566.
24 *Id.* at 565.

Justice Holmes, in his separate dissenting opinion, declared that to him

the power of Congress seems absolutely free from doubt. The end, to remove conditions leading to ill health, immorality and the deterioration of the race, no one would deny to be within the scope of constitutional legislation. The means are means that have the approval of Congress, of many States, and of those governments from which we have learned our greatest lessons. When so many intelligent persons, who have studied the matter more than any of us can, have thought that the means are effective and are worth the price, it seems to me impossible to deny that the belief reasonably may be held by reasonable men. . . . I agree, of course, that a law answering the foregoing requirements might be invalidated by specific provisions of the Constitution. For instance it might take private property without just compensation. But in the present instance the only objection that can be urged is found within the vague contours of the Fifth Amendment, prohibiting the depriving any person of liberty or property without due process of law. To that I turn.[25]

Then, after enumerating many of the cases which had sustained interferences with freedom of contract, Holmes went on:

I confess that I do not understand the principle on which the power to fix a minimum for the wages of women can be denied by those who admit the power to fix a maximum for their hours of work. I fully assent to the proposition that here as elsewhere the distinctions of the law are distinctions of degree, but I perceive no difference in the kind or degree of interference with liberty, the only matter with which we have any concern, between the one case and the other. The bargain is equally affected whichever half you regulate. *Muller* v. *Oregon,* I take it, is as good law today as it was in 1908. It will need more than the Nineteenth Amendment to convince me that there are no differences between men and women, or that legislation cannot take those differences into account. I should not hesitate to take them into account if I thought it necessary to sustain this act. *Quong Wing* v. *Kirkendall,* 223 U.S. 59, 63. But after *Bunting* v. *Oregon,* 243 U.S. 426, I had supposed that it was not necessary, and that *Lochner* v. *New York,* 198 U.S. 45, would be allowed a deserved repose.[26]

Turning to Sutherland's contention that the law exacts payments from employers for the relief of poverty for which they are not responsible, Holmes said:

This statute does not compel anybody to pay anything. It simply forbids employment at rates below those fixed as the minimum requirement for health and right living. It is safe to assume that women will not be employed at even the lowest wages allowed unless they earn them, or unless the employer's business can sustain the burden.[27]

[25] *Id.* at 567–568. [26] *Id.* at 569–570. [27] *Id.* at 570.

Of course, the statute compels the employer to pay the minimum only if he sees fit to employ the worker. Even if he does, there is no compulsion to pay more than the services are worth—whether we are speaking of what they are worth to the particular employer or what they are worth on the market. The fixing of the minimum wage will increase the market value of the services of those women for whose services the market previously set a lower value. It will do so by keeping from the market women who previously sold their services for less. But if the new market value is more than the services are worth to any given employer, there is nothing to compel that employer to hire that worker at all. The employer's real grievance, if he has one, is not that he must pay more than the service is worth, but that the market value has itself been raised (that is, that the labor has been made more expensive), without increasing the value of the work to him. There is a narrower margin than before between the benefit which accrues to him from employing a woman and the market value which he must pay for doing so. If the statute violates any of his constitutional rights, it is a right not to have the government raise the market value of the labor which he wishes to employ. His grievance in this respect is like that of a customer of a public utility company, who complains that the rates fixed by a commission are too high. If they are, it is not because they exceed the market value of the service, but because the market value ought to be reduced by a reduction of the rates, so that the customer may have a wider margin between the benefits he derives from the service and the price he must pay for it. The distinction between "value in use" (or value to the buyer) and "value in exchange" (or market value) is at least as old as 1776, when Adam Smith published his *Wealth of Nations*. The margin between the two is what the economists call "consumer's surplus."

But while the amount which the employer must pay can scarcely exceed the value of the service, the amount which the worker accepts may well fall short of that value. The worker may have to make a forced sale. One who cannot wait to sell, or who is unskilled in bargaining, may accept less for what he has to sell than could be obtained in a market in which there was time for all potential buyers to make their bids and in which the seller was able to bargain with as much skill as the buyer. A law authorizing a board to fix minimum wages, with a provision that they be not fixed above the market value of the services, would, if properly administered, prevent the employer from taking this sort of advantage of the employee. It would not increase the market value of the services, as would the law in the *Adkins* case; it would merely require the employer to pay that value. It would in no way infringe an employer's constitutional right, if he has such a right, not to have the market value of the services he buys increased. Though the employer may have no peculiar responsibility, as Justice Sutherland insists, for the poverty of one to whom he pays the market value of the services, he would seem to have peculiar responsibility for some part of the poverty of one whose wages are below the market value because of the employer's outbargaining her. To hold that a law which takes this advantage from the employer is unconstitutional is equivalent to holding that the employer has a constitutional right to obtain services for less than their market value. So to hold would violate "the moral requirement implicit in every contract of employment, viz., that the amount to be paid and the service to be rendered shall bear to each other some relation of just equivalence"—a moral requirement which Justice Sutherland mistakenly thought that the law in the *Adkins* case ignored. Yet the decision rendered in 1936, in *Morehead* v. *New York ex rel. Tipaldo,*[28] in which Sutherland himself concurred, can be sustained only on the assumption that the employer has a constitutional right to pay a wage which bears no relation of equivalence to the service to be rendered.

In that case the Court had before it the New York minimum wage law for women. This law authorized the State Industrial Commissioner, after approving a report of a wage board and certain other preliminaries, to issue a mandatory order defining minimum fair wage rates, and violation of the mandatory order was made a misdemeanor punishable by fine, imprisonment, or both. The statute defined a fair wage as one "fairly and reasonably commensurate with the value of the service or class of service rendered." It could be put into effect only if the Commissioner found that any substantial number of women in any occupation are receiving "oppressive and unreasonable" wages. An oppressive and unreasonable wage was defined as one which is "both less than the fair and reasonable value of the services rendered and less than sufficient to meet the minimum cost of living necessary for health." If administered according to its plain terms, it will be seen, the mandatory order could never prescribe minimum wages in excess of what the services were worth before the order was

28 298 U.S. 587 (1936).

made, no matter how far that might fall below the amount sufficient to meet the minimum cost of living. The existing wage could never be raised merely because it was less than the minimum cost of living, unless it was also less than the value of the service. After finding that any wage being paid was as high as the value of the service, the board would have no occasion to apply the other standard of its sufficiency to meet the minimum cost of living. It was only when a wage was found to be less than the value of the service that the board would have occasion to apply the minimum cost of living standard, and then it would apply it in favor of the employer, for even a wage below the value of the service was not "oppressive and unreasonable" within the definition of the statute unless it was also less than sufficient to meet the minimum cost of living necessary for health.

The *Adkins* case held that a particular act of Congress violated the constitutional rights of the employer. The particular act, unlike the New York statute, authorized the fixing of a wage which might exceed what the service was formerly worth. As we have seen, this feature of the act was stressed in the majority opinion to prove its invalidity. From the holding itself we cannot say that the Court in that case authoritatively denied all power to regulate wages. The Court may, it is true, have assumed that since labor was not affected with a public interest therefore any regulation whatsoever of its price would be unconstitutional. Such a doctrine, however, was not expressly stated in the *Adkins* case, and if it was the position of the Court, it must be derived from other decisions. Any such doctrine was expressly repudiated by the Court in 1934, in *Nebbia* v. *New York,*[29] two years before the *Tipaldo* case reached it.

In the *Adkins* case the Court expressed one further objection to the law in addition to the objection that the wage might exceed the value of the service. It pronounced the standard based upon the necessities of life to be too vague. Would the vagueness of the cost-of-living standard furnish a fatal objection to the New York statute? Since under the New York statute there would be no occasion to investigate the cost of living except for the purpose of determining whether the employer might continue paying wages below the value of the services, it is hard to see why this vagueness in itself would invalidate the act.

In the New York Court of Appeals, however, Chief Judge Crane, speaking for the majority in *People ex rel. Tipaldo* v. *Morehead,*[30]

[29] 291 U.S. 502 (1934).

[30] 270 N.Y. 233 (1936).

insisted that the act was unconstitutional under the controlling authority of the *Adkins* case. The opinion quoted a passage from the brief of the State Attorney General which concludes with the statement that the New York law "provides that the worker is to be paid at least the value of the services rendered." The statement is accurate except in those cases in which the cost of living is lower than the value of the services. After quoting from the brief, the Court continued:

This is a difference in phraseology and not in principle. The New York act, as above stated, prohibits an oppressive and unreasonable wage, which means both less than the fair and reasonable value of the services rendered and less than sufficient to meet the minimum cost of living necessary for health. The act of Congress had one standard, the living wage; this State Act has added another, reasonable value. The minimum wage must include both. What was vague before has not been made any clearer. One of the elements, therefore, in fixing the fair wage is the very matter which was the basis of the congressional act. Forcing the payment of wages at a reasonable value does not make inapplicable the principle and ruling of the *Adkins* case. The distinctions between this case and the *Adkins* case are differences in details, methods and time; the exercise of legislative power to fix wages in any employment is the same.

It is curious that Judge Crane should have minimized the difference between the two statutes, since the difference means that the New York statute does not contain the feature which, according to Justice Sutherland, "perhaps more than any other, puts upon it [the Act of Congress] the stamp of invalidity." Judge Crane failed to appreciate the precise significance of the cost-of-living standard in the New York law when he said that the State act had merely added another standard to that contained in the act of Congress, and that "the minimum wage must include both." It is not true that the minimum wage must "include" both. The most that can be said in this regard is that the wage-fixing authorities must ascertain both the cost of living and the reasonable value. But the wage is to be fixed at whichever of these two standards is the lower. It is not fixed on both. If the Congressional standard was bad because it might require payment of a wage in excess of the value, there was no such requirement in the New York law.

When the case reached the Supreme Court, Justice Butler for the majority relied on this statement by Judge Crane as an authoritative construction of the New York statute, binding on the Supreme Court.

"There is no blinking the fact," said Justice Butler, "that the state court construed the prescribed standard to include cost of living." But the state court, in making the statement quoted, was not insisting that under the New York law the wage was to be fixed as high as the cost of living, regardless of how much less the value of the services might be. If it had meant this, it could scarcely have said that the minimum wage must include both standards, and on this construction the value of the service would be irrelevant. As Chief Justice Hughes said in his dissenting opinion, the State court, in the passage quoted, "is not construing the state statute. It is passing upon the effect of the differences between the two acts from the standpoint of the Federal Constitution. It is putting aside an admitted difference as not controlling. . . That, it seems to me, is clearly a federal and not a state question.' [31] In examining what construction it placed upon the statute, the Chief Justice could "find little more than a recital of its provisions." Then, after quoting from Judge Crane's opinion, Hughes continued:

> But the Court expressly recognizes that a wage is not denounced by the New York act as "oppressive and unreasonable" unless it is less than the fair and reasonable value of the services rendered. The statute also provides in explicit terms that the "fair wage" which is to be prescribed is one that is "fairly and reasonably commensurate with the value of the service or class of service rendered." Section 551 (8). I find nothing in the opinion of the state court which can be taken to mean that this definite provision of the statute is not obligatory upon the authorities fixing a fair wage. Certainly, the court has not said so, and I think that we must assume that the standard thus described is set up by the New York act.[32]

If Justice Butler meant that the New York court had construed the statute as requiring the payment of a wage equal to the cost of living, even if the value of the service should be less, he was attributing to Judge Crane a most astonishing procedure. Most courts, including the Supreme Court, have followed a canon of interpretation in pursuance of which they construe an ambiguous statute, when one construction would render it clearly valid, and another would raise serious doubts of its constitutionality, in such a way as to preserve its validity. If construed according to its plain terms, the New York statute would authorize the fixing of a minimum wage which in no event would exceed the value of the services. As so construed it would be at least arguable that it could be held constitutional without over-

31 298 U.S. at 622.

32 *Ibid.*

ruling the *Adkins* case. To construe it as requiring payment of a wage which might exceed the value of the services is to construe so as to increase rather than to diminish the doubts as to its validity. Even where the statute is so ambiguous as to be susceptible to such an interpretation, to construe it in this way would be to reverse the conventional canon of interpretation. But to construe it contrary to its clear meaning so as to render it invalid would be little short of judicial sabotage.

As Chief Justice Hughes pointed out, it is not likely that Judge Crane meant to construe the statute in this manner. But if he did not, his statement that it was indistinguishable from the act held void in the *Adkins* case was a construction of the ruling in that case, not of the New York statute, and would not preclude inquiry by the Supreme Court into the question whether it is distinguishable from the act of Congress. If such an inquiry is open, it is difficult to see the bearing of Justice Butler's insistence that the state court's construction was binding.

However, it would seem that Justice Butler thought the inquiry was open after all, for he did not rest his conclusion that the *Adkins* case was controlling on the decision of the New York court alone. After summarizing the statements in the *Adkins* case that legislative abridgment of freedom to contract can only be justified by the existence of exceptional circumstances, that the cases in which such abridgment had been sustained are distinguishable, that the liberty of women to contract may not be abridged where the liberty of men may not be, save when women's health requires special protection, and that decisions sustaining regulations of hours of labor "afford no real support for any form of law establishing minimum wages," the Court concluded in regard to the *Adkins case:* "The decision and reasoning upon which it rests clearly show that the State is without power by any form of legislation to prohibit, change or nullify contracts between employers and adult women workers as to the amount of wages to be paid." [33]

That decisions on distinguishable questions do not furnish authority for minimum wage laws does not prove that such laws are unconstitutional. That interference with freedom to contract about wages can be justified only in exceptional circumstances and that the needs of employees to obtain more than their service was previously worth

[33] *Id.* at 611.

do not constitute such exceptional circumstances do not prove that the power of employers, when it exists, to obtain services for less than they are worth is not one of the exceptional circumstances which would justify the abridgment of the employer's liberty to contract.

However, Justice Butler, purporting to apply the *Adkins* ruling that employers could not be compelled to pay more than the previous value of services even if the employee needs the additional amount to preserve health and morals, held that the employer cannot even be forced to pay the full value of the services received when that is less than the minimum living cost.

After asserting that the *Adkins* case decided that the state had no power to interfere with contracts as to the amount of wages, Justice Butler proceeded to dismiss the reasoning by which Justice Sutherland had denounced the federal statute for not taking into account the value of the services—"the feature of this statute which, perhaps more than any other, puts upon it the stamp of invalidity"—as superfluous and of subordinate consequence.

Summing up the argument that the *Adkins* ruling was not based on a discrepancy between the wage to be paid and the value of the services, Justice Butler said:

> Petitioner does not attempt to support the Act as construed by the state court. His claim is that it is to be tested here as if it did not include the cost of living and as if value of service was the sole standard. Plainly that position is untenable. If the State has power to single out for regulation the amount of wages to be paid women, the value of their service would be a material consideration. But the fact has no relevancy upon the question whether the State has any such power. And utterly without significance upon the question of power is the suggestion that the New York prescribed standard includes value of service with cost of living whereas the District of Columbia standard was based upon the latter alone. As shown above, the dominant issue in the *Adkins* case was whether Congress had power to establish minimum wages for adult women workers in the District of Columbia. The opinion directly answers in the negative. The ruling that defects in the prescribed standard stamped that Act as arbitrary and invalid was an additional ground of subordinate consequence.[34]

The result of the decision was thus to deny all power to regulate the price of labor regardless of whether the particular regulation was arbitrary or not. The decision was in line with those cases which had held that except in businesses affected with a public interest any regulation of price is forbidden by the due process clause, even if the

[34] 298 U.S. at 613–614.

regulation is the only remedy for an admitted evil and is in no way arbitrary. Indeed, Butler cited the most glaring of those cases (*Ribnik* v. *McBride* [35]) to support his statement in reference to the *Adkins* case that "we have adhered to the principle there applied and cited it as a guide in other cases." [36] But if that was, indeed, the doctrine of the *Adkins* case, it had clearly been overruled in the *Nebbia* case when in the opinion rendered there by Justice Roberts the Court had repudiated the doctrine (though not the decision) of *Ribnik* v. *McBride*. Yet Roberts now, two years later, subscribed to the opinion which revived the doctrine he had himself repudiated.

The explanation may be that Roberts agreed with Butler's contention that on the pleadings the Court was precluded from questioning the authority of the *Adkins* case. The case had been brought to the Supreme Court from the New York Court of Appeals on certiorari, and Butler said:

> The petition for the writ sought review upon the ground that this case is distinguishable from that one [the *Adkins* case]. No application has been made for reconsideration of the constitutional question there decided. The validity of the principles upon which that decision rests is not challenged. This court confines itself to the ground upon which the writ was asked or granted. . . . Here the review granted was no broader than that sought by the petitioner. . . . He is not entitled and does not ask to be heard upon the question whether the *Adkins* case should be overruled. He maintains that it may be distinguished on the ground that the statutes are vitally dissimilar.[37]

Thus, because the petition denied that the *Adkins* case stood for the proposition that *Ribnik* v. *McBride* precluded all regulation of wages, therefore the Court must pronounce a statute unconstitutional on the authority of the *Ribnik* v. *McBride* doctrine, although that doctrine had already been repudiated in the *Nebbia* case.

Justice Stone did not agree. In a dissenting opinion, in which he was joined by Justices Brandeis and Cardozo, he insisted that even if the New York statute had not been distinguishable from the one invalidated in the *Adkins* case, it should be sustained, and the *Adkins* case should be treated as no longer authoritative. After quoting some of the language in the *Nebbia* case, he said:

> That declaration and decision should control the present case. They are irreconcilable with the decision and most that was said in the *Adkins* case.

[35] 277 U.S. 350 (1928). *Cf.* Chap. XIII. [36] 298 U.S. at 617.
[37] *Id.* at 604–605.

They have left the Court free of its restrictions as a precedent, and free to declare that the choice of the particular form of regulation by which grave economic maladjustments are to be remedied is for the legislatures and not the courts.[38]

As to the contention that the petitioner's argument precluded the Court from overruling the *Adkins* case, Stone had this to say:

I know of no rule or practice by which the arguments advanced in support of an application for certiorari restrict our choice between conflicting precedents in deciding a question of constitutional law which the petition, if granted, requires us to answer. Here the question which the petition specifically presents is whether the New York statute contravenes the Fourteenth Amendment. In addition, the petition assigns as a reason for granting it that "the construction and application of the Constitution of the United States and a prior decision" of this Court "are necessarily involved," and again, that "the circumstances prevailing under which the New York law was enacted call for a reconsideration of the *Adkins* case in the light of the New York act and conditions aimed to be remedied thereby." Unless we are now to construe and apply the Fourteenth Amendment without regard to our decisions since the *Adkins* case, we could not rightly avoid its reconsideration even if it were not asked. We should follow our decision in the *Nebbia* case and leave the selection and the method of the solution of the problems to which the statute is addressed where it seems to me the Constitution has left them, to the legislative branch of the government.[39]

Chief Justice Hughes wrote another dissenting opinion, with which the other three dissenters concurred, devoted to showing that the New York law was distinguishable from that for the District of Columbia. While Stone agreed "with all that the Chief Justice has said,"[40] he did not base his own opinion on that distinction.

I attach little importance [he said] to the fact that the earlier statute was aimed only at a starvation wage and that the present one does not prohibit such a wage unless it is also less than the reasonable value of the service. Since neither statute compels employment at any wage, I do not assume that employers in one case, more than in the other, would pay the minimum wage if the service were worth less.[41]

Coming to the merits of the constitutionality of legislative interferences with the contract of employment, he remarked:

There is grim irony in speaking of the freedom of contract of those who, because of their economic necessities, give their services for less than is needful to keep body and soul together. But if this is freedom of contract no one has ever denied that it is freedom which may be restrained, not-

38 298 U.S. at 635. 39 *Id.* at 636. 40 *Id.* at 631. 41 *Ibid.*

withstanding the Fourteenth Amendment, by a statute passed in the public interest.[42]

After discussing decisions of the Court he went on:

> In the years which have intervened since the *Adkins* case we have had opportunity to learn that a wage is not always the resultant of free bargaining between employers and employees; that it may be one forced upon employees by their economic necessities and upon employers by the most ruthless of their competitors. We have had opportunity to perceive more clearly that a wage insufficient to support the worker does not visit its consequences upon him alone; that it may affect profoundly the entire economic structure of society and, in any case, that it casts on every taxpayer, and on government itself, the burden of solving the problems of poverty, subsistence, health and morals of large numbers in the community. Because of their nature and extent these are public problems. A generation ago they were for the individual to solve; today they are the burden of the nation. I can perceive no more objection, on constitutional grounds, to their solution by requiring an industry to bear the subsistence cost of labor which it employs, than to the imposition upon it of the cost of its industrial accidents. [Citing cases.]
>
> It is not for the courts to resolve doubts whether the remedy by wage regulation is as effective as many believe, or is better than some other, or is better even than the blind operation of uncontrolled economic forces. The legislature must be free to choose unless government is to be rendered impotent. The Fourteenth Amendment has no more embedded in the Constitution our preferences for some particular set of economic beliefs, than it has adopted, in the name of liberty, the system of theology which we may happen to approve.[43]

Chief Justice Hughes, as well as Stone, was aware of the fact that liberty can at times be protected only by restricting a conflicting liberty of someone else. Speaking generally on this point he said:

> We have had frequent occasion to consider the limitations of liberty of contract. While it is highly important to preserve that liberty from arbitrary and capricious interference, it is also necessary to prevent its abuse, as otherwise it could be used to override all public interests and thus in the end destroy the very freedom of opportunity which it is designed to safeguard.[44]

That the New York statute differed in some respects from the one held void in the *Adkins* case was admitted by everyone. The question on which the Chief Justice differed from the majority was whether the differences were sufficient to make the *Adkins* ruling inapplicable,

[42] *Id.* at 632. [43] *Id.* at 635–636. [44] *Id.* at 627.

on the assumption that it had not been overruled. Justice Butler, in construing the *Adkins* case to stand for a principle which would invalidate any regulation of wages whatsoever, had stressed the fact that in their dissenting opinions neither Taft nor Holmes had discussed the particular standard which Justice Sutherland had so strongly emphasized, but had criticized the majority opinion on the assumption that it "held that Congress was without power to deal with the subject at all." Hughes, on the other hand, after citing Sutherland's objection to the cost-of-living standard for ignoring the value of the services, said:

As the New York act is free of that feature, so strongly denounced, the question comes before us in a new aspect. The Court was closely divided in the *Adkins* case, and that decision followed an equal division of the Court, after reargument, in *Stettler* v. *O'Hara,* 243 U.S. 629, with respect to the validity of the minimum wage law of Oregon. Such divisions are at times unavoidable, but they point to the desirability of fresh consideration when there are material differences in the cases presented. The fact that in the *Adkins* case there were dissenting opinions maintaining the validity of the federal statute, despite the nature of the standard it set up, brings out in stronger relief the ground which was taken most emphatically by the majority in that case, and that there would have been a majority for the decision in the absence of that ground must be a matter of conjecture. With that ground absent, the *Adkins* case ceases to be a precise authority.[45]

Accepting for the purpose of the argument Justice Sutherland's insistence that the employer who pays a fair equivalent for the service rendered has neither caused nor contributed to the poverty of the employee, the Chief Justice insisted that the reasoning is inapplicable to the New York statute. After pointing out that the lack of adequate earnings must be made good out of the public purse, he continued:

Granted that the burden of the support of women who do not receive a living wage cannot be transferred to employers who pay the equivalent of the service they obtain, there is no reason why the burden caused by the failure to pay that equivalent should not be placed upon those who create it. The fact that the State cannot secure the benefit to society of a living wage for women employees by any enactment which bears unreasonably upon employers does not preclude the state from seeking its objective by means entirely fair both to employers and the women employed.[46]

The decision in the *Tipaldo* case was handed down on June 1, 1936, on the eve of the holding of the national conventions. The

[45] 298 U.S. at 624–625.

[46] *Id.* at 631.

result of the decision was so unpopular that even the Republican platform suggested a constitutional amendment to authorize minimum wage legislation. Apart from this, one of the principal targets of the Republican campaign was President Roosevelt's criticism of the Supreme Court. Despite these attacks on Roosevelt's irreverence, he was re-elected by the electoral votes of every state except Maine and Vermont. While his proposal in February, 1937, for a reorganization of the Supreme Court met a storm of opposition and was ultimately defeated, most of the opponents were careful to disavow any sympathy for the type of decision which the Court had been rendering under the due process clause. Against this background and before the final defeat of the "court-packing" plan, the Court, with its personnel unchanged, handed down a decision on March 29, 1937, in *West Coast Hotel Co.* v. *Parrish*,[47] reversing the position it had taken less than a year before, and overruling the *Adkins* case.

While the Court, however, reversed its position of the year before, the individual Justices did not, with the exception of Justice Roberts. Four of those who had been with the previous majority (Van Devanter, McReynolds, Sutherland, and Butler) now dissented, in an opinion by Justice Sutherland. Chief Justice Hughes, whose dissent in the *Tipaldo* case had been based on the ground that the New York statute was distinguishable from the one involved in the *Adkins* case, now wrote the majority opinion sustaining a Washington statute which was not distinguishable. As would be expected, Brandeis, Stone, and Cardozo, who had previously contended that the *Adkins* case was no longer law, were now with the majority. So, too, was Roberts, whose adherence to the previous majority can perhaps be explained on the theory that on the pleadings the question of the soundness of the *Adkins* case was not then before the Court, the petitioner for the writ of certiorari not having asked to have it overruled.

That theory, even if sound, could not be applied to the *Parrish* case, which was a suit by an employee to recover the difference between the wages she had been paid and the minimum wages fixed pursuant to the state law of Washington. The state supreme court, reversing the trial court, had sustained the statute and directed judgment for the employee. The case was brought to the federal Supreme Court on appeal—not certiorari. The question before the Supreme Court, accordingly, could not be narrowed to the grounds stated in any

[47] 300 U.S. 379 (1937).

petition for certiorari. On this point Hughes, after quoting from Justice Butler's opinion in the *Tipaldo* (*Morehead*) case, said:

We think that the question which was not deemed to be open in the *Morehead* case is open and is necessarily presented here. The Supreme Court of Washington has upheld the minimum wage statute of that state. It has decided that the statute is a reasonable exercise of the police power of the state. In reaching that conclusion the state court has invoked principles long established by this Court in the application of the Fourteenth Amendment. The state court has refused to regard the decision in the *Adkins* case as determinative and has pointed to our decisions both before and since that case as justifying its position. We are of the opinion that this ruling of the state court demands on our part a reexamination of the *Adkins* case. The importance of the question, in which many states having similar laws are concerned, the close division by which the decision in the *Adkins* case was reached, and the economic conditions which have supervened, and in the light of which the reasonableness of the exercise of the protective power of the state must be considered, make it not only appropriate, but we think imperative, that in deciding the present case the subject should receive fresh consideration.[48]

In discussing the general principles the Chief Justice said:

The principle which must control our decision is not in doubt. The constitutional provision invoked is the due process clause of the Fourteenth Amendment governing the states, as the due process clause invoked in the *Adkins* case governed Congress. In each case the violation alleged by those attacking minimum wage regulation for women is deprivation of freedom of contract. What is this freedom? The Constitution does not speak of freedom of contract. It speaks of liberty and prohibits the deprivation of liberty without due process of law. In prohibiting that deprivation the Constitution does not recognize an absolute and uncontrollable liberty. Liberty in each of its phases has its history and connotation. But the liberty safeguarded is liberty in a social organization which requires the protection of law against the evils which menace the health, safety, morals and welfare of the people. Liberty under the Constitution is thus necessarily subject to the restraints of due process, and regulation which is reasonable in relation to its subject and is adopted in the interests of the community is due process.[49]

After citing numerous decisions prior to the *Adkins* case which sustained interferences with freedom of contract, the opinion went on:

This array of precedents and the principles they applied were thought by the dissenting Justices in the *Adkins* case to demand that the minimum wage statute be sustained. The validity of the distinction made by the Court between a minimum wage and a maximum of hours in limiting lib-

[48] 300 U.S. at 389–390.

[49] *Id.* at 391.

erty of contract was especially challenged. . . . That challenge persists and is without any satisfactory answer.[50]

The Court then quoted the passages on this point from the dissenting opinions of Chief Justice Taft and Justice Holmes.

As to the point that the standard did not take account of the value of the services rendered, the Court apparently thought that the Washingon statute did require some consideration of the value, but that even if it did not, it would not be bad, since it compelled nobody to pay anything. "It may be assumed," said the Court, "that the minimum wage is fixed in consideration of the services that are performed in the particular occupations under normal conditions. Provision is made for special licenses at less wages in the case of women who are incapable of full service." [51] The Court then quoted Holmes's statement that the statute did not compel anybody to pay anything, and Taft's statement that legislatures which pass these laws may be presumed to believe that "when sweating employers are prevented from paying unduly low wages by positive law they will continue their business, abating that part of their profits, which were wrung from the necessities of their employees." The Court added: "We think that the views thus expressed are sound and that the decision in the *Adkins* case was a departure from the true application of the principles governing the regulation by the state of the relation of employer and employed." [52] After citing cases subsequent to the *Adkins* case, including *Nebbia* v. *New York,* as reinforcing those principles, Hughes went on to make the point which Stone had made in the *Tipaldo* case, saying:

There is an additional and compelling consideration which recent economic experience has brought into a strong light. . . . What these workers lose in wages the taxpayers are called upon to pay. The bare cost of living must be met. We may take judicial notice of the unparalleled demands for relief which arose during the recent period of depression and still continue to an alarming extent despite the degree of economic recovery which has been achieved. . . . The community is not bound to provide what is in effect a subsidy for unconscionable employers. The community may direct its law-making power to correct the abuse which springs from their selfish disregard of the public interest. The argument that the legislation in question constitutes an arbitrary discrimination, because it does not extend to men, is unavailing. . . . There is no "doctrinaire requirement" that the legislation should be couched in all embracing terms. . . . This familiar principle has repeatedly been applied to legislation which singles

[50] *Id.* at 395. [51] *Id.* at 396. [52] *Id.* at 397.

out women, and particular classes of women, in the exercise of the state's protective power. . . . Their relative need in the presence of the evil, no less than the existence of the evil itself, is a matter for the legislative judgment.

Our conclusion is that the case of *Adkins* v. *Children's Hospital, supra*, should be, and it is, overruled. The judgment of the Supreme Court of the State of Washington is affirmed.[53]

Justice Sutherland opened his dissenting opinion with a general discussion of the function of courts in passing on the constitutionality of statutes. Referring to the majority statement that the quesion here should receive fresh consideration because of "the economic conditions which have supervened," he maintained that "the meaning of the Constitution does not change with the ebb and flow of economic events." Furthermore, to say

that the words of the Constitution mean today what they did not mean when written—that is, that they do not apply to a situation now to which they would have applied then—is to rob that instrument of the essential element which continues it in force as the people have made it until they, and not their official agents, have made it otherwise.[54]

This reasoning is not easy to reconcile with the same Justice's statement in the *Adkins* case, which we have already quoted, that the line beyond which the power of interference with the liberty of the individual "may not be pressed is neither definite nor unalterable but may be made to move, within limits not well defined, with changing need and circumstances." [55]

Coming to the more specific question of whether this particular law is forbidden by "the words of the Constitution," he added little to what he had written in the *Adkins* case, from which he quoted copiously. Among other passages, he quoted in full his remarks about the failure of the statute to take account of the value of the services, without any reference to the subordinate position to which Justice Butler had relegated those remarks. He concluded with a repetition of his contention that the power to fix minimum wages connotes a like power to fix maximum ones, making no attempt to refute Taft's criticism of that contention. With this contention as a basis, he ended with the warning that if both powers be exercised in such a way that the minimum and the maximum so nearly approach each other as

[53] 300 U.S. at 399–400.

[54] *Id.* at 403.

[55] 261 U.S. at 561. *Supra*, p. 435.

to be substantially the same, the right to make any contract in respect of wages will have been completely abrogated." [56]

However, as Justice Stone said in 1941, speaking for the unanimous Court in *United States* v. *Darby Lumber Co.*, since this decision in the *Parrish* case, "it is no longer open to question that the fixing of a minimum wage is within the legislative power and that the bare fact of its exercise is not a denial of due process under the Fifth more than under the Fourteenth Amendment." [57]

In the *Darby* case the Court sustained the federal Fair Labor Standards Act, which prohibited the shipment in interstate commerce of goods manufactured by employees whose wages were less than a prescribed minimum or whose weekly hours at that wage exceeded a prescribed maximum and which prohibited the employment of workmen in the production of goods for interstate commerce at wages below the prescribed minimum or at hours above the prescribed maximum. The policy as declared in the Act was in part to prevent the spread of "labor conditions detrimental to the maintenance of the minimum standard of living necessary for health, efficiency, and general well-being of workers."

COMPULSORY ARBITRATION AND "FAIR" WAGES

A minimum wage law, of course, does not preclude the parties from bargaining for a wage higher than the prescribed minimum. When a minimum is set, there is no implication that a higher wage would not be "fair." A different question arises when governmental authority not only sets a floor under wages, but substitutes its own conception of a "fair" wage (which may be well above any mere cost-of-living standard) for a wage determined by private bargaining. Are there circumstances in which such "fair" wages may be prescribed without violating the Constitution?

On March 19, 1917, in *Wilson* v. *New*,[58] the Court sustained the Adamson Act, which fixed railroad wages temporarily at a point well above what any mere cost-of-living standard would have called for. The Act was passed by Congress in 1916, at the instigation of President Wilson, to avert a threatened railroad strike, which would have paralyzed the business of the country. It provided that eight hours should be deemed a standard of a day's work for the purpose of reckoning the

[56] 300 U.S. at 413-414.

[57] 312 U.S. 100, 125 (1941).

[58] 243 U.S. 332 (1917).

compensation of employees engaged in the interstate operation of trains. The previous standard was ten hours. It provided for a commission to observe the operation of the law during a period of between six and nine months and to report its findings within thirty days thereafter. Section 3 provided

> that pending the report of the Commission herein provided for and for a period of thirty days thereafter the compensation of railroad employees subject to this Act for a standard eight-hour workday shall not be reduced below the present standard day's wage, and for all necessary time in excess of eight hours such employees shall be paid at a rate not less than the pro rata rate for such standard eight-hour workday.

Chief Justice White, speaking for himself and Justices Holmes, Brandeis, and Clarke, construed this section, unlike the time-and-a-half overtime provision in the Oregon statute, which was sustained shortly afterwards in *Bunting* v. *Oregon*,[59] as a temporary fixing of wages, not merely of hours. But he regarded it as supplementing, not restricting, the freedom of the parties to contract as to wages. In sustaining the law, he emphasized that Congress was asserting its admitted power to enforce on the railroads the duty of operation, and asked if this power did not extend

> to doing that which was essential to prevent operation from being completely stopped by filling the interregnum created by an absence of a conventional standard of wages because of a dispute on that subject between the employers and employees, by a legislative standard binding on employers and employees for such time as might be deemed by the legislature reasonably adequate to enable normal conditions to come about as the result of agreements as to wages between the parties? [60]

Justice McKenna wrote a concurring opinion, thus making up the five votes necessary for sustaining the law. While he doubted whether this law was properly to be construed as a wage-fixing one, he had no doubt of the legislative power to fix wages in a business affected with a public interest. In this connection he said:

> When one enters into interstate commerce, one enters into a service in which the public has an interest, and subjects one's self to its behests. And this is no limitation of liberty; it is the consequence of liberty exercised, the obligation of his un·lertaking, and constrains no more than any contract constrains. The obligation of a contract is the law under which it is made, and submission to regulation is the condition which attaches to one who enters into or accepts employment in a business in which the public has an interest.[61]

[59] 243 U.S. 426 (1917). See *supra*, pp. 388–389. [60] 243 U.S. at 351. [61] *Id.* at 364.

Justices Day, Pitney, and McReynolds wrote separate dissenting opinions, and Justice Van Devanter concurred in Pitney's dissent, as well as in that part of Day's which held the Act to be a violation of the Fifth Amendment.

Day thought the Act violated the Fifth Amendment, not because Congress lacked power to fix railroad wages, but because it lacked power to do so without first investigating the effects of its action. While every presumption exists that a power which Congress has was legitimately exercised,

> nevertheless Congress has in this Act itself declared the lack of the requisite information for definite action, and has directed an experiment to determine what it should do, imposing in the meantime an increase of wages peremptorily declared, the expense of which is to be borne entirely by the carrier, without recompense if the investigation proves the injustice or impropriety of the increase.[62]

Justice Pitney went further and denied the power of Congress altogether to regulate the wages of railroad workers. He thought the regulation of wages was not a regulation of interstate commerce, and so was not within the powers which the Constitution had conferred on Congress. Apart from this point, he thought the Act deprived the companies of property without due process, contrary to the Fifth Amendment. "The right to hire employees, to bargain freely with them about the rate of wages, and from their labors to make lawful gains" was, in his opinion, one of the essential rights of property, even when the property has been dedicated to a public use.[63]

Justice McReynolds's dissent was briefer. He construed the statute as commanding the railroads, for a temporary period, to pay for eight hours work what they had previously been paying for ten, and remarked:

> I have not heretofore supposed that such action was a regulation of commerce within the fair intendment of those words as used in the Constitution; and the argument advanced in support of the contrary view is unsatisfactory to my mind. I cannot, therefore, concur in the conclusion that it was within the power of Congress to enact the statute.[64]

He did not elaborate these grounds, nor did he invoke the Fifth Amendment. He merely pointed out in a concluding paragraph what he thought were the consequences of the Court's decision:

> But, considering the doctrine now affirmed by a majority of the Court as established, it follows as of course that Congress has power to fix a maxi-

62 *Id.* at 370. 63 *Id.* at 386. 64 *Id.* at 388.

mum as well as a minimum wage for trainmen; to require compulsory arbitration of labor disputes which may seriously and directly jeopardize the movement of interstate traffic; and to take measures effectively to protect the free flow of such commerce against any combination, whether of operatives, owners, or strangers.[65]

But four of the five judges who voted to sustain the act promulgated no such doctrine as McReynolds attributed to the Court. In sustaining the Act they did so on the ground that the temporary wages which it established did not override any which the parties themselves might have set by agreement. It did not require the railroads to pay wages higher than any which they could induce the men to accept. In this respect it differed from the minimum wage statutes with which the Court dealt in the cases we have examined. The doctrine of these four judges would seem, however, to lend support to the validity of statutes providing for compulsory arbitration of railroad labor disputes, with wages set by an administrative board, when the parties have been unable to agree, but the Court has never been called upon to pass directly on the validity of such statutes.

In 1923, however, in *Wolff Packing Co.* v. *Court of Industrial Relations*,[66] it did pass on a Kansas statute which provided for compulsory arbitration and wage-fixing and held it invalid as applied to the wages paid by a meat packing business. The statute declared certain businesses, including the manufacture and preparation of food for human consumption, to be affected with a public interest, and set up a Court of Industrial Relations. This court was empowered to hear any dispute over wages or other terms of employment in any of the specified businesses, and if it should find the peace and health of the public imperiled by the controversy it was required to make findings and fix the wages and other terms for the future conduct of the business. The state supreme court might review the orders and could be appealed to for their enforcement. The industrial court made an order requiring the Wolff company to increase its wages, and the state supreme court granted a writ of mandamus requiring the company to comply. On error, the United States Supreme Court reversed.

Describing the statute, Chief Justice Taft, speaking for the unanimous Court, said:

The necessary postulate of the Industrial Court Act is that the state, representing the people, is so much interested in their peace, health and comfort

[65] 243 U.S. at 389.

[66] 262 U.S. 522 (1923).

that it may compel those engaged in the manufacture of food and clothing, and the production of fuel, whether owners, or workers, to continue in their business and employment on terms fixed by an agency of the state, if they cannot agree. Under the construction adopted by the State Supreme Court the Act gives the Industrial Court authority to permit the owner or employer to go out of the business, if he shows that he can only continue on the terms fixed at such heavy losses that collapse will follow; but this privilege under the circumstances is generally illusory. . . . A laborer dissatisfied with his wages is permitted to quit, but he may not agree with his fellows to quit or combine with others to induce them to quit.[67]

Taft then entered into his analysis of businesses affected with a public interest, which we examined in Chapter XIII. These, as we saw, he divided into three classes—first, those carried on under public grants, such as railroads and utilities; second, exceptional occupations, such as innkeepers, as to which common law regulation had survived from earlier times; and third, "businesses which, though not public at their inception, may be fairly said to have risen to be such and have become subject in consequence to some government regulation." The meat packing business clearly did not fall in either of the first two classes, and Taft strongly intimated that (because of competitive conditions) it did not fall in the third. But he was "relieved from considering" whether it should be put in the third class, "because, even so, the valid regulation to which it might be subjected as such, could not include what this Act attempts." [68] Since businesses of the third class, unlike those enjoying public franchises, might at common law discontinue at will, Taft distinguished the case from *Wilson* v. *New,* saying:

The power of a legislature to compel continuity in a business can only arise where the obligation of continued service by the owner and its employees is direct and is assumed when the business is entered upon. A common carrier, which accepts a railroad franchise, is not free to withdraw the use of that which it has granted to the public. It is true that if operation is impossible without continuous loss [citing cases], it may give up its franchise, but, short of this, it must continue. Not so the owner, when by mere changed conditions his business becomes clothed with a public interest. He may stop at will, whether the business be losing or profitable.

. . . It is not too much to say that the ruling in *Wilson* v. *New* went to the border line, although it concerned an interstate common carrier in the presence of a nation-wide emergency and the possibility of great disaster. Certainly there is nothing to justify extending the drastic regulation sustained in the exceptional case to the one before us.[69]

[67] *Id.* at 533–534. [68] *Id.* at 539. [69] *Id.* at 543–544.

While it was an employer, not the employees, who challenged the constitutionality of the Act, the Court took the view that the joint compulsion of both was an essential part of its purpose. "The state cannot be heard to say, therefore, that upon complaint of the employer the effect upon the employee should not be a factor in our judgment." [70] And the effect upon the employee was apparently a factor to which the Court gave considerable weight. It pointed out that

the employer is bound by this Act to pay the wages fixed and while the worker is not required to work at the wages fixed, he is forbidden, on penalty of fine or imprisonment, to strike against them and thus is compelled to give up that means of putting himself on an equality with his employer which action in concert with his fellows gives him.[71]

It should be kept in mind that Taft's remarks were addressed to the question of legislative power over businesses in his third category of those affected with a public interest, and not necessarily to railroads or other businesses enjoying publicly granted privileges or to their employees. The Court did not overrule *Wilson* v. *New,* and made it clear in the following paragraph that there might be circumstances in which compulsory arbitration would be held to violate neither the constitutional rights of the employer nor those of the employee:

It involves a more drastic exercise of control to impose limitations of continuity growing out of the public character of the business upon the employee than upon the employer; and without saying that such limitations upon both may not be sometimes justified, it must be where the obligation to the public of continuous service is direct, clear, and mandatory, and arises as a contractual condition express or implied of entering the business either as owner or worker. It can only arise when investment by the owner and entering the employment by the worker creates a conventional relation to the public somewhat equivalent to the appointment of officers and the enlistment of soldiers and sailors in military service.[72]

Taft was not called upon to specify the circumstances in which such a conventional relation to the public would be created by investing in a business or entering an employment. But he clearly intimated that they might exist.

Where the circumstances do exist, a law forbidding interruption of the service would necessitate a governmental setting of a "fair" wage. The evil at which such a law is aimed is not an excess or a deficiency in the earning power of labor; the evil to be averted is

70 262 U.S. at 541. 71 *Id.* at 540. 72 *Id.* at 541.

simply the interruption of the service. But in forbidding strikes and lockouts, the compulsory arbitration law destroys the bargaining weapons of the parties. It was by the use, or threatened use, of these weapons that the market value of the labor was established. But if wages cannot be set by the usual bargaining process, some other means must be found for setting them. That is why a compulsory arbitration law involves the authoritative setting of "fair" wages.

The difficulty is that there is no generally accepted standard to determine what would be fair. It might be thought that the market value of the service would be a fair standard. This standard might be workable when there is a market for services of the type in question outside of those businesses subject to the arbitration law. If that law applied, for instance, only to railroads, the wages for stenographers employed by railroads might be fixed at what stenographers employed by other industries are getting. But what about locomotive engineers, for whom there is no market outside of railroads? Perhaps we should seek to ascertain what their services are worth on a hypothetical market. While forbidding strikes and lockouts, we might estimate what bargains would have been reached had they been permitted. If all could know accurately what wages would have resulted from a full use by each party of its bargaining weapons, then fixing wages at that point without allowing the strike or lockout to take place would harm no one. Why should workers strike or employers resort to a lockout if public authority is to fix the same wages that would result anyway? But if the outcome of a hypothetical bargaining struggle could be accurately predicted by all concerned, there would be no need for the compulsory arbitration law. The parties themselves would have no reason to undergo the hardships of strikes and lockouts. It is because the outcome is uncertain that the strike takes place. It is because the outcome of any war is uncertain that any two nations resort to war, instead of signing a treaty at once which embodies the terms in which a war would eventuate. Since the hypothetical outcome is uncertain, it does not offer a very satisfactory standard for fixing the wage.

If compulsory arbitration were applied to a few industries only, perhaps wages could be fixed with reference to some standard of actual or hypothetical market value, however unsatisfactory and elusive that standard may be. But the more widely extended the system, the less possible would it be to find any unregulated market for the services with which to make comparisons. The wage-fixing body would be largely creating its own market value for the laborer whose wages it fixes. In doing so it would be confronted with far-reaching problems as to how the wealth of the community should be distributed. A change of railroad wages may lead the Interstate Commerce Commission to institute a corresponding change in the rates to be charged the shippers of freight, and these changes may have further repercussions on the price level generally. Even when the prices charged by an employer are not regulated by public authority, an increase in the wages he pays may set in motion economic forces of an inflationary character. And any such inflationary force reduces the share of the community's goods going to the recipients of relatively fixed money incomes. As Professor Taussig pointed out some quarter-century ago, the ultimate problem of a fair wage "involves settlement by public authority of the distribution of wealth." While "this ultimate problem may be disguised and postponed," and while adjudicated wages when first fixed are not likely to exceed those previously current "to such an extent as to present a real question of principle," still

> finally the tribunal will be compelled to consider how far it can go in modifying the terms of distribution. Where stop? What are "fair" wages? That question cannot be settled without settling what is fair interest and fair business profits. Ultimately, the tribunal must determine what is fundamental justice; how much the owners of wealth are justly entitled to in the way of interest; what is a just rate to the employer in the way of business profits; why some laborers are to receive more than others, and what is justice as between the different groups.[73]

The baffling nature of such problems, as well as the practicable difficulty of enforcing any anti-strike law, may account in part for the failure to enact compulsory arbitration laws in this country since the demise of the Kansas attempt.

[73] Frank W. Taussig, 2 Principles of Economics (3d ed., rev., Macmillan, 1921), c. 59, § 6.

XV

THE "FAIR VALUE" FALLACY IN RATE-MAKING

THE ultimate problem in the regulation of railroad and utility rates, like the ultimate problem in the fixing of fair wages, "involves settlement by public authority of the distribution of wealth." [1] Yet for years this ultimate problem was "disguised and postponed" in an attempt by the regulating authorities to conform to an artificial rule which bound them like a straitjacket, a rule which the Supreme Court had read into the Constitution.

CIRCULAR REASONING AS EXEMPLIFIED BY THE RULE OF SMYTH V. AMES (1898)

One of the principal grounds adduced for holding the very existence of the rate-regulating power valid was that without such power

[1] FRANK W. TAUSSIG, 2 PRINCIPLES OF ECONOMICS (3d ed., rev., Macmillan 1921), c. 59, § 6. Quoted *supra*, p. 460.

the public might be subjected to exorbitant charges.[2] But if before regulation is called into play the owner of any kind of property has the power to make exorbitant charges, that very fact will add to the value of the property whose ownership gives it to him. If deprived of the power to make the exorbitant charges, he will likewise be deprived of some part of the value of his property. Yet for half a century the Supreme Court insisted that regulation, like the exercise of the power of eminent domain, must never deprive the owner of any part of the value of his property without compensation, and imagined that such a guaranty to the owner was compatible with a power to reduce rates which yielded too much. Under the influence of this illusion, it read into the due process clauses in 1898 what came to be known as the rule of *Smyth* v. *Ames.*[3] Under this rule rates fixed by public authority were valid if, and only if, they permitted the company to earn a fair rate of return on what was called the value (or the "fair value") of the property. This so-called value was to be measured, not by what really gave the property its value (namely, its earning power under the rates it had been charging), but by a "consideration" of various factors unrelated to earnings. Chief among them were the actual cost of the property and the hypothetical cost of replacing it at the time of the regulation.

The attempt to apply this rule in practice resulted in such difficulties and irrelevancies that in 1942 Justices Black, Douglas, and Murphy, in a concurring opinion in *Federal Power Commission* v. *Natural Gas Pipeline Co.*, deplored the fact that the majority had not seized the "occasion to lay the ghost of *Smyth* v. *Ames* . . . which has haunted utility regulation since 1898."[4] Two years later, in an opinion which Justice Douglas delievered for the majority in *Federal Power Commission* v. *Hope Natural Gas Co.*,[5] the Court seems definitely to have laid the ghost. While it did not declare in express terms that *Smyth* v. *Ames* was overruled, it rejected the doctrine of that case in no uncertain terms. Some of the notions generated by *Smyth* v. *Ames,* however, still linger in the minds of state courts and commissions, and some of the techniques developed in the application of the rule of that case still persist. It may be well, therefore, to examine the doctrine and its history more fully.

It had its origin in a concept appropriate to the exercise of the

[2] *Cf.* TAFT, C. J., in Wolff Packing Co. v. Court of Industrial Relations, 262 U.S. 522, 538 (1923). See *supra*, p. 413.

[3] 169 U.S. 466, 546–547 (1898).

[4] 315 U.S. 575, 603 (1942).

[5] 320 U.S. 591 (1944).

power of eminent domain. While Chief Justice Waite declared in 1877, in *Munn* v. *Illinois*,[6] that if the legislative power to regulate prices was abused, "the people must resort to the polls, not to the courts," he had apparently changed his mind by 1886. Delivering the majority opinion in *Stone* v. *Farmers' Loan & Trust Co.* (sometimes cited as *Railroad Commission Cases*), he sustained the validity of a Mississippi statute which set up a commission to regulate and "limit" local railroad rates, but added the caveat that

> this power to regulate is not a power to destroy, and limitation is not the equivalent of confiscation. Under pretense of regulating fares and freights, the state cannot require a railroad corporation to carry persons or property without reward; neither can it do that which amounts to a taking for public use without just compensation, or without due process of law.[7]

It is true enough that the power of eminent domain is not a power to destroy or to "confiscate" (in the sense of depriving a person of anything of value without awarding him the exact pecuniary equivalent by way of compensation). But this is not true of the police power, which, like the power to tax, is indubitably a power to destroy without compensation. The power to condemn is not exercised for the purpose of correcting any economic maladjustment, and its purpose is therefore not thwarted by the requirement that it must be so exercised as to leave the owner's economic relationship to the rest of the community undisturbed. The purpose of "just compensation" in eminent domain was thus stated by Justice Butler in *United States* v. *New River Collieries Co.*: "The owner was entitled to the full money equivalent of the property taken, and thereby to be put in as good position pecuniarily as it would have occupied, if its property had not been taken." [8] But the purpose of regulating utility rates, unlike that of condemning property, is to correct an economic maladjustment whereby the company owning the property is adjudged to have an undue advantage over the rest of the community. If its economic relations to the rest of the community may not be disturbed,

[6] 94 U.S. 113, 134 (1877).

[7] 116 U.S. 307, 331 (1886).

[8] 262 U.S. 341, 343 (1923). But in United States v. General Motors Corp., 323 U.S. 373, 378–379 (1945), Justice Roberts, speaking for the Court, said that "the Fifth Amendment concerns itself solely with the 'property,' i.e., with the owner's relation as such to the physical thing and not with other collateral interests which may be incident to his ownership.

"In the light of these principles it has been held that the compensation to be paid is the value of the interest taken. Only in the sense that he is to receive such value is it true that the owner must be put in as good position pecuniarily as if his property had not been taken."

and if it is to be left in as good position as if it were permitted to continue taking undue advantage of the rest, it is obvious that the regulation cannot accomplish the very purpose which justifies its exercise.

Even when the purpose of an exercise of the police power is something other than any correction of an economic maladjustment, the fact that it incidentally results in an uncompensated loss of value is not necessarily fatal to its validity. The only guaranty the owner has is that the legislation which deprives him of value must not seem "arbitrary" to the Court; and the resulting loss of value is never conclusive of arbitrariness. A state prohibition law,[9] a state conservation law prohibiting the continued use of natural gas for the purpose for which an owner was using it,[10] a federal requisition of the output of a steel plant which frustrated a contract of a purchaser, thus destroying the value of that contract which was recognized as the purchaser's property,[11] and a municipal zoning law[12] have all been sustained, though in each case the value of the property owned by the party who challenged the governmental action was diminished by it. If a value which is not based on any economic maladjustment may be destroyed without compensation by an exercise of the police power, it would seem to follow *a fortiori* that a value based on a maladjustment may be destroyed by an exercise of the regulatory power.

Regulation, we have seen, was regarded by Justice Roberts in the *Nebbia* case as an exercise of the police power,[13] and he emphatically denied that there was anything so "peculiarly sacrosanct about the price one may charge for what he makes or sells" as to distinguish the regulation of the price from the regulation of other aspects of one's business and that there is no constitutional principle which "bars the state from correcting existing maladjustments by legislation touching prices."[14] But the principle enunciated by Chief Justice Waite does just that, if logically applied. It precludes destruction of the advantage which an owner has by reason of the maladjustment. Roberts, however, seemed unaware that Waite's principle would bar the correction of maladjustments, for little more than a year after the *Nebbia* decision he adopted that very principle himself in deliver-

9 Mugler v. Kansas, 123 U.S. 623 (1887).

10 Walls v. Midland Carbon Co., 254 U.S. 300 (1920).

11 Omnia Commercial Co. v. United States, 261 U.S. 502 (1923).

12 Euclid v. Ambler Realty Co., 272 U.S. 365 (1926). See the illuminating discussion of these cases by Charles Warren, *What Is Confiscation?*, 140 ATL. MONTHLY 246 (Aug., 1927).

13 291 U.S. 502, 534 (1934).

14 *Id.* at 531–532.

ing the majority opinion in *West* v. *Chesapeake & Potomac Telephone Co.*, saying:

The established principle is that as the due process clauses (Amendments 5 and 14) safeguard private property against a taking for public use without just compensation, neither Nation nor State may require the use of privately owned property without just compensation. When the property itself is taken by the exertion of the power of eminent domain, just compensation is its value at the time of the taking. So, where by legislation prescribing rates or charges the use of the property is taken, just compensation assured by these constitutional provisions is a reasonable rate of return upon that value.[15]

So, while the state has power to correct a maladjustment through price regulation, by this reasoning it would seem to have no power to deprive the owner of any of the fruits of that maladjustment. Or, as Chief Justice Waite would have it, the power to reduce excessive net earnings is not a power to destroy any part of the value produced by those excessive earnings. But why is it not, if the police power as applied to other aspects of property is a power to destroy even a value which is not the fruit of maladjustment and the taxing power is a power to destroy? Walton H. Hamilton, commenting on Waite's dictum in a law review article, said:

Note the easy and all but unconscious carry-over of a doctrine from one domain of the law to another, and note what the mind does to it in metamorphosis. "The power to tax involves the power to destroy" of Mr. Chief Justice Marshall, in McCullough v. Maryland, 4 Wheat. 316, 431 (U.S. 1819), becomes "the power to regulate is not the power to destroy" of Mr. Chief Justice Waite's more radical colleagues; and he allows them to have their way with his rhetoric. The subtlety is that of the Lord Chancellor in W. S. Gilbert's Iolanthe who by inserting a "not" in a perpetual decree provided the deus ex machina which alowed the action of the play to come to rest. The powers to tax and to regulate rest upon the same constitutional foundations and such a distinction between them has no constitutional warrant.[16]

To the mind of Justice Field, as long ago as 1877, it was apparent that the power to regulate *is* the power to destroy. And because he thought that the state has no power to destroy any part of the value of property, except in cases in which that power exists as an implied condition of a governmental grant, he denied the power to regulate grain elevator charges altogether. To allow the legislature to fix the

15 295 U.S. 662, 671 (1935).
16 Hamilton, *Price—By Way of Litigation* (1938) 38 COL. L. REV. 1008, 1014, n. 12.

amount of compensation which the owner may obtain from his customers, he insisted in his dissenting opinion in *Munn* v. *Illinois,* "will operate as a partial destruction of the value of the property, if it fall below the amount which the owner would obtain by contract * * *" [17] In so far as the power to regulate involves the power to reduce net earnings, it must involve the power to destroy. Yet for a long time the Court persistently ignored the truth of Field's statement and adhered to the self-contradictory position that excessive earnings could be reduced, but no value could be destroyed. And whether any particular reduction of earnings involved a destruction of value was declared to be a judicial question.

The first definite holding that the question of reasonableness is a judicial one was in 1890. In *Chicago, Milwaukee & St. Paul Ry. Co.* v. *Minnesota* [18] a state statute, as construed by the state supreme court, authorized a commission to fix rates without a hearing and required railroads to observe those rates, without opportunity for judicial review. The statute was held unconstitutional by a divided Court, speaking through Justice Blatchford, who said:

> If the company is deprived of the power of charging reasonable rates for the use of its property, and such deprivation takes place in the absence of an investigation by judicial machinery, it is deprived of the lawful use of its property, and thus, in substance and effect, of the property itself, without due process of law and in violation of the Constitution of the United States.[19]

The company, it was implied, may be deprived of the power of charging unreasonable rates, but some court must pass on the reasonableness.

Justice Miller wrote a concurring opinion, in which he maintained that while a state may, through its legislature or through a commission, establish transportation rates, still neither body

> can establish arbitrarily and without regard to justice and right a tariff of rates for such transportation, which is so unreasonable as to practically destroy the value of property of persons engaged in the carrying business on the one hand, nor so exorbitant and extravagant as to be in utter disregard of the rights of the public for the use of such transportation on the other.[20]

[17] 94 U.S. 113, 143, (1877). *Cf. supra,* p. 405.

[18] 134 U.S. 418 (1890).

[19] *Id.* at 458. Concurring in Blatchford's opinion were Chief Justice Fuller and Justices Field, Harlan, and Brewer.

[20] 134 U.S. at 459–460.

And while the commission could establish rates without giving previous notice, the question whether it had acted arbitrarily was a judicial question. Whether he meant to preclude any destruction whatsoever of the value of the property or only a practically complete destruction he did not say.

Meanwhile Justice Bradley wrote a dissenting opinion, in which Justices Gray and L. Q. C. Lamar concurred. He maintained that the reasonableness of rates "is a legislative question, not a judicial one, unless the legislature or the law, (which is the same thing), has made it judicial, by prescribing the rule that the charges shall be reasonable, and leaving it there." [21] And again:

> Deprivation of property by mere arbitrary power on the part of the legislature, or fraud on the part of the commission, are the only grounds on which judicial relief may be sought against their action. There was, in truth, no deprivation of property in these cases at all. There was merely a regulation as to the enjoyment of property, by a strictly competent authority, in a matter entirely within its jurisdiction.[22]

However, the case established the proposition that legislative rates are subject to judicial review, but without expressly invoking the limitations which apply to the power of eminent domain. Those limitations were invoked in 1894, in *Reagan* v. *Farmers' Loan & Trust Co.*,[23] in which certain rates fixed by a Texas commission were held unconstitutional. They were so low that they did not permit the railroad to pay the interest on its bonds, which were outstanding in the amount of $15,000,000. The cost of replacing the property was $25,000,000, and the actual cost which had been incurred was $40,000,000. The regulation might therefore have been held invalid, not on the ground that it destroyed part of the value, but on the ground that it was wholly arbitrary. Justice Brewer, however, speaking for the unanimous Court,[24] invoked the principles which limit the power of eminent domain, saying:

> If the State were to seek to acquire the title to these roads, under its power of eminent domain, is there any doubt that constitutional provisions would require the payment to the corporation of just compensation, that compensation being the value of the property as it stood in the markets of the world, and not as prescribed by an act of the legislature? Is it any less a

[21] *Id.* at 462. [22] *Id.* at 466. [23] 154 U.S. 362 (1894).

[24] The other members were Chief Justice Fuller and Justices Field, Harlan, Gray, Brown, Shiras, Howell E. Jackson, and White.

departure from the obligations of justice to seek to take not the title but the use for the public benefit at less than its market value? [25]

If the Court conceived the use to be taken each time a service is rendered, it must be obvious that any reduction in any rate results in a taking at less than the previous market value. The rate charged is the market value of the service. The power to regulate is necessarily a power to reduce the market value. Perhaps, however, the Court's idea was that when a state prescribes a rate schedule it is taking the use in its entirety. In the *Reagan* case Brewer did not explain what he meant by the market value of the use. Later in the same year, however, he apparently translated the term so as to measure the market value of the use by the revenue required to pay operating expenses and in addition to yield a fair rate of return on the market value of the property. The legislature of Nebraska had prescribed intrastate rates for freight on the railroads. Certain security holders sought to enjoin compliance with the legislation, and the case reached the Circuit Court for the District of Nebraska, in which Brewer sat as a Circuit Judge, in 1894, in *Ames* v. *Union Pacific Railway Co.*[26] The Court enjoined the enforcement in an opinion by Brewer. The decision is the one which the Supreme Court later affirmed in *Smyth* v. *Ames*.

In the Circuit Court Brewer cited the *Reagan* case as authority for the proposition that "the protection of property implies the protection of its value." "The power which the legislature has," he said, "is only to prescribe reasonable rates, not any rates. . . . But the foundation of the idea of reasonableness is justice. . . . There can be no justice in that which works to such investors a practical destruction of their property thus invested." [27] By a "practical destruction," Brewer seems to have meant any uncompensated diminution of value.

He was not always clear on this point, for in 1901, in *Cotting* v. *Kansas City Stock Yards Company*,[28] in suggesting that the rule ap-

25 154 U.S. at 410.

26 64 Fed. 165 (C.C., D. Neb. 1894).

27 *Id.* at 176–177.

28 183 U.S. 79, 93–94 (1901). Although the official report prints "Opinion of the Court" over each page of Brewer's opinion, it is clearly not the opinion of the Court. Harlan, Gray, Brown, Shiras, White, and McKenna concurred in the result "upon the ground that the statute of Kansas in question is in violation of the Fourteenth Amendment of the Constitution of the United States in that it applies only to the Kansas City Stock Yards Company and not to other companies or corporations engaged in like business in Kansas, and thereby denies to that company the equal protection of the laws. Upon the question whether the statute is unconstitutional upon the further ground that, by its necessary operation, it will deprive that company of its property without due

plicable to regulations of those performing a public service (such as railroad transportation) might differ from that which applies to regulations of other businesses which have come to be affected with a public interest, he said in regard to one rendering a public service:

> While we have said again and again that one volunteering to do such services cannot be compelled to expose his property to confiscation, that he cannot be compelled to submit its use to such rates as do not pay the expenses of the work, and therefore create a constantly increasing debt which ultimately works its appropriation, still is there not force in the suggestion that as the State may do the work without profit, if he voluntarily undertakes to act for the State he must submit to a like determination as to the paramount interests of the public?

The suggestion that there is no confiscation if the rates yield no profit, provided only that they pay the expenses of rendering the service, was only a dictum. Brewer was making the point that in the case of a business which is not technically a public service, the state cannot reduce rates which are reasonable in comparison with those charged elsewhere merely because the profits from a large business are high.

Whatever conception Brewer may have had of the term "confiscation" in 1901, however, the fact remains that when he decided the *Ames* case he regarded any destruction of value as unconstitutional. He assumed, nevertheless, that reductions in net earnings did not necessarily destroy value. The test in his mind was whether the reduced earnings amounted to a fair return on the value. He ignored the obvious fact that the reduced earnings could not possibly amount to a fair return on the previous value. This is somewhat strange in view of the fact that he was well aware that the value of property depends on its earnings. In 1893 he had written the opinion of the Court in the case of *Monongahela Navigation Co.* v. *U.S.*,[29] in which he held that on condemnation the owner must be compensated for all the property taken, including the franchise. The Government was appropriating a lock and dam, together with a franchise wherein a state had authorized the exaction of tolls for the use of the canal. Speaking of the value for which the Government must make compensation, he said, "The value of property, generally speaking, is determined by its productiveness—the profits which its use brings to

process of law, we deem it unnecessary to express an opinion." Apparently only Chief Justice Fuller and Justice Peckham concurred in Brewer's opinion.

29 148 U.S. 312, 328–329 (1893).

the owner. . . . These tolls, in the nature of the case, must enter into and largely determine the matter of value." Moreover, on the same day on which the *Reagan* case was decided, Brewer handed down the decision of the majority in *Cleveland, Cincinnati, Chicago & St. Louis Ry. Co.* v. *Backus.* This case involved a question of the value of property for the purposes of assessing a tax on it. Brewer declared that "the value of property results from the use to which it is put and varies with the profitableness of that use, present and prospective, actual and anticipated. There is no pecuniary value outside of that which results from such use." [30] This being true, it must be evident that a fair return on the present value of the property is exactly what the company has been earning before regulation and that any reduction of earnings must necessarily result in less than a fair return on that value.

A fair rate of return means the rate sufficient and necessary to attract capital, as several cases have expressly defined it.[31] But if in a given case 8 percent, for instance, is the rate needed to attract capital, this means that for every eight dollars of prospective earnings, one hundred dollars can be obtained in the market—in other words, that the property of this particular company will have a market value of one hundred dollars for every eight dollars of anticipated earnings. Ascertaining value by this method is known as "capitalizing the earnings." If the rule were that rate reductions are always invalid when they reduce net earnings to less than a fair return on market value, then we should know in advance that any reductions in net earnings would be invalid and there would be no occasion to measure the value in order to ascertain what we already know. The value is simply that amount on which the net earnings before regulation constitute, in our given case, 8 percent. Any reduction in them will, of course, amount to less than 8 percent on that value. To go through an elaborate process of measuring the value in order to ascertain whether a given reduction of earnings will amount to less than a fair return upon that value is like taking careful measurements to determine whether a proposed reduction in the length of a circular race track would result in a circumference as great as 3.1416 times the previous di-

[30] 154 U.S. 439, 445 (1894).

[31] *E.g.,* Bluefield Waterworks &c. Co. v. P.S.C., 262 U.S. 679, 692–695 (1923); McCardle v. Indianapolis Water Co., 272 U.S. 400, 419 (1926); United Railways & El. Co. v. West, 280 U.S. 234, 249–252 (1930).

ameter. If the measurements indicate that it would, we can be sure that there has been a miscalculation somewhere.

Yet Brewer, in the *Ames* case, despite his knowledge that value depends on profits, assumed that a reduction of earnings would be possible which would still leave a fair return on the pre-existing value. He suggested that such a result might be unfair to the company if the investors had actually contributed a sum greater than the present value. This suggestion, which was not followed when the case reached the Supreme Court, Brewer did not press; but in stating the argument he revealed that he thought a power to reduce net earnings was compatible with the rule requiring a fair return on the value and compatible likewise with the complete protection of the value from destruction. He said:

> Now, if the public was seeking to take title to the railroad by condemnation, the present value of the property, and not the cost, is that which [it] would have to pay. In like manner, it may be argued that, when the legislature assumes the right to reduce, the rates so reduced cannot be adjudged unreasonable if, under them, there is earned by the railroad company a fair interest on the actual value of the property.[32]

He reached his conclusion that the rates in this case were invalid, not on the ground that all reductions of earnings are necessarily so, but on the ground that the earnings from these particular rates yielded less than a fair return on the value of the property. In coming to this conclusion he examined figures as to the actual cost as well as the lower cost of reproducing the roads.

Before the case reached the Supreme Court that body held that certain turnpike tolls prescribed by a Kentucky statute were unconstitutional. At the suit of travelers the state court had granted an injunction restraining the company from exacting tolls in excess of those fixed by the statute. The company had filed an answer in which it claimed a contract right to charge higher tolls and also set forth figures showing that under the statutory rates it would be unable to keep the road in proper repair or to earn any dividends whatsoever. The state court had sustained a demurrer to this answer. Its decision was reversed by the Supreme Court in 1896 in *Covington & Lexington Turnpike Co.* v. *Sandford.*[33] In the unanimous opinion rendered by Justice Harlan it was held that while the legislation did not impair the

[32] 64 Fed. at 177.

[33] 164 U.S. 578 (1896).

obligation of any contract, it did nevertheless, if the facts alleged by the company were true, deprive it of property without due process of law, and the case was remanded to the lower court so that the company should be allowed to prove its allegations. Harlan quoted copiously from previous opinions, including the passage in the *Reagan* case which invoked eminent domain principles. While maintaining that "the public cannot properly be subjected to unreasonable rates in order simply that stockholders may earn dividends," [34] he declared that

> when a court, without assuming itself to prescribe rates, is required to determine whether the rates prescribed by the legislature for a corporation controlling a public highway are, as an entirety, so unjust as to destroy the value of its property for all the purposes for which it was acquired its duty is to take into consideration the interests both of the public and of the owner of the property, together with all other circumstances that are fairly to be considered in determining whether the legislature has, under the guise of regulating rates, exceeded its constitutional authority, and practically deprived the owner of property without due process of law.[35]

The statement is vague, but in this case it was clear that the legislation would have completely destroyed the value of the property. But if the passage quoted from the *Reagan* case is to govern, even a partial destruction of the value of property would have to be held void. How the legislature could still protect the public against exorbitant rates is not indicated.

Smyth v. *Ames* [36] was decided in 1898, affirming Brewer's injunction against the statutory rates. While Harlan, who rendered the unanimous opinion, did not expressly invoke eminent domain principles, nevertheless, he asserted that "a corporation may not be required to use its property for the benefit of the public without receiving just compensation for the services rendered by it." [37] But the government had power, he said, to "protect the people against unreasonable charges for the services rendered by" a railroad. Without noting any incompatibility between this power and the assurance of a fair return on the value of the property, he proceeded to lay down the doctrine by which courts long professed to be governed in most subsequent cases:

> We hold, however, that the basis of all calculations as to the reasonableness of rates to be charged by a corporation maintaining a highway under

[34] 164 U.S. at 596. [35] *Id.* at 597. [36] 169 U.S. 466 (1898).
[37] *Id.* at 546.

legislative sanction must be the fair value of the property being used by it for the convenience of the public. And, in order to ascertain that value, the original cost of construction, the amount expended in permanent improvements, the amount and market value of its bonds and stock, the present as compared with the original cost of construction, the probable earning capacity of the property under particular rates prescribed by statute, and the sum required to meet operating expenses, are all matters for consideration, and are to be given such weight as may be just and right in each case. We do not say that there may not be other matters to be regarded in estimating the value of the property. What the company is entitled to ask is a fair return upon the value of that which it employs for the public convenience. On the other hand, what the public is entitled to demand is that no more be exacted from it for the use of a public highway than the services rendered by it are reasonably worth.[38]

The enumeration of so many elements to be considered in order to ascertain value closed the eyes of the Court for forty years to the fact which Brewer had pointed out in the *Backus* case that value "varies with the profitableness of that use, present and prospective, actual and anticipated. There is no pecuniary value outside of that which results from such use." If value depends in fact on elements which are independent of earnings, then of course the insistence upon a fair return on that value may be compatible with the power to reduce net earnings. But if there is a value other than one depending upon the profitableness of the use, a regulation which reduces profits cannot impair such an independent value. If such be the case, the rule of *Smyth* v. *Ames* does not perform the function for which it was invoked—namely, to prevent any uncompensated destruction of value. After forty years, however, as we shall see, the Court finally recognized in the *Denver Stockyards* case in 1938 that the elements listed in *Smyth* v. *Ames* indicate value only when they result in a figure dependent upon profitableness. If the value is indeed to be measured by profitableness under existing rates, we come back to the incompatibility of the power to regulate with the assurance of a fair return on the value. If, on the other hand, the value is to be measured, as suggested in 1938, by profitableness, not under existing rates, but under rates that are just and reasonable, it is impossible to determine what the value is without first determining without the aid of value what rates are just and reasonable. If we have determined this, we need no other test.

[38] *Id.* at 546–547.

THE ILLUSORY ESCAPE FROM THE VICIOUS CIRCLE BY IGNORING THE DEPENDENCE OF VALUE ON THE RATES

Meanwhile, however, in a long series of cases the Court found what it called value by giving consideration to the elements suggested in *Smyth* v. *Ames* rather than by capitalizing the earnings. The Court itself was at times dubious whether the value on which it insisted that the company must be allowed a fair return was the same thing as the value in the ordinary sense, as used in condemnation, damage, and tax cases. In 1910, for instance, in determining the amount to be paid by a city under a contract for the sale of a water plant, in *Omaha* v. *Omaha Water Company*,[39] Justice Lurton distinguished two rate cases on the very ground that they "were rate cases and did not concern the ascertainment of value under contracts of sale." Indeed, one clear-sighted commissioner, noting the incompatibility between the power to regulate and the assurance of a return on value and the reliance of the Court on the elements enumerated in *Smyth* v. *Ames* for the ascertaiment of what was called value, seemed to think that the Court must have been using the word in some different sense. Chairman Frank W. Stevens, of the New York Public Service Commission for the Second District, declared in 1913, in *Fuhrmann* v. *Cataract Power and Conduit Co.*,[40] that since exchange value depends upon the earnings

> there would seem to be no escape from the conclusion that, when courts have used the term "fair value" in rate cases they had something in mind different from "exchange value" or in other words, "value." It is not to be supposed that they did not comprehend that value depends upon the rate and that a change in rate means a change in value if it affects net income.

Then, after quoting the language of *Smyth* v. *Ames*, he went on:

> This enumeration of matters to be considered may be regarded as a demonstration that the Court did not have in mind "value" in its economic sense of "exchange value," since the matters enumerated do not lead logically or otherwise to a fixing of exchange value. It would be too much to say that anyone ever arrived at a conclusion as to how much he would be willing to part with for a given piece of property by any such process as is here indicated. If, however, the court was endeavoring to point out a method of reaching a just and reasonable conclusion as to the just and reasonable

39 218 U.S. 180, 203 (1910). 40 3 P.S.C. (2d Dist. N.Y.) 656, 680–682 (1913).

amount upon which the return should be allowed, it could not well have used better or more comprehensive language.[41]

Stevens here assumed that at the time it enunciated the rule of *Smyth* v. *Ames* the Court was aware that value depends upon the rate. But, though Brewer had shown his awareness of that fact in condemnation and tax cases, he apparently forgot it when discussing rate cases. The entire purpose of the rule, in his mind, would have been frustrated if the meaning of "value" in a rate case differed from its meaning in a case involving condemnation, or taxation, or sale. But if, as in a condemnation case, value depends on profitability, the power to reduce earnings is gone. That power was preserved only by pretending that the same value which, in eminent domain, depends on earnings, depends in a rate case on something independent of earnings, such as actual or replacement cost. That the Court, despite the doubts which it entertained in the *Omaha Water* case, conceived of rate-making value as the same as value for other purposes was made clear in several cases decided after Mr. Stevens had written. In a case involving the value of a vessel which had been sunk in a collision, Justice Butler, speaking for the Court in *Standard Oil Co.* v. *Southern Pacific Co.*,[42] in 1925, cited rate cases as authority for certain methods of ascertaining value. In 1926, in *McCardle* v. *Indianapolis Water Co.*,[43] the same Justice cited this damage case to support his conclusions as to rate-making valuation. And in 1936, in *Great Northern Railway Co.* v. *Weeks,* speaking for the majority concerning tax valuations, he said: "The principles governing the ascertainment of value for the purposes of taxation are the same as those that control in condemnation cases, confiscation cases, and generally in controversies involving the ascertainment of just compensation." [44]

[41] After leaving the Commission, Mr. Stevens became counsel to the New York Central Lines, and in that capacity sought to give currency to the view which he had rejected as Commissioner. In a pamphlet published in 1914, THE VALUATION OF RAILROAD RIGHT OF WAY, No. 3, commenting on the language of Smyth v. Ames, he said (p. 30): "The Court lays down certain matters which must be considered in ascertaining value. The consideration of all these matters and the giving to each of them such weight as may be just in a given case is wholly inconsistent with the investment theory of value and entirely consistent with the ascertainment of exchange value." Acceptance of this contention would of course lead to inclusion in the valuation on which rates were to be permitted of something considerably higher than what the railroads had actually invested in right of way.

[42] 268 U.S. 146, 156 (1925).

[43] 272 U.S. 400, 411 (1926).

[44] 297 U.S. 135, 139 (1936). Justice Stone wrote a dissenting opinion in which Justices Brandeis and Cardozo concurred.

So, it would seem that value on which a fair return is to be allowed varies with profitableness, and at the same time it depends on factors which have nothing to do with profitableness. There was no exaggeration in Gerard C. Henderson's statement in 1920 that:

The whole doctrine of *Smyth* v. *Ames* rests upon a gigantic illusion. The fact which for twenty years the court has been vainly trying to find does not exist. "Fair Value" must be shelved among the great juristic myths of history, with the Law of Nature and the Social Contract. As a practical concept, from which practical conclusions can be drawn, it is valueless.[45]

But the Court continued its vain search for a "value" defined as the same value which in eminent domain and tax cases varies with profitableness, but which is to be measured by factors other than profits. Indeed, this most relevant of all factors in the ascertainment of value had to be ignored, or the incompatibility of *Smyth* v. *Ames* with the power to reduce would have become apparent. As Chief Justice Hughes said in 1933, in *Los Angeles Gas & El. Corp.* v. *Railroad Commission,*

the criteria at hand for ascertaining market value, or what is called exchange value, are not commonly available. The property is not ordinarily the subject of barter and sale and, when rates themselves are in dispute, earnings produced by rates do not afford a standard for decision.[46]

But earnings produced by rates are what give the property the only kind of value which might be impaired by regulation. By ignoring this fact and by assuming that a value could be "ascertained" by a consideration of such factors as actual and reproduction cost, the Court frequently arrived at a figure which it called "value," on which the earnings under the old rates amounted to more than a fair return; reduced rates which reduced those earnings were accordingly sustained, with a pronouncement that there had been no "confiscation"—meaning no impairment of value. In fact, however, there must necessarily have been. Although the rule of *Smyth* v. *Ames* professed to require a fair return on the value of the property, still,

[45] Henderson, *Railway Valuation and the Courts* (1920) 33 HARV. L. REV. 1031, 1051. Justices Black, Douglas, and Murphy quoted these remarks with approval in their concurring opinion in Federal Power Commission v. Natural Gas Pipeline Co., 315 U.S. 575, 605, n. 6 (1942). Justice Stone, in his dissenting opinion in West v. Chesapeake & Potomac Tel. Co., 295 U.S. 662, 691, n. 7 (1935), cited with apparent approval a comment which paraphrased this thought from the minority report of the Commission on Revision of the New York State Public Service Commission Law (1930).

[46] 289 U.S. 287, 305 (1933).

as the Court applied it in practice, it required a fair return on something that was not value at all.

What that something was, however, remained shrouded in mystery. Its ascertainment, said Justice Hughes, as long ago as 1913, in the *Minnesota Rate Cases,* "is not a matter of formulas, but there must be a reasonable judgment having its basis in a proper consideration of all relevant facts"[47]—all, that is, except the most relevant fact of all, the earnings. *Smyth* v. *Ames* enumerated several facts to which consideration was to be given in order to ascertain "value." Two of these, "the probable earning capacity of the property under particular rates prescribed by statute," and "the sum required to meet operating expenses," have to be considered in order to determine whether the prescribed rates are valid, but not in order to ascertain the value of the property. After determining a standard to which the rates must conform (by calculating what would be a fair return on the value), the next step was to determine whether the prescribed rates did in fact conform to the standard. It was in taking this step, rather than in calculating what the "value" was, that the probable gross earnings from the prescribed rates must be determined and the operating expenses subtracted from them. It is doubtful whether Justice Harlan, despite the looseness of his language, really meant them to be considered in the process of ascertaining value.

Two other items which Harlan enumerated for consideration in the ascertainment of value never played any significant role in subsequent cases. These are "the amount and market value of its bonds and stock." The reason is, perhaps, that the "amount" (the par value) may have been thought to result from stock watering, and the market value from manipulation. Another reason for ignoring them is that a rate case often concerns rates for only part of the entire service rendered by a company, and it is only on the value of the property used in the rendering of the particular service that the company was supposed to be entitled to a fair return. The stocks and bonds generally cover the company's entire property. It was because of the difficulty of determining what proportion of the securities represented the property used in rendering the service for which the rates were fixed that the Court sustained the master's refusal to give consideration to the market value of the securities of the Northern Pacific Railway in the *Minnesota Rate Cases.*[48]

[47] 230 U.S. 352, 434 (1913).

[48] *Id.* at 440.

The remaining matters which Harlan enumerated are the ones to which the Court for a long time directed its attention. They are "the original cost of construction, the amount expended in permanent improvements, . . . the present as compared with the original cost of construction." It is from these ingredients, principally, with the addition sometimes of an item called "going value," that the Court produced the figure which it declared to be the value of the property upon which the rates must yield a fair return. "The original cost of construction" and "the amount expended in permanent improvements" are added together to form what came to be called "actual cost" or "historical cost." "The present as compared with the original cost of construction" came to be designated "reproduction cost" or "replacement cost," and from it is subtracted an allowance for accrued depreciation. "The cost of reproduction," said Justice Moody for the Court in 1909, in *Knoxville* v. *Knoxville Water Co.*, "is one way of ascertaining the present value of a plant like that of a water company, but that test would lead to obviously incorrect results, if the cost of reproduction is not diminished by the depreciation which has come from age and use." [49] Included in reproduction cost is supposed to be the "present value" of the land.

Ascertaining the reproduction cost is a long and expensive process, and the resulting figures are highly speculative. Expert witnesses reach widely divergent conclusions. As Justice Stone said in his dissenting opinion in *West* v. *Chesapeake & Potomac Telephone Co.*: "In assuming the task of determining judicially the present fair replacement value of the vast properties of public utilities, courts have been projected into the most speculative undertaking imposed upon them in the entire history of English jurisprudence." [50]

Nor was this all. Once the difficulties of ascertaining replacement cost were surmounted, the problem was not solved. Replacement cost was not the only factor to be "considered." There were other factors, including actual, or "historical," cost. For a long time the Court declined to indicate how much weight should be given to each factor. On a single day in June, 1923, two decisions were handed down passing on the validity of rates fixed by two state commissions. One sustained the regulation; the other held it invalid. In each case the commission had made findings of the actual cost and of the replacement cost. In each, the commission made a "finding" of fair value, which

[49] 212 U.S. 1, 9 (1909).

[50] 295 U.S. 662, 689 (1935).

slightly exceeded the actual cost, but fell considerably below the replacement cost. In *Bluefield Water Works & Improvement Co.* v. *Public Service Commission*[51] the rates were held invalid, in an opinion by Justice Butler, because, in fixing the valuation so far below replacement cost the commission could not have given any "real consideration" to that factor. On the other hand, in *Georgia Railway & Power Co.* v. *Railroad Commission*,[52] the rates were sustained, because, although the commission had "found" the value to be far below replacement cost, it had nevertheless "considered" that item, and "value" was not synonymous with replacement cost. Justice Brandeis's opinion had the concurrence of Butler and all the other Justices except McKenna.

By 1926, however, the Court had become more definite as to the relative weight to be given to those two factors. In *McCardle* v. *Indianapolis Water Co.*[53] it was held, in an opinion by Justice Butler, that while actual cost was good evidence of "value" at the time of construction, it ceased to measure value when the level of prices which enter into construction has advanced to a position where it seems likely to remain for a reasonable time in the future. The rule of *Smyth* v. *Ames*, he said, "does not mean that the original cost or the present cost or some figure arbitrarily chosen between these two is to be taken as the measure." Cost of reproduction (less depreciation) seemed to be the factor which would measure the value to be attributed to the physical assets, actual cost being considered only (if considered at all) for the purpose of checking the accuracy of the reproduction cost figures. When, in 1933, the Court accepted the commission's findings of actual cost (in *Los Angeles Gas & El. Corp.* v. *Railroad Commission*[54]) as the maximum that could be attributed to the "value" of the physical plant, it was because most of the construction had taken place in periods of high price levels, and the accuracy of the figures which the company submitted of reproduction cost was impugned by the erroneous assumption on which they were based, that the drop in price levels at the end of 1929 was ephemeral.

51 262 U.S. 679 (1923).

52 262 U.S. 625 (1923).

53 272 U.S. 400, 411 (1926). Justice Holmes concurred in the result. Justice Brandeis wrote a dissenting opinion, in which Stone joined.

54 289 U.S. 287 (1933).

ESCAPE FROM THE VICIOUS CIRCLE BY GUARANTEEING PHYSICAL VALUE ONLY

But replacement cost would not necessarily measure the value of the property as a going concern, or even the value of the physical elements. If it did, the value would remain as high, even after the most drastic reduction of rates, as before, and there would be no need to protect that value from impairment at the hands of the regulatory authority. And the Court at times recognized that the value, even of physical property, is not necessarily identical with the cost of replacing it. As Butler himself said for the Court in *Brooks-Scanlon Co.* v. *United States,*[55] a case decided in 1924 involving the compensation due for a contract requisitioned by the Government, "this court has held in many cases that replacement cost is to be considered in the ascertainment of value . . . , but that it is not necessarily the sole measure of or guide to value." And in another case the Court recognized that replacement cost would cease to be a measure of value if the company's earning power were sufficiently reduced. In sustaining the failure of the Interstate Commerce Commission to include in a valuation of the New Haven Railroad separate items for the road's interests in the Harlem Railroad's tracks from Woodlawn to the Grand Central in New York and its interests in the Grand Central Terminal itself and in the Boston Terminal, when the New Haven's trackage had been valued at reproduction cost, the Court said in 1932, in *Interstate Commerce Commission* v *N.Y.N.H. & H.R. Co.:*

> Not a mile of track would be worth the cost of reproducing it, not a trackage right the rental, if there were not stations at either end. Not a station would be worth the cost of building it anew if there were not roadbeds or trackage rights beyond . . . . Every trackage contract and every terminal use, in so far as it contributes to the unity of the system, is reflected in the final value ascribed to the physical things that are listed in the inventory. The Harlem trackage contract is there reflected, for the reproduction cost would cease to be a measure of the value if the trains stopped short at Woodlawn.[56]

While this statement by Justice Cardozo was in a four-to-three decision (Hughes and Butler taking no part, and Van Devanter, McReynolds, and Sutherland dissenting), Butler recognized the same fact in 1938 in *Denver Union Stockyard Co.* v. *United States.*[57] "Appel-

55 265 U.S. 106, 125 (1924).

56 287 U.S. 178, 201–202 (1932).

57 304 U.S. 470, 479 (1938).

lant's plant," he said, "without business, present or prospective, would be worth much less than the cost figures found by the Secretary to represent value." The "cost figures" were those for replacement cost.

If low earnings can make the value of a plant less than replacement cost, can high earnings make it more? Unquestionably they can, if we are speaking of its worth as a going concern. It is only a coincidence if replacement cost measures such value. True, in a world such as that visualized by the classical economists, with perfect competition and perfect mobility of capital, replacement cost would supposedly constitute the standard to which value based on capitalized earnings would conform. If for a moment a plant were earning more than a fair return on replacement cost, new capital would supposedly take advantage of the situation by building competing plants; the effect would be to increase the output of similar products and hence to reduce prices and earnings; the process would supposedly continue until the earnings fell to the level at which the plant would have a value equal to replacement cost. Conversely, if for a moment plants were earning less than a fair return on replacement cost, capital would flow out of that industry to more profitable fields, until the total output of the remaining plants fell to the point where the products could be sold at prices yielding a fair return on replacement cost. The process of withdrawing capital would take the form of a failure to restore plants as they wore out. In a world of such complete mobility, replacement cost would measure the value of going concerns only because it would measure the capitalized earnings. The moment, however, that we know that a public utility plant will be able (if not regulated) to continue to earn more than a fair return on replacement cost, we know that replacement cost has ceased to be a measure of its value as a going concern, and any reduction of the earnings will impair that value.

While high earnings, however, can make the value as a going concern more than replacement cost, there is a sense of the word in which they cannot make the value of the physical property more, though low earnings can make it less. If a plant is capable of earning appreciably more than a fair return on the cost of replacing its physical elements with equally efficient substitutes, the ability to earn the additional amount may be attributable to patent rights, franchise rights to prevent competition, or a right to prevent others selling under the same name (good will), not solely to ownership of the physical elements. In that case the value of the physical elements will obviously not comprise the entire value of the going concern. But it may well be that a plant can earn more than a fair return on replacement cost even if there are no patent rights, no right to exclude competition, and if customers are indifferent to any good will of the concern from which they buy service. Even in such a case competition may be impotent to force earnings down to a fair return on replacement cost, not because the law forbids competition, but because every would-be competitor knows that the establishment of a competing plant on a scale large enough to produce efficiently will result in such an oversupply of the service as to be ruinous to all the plants. In such a case the earning power of the business is attributable solely to the ownership of the physical equipment—the legal privilege to use it for the production and sale of the service in question, and the right to prevent others from using that particular equipment. The owner would presumably refuse to transfer his ownership to another for an amount as low as replacement cost, when the value of the business as a going concern is more, for he could not restore his business by replacing the physical units, since competition with the purchaser would be ruinous. And presumably a purchaser would find it worth while to pay the full value as a going concern, for he could not acquire an equally profitable business by building a similar plant to compete with the present one. In this sense the value of the physical elements is indistinguishable from that of the going concern.

There is another perfectly legitimate sense of the word, however, in which the value of the physical property in a case like the above may be said to be less than that of the going concern. While the transfer of the physical property to another would involve the owner in a loss equivalent to the value of the going concern, a mere loss of the physical property (as by a physical destruction), without its acquisition by anyone else, would not involve loss of the business. The owner could restore his business at the expense of the smaller amount needed to replace the physical property. This cost of replacing includes, of course, any loss of earnings incidental to the delay.[58] In this sense

[58] "Replacement cost" means the cost of substituting for the existing physical units others of equal desirability. If, by reason of technological progress, a different type of plant would now be substituted, replacement cost is the cost of acquiring the improved type of plant, less an allowance by reason of the inferiority of the existing one; for the new plant would not be one of equal, but of superior, desirability to the existing one. If there has been no technological change, the cost of a new plant of a type similar to the existing one would also be the cost of a superior plant. An old plant is worth less than a new one of similar type, not only if, by reason of its age, it gives poorer or more

the value of the physical property cannot exceed the cost of replacement, however high the earnings may be. It can, however, fall short of replacement cost. If the plant could not earn as much as a fair return on replacement cost, then the latter would cease to be a measure of its value; for, should it be destroyed, there would be no occasion for the owner to incur the cost of replacing it. He has the option to suffer the smaller sacrifice of losing the business. Earnings above a fair return on replacement cost, therefore, can be reduced to such a fair return, without impairing the value of the physical property in the sense in which we are now using "value." Its value would still be measured, as before, by replacement cost. But any further reduction of earnings would impair physical value, for it would bring about a situation in which physical value would be less than it was before. By defining physical value in this way, one could employ the rule of *Smyth* v. *Ames* to safeguard the owner against any loss in physical value, without at the same time completely nullifying the regulatory power. In so employing the rule, the "consideration" that would be "just and right" to give to the element of actual cost would be such consideration only as aids in the ascertainment of replacement cost.

While the rule of *Smyth* v. *Ames* could be used to safeguard against loss of physical value (so defined), such a use would not fulfill the purpose for which the Court professed to invoke the rule. If the property were taken by eminent domain, the owner would be entitled to compensation not only for the physical value as we have defined it, but for the total value of what it lost—that is, the value as a going concern. This sum exceeds the replacement cost by an amount which may be designated as the intangible value if we insist on defining physical value so as to make it distinguishable from the value of the going concern. And as we have seen, the owner would be entitled, on condemnation, to the value of the franchise, as the *Monongahela* case held.[59] However, if regulation is permitted to reduce the earnings to a fair return on replacement cost, it may subject the owner to uncompensated loss of all the intangible value.

expensive service, but even if it does not. Being nearer the end of its useful life, the amount that has to be set aside from its earnings to provide for replacing it has to be spread over a shorter number of years. In other words, a larger amount has to be subtracted each year from the gross earnings, by way of depreciation, than would be necessary if it had a longer life before it. Hence its net earning power is less than that of a new one. So the cost of replacing with an equally desirable substitute is the cost of reproduction new, less an appropriate deduction for depreciation.

[59] 148 U.S. 312 (1893). *Cf. supra*, pp. 469–470.

While insistence on a fair return on physical value (in one sense of the word) is consistent with a power to reduce net earnings, it is difficult to understand upon what theory it can be maintained that an owner may be deprived, without compensation, of the value of intangible property under the police power, while he may be deprived of the value of physical property only by the exercise of the power of eminent domain, which requires compensation. The due process clauses contain no language which recognizes any distinction between physical and intangible property.

But the Court did not always protect the full physical value (measured by replacement cost) from impairment, and in some cases it protected intangible as well as physical value. In 1915, in *Des Moines Gas Co.* v. *Des Moines,*[60] it rejected the company's claim to include in the valuation of its gas mains the sum which it would cost at the time of the regulation to cut through the pavements in order to lay the mains, on the ground that the mains had in fact been laid before the streets had been paved, and that the actual cost of laying them had been less. But the mains, being in place, surely had a value greater than they would have on the surface, and the additional value due to their being in place would surely be measured by what it would cost to place them there. It may be, however, that the Court did not intend to permit the physical value to be reduced and merely misconceived what would have that effect. But in 1921 Justice Holmes, who spoke for the majority in sustaining the emergency rent laws for the District of Columbia in *Block* v. *Hirsh,* was well aware that those laws would impair the value of physical property. He said:

> The fact that tangible property is also visible tends to give rigidity to our conception of our rights in it that we do not attach to others less concretely clothed. But the notion that the former are exempt from the legislative modification required from time to time in civilized life is contradicted not only by the doctrine of eminent domain, under which what is taken is paid for, but by that of the police power in its proper sense, under which property rights may be cut down, and to that extent taken, without pay.[61]

The regulation of rents was sustained despite the fact, which Holmes recognized, that it might deprive the landlord "in part at least of the power of profiting by the sudden influx of people to

60 238 U.S. 153, 171–172 (1915).

61 256 U.S. 135, 155 (1921). Justice McKenna wrote a dissenting opinion with the concurrence of Chief Justice White and Justices Van Devanter and McReynolds. Concurring with Holmes were Justices Day, Pitney, Brandeis, and Clarke.

Washington . . . , and thus of a right usually incident to fortunately situated property—of a part of the value of his property." [62]

The regulation was justified, however, by reason of an emergency. It may be that, apart from emergency, the Court had no intention of permitting the physical value to be reduced.

THE ADDITION OF "GOING VALUE" TO PHYSICAL VALUE

But if the Court did not mean to expose the physical value to impairment at the hands of the regulatory authorities, it soon became clear that it did not intend to confine its protection of value to the physical assets alone. In reaching a rate base, on which the rates must be permitted to yield a fair return, the Court came to hold that certain intangible elements must be added to the physical value. If they were to include all of the value which the going concern had, over and above the value of the physical property, there would be no occasion to ascertain the physical value separately; replacement cost would be irrelevant, and we would be right back in the vicious circle—the earnings to be adjudged with reference to a value which itself depended upon the earnings. For a time, however, it seemed that the Court did not mean to include in the rate base the entire intangible value.

When, in an opinion rendered by Justice Peckham in 1909, in *Willcox* v. *Consolidated Gas Co.*,[63] it sustained a statutory reduction of gas rates, good will was excluded from the valuation. But this was on the questionable ground that good will represents an advantage over competitors and could not exist in the case of a monopoly.[64] Though good will was excluded, the Court approved the inclusion of as much of the value of the franchise as existed at the time of the consolidation of the companies in 1884, on the ground that this value actually existed in 1884 because of the earnings the company was then making from rates which the Court characterized as excessive, that it had been approved by a legislative committee which had been set up to investigate the circumstances of the consolidation and that the stock had since been bought and sold on that basis. The approval of the inclusion of this value was based on the peculiarity of the circumstances, and the Court warned that it should not be taken as a precedent in other cases in which the circumstances were different.[65]

[62] *Id.* at 157. [63] 212 U.S. 19 (1909). [64] *Id.* at 52.
[65] *Id.* at 48.

The Court rejected, however, an increase which the lower court had assigned to the value of the franchise as of the time of the hearing.

Since the value as of 1884 was said to be founded on excessive earnings, since it would be unfavorably affected whenever the legislature "reduced the earnings to a reasonable sum" and "would most certainly not increase," and since the rates actually were finally reduced by the acts under review which, said Justice Peckham, "were in existence when the court below found this increased value of the franchises," the Court was unable to concur in that finding.[66] The regulation itself was thus permitted to destroy whatever increase had taken place in the value of the franchises, and on the basis of its nonexistence at the time of the decision, it was held that there was no such increased value to be protected from regulation. By this circular reasoning the Court was able to permit destruction of part of the franchise value, while still maintaining, on the authority of the *Monongahela* case, that "franchises of this nature are property and cannot be taken, or used by others without compensation. . . . The important question is always one of value." [67] Subsequent rate cases, however, did not include in the valuation anything by reason of franchise value, under that name.

But before long the Court declared that an item called "going value" or "going concern value" must be included whenever its existence has been shown, though good will and franchise value should be kept out. The groundwork for the distinction had already been laid in two cases involving the purchase of utility plants. In the Circuit Court of Appeals, in 1894, Brewer wrote the opinion in *National Waterworks Co.* v. *Kansas City*.[68] The question at issue was the compensation to be paid by the city for the purchase of a plant. Because the franchise had expired, Brewer awarded appreciably less than the capitalized earnings. He insisted, however, that something must be added to cost of reproduction, in order to distinguish "a living and going business" from "a dead structure." The added value, he said, 'was created by the fact of many connections with buildings, with actual supply and actual earnings," and the connections depended upon the will of the owners of the buildings and was "not represented by the mere cost of making such connections." While this added value

[66] 212 U.S. at 47.
[67] *Id.* at 44.
[68] 62 Fed. 853, 865 (8th Cir. 1894). The other members of the court were Sanborn, Cir. J., and Thayer, D.J.

of the "going" business may be distinguishable from that of the franchise, it seems to be nothing other than good will.

The other purchase case, *Omaha* v. *Omaha Water Co.*,[69] was decided in 1910, soon after the *Willcox* case had held that good will could not exist in the case of a monopoly. The purchase was made under an option in the franchise which contained a proviso "that nothing shall be paid for the unexpired franchise of said company." [70] Thus, it would seem that the appraisers appointed under the terms of the franchise should include nothing either for good will or for franchise value. They did, however, include in their award an item for "going value." In sustaining their award, Justice Lurton, referring to this item, said it represented "the difference between a dead plant and a live one." [71] It was, he said, "independent of any franchise to go on, or any mere good will as between such a plant and its customers." While the option, he said, "excluded any value on account of unexpired franchise," still "it did not limit the value to the bare bones of the plant." In the same passage, however, he referred to the allowance for going value as representing the difference between "the cost of duplication, less depreciation, of the elements making up the water company plant, and the commercial value of the business as a going concern." How this commercial value could be thought to be "independent" of the franchise or good will he did not explain. Surely those items form part of the value of the business as a going concern.

Both Brewer and Lurton assumed that replacement cost would measure the value of a dead plant, the "bare bones." But this is not true. A dead plant would be worth much less than the cost of replacing it. It would have only a scrap or salvage value.

In 1912, however, in *Cedar Rapids Gas Light Co.* v. *Cedar Rapids*,[72] the Court, of which Lurton was still a member, seems to have taken the position that in a rate case sufficient consideration is given to going value when the plant is valued on the assumption that it is operating successfully; and that when so valued a claim for the inclusion of an additional element is in effect a claim to good will or franchise value, which should be rejected on the authority of the *Willcox* case. The Court did not feel called upon to make any very thorough analysis, since the state court had dismissed the bill for an

[69] 218 U.S. 180 (1910).

[70] *Id.* at 191.

[71] *Id.* at 202–203.

[72] 223 U.S. 655, 669–670 (1912).

injunction "without prejudice to a later suit after it [the rate-fixing ordinance] should have been given a fair test." On the subject of going value, Justice Holmes, speaking for the Court, said:

Then again, although it is argued that the court excluded going value, the court expressly took into account the fact that the plant was in successful operation. What it excluded was the good will or advantage incident to the possession of a monopoly, so far as that might be supposed to give the plaintiff the power to charge more than a reasonable price. *Willcox* v. *Consolidated Gas Co. of New York,* 212 U.S. 19, 52. An adjustment of this sort under a power to regulate rates has to steer between Scylla and Charybdis. On the one side if the franchise is taken to mean that the most profitable return that could be got, free from competition, is protected by the Fourteenth Amendment, then the power to regulate is null. On the other hand if the power to regulate withdraws the protection of the Amendment altogether, then the property is nought. This is not a matter of economic theory, but of fair interpretation of a bargain. Neither extreme can have been meant. A midway between them must be hit.

In 1915, in *Des Moines Gas Co.* v. *Des Moines,*[73] the Court again took cognizance of the fact that replacement cost represents more than the value of a dead plant. While Justice Day, speaking for the Court, conceded that consideration should be given to the "element of value in an assembled and established plant, doing business and earning money, over one not thus advanced"—an element whose existence he said was "self-evident" [74]—he held at the same time that there was no occasion to include the separate item which the master in the court below had appraised as going value and for which the master had found that a purchaser would be willing to pay. The master, said Day, "had already valued the property in the estimate of what he called its physical value, upon the basis of a plant in actual and successful operation; for he said that otherwise its value would be much less." [75] Day pointed out that the master, in estimating the physical value, had added 15 percent as overheads to the cost of reproducing the separate items. It is not clear whether these overheads were meant to represent what it would cost to assemble the separate items once they were reproduced, or whether they were meant to represent something to be added to replacement cost. Possibly they represented that part of replacement cost which would be caused by the delay in replacing the

[73] 238 U.S. 153 (1915). Lurton had died in 1914. The Court consisted of Chief Justice White and Justices McKenna, Holmes, Day, Hughes, Van Devanter, J. R. Lamar, Pitney, and McReynolds.

[74] 238 U.S. at 165.

[75] *Id.* at 171.

physical plant, over and above the cost of reproducing and assembling the separate elements. The Court did not have to elucidate the matter, for even when the 15 percent was included in the valuation, the rates were held to be valid.

As to the company's claim that the rejected item of going value was based on the costs (long since incurred in the past) of organizing and establishing the business, the Court said that "for aught that appears in the record, these expenses may have been already compensated in rates charged and collected under former ordinances." [76] But if the search is for value, not cost, the question whether costs had been incurred and the question whether they had been compensated would both seem irrelevant. As Justice Brandeis remarked for the Court in 1922, in *Galveston Electric Co.* v. *City of Galveston,*[77] in rejecting a claim for going value based on losses incurred while the business was being developed, "past losses obviously do not tend to prove present values." However this may be, it seems clear that in the *Des Moines* case the Court did not mean to include, under the head of going value, the entire difference between the cost of replacing the physical property and the "commercial value of the business as a going concern." Just what it did mean to include is not so clear. Nor was it made clearer in 1918, in *Denver* v. *Denver Union Water Co.,*[78] where the master below was sustained in apparently including a separate item for going value. It is not certain that the master did in fact add this item to replacement cost, for Justice Pitney referred to a finding that a new plant could not be built for $13,415,899, which is a figure that includes the going value item. And Pitney said that the master "made no allowance for franchise value."

In 1926, however, Justice Butler's opinion for the majority in *McCardle* v. *Indianapolis Water Co.*[79] would lead to the inference that every bit of the commercial value should be included, whether based on the franchise or good will or not, and that the company was entitled to a return on a value measured by profitability, at least if that profitability resulted from rates which, judged by some standard in-

[76] *Id.* at 166.

[77] 258 U.S. 388, 395 (1922).

[78] 246 U.S. 178, 192 (1918). Day was still a member of the Court. The personnel was the same as in the Des Moines case, except that Lamar had been succeeded by Brandeis, and Hughes by Clarke. Brandeis and Clarke concurred in Holmes's dissenting opinion, which was based on the ground that since the franchise had expired the company had no right to be permitted to charge any rates other than whatever the city might prescribe; it had the alternative of going out of business and selling its property as scrap.

[79] 272 U.S. 400, 413-415 (1926).

dependent entirely of the return which they yielded, were reasonable. The commission had reduced the figure for going value considerably below the figure which it had itself assigned to that item, in an opinion rendered less than a year earlier. Holding that there was no warrant for making the reduction, Butler quoted with approval the commission's earlier opinion, in which it referred to going value as the amount which a purchaser would be willing to pay over and above the value of the physical property, in view of "its earning power with low rates, the business it has attached, its fine public relations," and so forth. But any value based on fine public relations would seem to be good will, which earlier cases had held must be excluded. And if value based on earning power is to be protected whenever that earning power comes from rates that are low, we must have some criterion to determine whether they are so "low" than any reduction will be invalid. If we have such a criterion apart from the question whether they yield more than a fair return on value, then the rule of *Smyth* v. *Ames* becomes superfluous. If, on the other hand, they are adjudged low because they yield a low return on value, we are again in the vicious circle: they yield a low rate of return on value, because that value is high; that value is high because the earning power with the rates the company has been charging is great; that earning power is an "earning power with low rates" because the rates yield a low return on a value which they themselves create.

While Butler's conception of going value, however, would involve this circular reasoning, that fact was more or less obscured in this case by the fact that he did not measure it by capitalizing the earnings. The commission, in its earlier opinion, had added to the amount assigned to the physical property 9.5 percent of that amount to cover water rights as well as going value. Butler objected to the commission's subsequent reduction of this percentage, saying:

> The evidence is more than sufficient to sustain 9.5 per cent for going value. And the reported cases showing amounts generally included by commissions and courts to cover intangible elements of value indicate that 10 per cent of the value of the physical elements would be low when the impressive facts reported by the commission in this case are taken into account.

But if the item to be measured is what a purchaser would pay for the property over and above the physical value, in view of its earning power with low rates, why should it be assumed that any conventional percentage of the physical value would measure it? It was, perhaps, to indicate rejection of any such rule-of-thumb measurement that Chief Justice Hughes, when discussing going value in 1933 in *Los Angeles Gas & El. Co.* v. *Railroad Commission*,[80] declared that the function of a court in a confiscation case is "not to lay down a formula, much less to prescribe an arbitrary allowance," and that Justice Cardozo declared in 1934 in *Dayton Power & Light Co.* v. *Public Utilities Commission* [81] that "going value is not something to be read into every balance sheet as a perfunctory addition."

In the *Los Angeles* case the Court sustained an order reducing rates, which was assumed to reduce the company's net revenue by more than a million dollars. The reduced earnings, however, amounted to a fair return on the rate base of $65,500,000 adopted by the commission. In arriving at this rate base the commission included no separate item for going value, although the company contended that more than nine million should have been added. The Court held that the $65,500,000 overestimated the amount attributable to the physical property by at least $5,500,000, and, said Hughes, "the entire excess may be regarded as applicable to whatever intangible value the property had as a going concern." [82] Accordingly, unless the company could show that the going value exceeded $5,500,000, the rate order must be sustained.

Repeating previous assertions of the Court, Hughes agreed that "the element of value in an assembled and established plant" must be considered. It is not likely that he meant this item to include all the intangible value the property might have as a going concern, for, apart from the circular reasoning such an assumption would involve, this would include good will, and Hughes said:

> The going value thus recognized is not to be confused with good will, in the sense of that "element of value which inheres in the fixed and favorable consideration of customers, arising from an established and well-known and well-conducted business," which, as the Court has repeatedly said, is not to be considered in determining whether rates fixed for public service corporations are confiscatory. [Citations.] Nor does this recognition of going value countenance a mere attempt to recoup past losses. *Galveston Electric Co.* v. *Galveston, supra.* . . . The concept of going value is not to be used to escape the just exercise of the regulatory power in fixing rates, and, on the other hand, that authority is not entitled to treat a living organism as nothing more than bare bones.[83]

80 289 U.S. 287, 314 (1933).
81 292 U.S. 290, 309 (1934).
82 289 U.S. at 317.
83 *Id.* at 313–314.

But, as we have seen, no addition to replacement cost would be required in order to avoid treating the property as bare bones. The physical property would not be worth the cost of replacing it if it were so treated.

Hughes seemed to think that some item, however, must be added to replacement cost under the name of going value. But what that item is he did not specify. Its determination "calls for consideration of the history and circumstances of the particular enterprise, and attempts at precise definition have been avoided." [84] No definition, precise or otherwise, is given in the opinion. It was merely held that the company had not proved that it exceeded $5,500,000 in this case. One of its two witnesses who sought to prove a higher value based his calculations on certain arbitrary rules-of-thumb to indicate what a purchaser of the property would be likely to pay above the physical value. The other apparently sought to measure that part of the cost of replacing the property which would represent the loss to the company because of the necessary delay in replacing it. He calculated how much the hypothetical earnings would fall short of 8 percent of the value of the property each year of the hypothetical period during which the hypothetical reproduction would last. But the Court found it "unnecessary to analyze the testimony of these witnesses, as it is obviously too conjectural to justify us in treating the failure to include their estimates as a sufficient basis for a finding of confiscation." [85]

While the majority refrained from defining this item of "going value," which it conceded should be included if it could be proved, Justice Butler in his dissenting opinion [86] reverted to the conception of it which he had expressed in the *McCardle* case, as based on earning power under low rates. The rates which the company had been charging before they were ordered reduced were "low in comparison with those generally collected for like service" and much lower than those which the company had itself previously charged. Knowing for these or other reasons, without the aid of *Smyth* v. *Ames,* that any lower rates would be confiscatory, he declared that "if permitted to charge

[84] 289 U.S. at 314.

[85] *Id.* at 319. In St. Joseph Stock Yard Co. v. United States, 298 U.S. 38, 62–63 (1936), the Secretary of Agriculture was sustained, in an opinion by Hughes, in treating a calculation of going value, which the company's witness made by a somewhat similar method, as "in no real sense evidence."

[86] 289 U.S. at 324–326. Justice Sutherland joined in this dissent. Those who concurred with Hughes were Justices McReynolds, Brandeis, Stone, Roberts, and Cardozo. Justice Van Devanter took no part in the case.

reasonable rates, or those merely high enough to be non-confiscatory, plaintiff will continue to be able to earn an ample rate of return upon the value of the property." Hence "millions should be added to the cost figures applicable to the physical items in order to find the value of plaintiff's property, the amount protected by the Constitution." So, after making an expensive and meticulous calculation of the replacement cost of the physical items, we subtract that figure from the value based on earnings from rates which we already know to be "merely high enough to be non-confiscatory" in order to find the item of going value. Having found this item by subtracting physical value from the capitalized earnings, we proceed to add it to the physical value we have just subtracted. The procedure obviously makes the physical value, or replacement cost, irrelevant. We might as well adopt once and for all as a rate base the value based on earnings from the rates just high enough to be non-confiscatory. But we cannot arrive at this figure unless we know in advance what such rates would be. And if we know in advance what rates would be confiscatory, why do we have to resort to the rule of *Smyth* v. *Ames* in order to reach a conclusion with which we started out? To Butler, however, though the conclusion could be reached in advance, it still seemed necessary to go through all the motions.

CIRCULAR REASONING AS EXEMPLIFIED BY THE DENVER STOCK YARD CASE (1938)

In 1935, in *West* v. *Chesapeake & Potomac Tel. Co.*,[87] although there was no discussion of going value, the Court suggested that there it was unnecessary to value the different elements in a company's property piecemeal. "It is to be remembered," said Justice Roberts, "that such a property as that here under consideration is a great integrated aggregate of many and diverse elements; is not primarily for sale in the market, but for devotion to the public use now and for the indefinite future; and has, so far as its market value is concerned, no real resemblance to a bushel of wheat or a ton of iron." What he said is undoubtedly true, for while cost of reproduction might measure the value of a bushel of wheat or a ton of iron, it would be only by the merest coincidence that it would measure the value of such an "in-

[87] 295 U.S. 662, 672 (1935). Justice Stone wrote a dissenting opinion, in which he was joined by Brandeis and Cardozo. Those concurring with Roberts were Chief Justice Hughes and Justices Van Devanter, McReynolds, Sutherland, and Butler.

tegrated aggregate." Yet the criticism which Roberts leveled at the commission was for its failure to base the valuation on "such factors as historical cost and cost of reproduction."

In 1938, however, in *Denver Union Stock Yard Co.* v. *United States*,[88] Justice Butler, speaking now for the Court, applied the same reasoning which he had applied in his dissent in the *Los Angeles* case, though without making separate appraisals of the different items of property. Charges fixed by the Secretary of Agriculture were sustained, which resulted in a considerable reduction of earnings. The reduced charges would yield a fair return on what the Secretary called "the fair value of the property of respondent as a going concern." This "value" was found by ascertaining the replacement cost—the present value of the land plus the cost of reproduction new of the structures less depreciation. In reaching this figure, according to the Court, "consideration was given to the element of going concern value." [89] The meaning of this is somewhat obscure. The idea is, perhaps, that the Secretary assumed that the physical property would be worth the cost of replacing it only because the company was a going concern. But the reason given by the Court for sustaining the rates was not based on any distinction between physical and intangible property. In fact, the Court's reasoning would seem to make replacement cost wholly irrelevant. Rejecting the company's claim that the valuation should have included a separate item for going concern value, Butler cited the *Chesapeake & Potomac Telephone* case as authority for the proposition that "the value of the going concern" (on which it was said the company was constitutionally entitled to a fair return) is "single in substance" and "not necessarily to be appraised by adding to cost figures attributable to mere physical plant something to cover the value of the business." He went on to say:

> Value depends upon use and is measured, or at least significantly indicated, by the profitableness of present and prospective service rendered at rates that are just and reasonable as between the owner of and those served by the property. [Citing cases.] It is elementary that value of a going concern may be less than, equal to, or more than, present cost of plant less deprecia-

[88] 304 U.S. 470 (1938). Justice Cardozo took no part in the case. Justice Black concurred in the result, without opinion. Chief Justice Hughes and Justices McReynolds, Brandeis, Stone, Roberts, and Reed would appear from the report to have concurred in Butler's opinion. It is possible, however, that some of them may have thought it inopportune to register dissent from the reasoning, for it is difficult to believe that Hughes, Brandeis, or Stone could have failed to recognize the fallacies in it.

[89] 304 U.S. at 478.

tion plus necessary supplies and working capital. [Citing cases.] Appellant's plant without business, present or prospective, would be worth much less than the cost figures found by the Secretary to represent value. Appellant's claim that the rate base includes nothing on account of going concern value is without foundation in fact.[90]

After the reduction, the value of the going concern must have been measured by the profitableness under the reduced rates. Before the reduction, the profitableness was greater, and so too was the value of the going concern, for that value is measured by profitableness, not merely under rates that are just and reasonable, but under whatever rates can be reasonably expected. And the previous rates, however unjust and unreasonable they may have been, were entirely lawful until the order was made which reduced them.[91] By pretending that

[90] *Id.* at 479.

[91] Of course, there is no constitutional protection, even as against the power of eminent domain, for any element of value which depends on the continuance of unlawful practices. If rates higher than "just and reasonable" ones were unlawful before the Secretary ordered their reduction, then the establishment of just and reasonable rates would not destroy any lawful element of value. But on this assumption we could not, without reasoning in a circle, pronounce any given rates to be just and reasonable, merely because they yielded a fair return on a value based on just and reasonable rates. For an early and (in the view of the present writer) unsuccessful attempt to avoid the vicious circle, see the opinions rendered by Justice Savage in the Supreme Judicial Court of Maine, in two purchase cases in which it was assumed that water companies were under a common-law duty to charge only just and reasonable rates. Kennebec Water District v. Waterville, 97 Me. 185 (1902); Brunswick & Topsham Water District v. Maine Water Co., 99 Me. 371 (1904).

There was a common-law notion that a few special businesses, such as common carriers (but not stockyards) were under a duty to charge only just and reasonable rates. At the suit of a shipper a court, finding the rate charged by the carrier to have been unlawful, would award reparation for the overcharge. The court had to make some determination as to whether the rate was reasonable. And in 1894 Justice Brewer assumed that a court was to apply the same criterion of reasonableness when determining whether a statutory rate is valid. "The province of the courts is not changed," he said in Reagan v. Farmers' Loan & Trust Co., 154 U.S. 362, 397, "nor the limit of judicial inquiry altered, because the legislature instead of the carrier prescribes the rates." In other words, the legislative rate is valid only if it is declaratory of the obligation which the common law already imposed on the carrier.

It still seems to be the theory of the law that when, under the Transportation Act, the Interstate Commerce Commission awards a shipper reparation for an overcharge, it is acting judicially and declaring that the rate paid was unlawful when charged. But when the Commission itself prescribes a rate for the future, it is now the accepted theory that it is legislating—making that lawful which was hitherto unlawful, or making that unlawful which was hitherto lawful. See the discussion by Justice Roberts for the majority in Arizona Grocery Co. v. Atchison &c. Ry. Co., 284 U.S. 370 (1932). See also Hale, *Commissions, Rates, and Policies* (1940) 53 HARV. L. REV. 1103, 1105–1108. The power to regulate is more than a power to declare what was already lawful. It includes a power to change the law as to what it is lawful to charge. There would seem to be no question that the rates which the stock yard company had been charging were lawful until the Secretary ordered their reduction.

this greater element of lawful value did not exist, because it was the product of unjust and unreasonable rates, the Court permitted its destruction without compensation and was apparently unaware that it was thus denying to the company the protection to which it would have been entitled had its property been appropriated by eminent domain. It is only as much of the value as depends upon profitableness under just and reasonable rates that it protected. And this value depends in no way on replacement cost—since it "may be less than, equal to, or more than" such cost. The two principal "matters for consideration" enumerated in *Smyth* v. *Ames* are to be ignored—actual cost and replacement cost.

But if value measured by profitableness under just and reasonable rates is to be protected,[92] we must have some way of knowing what rates are to be considered just and reasonable. In *McCardle* v. *Indianapolis Water Co.* Justice Butler would protect a value based on earning power at rates which were characterized as "low"—apparently as judged by rates charged by comparable companies. And in his dissent in the *Los Angeles* case he was more explicit in pronouncing the rates which the company had been charging just and reasonable on the basis of a comparison with those charged elsewhere. In the *Denver Stock Yard* case he found the evidence for making such a comparison lacking. Since the Secretary's order would obviously leave intact a value measured by profitableness under the Secretary's rates, Butler would seem to place on the company the burden of proving by comparison with other companies that such rates were less than just and reasonable.

Appellant does not claim [he said] that its past operations clearly reflect excellence of service at low cost per unit in comparison with results attained by other stockyards, or that conditions affecting performance give dependable assurance of future growth and capacity to earn net returns at relatively low rates. See e.g., *McCardle* v. *Indianapolis Water Co.*, ... Its evidence falls far short of condemning as arbitrary and confiscatory the

[92] In 1925 Butler had maintained that the fact that rates might be just and reasonable did not preclude a finding that substantially lower ones might be constitutional. In Banton v. Belt Line Ry. Corp., 268 U.S. 413, 423, he asserted that "rates substantially higher than the line between validity and unconstitutionality may be deemed to be just and reasonable, and not excessive or extortionate." Perhaps, in the Denver case, he meant to imply that the value of the going concern was to be measured by profitableness of service rendered at the lowest of the several rates that could be deemed to be just and reasonable, within what has been characterized as the "zone of reasonableness." *Cf.* Cardozo, J., in United States v. Chicago &c. R.R., 294 U.S. 499, 506 (1935).

Secretary's refusal to add a separate amount to his rate base to cover going concern value.[93]

If the reasonableness of rates can be judged by comparison with those charged elsewhere, and if a value measured by profitableness under reasonable rates is to be protected, then any rate order which reduces the profits from rates already determined to be reasonable is invalid. No ascertainment of value is needed to reach this conclusion. And the statement in *Smyth* v. *Ames* must be rejected, that the basis of all calculations as to the reasonableness of rates "must be the fair value of the property used." On that basis we cannot determine fair value, if it is measured by profitableness under just and reasonable rates, without first determining the reasonableness of rates on some entirely different basis. And, on Butler's reasoning, once we have found what rates would be reasonable on this other basis, we know without further inquiry that any rates yielding less profit would be invalid. No room is left for invoking *Smyth* v. *Ames*.

RECOGNITION OF THE "FAIR VALUE" FALLACY IN THE HOPE NATURAL GAS CASE (1944)

So powerful, however, was the hold of the superstition which supported *Smyth* v. *Ames* that the majority of the Court went slowly in defying it. In 1939 a reduction by a state commission was sustained in *Driscoll* v. *Edison Light & Power Co.*,[94] but on the ground, in Justice Reed's opinion for the majority, that the reduced rates yielded a fair return on a "value" at least as high as depreciated reproduction cost. Justice Frankfurter, in a concurring opinion in which Justice Black joined, complained that "the Court's opinion appears to give new vitality needlessly to the mischievous formula for fixing utility rates in *Smyth* v. *Ames*." [95] Again, in 1942, a reduction of natural gas rates by the Federal Power Commission was sustained, in *FPC* v. *Natural Gas Pipeline Co.*[96] The Commission had fixed the rates on the basis of a valuation measured by reproduction cost. Chief Justice Stone, for the majority, declared that "the Constitution does not bind rate-making bodies to the service of any single formula or combination of formulas," that these bodies are free "to make pragmatic adjustments,"

[93] 304 U.S. at 480–481.

[94] 307 U.S. 104 (1939).

[95] *Id.* at 122. The other members of the Court who presumably concurred in Reed's opinion were Chief Justice Hughes and Justices McReynolds, Butler, Stone, Roberts, and Douglas.

[96] 315 U.S. 575 (1942).

and that "if the Commission's order, as applied to the facts before it and viewed in its entirety, produces no arbitrary result, our inquiry is at an end." [97] The concurring opinion of Justices Black, Douglas, and Murphy interpreted these statements as freeing the Commission "from the compulsion of admitting evidence on reproduction cost or of giving any weight to that element of 'fair value.' " [98] Nevertheless, the majority opinion was hardly as explicit as this. The rates were sustained largely on conventional grounds, and cases stemming from *Smyth* v. *Ames* were cited as authoritative.[99]

It was in the concurring opinion that Black, Douglas, and Murphy thought this an appropriate occasion to lay the ghost of *Smyth* v. *Ames*. After quoting Harlan's dictum in that case, they said:

> This theory derives from principles of eminent domain. [Citations] In condemnation cases the "value of property, generally speaking, is determined by its productiveness,—the profits which its use brings to the owner." *Monongahela Navigation Co.* v. *United States*, ... *Cf. Consolidated Rock Products Co.* v. *Du Bois*, 312 U.S. 510, 525, 526. But those principles have no place in rate regulation. In the first place, the value of a going concern in fact depends on earnings under whatever rates may be anticipated. The present fair value rulc creates but offers no solution to the dilemma that value depends upon the rates fixed and the rates upon value. [Citations] In the second place, when property is taken under the power of eminent domain the owner is "entitled to the full money equivalent of the property taken, and thereby to be put in as good position pecuniarily as it would have occupied, if its property had not been taken." *United States* v. *New River Collieries Co.*, ... But in rate-making the owner does not have any such protection. We know without attempting any valuation that if earnings are reduced the value will be less. But that does not stay the hand of the legislature or its administrative agency in making rate reductions.[100]

This clear exposition of the fallacy of the "fair value" rule of *Smyth* v. *Ames* is contained in a minority opinion. The majority said nothing to contradict it or, for that matter, to endorse it. Since the rates could be sustained without overruling *Smyth* v. *Ames*, the majority seemed to think the time not ripe for overruling it. However, when *Federal Power Commission* v. *Hope Natural Gas Co.*[101] was decided, on January 3, 1944, this easy course was not open. The Commission, instead of basing rates on reproduction cost, as in the *Pipeline*

97 315 U.S. at 586.

98 *Id.* at 606.

99 For a discussion of the case see Hale, *Does the Ghost of Smyth v. Ames Still Walk?* (1942) 55 HARV. L. REV. 1116.

100 315 U.S. at 603.

101 320 U.S. 591 (1944).

case, had professed to base them on the actual prudent investment and had refused to place any reliance on reproduction cost. It was for this reason that the Circuit Court of Appeals had set the order aside. No one contended that the rates fixed would yield a fair return on "present value." Yet the Supreme Court sustained them, in an opinion written by Justice Douglas, who was one of the authors of the concurring opinion in the *Pipeline* case. This time he had the concurrence not only of Black and Murphy but also of Rutledge, who had succeeded Byrnes since the *Pipeline* decision was rendered, and of Stone. Without mentioning *Smyth* v. *Ames*, the "fair value" rule was definitely repudiated,[102] as was the notion that rate regulation must refrain from reducing the value of the property. And, as in the *Pipeline* minority opinion, it was recognized that Justice Butler's notion was wrong, that value depended only on earnings from just and reasonable rates, rather than on those from whatever rates might be anticipated. The Court said:

> The fixing of prices, like other applications of the police power, may reduce the value of the property which is being regulated. But the fact that the value is reduced does not mean that the regulation is invalid. [Citations] It does, however, indicate that "fair value" is the end process of ratemaking not the starting point as the Circuit Court of Appeals held. The heart of the matter is that rates cannot be made to depend upon "fair value" when the value of the going enterprise depends on earnings under whatever rates may be anticipated.[103]

The decision was not unanimous. Justice Roberts took no part. Justice Reed's dissent was based on the ground that the Commission departed, not from the constitutional, but from the statutory standard "added by" the Natural Gas Act of 1938.[104] That Act provided that the rates should be "just and reasonable." Congress legislated, thought Reed, "in the light of the relation of fair and reasonable to fair value and reasonable return." And, "until Congress changes the standards for the agencies, these rate making bodies should continue the conventional theory of rate making." Reed would, however, permit a somewhat unconventional use of the conventional theory, for he had no objection to the Commission's use of actual cost as the rate base in this case. Its determination of the rate base on actual cost "is to me a

102 "Rates which enable the company to operate successfully," said Justice Douglas at 605, "to maintain its financial integrity, to attract capital, and to compensate its investors for the risks assumed certainly cannot be condemned as invalid, even though they might produce only a meager return on the so-called 'fair value' rate base."

103 320 U.S. at 601.

104 *Id.* at 620.

determination of fair value." His objection to the Commission's rate base was only that it failed to include the cost of certain property which, before the period of regulation, had been charged to operating expense. He seemed to recognize that as far as the Constitution is concerned Congress is free to depart from "the conventional theory" of *Smyth* v. *Ames*.

Justice Jackson, who wrote a more elaborate dissenting opinion, based on his interpretation of the statutory standard of "just and reasonable," did not believe that even the statute required conformity to *Smyth* v. *Ames*. In fact, he commenced his opinion with the statement: "Certainly the theory of the court below that ties rate-making to the fair-value-reproduction-cost formula should be overruled as in conflict with *Federal Power Commission* v. *Natural Gas Pipeline Co.*" [105] And Justice Frankfurter, whose briefer dissent was largely an endorsement of Jackson's views, spoke of "the hodge-podge of the rule in *Smyth* v. *Ames*." [106]

Thus, in the view of the minority, as well as the majority, of those who participated in the *Hope* case, the doctrine that governments are powerless to reduce rates below the point where they yield a fair return on present value, a doctrine which judicial casuistry had inserted in the Constitution, is no longer there. As in the case of other exercises of the police power, courts and commissions no longer have to pretend that regulations of rates, to be valid, must leave the owner in as good a pecuniary position as if he were unregulated. Limitations which are appropriate to an exercise of the power of eminent domain no longer have to be applied illusively to the exercise of a power designed to correct an economic maladjustment. The *Hope* case has authoritatively removed a spurious constitutional barrier to intelligent rate regulation—a barrier which could not serve its professed purpose of protecting value from impairment, but merely served to obfuscate the whole process of regulation, to make it needlessly expensive and time-consuming, to divert attention from a realistic appraisal of the conflicting interest of investors and consumers, and to stultify the reasoning processes of the judiciary. Since the removal of this constitutional barrier commissions and legislatures have been free to formulate realistic economic policies to govern the relations between public utilities or other properties and the public.

[105] 320 U.S. at 628.

[106] *Id.* at 627.

XVI

UTILITY REGULATION AND TAXATION AS CORRECTIVES OF ECONOMIC MALADJUSTMENTS

DISSIPATION of the fog generated by *Smyth* v. *Ames* makes it possible to take a fresh view of the problems of economic policy involved in determining how much the owners of public utilities, and indeed of other property as well, should be empowered to earn.

SCRUTINY OF PROPERTY-INCOMES NECESSITATED BY UTILITY REGULATION

Despite the early position of the Supreme Court, described in the preceding chapter, it must now be clear that the regulation of public utility rates involves a readjustment of the values of utility properties. To be intelligent, the readjustment must be based on policies of some kind concerning the proper economic relationship between the owners of utility property and the rest of the public. It cannot be based on the assumption that the relationship which now exists is a proper one, or there would be no need for regulation. Nor can it be based on the assumption that the relationship between the general public and the owners of property which has not yet been placed in the "public utility" category is necessarily a proper one, for, as was said in the *Nebbia* case, "there is no closed class or category of businesses affected with a public interest." [1] Until 1944, however, when the *Hope* case [2] was decided, commissions were hampered in any inquiry into property relationships by the supposed necessity of making rates conform to the fallacious and elusive formula of yielding "a fair return on the fair value of the property"—a formula originally designed to preclude any readjustment whatsoever of property values. But the *Hope* decision would seem to render the legislative branches of government, federal and state, as free within their respective spheres "to adopt whatever economic policy may reasonably be deemed to promote public welfare," when they determine what the rates of a regulated company should be, as they were said to be in the *Nebbia* case, when they determine whether any regulation at all of the prices of any given business is called for. In either case, the chosen policy might be set aside on constitutional grounds, if it seemed to the courts arbitrary beyond the limits of judicial tolerance. Meanwhile, if the legislature has proclaimed no policy more precise than that the rates should be "just and reasonable," and if the courts of the jurisdiction have read no specific economic policy into those words, it would seem incumbent on the regulatory commission to formulate economic policies itself and to apply those policies to the regulation of the rates entrusted to it, unless and until the court gives a different interpretation to the statute or the legislature revises it to embody a different policy.

What do considerations of economic policy suggest as to the return that utility companies should be permitted to earn?

CURRENT AND CAPITAL COSTS OF THE SERVICE

There seems to be general agreement on the policy that the rates should at least cover the costs of operating the plant.[3] Controversy

1 Roberts, J., in Nebbia v. New York, 291 U.S. 502, 536 (1934), discussed in Chap. XIII, *supra.*

2 Federal Power Commission v. Hope Natural Gas Co., 320 U.S. 591 (1944), discussed in Chap. XV, *supra.*

3 However, Frederic G. Dorety, in *The Function of Reproduction Cost in Public Utility Valuation and Rate Making* (1923) 37 HARV. L. REV. 173, advanced a theory under which rates would not necessarily be set high enough to cover the operating costs of the existing utility. His theory would fix for the existing utility the rates which would have to be charged by a hypothetical utility, entering the field at the time of regulation,

arises over the amount they should yield in addition. A company which could not collect from its customers the current cost of operating would soon have to go out of business. But the cost of operating the plant is by no means the only cost involved in supplying the service. The plant has to be constructed in the first place, and large portions of it have to be retired at intervals and replaced with new units. Unless the cost of making these replacements is fairly uniform from year to year, we cannot expect it to be met entirely by those who happen to buy the service in the particular years when the replacements are made. Provision for future replacements is customarily made in advance in the form of an annual depreciation charge, which is included in the operating expenses.[4] As with the other operating expenses, there is general agreement that an appropriate allowance for depreciation should be covered by the rates, though there has been some controversy as to how much of an allowance would be appropriate.[5]

The principal controversy, however, revolves about the amount of net earnings, over and above the operating expenses and depreciation, which a company should be permitted to obtain from its customers. It is only by providing the company with net earnings that the customers pay anything toward the initial cost of constructing the plant. This cost is as truly part of the cost of furnishing the service as are the

---

in order to meet the operating costs which that new utility would incur, plus a return sufficient to attract the capital which that new utility would require. If technological progress has been rapid since the existing plant was built, the cost of operating a new utility might be greatly reduced, and the rates sufficient for that new utility might not suffice to cover even the operating costs of the existing one, let alone yield it any return on its investment. This effect Mr. Dorety's proposal might minimize in practice, for "In the absence of an affirmative showing that equally efficient service would be rendered by a more economical substitute, the presumption should be that the existing plant would have to be reproduced." *Id.* at pp. 187–188.

[4] In large complex plants, after an initial period in which few, if any, major replacements have to be made, the cost of such replacements year by year may be fairly uniform. It has been argued accordingly that in such cases there is no need to provide in advance for replacements, since such costs can be charged to the operating expense of the year in which they occur, the only function of a depreciation allowance being to spread uniformly over the years those costs which occur at irregular intervals.

[5] In 1930 the Court held in United Railways Co. v. West, 280 U.S. 234, that the annual depreciation allowance must be based on the present cost of replacement or on "present value" (which the Court erroneously assumed to be the same thing), in order that the company might be able to keep its plant intact; and that if the original cost of the depreciable property was less than the present cost of reproducing it, an allowance calculated only to return the original cost at the termination of the property's useful life was insufficient. This holding was expressly overruled in the Hope case, 320 U.S. 591, 606 (1944), and an allowance based on original cost held sufficient.

operating expenses. Unlike the operating expenses, however, the customers cannot be expected to pay this cost in the years when it is incurred nor can they pay for the original construction in advance, as they can for future replacements of retired property. The cost of the original construction must be met from capital contributed by the investors, who can be induced to contribute it only if they can hope to obtain deferred payments from the customers. These deferred payments, which reach the investors in the form of interest on the bonds and dividends on the stock, can only come from the company's net earnings.[6]

It is not necessary for the company to pay back any of the principal from its earnings. When bonds mature, it can redeem them from the proceeds of a new issue, while continuing to earn enough to pay the interest on these new bonds, in lieu of that which it no longer has to pay on those which have matured. And the company never has to pay the stockholders the principal of their investment, unless it goes out of business. A stockholder who wishes to recover his capital must do so by selling his stock to a new investor, at a price depending upon the market estimates of future dividends. He cannot get it from the company. In the case neither of bonds nor of stock, then, is it incumbent on the company to exact anything from its customers to repay any part of the principal. It is incumbent on it to exact only enough to pay the investors a continuous series of annual returns on their investments. It is the prospect of obtaining these annual returns which gives to the property whose ownership enables them to accrue, whatever market value it may have. If we ignore for the present any change in the purchasing power of the dollar, we can say that the consumers have been and are paying the full annual cost of serving them if the returns suffice and have continuously sufficed to give the property a value equal to what the investors contributed.

Under the rule of *Smyth* v. *Ames*,[7] however, the permissible net return was not determined with a view to make it conform to the annual equivalent of the capital cost of the plant. The process of determining the number of dollars which the rates must be permitted to yield consisted of taking a percentage (called the fair rate of return), not of the capital cost, but of the "fair value." The resulting figure would

[6] The term "net earnings" in utility regulation does not imply (as it does in some other usages) a deduction of interest charges from the gross. The interest on the bonds is paid out of the net earnings, not deducted from the gross in order to ascertain the net.

[7] 169 U.S. 466, 546 (1898), discussed at length in Chap. XV.

only by accident indicate the annual capital cost of rendering the service unless both the percentage and the rate base were determined with the view of arriving at that cost. But while the percentage (the fair rate of return) was chosen with that aim in view, the rate base was not. Thus, Justice Butler was discussing only the fair rate of return when in 1923 in *Bluefield Water Works &c. Co.* v. *Public Service Commission,* he said:

> The return should be reasonably sufficient to assure confidence in the financial soundness of the utility and should be adequate, under efficient and economical management, to maintain and support its credit and enable it to raise the money necessary for the proper discharge of its public duties.[8]

But this rate of return he did not apply in this case to "the money necessary for the proper discharge of its public duties." That would be measured by the actual cost of its property. The rate of return was applied to a rate base considerably higher. The higher rate base was adopted because there had been an increase in the hypothetical cost of reproducing the property. There is no reason to suppose that this increase in a cost which the company never had to incur, and never will have to,[9] would necessitate a higher return than otherwise, in order to enable the company to maintain its credit and to raise the necessary money or to assure confidence in the financial soundness of the utility. The use of the *Smyth-Ames* rate base is inconsistent with any attempt to make the net earnings conform to these criteria. These indicate the annual equivalent of the capital costs, but they were not the ones applied under the *Smyth-Ames* regime for arriving at the final amount of net earnings to be permitted. They were applied in arriving at only one of the factors from which that final figure was derived, but were ignored in arriving at the other factor.

DIFFERENTIATION BETWEEN PAST AND FUTURE INVESTORS

There may be sound reasons of policy, however, for permitting the earnings, in some circumstances, to exceed what would be necessary to cover the costs of rendering the service. Those who will be adversely

[8] 262 U.S. 679, 693 (1923).

[9] Of course, the company will have to replace portions of the property when their useful life ends; but the cost of doing so will be met from the depreciation fund, or, if that proves insufficient, from additional capital, which will from that time on constitute part of the actual cost (not reproduction cost). Justice Butler was speaking, not of the proper allowance for depreciation, but of what should be permitted over and above that allowance.

affected by a reduction of net earnings are the present stockholders, not necessarily the ones who originally contributed the capital for the acquisition of the plant. The company may have been permitted for a long time to charge rates well above the costs of the service. As a result, its securities may have been selling at prices much higher than the amounts originally contributed. This would not have been so had the recent purchasers been warned that the rates would be reduced to the level of costs (including the annual equivalent of the capital costs). The rates may have been high enough to attract much more capital than the amount originally advanced. But the additional capital which the recent purchasers of the stock invested did not go into the hands of the company to be used for adding to its equipment. It was no part of the necessary cost of the service. It overflowed into the pockets of those who sold their stock at the advanced prices. To allow a return sufficient to attract this overflow capital is to compel the customers to pay investors for more than any costs which the investors have incurred for the benefit of the customers. In this respect it differs sharply from returns commensurate with investments made directly to the company to enable it to perform its duties.

However, while the premium paid for stock by recent purchasers, based on the expectation that returns in excess of those needed to attract the company's capital will continue, is a cost which has conferred no benefit on the customers, it is nevertheless a cost to these recent purchasers. Many of them made bona fide investments in this stock in the expectation that the rates would either not be regulated at all or would be regulated pursuant to a policy which would permit continuance of most of the accustomed earnings. They had no warning, at the time when they made their investments, that a different policy would be pursued. To apply such a policy now would work a real hardship on them. The benefit it would confer on the customers would be at the expense of those who had paid full value for their shares, not at the expense of those earlier investors who had reaped the benefit from the excessive rates which had been permitted without paying anyone for that benefit and will not now be affected by any regulation of the rates. Moreover, if savings banks and insurance companies have invested heavily in the stocks, any drastic reduction in their values may spread widespread havoc.

Such a situation presents the regulatory authorities with a dilemma. If the return is to be made commensurate only with the capital cost of supplying the service, there will be hardship to the unwarned bona fide investors. If, on the other hand, the hardship is to be mitigated at the expense of the customers, the latter will be required to pay more than would otherwise be necessary in the future, because they have been overcharged in the past. As to properties with respect to which such a situation has already arisen, there is no ideally satisfactory escape from the dilemma. We cannot go to the extreme of assuring investors that what they have paid in good faith for their investments will under no circumstances be reduced in value. All buyers of property have to take some risks that its value may be reduced by an exercise of the police power, and in this respect the regulation of rates does not differ from other exercises of that power. Even under *Smyth* v. *Ames,* reductions of net earnings were not held to be conclusive of invalidity. Some compromise has to be reached.

The rule of *Smyth* v. *Ames* is not a satisfactory compromise, nor is the basing of rates on replacement cost even without the other elements whose "consideration" was called for by that rule. In many instances, it is true, the replacement-cost principle would protect investors from the full force of the hardships which an actual cost principle would involve. But in case replacement cost had declined, it would subject them to even greater hardships, and the hardship inherent in an actual cost base would be just as great if replacement cost had remained stationary as if it had advanced, provided the expected net earnings were as great which had induced the investment. When a given proportion of the value of the property is wiped out, it is of no comfort to the investor to be told that what was destroyed was only the value of the intangibles and that the value of the physical property remains intact. It makes no difference to him what part of the value of the stock he purchases is physical, what part intangible. He makes his investment in view of the earnings he hopes to get, without making any such unrealistic distinctions. Moreover, if replacement cost were adopted, the company would in many cases be permitted to obtain returns sufficient not only to avoid inflicting hardship upon those who had already invested but also to increase the value beyond what they had paid. Then, if they were to sell out at the higher price, there would be a new crop of innocent investors to be protected.

The most satisfactory way out would be to announce a principle which would warn investors that the companies would be permitted from now on to earn only enough to pay stated returns on some compromise rate base for their existing property, plus sufficient on new investments to attract the capital—sufficient, that is, to add to the market value of the property, at the critical time when the decision to invest is called for, a sum equal to the amount to be attracted. Companies established after the announcement of such a policy would be permitted to earn a return based on cost. Companies already established would be permitted a return on the compromise rate base, plus the cost of any subsequent additions to the plant. Neither old nor new investors would thereafter obtain increments in value merely because hypothetical replacement costs might rise in the future. The customers' freedom to enjoy the service would be limited only by the requirement that they pay its cost, plus the return on the compromise valuation of the pre-existing properties. They would not meet the additional impediment of a requirement to pay in the future a return on a rate base which expands without reference to any additional cost of the service.

The denial of such an increment will work no hardship to new investors comparable to that which would often result from the application of the cost principle to properties whose present owners had bought in the expectation that present earnings in excess of cost would be permitted to continue. The new investors would have ample warning before making their investments that their returns would be limited to what was necessary to attract their capital. As to those who bought stock in the existing companies before the new principle was announced, if the compromise valuation exceeds what would be required by the cost principle they may continue to enjoy part of the increments already accrued for which they have paid. They may not enjoy it all if that compromise valuation falls short of the market value which resulted from the expectation of larger earnings. The denial to them, as to new investors, of the future speculative increment from their utility investments which might accrue to them under the replacement cost rule should replacement cost rise, or of an increment comparable to that which fortunate owners of land in unregulated uses may get, will place them in no worse position than anyone else with money to invest, who does not already own land destined to increase in value. If they prefer a more speculative investment, they can readily sell their utility stocks in the market and buy land with the proceeds.

The desirability of thus making a separation between the past and the future has been strongly urged by several writers.[10] Some commissions made attempts, after price levels had risen during the First World War, to give differential treatment to property installed before, and property installed after, the war. The Wisconsin Railroad Commission adopted in some cases what it called the "split inventory" method, which it described in 1921 as consisting "in applying pre-war normal prices to property installed before the war and investment cost on all property installed since." [11] But while a valuation made by this method was sustained by the state supreme court in 1923, that case was overruled in 1927,[12] on the authority of the *McCardle* case.[13] In the test case of the St. Louis & O'Fallon Railway,[14] the Interstate Commerce Commission made a valuation of the railroad's property as of December 31, 1920, 1921, 1922, and 1923, for the purpose of determining how much the earnings in each of those years exceeded 6 percent on the "value" of the property "for rate-making purposes"; for under the so-called recapture clause of the Transportation Act of 1920, one-half of the excess was to be paid over to the United States. The commission started with a valuation as of 1919, made up of the 1914 reproduction cost of structures existing in 1914, plus the actual cost of structures installed since that time, plus land valued as of 1919. This initial valuation it brought up to date for each of the years in question by adding at cost the net additions to the structures and revising the land values to conform to the current values of adjacent lands. Had it not been for the inconsistency of treating land differently from structures,[15] the case might have been taken as the announcement of a policy to allow a return on the cost of all investments made after

10 See, for example, I. L. SHARFMAN, THE AMERICAN RAILROAD PROBLEM (1921), pp. 301–305; JOHN MAURICE CLARK, SOCIAL CONTROL OF BUSINESS (1926), p. 381; James C. Bonbright, *Progress and Poverty in Current Literature on Valuation* (1926) 40 Q.J. OF ECONOMICS 295, 297–302.

11 City of Tomahawk v. Tomahawk Light, Tel. & Imp. Co., P.U.R. 1922A, 259, 262–263 (1921).

12 Waukesha Gas & El. Co. v. Railroad Commission, 181 Wis. 281 (1923), overruled in case of same name, 191 Wis. 565 (1927). Meanwhile another valuation made by this method had been rejected in Ashland Water Co. v. Railroad Commission of Wisconsin, 7 F. 2d 924 (D. Wis. 1925), on the ground that the valuation so made failed to give to reproduction cost the consideration required by the United States Supreme Court.

13 272 U.S. 400 (1926), discussed in Chap. XV.

14 Excess Income of St. Louis & O'Fallon Ry. Co., 124 I.C.C. 3 (1927).

15 The Commission's inconsistency was forcefully pointed out by Professor I. L. Sharfman in his treatise, 3a THE INTERSTATE COMMERCE COMMISSION (1935), 292, especially footnote 347.

1914, with the freezing of investments made prior thereto at the 1914 reproduction cost figure. Reproduction cost of the structures installed after 1919 probably did not exceed the actual cost figures taken, but the cost of reproducing in the twenties the structures which existed in 1914, if we assume that identical structures would have been reproduced, doubtless exceeded the 1914 figures, because of the advance in the price level. Largely for this reason the Supreme Court upset the commission's order in 1929,[16] as deviating from the statutory directions, in not giving weight to the cost of reproducing that part of the property. The intimation, however, was, not only that "consideration" must be given to post-war reproduction cost of the property existing when the 1920 statute took effect, but that in calculating the value for each subsequent year the commission must ascertain the current reproduction cost of all the property again each year, and give it "consideration"—though "no doubt there are some, perhaps many, railroads the ultimate value of which should be placed far below the sum necessary for reproduction." [17] The Transportation Act directed the commission, in determining "value" for recapture purposes, to "give due consideration to all the elements of value recognized by the law of the land for rate-making purposes," and ever since *Smyth* v. *Ames,* said Justice McReynolds for the majority, reproduction cost has been recognized as one of the "elements." Under this interpretation the commission was precluded from inaugurating any cost principle to determine what returns a railroad might retain, under the recapture clause, on investments made subsequently. And since a reappraisal of reproduction cost every year was administratively impossible, the recapture clause was, on the commission's recommendation, later repealed.

However, a statute freezing the rate base for existing investments at some reasonable level and providing a cost basis for future investments might have passed muster even under *Smyth* v. *Ames,* since its chief effect would have been, not to reduce values, but to limit their increase; [18] such a statute would clearly be held valid after the *Hope* decision. Legislation was urged for this purpose by Dr. John Bauer as

16 St. Louis & O'Fallon Ry. Co. v. United States, 279 U.S. 461 (1929).

17 *Id.* at 487.

18 See *The Bauer-Bonbright Proposal for the Revision of the New York Public Service Commission Law and Its Constitutionality* (1930) 30 COL. L. REV. 548; R. L. Hale, *The Courts and the Attraction of Capital* (1930) 14 Proceedings Academy of Political Science 96.

early as 1916 and has been urged since by many writers.[19] Even without legislation, it would still seem appropriate for commissions to institute such differential treatment of past and future investments. As Professor Bonbright pointed out in an illuminating article published in 1926,[20] the problem of fairness to those who made their investments without notice of what was in store for them differs sharply from the problem of the proper treatment of investors who are forewarned. Even though it should be concluded that the same rate base would be appropriate for both old and new investments (which he doubted), still he insisted on

> the necessity of breaking up the subject along functional lines for purposes of analysis. If, after doing so, we still decide to compromise on a single rate base, our compromise may then rest on an intelligent choice instead of resting, as it does now, on an uneasy, half-conscious awareness of the presence of conflicting considerations.

The substitution of replacement cost for actual cost would not aid in the solution of either of these two distinct problems. Fairness to those who invested without notice may require the use of a rate base for old investments which exceeds the actual cost to the company of the property originally acquired, because of the hardship which use of the original cost rate base would work to those who purchased their stock for more, in reliance on continued high earnings. But the hardship is no greater and no less (in the case of a company whose property as a going concern has attained a market value which exceeds actual cost) when the cost of replacing its structures and its land has advanced than when it has remained stationary. The hardship in applying the actual cost principle to such investments would be measured by the gap between the actual cost to the company per share of stock, and what the present investor paid for his share, and the latter has nothing to do with replacement cost.

Perhaps, even from the point of view of the customers, it would be well when announcing a new policy to treat the existing investors generously by telling them that they will be permitted to earn a specified rate of return on a rate base little if any below the market value at the time of the announcement—the rate of return being such

[19] Bauer, *The Control of Return on Public Utility Investments* (1916) 31 Pol. Sci. Q. 260. See other authors cited in Note 10, *supra*.

[20] Bonbright, *Progress and Poverty in Current Literature on Valuation* (1926) 40 Q.J. of Economics 295. The ensuing quotation is the concluding portion of the article. It appears on p. 328.

as to give the existing property a market value equal at the time of the announcement to the rate base. The market value might thereafter fluctuate slightly, as the risk of actually earning the permitted return might vary. Such a treatment would preclude any great reduction of earnings, but by freezing the existing investment and applying a different principle to future investments it would preclude the necessity of increasing them more than the capital costs of rendering the service necessitate. Such treatment may, perhaps, be too generous to the investors and not generous enough to the customers. Whether it is may depend on whether the stock is largely held by small investors who themselves paid the market value for it and by insurance companies and savings banks as a basis of credit or whether it is still largely in the hands of the original investors, who paid for it only on the basis of the original cost of the property acquired from their investments. If the announcement of a new policy is made at a period when the companies are mostly earning only enough to give their properties a market value which does not deviate widely from the actual cost, the announcement of an actual cost rate base to be applied to both past and future investments may be as good as any other makeshift solution for the problem of fairness to those who invested without notice. The important thing is that some announcement be made to future investors of what they may expect from the rate-making authorities. These authorities could thereafter confine their attention to determining what should be allowed by way of return to future investors with full notice.

THE ANNUAL COST OF ATTRACTING CAPITAL

Whether or not future investors should be denied an opportunity for speculative gains unrelated to the costs they have incurred, it may be assumed that the net earnings should be permitted to be at least as high as the annual equivalent of the capital cost. In other words, the annual returns should be sufficient to attract the necessary capital; otherwise the customers would be paying less for the service than it cost. However, it is not always clear what this requirement calls for. As already observed, if we disregard any change in the purchasing power of the dollar, customers can be said to be paying the annual capital costs if they continuously pay the investors enough to keep the value of the investment equal to the amount invested. But there is no guaranty that they will pay this amount every year. To induce the investors to part with the necessary money, we can hold out only a prospect, not a guaranty, that they will receive any given return. The greater their risk of not getting it, the greater must be the permissible rate of return on their investment. Moreover, there may be some years in which the prospective returns, regardless of what the regulators permit, may be too small to keep the value up to the amount invested. If in later years the value reaches this sum, but goes no higher, can it not be said that the customers have failed to pay the full cost of the service?

INITIAL RISKS AND INCREMENTS IN VALUE

Whatever prospect is held out to the investors must be held out at the time for making the investment. If the risk at that time is great, the prospect of a high rate of return must be held out in order to attract the investment. Should the risk subsequently lessen, the continuance of the same rate of return on the original investment would attract a larger amount of capital to the investor than what he had put into the business—it would enable him to sell out at a profit. Yet the prospect of the continued high rate and of the consequent increment in value (in case of success) might serve to offset the initial risk and thus to induce the investor to part with his capital in return for the prospect of a lower rate than otherwise during the years when the greater risk continues. Indeed, there may be cases in which the prospect of an increment in value is the only means of inducing the investor to take the initial risk. It may be that at the moment of investment the risk is very great, but that the crisis in the company's affairs is expected to be reached very soon after the initiation of the enterprise. After the crisis is passed, the business will either be a complete failure or an assured success. The shortness of the period before the crisis reduces the effect which the permitted earnings during that period will have on the attraction of capital; it may be commercially impossible to earn enough during this period, no matter how much may be permitted, to induce the taking of the initial risk. The prospect of a subsequent return in case of success sufficient only to attract, under the subsequent conditions of lessened risk, the amount of capital originally required would be insufficient to attract it at the crucial time when the success of the enterprise is so problematical. A return sufficient for this purpose would be a return which, would subsequently, should the success of the enterprise then be assured, attract a larger sum to the stockholders (should they choose to sell) than they were required to invest in the plant. It would result in an increment in the capital value. But under these conditions that increment would not indicate that the rates exceeded the cost of the service. It would not be an "unearned" increment. It would not by any means, however, be identical with the increment which might accrue if the company were allowed a fair return on the present cost of reproducing the structures and the present value of land adjacent to that owned by the utility. To permit an increment to accrue sufficiently large to offset the initial risk it would only be necessary to adopt the method proposed by Justice Brandeis in his well-known minority opinion delivered in 1923 in *Southwestern Bell Telephone Co.* v. *Public Service Commission.*[21] He would apply to the actual prudent investment a rate of return sufficient at the time the investment is made to attract the necessary capital and would continue that return in the future, regardless of what other rate of return might later be sufficient or necessary to attract capital. The increment which would in some circumstances accrue as a result of the adoption of the Brandeis suggestion corresponds only by accident to that which would accrue if returns were based on replacement cost.

When the period before the crisis in the company's affairs is not expected to be so short, or when no particular crisis is expected, the Brandeis method might serve to attract the capital, but it would not be the only method. The rate of return on the prudent investment might instead be adjusted from year to year according to what would currently be needed to attract capital. If this were done, the value of the property would remain stable. At no time would rates be high enough to enhance the value, and this fact might necessitate higher returns in the early years than would suffice if the investor could look forward to future returns sufficient to increase the value of his capital. It is the method advocated by Commissioner Eastman for application to the railroads, in a most illuminating dissenting opinion delivered shortly after the discussion by Justice Brandeis.[22] It might not make much difference whether the Eastman or the Brandeis method were chosen, provided advance notice were given of the choice.

21 262 U.S. 276, 304–306 (1923).
22 Re San Pedro, Los Angeles & Salt Lake R. Co., 75 I.C.C. 463, 523 (1923).

CHANGES IN THE BUYING POWER OF THE DOLLAR

So far we have disregarded any change in the purchasing power of the dollar. But, as we have been made painfully aware in recent years, such changes occur. A dollar is worth having only because of what one can buy with it. If an investor parts with a hundred dollars in the hope of obtaining thereafter six dollars a year, he very likely takes it for granted that each of the six dollars he receives will buy as much as each of the hundred which he invested. But if at the time when his dividend comes in the price level is only half what it was when he invested, the six dollars he receives will be equivalent in terms of real value to twelve of the dollars he invested; and if the price level has doubled, the six dollars of his dividend will be equivalent to only three of those he invested. If he is to receive an annual return commensurate in purchasing power with what he invested, his permissible return must be translated into dollars of current purchasing power. If the investors were all common stockholders this could be done by applying to the number of dollars comprising the original investment an index number reflecting the change in the general price level. Thus, if the price level is half as high as when he invested, an index number of 50 percent will result in a rate base of half as many dollars; if the price level has doubled, an index number of 200 percent will give a rate base of twice as many dollars. But in terms of purchasing power, the rate base will be the actual cost; for it will be measured by the number of current dollars equal in buying power to that of the number of dollars originally invested. If the price level has risen, the investors will get more dollars than if it had not, but they will make no real gain, for they will be paid in cheaper dollars; and while the customers will be paying more dollars for the service, they will be sacrificing no more than if the price level had been stable and they had been paying only a fair return on the number of dollars originally invested, for they will be paying in cheaper dollars.

Judge Learned Hand, basing an argument on such considerations in an opinion delivered in 1920, drew the erroneous conclusion that "the rule of the present reproduction cost . . . is a necessary consequence of the foregoing argument." [23] If a change in price levels were the only factor which makes present reproduction cost deviate from

[23] Consolidated Gas Co. v. Newton, 267 Fed. 231, 236–239 (S.D.N.Y. 1920).

the original dollar-cost, the conclusion would be sound. But it is by no means the only factor. Changes in land values (included in reproduction cost) take place even when general price levels do not change. Gas mains that were laid in dirt streets at comparatively small expense would cost much more to lay today because the streets have since been paved.[24] Technological changes or changes in the price of materials entering into the company's equipment, if they do not correspond to changes in the general cost of living, will cause a serious discrepancy between current reproduction cost and actual cost translated into dollars of current purchasing power.

Even the latter rate base, if applied to the entire investment, would not be appropriate for the purpose of making the return commensurate in buying power with what was invested. In many utilities, two-thirds or so of the investment represents capital contributions made by bondholders. No scheme of regulation can adjust the bondholders' returns to changes in the buying power of the dollar. Their return in dollars is fixed as long as the company remains solvent. Suppose that the holders of 5 percent bonds invested $200,000,000 in a given company, and common stockholders $100,000,000, and that it took the prospect of a 14 percent return to attract the stockholders' capital. In that case, 8 percent on the total rate base of $300,000,000 (or $24,000,000) would suffice to pay the $10,000,000 interest on the bonds and to pay the stockholders the necessary $14,000,000 in dividends. Now suppose that the price level is doubled, and we were to allow the company 8 percent on a rate base of $600,000,000. This would amount to $48,000,000; but only $10,000,000 of it, as before, would go to the bondholders, the remaining $38,000,000 to the stockholders, while $28,000,000 would suffice to compensate them for the loss in buying power. If the price level, instead of rising, had fallen to one-half of what it was before, and we consequently used a rate base of $150,000,000, 8 percent of that would amount to $12,000,000. Out of this the bondholders would still get their $10,000,000 of interest, and there would be only $2,000,000 left for the stockholders, who would need

[24] Even while Smyth v. Ames held sway, courts generally included only the cost that had actually been incurred in laying the mains in the dirt streets, for reasons hard to reconcile with their "present value" premise. See Miller, J., in Peo. ex rel. Kings County Lighting Co. v. Willcox, 210 N.Y. 479, 495 (1914), and Day, J., in Des Moines Gas Co. v. Des Moines, 238 U.S. 153, 172 (1914). Judge Hand cited the Des Moines case as authority for his seemingly reluctant omission from the rate base of the cost of tearing up the streets.

$7,000,000 to give then the same buying power that their $14,000,000 would have given them under the original price level. If adjustments are to be made in the actual dollar-cost rate base, to compensate for changes in the buying power of the dollar, they should be made only in that part of the rate base which represents the stockholders' contribution.

As Commissioner Eastman observed in his dissenting opinion in the *San Pedro* case, commenting on Judge Hand's argument for reproduction cost:

> This ingenious argument has only of late been summoned to the aid of reproduction cost. It assumes that such cost is equal to the original investment translated into terms of depreciated dollars, which is seldom if ever the case. It also assumes that justice to investors in railroads or other public utilities requires that their income from money so invested should at all times have the same purchasing power. Inasmuch as the return on much of this money, where bonds have been issued or property leased, is fixed, the result of Judge Hand's doctrine would be to give the owners of the equity in the property a wholly unwarranted return and one which, if brought sharply unto the limelight, would impress any court as "manifestly unfair to the public." [25]

Then, turning to the supposition that wages and prices, instead of rising, had fallen in equal proportion, he asked:

> Is it not clear that the application of the reproduction-cost theory under such circumstances would be wholly destructive not only of the interest which the stockholders have in the railroad properties but of much of the interest of the bondholders and other creditors? And is it not equally clear that under such circumstances the flow of capital into railroad and other public-utility enterprises would wholly cease?

Fluctuations in the value of the dollar, then, do not warrant the substitution of reproduction for actual cost as the rate base in order to induce the investment of the necessary capital. The most that they require is an adjustment of the stockholders' share of the return to compensate for changes in buying power. No theory of regulation can compensate the bondholders for such changes. Those who contribute capital by buying bonds have to assume the risk that their stipulated dollar-returns will buy less than they had expected, a risk which is compensated, in part at least, by the possibility that their returns will buy more. If subscribers to stock were warned in advance that they must incur similar risks, while at the same time they would be per-

[25] Note 22, *supra*. 75 I.C.C. at 532, 534.

mitted an increase in the buying power of their returns should price levels fall, it is doubtful whether an appreciably higher rate of return would be needed than otherwise in order to attract their capital. Whether it be considered wise to ask stockholders to incur such risks, or instead to adjust their returns to the current buying power of the dollar, it would be desirable in either case that they should be notified before they invest which principle is to be applied to them.

EXCESSIVE OR DEFICIENT EARNINGS IN THE PAST

The foregoing discussion is based on the assumption that advance notice be given to investors of the returns that will be permitted. But when a commission issues a rate order, there is no assurance that the returns will be those which the rates were intended to yield. It is impossible to predict with accuracy the return from any given rates. If they yield more or less than the amount intended, they can be readjusted; but it will always be a number of years before the readjustment can take place. Meanwhile the company will be receiving for some time either more or less than was intended. In other words, there will be a considerable period during which the customers will be paying more or less than the portion of the cost of the service imputable to those years, and the investors will not know in advance just what returns the company will obtain. They will know only what the commission intends the rates to yield. The advance notice might be made more precise, however, if any failure of the investors to obtain the specified return were treated as an additional cost and added to the next year's rate base; while any receipt by them of more than the specified return were treated as a return of so much of their capital and deducted from the next year's rate base. Under such treatment, one possibility of a speculative gain would be denied to prospective investors, and its elimination might tend to necessitate a higher rate of return to induce them to invest; on the other hand, the risk of obtaining for a time less than the permitted return would be minimized, though not entirely eliminated, and the minimization of this risk would tend to induce them to invest for a lower return than otherwise. Their investments would be less speculative. If notified in advance that regulation would follow this principle, they would have assurance that any temporary failure to collect the full annual cost of the service would be made up to them if the traffic should eventually bear the rates sufficient to do so. And they would know that they could expect no benefits received in excess of the annual cost, since the excess would be treated as a repayment of part of their principal. Their position would resemble somewhat that of the holder of cumulative preferred stock.

Such a treatment of excessive or deficient earnings in the future would simplify the problem of dealing with existing property whose costs the company has met, not out of the proceeds of security issues, but out of earnings. If excessive earnings, accruing before a rate adjustment can be made, are not deemed to be a return of so much of the capital, the investors would have a choice between obtaining the full benefit of such excess by taking it out as dividends and perhaps investing it elsewhere or turning it back into the plant to make additions to the equipment which would be of benefit to the customers. If they are to be induced to make the latter choice, the company must be permitted to earn an additional return on the cost of this new equipment comparable to the amount the investors could have obtained had they taken the money out and made other investments with similar risk. If, on the other hand, excessive returns received by investors are to be treated as a return of part of their capital, then no return on the cost of the company's property defrayed from these excess earnings would be necessary in order to induce the investors to plough them back. Taking the excess earnings out would involve as much of a sacrifice to the investors as putting them back, for what they would gain in the form of a return on the alternative investment would be offset by the reduction of the utility's rate base on which they would thereafter be allowed a return. Under the proposed system, if the entire excess were ploughed back, there would be no reduction of the rate base, for the investors (as distinguished from the company) would be receiving no excess earnings; by preventing a reduction in the rate base, the investors would be making as good an investment as if they had taken the excess out and invested it elsewhere.

Suppose, however, that in a given year the company earns enough, but no more than enough, to pay the investors the appropriate fair return for that year; but instead of paying it, it takes part of the money available for the return and puts it into the plant. The result will be that the investors will receive that year less than a fair return, and the deficiency below it will be the exact amount of the ploughed-back earnings. Had they taken this amount out, instead of ploughing it back, there would have been no reduction of the rate base. To make it equally attractive to them to plough the earnings back, the company must be permitted an additional return on the cost of the property defrayed from these nonexcessive earnings. This will result if the deficiency below the investors' fair return is added to the rate base. Under our suggested method, in short, the company will be permitted a return in the future on the cost of property defrayed from earnings that are not excessive, but not on the cost of property defrayed from earnings that do exceed a fair return. It is only when this method of treating excessive and deficient earnings is applied, that the announcement made by the Nebraska Commission in 1919 would seem appropriate, when it declared that utilities subject to its power

> will not be permitted to earn a return on accumulations of property made from excessive rates, but, where the rates have been insufficient to provide a reasonable return to the investors, or where this reasonable return has been invested in property rather than taken as dividends, such company in a readjustment case will be authorized to earn on such investment or will be given opportunity to capitalize the dividends due and unpaid.[26]

The investors would thus be permitted returns on all the financial sacrifices they have made for the benefit of the customers, except in so far as they have already been compensated by the receipt of excessive dividends. These sacrifices include not only the money they have from time to time contributed to the company in the form of purchases from it of its securities; they also include subsequent sacrifices which have taken the form of failure in any year to receive adequate dividends. The latter sacrifices may result from decisions to reinvest earnings which were not excessive or from the fact that in some years the rates charged were insufficient to provide the full annual cost of the service. In either case the customers have benefited from the investors' sacrifice. The original contributions made by the investors when they invested in the company, except to the extent that they have recouped part of their principal, still constitute part of the sacrifice on which a return would be permitted, regardless of whether some of the property acquired from their investments has been retired or whether portions of it have deteriorated. There would be no occasion to deduct accrued depreciation as such. The only deductions would be for capital costs which the customers have already defrayed in the form of excessive earnings which have not been re-

[26] In re Scotia Independent Telephone Co., P.U.R. 1919E, 217. For an illuminating discussion of property acquired from surplus earnings see the Eastman dissent in the *San Pedro* case, 75 I.C.C. at 558–61.

invested. The rate base would be the net investment made by the investors—that is, the total sacrifices less as much of them as have been repaid. This is not the same thing as the cost which the company has incurred for the property now in existence. That figure fails to include property which has been retired and fails to exclude property bought from excessive earnings or to account for excessive earnings which have been taken out by the investors rather than reinvested.[27]

The addition to the rate base of deficiencies below the investors' fair return and the deduction from it of their receipts in excess of it is a technique suggested by the computations made by the Wisconsin Railroad Commission in its early days for determining what it unfortunately called "going value." Confining its attention to the early years of an enterprise before it could get going as an established business and recognizing that in those years it was most likely that a utility would be unable to obtain a fair return, the commission in come cases added the deficiencies to the rate base and called the addition "going value," while recognizing that it was not the same thing as the "going value" claimed by the companies; [28] and if surpluses had accrued subsequently, they were sometimes deducted from any "going value" which had been built up by adding deficiencies.[29] The com-

27 When the annual depreciation allowance, instead of being set aside in cash, is used to acquire new property in anticipation of the future need to retire part of the old, the cost of the property so acquired is ordinarily entered in a capital account called "depreciation reserve," and when any property is retired its cost is deducted from that account. If the rates in the past have exactly sufficed to cover the operating expenses and the annual depreciation allowance, and to yield a fair return to the investors, the net investment could be ascertained by subtracting the amount shown in the depreciation reserve from the actual cost of the existing property. In such a case, the property acquired by investing the depreciation allowance would represent a cost, not to the investors, but to the customers. The depreciation reserve does not state the full cost of that property, for the cost of retired property has been deducted; but the actual cost of the existing property understates the cost incurred by the investors to precisely the same extent. Accordingly the result will be the same as if we had started with the total cost for all the property, existing and retired, and had subtracted from it the total cost of all property (including what has been retired) purchased with depreciation funds. Further adjustments would have to be made to account for excessive or deficient earnings in the past and for the acquisition of property from earnings other than those charged to depreciation. For an analysis of what the commission deducted from the cost of existing property in the Hope case (44 P.U.R. [n.s.] 1) see R. L. Hale, *Utility Regulation in the Light of the Hope Natural Gas Case* (1944) 44 COL. L. REV. 488, 503–520. For a criticism of the commission's treatment of depreciation see Henry F. Lippitt II, *Net Investment Rate Making—the Deduction for Depreciation* (1949) 62 HARV. L. REV. 1155.

28 *Cf.* State Journal Ptg. Co. v. Madison G. & E. Co., 4 Wis. R.C.R. 501, 585 (1910); Hill v. Antigo Water Co., 3 Wis. R.C.R. 623, 720–23 (1909); Payne v. Wis. Tel. Co., 4 Wis. R.C.R. 1, 60–61 (1909); City of Milwaukee v. Milwaukee Gas Lt. Co., 12 Wis. R.C.R. 441, 459 (1913).

29 *Cf.* City of Green Bay v. Green Bay Water Co., 11 Wis. R.C.R. 236, 243 (1913).

mission stopped there, however, perhaps because of the appellation it had given to the procedure. Deficiencies incurred in the later years of the enterprise could not readily be referred to as "going value," and they were not added.[30] And treatment of surpluses as an amortization of anything other than the "going value" would suggest that there was a negative going value. If one should forget that "going value" in the Wisconsin sense is not value at all, but a cost, the suggestion that a prosperous concern might have a negative going value might seem absurd. Whether for this reason or not, the commission treated the surpluses as an amortization of the going value alone, not of the original investment.[31] It would seem to be only the use of the term "going value" which would prevent one from seeing that the same reasoning which would justify the Wisconsin commission's treatment of the early deficiencies and offsetting surpluses would also justify adding later deficiencies as well and treating surpluses as recoupments of part of the original investment.

Inevitable errors in predicting just what any given rates will yield will necessarily result in deficiencies and surpluses. One specific error lies in the estimation of the proper annual charge required to care for depreciation. In two dissenting opinions Justice Brandeis suggested that under the prudent investment principle adjustments like those we have been discussing could be made to prevent the company from suffering by underestimates of the necessary depreciation charge and consumers from suffering by overestimates.[32] In 1924, in *Pacific Gas & El. Co.* v. *City & County of San Francisco,* he alluded to the principle of mutual life insurance, under which "the premium charged is made clearly ample, and the part thereof which proves not to have been needed inures in some form to the benefit of him who paid it." He then went on:

Legal science can solve the problem of the just depreciation charge for public utilities in a similar manner. Under the rule which fixes the rate base as the amount prudently invested, the inevitable errors incident tc fixing the year's depreciation charge do not result in injustice either to the utility or to the community. If, when the plant must be replaced, the amount set aside for depreciation proves to have been inadequate, and in-

30 *Cf.* City of Marinette v. City Water Co. of Marinette, 8 Wis. R.C.R. 334, 345–46 (1911).

31 Unless the surplus was collected under the name of "depreciation." *Cf.* In re Appl. La Crosse G. & E. Co., 8 Wis. R.C.R. 138, 163 (1911).

32 Pacific Gas & El. Co. v. City & County of San Francisco, 265 U.S. 403, 416 (1924); United Railways & El. Co. v. West, 280 U.S. 234, 255 (1930).

vestment of new capital is required, the utility is permitted to earn the annual cost of the new capital. If, on the other hand, the amount set aside for depreciation proves to have been excessive, the income from the surplus reserve operates as a credit to reduce the current capital charge which the rates must earn. . . . Thus justice both to the owners of the utility and to the public is assured.[33]

The same reasoning which would protect investors and customers, respectively, from permanent loss due to inevitable errors in estimating the adequacy of the annual depreciation charge would seem to justify protecting them as well from permanent loss due to any other inevitable errors in estimating the net earnings which the rates fixed are likely to yield. And this protection would be afforded by adding temporary deficiencies in earnings to the rate base and subtracting from it any excess returns which the investors have received. The assumption is that the excess returns resulted from the rates being set, though unintentionally, too high.

EXCESSIVE EARNINGS FROM REASONABLE RATES

That assumption, however, is not always correct. There are circumstances in which a price may be reasonable even though it yields an excessive return. A price or rate plays a twofold role in our economy. It yields a return to the seller, and at the same time it restricts or regulates the freedom of potential consumers. A price which gives the seller an unjustifiably high return may or may not constitute an unjustifiable restraint on the liberty of consumers. If reduced to the point where the seller receives no more than a proper return, there will most likely be a demand for more of the product or service than before. If the output can be expanded to take care of the additional demand, a reduction in the rate would seem proper; it would give the seller all that he can properly claim, and would increase the liberty of consumers. But the output cannot always be expanded to take care of the additional demand. The present rate may yield an excessive return; but any lower one might call forth a demand which the company could not satisfy except at a cost which would be prohibitive. Under the present rate freedom to enjoy the service would be accorded to

[33] 265 U.S. at 423. *Cf.* Pincus M. Berkson, *Excess Depreciation Reserve and Rate Control* (1936) 36 COL. L. REV. 250. Mr. Berkson, invoking a principle similar to that of Justice Brandeis, suggested the enactment of a statute under which companies would be required to hold in trust for their patrons any excess of future depreciation reserves over actual requirements, and commissions would be empowered to order the equitable distribution of the excess to customers in future rate proceedings.

those who are willing and able to pay it, but not to others. If the rate were reduced, service would have to be denied to some of those who would be willing and able to pay the reduced rate, for there would not be enough to go round among them. Those who could obtain the service at the lower rate would have a freedom to enjoy it which would be denied to others equally willing and able to pay for it. They would enjoy a special privilege unless rationing in some manner could assign equitable shares of the limited supply to all. But rationing is a difficult thing to administer and except in times of war or other emergency may be deemed undesirable. In ordinary circumstances fixing the rate high enough to discourage any excess demand may seem preferable, even if that rate yields an excessive return. The result may not be ideally fair to some of those who are unable to pay that price; but it is fair enough to those who do pay it, for if they could obtain the service for less they would have an unfair advantage over others. In these circumstances the rate which yields an excessive return may well be called for; and while subtracting the excess from the rate base would permit a still lower rate in the future without depriving the company of a fair return, that lower rate in the future would be objectionable for the same reasons. However, the rate was not fixed high in order that it might yield the excess return, but in spite of the fact that it would do so. Is there any reason why a resulting windfall should come to the investors? If they are getting more than is justified, but if at the same time the customers are not being overcharged, why should not the excess be taken away by taxation to be used for the benefit of the public in general, instead of making either the customers or the investors into a privileged class?

Sometimes when a customer could not obtain service from a given company if it were to charge only a compensatory rate, he would not have to be denied service altogether, but could obtain it from another company whose rates are higher. This is the situation when several competing railroads, whose costs differ, are rendering the same service. The "strong" roads could obtain a fair return at a rate which would not yield enough to their "weak" competitors. But if the former were to charge lower rates than their competitors, congestion on their lines would result. Shippers and passengers would apply for more service than the strong lines could supply, and many would have to patronize the weak lines at higher rates. Congress sought to deal with this situation when it enacted the Transportation Act of 1920. It provided that rates for competing roads should be uniform. The Interstate Commerce Commission was told to fix rates for groups of railroads sufficient to yield a fair return on the aggregate value of the property of the group, rather than on the separate property of each road. The Act went on to declare that since it would be impossible to do this without giving some of the carriers a net income in excess of a fair return therefore any carrier receiving such excess should hold it in trust for the United States, and half of it should be paid into a revolving fund to be administered by the commission for the purpose of making loans to weak roads.

In the test case brought by the Dayton-Goose Creek Railway, the strong roads challenged the constitutionality of this "recapture clause." They contended "that the Government has no right to retain one-half of the excess, since, if it does not belong to the carrier, it belongs to the shippers and should be returned to them." Chief Justice Taft, however, speaking for the unanimous Court, rejected this contention. The rates, he said, "are reasonable from the standpoint of the shipper . . . though their net product furnishes more than a fair return for the carrier." [34] If the rates on the different roads were not uniform, there would be congestion of traffic on the strong roads, the shipper on which

> with every other shipper similarly situated in the same section is vitally interested in having a system which can do all the business offered. If there is congestion, he suffers with the rest. He may, therefore, properly be required in the rates he pays to share with all other shippers of the same section the burden of maintaining an adequate railway capacity to do their business.[35]

But while the rates are reasonable from the standpoint of the shipper, lower ones would be reasonable from the standpoint of the strong carrier, and "the reduction of the net operating return provided by the recapture clause is, as near as may be, the same thing as if rates had all been reduced proportionately before collection." Since the carrier could have no valid constitutional objection if the rates had been so reduced,

> the excess caused by the discrepancy between the standard of reasonableness for the shipper and that for the carrier due to the necessity of maintaining uniform rates to be charged the shippers, may properly be appropriated

[34] Dayton-Goose Creek R. Co. v. United States, 263 U.S. 456, 484 (1924).
[35] *Id.* at 480.

by the Government for public uses because the appropriation takes away nothing which equitably belongs either to the shipper or to the carrier.[36]

The reason the recapture clause proved unworkable and was eventually repealed was, as we have seen, that what was to be recaptured was one half the excess above a fair return on the "value for rate-making purposes," and the Court in the *O'Fallon* case construed that phrase as necessitating a reappraisal of reproduction cost each year. But there is no reason for thinking that it would have been unworkable if the statute had referred to the excess above a fair return on cost or on a frozen compromise rate base as of the date when the statute took effect plus the actual cost of property acquired thereafter. The principles so clearly enunciated by Chief Justice Taft are eminently sound, but have been largely ignored.

Justice Jackson, for instance, in his dissenting opinion in the *Hope* case, objected to the use of prudent investment as a rate base for the gathering (as distinguished from the transmission) of natural gas, because of the wide variation in the amount which would have to be invested by different producers to obtain the same amount of gas.

Let us assume [he said] that Doe and Roe each produces . . . the same quantity of natural gas per day. Doe, however, through luck or foresight or whatever it takes, gets his gas from investing $50,000 in leases and drilling. Roe drilled poorer territory, got smaller wells, and has invested $250,000. Does anybody imagine that Roe can get or ought to get for his gas five times as much as Doe because he has spent five times as much? The service one renders to society in the gas business is measured by what he gets out of the ground, not by what he puts into it, and there is little more relation between the investment and the results than in a game of poker.[37]

A similar argument is made by a recent writer in the *Yale Law Journal,* who cites (with apparent approval) the industry's argument that the use of net investment "achieves unjust results" in the regulation of field prices for gas.

Producer A, who spends $10,000 and hits gas on his first drilling, receives a 6 per cent return on his rate base of $10,000. But Producer B, who drills several dry holes and spends $50,000 before striking gas, perhaps in the same pool, receives a 6 per cent return on his $50,000. This rewards individuals for their efforts instead of their achievements.[38]

[36] 263 U.S. at 484.

[37] FPC v. Hope Natural Gas Co., 320 U.S. 591, 649 (1944).

[38] *Federal Price Control of Natural Gas Sold to Interstate Pipelines* (1950) 59 YALE L.J. 1468, 1505–1506.

Such comments ignore the point made by Taft that a price which it may be reasonable to make the customer pay may exceed what it would be reasonable to allow the seller to keep. It is reasonable enough to make Doe's customers and those of A pay for their gas as much, respectively, as Roe's or B's customers have to pay. To charge them less would extend to them a special advantage not open to other members of the community who are no less deserving of it. It is true that Doe's service to society is as great as Roe's, though it cost him only one-fifth as much to render it; and A's "achievement" is as great as that of B, which cost five times as much. Both Doe and A may reasonably charge their customers prices which yield a large excess over a fair return on their respective investments. But because that excess does not "equitably belong" to the customers, it does not follow that it equitably belongs to the producers, as the railroads argued in the *Dayton-Goose Creek* case. The services rendered to society by the strong roads (or their "achievements") in that case were equal to those of the weak roads, and it was thought that shippers should be made to pay as much for them. But the Court distinctly repudiated the notion that the strong roads should be rewarded for their "achievements" when their "efforts" would justify a smaller reward. It declared that the excess resulting from the discrepancy between their achievements and their efforts did not equitably belong to them and could properly be appropriated by the government for public uses.

After all, as John Stuart Mill said long ago, "the proportioning of remuneration to work done [that is, to "achievements"], is really just, only in so far as the more or less of the work is a matter of choice," [39] though, as he went on to say, that method of remuneration may in many circumstances be highly expedient. If the service is not likely to be rendered without special remuneration, such special remuneration may be called for. But when one person is in a position to render more valuable services to society than another can render, because the law has endowed him with special property rights or because of sheer luck, much of that justification disappears. One who happens to observe a fire in a valuable building and notifies the fire department may be rendering a service of great value. But no one would think him entitled to remuneration proportionate to his

[39] PRINCIPLES OF POLITICAL ECONOMY, Bk. II, c. 1, § 4. Quoted at more length *supra*. p. 34.

"achievements." If natural gas is to be produced, many dry wells will have to be drilled, and the efforts of drilling them must be rewarded. If Roe's efforts, in Justice Jackson's illustration, are required for the satisfaction of society's needs, the price must be high enough to induce him to make the efforts, and, for reasons we have adduced, those whose efforts would have been forthcoming at a lower price must nevertheless be permitted to charge the same price as Roe. When Doe, in the illustration, charges a price which is essential for rewarding, not his, but Roe's efforts, that may well be regarded as a reasonable price for Doe to charge; but its reasonableness is not based on any judgment as to what it would be reasonable for him to get. To paraphrase Taft's reasoning, there is a discrepancy between the standard of reasonableness for Doe's customers and that for Doe himself. It may be that in view of the speculative character of the enterprise it would be reasonable to let him keep more than a fair return on the actual cost of his well-drilling in order to induce others to take chances. But there is no reason at all to suppose that the standard of reasonableness for Doe would justify him in keeping all that would come to him by charging a price which is fixed with a view, not to his, but to Roe's costs. There is still a discrepancy between the two standards of reasonableness for his prices, and no reason to suppose that the excess caused by that discrepancy could not "properly be appropriated by the government for public uses" or that the appropriation would take away anything which equitably belongs either to his customers or to Doe himself.

A VARYING RETURN TO STIMULATE EFFICIENCY

But if a company is to be permitted a specified return on its actual investment, while any deficiency below that return is to be added to its rate base and any excess either deducted from its rate base or taxed away, it may be asked what incentive it would have to invest economically or to operate its plant with economy and efficiency. Wartime production under cost-plus contracts was characterized by notorious waste. This objection is only partly met by basing returns on the "prudent," rather than the actual, investment and by confining the operating expenses which the rates must cover to those which are "reasonable." Justice Brandeis himself would apply the term "prudent" only to exclude "what might be found to be dishonest or obviously wasteful or imprudent expenditures. Every investment may be assumed to have been made in the exercise of reasonable judgment, unless the contrary is shown." [40] And the exclusion of operating expenses which are shown to have been "unreasonable," though long sanctioned by court decisions even under *Smyth* v. *Ames*,[41] is hardly sufficient to induce the company to practice any but the most obvious economies. To stimulate more than ordinary alertness on the part of the company, it may be in the interest of the customers to allow the company some advantage from its own efficiency.

But what is meant by "the company" which practices the efficiency and gets the reward? In the case of a giant utility corporation it is the management personnel (not the stockholders) whose efficiency matters, but the stockholders who will get the rewards. The managers of such a corporation may own a few shares of the stock, but ordinarily not enough to make their total income vary appreciably with the earnings of the company. Nevertheless, if stockholders are permitted to benefit from efficiency and compelled to suffer from inefficiency, they or the investment house which represents them may be more likely to see to it that those officers who show the most efficiency receive suitable rewards in the form of promotions. Moreover there may be something in the psychology of many managers, apart from any consideration of pecuniary advantage to themselves, which causes them to be more interested in bringing gains to the company they serve than they would be in bringing gains to the public. For these indirect reasons it may be necessary to let the stockholders obtain from the customers not only enough to pay them for their services in making the investment, but something more as the indirect cost of efficient management. The reasons for this are stronger in the case of small companies in which the managers are themselves the principal stockholders.

These considerations, however, do not require that the stockholders be permitted to keep the entire amount by which the return in any one year may exceed the amount intended when the rate was fixed or that they should receive no credit at all for deficiencies below the intended return. Part of the excess or deficiency may be plainly the result of circumstances over which the management had no control,

[40] State ex rel. Southwestern Bell Tel. Co. v. Public Service Comm., 262 U.S. 276, 289, note 1 (1923).

[41] See Chicago & Grand Trunk R. Co. v. Wellman, 143 U.S. 339 (1892); Aetna Ins. Co. v. Hyde, 275 U.S. 440, 448 (1928); United Fuel Gas Co. v. Railroad Commission, 278 U.S. 300 (1929); Smith v. Illinois Bell Tel. Co., 282 U.S. 133, 151–57 (1930); Western Distributing Co. v. Kansas, 285 U.S. 119 (1932); Columbus Gas & Fuel Co. v. Pub. Utils. Comm., 292 U.S. 398 (1934).

as when the price which the utility has to pay for coal or labor fluctuates. If these circumstances could be identified and eliminated, it would still not follow that all the remaining excesses and deficiencies would indicate efficiency or inefficiency on the part of the management. They may result largely from inevitable errors made by the commission in predicting what the rate it fixed would yield. Nevertheless, it may stimulate alertness in the management if a certain margin above or below the intended return be permitted. If it be thought, for example, that 8 percent on the investment would be the amount required to attract the capital, the commission might fix a rate designed to yield that return. Then, if the yield turned out to be 10 percent, it might be assumed, in the absence of a contrary showing, that the excess was due to superior efficiency. Only returns above 10 percent would then be subject to recapture, or, if not recaptured, deducted from the rate base. At the same time, if the return in any year amounted to 6 percent, it might likewise be assumed, in the absence of a contrary showing, that the deficiency was due to bad management. Only deficiencies below 6 percent would then be added to the rate base. Or again, sufficient flexibility in earnings to stimulate efficiency might result, if something less than 100 percent of the excesses and deficiencies were debited or credited to the company. Instead of recapturing (or deducting from the rate base) the entire amount of the returns in excess of a given figure, 50 or 75 percent of the excess might be recaptured. The company would then derive some pecuniary advantage should it by efficient management be able to push the earnings up beyond the level which the rate was designed to meet, and the public would derive benefit from that efficiency too. It will be recalled that the recapture clause of the Transportation Act called for the recapture of only one half of the excess earnings.

Permitting a certain flexibility in the returns will prevent giving to future investors as precise a notice of the return to be allowed them as would be possible if a definite figure could be stated. Investors would be taking somewhat greater risks. But the variations in what would be permitted would probably be narrow enough to prevent the investments from being unduly speculative. If advance notice were given to future stockholders of the percentage of the actual investment which would be regarded as excessive and of the proportion of the excess which would be recaptured or deducted from the rate base (if not reinvested), the uncertainties would be mild, indeed, compared to those which prevail when no correction at all is made for excessive or deficient earnings during long intervals before rates can be adjusted or when the return is based on the wild fluctuations of replacement cost.

Even though a flexible rate of return may be desirable, there is no reason why that return should be based on anything other than the prudent investment, except in so far as a compromise has to be made on behalf of unwarned investors and except as adjustments may be thought desirable to changes in the buying power of the dollar; and neither of these exceptions calls for any consideration of reproduction cost. Moreover, there is no reason for not recapturing at least a large proportion of such excess earnings as result, like those of the strong railroads, from the necessity of fixing rates high for reasons unconnected with their yield. The philosophy of the *Dayton-Goose Creek* case is by no means impaired by any necessity there may be for permitting a certain variation in earnings as a stimulus to efficiency.

THE BROADENING OF THE UTILITY CONCEPT BY THE DAYTON-GOOSE CREEK PHILOSOPHY

That philosophy broadened the concept of public utility regulation. Regulation had been justified as a necessary corrective for economic maladjustments. Those maladjustments were thought of in terms of the relationship between the utilities and their customers. It was thought that regulation was required where without it the customers might be subjected to exorbitant charges.[42] But in the *Dayton-Goose Creek* case it was recognized that regulation of exorbitant earnings might be called for even when the rates were not exorbitant. Though there was no maladjustment in the relations between the strong roads and their customers, it was thought that recapture of the excess earnings was required, since otherwise the strong roads would be in a position to appropriate what the Court said did not "equitably belong" to them. This would have been a maladjustment in their relations, not with their customers, but with the general public. It would put their owners in a position to command a share of the products turned out by society larger than was justified, to the detriment of those who would in consequence have to be content with smaller shares.

[42] See the discussion in Chap. XIII, *supra*.

EQUAL TREATMENT FOR UTILITY OWNERS AND OTHERS

But if the earnings of railroads and utilities are to be limited in accordance with the principles we have been discussing, investors in such businesses will be denied gains similar to those which certain other members of the community may enjoy. The market value of utility investments will not be permitted to rise above the amount that was invested, except in so far as adjustments may be called for to mitigate the hardship to those who invested without having been warned of the regulation, or to offset early risks, or to compensate for changes in the buying power of the dollar, or to stimulate efficiency on the part of the management. Meanwhile owners of property in unregulated businesses, particularly owners of land and other natural resources, may be profiting from increments in value far beyond any which accrue from any such adjustments. It is sometimes thought that the railroad or utility must be permitted similar increments, not because they are necessary for the attraction of capital or to mitigate hardships, but simply that they may share in the general prosperity of the community or may enjoy equality of treatment with others. In the *Minnesota Rate Cases,* in 1913, Justice Hughes, speaking for the Court, while rejecting the high valuation which the lower court had placed on the railroad's right of way and terminal lands, intimated that the company might be "entitled to a reasonable share in the general prosperity of the communities which it serves, and thus to attribute to its property an increase in value," this increase, apart from improvements, to extend to "the fair average of the normal market value of land in the vicinity having a similar character." [43] As to this theory, which Justice Hughes "merely suggested but which was thereafter enthusiastically adopted by the carriers," Commissioner Eastman asked, in the dissenting opinion to which reference has already been made in the *San Pedro* case:

> But what is the "general prosperity" of a community? Is it the prosperity of favored landholders? Because certain owners of real estate reap profits which have universally come to be known by the designation "unearned increment," is that a reason why railroads should have such an increment also? Are there not communities where such profits have been realized but where no "general prosperity" has visited the bulk of the inhabitants? [44]

[43] 230 U.S. 352, 455 (1913).

[44] 75 I.C.C. at 536.

Unless everyone is a landowner, a system which distributes the fruits of prosperity to landowners alone can scarcely be characterized as a system of equality of treatment.

Nevertheless, Professor Nelson Lee Smith (at the present writing a member of the Federal Power Commission) contended, in a book published in 1932, that utilities should be given the benefits of unearned increments in land values, on the ground that

> the ethics of discriminating against one group of owners of property in such fixed goods as land at the same time that others are allowed to enjoy the fruits of appreciation in the value of such goods may be seriously questioned. To call returns of this sort "fair," if that term implies equality of treatment, would involve a somewhat wry humor; the modification of competitive distribution is not a problem peculiar to public utility regulation.[45]

Mr. Smith is here pursuing a will-o'-the-wisp. Equality of treatment will not result from giving utilities the benefit of unearned increments. Land values are themselves symptoms of inequality of treatment. As pointed out more fully in Chapter II, the law intervenes to protect the property rights of each owner against the rest of the world; it assigns, or provides rules for assigning, the particular property rights which it will protect for each owner, and these particular rights which it assigns are not, and cannot be, equal, nor do they result from equality of opportunity. The law, through control of utility earnings, cannot possibly accord to utility investors a treatment equal to that which it accords to all other persons, when it does not treat the others alike. You cannot make one thing equal to a number of other things which are themselves unequal.

It is very true, as Mr. Smith asserts, that "the modification of competitive distribution is not a problem peculiar to public utility regulation." But it does not follow that commissions must avoid facing the problem or that they must assume that utility investors should be permitted to enjoy economic advantages which cannot be justified on their own merits merely because the law has not yet got around to withdrawing similar unjustified advantages which it confers on another group of privileged persons. What does follow is rather that economic maladjustments should be corrected wherever they may be found, not alone in the field to which the label "public utility" is

[45] Nelson Lee Smith, The Fair Rate of Return in Public Utility Regulation (1932), p. 44.

now attached. As long as the law empowers certain people outside that field to appropriate from the general mass of goods produced by the collective efforts of the community a share which cannot be justified as an incentive to thrift or efficiency or as a relief from peculiar hardship, the less favored will receive a smaller share of such goods than they would otherwise receive. But it does not improve the situation of the less favored to diminish their shares still further by enhancing those of utility investors. Utility commissions have no power to correct maladjustments other than those pertaining to the property of the small class of businesses over which they have statutory control. Within their sphere of control, however, they should not hesitate to recognize and remove maladjustments merely because similar ones still exist outside that sphere. As Justice Stone said in another connection, a determination of the reasonableness of prices "can be satisfactorily made only after a complete survey of our economic organization and a choice between rival philosophies." [46] Regulatory authorities, though without power to correct them, cannot properly avoid passing judgment on the relationships of other property owners to the public before determining whether or how far similar relationships between utility companies and the public demand correction. Then the judgments made by the regulatory authorities may throw light on the extent to which these returns from other forms of property should be subjected to similar control and correction. As the Court recognized in the *Nebbia* case, economic maladjustments calling for price control may exist outside of any "closed class or category of businesses affected with a public interest." [47] And the maladjustment, as was recognized in the *Dayton-Goose Creek* case, may call for correction by means of public appropriation of excess earnings rather than by price control; for maladjustment may exist in the relationship of the property owner to the public at large even when there is no maladjustment in his relationship to his customers. In other words, taxation must at times be used as an instrument for the readjustment of economic relationships.

TAXATION AS A CORRECTIVE OF ECONOMIC MALADJUSTMENTS

The use of taxation as an instrument for correcting economic maladjustments, like the regulation of prices, involves "a complete

[46] United States v. Trenton Potteries Co., 273 U.S. 372, 398 (1927). See *supra*, p. 130.
[47] 291 U.S. 502, 536 (1934).

survey of our economic organization and a choice between rival philosophies." More specifically, it involves a scrutiny of our present unequal distribution of economic power and a determination of what economic inequalities are justified and what are not. The relevant question would be how much the taxpayers should be permitted to keep as a result of their bargaining power. A corrective tax, unlike many of those now in force, would fall only on what they are receiving in excess of this amount.

Should a corporation, for example, be permitted to keep untaxed and to distribute to its stockholders a "fair return" on the cost of its plant, or is more needed to attract the necessary capital? If it has long been earning more than is necessary for this purpose, how much of the excess should go untaxed in order to avoid undue hardship to those investors who bought their stock at high prices? What adjustments should be made for changes in the buying power of the dollar? How much should it be permitted beyond what is needed to attract capital in order to stimulate efficient and economical management and the taking of risks? Questions such as these, which arise in public utility regulation, would properly arise in the formulation of any excess profits tax designed to redistribute corporate earnings. Furthermore, it might be asked whether any such tax can surmount the practical difficulties of administration, including those inherent in the wide variations in the rate of return required for the attraction of capital in industries with different degrees of risk.

Taxation to alter the distribution of wealth need not be confined to corporations. To what extent should a person be enabled to profit from an increase in the value of his property which does not correspond to any cost he has incurred as a contribution to the productive activities of the community? How much of the increment can be taxed away without weakening the incentive to incur risks whose incurrence may be beneficial to society? How much property should a person be permitted to inherit or a testator be permitted to assign to others at his death? Complete expropriation of a decedent's property would, of course, work great hardship on those of his dependents whom he has been supporting; it would also take away much of his incentive to engage in productive work. One important motive for economic activity and for investing rather than spending one's income (thus indirectly adding to the community's productive capacity) is the expectation that at death the property so acquired can be passed on to one's children. How far would this motive be weakened by a heavy tax on that part of one's estate which exceeds a liberal allowance for one's beneficiaries? or by a tax to be imposed a generation or so after one's death?

Does a graduated tax on personal income seriously weaken the taxpayer's motive to use his money and his energies productively? Money invested in an enterprise paying 6 percent will not yield 6 percent to a person in the higher taxable brackets, for the added income which his investment brings him will be partly taken from him by the added tax which it involves. Investment in the same enterprise will yield the full 6 percent only to the investor whose total income is low enough to exempt him from the income tax. It does not necessarily follow that the tax causes the man in the upper bracket to invest less. A rate of return which is essential to induce the marginal investor with a low income to sacrifice his present enjoyment for the sake of a future return may greatly exceed the rate needed to induce the rich man to invest his money, since the rich man's investment of it means a much smaller sacrifice of present enjoyment. Nor would the higher tax on that portion of a rich man's income which comes from his personal services necessarily reduce the incentive to render them. If the taxpayer's earnings from his services are high enough to put him in an upper bracket, it is presumably because the market places on those services a value that is high by reason of their scarcity, not because a lower reward would fail to bring them forth. How far the principle of a graduated tax on personal income can be pushed without seriously impairing the incentive to invest and to work would be difficult to determine. There is, of course, a limit, but whether our present taxes have reached it we cannot say with assurance.

The purpose of corrective taxation is not to punish the taxpayer. The only objection to his deriving what enjoyment he can from all the material goods which his income enables him to buy is that he may be unduly diminishing the share of goods available to others. The corrective tax is justified only in so far as what is taken from the person with "excess" income is used so as to spread the material benefits more widely or to those more in need of them. A dictatorial government might merely divert the excess wealth of some to increase the excess wealth of another class in favor with the dictator or to build up armaments for aggressive purposes or a secret police to repress the liberties of all its people. But if the proceeds of a tax on excess wealth are employed to promote public health, or to conserve natural resources, or to reduce unemployment, or to provide educational opportunities to those whose latent abilities would otherwise be undeveloped and who would thus be barred from making the economic contributions of which they are inherently capable, or for a thousand other useful purposes, then the corrective tax, while reducing somewhat the liberty of those who pay it, will enhance the economic freedom of others who now have less of it—freedom in the choice of their work and freedom to enjoy the material products of society. It will bring about a net increase in individual liberty.

One important way in which taxes on excess wealth may increase economic liberty is by displacing other taxes which discourage production. Taxes on buildings and factories act as impediments to their construction. Unlike taxes on land values, they tend to keep down the supply of buildings and of their products, and thus keep up the prices which their owners can charge. The higher price which the tax enables him to charge may compensate the owner for what he has to pay to the Government, but it keeps others from building, and it increases the prices which consumers must pay for the freedom to consume, without in any way increasing the funds out of which they must pay for it. Taxes on business income which fail to discriminate between income which is essential as an incentive to production and income which is not have a similar repressive effect on production and fall ultimately on consumers in the form of higher prices and less freedom to consume. So too, of course, do sales taxes and excises.

Taxes which in some degree repress production may perhaps be unavoidable. The revenues obtainable from corrective taxes alone may be insufficient to meet all public needs, particularly at a time which calls for large appropriations for defense. The benefit which even those with low incomes derive from public expenditures may offset the loss which they suffer from decreased private production. To the extent, however, that the public expenditures are defrayed from taxes which do not repress production, this benefit is, of course, greater. It is doubtful whether nonrepressive taxation has been pushed at all closely to the limits of its possibilities. Inheritances and windfall gains from the exploitation of natural resources can surely be taxed much more heavily than at present without impairing the incentives for production.

This is not, of course, the whole story. Not all of the revenue derived from taxation is used for the benefit of the public, even in governments like ours which are subject to a large degree of popular control. Nor is all the wealth which our system bestows on the rich, even when it exceeds what is required as an incentive, employed for the exclusive benefit of its owners. A considerable amount goes to various private philanthropies, many of which confer benefits on the public which government might be less likely to confer. This fact may justify exempting money from taxation which is devoted to charity or education, as our present tax laws do to a large extent. It hardly justifies complete failure to revise a system which diverts a larger proportion of the community's wealth than can be justified on other grounds into the laps of a favored few and fosters the existence of hereditary privileged classes, merely because some of those so favored may choose to confer part of their wealth on the less favored. It is true that even when gifts are exempt from taxation, the heavy tax on the remainder of his income may cause the rich man to feel that he cannot afford to make as large gifts as if he were more lightly taxed. A heavy tax on large incomes and estates does undoubtedly diminish the amount of money devoted to private philanthropy. This is a price which has to be paid if surplus economic power which the law has indirectly delegated to persons who may or may not use it for the public good and are responsible only to themselves is to be transferred to governmental bodies which can be held to account by the voters. The price to be paid does not involve complete drying up of the sources of private philanthropy, for many inequalities in fortune would be left undisturbed by corrective taxation which would avoid the weakening of productive incentives. Such as it is, however, the price for making the transfer of power to the Government will seem too great to those who believe that all governmental expenditures of tax revenue will be of the pork barrel variety. To those who have more faith in democratic processes and who believe that this surplus wealth will be more likely to benefit the general public when its disposition is entrusted to those who are responsible to the voters than when entrusted to those who are not, on the other hand, the price will seem worth paying.

PART FIVE

CONCLUSION

XVII

ECONOMIC LIBERTY IN A DEMOCRACY

THE various attempts we have been discussing for eliminating economic maladjustments—price and wage control and corrective taxation—require government to choose between different principles for determining how the wealth of the community should be distributed. But by leaving present inequalities undisturbed, government would be making a choice, too; for these inequalities are dependent upon governmental intervention in the relations between different individuals.

Government, by its very nature, involves some control of the freedom of individuals. But without government no one would have much liberty in the ensuing chaos. While government, however, is essential to liberty, it is also capable of destroying liberty, as in totalitarian systems or other tyrannical states. Much depends upon the persons who control the government and their motives.

Some of the restraints which in our own society the law places on the liberty of each of us take the form of legal obligations to respect the legal rights of others. At the same time the law confers on each of us legal rights which others are bound to respect. On the whole, our rights against others expand our liberty in a way which more than compensates for the restrictions which our obligations impose upon it. Many of these rights and obligations have been evolved in the long development of the common law by the courts of England and of this country. These common law rights are important ingredients in whatever freedom each individual has from restraints imposed upon him by other individuals, while common law obligations, particularly in respect to property, are important factors in subjecting the liberty of some to the economic control of others. The liberties which result from the network of common law rights and obligations, though real, are very unevenly distributed among the members of the community. Some have much more freedom than others, both in their choice of work and in their enjoyment of the material products of society. Courts occasionally modify some of the legal rights and obligations to bring about what seem to them a more equitable balance of liberties. But it is to legislation that the individual must look for any thoroughgoing changes.

Legislation can either enhance or diminish the liberty of given individuals. It may give greater protection than the law previously gave against the harmful acts of other individuals, or it may take away protection which the law previously gave. It may impose new obligations, or release from old ones. It may indirectly accord to those who are less well off more freedom to enjoy the material fruits of society by removing obstacles to their production, such as repressive taxes, or by reducing the prices exacted for them when this can be done without impairing the incentives to produce, or by levying taxes on wealth which does not function as an incentive to produce, and employing the proceeds to distribute wealth more widely. On the other hand, legislation may accentuate the inequalities in wealth and in economic liberty which now exist by increasing the power of monopolies, or by levying taxes of the kinds which fall most heavily on the poor, or by spending public funds for the benefit of privileged classes, or by deficit spending at a time when production cannot be increased, thus placing more dollars in the hands of some classes, enabling them to bid up the prices of the limited supply of goods and by this inflationary process subjecting those whose money incomes fail to keep pace to what is in effect a sales tax. Even legislation which tends to equalize wealth may diminish the economic liberty of those who have least if it is so unwisely drawn that it decreases greatly the total output of society. All legislation which effects economic changes will be restrictive of some liberties. If it accentuates economic inequality it will, unless it causes a sufficient increase of the total output of society, reduce the liberty of the least fortunate while enhancing that of the more fortunate. If it mitigates inequality it will reduce the liberty of the more fortunate, and it may, by reducing production, diminish the liberty of all. If wisely drawn, on the other hand, it may greatly increase the liberty of those whose freedom is now the most restricted.

Since the liberties of different individuals frequently conflict, and since a choice between them must necessarily be made by some governmental authority, the question arises whether democratically elected legislative bodies should be the ones to make the final choice. Is this what the principles of democracy call for, and if so, does democracy produce the best distribution of individual liberties?

The concept of democracy is somewhat ambiguous. From one point of view democracy rests on the doctrine that "all men are created equal," in the sense that each person's welfare (of which his liberty is a part) is as sacred as that of every other person and should never be sacrificed except when necessary to avoid a worse harm to someone else or an equal harm to a greater number of persons. This doctrine seems to me to express the fundamental value in democracy. It is a doctrine which accords with the tenets of some, but not of all, religions; and it is accepted by many who regard individual welfare in this life as a good in its own right, rather than by virtue of any divine decree.[1] The word "democracy," however, carries another connotation closer to its etymological derivation—namely, rule by the people. The value of democracy in this sense must rest on a belief that government by the people is more likely than other forms of government to serve the values of democracy in its less literal, but more basic, sense.

To support such a belief it is not necessary to assume that the people *en masse* are necessarily wiser or juster than any small group that might conceivably control the Government. More convincing is the argument that they are more likely than anyone else to recognize their own interests and, if holding governing power, to promote them, and that promotion of the individual interests of the most people accords

[1] The idea that because all Communists profess to be atheists and seem to have no regard for individual well-being, therefore all atheists must be Communists and can have no regard for the welfare of other individuals, is one of the crudest of fallacies. In fact, an atheist may well regard the welfare of individuals in this life as all the more precious because of his belief that there is no after life to compensate for the evils of this.

with the basic tenets of democracy. Even this contention, however, requires some qualification.

It would, of course, be impossible for the people to do all the governing directly. They can, however, if they have the vote, choose legislators and other officials to do it. But control over legislation would not give the people unlimited power to govern, if legislation can be set aside by the Supreme Court. It is true that in setting aside legislation it has often been said that the Court is not thwarting the will of the people, but giving effect to it, since the people have expressed their will in the Constitution, while a statute expresses only the will of the people's legislative agents. But if the "will of the people" means anything, it must mean the will of the majority of the people. The will of a minority, when opposed by that of the majority, cannot be said to be the will of the people themselves. Nor can it be said that the concrete meanings which nine life members of the Supreme Court, or five of the nine, have read into the vague texts of the Constitution necessarily reflect the will of the majority of the people. Even the texts, other than the most recent amendments, were adopted by people long since dead, not by the people now alive. If the majority of the people could at any time amend the Constitution and reject the Court's interpretations, there would be some reason for saying that failure to amend indicates popular approval of the judicial decisions. But since adoption of an amendment requires ratification by three-fourths of the states, regardless of population, legislatures in our thirteen most sparsely populated states, representing far less than one-fourth of all the people, can defeat the will of a vast majority. This is, of course, an extreme case, for the opponents are not likely to be concentrated in the smallest states. Nevertheless, when the Court has held state or federal legislation invalid as in conflict with the judicial interpretation of the Constitution, it is less likely that the Court was reflecting the will of the people when it rejected the legislation than that Congress or the state legislature was voicing it when it legislated. After all, the majority could vote for a new legislature to repeal any laws which it felt to be obnoxious, while it could not vote for new Justices of the Supreme Court; and the process of amending the Constitution is at best cumbersome.

However, even though judicial invalidation of legislation limits control over their government by a majority of the people, it does not always impair the fundamental values of democracy. The chief virtue of majority rule lies in the assumption that when a choice has to be made between the welfare of some individuals and the conflicting welfare of others, it is better that the welfare of relatively few should be subordinated to that of a greater number. A disaster to ten persons is less of an evil than a similar disaster to a thousand. If one choice will inflict the same degree of harm on each member of the majority that the opposite choice will inflict on each member of the minority, it is better to allow the majority to make the choice. This principle applies, however, only to majorities and minorities of those affected by the choice. If a certain legislative proposal affects only the conflicting interests of a thousand persons, there is no assurance that the interests of a majority of those affected will prevail if the matter is to be decided by a legislature responsible to millions of voters who have no concern in the matter; nor is there, on the other hand, any such assurance if any appreciable proportion of the thousand have no votes for that legislature.

There is no practicable way to guarantee that legislation shall be enacted by bodies in the choice of which only those affected or all of those affected shall have a voice. But our constitutional demarcation of the spheres of state and federal control brings about a rough approach to such a condition. If Congress were to legislate on matters which affect only the inhabitants of Massachusetts, the vote of a majority of those inhabitants might well be outweighed by the votes of persons outside the state who are not concerned with the matter. For the Court to hold such federal legislation unconstitutional as a violation of the Tenth Amendment would be to restore the power of those concerned to make the decision. On the other hand, if Massachusetts could enact a tariff on goods imported from other states, or could establish its own currency, or could regulate the rates charged in Boston for the shipment of goods to Chicago, the interests of many outside of Massachusetts would be controlled by a legislature in which they would have no representation. A judicial holding that such state legislation violates the commerce clause or some other provision of the Constitution would again bring about a closer approximation to control of legislation by a majority of those affected.

Of course, the approximation cannot be made perfect. Many acts of the Federal Government, while affecting people in more than one state, affect only a fraction of those who can vote for Congress; and many acts of state governments are valid which have some effect on the interests of persons who live in other states. Moreover, many acts of sovereign nations have a serious effect on the economic interests of foreigners, and we have no international legislative bodies to handle such matters. Nevertheless, majorities of those affected have more control over governmental adjustments of their conflicting interests than they would have if the Supreme Court had no power to stop the less appropriate legislative bodies from encroaching on the sphere of the more appropriate.

There is another way in which judicial invalidation of legislation promotes, rather than obstructs, majority rule. A state may determine who may vote for its legislature and in doing so, who may vote for members of the United States Congress. But if a temporary majority were to disfranchise large numbers of its inhabitants, it might be impossible for some future majority, composed partly of the disfranchised, to prevail. Qualifications for voting, however, if based on race or color, would be held to violate the Fifteenth Amendment, and if based on a classification which the Supreme Court should find arbitrary, to violate the equal protection clause. Though the constitutional right to vote is not absolute, court review in such cases gives some support to majority rule. It is, perhaps, unfortunate that the Court has seen fit not to interfere with other schemes which thwart the power of majorities, such as the county unit system in Georgia and the distorted apportionment of legislative and congressional districts in Illinois, which give far more weight to the votes of rural voters than to those of urban voters. The Constitution itself, by giving a small state the same representation in the Senate as a large one, gives to voters in the small states an influence over legislation that is disproportionate to their numbers.

Even the vote, however, will not enable the majority to promote its own interests unless the voters can participate in discussions and other political activities, listen to speeches, attend meetings, and acquire information from the press. By denying these opportunities, a temporary majority might, without denying the ballot, render it impotent. When the Court strikes down statutes which abridge freedom of speech, of the press, or of assembly, it is keeping the channels open for majority control in the future.

But keeping the channels open for majority control does not suffice to protect minorities from measures which may harm them out of all proportion to any benefit they confer on majorities. When legislation deals with conflicting economic interests, it may be impossible to determine whether the harm to each member of the minority outweighs the good to each member of the majority. Hence, it may be a safe working assumption that if it benefits more people than it harms, it should stand, and that when enacted by a legislature which represents the majority, even roughly, it presumably does benefit more people than it harms. If such turns out not to be the case, reliance can better be placed on political than on judicial processes for a remedy. Those in the majority, after experiencing the working of a measure, may be better able than any court to determine whether it benefits them or not. When on the other hand the majority curbs the liberties of distinct minorities which can never hope to become majorities, the chances are greater that these liberties were not curbed in order to promote any legitimate interests of the majority, but merely to satisfy its prejudices. For reasons such as these, Justice Stone suggested in a notable passage that the Supreme Court should keep a closer rein on legislation which affects distinct minorities, as well as that which clogs political processes, than on that which affects economic matters alone. In sustaining the validity of the federal Filled Milk Act, in *United States* v. *Carolene Products Co.*, he declared that "regulatory legislation affecting ordinary commercial transactions is not to be pronounced unconstitutional unless in the light of the facts made known or generally assumed it is of such a character as to preclude the assumption that it rests upon some rational basis within the knowledge or experience of the legislators." [2] Then in a footnote he added:

> It is unnecessary to consider now whether legislation which restricts those political processes which can ordinarily be expected to bring about repeal of undesirable legislation, is to be subjected to more exacting judicial scrutiny under the general prohibitions of the Fourteenth Amendment than are most other types of legislation. [Citing cases dealing with restrictions upon the right to vote and upon the dissemination of information, with interferences with political organizations and restrictions upon peaceable assembly.]
>
> Nor need we enquire whether similar considerations enter into the review of statutes directed at particular religious . . . or national . . . or racial minorities . . . whether prejudice against discrete and insular minorities may be a special condition, which tends seriously to curtail the operation of those political processes ordinarily to be relied upon to pro-

[2] 304 U.S. 144, 152–153, and n. 4 (1938). See George D. Braden, *The Search for Objectivity in Constitutional Law* (1948) 57 YALE L.J. 571, 579–582, especially n. 28, for a discussion of this passage.

tect minorities, and which may call for a correspondingly more searching judicial inquiry.

Judicial review of legislation, then, may frequently serve better than unlimited legislative power to preserve the more basic democratic values—by invalidating legislation directed against "discrete and insular minorities" and legislation which restricts the power of future majorities. But courts which have this power can use it to prevent majorities from protecting their legitimate interests against the oppressive economic power of minorities. As far as individual liberty is concerned, it is just as important that legislative bodies should be able to protect persons from oppression at the hands of private groups which exercise power indistinguishable from that exercised by government as it is that courts should be able to protect them from oppression by officials whose power is more generally recognized as governmental.

The power of the Supreme Court to invalidate legislation does not guarantee that the Court will prevent all legislative attempts which impair democratic values, or that it will sustain all legislative measures which promote them. Much depends on the wisdom, integrity, and self-restraint of the judges. Nor would the removal of all judicial restraint on legislation guarantee democratic values. Apart from the fact that legislation may be passed by bodies representative of many others than those affected by it, or not representative of all who are, and, apart from legislation which restricts political processes or which is directed at insular minorities, there can be no absolute assurance that legislation will promote the greatest individual welfare of the greatest number of people.

In the first place, the ballot gives a very incomplete control over the details of legislation. The electors vote for legislators to represent them, not for individual measures. In choosing a representative whose legislative views on the whole appeal to them more than do those of his rival, they frequently have to swallow unpalatable legislation on matters they regard as less crucial in order to obtain legislation which they desire on matters about which they are more concerned. In states which have the initiative and referendum it is possible for the voters, without turning out the legislators, to overrule them by enacting laws which the legislature has failed to pass and by rejecting those which it has passed. Even so, it is not possible for even the most alert and intelligent voter to form an opinion on the merits of all the detailed proposals, many of them technical, which come before the legislature. Voters have their own business to attend to. One of the chief reasons for the existence of legislatures is to enable their members to devote time, which the voter himself cannot spare, to a study of legislation. And the legislators themselves have to confine most of their study to matters which come before their respective committees and have to delegate the making of policies on many technical questions to administrative commissions. It is only on matters in which a large part of the public takes a serious interest that the majority of the voters can insist on legislation which reflects their wishes. For the rest, they can do no more than insist on being represented by legislators of character and intelligence. Despite all these shortcomings, however, the ballot seems more likely than any other device to secure legislation which shall not deviate far from what the majority of the voters desire. And since by the suffrage laws of all the states almost every adult citizen has the right to vote, the desires of the voters are likely to reflect the desires of the people in general.

The desires of the people, however, do not necessarily turn to legislation which will enhance their own liberty and welfare. Many voters have no desires at all in respect to legislation, but vote for this or that candidate out of traditional party loyalty or personal devotion, or because he is a member of their own religious or racial or national group, or for any one of a dozen reasons which have nothing to do with his legislative program. Some fail to respond to suggestions for legislation which would benefit them because unaware that it would do so; others favor quack legislative remedies for their ills without realizing that the cure may be worse than the disease. Nevertheless, as long as there are enough alert and intelligent voters, universal adult suffrage would seem to give greater promise of a desirable distribution of liberties than would government by any self-chosen elite. Any such elite would be tempted to subordinate the liberties of the great mass of the population to those of the elite themselves and of the class from which they spring, and even if conscientious would be less acutely aware of the grievances of the majority. Popularly elected legislative bodies would thus seem to be the organs best suited to make the final choices which government at times has to make between conflicting liberties, subject to whatever judicial control may be necessary to secure the proper degree of centralization and decentralization as between national and state legislatures, and to prevent legislatures from crippling the power of future majorities and from promoting majority interests at a disproportionate cost to minorities.

Popularly elected legislatures, however, do not furnish an absolute guaranty that the best choices between liberties will be made. Such choices involve choices between various principles as to the best distribution of the community's wealth. The choices which our laws now effectuate cannot be regarded as ideal. Though the standard of living of the average American may be the highest in the world, and his economic liberty consequently the greatest, many economic maladjustments remain to be corrected. The hope is that public officials, with the approval of the voters, may manage to devise methods to distribute wealth more widely without checking its production or so regimenting its producers as to discourage their productive activities. In this way it is believed that under our system of government, the liberty of individuals can be greatly expanded where its expansion is most called for. This requires a high type of statesmanship, but without it the beneficent results which a democratic system of government makes possible cannot be realized in fact. The best institutional machinery depends on men of character and intelligence for its successful operation.

TABLE OF CASES

INDEX

For cases, see separate Table of Cases

Bei Fragen zur Produktsicherheit wenden Sie sich bitte an:
If you have any questions regarding product safety,
please contact:

Walter de Gruyter GmbH
Genthiner Straße 13
10785 Berlin
productsafety@degruyterbrill.com